LADINO-ENGLISH
ENGLISH-LADINO

Concise Encyclopedic Dictionary
(Judeo-Spanish)

LADINO-ENGLISH
ENGLISH-LADINO

Concise Encyclopedic Dictionary

(Judeo-Spanish)

DR. ELLI KOHEN AND
DAHLIA KOHEN-GORDON

HIPPOCRENE BOOKS
New York

Acknowledgement

The authors thankfully acknowledge the magnificent contribution of Nadia Hassani, who as editor has gone beyond the call of duty in her task to help in the shaping and finalization of this dictionary. She fully deserves commendation for enthusiastic and superb effort. The authors also thank Dr. Joseph G. Hirschberg, Professor Emeritus of physics, University of Miami, for his help with reviewing and editing the introduction. Mrs. Cahide Cohen and Mr. Albert Barouch helped the authors to compile folkloric words used among Sephardic Jews.

ISBN 0-7818-0658-5

For information, address:
HIPPOCRENE BOOKS, INC.
171 Madison Avenue
New York, NY 10016

Printed in the United States of America.

For Sylvester with eternal love

TABLE OF CONTENTS

INTRODUCTION

Is there a Ladino language? In reality, Ladino comprises three separate languages:

Ladino is the liturgical language of the Old Testament, prayer books and religious texts. It is not a spoken language. The ancient texts are in Rashi* characters. After their expulsion from Spain, the only language that the Sephardim in the Ottoman Empire could read fluently was the Spanish written in Rashi characters. This Ladino has been adulterated with local words. In the Ladino of the earliest translations made in the Ottoman Empire, there are Turkish and Hebrew words. Ladino is an archaic and artificial language which has been a vehicle bringing the Bible, the prayers and all the compositions which were more or less ritualistic to the ordinary, Spanish-speaking Jew. Ladino renders a word by word juxtaposition of the Hebrew original with total disregard for Spanish syntax, the appearance and interpretation of phrases.

Judeo-Spanish, the spoken language which does not have any trace of the Hebrew syntax is the language of romances, fictional and folk stories, popular Jewish history books such as *Istoria Santa* (Sacred History), and Sephardic newspapers which appeared throughout Jewish communities. The unschooled called it "muestro espaniol" (our Spanish). It is a vernacular language which follows Spanish grammar and Spanish syntax along with a flurry of Turkish, Judeo-Spanish and Hebrew words. It also includes some Greek, Italian and Portuguese words, as well as French words—due to the influence of the Alliance Israélite Universelle schooling, and more recently a few fashionable English words. One can find in the same sentence Spanish, Turkish, Hebrew and French, which makes it quite difficult to speak of a unified Judeo-Spanish syntax.

Finally, there is a purified, solemn, noble Judeo-Spanish used for speeches, declarations, and high-style showcase meetings which is preserved by the

---

*Rashi is a special Hebrew alphabet used by Rav Shelomo Itshaki (11th century) for the publication of his commentaries on the Bible and the Talmud., cf. *Rashi* in the Ladino-English section of the dictionary.

1

cultivated male elite. This language, at least until the modern days of women's liberation, has never been spoken by women and would bring ridicule upon them.

There is a popular Judeo-Spanish script, a cursive called Soletreo, which in the late Ottoman years was also called "ganchos" (hooks). One of the setbacks of Soletreo is the lack of punctuation. The comma, period, question mark, exclamation mark, and quotation marks—they all can alter the meaning of the word preceding the punctuation mark. This is so, unless such punctuation is placed at some distance away from the end of a sentence and the beginning of the next one. Confusion of punctuation with a letter of the alphabet is not unlikely. Any correspondence written in Soletreo is just one long sentence from beginning to end, with the conjunction "y," placed instead of periods or commas.

In earlier times, Judeo-Spanish documents were written in Aljamiado, that is, in the Judeo-Spanish language, but using Hebrew characters. In recent years, Yolanda Moreno Koch, of the Universidad Complutense in Madrid, has published an annotated transcription in the Roman alphabet of the "Taqqanot Laws," written in Valladolid in 1432 to govern the Jewish communities in Castile.

The Hebrew alphabet consists of consonants only; vowels are represented as dots or dashes above, below or besides the consonants. However, vowels are quite significant in Spanish and Judeo-Spanish. The Aljamiado written system, which was formalized after the advent of printing presses in the Ottoman Empire, partially resolved the problem, by co-option of a limited number of consonants which would serve as vowels. Other difficulties in Aljamiado were consonantal sounds in Judeo-Spanish which did not exist in Hebrew, and single sounds represented by more than one Hebrew consonant.

The Judeo-Spanish is only one among a broad variety of Judeo-Iberan-Romance languages: Judeo-Italian, Judeo-French, Judeo-Provençal, Judeo-Portuguese, the Judeo-Castilian and Judeo-Aragonese varieties, Iberian Judeo-Arabic and North-African Judeo-Arabic (Haketia). Within the Judeo-Spanish itself there are different variants due to the broad territorial extensions of the Ottoman Empire, particularly in the Balkans: the Judeo-Spanish of the Istanbulis, Adirnalis and Izmirlis; the

Salonician version of Judeo-Spanish, the Judeo-Spanish dialect of Monastir, the Judeo-Spanish of Sofia.

In using Roman characters for Judeo-Spanish, one basically has two approaches: transcription which reproduces the phonetic, and transliteration which rewrites the Aljamiado texts in the Roman alphabet letter by letter. According to Professor Moshé Lazar from the University of Southern California, reading a transliterated text is more work than reading the text in the original Aljamiado version. As stated in Joseph Nehama's *Dictionnaire du Judéo-Espagnol*,

> "the adoption of a system of transcription for Judeo-Spanish is a rather delicate problem. One is tempted to use the so-called international alphabet. However we consider that such an alphabet disfigures too much the spelling of the Spanish and gives a strange aspect to the Judeo-Spanish. We have preferred to adopt the system of the Spanish Romanists with some modifications. . . . On the other hand any system of transcription is in principle acceptable, if it is consequent."

Despite the tremendous effort at the Instituto Benito Arias Montano in Madrid to produce a consistent Judeo-Spanish-French dictionary, Professor Jack Levy from the South Carolina University comments: "I've just finished translating many, many poems on the Holocaust, and when I didn't know a word, half of the time I couldn't find it in Nehama, because I didn't know how he spelled it. It is a labyrinth". It is not so easy to advance any proposal for transcription which would be found acceptable on a nearly universal basis. The system would have to take into account the various native languages of the transcribers and readers for whom the transcription is being made, and some amount of transliteration may have to be included.

Thus a few questions remain.

1. Should a single system be used for texts destined to a non-technical audience and for historical or liturgical and rabbinical texts?
2. What current dialect of Judeo-Spanish should be used for transcription?
3. Should the transcription attempt to approximate current Spanish pronunciation?

Perhaps what is needed is not one, but rather several separate systems, each of them consistent within itself. To create some order in this chaos, what seems to be needed is, as suggested by George K. Zucker, the convening of an interdisciplinary Sephardic studies conference whose specific topic will be the problem of transcription of Judeo-Spanish texts into Roman characters.

In this area a proposal by Professor Jacob Hassan, of the "Instituto de Estudios Sefardies" could help to provide an auspicious start. Just before the *Dictionnaire de Judéo-Espagnol* was going to press, but too late for adoption in the Nehama dictionary, Professor Hassan had come up with the elaboration of what Nehama had considered a very successful system of transcription.

Until then the choice is open. The authors of the current dictionary have adopted for convenience separate systems for transcription according to the origin of the word listed in the dictionary, whether from:
• popular and folklore language
• biblical or liturgical sources
• novels and other Sephardic publications.

Consistency within each system was attempted. At time different possible spellings of the same word are entered. For reminiscences from language used in the family, the uncle's table or the aunt's kitchen, transcription in Roman letters as close as possible to the phonetics recalled has been used; in some cases recourse was made to Turkish spelling and in limited instances the transcription system of the *Dictionnaire du Judéo-Espanol* was used.

4

ABBREVIATIONS

adj	adjective
adv	adverb
arch	archaic
Bab	Babylonian origin of a month's name
Bulg	Bulgarian
coll	colloquial
Engl	English origin
F	French origin
fem	feminine
Fer Bib Gen	The Ladino Bible of Ferrara (1553)
fig	figurative
Gal	Galician origin
Gr	Greek Origin
H	Hebrew origin
Haketia	Moroccan Judeo-Spanish
imp	imperative
inter	interjection
iron	ironical
Ital	Italian origin
kanunn	Ladino translation of Kanun Name (Ottoman Penal Code)
lit	literally
masc	masculine
n	noun
Port	Portuguese origin
prep	preposition
rel	religious
Sl	Slavic origin
Spanish	Spanish origin
T	Turkish origin
v	verb
vulg	vulgar

LADINO-ENGLISH DICTIONARY

A

a to; as
a has; has performed
a caso in case
a cerca next to
A Lahmania Passover Prayer; Bread of Affliction (H)
a l'aznedad (adv) stupidly (T *eshekçasina*)
a mucha dulseria afita excess of sweets constipates
a quien him
abaca dormer; dormer-window; garret-window; ventilation duct; air
    hole; vent-hole; hole in the roof (from T *baca* chimney)
abacho down
abafado braised
abafar suffocate; extinguish (v, Port)
abafyamento suffocation; extinguishing by lack of air (Port)
abarabar to become too familiar with a subordinate; bring oneself
    down to the level of an inferior (T *beraber* together)
abashada descent; common cold
abashár go down; lower; (el) abashan (he) descends; (el) abashan por
    veyèr (he) condescends to look down
abastado all present
abastadrear bastardize; degenerate; corrupt (v)
abastansa sufficiency
abastava would have been sufficient
abastessir supply the necessary (v)
abastissiar have enough; have enough time
abatir soothe; diminish
abaxo down
abazur lampshade (F *abat-jour*)
abdal imbecile; rude; badly groomed (T *aptal*)
abdest ritual ablution practiced by the Muslims five times a day (T)
abediduarédech - (la) abediduarédech you shall save alive (every girl);
    Pharaoh's command in the Haggadah (Passover story)
abes vain; useless; absurdly useless; futile; pointless (T)
abestruz ostrich

7

abidugar almas save souls
abiendo having
abiguar conserve (v); **abiguiaremos de nuestro padre semen** (let us lay
    with our father so that) we can conserve the race, the heredity of
    our father—Lot's daughters (Fer Bib Gen)
Abisinya Abyssinia
abitante inhabitant
abitar inhabit
abiuiguar conserve (v)
ablasyon removal
Ablón Absalon David's rebellious son (Moroccan Sephardic ballad)
abogador advocate; defender; someone who speaks in favor of
    someone else, who supports another person, speaks well of
    him/her
ablusyon ablution
abokar bend (v); **abokar (se)** bend one's head
abolcear put at the disposition of a person, a household, an enterprise
    money, food supplies or merchandises in sufficient or even large
    quantities (from T *bol* abundant)
aboltar (se) turn oneself
abolto a pleto turned into a fight
abominavle abominable
aboniguares if you have done good (Fer Bib Gen)
aborresido hated; universally detested; held in horror by everybody
aborriciente abhorrent
abot patriarchs; fathers (Haketia)
abrasar embrace (v)
abreuar irrigate (Fer Bib Gen); **abreuaua** irrigates (Fer Bib Gen)
abreuuamos let us quench our thirst; let us drink
abrikok apricot (Port *albricoque*)
abrir open (v)
abrirsean they opened themselves
absencia absence
absolusyon absolution
absoluto absolute
abu (Bab) April
abudaraho smoked and salted fish roe (Mediterranean specialty) often
    coated with wax; **abudaraho hoho** funny way to speak about
    abudaraho
abujero hole

abutargo same as *abudaraho*, made of mullet egg sacs; it is highly appreciated in the Orient as an aperitif or at the end of a meal as a food complement. Traditional families used to prepare their own *abudaraho*.

abuzar abuse (v)

abuzo abuse (n)

abysmo abyss

acaba Is it so? Is it possible that it is so? Could it be so? (T)

acabamiento end; termination

acabár end (v)

acaescimiento rare event (Ferrara Siddur)

acavidar warn; advise (v, Port *cavidar*)

acazàyito weight of nine drachmas

açecalan forged; açecalan toda maestria forged all sorts of tools (Fer Bib Gen)

aceytùna olive

achadu found (Port *achado*)

achetar accept; give one's agreement (Ital *accettare*)

achilear emancipate; inculcate to someone self-confidence and open manner (v, from T *açilmak* open oneself)

achunkar sit on one's knees with the legs folded inside, like a camel (from T *çökmek* collapse, fall down); sit down in a collapsing way (neg)

acimentar lay the foundation (v, Fer Bib Kings I)

acompañar accompany

aconsejar tell; mean (v Fer Bib Kings I)

acontesser happen

acontissio happened

acusar scratch (v, Port *coçar*)

adalet justice (T); musculature (T)

adanear sustain; support (from T *dayanmak* resist)

adaptasyon adaptation

adar March. Sixth month of the Hebrew calendar

addaru March (Bab)

ade Go! Go forward!

adéfla bile

adelantamiento progress (n)

adelantar move forward; progress

adelantre forward; before

adepto adept

aderechere I shall put right
adet custom; habit (T)
adisyon addition
adjaib surprising; astonishing; strange (T *acaib*)
adjami beginner; unskilled; neophyte; inexperienced (T *acemi*)
adjamilik inexperience; state of being unskilled (T *acemilik*)
Adjem Persian (T *acem*); adjem oilav rice prepared in the Persian style, mixed with small pieces of meat
adjidear pity (v); take be compassionate; pity one's condition (T *acimak*)
adjile haste; precipitation (T *acele*)
adjileli person who acts hastily, with precipitation
adjiorno like in full day; being brightly lit; having plenty of light (Ital *a giorno*)
adjunta reunion; assembly
adjuntamyento coming together
adjustar adjust; arrange
admeter admit
administrador administrator
administrar administer
admirar admire
admirasion admiration
admisyon admission
ado tu Where are you?
adobar arrange; repair (v)
adobe por piedras bricks instead of stones
adobemos let us make
adobes he makes
adolme violence; (mi) adolme sobre ti the outrage they did on me will befall upon you (Fer Bib Gen)
adolôria (se) shrunk back
adón master
Adonay God; the Lord; the Eternal
Adoniah Adonija (Fer Bib Kings I)
adopsyon adoption
adoptivo adoptive
adorado adored
adormeçimiento deep sleep
adormeciose fell asleep
adormidura (echo) laid asleep
adornar adorn; decorate

adotrinar indoctrinate; teach
adovador repairman
adovar repair (v)
adôves bricks
adquéri I have acquired
adquirir acquire
adredor Seraph
adres address (n)
adresar (se) address oneself
adulsado made sweet
adúltera adulteress
adúltero adulterer
adurmeser put asleep; benumb; make numb
adverbo adverb
adversidad adversity
adyar delay; postpone; save time (Port)
adyentro inside
adyo/adyo Señor del mundo! scream of terror; of horror
aeradji someone who receives a sum of money for conceding his right
    to occupy an apartment
aezyte de oliva olive oil
afalagár console
afamado famous
afanamyento illusion; chimerical idea
afartado satisfied
afatigar constipate; cause an indisposition, a malaise
afavle friendly
afeador accuser
af-edersin excuse me
afera outside
aferado amorous; in love
aferar catch (v)
aferin Congratulations! (T)
afermoziguar glorify
aféyto ornament; adornment
affincar drown (from Salonician Passover Haggadah)
affliciaran a ellos they will be afflicted (Fer Bib Gen)
afikomim half of a Passover unleavened bread which is saved for the
    end of the meal in the first night of Passover and which is eaten
    while pronouncing the last prayer by which the meal is blessed

afillu even if
afilou/afilu even; even if (H)
afim so that; to that end
afinkar/affinkar pierce (v); make enter by the tip; introduce a pointed
    object into the soil, into the flesh; get fixed; settle in a place
afirmare I shall establish
afitar constipate; happen
aflakar lose weight
afliçion affliction
afligete de baxo sus manos humiliate oneself in front of her (injunction
    to Agar to humiliate herself in front of Sara) (Fer Bib Gen)
afofado spongy; without consistency; soft
afrentar inflict an affront
afreskar refresh
afriir/affriyar afflict; inflict deprivations; cruelly deprive of something
    ardently desired, which is needed to live
afriisyón/afriission/affrisyón hard deprivation; intense suffering which
    lasts
afrisyonado to be cruelly deprived of indispensable and desired things
afuera outside
afueras outside of; except
afuere - (di) afuere exterior (Monastir dialect)
agam - (ke) agam let them do
agáya tonsillitis
agencia agency
agenda agenda
agente agent
agidear to have pity with; to have compassion (T *acimak*)
agil/aghil sheepfold (T kanunn)
agir mushteri (lit: heavy client) serious client (T *agir mushteri, aghir
    mushteri*)
agonia agony
agóra now
agorar augur; presage (v)
agosto August
agradavli amicable (Monastir dialect)
agradecer thank (v)
agraz green grape
agrear make sour; irritate
agristada boiled mayonnaise

agro sour
agua water; **agua de dulse** sweet water; **aguas** waters
aguada very clear soup
agudo pointed; sharp
agüelo grandfather
aguentado liquidized; mixed with lots of water; without consistency
  and solidity
aguila eagle
aguita a very simple, harmless potion; very light medicine
aguja needle
aguntar unite; reunite (v, Monastir dialect)
agunte reunion
aguzero merchant of needles
agyar drive; conduct; direct (v)
ahali population; crowds
ahalidje in keeping with the needs of the population (T *ahâlice*,
  kanunn)
aharvar beat up (from Arabic *harb* strike, war)
ahbár rat
ahi there (Moroccan Sephardic ballad)
ahijada (sere)(I shall) have children by her
ahir stable (n, T)
ahlat eat; glutton (from H *ahal*)
ahora now
ahtar small retail dealer; druggist; herbalist; dealer in small wares and
  notions; haberdasher; mercer (T *aktar, attar*). In Turkey, this shop
  used to be a quite folkloric place, a hangout for children, place
  to buy candies, or candied sugar, or mastic, a forerunner of
  chewing gum.
ahuecada hollowed
ahuecar hollow out (v)
ai there
ai y uy subject of sorrow and anxiety; deeply sunken in regrets,
  sorrows, and anxieties; continuous complaints and moaning
ai! Ah! alas!
aidado advanced in age
ainda still (Port)
aindamas and still more
ainde even; even though; in any case; still; as yet (Port *ainda*, Monastir
  dialect)

airado prone to anger; irritable; irritated
aire air
airi air (Monastir dialect)
ajada garlic sauce
ajalú non-existent place; place which has never existed (H *ahel*)
ajana preparations; simulated efforts; spectacular gestures executed to make believe that someone is really busy, that he/she is unsparingly working to prepare something important (H *ahana*)
ajarvar hit; beat; strike with a stick to cause pain; mistreat; brutalize (from H *herev* short sword)
ajay ah; oh (Haketia)
ajeno alien
ajero garlic vendor
ajitador agitator
ajitar agitate
ajo garlic
ajtche one third of a para, para being one fortieth of piaster and piaster being one hundredth of a lira, the Turkish gold pound (T *akçe*)
ajtchi cook (n, T *ashçi*)
ajugar dowry
ajur visible from the exterior; disheveled clothing; a little indecent or audacious female not properly dressed (F *à jour*)
ajustar add
ajyo, agio a premium on money in exchange; fund transfer
aka here
akadir capable; endowed with the qualities required to run an enterprise (T *kadir* capable)
akatar honor; respect; render homage (v)
akavidar recommend caution; put in guard (v, Port)
akavido prudence; caution
akayado who does not talk anymore; silenced
akdama prologue; preface; introduction; foreword (H)
akedado tranquil; who does not move; apathetic; silent
akel this
aken to whom; at whom
akerensyado nurtured; object of affection
akeyar verb used as a pass-key which substituted for any verb which momentarily escapes the memory
akeyo that

aki abasho down here
aki here
akishear to become suited; proper; fitting; right; convenient; harmonize
      (T *yakishmak*)
aklimatar acclimatize
akolyo greeting; welcome (Ital *accogliere, accoglienza*)
akomodar arrange; adapt; accommodate
akompanyado accompanied
akondjurado someone who has taken the obligation; under oath
akonsejar advise
akontentar content; satisfy (v)
akonteser happen
akontesimyento event; happening
akorar languish; make languish; exasperate by making wait
akordar accord; determine by a common accord; put musical
      instruments in tune with each other; tune the sounds of musical
      instruments with a diapason; tune a piano; set watches and clocks
      all to the same time
akordar remember
akordeon accordion
akorrer run to bring help; come at full speed
akorrido very much in rush; very pressed for time
akostar approach the coast
akostumbrado accustomed
akostumbrar accustom; give the habit; habituate
aksadear create an obstacle; compromise the progress of a business
      (T *aksamak*)
akseptar accept
aksesoryo accessory
aksi angry; grouchy; mean (T)
aksidental accidental
aksidente accident
akulpar inculpate
akurtar shorten
akuturu at a fixed price; **dar un fecho akuturu** get a job done at a
      fixed price; **favlar akuturu** speak without thinking
akuzasyon accusation
al the
al lado on the side
al lugar because of; instead of

Alá Allah; God
ala to, to the
ala wing
ala prefix signifying in the manner of
ala franka in the Frankish manner; in the European manner
ala maghna the manna
alabaron a elle they praised Him (Fer Bib Gen)
aladinan someone who speaks a language understood by all people
aladinar translate from a foreign language into Judeo-Spanish
aladja sort of inferior quality cotton tissue dyed with bright colors
    (T *alaca*)
Aláh bilir God knows (meaning only God knows about a doubtful sit-
    uation of which there is no accurate information)
alaja closet in which the Torah scrolls are locked at the synagogue
    (H *alaha*); alaja kon melaja "the theory must be followed by the
    practice without any failing; it is certainly interesting to comment
    about, discourse and interpret, but under the condition that prac-
    tice follows"(H)
alak bulak in great disorder; all upside down (T *allak bullak*)
alakran scorpion
Alalabanza to the praise of
alanceado pierced by spear
alancear spear (v)
alargar make long; prolong a speech, a conversation
alarmado alarmed
alárze copper; brass
Alav a shalom Peace upon him (this expression always accompanies
    the name of a deceased beloved and cherished, H)
Alavàd a Adonay Hallelujah
Alavàd Hallelujah; praise (n)
alavádo praiseworthy
alavàr praise (v)
alay band of people; cohort of people; a heap of rowdy people
alay irony (T); tomar al alay make fun of
albadrar saddle a donkey
Albanez Albanian
Albania Albania
albasha distribution of clothes to needy students (H)
albergo inn (Ital)

albondiga meatball; cheese ball; **albondigas con ajo** chicken breast
    meatballs with garlic; **albondigas con kaartofia i ajo** chicken
    breast meatballs with garlic and potatoes; **albondigas con**
    kalavasikas meatballs with zucchini; **albondigas con limon**
    small chicken breast meatballs in lemon sauce; **albondigas con**
    merendjena meatballs with eggplant
alborear dawn (v)
albornia large earthen vase; large porringer or pot made of varnish
    coated earth; large nose; burnoose, hooded cloak or mantle worn
    by Arabs; large sleeved towel worn at exit from Turkish bath
albrisyas present offered to the first one who brings good news
alçaron they elevated
alçe mi mano I raised my hand
alchak vile; contemptible; licentious; dissolute; shameless (T *alçak*)
alchin plaster; gypsum (T *alçi*)
alço alçaciones made sacrifices (Fer Bib Gen)
Alcorán the Koran
alçosse was elevated
alcuñe name; last name (from T *künye*)
alderedór around
aldikera pocket
aldurear invent something which is not true (T *uydurmak*)
alechadera nursemaid
alechuga lettuce
alef (aleph) (first letter of the Hebrew alphabet)
alef bet A, B; alphabet
alegoria allegory
alegre joyful
alegri happy
alegria de Purim rejoicing of Purim
alegria grande great rejoicing
alegria rejoicing
Aleman German
alenguar make longer (skirt, pants)
alenguaziko a little long; tiring; boring
alerta alert; alarm (n)
alesensyado authorized; someone who has received authorization;
    licensed
aleshado far away; away from the world; solitary

aleskuro dark
alesta promptly; prompt to obey; prompt to devote oneself to work
alevantàn (He) raiseth
alevantar lift
alevantar uplift
alevantar (se) get up; make oneself rise; raise oneself
alevdado fermented
alevo student
alezar de take distance from; go away from; separate from
alfabé alphabet
alfabeta alphabet
alfinete pin (Gal *alfinete*)
alfineti pin (Gal *alfinete*)
alforria franchising; liberation
alforria freedom
alga alga
Algeria Algeria
algo a little; something; a little something
algodon cotton
alguaya lamentation; moaning
alguenga tongue
alguja needle
algun some
algune coze something (Monastir dialect)
alguno any; anyone; someone
algunu some
algunu someone (Monastir dialect)
alhad Sunday
aliado ally (n)
aliansa alliance
aliar ally (v)
alibé alphabet
alichverich business deal; commercial transaction; give and take
     (T *alishverish)*
alidji buyer; client; taker (T *alici)*
aliento respiration (Fer Bib Gen)
alikodear keep; detain (T *alikoymak* kanunn)
alikudear delay; cause to delay; cause loss of time that could have
     been used to execute a determined task (T *alikoymak)*
alilá calumny; false accusation (H)

alimár use file to polish
alimpiadéro obsession with cleaning
alimpiar clean (v)
Alina woman's name
aliniaron were diminished (the waters of the Flood) (Fer Bib Gen)
alisar polish; make even (v)
alishik social relations commercial or else; acquaintances (T *ilishik* connection)
alishterear make accustomed; practice the handling of an instrument or technique; help to gain proficiency (T *alishtirmak*)
alivyanar soothe; facilitate; render lighter, less tiring; simplify
aljamóras heat flashes which rise to the head producing nausea and vertigo
aljashu sort of nougat made of powdered biscuits or scrapings of Passover's unleavened bread, almonds, nuts, and other grilled fruits, spices, all of it well piled and cooked in honey
aljavaka basil
aljeña henna
alkadrúz tube; pipe; duct (Port)
alkanfór camphor
alkansar reach (v)
alkaparra caper
alkatchi, malkatchi Turkish children's game where the child running the game stands at the center of a half circle made by the other participants in the game; he holds between his clasped hands the token which is the object of the game: a pebble or a small coin. He slides the token from hand to hand each time pronouncing one of the keywords of the game, such as "take and run," "take well this and run," "take this also and run fast." The one who actually receives the token waits a little while to distract the attention and suddenly he starts running, pursued by others. The winner is the one who catches him, and it is now his turn to lead the game.
Alkatran tar
alkavo in the end
alkilar rent (v)
alkímiko alchemist
alkonfites white Jordan almonds given in weddings wrapped in little lace bags
alkoóliko alcoholic

19

alkunya last name; surname (from Turkish *künye* register of names)
allado next to
Alláh kyerim God the Almighty (formula of hope and trust in God, which is invoked each time the resolution of a difficulty is postponed to a later date in the hope that divine goodness will inspire the solution when the time comes) (T)
Alláh versin may God give you, help you (said when someone wants to get rid of a beggar) (T); may also mean "may God will," "let it be so," "I wish it" or "I will be more than happy if you get what you want."
allegán (el) the one who reaches at (Ferrara Siddur)
allegaronse they reached; they arrived
allegria joy; festivity
allegria de Purim festivity of Purim
alli there
alma soul; person
almadén mineral deposit
almadraque mattress
almanak almanac
almaryiko small chest (furniture)
almaryo chest (furniture)
Almashiah the Messiah
almasiga mastic
almasjear aromatize by adding a little mastic
almemdro almond tree
almenara candelabra
almendra almond
almendrada drink made with almond milk and sugar
almendral almond tree
almendro/almendrero almond tree
almenos at least
almirez mortar
almizklár perfume with musk (v)
almoáda pillow
almodrote baked chopped eggplant
almohada cushion
almoneda - (fazer) almoneda (to be) auctioned
almoneda auction
almorrána hemorrhoids
almorzar have lunch

almudroti baked chopped eggplant baked with cheese
almusama evening entertainment (T *müsamere*)
alokado maddened; someone who has a disorderly conduct
alondjar make go farther away; push to a further date
alongar prolong (v, Fer Bib Kings I)
alora then (Ital)
alpáka alpaca
alsar heighten; elevate (v)
alsayon sacrifice; holocaust
altar altar; high place
altarrassa terrace
alterear alter; drive to adopt a disorderly and irregular conduct (v)
alternar alternate
alteza height
alti ostu upside down; completely in disorder (T *altüst*)
altiuo elevated (Ferrara Siddur)
alto high
altraménte in the opposite case; if it is in another way; if it is
      differently (Ital)
altramúz lupine
altretánto similarly; likewise; as much; as well (Ital, is only used to
      reciprocate when someone receives a vow, a salutation or a
      compliment)
altro ke (adv) it is just the contrary (Ital)
altrónde anyway; moreover (Ital)
altruista altruist
altura height
aluengadura piece used to lengthen a cloth or a carpet; divine
      clemency at the last hour, when everyone's fate is finally
      determined by God
alumbrar illuminate; lighten
aluminyo aluminum
alviyána hazelnut
alviyanéro hazelnut tree
alvoráda sunrise; first lights of the morning before sunrise; dawn
ama but (T)
amaáres illiterate; ignorant (H *am aaretz*)
amabilidad friendliness
amadór amateur; music lover
Amalék Amalecite

amalgama amalgam
amalgamar amalgamate
aman Mercy! Alas! For goodness sake! Have mercy on me!
    (expression of unhappiness at being relentlessly disturbed by
    someone or something that is at hand's reach)
amanat entrusted for safe keeping; deposit (T kanunn)
amané sentimental Turkish song
amanecer rise (of the sun, v)
amanét object left in trust; confided in trust (T emanet)
amánte lover
amanyana tomorrow
amar love (v)
amargar embitter
amargàron they (the Egyptians) embittered
amargór bitterness
amargura bitterness
amariya - (una) amariya a Turkish or English gold pound (slang
    expression, like U.S. "buck")
amariyar dye in yellow (v)
amariyo yellow
amasa knead (imp)
amaskanta placing in mortgage (H)
amatar tune off; extinguish
amatô extinguished
amator amateur; fan; enthusiastic about; fond of; keen on (Monastir
    dialect)
amavdil amavdil cautious formula announced when someone dares to
    compare two things or persons which have qualities or
    destinations of the same order but of a different rank, for
    example mayor and emperor; humble provincial journalist and
    world famous writer
amavle friendly
ambar granary; storehouse (T)
ambára amber
ambarika small false pearl
ambér amber
ambezado learned
ambezar learn
ambicioso ambitious
ambientación background

ambiente environment
ambierto hungry
ambisyon ambition
ámbito ambit; field; ground
ambizar notify (v, Monastic dialect)
ambos both
ambre hunger
ambrera starvation
ambriyénto famished
ambulansya ambulance
ambyente ambient
amedia noche at midnight
amele workman (T kanunn)
amelyorar ameliorate
amen amen; let it be so
amenáza threat
amenguar diminish
Amerika America
Amerikano American
amezurar measure (v)
amida part of a religious service which is recited sotto voce, standing
    up and facing Jerusalem (H)
amigito boyfriend in a flirting and innocent relationship
amigo friend
amintar mention (v, Monastir dialect)
amiral admiral
amistad friendship
ammal porter (T *hammal*)
ammalik hard work
ammaliko man doing any kind of hard work; porter
ámo boss; chief
amofado rotten
amofar rot (v)
amofeser rot (v)
amohado wet (adj)
amojado wet (adj)
amokar (se) wipe one's nose
amoldar adapt; recourse to a good way (v)
amontonar pile up
amor love (n); (de) amor caught by love

amor platonik platonic love
amor propryo self-esteem
amóra mulberry
amoréro mulberry tree
amortazyamento preparation of the dead for burial
amortízir allay; liquidate a date; pay off; pay by annuity (v)
amosi blessing; action of grace performed by every pious Jew from
    taking a small piece of bread dipped in salt before the first
    mouthful of the meal (H)
amostrar a si mesmo show to himself; regard himself
amostrar show (v)
amostrare I will show
amparo help
ampula lightbulb
amuchiguaronse they were multiplied
amurchár fade; deteriorate; wither (v, Port *murchaer-se*, Monastir
    dialect)
amustrar indicate (v, Monastir dialect)
anachar broaden
añada one year duration
anadan babadan (lit: from mother from father) from all times; since
    always; traditionally (T)
añader add (arch, still used for needle work in the meaning of adding
    rows)
añadio - (y) añadio (por parir a su hermano a Heuel) (and) she (Eve)
    did (give birth to his brother Abel) (Fer Bib Gen)
añadio - (y) añadio (por hablar a el) (and) he did (continue to speak to
    him) (Fer Bib Gen)
añadira - (no) añadira (su fuerça ele a ti) (it) will not yield (its fruit to
    you you anymore)
añadire - (no) añadire (mas por herir a todo biuo como hize) I surely
    shall (not destroy anymore all that lives as I did) (Fer Bib Gen)
añadire - (no) añadire (por maldezir mas a la tierra por el hombre) I
    surely shall (not curse anymore the earth because of man) (Fer
    Bib Gen)
anádo to be saved from a great danger; saved from sinking ship, from
    death; saved from a precarious situation and become rich; entered
    in a path of security and prosperity; fortunate by a stroke of
    good luck, by protection or favor
análes annals

analiz analysis; **analiz de sangre** blood analysis; **analiz de urina** urine
   analysis
analizar analyze
analogia analogy
analysta chronicler; historian
anarchia anarchy
anatomia anatomy
anatomiko anatomical
anatomista anatomist
añazme ring of precious metal which used to be hooked at the bottom
   of the median nasal cartilage as an ornament
anbar storehouse; granary (T)
anchadizo ganglion; goiter
ancho wide; broad; (fig) easy-going; somewhat negligent
anchura width
anchúya anchovy
andalavizo name given by the Turks to the first Jews expelled from
   Spain who landed in Salonica. The appellation was the result of a
   misunderstanding. The Sublime Porte had ordered by way of
   posters (*avizo*) the subjects of the Empire to receive with benevolence the incoming Jews. As the Jews arrived they were greeted by
   Spanish-speaking Turks who addressed them in the language of
   their country of origin. As they were asked their names and place
   of origin, the Jews invariably responded by the words: "anda el
   avizo" (go see the poster). This made the Turks believe that the
   incoming foreigners were called *andalavizos.*
Andalúz Andalusian
andán (en el) huerto (Adam and Eve) walked (in the Garden of) Eden
andante going
andar go (v)
andaras you will go
andaréte person who cannot stay in one place; vagabond; person who
   drifts from one place to another
ande saves - (d')ande saves From where do you know, how do you
   know?
ande where (Haketia)
andi where
andjak anyway; but; however; moreover (T *ancak*)
Andrinopoli Adrianopolis
anduuieron atras they walked; went backward

anduuieron they went

anduuo - (y) anduuo (con el Dio) (Anoch and Enoch) went (with God) (Fer Bib Gen)

anduuo (la arca) (Noah's) ark was floating

anduuo went with; walked with (Fer Bib Gen)

angarya (T) forced labor; drudgery; useless; superfluous task which is imposed (an unpleasant imposition; a task which someone must do because he has to); in the Ottoman Empire *angarya* was a kind of forced labor, like digging trenches, building fortifications, imposed on the Dimmis (the non-Muslim subjects), but it could also be some kind of semi-punitive labor imposed on Muslims.

angel angel; **angeles** angels

anginara artichoke

angustia anguish; disgust; repugnance; something that inspires disgust; trouble

angustiador oppressor

angustiadores enemies (Fer Bib Gen)

ani poor (H)

anillo ring (n)

animado animated

animal animal

ánimo courage

anio aqui siervos slaves in the year here (from Passover song A Lahmania)

anio el vinien coming year; next year (from Passover song A Lahmania)

anio year

añir indigo

añireár dye with indigo

aniversaryo anniversary

aniyá (interj) Oh! If it could be so ! (T *haniya*)

aniyo ring

aniyut poverty (H *ani* poor)

ankora anchor

annáv humble; modest

ano year

año year

anocheser start to become night

anomalia anomaly

anonimo anonymous

anormal abnormal
añóryos numerous years
anos de alkavos last years; last years of life
anotár take note
ansi so
ansia anxiety; mourning
ansina so; in this way; (y) ansina se paso (and) so it came to pass
ansine so (Monastir dialect)
ansya sorrow; anxiety
ansyozo anxious
antanyus in the past
antari sort of toga or robe, male or female dress without sleeves and
   with non sewn fringes which are crossed on the front. The
   Sephardic women's antari was broadly hollowed on the chest and
   left the throat and the breasts simply veiled by a flap of muslin.
antedatar antedate (v)
antena antenna
antender understand
anteryor anterior
ántes before
antes de todo before everything
antesedénte antecedent
antigo antique (adj)
antiguedad antiquity (Ferrara Siddur)
antika antique (n)
antikadji antique dealer
antiko di portokal orange peel marmalade
antinotche the night before
antipatia antipathy
antisemita anti-Semite
antisipar anticipate
antiuo antique (adj)
antiyer the day before yesterday
antojos eyeglasses
antrakto intermission
anujar annoy (Port)
anulamyento cancellation
anulasyon annulation
anunsyar announce
anunsyasyon annunciation

anyo year
aogando drowning
aogar (se) drown
aogar choke; strangle (v)
aonde where
aora now
apalpadura groping; feeling one's way
apalpar - (ay k') apalpar there is something to touch; it is the occasion
    to profit from a bargain; abandon oneself to inappropriate, lurid
    touchings
apalpar feel one's way; grope; receive money (that can be groped)
apalpar grope; palpate; touch (v, Monastir dialect)
apañar seize hastily, often violently or by cunning
apañaras you will store, assemble, keep as provision
apañense they assemble
apansiz sudden (T)
aparadór pencil sharpener (Port)
aparar (se) show oneself from an elevated position; appear from a
    balcony
aparár sharpen a pencil; sharpen a rod to use it as a pen; spread; dis-
    play in public; raise the Torah Scroll in the Sabbath service to
    show it to the congregation; display the bride's trousseau to have
    its quantity and quality appreciated by relatives and friends (v)
apareár arrange by pairs; sort gloves or shoes by pairs
aparecido (adj) young person of good height and of a stature beyond
    what could be expected considering the person's age; person of
    imposing behavior
Aparecido (el) (the One who) appeared (Fer Bib Gen)
aparecisiosse appeared
aparejar get ready; prepare
aparejar prepare; set the table; prepare a war
aparejo preparation
aparensya appearance
aparentar associate with good families (v)
aparente apparent
aparescer appear
aparesimyento apparition
apariguar compare to a model or standard
aparijar get ready; prepare (v, Monastir dialect)
aparisyon apparition; specter; ghost; phantom

apariyar assort by pairs
apartadu distinct (Monastir dialect)
apartaduos retire yourselves; withdraw yourselves (imp) (Fer Bib Gen)
apartamento apartment (F *appartement*)
apartamyénto action of separating something from its surroundings;
    put aside
apartante separation
apartar separate; put aside (v)
apartarense - (y porfio con elles mucho, y) apartarense (a el, y vinieron
    a su casa) (and he pressured them so much that) they withdrew in
    his house (Fer Bib Gen)
apartenénsya pertinence
apartenér pertain
apartidizo small portion of a building separated from the rest
aparyentamento parenthood
apasensyár tranquilize; convince to be patient
apasentár make the animals graze
apasénto pasture
apedrear stone (v)
apega a la naris stick to the nose
apegado stuck; glued; inserted
apegadozo sticky; glutinous
apegar to stick; to glue
apegarse en ti stick to you; stay glued to you
apégo attachment; contagion
apegue - (no se) apegue el mal let no evil stick to me; may no evil
    reach me
apélo appeal (n); recourse to a superior court for revision of a lawsuit
    or sentence
apena barely
apeñar punish
apenas as soon as
aperreado someone who incurs universal disdain; who is proscribed
    and banned from everywhere
aperreamyento public disdain; debasement; degradation in the eyes of
    everybody
aperrear launch the dogs on; (fig) despise someone deeply; expose to
    public contempt
apesgar (se) make oneself heavy; insist heavily; multiply the arguments,
    the solicitation, the recommendations

apesgar make heavy
apesguo mucho it became very heavy (Fer Bib Gen)
apetito - (que) apetito (del hombre es malo de sus moçedades) (that)
the imagination (of man's heart is bad from the time of his youth)
(Fer Bib Gen); (todo) apetite (de pensamiento de su coraçon) (all
the) imagination (of the thoughts of his heart)
apetitózo appetizing
apezadumbre heaviness; aggravation; deep unhappiness; remorse; bad
conscience
apezadúmbre imposed heaviness; aggravation; sorrow; sense of heaviness; remorse; bad conscience
apezgár weigh heavily upon; aggravate; make more difficult; more
austere
apiadador someone who feels compassion, who is accessible to
compassion and strives to relieve the pains of others
apiadar have compassion; manifest compassion; share the pain; come
to help
apiadar to have pity
apikorós epicurean
apio celery; apio hado celery in lemon sauce
apititi appetite (Port *appetite*)
aplanar straighten
aplaudir applaud
aplaynár plane down; polish (v, Port)
aplikado attentive; dedicated
apoko apoko slowly slowly; step by step; gradually
aporey (adj) to the garbage; to be discarded
aporfizar adopt a child
apostolato apostolate
apotropos guardian (kanunn)
apozador someone who positions someone else or something
apozantado (adj) forming a layer
apozar put on; place on; lay on; put in position (v)
apozento sediment of wine or vinegar
appartadura separation
appodearon (se) (they) environed (Fer Bib Gen)
appresuraron los angeles con Lot the angels pressured Lot
appretar oppress; squeeze (v)
appréto oppression
approntar prepare; make ready

approprinquidad proximity (Ferrara Siddur)
apransado someone in the honor of whom a banquet is offered
aprekantado exorcised
aprekantar exorcise
aprematare I will exterminate (Fer Bib Gen)
aprendeár leave in pawn; put on mortgage
aprender learn
aprendisaje apprenticeship
aprendista apprentice
apressura go in haste (imp)
aprestaese serve; to be useful; temporarily devote oneself to help
apresura hasten (imp)
apresuro went in haste (Fer Bib Gen)
apresyado appreciated
apresyar appreciate
apretamyento pressure; compression; anxiety
apretár squeeze (v)
apreto distress; anxiety
apreton de mano handshake
apretón pressure; squeeze
apretura misery; material distress; poverty
aprevar test; put to the test; make suffer to test the degree, and/or the quality of courage, faith; faithfulness
aprezado jailed
aprezamyento imprisonment
aprezar jail (v)
aprimir oppress
aprobasyon approval
aprofondar deepen
aprofondir examine in full; submit to a minutious examination
aproksimasyon approximation
aprometido fiancé; engaged to marry
aprontamyento readiness; preparation
apropriar appropriate; take possession
aproprincar approximate; approach (v)
aprouechar (se) benefit; take advantage (from Ferrara Siddur)
aprovar try (v)
aprovasyon approval
aprovechamyento profit; advantage; utilization (n)
aprovechar profit; to be useful (v)

apuçar cease (Monastir dialect)
apuestar engage in a bet; bet (v)
apuesto bet (n)
apuntamyento rendezvous; appointment
apuntar point to
apurar (se) concentrate oneself; get weakened; anxious; afflicted; give
  pain to oneself
apurar concentrate by boiling; by evaporation; by blowing over an
  airstream; concentrate broth over the fire; purify; condense;
  reduce
apuro sense of uneasiness; oppression; anxiety
apyo celery
aquedarse stopped
aqueilla that (fem)
aquel this
aquello this
aquesto this
aqui here
àra altar
arà will make
araba Turkish carriage; wagon; horse or ox driven carriage (T)
arabadji coachman; charioteer (T arabaci)
arabeka wheelbarrow; barrow
arabi Arabic language
Arabia Arabia
aradera plug (n)
arado tilled land
arador husbandman; tiller; plough-man
Aragón Aragon
arakshamma November (Bab)
aralik space; interval (T)
Arami Syrian; Aramaean
araña spider
arañero spider web
aranjamiyento arrangement
aranjar arrange
Arap Arab
arapar shave (v)
aràs thou will perform
araskar scratch (v)

arastado dragged
arastar drag (v)
aravle arable
arbaamót (lit: four cubits) in a very short time; the very short time
    required to cross four cubits (H); (no dechar) arbaamot press;
    harass so that something is done immediately, relentlessly (every
    Jew who is a faithful observant of the Law must not take more
    than four steps, cross a distance longer than four cubits when
    coming out of his bed before proceeding to his first ablutions)
arbaáveestrim twenty-four; the twenty-four books of the Bible; the
    Bible (H)
arbánte very rough person; brutish person; boor
arbito arbiter
arbitrar arbitrate
arbol de las vitas tree of lives
árbol tree
arbolikoltúra arboriculture
arca chest; ark
arcu circle (Monastir dialect)
ardedura bricks baked in fire
ardiye storehouse; time spent in storage at the customhouse; tax paid
    for prolonged stay of merchandise at customs (T)
ardor ardor; zeal
ardyente ardent
aré I will execute
arebachar humiliate
arebiver (se) revive oneself; revitalize oneself; invigorate oneself (T)
arekojer collect; pick up (v); (las) arekoji I collected them; I picked
    them up
arel non-Jew; not circumcised
aremedji - (me) aremedji I took advantage of
aremos may we do it; we will do it
arena sand
arenadji vendor of sand
arenal sandy beach; sandy terrain; trail of sand left by a torrent
arenar (se) get caught in quicksand
arenar cover with sand
arenozo sandy
areskovdado reclined
areskuniado/areskunyado scratched

aretar stop (v)
arezvalar upturn; fall from a stairway
argat unqualified worker; non-specialized worker; handyman (Gr)
argatlik simple handyman's work; work which does not require special
    skills (example of Turkified Greek used in Judeo-Spanish)
aribivio resuscitated
arientro inside
arina flour; wheat
arinero someone who makes flour
aringa herring
aristokrasya aristocracy
aristokrata aristocrat
aritmetika arithmetic
ariva on top
arivar arrive
arjanteria silverware
arka - (la) Arka de la Aliansa The Ark of Alliance, The Ark of
    Covenant, the precious chest in which were saved the Tables of
    the Law
arka - (la) arka de Noaj Noah's ark; (fig) a place where people of all
    classes, races, and professions are gathered; very mixed
    environment
arka - (tener) arka enjoy high protection, protection in high place)
arka arch
arká charge that someone holds on the back; (fig) protection,
    protector (T)
arkada arcade; arc shaped opening in the superior part of a wall;
    covert gallery with roof supported by pillars surrounded by
    arcades)
arkadash friend (T *arkadash*)
arkali someone who feels strong and is full of audacity because he
    counts on protection from high place
arkeologo archeologist
arkeolojia archeology
arkilar rent (v)
arkilo rent (n)
arkitekto architect
arkitektura architecture
arko/arkol arc; rainbow
arktiko arctic

arli afflicted with a sentiment of bitterness in the aftermath of failure, mishap, deception (T *agrili, aghrili*)

arlilik feeling of bitterness caused by a failure, a deception, a betrayal, a frustration, an insult, a rejection; feeling of oppression due to an unexpected bad turn of events, a gesture of ungratefulness, a denial, a betrayal of given word (T *agrilik, aghrilik*)

arma weapon

armada army

armado armed

armado de bilibiz acting very threateningly, but in reality quite powerless having neither the strength nor the authority to put the threats in execution

armamyento armament

armar arm (v)

armáryo closet

armatura frame; brace; fencing; tressing

Armenia Armenia

Armeno Armenian

armi di gaina chicken with onions

armi quartered tomato cooked with rice

armistisyo armistice

armo arm; weapon

armonia harmony

armonika harmonica

armonizar harmonize

armonyozaménte harmoniously

arnánsyo/arnancio/arnásyo generation

Aron Aaron

arón coffin; bier

arondjar push (v)

arope grape syrup spread on pancakes

arostokratiko aristocratic

arovada stolen

aroz di domates i pipiritzas pilaf of tomatoes and peppers

arozár perfume with rose water (v)

árpa harp

arpista harpist

arrafganeár relax; unbend; loosen; slacken (v, T)

arrajlaneárse relax; strut (T *rahatlik*)

arrancár tear out; uproot

asada grilled; broiled
arranjamiento arrangement
arrankado extirpated; torn off
arrankar brutally pull; extirpate; uproot (v)
arrankar extirpate; tear off
arrapada shaving; shaving executed with a few strokes of the razor
arrapador barber (Monastir dialect)
Arrapados (los) one of the three sub-sects of the Salonician Judeo-Muslim sect of the Deunmes (Dönmes); it was the sub-sect which externally affected the most by Muslim customs
arrapadura (la primera) cutting of the hair on the thirty-third day of Omer (forty-nine day period between the second day of Passover and Pentecost); on this day called Lag laomer, upon the specific recommendation of the scholar Rabbi Simon, the anniversary of his death is celebrated in joy with banquets and entertainment. On that day all signs of mourning are abolished, and marriages can take place. Among other things, one can have a haircut, from which one must abstain for reasons of contrition in the other days of Omer.
arrapar shave; to get a shave (v, Monastir dialect)
arrasgada tearing accomplished with a single stroke of the hand
arrasgar tear (v)
arraskador stick for scratching the back
arraskar scratch (v)
arraskatina pruritus; very persistent itching
arrasladéar encounter by accident; coincide by chance (v, T *rastlamak*)
arrastakáño individual deprived of any moral or intellectual value, who has no merits whatsoever; who roams around the shallowest dens
arrastár drag (Port)
arrastrar drag (v)
arravdón ravage caused by a torrent or flood
arraviado angry with; confused; someone to whom everything appears strange
arraviar (se) get mad with; get angry with; annoyed by; not being in friendly terms with someone any more (Monastir dialect)
arraviar get angry with
arravyadéro unending anger
arravyar get angry
arravyatina violent bout of anger

arravyon person who gets angry easily; irascible
arrayarte ceruse (a pigment composed of white lead)
arraygádo rooted
arraygar take root
arrayyarse get angry
arrebividor someone who rescutitates, brings back to life, to health, to
    trust
arrebivimyento revival; return to life, vivaciousness, hope
arrebivir revive; bring back to life
arreboltear perturb; turn upside down
arredondear make round
arrefinar refine
arrefregar make a friction; rub against
arrefreggádo friction (n)
arrefreskar refresh
arrefulgar relax; rest (v)
arregáda rain shower; light rain
arregado someone who gives excessive credit to an extended group
arregador watering can
arregadúra watering; irrigation
arregaladór caressing; someone who cajoles, who manifests a constant
    affection; someone who lavishes presents
arregalar give presents
arregár irrigate
arreglado regular; moderate; someone who has habits of order and
    economy
arreglamyento arrangement; friendly agreement
arreglar (se) regulate one's expenses; spend with order and measure;
    put order in one's conduct; draw a program of one's life; impose
    upon oneself a rhythm for one's meals, sleep; regulate one's body
    functions
arreglar draw parallel inches on paper or cardboard; regulate; put in
    order (v)
arréglo arrangement; conclusion of an arrangement or agreement
arrekamádo embroidered
arrekavdadór clerk for collecting money; cashier
arrekavdár cash; recuperate; recover
arrekayentar heat up again what has become cold
arrekodrar remember; reminisce
arrekojer collect; gather; assemble together

arrekojido dressed; someone who is wearing his clothes; concentrated; gathered in a reduced space which keeps everything within reach

arrekojimyento concentration

arrekolmádo enriched

arrekolmar make rich

arrekuxir sew again; darn; darn up; patch up (v)

arrelumbrar lighten; illuminate

arrelumbre let it shine

arrelustrear put luster; make shine; varnish; wax (v)

arremanear agitate; revive; bring back as remembrance; bring back to light

arremangada action of pull up one's sleeves to resolutely put oneself to work; brief and vigorous effort to complete a task fast and well

arremansevádo someone who has become young again; someone who has become younger

arremar raw; maneuver a raw (v)

arrematado ostracized; destroyed

arrematar destroy; eradicate; give the stroke of grace

arrematar exterminate; annihilate

arrematare criatura I will destroy the creatures

arrematasyon total destruction; deliverance of an individual who was in trouble after the destruction of the party causing the trouble

arremedyado assisted; helped

arremendado patched up; vamped up; revamped

arremeterse put oneself back on feet; regain health; return to a satisfactory state of wealth

arremiransa resemblance

arremirante resembling; similar; something which has almost the shape of something else

arremojado dipped in water; wetted with water; revived by water; irrigated

arremojar dip in water; wet; impregnate with water

arremoshkar ferret; ferret out; rummage; search out (v)

arrempushar push violently (v)

arrenovar renovate

arrenpentidizo taking back a given promise; unilateral cancellation of agreement; refusal to abide by agreement

arrepellador sponger; someone who tries to get into a place without paying the entrance fee; someone who arranges swiftly but without dignity; to be given low-value gifts here and there

arrepensar rethink
arrepentirse give up; retract agreement; step back from an agreement;
    refuse execution of an agreement
arrepintiosse he repented (Fer Bib Gen)
arrepintir (se) repent
arrepotreador nice kind of chap who likes to enjoy life and feast all
    the time; man of happy humor
arrepotrear lead a pleasant life; act merrily; enjoy oneself; feast (v)
arrepozadiko quiet; tranquil; Kedate arrepozado Stay quiet!
    (recommendation given to an excited child)
arrepozar rest; sleep (v)
arrepudyado banished; gravely humiliated in public
arrepudyar show public disdain to someone; humiliate in front of
    others
arrescovdado reclined
arresekado dried; shrunken; wrinkled to the extreme
arresentado ordered; regulated without excess; without occupation
arresentar arrange; put in order (v)
arresentyamento arrangement; tranquillity of mind of someone who
    before was uncertain, unstable, slightly wandering, and now has
    settled in a definite job or lodging
arresevir receive
arresgatádo bought back against a (slave's) ransom
arreskaldáda remainder of fire under the ashes
arreskaldár gently heat under the ashes (v)
arreskovdades reclined
arresvalada sliding
arresvaladera place where one can slide (easily)
arresvaladero continuous series of slidings
arresvalado someone who has slided; someone who has managed to
    escape from a torture that would bring immediate death;
    metaphorically: someone who is capable of a highly loosened
    dialectic. The Turks used to condemn certain criminals to
    impaling in a public place. Sometimes a condemned individual
    could take advantage of the chaos and uproar around the place
    of execution to escape his tormentors.
arresvalar slide; eat as a glutton
arresvalarse fall in sliding; die (v)
arretornar bring back to oneself; bring back to one's senses
arretratador portraitist; photographer

arretuuerser twist (v)
arrevanador glutton
arrevánso savings
arrevantar burst; splinter; fly into pieces; stave (v)
arrevatado stolen; taken brutally
arrevatar take possession brutally; plunder (v)
arrevatarse cook a dish too fast and badly; burn before cooking,
    before letting it marinate in its juice; devour, eat as a glutton (v)
arreverter spill over
arrevés upside down
arrezikar risk (v)
arrezistado timid; bashful; someone who feels shame; someone who
    lacks assurance
arrezistarse lack of self-confidence (v)
arriba up; on top
arriftar take back; redress; correct a reading mistake,a spelling
    mistake; a linguistic mistake or a misconduct
arrijado wrinkled; rugged
arrimar rest on; push on; put his back on (v)
arripuzadu rested; tranquil (Monastir dialect)
arriva (la de) arriva the matzoh which is on top (Passover Haggadah)
arrivar arrive
arrivo arrived
arrizgatar save (v, Port *resgatar*)
arrizintar regulate (v, Monastir dialect)
arrodeamyento long and painful research; trouble when looking for a
    object which has been misplaced
arrodeante something that flows (Fer Bib Gen)
arrodear turn in circles
arrodeo turning; turn; winding of road or river
arrodiyarse kneel; squatter (v)
arrogansya arrogance
arrogante arrogant
arrogar pray (v)
arrojada whim; freak; humorous answer; wanton insult; frolic; prank
arrojador prankster; someone who praises himself and mentions large
    sums of money to draw attention upon himself; person able to
    drink a lot without losing continance
arrojatina jet of water thrown or gushed violently

arrovar steal; take by cunning or force what belongs to someone else
arrovvón someone who commits petty larceny
arróyo torrent
arroz rice
arrozal rice field
arroziko sophisticated rice dish
arrufyáda light cloud of fine droplets coming out of a vaporizer, atomizer or from the mouth
arrufyar spray; slightly wet underwear before ironing
arrujarse to be covered with wrinkles; get wrinkled
arsenal arsenal
arshin Turkish measure of length; 75 cm for terrain; two thirds of a meter for tissues and ropes
arsiz wild; insolent (T)
arsizlik impertinence; cynicism (T)
artadura satiety; fullness
artar to be full; satiated
artaron (se) they got fed well enough, they got satisfied
artche something which is "in," which is liked, which is searched for or for which there is an inclination (T *arz*)
arte art
artero the finest; the thinnest of the animals
artezaneria craftsmanship; workmanship
artezáno artisan; operative; mechanic; workman
articho artichoke; **articho alaturca** artichoke Turkish style; **articho con bitela** veal with artichoke hearts; **articho lenos fritos** fried stuffed artichokes; **articho lenos con karne** artichokes stuffed with meat
artifisyal artificial
artik! well now! come now! enough! not anymore; I cannot anymore; this is too much; this has gone beyond the limits! stop there! the measure is full! (T)
artikolista journalist; chronicler
artikolo article in a newspaper; kind of merchandise
artikular articulate
artista artist
artistiko artistic
artiyeria artillery
arto well fed; satiated (Fer Bib Gen)
artritismo arthritis

Arvanit Albanian

arvit - dizir minha y arvit evening prayer (H) recite the double prayer
that every practicing Jew pronounces in the middle of the
afternoon and at sunset to prove his rigorous piety

arvole tree

arvolear cover with trees (v)

arvolero alley of trees

arvoliko small tree

arvolina disagreeable accumulation of trees in a way which hides the
horizon and increases unpleasant humidity

aryénto inside

aryentro inside

arzoal request; petition (T *arzuhal*)

arzuhal petition; written application (T kanunn)

as asper; old Turkish coin; one third of a para (one fortieth of a
piaster; a piaster is one hundredth of a lira, the Turkish gold
pound)

asabi nervous; extra nervous (T)

asaborar savor; relish; enjoy

asada roasted

asaderia rotisserie

asaetár throw arrows

asafran saffron

asafranado cooked with saffron

asafranar cook with saffron, especially rice

asaltar assault (v)

asalto assault (n)

asana bukata beating up like plaster; the kind of beating that took
place in Turkish police stations (*alsana bukadar* take that much:
take that much beating)

asar roast; grill (v)

asarabatlanism (lit: the ten idle) group of ten idle men who for a
modest salary stand daily in a place of prayer or rabbinical
studies to make sure that there is a *minyan* (ritual quorum)
required for recitation of prayers as well as for dedication to
Holy Scriptures, or at least, for daily recitation of the one
hundred and fifty psalms. According to beliefs the world cannot
subsist unless one continues uninterruptedly the study of Holy
Scriptures; (asentarse a) asarabatlanism to definitely install oneself

in idleness; to do nothing in life; to get caught by laziness; to live
from discrete alms; to live in perpetual idleness

asararse to be in distress, anxiety

asarse (lit: to be grilled) resent; feel through oneself

asasinar assassinate

asasino assassin

asaventár inform; keep informed

asedár make thirsty; deprive of water, of drink (v)

asedyar besiege

asédyo siege (n)

asegitina feverish speed when someone is harassed

asegiyir pursue; run after someone to seize him/her

asegun like; according to

asegundar second (v)

asegundear repeat; start again; say again; accomplish a second time the
same act

asegurar assure; certify

asekar to be a first-grade pupil; read each letter separately

aselada trap; ambush

asembrado seeded

asembrar seed (v)

asemejado compared; assimilated; brought together to compare

asemejansa similarity; resemblance

asemejar resemble; find a resemblance between two persons, two
things, two events

asementar initiate; fund; establish the fundament; take the initiative to
fund something

asendedór person in charge of lighting the street-lamps; lighter (Port
asendeór)

asender lighten up

aseñorado someone who has been able to dominate; who has become
lord and master

asensor elevator

asentadera buttock

asentador buttocks

asentar (se) sit down

asér (adv) lest; must know that (conj); it is indispensable to take in
view that (to introduce an explanation, a restriction, an objection,
a contradiction) (from H *aser* misappropriation, taking away)

aserenado serene; calm (adj)
aserkar approach; come close to
asetensyado decided by destiny; written in the sky
asetensyar render a decision, a sentence, a judgment; pronounce a condemnation
asfalt asphalt
asfiksyar asphyxiate
ashar one tenth; tithe (T kanunn)
Ashem ishmeru May God have him in his protection
Ashem yishmereu (a) May God guard him/her (formula which accompanies the name of living persons held in affection and consideration)
ashikyar openly; publicly (T kanunn)
ashikyare clearly; with no reticence (T *ashikâr*)
ashirear pass over; trespass (v, T *ashirmak*, kanunn)
ashkina to the health; to the honor of; in consideration of (T *ashkina*)
ashkulsun bravo; felicitations (expression of admiration, sometimes of irony, of disapproval or disdain) (T *ashkolsun*)
ashlama grafted tree (T kanunn)
ashlama iced; frosted (T)
ashlama vaccine; graft (T *ashilamak*)
ashlik pocket money; money reserved for menial pleasures
    (T *ayyashlik*)
ashugar dowry
ashure holiday of plants and trees which is celebrated on the fifteenth of the Hebraic month of shevat, at the beginning of spring, when people splurge on all kinds of fruits and new wine (H); a kind of fruitcake
ashure wheat boiled in milk, assorted with seeds of pomegranate and all kind of broiled dried fruits (T *ashure*); mix of all sorts
asi ... asi idiomatic expression to introduce a solicitation, a request for a service, a favor (accompanied by a vow, a benediction which will be the reward of the expected favorable response to the solicitation)
asi rebel (n, T kanunn)
asi so; like this
asibiva me I swear on my life
asibiva tus pulgas! (lit) So may live your fleas! Exlamation of disbelief
asibiva tus piojos (lit) So may live your lice! Exclamation of disbelief
asigiyir pursue; harass; stimulate

44

asigurador insurer
asiguransa certification
asigurar assure; certify; insure against fee
asikomansi expression
asilik rebellion (T, kanunn)
asimentán they bring seed; they place seed; they fertilize; they carry
  seed (Fer Bib Gen)
asimetria assymetry
asímijar (se) imagine oneself; make oneself see something in a certain
  way; seem to oneself (v, Monastir dialect)
asimilar assimilate
asimilasyon assimilation; a doctrine which recommends the
  assimilation of the Jew to his environment to the detriment of his
  special characteristics
asimyente seeding
asiñálar marked with a special sign for recognition
Asiria Assyria
asiryolojia Assyriology
asistir assist
asistyente assistant
asivar aloe
asiviva tu by the life of your son, daughter, etc.
askama decision; ordinance taken and proclaimed by a rabbinical
  body (H)
askava prayer for the soul of a deceased (H)
askeado someone who is repelled with disgust
askear cause disgust
askeozo repellent; dirty; someone who feels or manifests disgust
asker soldier (T)
askerlik military service (T)
askolsun! (T) Bravo, felicitations! (expresses admiration, but it could
  be as well irony,disapproval and disdain)
askultar auscultate; medically examine
askultasyon auscultation
askyer soldier (T asker)
askyeriko (coll) young conscript; young soldier
askyerlik military service; duration of military service (T *askerlik*)
asma asthma
asnas female donkeys
asno ass

asno donkey
asnos donkeys
aso peruta aharona till the last cent; integrally (H)
asobrevyado subject to anger; irascible; irritated
asodesér come suddenly; take place; happen; arrive
asodreser cause death
asofayfa/asofafya jujube
asoflamado slightly feverish
asoflamar give a slight fever
asoládo devastated
asolambrado shady
asolapado uninhabited desert; far away from any inhabited place
asolombrado umbrageous
asolombrar give shadow; cover with shadow
asoltado relaxed
asoltador braggart; swaggerer; braggadocio; blusterer
asoltar relax
asonadero tendency to blow nose too frequently
asoplada action of blowing
asoplar blow on
asortido assorted
asosyado associated
asosyar associate (v)
asotada stroke of a whip
asotar whip (v)
asote whip (n)
asotir assort; sort (v)
asovrindado being relatives; someone who belongs to a rich powerful
    family; a numerous and important family
asovrindar cultivate family relations; maintain relations with people of
    one's parenthood; acquire a numerous and important parenthood
aspaka salary; honorarium (H)
asped religious ceremony celebrated at the anniversary of a death
aspekto aspect
asperar wait
aspro rugged; sharp; rough in taste
aspro small coin in the Ottoman Empire
aspur ruined; put in pieces (adj)
assar roast (v)
assaventér deal wisely

assituado situated; precisely located
assortimento assortment
asta until; before
asta onde unto
asufre sulfur; color of sulfur
asufreado sulfured; covered with sulfur; someone who has taken the
    color of sulfur
asufridor someone who embodies and relieves the suffering of others
asufriduos de baxo del arbol you rest under the tree
asukar kande candy sugar; crystallized sugar
asukarado with sugar on one side; separated from a bulk of sweets or
    candies, like in old times
asukarear add sugar; coat with sugar
asumar totalize
asumir assume
asunar touch; play a musical instrument (v, Monastir dialect)
asur prohibition; forbidden by religion (H)
asustar scare
asyento sit
asyertar certify
atabafar la lumbre extinguish the fire by preventing air contact
atabafo de paron silence to which one is constrained by fear or threat
atabafo suffocation
atadero tie; bond
atadijo lasso; ligation
atado someone who has made a promise, who has taken an
    engagement
atadrar delay (v); to be late
atadreser begin to dawn; go down (the sun, the day)
atadura tie; ligation
atajeado - (lavoro) atajeado assigned task
atajeado - (ya lo tenia) atajeado it was written by fatality; he was
    condemned to it by a decree of destiny; the fate had been
    decided, the dice had been thrown (said for an accident, a
    death, a big loss)
atajseado received in partaking (a task)
atakanádo ordered
atakar attack (v)
atamarales pillars
atamyento attachment

atán as much; also
atansion attention
atansyon attention
atar tie (v)
atardado delayed; late
atardamyento delaying; extreme conservatism
atavanado so crazy as to walk on the ceiling (from T *tavan* ceiling)
atavismo atavism
atejeadór distributor of tasks and foodstuff
atelyé craftsman's workshop
atemár make lose strength and courage
atemo completed; had ceased (Fer Bib Gen)
atemo de - (y) atemo de farlar con el (and) he terminated to speak
    with him (Fer Bib Gen)
atemorense achieved (Fer Bib Gen)
Atena Athens
atendeo dressed (moved) his tents (Fer Bib Gen)
Ateneo Athenian
atension attention
atentivo attentive
atenuado attenuated
aterceada of three years
atermar annihilate
atestar to be a witness
atestiguar attest (v); to be a witness to; testify
athesorar consecrate as a treasure (Ferrara Siddur)
atirar attract
atlas atlas
atléta athlete
atletismo athleticism
atmosferiko atmospheric
atmosfero atmosphere
atolontrado wounded at the forehead, at the head
atontar render stupid (by executing an automatic task which does not
    require any intellectual effort)
atontarse to become stupid
Atorá the Torah
atorgár confess; recognize one's faults and sins
atormentado tormented
atormentar torment (v)

atormentarse torment oneself

atornada return; return to life after death (for those who believe in reincarnation). It is used humorously when speaking about something that someone has not been able to realize in his/her lifetime; also said with bitter irony, to express that a lifetime dream cannot be realized.

atornar return on one's step; atornar en si come back to oneself; recover one's senses and spirits; atornar en teshuva expiate

atorsar twist (v)

atorvar frighten; scare

atrabularse look lost; lose one's head; look haggard

atraer attract

atraksyon attraction

atramuz lupine bean; lupine seed

atrás back (in time); backward

atras on the back of

atrasmano (lit: behind the hand) secretly; under the hand; without somebody suspecting; under the counter

atrazado backward; late

atrazante someone who delays progress

atrazar delay (v)

atrazarse to be late; to be delayed

atrazo something that remains owed; what should have been done and has been delayed

atrensar plait one's hair

atribuir attribute (v)

atribusyon attribution

atrisrarse to become sad

atristar sadden

atriviar dare

atrivido audacious; daring; shameless; (no so) atrivido I am not shameless

atróche atrocious (Ital)

attakado attacked; having caught tuberculosis or an infection; cloth which takes the shape of the body

atudrimyénto numbness

atudrir make numb

atuenderio excess of preparation and attire

atuendos preparations to show oneself in the best light

atufar to have an odor of mold

aturnar return; return to someone (v, Monastir dialect)
audencia audience
auergonçauan they did not feel ashamed (Fer Bib Gen)
auflado swollen
auflár puff; blast (v)
auflar swell
aumentar augment
aun all that; still more; even
aun él está adelante he is still in front
aún still
aunque even if
Australia Australia
Austriako Austrian
Austriya Austria
auto car; automobile
autodeteminasyón self-determination
automobil automobile
autór author
autoridad authority
autoritaryo authoritarian
autúño autumn
av April. (H) Ninth month of the Jewish calendar; the first days of av
    are days of mourning and also a period in which accidents are
    frequent
ava bean
avagar slow
avagareza slowness
avagariko very slow
avagarozo someone who goes without haste
avagazi lighting gas; natural gas (T *havagazi*)
avait fee, revenue (T kanunn)
avaliado valorized; put in value; presented in its best aspect
avaliar put in value; make it stand; put in relief (v)
avalorar valorize; present a thing in such a way that its full value
    stands out
avanado confused; like half asleep; (esta) avanado someone who is
    talking senseless; senile
avanamyénto dementia; madness
avansado advanced
avansador someone who makes savings

avansar advance; move forward; progress (v)
avansar save; economize
avantadji someone who dips in the dish of somebody else; who tries to
    gain admission without paying the entrance fee
avantajar give preference to, favor (v)
avantajozo advantageous
avantar praise; laud (v)
avante - (travar) avante live at the expense of someone else; abuse of
    the kindness and naiveness of others; live at their expense without
    paying
avaria damage a ship or its cargo
avaro stingy
avaya (adv) in the air (T *havaya*)
avaynár hem (v)
avdala ceremony; prayer which marks the end of Sabbath and the
    beginning of a new week. It is celebrated on Saturday, after the
    apparition of the first star, when the lamps are lit for the blessing
    of a vegetable with a pleasant smell (lemon, coffee). All family
    members contemplate the reflection of light on the nails.
    According to popular belief, the absence of such reflection is a
    bad omen, a forewarning of death.
ave flying creature; bird
avedredear verify
avél mourning; one-week mourning which is observed after the death
    of a close relative
avena oat
avenenar poison (v)
avenimyento accord; conciliation; reconciliation
avenir future; future time (F)
avenivle conciliatory; accommodating; someone who has a good char-
    acter
aventador fan
aventurado audacious; hardy
aventurarse adventure oneself; expose oneself; hazard oneself; take a
    risk
aventurero adventurer; someone who does adventurous business;
    sharper; swindler
aver air; climate (Monastir dialect)
averdadear control (v); verify the facts of a story, of an affirmation
averé at a slant; across; crookedly

averguensar (se) to be ashamed; (me) averguenso I feel ashamed
averiguar verify; inquire; research the truth
avezindar neighbor (v); frequent the neighbors; to have contact with
    the neighbors
aviasyon aviation
avis so
avismo abyss
avizar give notice; inform
avizo notice (n); posted notice; poster
avla talk (n)
avladero too much talk
avlador speaker; conference speaker
avlar speak; talk
avlastina much talk
avlastina muncha too much empty talk
avóda work; task
Avodà Zarà idolater; is said about an act of dissipation; abuse which
    is condemned by religion as well as common sense
avokado/avokato lawyer
avokateria profession of lawyer
avokato lawyer
Avraám/Avrám Abraham
Avramatchi/Avramucho affectionate or honorary form of the name
    Avram
avrigo refuge; shelter
avril April
avrir open (v)
avtajá hope; confidence (H)
avtajali optimistic; someone who does not lose hope or courage; who
    has confidence in the future
avyerdo open (adj)
avyertamento openly; in the eyes and knowledge of all
avyertura opening; crack in the wall
avyon airplane
ay ay ay alas! it is desperate!
ay ay! scream of deception and pain
ay there is
aya in children's language, cry of satisfaction professed in the intention
    to provoke the feeling of envy or anger in another child
aya there

aya, yo tengo vestido nuevo, tu no aya! I have new clothes, and you don't.

ayaktash (lit: foot companion) companion; comrade (T *ayaktash*)

ayar standard of purity (T); title of money, jewelry, gold and silver objects

ayaru May (Bab)

ayde (interj) let us go; hurry up; come on; move on (T *haydi*)

aydear push (an animal—a donkey or a horse); push by picking with a pointed object (T *haydamak*)

ayegamyento approach (n)

ayegar reach to

ayegava - (mos) ayegava had brought (us) (Passover Haggadah)

ayéges - (mos) ayéges mayest thou bring us to enjoy in peace (Passover Haggadah)

ayegô - (mos) ayegô brought us to the enjoyment of (Passover Haggadah)

ayego - (mos) ayego He let us reach; we were bestown

ayego approach; come close; come within reach

ayego arrived; reached (Fer Bib Gen)

ayeguaran will reach to

ayer yesterday

ayi there

Ayifto Egypt

ayin sixteenth letter of the Hebrew alphabet (numerical value: 70).

ayinda still

Ayissiano Egyptian

Ayisyano Egyptian

Ayiteken baolam Is it, God, possible? It is unbelievable; I cannot believe it; It is entirely strange.

aylak doing nothing; idle (T)

aylik monthly pay (T)

aynara evil eye (H *ayin ara*)

ayno it means; almost; approximately

ayom arad olam let us make abstraction of everything; let us say that nothing has happened; we shall not take any account of the past; it is today that the world is born (H, taken from a Kippur prayer)

ayrada appearance; air; aspect; resemblance

ayre air; emptiness; (a) ayre (del dia) to the wind of the day

ayreasyon aeration

ayregina winds that blow non-stop; permanent wind

ayregozo ventilated
ayres winds
ayshe green bean
ayuda help
ayudante helper; assistant
ayudar help (v)
ayunar fast (v)
ayuno fast (n)
ayuntaron (se) they met (joined) each other
az in small amounts; in a little amount; insufficient (T)
áza cup holder
azar hazard; adventure
azardar hazard; risk (v)
azardózo hazardous
azardu - (pur) azardu by chance; by coincidence; incidentally
    (Monastir dialect)
azat free (adj and adv); with no restraint (T azat); (deshar) azat let
    free; let without restrain; let loose
azerse - (su pecado se) aze your sin has become very heavy
azeite oil (often olive oil)
azeitunas olives
azer do; make
azer estàr make stay; assign a seat
azero steel
azete ermosa make oneself beautiful
azeytadura act of covering with a layer of oil; oiling
azeytar oil (v)
azeyte de moruna cod liver oil
azeyte de rizino castor oil
azéyte oil (n); freirse en su azeyte fry in its own oil (fry meat or fish
    without addition of any fat)
azeytero oil merchant
azeytozo impregnated with oil
azeytuna olive
azeytunero olive tree; olive merchant
azia - (se) azia pagar he made something paid to him; he required the
    payment to himself
azia justicia had executed judgment (from the Passover Haggadah)
aziendas wealth
azlaha prosperity; success; happiness; chance (H)

azneria group of donkeys; figuratively: stupidity; imbecility; words deprived of common sense

aznesko language of a donkey

azniko small donkey; (el) **azniko del sinyor haham** (lit: the donkey of the lord rabbi) this is said in sarcasm against the chiefs, the powerful who multiply the interdictions and the taboos for the common people, while for themselves everything is permitted)

azno donkey; figuratively: stupid; idiot; (un) **azno** emphatically: a completely incompetent person

azo ace in card and dice games

azógre mercury

azpan cynical; rude; insolent; shameless

azúl blue; dark blue; indigo

azulear make blue; dye in blue

azyenda fortune; riches

azytunal olive grove

azzeite oil

B

baak anesh someone in favor of whom God accomplishes miracles; recipient of miracles (H)

baal adavár suitor; litigant; demander of justice (H)

baal aftaja optimist (H)

baal din litigant; someone who is part of a lawsuit (H)

baal jalamot someone who often has dreams in which the future is announced to him; someone who has premonitions; fortuneteller who knows how to interpret dreams, who has the key to dreams (H)

baal teshuva repentant sinner; penitent (H)

baavonót arabim (adv) having caused many sins (said so as a resignating acceptance of misfortune and mishap (H)

baba duck; cry of the goose; (ya lo saven las) **babas del kortijo** even the geese of the courtyard know it; Pagliacio's secret; a secret everyone knows

baba father (T)

bábachko robust; well-built; solid; firm; in good health; in excellent form

babadján feeling well despite old age: joyful; full of life (T *babacan*)

babarúto imaginative person to scare misbehaving children (derived
from *pan barato* cheap bread, the cry of the baker who, all black-
ened by the smoke of his oven, walks down the street to sell his
bread)
babayamin advanced in age
babayit robust; in excellent health (T *babayigit, babaghit*)
babéka de mar seagull
Babilóna Babylon
bábo Macedonian peasant advanced in age
babóta large prune; tumor; excrescence; induration on the forehead,
the head, the arm
bábu father (in the language of children and adolescents)
babúla - (a la) babúla lightly; devilishly, deucedly bad
bacál grocer
bachikón three of the same cards in a card game; group of three
persons baring resemblance between themselves; derisively, a trio
of liars
badana wall painting with lime (T); proceed to a superficial repair in
the most visible parts; paintings which create an illusion to fool
the eye; hasty maquillage; make-up
badéla portable bidet
baderear bother
badja chimney; opening for the escape of smoke; dormer; dormer-
window; garret-window (T *baca*)
badjanak brother-in-law (T *bacanak*)
badkár examine in depth (H)
badkol echo; divine voice; order coming from the sky (H)
badyavá gratis; gratuitously; in vain, without result (T *bedava*)
bafo breath (Port)
baforada puff (n); whiff; hot whiff bringing generally an unpleasant
odor .
bagaje luggage
bagaláu cod
baganeár condescend with a disdainful attitude; display haughtiness;
accept with a faint heart (from Turkish *begenmek, beghenmek* to
like)
bagatella trinket; trifle thing
Bagdad Baghdad
Bagdadi (El) surname of Yehezkiel Gabay, famous Jewish banker at
the time of Sultan Mahmud II. He became the favorite of Haled

Pasha, Vali (Governor) of Baghdad, after helping him in a
successful plot to eliminate Haled's rival for the governorship.
While his power base was in Baghdad (which explains his
surname) next to Haled, surprisingly he gained considerable influence at the Seraglio in Istanbul, being at one time a maker and
unmaker of even vizirates. He used to parade on horseback in
Istanbul exhibiting a sword with his name incrustated with letters
in Hebrew. He lost all influence after the disgrace of his protector
Haled Pasha. He was arrested, first locked in a dungeon in Ana-
tolia, finally strangled with the customary horsehair knot
tightened on his throat and subsequently decapitated. All his
property was first confiscated; but when his son-in-law Shemtov
who was a British citizen placed a claim supported by English
authorities, part of the property was returned to the family. His
similarly named grandson was an author and a journalist at the
Sephardic journal Journal Israelite, and he translated the
Ottoman Penal Code into Ladino ("Kanun Name de Penas"). He
also played a significant role as a Jewish notable during the visits
to Istanbul of Empress Eugenie, the wife of Napoleon III of
France and Emperor Franz-Joseph of Austria. Eugenie who was a
Spaniard was pleasantly surprised to find a Spanish-speaking
community in Istanbul.

bagdadi light construction made of wood and plaster lathes; lattice
bagshaván gardener (from Turkish bahçivan)
bahshish, bakshish tip (n) (T *bakshish)*
bailador dancer
bajotirké beginning of the second verse in the Lamentations of
     Jeremiah: "She was crying with hot tears;" whiner; squinny
bajtina chance (T *baht)*
bajúr adolescent; young; unmarried man (H *bahur)*
bakal grocer
bakalum (interj) we shall see! (can imply doubt, hesitation, threat,
     encouragement) (T *bakalim)*
bakir copper; copper money (of little value) (T)
baklava pastry filled with pistachios, or walnuts and honey, flavored
     with cinnamon (T); **baklava di almendra** baklava with almonds
     (in this variant of the Middle Eastern baklava, almonds replace
     the walnuts or pistachios)
bakrach bucket of copper; copper pitcher; small caldron
bala ball; bale; package; **bala de papeles** paper ball

balabay master of the house; father of the family (H)
balabaya homemaker; mistress of the house; mother of the family
balabusha mistress of the house who is careless
balabústro unscrupulous father and mother who are failing in their duties
balansa balance (n)
balansar balance; rock the child; rock the cradle
balasto ballast
baldadúra abrogation
baldajón gratis (adv); paying no charge; komer de baldajon eat without paying
baldakino baldaquin
baldar abolish
balderan - no se balderan they will not cease
baldes gratis; gratuitously; (de) baldes gratis
baldez - en baldez in vain
baldo - a mi firmamiento baldo he has violated (my alliance) (Fer Bib Gen)
balebatim homeowners
balena fin of the whale
balena metal rod having the same use as the fin of the whale; (las) balenas del korsé whale fins used as support for women's corsets; (las) balenas del solombrero whale fins or metal rods forming the rays of the umbrella
balena whale
balgam sputum (T)
balgamoni decalcomania the art or process of transferring images or designs from specially prepared paper to metal, wood or grass
balgamún caramel; candy aromatized with bergamot (fruit of small citrus tree with rind that yields a fragrant oil; the fruit is an intermediate between orange and citrus)
balkone balcony
balo bale
balón balloon; kite
balsa paddle (n)
bálsamo balsam
balta ax
baltadji woodcutter; woodsman
bambarúto boogeyman who is supposed to roam the street at night to punish misbehaving children (see *babarúto*)

bambashka strange; unusual; who does not resemble anyone or
   anything (T *bambashka*)
bambula scarf; silk handkerchief; neck-handkerchief
bamia okra (Turkish *bamya*); **bamya hada con domates** okra in
   tomato sauce
banabak (lit: look at my face) rough and rude person (T)
banámelolololó vain words by which it is attempted to lure someone
banana banana
bañar take a bath
banco bench
band tape
banda band; reunion
bandaje bandage (F)
bandido bandit
bandiera flag
bañéro bathtub
banios hot thermal springs
banka bank
banketa stool
banketo banquet
banko bench
banquiero treasurer
banyo/banyu bath
bar aroma; scent; perfume (T *bahar*)
bar bar; stand where drinks are served
Bar Yojáy half-holiday celebrated on the thirty-third day of Omer
   which interrupts the 49 days between Passover and Pentecost;
   decorating a place for the celebration of a party
bára swamp; red-light district (in Salonica the red light district was
   located in the northern part of the city which was infested by
   swamps)
baraber together; in concert; in company (T *beraber*)
baraja quarrel (n)
baraka barracks
baratero someone who sells cheap; opposite of carero
barato cheap
baratura cheap quality
barbaria barbarism
barbút dangerous game of dice in which the stakes are high and one
   risks to make great losses

barbuzáen rude; clumsy
baréto beret; cap
bari at least (T)
barir sweep with a broom
barka rawboat
barkero ferryman
barmimam alas; unhappily; by misfortune (H)
barmitzva bar mitzvah (ceremony of religious initiation which is cele-
    brated when the male child has reached thirteen years and is con-
    sidered responsible for his actions)
barometro barometer
barragan powerful
barragan hero (H)
barraganes powerful men
barragania heroism
barragania muscular strength; indomitable courage combined with
    physical strength
barredéro manic behavior which consists in needlessly sweeping the
    floor all the time
barrer sweep the floor
barrida a very thorough sweeping of the floor
barridika swift sweeping of the floor with a broom
barril barrel
barril very fat person
barriléro barrel maker
barro mortar; clay; bitumen
barruga wart
barrugita small wart
barsak intestine (T)
baruez ram
baruh a shem may God be blessed
baruh aba welcome
Baruh dayan aemed formula of condolence rendered in front of a
    deceased (Blessed be the Judge of Truth, Blessed be the One Who
    Renders Sentences of Truth)
barút explosive (from T barut gunpowder, cannon powder)
barva beard
barvés individual with a beard having rare, long hair
barvéze ram

barviáácho double chin
barvika short beard
barvúdo bearded; slang: twenty franc gold coin bearing the profile of
   Napoleon III (who had a typical beard)
baryón turbulent and noisy individual
bás bet (n, T *bahis*)
basáar vadám (lit: flesh and blood) human being made of flesh and
   blood and therefore accessible to human weaknesses, temptations
   and envies (H)
basaménto basement; foundation
basar - (k'es el) basar vadam! how little counts the human being! (told
   each time the weakness, the powerlessness of man against death
   and the forces of the nature becomes obvious)
basár meat (H)
basbayá (adv) quite simply! quite obviously! (T *basbayaghi*)
baseár attack by surprise; search the pockets of someone; conduct
   searches in an apartment, an office, a store to find the valuables
   and grab them; police raid and search (v, T *basmak*)
baséter secretly; under the mantle; discretely
bash ladrón chief thief
bash mentirozo chief liar
bash someone with superior skills in a certain field (T)
basharisi headache (T *bashagrisi, bashaghrisi*)
bashéa lowliness; vile character; villainy
bashetiko abortive child; homunculus
bashiboósh rough, uneducated individual (T *bashibosh*)
bashibuzúk irregular soldier (in opposition to the Janissaries who con-
   stituted the regular military corps until their gunning down by
   Sultan Mahmud II because they had become overtly rebellious)
   (*bashibozuk*)
bashiko short-bodied
basho low; (fig) vulgar
bashúra state of what is low; little elevated
bashustune (lit: over the head) (T *bashüstüne*); equivalent of the
   Spanish "a sus ordenes," the French "à vos ordres," or the
   English "at your orders," meaning that a request will be done
basin chamber pot
basina circular metal container with low edges used for laundry
baskeár to have heat flashes

báskula swing (n)
basma kind of linen with printed designs used for simple dresses, children's clothes and curtains (T)
básta enough! that is enough
bastádro bastard
bastánte enough; sufficient
bastár suffice; to be enough
bastereár press; press the wool of mattresses; admonish; address strong reproaches (v) (T *bastirmak*)
baston cane; also colloquially: long French bread
bastonáda cane strokes
baták disorganized; unreliable individual; swindler (T)
batakaná quagmire; mire; slough; muddy place; fraudulent, dirty business; bad district of a town (T *batakhane*)
batakchi someone who does not pay his debts; swindler (T *batakçi*)
batal - (asentarse) batal settle in idleness; do nothing
batál idle; without work; useless; invalid
batálya battle
batán thistle head; pressing under the feet; trampling
baté enayim eyeglasses (H, ironically used)
bater hit; knock (v)
batereaár cause sinking (v, T *batirmak*)
batidos heart beats; palpitations
batir beat (Port)
batiriko grouchy; moody (coll)
baúl small chest
bauleria workshop where small chests are made
bautizar circumcise; baptize; convert
bava foam at the mouth
bavadór piece of cloth placed over the chest of babies to protect the mouth from dribbles
bavajadas stupidities
bavajador someone who tells empty, meaningless stories
Bavél Babylon
bavón someone who talks but says nothing; says stupid words; makes fallacious promises; makes empty threats
bavóza slug; caterpillar
bavul trunk (T)
baxo - (de) baxo down; below

bayaleár pass out because of excess heat or lack of air (T *bayilmak*)
bayát stale; rancid (T)
baylacho dancer on a rope
bayladéra female dancer; very thin slice of bread (said ironically)
baylar dance (v)
bayle dance (n)
bazár base (v)
bazar market (T *pazar*)
bazarlik bargaining (T *Pazarlik*)
baziryán merchant (T *bazirgân*)
beáta beatitude; felicity
beáto happy
bebé baby
bebiendo drinking (Moroccan Sephardic ballad)
bed din rabbinical court (H)
bedajayim (lit: house of the living) cemetery (H *beth ahayim*)
bedakavód restroom (H)
bedakavod - (es un) bedakavod trashy man
bedakise - (boka de) bedakise rude person who is always ready to use
      trashy language
bedamikdash Temple of Jerusalem (H)
bedél tax in the Ottoman Empire paid to avoid military
      service (T)
bediká ritual examination of the beast before slaughter (H)
bedjereár succeed; overcome a difficulty (T *becermek*)
beduino Bedouin
beemá animal; beast (H)
befá good faith (T *vefa*)
behema domestic animal; beast
behor oldest son
beit ahayim (lit: house of health) hospital (H)
bejerear succeed (from T *becermek* to be able of)
bekaiyá arrears of a debt
bekar bachelor (T *bekâr*)
bekar odalari inn where rooms are let to provincialists who come to
      town for work (T kanunn)
bekdji night guard (T *bekçi*)
bekei drunkard; alcoholic (n, T)
bekleár guard; watch; exert surveillance (T *beklemek*)

bektchi guard; night guard (T *bekçi*); traditionally the night guard of a
    quarter in Istanbul was paid door by door by the residents of the
    quarter
bekyár bachelor (T *bekâr*)
bekyarlik celibate
bela calamity; troublesome person; pain in the neck (T); bela de los
    sielos calamity of the skies; misfortune from the skies; bela en la
    kavesa calamity (on the head)
belediye municipality (T)
bemazál tov (interj) let it be a propitious sign, a propitious event! let it
    be favorable! (felicitation at the birth of a girl)
bembriyo quince
ben ammi Ammon son of the Ammonite people
benadam (lit: son of a man) gentleman; mensch (H)
benadamlik being gentlemanlike (word is a combination of H
    benadam and the T ending *-lik* for nouns)
benayim raiti I have seen with my own eyes; I am an eyewitness (H)
bendigar bless (v)
bendision blessing
benditcho blessed
berahà blessing
berát patent; official authorization; document by which the Ottoman
    government acknowledged to residents of the Empire the privilege
    of a foreign consular protection and the prerogatives of the capit-
    ulations; impertinent arrogance of someone who has the certitude
    of being protected if circumstances call for a high power (T *berat*)
berbánte individual capable of committing all kinds of mischief
berbeliko little nightingale (T *bülbül*)
berber barber (T)
berbil nightingale (T *bülbül*)
Bercerano, Rav Hayim Moshe (1850–1931), Grand-Rabbi of Turkey
    from 1920 to 1931, befriended by Kemal Atatürk. A superiorly
    cultivated scholar, he knew Mustafa Kemal (Atatürk) from the
    time before World War I, when as a young Turkish officer
    Mustafa Kemal was invited to dine with the Grand-Rabbi. The ·
    friendship continued over the years when Atatürk became
    president. In later years, when the Grand-Rabbi became ill, it is
    reported by the historian Avraham Galante that Atatürk sent his
    yaver (assistant) to inquire about Becerano's condition and
    brought him a gift from the President.

berenjena eggplant
berit milá circumcision
beshlik old Ottoman copper coin worth ten piasters T *beshlik*)
besim eggs; testicles (H)
beso kiss (n)
béstya animal
betakiseé restroom (H)
betchi parasi night guard fee paid by each household in the quarter
Beth Amikdach Temple en tiempo que el Beith Amikdash firme during
    the existence of the Temple of Jerusalem (from Passover Haggadah)
beuio del vino he drank of the wine
bey lord; gentleman
beyefendi honorable gentleman; monsignor
beylik title of a Bey, a Turkish lord
bezadura de mano (lit: hand kissing) present that the relatives give to
    the bride when she visits them for the first time; kissing the hand
    of a person who gives a gift as a sign of respect and thankfulness;
    greeting addressed to a person who has not been seen for a long
    time (can be used also ironically for an unfriendly or even aggres-
    sive behavior instead of the expected friendship and affection)
bezadura kissing with the lips
bezar kiss (v)
bezbe bee (Monastir dialect)
bezerra heifer
bezo kiss (n)
biba turkey; **biba con kol agra** sweet and sour turkey with rice; **biba
    con kol dulse** turkey drumsticks and cabbage
biblioteka library
bic bull
Bicerano, Salamon. Contemporary Sephardic businessman, author and
    poet living in Istanbul. Laureate of Judeo-Spanish poetry, and
    member of the editorial board of *Shalom*, the Judeo-Spanish
    weekly published in Istanbul.
bicimsiz someone who acts pointlessly and strangely (from T *bicim*
    shape and *bicimsiz* shapeless)
bicu teat (Port *bico*)
bien good
bienvenido welcome
bijirear succeed
bilbil nightingale (from T *bülbül*)

bilgüzar probably derived from (T *güzar*, kanunn)
bilieto ticket
bilmejeke riddle (from T *bilmece*)
bilyon billion
bimuelo sort of sweet pattie
binadán human
binbriyo quince
binek saddle beast (T kanunn)
birit circumcised penis
birra rage
birra de Kohen rage of Kohen (in the Golden Horn Jewish district in Istanbul, Kohens were reputed to have a bad temper)
biscocho biscuit
biscocho de franzelera slightly anise-flavored toast
biskuchiku cookie
bitire(y)e finish (v, T *bitirmek*, kanunn)
bitirear finish (v, from *bitirmek*); achieve
bitpazar (lit: lice market) flea market (T)
biua alive (fem)
biuio lived
biuir live (v, Ferrara Siddur)
biuira will live (Fer Bib Gen)
biuo living (Ferrara Siddur)
bivda widow
bivdo widower
bivientes alive; living (pl, Salonica Siddur)
bivier drink (v); (nos) **bivientes** we drink; (se) **bivió** drank
bivir drink (v)
bizbon bee sting
bizelia green pea (T)
bjen good
blanko white
blóko block; street
blu blue (Monastir dialect)
boda wedding
bodear ruin; spoil (from T *bozmak*)
bodre border; edge
bohcha bundle of old clothes
bojor oldest son; oldest male child in a family

boka mouth; **boka por ermozura** (lit: mouth for beauty) person who
   speaks very little
bokal bottle; pitcher
bol bol very abundant (T)
bolando - (el se estaria) bolando he would be flying
bolante flying
bolar fly (v)
bolo (se) he flew
bolsa de oro bag of gold
bolsa purse
boltar return (v)
bonansa catch (n)
bonatchón of excessive goodness by simplicity of mind
boneka cap
booz ice (from T *buz*)
borá cold and violent northern wind
borása borax
bordélo brothel (It *bordello*)
bordo - (suvir a bordo) go on board the ship
bórdo side; flank of a ship; ship (n)
bordúra edge; contour lines or adornment of a carpet, bed, sidewalk
   painting, etc.
boreka turnover (food)
borekita small turnover or *boreka*
boréo corporation; syndicate; trust; cartel
boron old-fashioned cabinet; safe deposit; rear end
borózo marked by hot temper and easily provoked anger
borrachéz drunkenness
borracho drunkard (n); drunk; in the state of drunkenness
borráska short lasting strong storm; thunderstorm
borréka sort of puff pastry stuffed with cheese, meat, spinach and
   pumpkin
borrekíta small, puff pastry prepared in different ways and most often
   made with a stuffing of walnuts, honeyed almonds, sugar and
   cinnamon
borríko small donkey
borrón commercial record book; book of first records which includes
   sales, purchases and the day's operations
bórsa stock market

bos voice
boshbogaz someone who speaks nonsense (lit: from T empty neck)
boshnák Bosnian; very stubborn; unreasonable person
bósko plantation of trees; wood; small forest
bostejadór someone who yawns
bostejár yawn (v)
bostíjo yawning
bót whim; freak; sally; rudeness
bota - echár una bota, echar botes say insuitable things, allow oneself
    to go into wanton insult, frolic, pranks, language
bóta barrel
bota boot
botcha bottle
botcha de kura bottle of medicine
botika shop
bovankyón simple; candid; innocent (affectionate name for a kind
    person who, believing in the good faith of others, gets derided
    easily)
bovarrón same meaning as *bovankyón*
boveando - (estar boveando) do stupid things
boveár tell or make stupidities (s)
bovedad stupidity
bovo idiot; stupid person (n); stupid (adj)
boy size
bóya color; painting; make-up; meterse boya put on make-up
boyadeádo colored; painted
boyadeadór outdoor painter; wall painter
boyadeadúra action of painting, laying several layers of paint on a
    wall or furniture
boyadear paint (v, from T *boyamak*)
boyadji painter; shoe polisher (T)
boykót boycott (n)
boykotáje boycotting
boykotár boycott (v)
boylí tall; of beautiful stature (T *boylu*)
boyo brioche; sweet roll made of flour, sugar, olive oil and black
    pepper
boz voice
boza Turkish alcoholic drink made of fermented millet
bozadji vendor of *boza*

bozarrún thick; deep; unattractive voice
bozdear la fiaka (lit: spoil the ostentation) mock someone who is
    showing off
bozdear ruin; spoil (v, T *bozmak*)
boze voice
bozeado - guevo bozeado rotten egg
bozeádo destroyed; deteriorated; spoiled; decomposed; corrupted;
    deranged; indisposed; slightly sick
bozeadúra derangement; deregulation
bozear ruin; spoil (from T *bozmak*)
bozéo indisposition; upset stomach; diarrhea
bozúk destroyed; deranged; deregulated (T)
bozzezika very feeble, weak voice
bracheta - (tomerse a la) bracheta hold each other with intertwined
    arms; kaminar a la braceta walk with intertwined arms
brachéta - a la brachéta arm in arm (Ital *a braccetto*)
brága breeches; drawers; bragas de tabana puffing drawers in rough
    drape worn by men of low class; bragas de tarabulu breeches
    made in Tripoli drape; bragas con chikur breeches which were
    tied with a belt instead of being held by a button or an elastic
    string; person with a backward attitude; no tener ni bragas (lit:
    having no drawers) very poor person; no se save atar las bragas
    person without experience; incapable individual; se le estan
    kayendo las bragas he is losing his drawers
bragali (suffix) person who wears puffed drawers as in former times;
    individual of low descent (T)
bragil in rags; badly dressed; disheveled
bragita flap of pants; dainda va kon la bragita he is still dressed in the
    fashion of low-class people; he does not decide to conform
    himself to the modern style (although he has become rich)
bragón individual of low descent
brameár bellow; roar; to be carried away by anger; manifest one's
    anger or indignation by violent words and threats (v)
brasáda arms' full
brasso arm
bravo (interj) very good; bravo
brávo valiant; brave; honest; loyal
bravúra bravery; heroic action
bráza ember; ardent coal
brazéro brazier

brazika small piece of ember; **las brazikas** old womens' remedy against psychic troubles and obsessions caused by bad spirits. A metal plate containing three pieces of ember is rotated on top of the patient's head, while magic formulas are pronounced to attract good spirits which chase the bad spirits; then the embers are thrown into water. This whistling sound indicates that the bad spirits are leaving.

brazináda sparkling fire

brazo arm

brazón subterfuge; idle talk

brazonéro person who talks without thinking, makes fallacious promises and utters ridiculous threats

bre Now then! Hi you! (exclamation expressing indignation). It could be also used sometimes in admiration (T). Barbarossa's sailors would use it often to address people around; must have been used a lot also by Janissaries because the expression resounds so vehemently. Sultans must have been using it also when they get angry to their entourage

brélan (in certain card games) three cards of the same value; three aces; three jacks

brelók pendant (of watch, necklace, etc.)

brerekyét abundance; fecundity (T *bereket*)

breuedad brevity (Ferrara Siddur)

breváje drink (n)

bréve/en breve (prep) in summary

brézba buzzed; ignorant and stupid individual

bridj card game; bridge

brigáda brigade

brigánte brigand (Ital)

brigante brigand; bandit

bríl gold thread; glittering thread

brilánte brilliant; multifaceted diamond

brindár make a toast to the health of a person or the success of an enterprise

brindis toast; action of toasting

brio - (estar con) brio to be self-sufficient; ostentatiously display one's riches, power, beauty; **kaer el brio** lose somebody's favor; lose one's arrogance; look downcast; **abashar el brio** lose arrogance and haughtiness

brio arrogance; haughty attitude; boasting; bragging
briskéro peach tree
brisko inn
brisko peach
briyar shine; to be resplendent
briyando komo el sol shining like the sun
briyánte brilliant; resplendescent; multifaceted diamond
briyantína perfumed oil used to style hair and make it shiny
brizóla cutlet (T *pirzola*)
bróce brooch; jewel with a large pin
brodár embroider
brokádo brocade; vestido kargado de oro y de brokado richly
    decorated cloth adorned with gold and brocade
brónda nougat made with all sorts of sweets boiled in honey and
    sesame and then cut into lozenges
bronzádo bronzed
brónzo bronze; brass
bronzo - (komerla de) bronzo let oneself be derided in a gross manner
broshúra brochure; pamphlet
brumózo cloudy
brúna young girl; dark-haired woman; last moments of twilight before
    the fall of the night
brunácho brownish
brúno brown hair; dark hair
brúsha witch; old witch
bruskár act in a brisk way
brúsko brisk (adj)
brutál brutal
brutalidád brutality
brutalizár brutalize (v)
brúto ugly (It *brutto*)
brúya word used in the expression bruya bruya la kastaúa: bruya
    bruya la kastaña! a la bruya cry of the chestnut vendor who
    roasts or boils his chestnuts at the street corner, fig for: swiftly
    seize a good opportunity
bruyón rough first draft of letter, contract, dissertation etc.; (echar,
    meter en) bruyon rapidly note a commercial operation in the cur-
    rent register, jot down phrases and ideas
buchicha pouch; swimming pad (Port *bochicha* cheek)

buchúk twin (from T *buçuk* half)
buchukchulukes - (estar metido en) buchukchulukes to be engaged in
     insignificant things, waste one's time with trifles
buchukchulúkes stupidity; childishness; trifles (T *buçuk*)
budalá crazy (T)
buélta turn; return (n); (una) buélta de yave a turn of the key; (en una)
     buelta de mano in one turn of the hand; (a la) buelta to the con-
     trary
bueltezika - (dar una) bueltezika make a short round, a small walk
bueltezíka short walk
buen good (Moroccan Sephardic ballad)
buen senso good sense
buenácho (adj) of excessive goodness because simple-minded
buendad goodness
bueneziko a little good; a little bit good
bueniko not so bad; good enough
buenissimo excellent; entirely good (It *buonissimo*)
buenivle innocent; candid; simple-minded
bueno good
buenos favors; grandes buenos big favors
buey beef
bueyeziko small beef
búfalo buffalo
búfano buffalo; ox; venir kon araba de bufano (lit: arrive with a
     carriage of oxen) arrive very late
bufé buffet (furniture); buffet; railroad station restaurant; restaurant in
     a casino; feast; reception
bufedji buffet holder in a café or restaurant
bufetûn - (echar a bufeton) slap on the face; physical aggression
bufón buffoon
bufonáda buffoonery
bufonería buffoonery
bugrán gummed strong cloth placed between fabric and lining
buirum welcome
buják lost corner; lifeless, boring place (T *bucak*)
bujéto budget
bukéto bouquet
buketyéra flower shop
buklé hair clip; buckle; metal ring with cross-bar carrying one or more
     buckle tongues

bula - (la) bula spouse, my spouse (popular)

Bula Klara popular person who did not chew her words and squarely told everyone the full truth, fig for: matron with lucid mind who bluntly tells the truth, even to powerful people; (todo se la dize) **Bula Klara** he does not hide anything; he tells it to everybody

Bula Oro ke se le dize todo person incapable of keeping a secret

Bula Sete (kita y mete) said of a person who moves relentlessly, changes the places of objects, brings disorder and confusion where ever he goes; a blundered, a disorderly person who does not have any method of work and whose business is messy

búla title for a woman of a certain age

bulama very sweet paste made of raisins

bulanayar feel nauseous

bulandereádo disturbed; nauseous

bulandereár make turbid by agitating water, wine or oil (v, T *bulandirmak*); cause trouble, anxiety, awaken suspicion, upset (v)

bulanear nauseate to become turbid by agitation; cause trouble, anxiety (from T *bulanmak*)

bulanik - (syelo) bulanik cloudy, threatening sky

bulaník thick; turbid; opaque (T); (vino) bulanik opaque wine

buléma round, stuffed fritter; esta entero una bulema he is plump, rebounding of fat

bulevár boulevard

bulgarésko Bulgarian

búlgaro Bulgarian

bulísa, bulisú an alternative form of *bula* wife, spouse

bulisú - (kayades) bulisú attention! you are making a blunder; you are putting your feet in the dish, fig: a warning to be silent

bulluk gathering of crowd; (military) company (T *bölük*)

bulma - (se l'enklavó) bulma he has been the victim of a gross fraud; he is trapped in a business in which he will get cooked

bulmá deception; fraud which causes great loss

búlma furuncle; tumescence

bulmá shape as a spiral (v, T *burmak, burulmak*); screw, nail with screw

bulmalí (adj) construction or furniture held by screws

bultéro - (fazer un) bultéro poorly, sloppily tied large package; pack something by throwing things in a hodgepodge and tie it sloppily

bultero small lump

bultero - (fazerse un) bultero bundle up oneself

bulto - (fazer) bulto present something considerable; give the impression of something voluminous; (kosta un) bulto de moneda, de oro this costs a fortune

bulto - (no tyene) bulto it is too small

búlto lump; volume; something that occupies space; body, or object with poorly distinguishable contours; indistinct appearance or face

bultózo voluminous

búm onomatopoeia for a sound made by a falling large object or person

búmba large glass marble for children's game

bumuelo crêpe; fritters; Passover pastry (crêpe made of mashed unleavened bread, butter, beaten eggs and sugar fried in a pan and eaten with honey)

burakáda piercing stroke to make a hole

burakadéro tendency to perforate, to make a hole; persistent, indiscret questioning; minutious and stubborn interrogation

burakado es poko (malediction) if he is pierced it is too little; may he be pierced by the stroke of a dagger, fig for: being pierced by the strokes of a dagger is not enough punishment for the mischief he has done

burakádo pierced; perforated

burakador - (ojo) burakador evil eye

burakadór someone who pierces, makes a hole, perforates

burakar make a hole (v)

burakito - (el) burakito de l'aguja the eye of a needle

burakíto small crack; small hole; la kyerriya ver por un burakito (I do not believe in any of it and I would like to be able to watch him through a small hole) fig for: he is boasting about his courage, patience, etc.

burako - en mi lugar burako lit: it-the rowboat—has a hole only in my place. But since in a rowboat there were are also other passengers, they will all sink together with the boat. Fig for: someone who stupidly insists on doing a thing which may also hurt other people, and who does not have enough sense to realize that

burako nostril; hole; (no deshar) burako carefully search everywhere

burék little pie stuffed with cheese and ground meat in a paste of pumpkin or eggplant (T börek); burekas di kartof meat-filled potato turnovers

burla act of making fun of; mockery
burlar make fun of
burleskas burlesques
burlésko burlesque
burlón joker; prankster; jocular; droll
burnú tutún snuff (pulverized tobacco inhaled through the nostrils)
burnús burnoose (a long hooded towelcloth worn when leaving the
    hot bath)
burnusuz (adj) (lit: someonewho has a cut nose) despicable; a morally
    and physically ugly person without money, education, friends or
    protector (T *burunsuz*) In Turkey, some crimes were punishable
    by amputation of the nose, which disfigured the delinquent
    rendering him grotesque and despicable.
buro office
burokrásya bureaucracy
burokrátiko bureaucratic
burráska thunderstorm, violent storm which passes rapidly; intense
    and short-lasting access of anger and bad temper
Bursa city south of the Sea of Marmara in Northwestern Turkey,
    famous for its hot baths and thermals. Istanbulli Jews often used
    to go to Bursa for thermal and highly sulphurated water cures.
bushka - (la) bushka looks for her, searches for her
bushkadór researcher; investigator
Bushkáldo imaginary person to whom are pleasantly attributed unpre-
    dictable, bizarre and burlesque acts (he is often called Jan
    Buskaldo)
bushkamos - (ke) bushkamos aki what are we looking for here? what
    are we doing here?
bushkapléytos quarrelsome; bad pal
bushkár search (v)
búshkita research; investigation
busqueda - (en) busqueda (in) search (Moroccan Sephardic ballad)
bustejar/bustijar yawn (Port *bocejar*)
but leg of mutton (T *bud*)
butárgo fish eggs (of mullet, sturgeon, etc.) The eggs are dried, assem-
    bled in the shape of fingers, covered by a layer of wax. Fish eggs
    are a delicacy highly appreciated in the orient. They were home-
    made in Istanbul's Sephardic households, and have become highly
    expensive in Turkey, but can be bought at the Rue des Rosiers, in
    the Jewish quarter of Paris.

buticariu shopkeeper (Monastir dialect)
butika shop; store
butikáryo shop owner; storekeeper
butique shop (Monastir dialect)
búto goal; aim
buto purpose; object
butu object
butuñere buttonhole (Monastir dialect)
buxcar search (v)
buyéndo very hot; boiling; el kave turko se beve buyendo the Turkish
     coffee is served boiling
buyida - (pita) buyida cake made of a boiled paste
buyído boiled; breathless; weak; debile; harassed; (medyo) buyido
     prostrated; extremely downcast
buyidór boiling ware
buyir boil (v)
buyitína boiling; itching; pruritus
buyór boiling
buyót hot water pad
buyrún (interj) welcome! please come in! sit down! I beg you!; **buyrún**
     cream parlor; vendor stand for various kinds of fritters and dairy
     products such as milk, *kaymak* (clotted cream) yogurt
buyurultu mandate; nomination paper for a lower official (T kanunn)
buz ice (T); person incapable of enthusiasm, who remains aloof and
     does not manifest any sentiment; **eskrivir enriva el buz** (lit: write
     on the top of ice) make promises that the person who made them
     rather prefers to forget quickly; **un kalip de buz** an ice cube
buzaná ditch high up in the mountains where water freezes and forms
     a reserve of ice which is used in the hot season; ice stand where
     refreshments are sold; cabinet where refrigeration is provided by
     ice; very cold place
buzdjí vendor, distributor of ice (T *buzcu*)
búzdro brisk; harsh; bad-mannered
byambali licorice (T *meyan bali*)
byambali - (ya dio savor de) byambali (lit: it already gave the taste of
     licorice) this is becoming insupportable and disgusting
byankería body linen; part of the trousseau consisting of intimate
     apparel, bed sheets, pillowcases, table cloths and napkins (Ital
     biacheria)
byén good; conform to duty

byenaventurádo happy; blessed
byenazedór benefactor
byenfezénsya charity
byenintézo it's understood; surely; it goes without saying (Ital
    beninteso)
byenkyerénsya benevolence; friendship; affection
byenkyérer affection; friendship; cordiality
byenkyísto estimated; considered with favor
byenvenída welcoming (n)
byenvenido sea el mal quando vyene solo (lit: let the evil be welcome
    when it comes alone) the evil that comes without a string and
    accompanied by other pains can be sustained with resignation
    because, as a rule, misfortune never comes alone
byenvenído welcome!
byervezíko - (tengon un) byervezíko very short word; very rapid
    conversation
byerveziko a dezirte I have a word to tell you (reply to reproaches or
    threats)
byérvo word; (no pepitar) byervo do not say even one word
byervos feos ugly words
byóndo blond

C

caballero young man
cabdillo caudillo; great leader
cabeça head
cabeças (heads of) flowers
cabra goat
cabrito kid
caça hunt (n)
cada each
cada ferida every plague (from the Passover Haggadah)
cahale community
caientó (quién se la) (someone who has) heated (Ital *quién* for him)
cal bitumen
calá bride
calade cold (adj, Monastir dialect)
calar (si) refresh oneself (v, Monastir dialect)

calcañar heel
calma calm; quiet (Port *calmo*)
calor heat (n)
cama bed
camellos camels
caminar walk (v)
camino road
caminu path (Monastir dialect)
camisa shirt
campion sample
campo field; country
canape sofa
cancionero singer
candelabre candlestick
cansar (se) get tired
cantador singer
cantàr hymn
canto song
caño gutter, drain, sewer
capache able; capable (Monastir dialect)
capu chief (Monastir dialect)
cara face; cara pintada (lit: painted face) beautiful face
carapicado wrinkled; carapicado (el) someone with a wrinkled face
cardo thistle
care cheek; face (Monastir dialect)
caridad charity
caritativa charitable
carne mala bad meat (fig for cancer, malignant growth)
carne meat
carnéro holy paschal offering (lamb, mutton)
carpintero carpenter
carrera road
carriar change house (v, Monastir dialect)
carrose coach; carriage (Monastir dialect)
carru wheel; tire (Monastir dialect)
carruseru coachman
carta letter
carte card
casa house; casa de Yaakov house of Jacob
casamiento marriage

casca shell (n)
cáscara peel (n)
cásha box
caso case
casole bread (Port *cassoula, caçoula*)
ca_que peel (n, Monastir dialect)
castania chestnut
castigo punishment
castillo castle
cata raise your head towards (imp, Fer Bib Gen)
catiuado taken prisoner (Fer Bib Gen)
cato had regarded
caualgadura cavalcade (Ferrara Siddur)
causa - (tu) causa a tu considéracion (your) case for your
    consideration
cautiva cavayo captive
cavenádo lock (n)
cavesa head
cavevas di Aman vermicelli in oil and lemon sauce
cavretico small goat
cavrito small goat
cavso cause (n)
cayadés silence (Monastir dialect)
cayente he who falls upon himself
cayente warm
cayer fall (v)
cayeron sus façes he fell on his face; his face was downcast
cayo adormeciente (was surprised to) have fallen asleep
caza house
cazal hamlet; small village (Monastir dialect)
cazalinu resident of a hamlet (Monastir dialect)
centenaryo centenary
cercado fenced
cercucido circumcised
cercucir circumcise
cerrado closed; cerrado mocho que no se circuçua a carne de su
    çerradura, y sera tajada la alma essa de sus pueblos the uncircum-
    cised man who will not circumcise his foreskin, and his person
    will be removed from the midst of his people (Fer Bib Gen)
cerraronse they closed

cerro closed
ceso cheese; ceso blanco asado grilled white cheese
Chabath Salonica Haggadah's spelling for *Sabbath* chachuta with
    squinty eyes (fem)
chadir umbrella (from T *çadir* tent, umbrella)
chafteyar knock on something (T *çarpmak*)
chaketon slap in the face (n)
chakshir pants
chanaka pot; bowl
chantika canticle
chapa lock (n)
chapachul sloppy; shabbily dressed; untidy
chapeyo hat
chapeyu hat (Monastir dialect)
charif prince
charshi market; marketplace (T)
charsí market (T *çarshi*)
chastre tailor
chehina Divine Presence (H)
Chenaan Canaan (Fer Bib Gen)
Chenaani Canaanites
cherubim cherubs
cheshme fountain (T *çeshme*)
chetrefil someone who is quite thin; colloquially: a person with quite a
    character—thin like a match but buzzing like a mosquito
chichek flower (from Turkish *çiçek*)
chico small; little; young
chicu small (Monastir dialect)
chicuy - (más) chicuy smaller
chilibi gentleman (from T *celebi* a royal prince)
chincha bedbug (Gal *chincha*); figuratively and colloquially someone
    who is quite stingy; a miser; **agua de chinchas** lit.: bedbug's water.
    Colloquial name for whisky, because it was said to smell like a
    squeezed, blood-filled bedbug.
chingirák bell (n, from T *çingirak*)
chiquito small
chirak apprentice (T)
chiyo a piercing scream
chizo sorcery
chofer car driver (F *chauffeur*)

chohét butcher who slaughters according to the ritual laws
cholpa sloppy; shabbily dressed
chop garbage (T *çöp*)
choque brood hen (Port *gallinha choca*)
chorap stockings; socks (from T *çorap*)
chorba soup (T *çorba*)
choron whiner
chosa hut; cabin; cabana; shack; very poor living quarter
christiandat Christianity
christiano Christian
chufa - orchata de chufa a very popular Oriental syrup prepard with
     chufa, almond of the earth (Judeo-Spanish)
chuflár whistle (v)
chufletes lit: whistles; Passover meal made of carved and fried leek
     stems
chukal chamber pot; fig: an ill-fitting, ugly, ridiculous woman's hat
chukalito (coll) ridiculous woman's hat
chupamoko someone who sucks his bogers; unclean person
chupar suck (v)
ciego blind (adj)
cien hundred
ciento one hundred
ciento y cinquenta hundred and fifty
cientos hundreds
cierto certain; (de) cierto certainly; however; in effect; effectively
cimiento cement
cinco five
cinquenta fifty
cinturas belts
circuçir circumcise
circuncidado circumcised
circundar surround
ciudá city
ciudad city
combatido fought
comer eat; (lo que) comieron los moços what the young men ate (Fer
     Bib Gen); (au) comer the food; the nutrition
comida food; comida di mirindjina con kalavasa mixture of egglant
     and zucchini
cómo how

como like; as if

como nombre as a name

como todo que all the things that ...; like all the things

compañero companion

compañia company

compás rhythm

complido complete; completed; someone who lacks nothing; **(que no) complido peccado de Hemori fasta aqui** (since) the impunity of the Amorrheans has still not come to its term (Fer Bib Gen)

complir carry out

compra de plata purchased with money; slave (Fer Bib Gen); **compra de plata de todo hijo de estraño que no de tu semen** someone who is bought with thy money; the slave bought for money; every alien who is not of your race

compuesto made of

con with; **(y lo que) con el en la arca** (and what is) with him (Noah) in the Ark (Fer Bib Gen)

concebido conceived

concluission community

confesar confess

confetti white sugar-coated Jordan almonds served at weddings, traditionally in little lace bags

conocer know

conoçio knew

conortora - (no) conortora de nuestros echos he will not comfort himself with works; he will not profit from our works

conosçio Cain a su mujer (lit: Cain had known his wife) Cain had intercourse with his wife

consejer advise

consejero adviser

consejo counsel (n)

constar certify; state on a record

contador accountant

contar count; recount (v)

contee en count on someone or something (Ferrara Siddur)

contenér pretend

contigo with you

conto lo el por justedad and (the Lord) attributed this to justice, counted it as justice

convente convent

conversos Western Jews
convite invitation
copo/copu cup (Port *cup*)
coraçon/corazón heart
corcova hump
cordéla ribbon
cordele rope
cordero lamb; fig for angel
cornado coin
corona crown
correa leather strip
corrençias verbosity
correr run (v)
corrio ran
corrumpio - (se) corrumpio he (it) corrupted (himself, itself)
corrupto corrupt (adj)
corte frontyard
cortesia courtesy
cortíjo neighborhood
cortijo patio
cosa thing
cosieron they had it sewed together, they sewed it together (Fer
　　Bib Gen)
costilla rib
creer believe
creyo believed
criado creature; someone created by God; human being
Criador Creator
criar childbearing
criatúra child; the created (the creatures); something that is created
criminalidad criminalilty
crio - (que) crio the one (who) created
Cristianos Christians
crize crisis (Port *crise, crize*)
cruz cross (n)
cruzada crusade
cual (dil) - whose; of whom; of which
cuando when
cubiertos covered
cubrir cover (v)

cuchara spoon
cuellu graceful
cuento account
cuero skin
cueru skin (Monastir dialect)
cueruo/cuervo crow
cuesta hill
cuiziér cook (v)
culantro cilantro; coriander
culebra snake
culebros snakes
cumerchu customs (Monastir dialect)
cumier eat (v); (nos) cumientos we eat
cumplió fulfilled
cumplir fulfill; comply
cumpuzadu composed (Monastir dialect)
cumpuzar compose
cuñada sister-in-law
cuñado brother-in-law
cunisensje knowledge (Monastir dialect)
cunsejo story; tale (Monastir dialect)
cuntenti happy (Port *contente*, Monastir dialect)
curtar interrupt
custo cost (n)
custumbre custom
cutchiyada stab wound
cuvá bucket (Monastir dialect)
cuvio - (ya lo) cuvio he bored me (us) by being too repetitive, insistent,
   pushy
cuzír sew

Ç

çaça nanny
çaças insignificant words; vain excuses
çaço insignificant young man
çadir mavi blue sky; fig for: God's residence

çadir tent; umbrella (T)
çadirdji vendor and repairman of umbrellas
çadrak terrace; pergola (T *çardak*). In former times every house had a
    terrace where the laundry was dried and the family slept in hot
    summer nights.
çair prairie (T *çayir*)
çakal jackal (T); bully fellow; blusterer; bad-mouthed person;
    aggressive individual
çakeada shock; sudden knock; blow (n)
çakear shock; knock on furniture or an object; give a blow
    (T *çarpmak*)
çakeo knock; blow; rebuff; rebuke; fight; quarrel (n)
çaketon blow; slap in the face; spanking
çakmak lighter
çakon boaster; braggart; brawler; fem form: çakona
çaktear furtively look from the corner of the eye; throw an eye on
    something; glance with curiosity and envy (T *çaktirmak*)
çalgi Turkish orchestra; (no boda sen) çalgi no wedding without music
çalgici Turkish musician; minstrel
çalik bedfellow; debauchee
çalishear make an effort; work hard (T *çalishmak*)
çalishkan hardworking; industrious; active, laborious person
    (T *çalishkan*)
çalum arrogance; self-sufficiency; self-assurance;(T *çalim*)
çamashir laundry; linen for bathwear; underwear or tablecloths (T)
çamsakiz resin of the pine tree (T *çam sakizi*)
çamurluk quagmire; sulfurous hot mud used to treat rheumatism
çamushkado - (komer) çamushkado badly cooked dish which smells
    smoky
çamushkado disagreeable odor of imperfectly burned material; imper-
    fectly reddened material
çamushkar redden; to be in flames; burn imperfectly (v)
çamushkina smell of something that was burned imperfectly
çanaka cooking pot; porringer; earthen pan (T *çanak*); avrir los ojos
    çanaka keep the eyes wide open
çanakaada content of an earthen pot
çanakita small earthen pot
çanta bag; small piece of luggage; student's bag (T)
çapa pick; holly (T)

çapaçullo a person in rags; unclean person; someone going shoeless; bad-mouthed individual without education; person without character (T *çapaçul*)

çapato shoe

çapeo hat

çapeo melon; melon hat

çapeo top hat

çapeudo In times of the Ottoman Empire, the authorization to wear a European-style hat other than the traditional headgears such as the fez or the man's cap without a shade (the latter would hamper the touching of the forehead to the earth or the floor of the mosque during the prosternation which is part of the Muslim prayer). Since wearing a hat was a privilege, the word had an ironical and jealous implication. In 1922, when the Turkish army was about to reenter Istanbul under the command of Refet Pasha and the last units of the British occupying forces were preparing to leave, there was a rush among the Jewish, Armenian and Greek minorities to throw away their hats and buy fezes. At that time, the non-Muslim minorities could not anticipate the modernist views of Mustafa Kemal, the leader of the War of Independence and Turkish Revolution, who surprisingly enough would ban the fez and adopt the hat as national headgear a few years later.

çapeyera hat box; modist who makes and sales women's hats

çapeyero manufacturer and merchant of hats men's and boys' hats

çapin patent leather shoes; ball shoes (Port *chapin*)

çapkin outcast boy in the streets of a city; worthless scamp; womanizer; ladies' man

çapozo having overdeveloped canines and incisives which give an unsightly appearance

çaptear see *çaktear*

çarabara (adv) a street vendor's loud cries to attract buyers; fig for: at the sight and knowledge of everybody (T *çagirmak bagirmak*)

çaramella weed; individual who is unable to keep a secret, who speaks without thinking and stupidly repeats all he hears; arch: bagpipe

çare remedy; expedient (T)

çarika sandal of raw-hide or rope worn by peasants (T); **(perder) fina las çarikas** to be totally ruined by gambling or bad business

çark wheel; paddle-wheel; fly-wheel; anything that revolves; machinery; hydraulic which raises the water of a well; the celestial sphere; fate, destiny (T)

çarla conversation; chattering; talkativeness
çarlar/çarlear talk, chatter (v)
çarlatan charlatan; boaster
çarpara slap on the face given with the back of the hand; box on the
    ear
çarshaf usually dark-colored mantle in which the Muslim women (and
    in former times Jewish women as well) wrapped themselves from
    head the toe. It was banned by Mustafa Kemal Atatürk, the
    founder of the Turkish Republic. However, with the resurgence of
    fundamentalism in modern Turkey, it has gained some popularity
    again. Its wearing has been supported by the conservative Refah
    Party and in a somewhat more cautious way by its successor, the
    Fazilet Party.
çarshamba Wednesday (T *çarshamba*); pedrer el çarshamba y el
    pershembe (lit: lose the Wednesday and Thursday) fig: lose the
    notion of time; to be confused
çarshi non-food market; (el) çarshi eskuro (lit: the dark market)
    covered market; kapali çarshi (lit: closed market) the famous
    Grand Bazar in Istanbul, located beyond the Galata bridge at the
    entrance of old Istanbul, where bazaar-style bargaining has been
    brought to the level of an art; misir çarshishi Egyptian bazaar
    (spice market with a great variety of spices)
çata chamber pot
çati framework; skeleton; roof (T); (eçar) çati a roof under
    construction. Usually a festivity bringing together the owner, engi-
    neers and construction workers.
çatla crack; stripe; slit; rent (n, T *çatlak*)
çatladear crack; cleave; cut open; rip up; chip; burst; rent; (v, T
    çatlatmak)
çatlak skeptic; heretic (T); someone who doubts the value of the Holy
    Scriptures and the doctrines of religion; someone who is
    suspected of heresy
çatleado cracked
çatleadura crack; rent (n)
çatra patra about; approximately; not very precise; not very correct;
    grammatically poor; se desbroya en cinko linguas çatra patra he
    knows enough to get by in five languages (Sephardic merchants
    who did a lot of international business often had basic knowledge
    of many foreign languages)
çaush (military) sergeant (T *çavush*); guardian; bailiff

çavdar rye (T)
çay tea (T)
çaylik teapot; tea service (T)
çedaquá tsedaka righteousness, saintliness (H)
çedros cedars
çek check (n)
çekenbilir only someone who has endured the sufferings can realize
their seriousness (proverb)
çekil Turkish weight measure; a bundle of firewood branches (approx.
550 pounds)
çekinearse to be ashamed; hesitate; hesitate to claim one's due;
withdraw
çekineo timidity; reserve; hesitation
çelebi deskalso shoeless; someone who wants to be respected by others
but lacks the qualities of a respectable person
çelebi title given to someone of good family, education and wealth
çeleste sky blue (adj); color of the sky
çemimea chimney; someone who smokes nonstop
çengel/çingel hook (T *çengel*); artful; crafty; cunning; someone who
tries to seize any opportunity to shuffle a commitment or task
çentro center; cabaret; nightclub (Ital *centro*)
çentura/çintura belt
çerçeve frame; framework
çerkes Circassian (inhabitant of the northerwestern Caucasus) fig for:
vicious, voracious, sanguinary bandit
çerkes tavughu chicken with walnuts
çerradura foreskin
çertifikato certificate
çeshke (adv) regret for an action which has not been accomplished,
words that were not said; what a pity that... (T *keshke*)
çetrefil speaking Turkish with many mistakes and bad pronunciation;
badly spoken language; someone who speaks a foreign language
badly
çevireada skillful interrogation during which a full confession is
obtained (T *çevirme*)
çevirear rotate; turn in circles; skillfully interrogate someone to make
him confess
çevirme piece of meat roasted on a spit or skewer; kebab; a kind of
thick marmalade (T); encircling movement (of the military); translation

çi tengo I want it very much; I want it badly; it is indispensable for me; sine qua non

çibuk cigarette holder; pipe; **çibuk i kave** water pipe and coffee offered to a visitor of importance who comes with the intent to stay for a long period; repose; serenity; relaxation; daydreaming in the very Turkish way *kief* or *keyif*—enjoying oneself, smoking water pipe, sipping from often beautifully decorated coffee cups and nibbling lokum (Turkish delight)

çiça maçiça children's game. Two ends of a string are tied together to form an endless chain, which is skillfully twisted, forming some sort of cross. The game is played by two children, who hold the two ends of the cross with both their index and middle finger of each hand and alternately pull on the string in a back and forth movement

çiçaron brawler; someone who screams and protests loudly

çiçek flower (T); (komo) **çiçek enriva de mi kavesa** I will welcome you like a flower on my head

çiçekli flowered; someone who wears a flower in the buttonhole; tissue, paper or tapestry decorated with flowers

çiçigaya - (savor de) **çiçigaya** tasteless, insipid; **jasbon de çiçigaya** erroneous calculation; badly made repartition; faulty sales' license

çiçigaya cicada; grasshopper

çiegedumbros blinded by very bright light

çiego blind

çielos skies

çient hundred; a hundred

çif cost-freight-insurance (Engl, commercial formula indicating that the quoted price for merchandise includes freight and insurance charges)

çifçi farmer (T *çiftçi*)

çiflik farm (T *çiftlik*); benefits acquired with no work or effort; **çiflik de su padre, se lo fizo çiflik** he took it over, he acquired it arbitrarily (indignantly said of an undue appropriation, of unwarranted treatment of a good as if it was legitimate property)

çifut (T, *çifit*, deformation of *gihud* Jew) derisive name that the Turks gave to Jews; mean; **çifut çarshisi** like a junk sale; **çifut yahudi** insulting term used by the Turks to address Jews. **içi çifut çarshisi** evil-minded; malevolency

çigaro cigarette

çijifyongo coquette; dandy (ironical)

çikez childhood

çikibilik masterful, domineering attitude; someone who wants others to work for him (T *çelebilik*)

çikidumbre smallness; exiguity

çikitiko diminutive of *çikito*

çikito young child; young boy

çikitura smallness

çikma pretext; excuse; way out; twisted way (T)

çikma sokak dead-end street (T *çikmaz sokak*)

çiko small; çiko de grande d'afferezia boy; small of size and age, but big by the experience acquired

çikolata chocolate

çikolatero chocolate vendor

çikur drawer (underwear for the lower body) holding cord; no saverse atar los çikures (lit: he does not know how to tie his underpants) he is very clumsy to the point of not knowing how to tie the cord of his underpants

çil brilliant; resplendescent; entirely new; brand new; unedited

çilik steel

çilindro top hat; yellow dwarf (game in which the betting is insignificant); fortuitous occupation which only brings worries; gratuitous work; annoyance; nonsense; nothing; ganar el çilindro waste one's time; lose when the hope was to win; kada punto nos sale con un çilindro he was disappointed; repeatedly deceived hopes and annoyance

çima despisive term for a poorly dressed woman; disgracious; unskilled

çimento cement

çinar plane-tree. The site of the immemorial plane-tree of Emirgân, on the European side the Bosphorus, is a popular place to enjoy the traditional Turkish art of relaxation keyif: smoking the water pipe, sipping coffee and eating sweets

çinça bedbug. In former times the wooden bed frames of Sephardic households were infested with legions of bedbugs whose multiple bites created tormentous itching. The word is often used as a synonym for a stingy person; agua de çinças (lit: bedbug water) among Istanbul's Sephardim, ironical name for whisky; no da ni çinças (lit: he would not even give bedbugs) he does not give anything to the poor; sangre de çinças (lit: bedbugs' blood) something or somebody very unpleasant and disgracious; çinça de

90

tamuz y av (lit: bedbug in the two hottest months of the year,
July and August) a very irritating person

çinçero invasion of bedbugs

çinco five

çincuenta fifty

çines Chinese

çinesko Chinese language; incomprehensible language

çingene/çingane Gypsy (T); avaricious; petty; shabby; paltry

çingenelik sordid avarice (T)

çini china; dish; plate; **çini tano** flat dish; **çini fondo** hollow dish

çio/çiyo piercing scream

çioe (adv) it means; meaning; otherwise said (Ital *cio e*)

çip lowest chip in game

çiplak naked; bare of everything (fortune, consideration, education) (T)

çipro brandy from the island of Cyprus

çipura dorado (fish)

çira resinous wood (T); torch; kindling wood

çirak apprentice; student; disciple; **salir çirak de** to be indebted to
someone for one's fortune and knowledge

çiraklik outstanding service; highly appreciated service

çirek green or gray muslin ribbon attached to the front part of the
tokado, the traditional ceremonial headgear of the married
Sephardic woman. It has its origin in the Latin rotello (Lat), the
yellow badge imposed on Jews. Ironically it has remained on the
tokado by routine and tradition, and many people are not aware
of its origin.

çirek quarter; fourth part (T çeyrek)

çirka about; almost; more or less (Ital *circa*)

çirko circus (Ital)

çirkolar circular (letter)

çiro dried mackerel (Gr), usually broiled, cut in chunks and served as
a salad with olive oil and dill. This is a delicacy in Istanbul's open
air restaurants along the shore of the Marmara Sea and the
Prince Islands; a very thin person

çispa sparkle; cinder (which penetrates the eyes and nostrils); **entrar
çispa en el ojo** standing far away the others in a corner, as if a
foreign body has entered the eye

çitener I want it badly (Ital); give big importance to a thing; want
something very badly

çivit indigo (T)

çiyon brawling; squalling; big screamer

çizmez top boot; Wellington

çoban shepherd; person wearing ill-fitting, excessively broad, and disgracious clothes

çoka incubation; brooding over eggs; meter çoka settle comfortably, giving the impression of not intending to leave soon; accommodate oneself to a lazy lifestyle; chicks coming from a single covey; name of a game

çokada brood; covey; hatch (n)

çokal chamber pot

çokar brood over eggs; cover (v)

çokluk bokluk (adv) (lit: too much abundance and too much excrement) superabundance; exaggeration; excess bringing only disorder. Idiomatic expression for: a good measure in all is the sole source of true enjoyment.

çokolata chocolate

çokolateria chocolate factory; distribution counter

çokolatero chocolate vendor

çolak one-armed person (T)

çomak someone who is unconscious about and unsensitive to the harm he causes; rude, uncouth, ill-bred person; boor (T)

çomlek earthenware pot (T çömlek); dish in which all sorts of vegetables are mixed; heterogeneous mixture of objects and people

çon honorary title; suffix added to the name of notable Jewish citizens in the Orient, for example: David-Daviçon, Juda-Judaçon)

çop hay; garbage (T); eçar çop draw a lot

çorap socks; stockings; socks worn over stockings (T)

çorba soup

çorbadji head of a military unit of the Janissaries (T çorbaci), the standing Ottoman Turkish army. The word comes from a gigantic cauldron which was the emblem of the Janissaries. The Janissaries used to lift the cauldron when asing for higher pay, or when they attempted to remove the Sultan. In 1826, after revolting against Sultan Mahmut II, the corps was dissolved and many Janissaries killed. The relationship between Jewish merchants and Janissaries was rather friendly, but occasionally Jewish properties were plundered by Janissaries. After the eliminiation of the Janissaries, such Jewish-Janissary connections may have arisen the suspicion of

Mahmut II, and this would partly be a possible explanation for the execution of the prominent Jewish financiers Aciman and Karmona.

çorbadji title given to prominent non-Muslim citizens who used to periodically distribute soup and other food to the poor

çorbatina very clear soup; muddy pond which forms in the street after the rain; quagmire

çorça name given to the Catholic church and the papacy

çorreadura something that flows and drips

çorrear flow; drip (v)

çorredero continuous flowing; dripping

çorreo flow; dripping

çorreteo/çorretero flowing; continuous dripping (Haketia)

çorretear flow; drink intemperately; tolerate drinking

çorretina abundant flow from a faucet, a pipe, an artery, or the nostrils

çorriko weak, continuous, permanent flow of liquid; draft coming from a crack; maleficient; sly; treacherous; **tyene çorriko, le korre el çorriko** he has steady income without making any effort

çorro steady flow; **çorro de agua** water flow; **çorro lagrimas** flow of tears; **çorro de liras** flow of gold pounds (of gains); **çorro de sangre** blood flow; **çorro de sudor** flow of sweat; **se korre a çorros** something that lets a liquid (water, oil, petroleum) flow steadily

çorron large flow of liquid gashing out violently

çosa hut; log cabin; shack

çuço caressing name for young children

çuçu/çççuçu (onomatopoeia) unending blabber; chatter; continuous whispering; **estar çuçuçu** uninterrupted whisper

çuçutear whisper (v)

çuçuteo whispering

çueta name given to the Jews of the Balearic Islands, who converted to Christianity after the Reconquista

çuflar seco drink a lot without giving signs of drunkenness; drink with a merry manner

çuflar whistle; blow (v)

çuflet whistle; small whistle

çufletes Sephardic Passover dish consisting of fried, carved leek stems (looking like whistles)

çufletiko small whistle; **tomar çufletiko en** (lit: take the little whistle in the hand) repeat everywhere and to everyone the news that were supposed to remain secret

çufliko insidious aircraft

çuflo blowing the whistle; air draft

çul rough carpet (T); bed cover made of raw tissue

çunko rush; rattan

çupa - estar çupa çupa kiss non-stop; peck without interruption

çupada sucking; amount of liquid drawn into the mouth by strong suction

çupadero continuous sucking; strong desire to suck

çupadika short and rapid sucking; short puff taken from the cigarette; short sip

çupado depleted of flesh, of fat; **gueso çupado** a very skinny person

çupador sucker; heavy drinker; spot made by sucking

çupadura sucking

çupar a uno/çupar la pull out of someone as much as possible; exhaust somebody

çupar suck (v); drink alcoholic beverages very hastily; give a kiss

çuparse los dedos lick one's fingers after eating a succulent dish

çupetada sucking in which a large quantity of liquid is absorbed at once

çupetear suck longly; keep a sweet, etc. in the mouth to prolong the pleasure

çupon de agua rozada gain; advantage; profit which comes without difficulty; sent by God; **tener çupon en la boka** to be at the source of easy and abundant gains

çupon pacifier

çurek a kind of shortbread in the shape of a ring (T *çörek*)

çurro dirty; unkept; poor; wretched; miserable; mean; shabby; paltry; unappealing; unpleasant; **caldo çurro** very lean broth; **agua çurra** insipid beverage; purely and simply water; **un kave çurro** bad coffee; coffee with no milk, sugar, etc.; **un ayudo çurro** insignificant; very weak; inefficient (epithet which expresses disdain)

çuruk rotten; ready to fall into pieces, for example wooden plank, wooden beam of a building, wooden furniture (T *çürük*); **pizar, no pizar en tavla çuruk** (lit: step or not to step on rotten plank) count on a reliable person and do not count on a person who is little secure or on a business which is contingent; **no piza en tavla**

çuruk (lit: he does not step on rotten plank) he always acts know-
    ingly, willingly, and in good earnest
çurukluk dilapidation; state of being shattered; ruin (T *çürüklük*);
    worm-hole; state of wooden object gnawed by worms
çuska very pungent pigment; paprika (Gr)
çuspa bread; dry, hard cake
çutra pumpkin which, sliced in two and emptied, served as recipient
    for wine or water; bottle; gourd; imbecile, stupid person (T)
çutrea bueno he is an intrepid drinker
çutrear drink without measure; absorb wine and liquors
çuval jute sack; tener çuval de liras to be very fortunate

D

da he gives; da y fuy make a fleeting allusion, but then do not insist,
    do not push the point
daabeter worst (T *daha beter*)
dáath intelligence; lucidity of mind; understanding (H); en su daath
    esta he/she is in perfect equilibrium; he/she reasons justly. This is
    said about someone who is very conscious of what he/she does,
    and of its actions. It is usually used when others believe that this
    person is drunk, or just talks nonsense.
dabashamento in secret; slyly; on the side scene; under the mantle of,
    under the counter
dad let us go
dada hit; stroke
dada nanny
dadanear resist; tolerate; support help to stand up; stop; impeach the
    advance (v, T *dayanmak*)
dade stroke; punch (Monastir dialect)
dadear go here and there (in an office); look busy but in reality do not
    accomplish anything useful
dadika en la espalda small taps on the shoulder to express affection or
    approval
dadika light stroke; tap; pat
dadiva present; gift
dadivozo generous, charitable person
dado finger; thimble; dice
dador benefactor

dados - (son) dados are given
dainda still; yet
daka dakaki! dakaka! (exclamation) give it to me! (very colloquial
    expression for: if it would be so!)
daki - de aki from here; starting from here
dalavera trick; intrigues; disloyal maneuvers
dalaveraci tricky, deceitful person (T)
dalaveradji intrigant; swindler (T *dalaveraci*)
dalde! (interj) give it to him! strike him! Is said ironically and as a cruel
    joke to someone who, in front of a scene of brutality, refrains from
    intervening. It is also said sarcastically about the chastisement
    imposed in hell to the avaricious who did not enjoy their money
dale dale adv) at the most; at the maximum; admitting the most; given
    the most
dale kamino (lit: give him road) do not pay attention to him; do not
    do what he is asking for; just let him go
dalear plunge; dive in the water (v)
dalearse plunge oneself
dalga wave (n, T)
dalgitch plunger; diver (T *dalgiç*)
dalkauk parasite; flatterer who pretends to worship a person to the
    expense of whom he lives (T *dalkavuk*)
dalkaukluk flattery; fawning (T)
dalkavuk flatterer (T)
dalli of there; of that
dalyan enclosure of sets fixed as poles used for catching fish; fishing
    site where fish are abundant (T *dalyan*, archaic for *italyan*)
damajero person who creates damage because of clumsiness and the
    habit of touching everything
damar stripe or vein on marble; blood vessel; a tendency to madness;
    trait of character (T)
damarli striated (wood or marble) (T)
damasceno (adj) from Damascus
damasko silk tissue with arabesque thread design
dame a mi alma (lit: give me the people) give me my soul brother(s) or
    sister(s)
damgali stamped; marked by a title or sign to attract attention
damgua mark; imprint; puncheon or stiletto imprint to indicate the
    title of a jewel or any other object made of precious metal;
    official seal; post office stamp (Turkish *damga*)

damjana large narrow-necked bottle enclosed in wickerwork; jug (usually filled with water from the famous springs in the outskirts of Istanbul, such as Tashdelen, Kayishdagi), highly appreciated in Jewish households

damla drop (T); apoplexy; gout; circulation problems of the brain causing loss of consciousness and paralysis; intense gout pain in the toes

damladear drip; make drops fall (v)

damma/dama dame; lady; queen in chess game

damua seal; stamp (n)

damuali bearing the official pungeon or stiletto mark; awl's imprint; officially certified document; stigmatized

dán - (senal que yo) **dán** (signal that I) give

dañada corrupt woman (Fer Bib Gen)

dañado damaged; altered; spoiled; deteriorated

dañador ghost; phantom; wandering soul; soul from the kingdom of the dead bringing bad luck

dañadoriko surliness; crabbiness; anger ready to be manifested at the first occasion, with or without reason

dañar harm; damage; hurt (v); **que dañiantes al lugar este** we shall destroy this place (Fer Bib Gen); **que dañian** will destroy

dañaras you will destroy

dandana pomp; noisy display of luxury; ostentatiousness, pageantry; magnificence (T *tantana*)

dando i tomando give and take; deliberation; discussion; long and trifling conversation; exchange of ideas

danishear consult; approach for consultation; ascertain sentiments (v, T *danishmak*)

daño damage; ravage; devastation; havoc; prejudice; harm (n)

dañozo damaging; harmful

dantela lace

danyozo damaging; harmful

dar atráz return

dar give; give funds; deliver

dar palmadas clap (v)

dar te e por gentes I shall make you become (powerful) nations

darchó proved it

dare - ti la dare I shall give her to you

darom south (H)

darsan preacher; orator (H); **kyen es el darsan?** (ironical) who is holding the spittoon?

darsar preach (from Turkish ders lesson)
darsyo tax; en tyempo del turko los darsyos no se puedian a levabtar
    under in the Ottoman Empire, the taxes were heavy
data date (time)
datar date; put the date (v)
datlanal/datlanar date tree
datle date (fruit)
datli date (fruit, Port *datile*)
daul drum; large box (T *davul*); daul y zurna drum and clarinet. In vil-
    lages in Macedonia and and in the Balkans, these two
    instruments formed a little orchestra; un daul fazer la kavesa (lit:
    make the head a drum) fig for: exhaust someone by interminable
    speeches
daules drums; arresevir kon daules daul y zurna welcome with enthu-
    siasm (v); receive with reproaches and screams of anger
dava had given
dava lawsuit (T)
davadji plaintiff (T *davaci*, kanunn)
davagar slowly (Port)
davar ajer speak about something else (H)
davranear behave; sustain; support (v, T *davranmak*)
davranerarse get back on his feet (T)
davul drum
dayak spanking (T)
dayanak support; prop (n, T)
de adonde from whence; de adonde tenemos from whence can it be
    deduced
de agôra y asta siempre from henceforth and forever more
de assi in that way; like this
de cierto certainly; verily
de dentro from inside
de en basho en basho sly; perfidious
de from
de of; in consequence of; from
de onde from
de prendimiento therefore
de varon (of) man; (of) male
deazrimar deprive somebody from his foothold, lodging, etc. (v)
debacho down

debaldajon gratis; for free (adv); sarcastic: free loading
debaldes gratis (adj and adv)
debasho en basho sly; hypocrite
debasho under; below
debate debate; discussion
debil weak
debuxada portrayed (fem)
deceit said
december December (It *dicembre*)
dechar let (v); (te) dechar let yourself
decidido decided; resolved
decidir decide (v)
decierto certainly; surely
decierto verily
decindieron (de Ayifto) they came out (lit: down) from Egypt (Salonica
     Pesach Sidur)
decindir descend (v)
decizo resolved (Ital *deciso*)
decizyon decision (Ital *decisione*)
dedada quantity of a liquid
dedal thimble
dedikar dedicate; consecrate (It *dedicare*)
dedikas dedication
dediko small finger
dedo finger
dedyentro inside; within
dedyes Turkish coin of very little value
def (self-) defense
defekto defect
defendedor defender
defender defend (v)
defendido forbidden; prohibited
defensa defense
deferensya difference
defeto defect; imperfection
defeza defense (Ital *difesa*)
definisyon definition
definitivo definite
defter notebook; register (T)

defterdar Minister of Finance or treasurer in the Ottoman Empire; high-ranking official who was in charge of administering the high finances of a *vilayet* (Turkish province) or a department of the Ottoman Empire (T)

degoyador butcher, fig: merchant or other professional (physician, lawyer) who asks a very high price for his merchandise or services and who unscrupulously exploits his clients

degoyar slaughter by cutting the throat

degoyo he cuts his (its) throat

degueler to have pain; feel the pain (v)

dehaynu that is; viz. (H)

dehiyár hesitate

dejenerado degenerated

dejenerar degenerate (v)

dejiya pretext; subterfuge to slow down; impediment (n)

dejrea necessity; need (H)

dekagramo decagram

dekara coin worth ten cents (Gr)

dekaras (slang) money

deke why

deklamar declaim (v)

deklarar declare (v)

deklarasyon declaration

dekorador decorator

dekorasyon decoration; medal

dekorozo pompous; ornamental; which puts in value

del of the; from the (masc)

dela from the (fem)

delante in front of

delantre in front of; from the presence of

delantre in front; forward (prep and adv)

delegado delegate

delegasyon delegation

deletaçion satisfaction

deleyte delight (Ferrara Siddur)

delgado thin

delgádo thin

deliberasyon deliberation

delicto crime; **grande mi delicto de perdonar** my delict is too big to be
    pardoned; my pain (due to my sin) is too big for me to be carried
    (Fer Bib Ge)
delifesfes crazy; lunatic; someone who speaks incoherently (T)
delikado delicate
delikanli young man; lad (T)
deliryo delirium
delisya delight; great pleasure
delisyozo delicious
delivransa deliverance
delivrar liberate; free; make free (v)
delphin dolphin
demagogo demagogue
demañana morning
demanda interrogation
demandador claimant
demandar ask; demand (v)
demaniana morning
demanyanika early morning
demarkar demarcate
demas more; in addition
demasia in excess; too much
demasiado too much
demaskar unmask
demazya excess (n); excedent; surplus
demazyado excessive; more than owed
demenester by need; by necessity; obligatorily
demenester distress (n)
demirindi tamarind (T *demir hindi*, also *merendi*)
demisyonar resign (v)
demokrasia democracy
demokrata democrat
demokratiko democratic
demokratizar democratize (v)
demolisyon demolition
demonio devil; demon
demonstrativo demonstrative
demostrar demonstrate (v)
demostrasyon demonstration

démoudar distinguish
dempues after (prep)
demuazel young girl; maiden (F *demoiselle*); tutor for young children
demudadiko meddler; busybody; picky; difficult to satisfy; someone
    who finds an objection to everything
demudado pale; disfigured; meticulous; maniac; someone with an
    eccentric taste
demudamyento bizarre; strange habits; difficult to satisfy
demudar fade (v)
demudarse to become pale; to be pale because of an indigestion; illness
    or strong emotion
demudasyon particular exigencies regarding meals and cloths
den basho enbasho perfidious; plotting; having an angel's face and a
    devil's character
deñar condescend (v)
dende from where
denigrador someone who deprecates
denk bale; package; load; burden
dentrada all at once; from the beginning; prior to all discussion
denuncia denunciation
denunciar relate to (v); proclaim
denunçio denounced; reported
denuncio(a te) has shown; proclaimed (to you)
departamento department; administrative division
depedrér/depiedrer cause to perish; cause moral and material loss
depedrisyon total loss; ruin
dependensya dependency
depender depend
dependyente dependent
deperdar (se) disappear; get lost; to be ruined (v)
depistar track; hunt; ferret (v)
deploravle deplorable
deportado deported
deportar deport
deportasyon deportation
depozitar make a deposit; place in custody (v)
depozitaryo depository
depozito deposit
deprendér learn (v, archaic); inquire
depsiz insolent; bad-mannered (T)

deputado deputy
deputasyon deputation
deranjado incommodated; indisposed; someone with a slightly affected
    health
deranjamyento perturbation; slight indisposition
deranjar disturb; importune (v)
derasa speech; sermon; homily; furtive indication; discrete warning (T)
derbil binoculars; magnifying glass (T *dürbün*)
dere river; torrent; affluent of a river; ravine (T)
derecha right hand
derecha right side
derechedad righteousness
derechitud straightforwardness; rectitude; loyalty; probity
derecho legal science; disposal; claim (n)
derechura rectitude
derej eres good education; politeness; good manners (H)
derito legal sciences; study of law; legal body (Ital *diritto*)
dererokado demolish
derivado derived
derivar derive (v)
dermatolojia dermatology
derramar spill (v)
derredor ambience; parents; relative; family
derritidor squanderer; big spender
derritir dissolve; liquidize; melt
derrokador demolisher; destroyer; **derrokador de kazas** destroyer of
    families; someone who puts trouble in the family
derrokar demolish; put down; overthrow (v)
derrokar destroy
derrokiyo demolition; destruction; devastation
dert worry; pain (v); preoccupation (T *dert*)
dertes worries (T *dert*)
derush preach; preacherman; predication (H)
derusha dew; mist; fog (H)
derven mountain pass where a very strong wind is blowing (T)
dervish dervish; carefree, calm person who takes things as they come
    (T *dervish*). Jews maintained particularly friendly ties with the
    easygoing Bektashi dervishes and visited their monasteries.
    Dervish orders were banned in Atatürk's Republic
deryade libertine; someone who is much inclined to sexual excesses (T)

deryan very large place (T)
desaladura desalinization
desalar desalinize (v)
desamparado helpless
desarrollo development
desavido ignorant; badly informed
desbafamyanto ventilation
desbafar ventilate
desbafo depression; decompression
desbalar unpack a bale of merchandise (v)
desbarasar clear; clear off
desbarkador worker who unloads a ship
desbeder vagabond; tramp
desbelarse break one's back; tire out oneself (v, T *bel* back, backbone)
desbilamyento violation of a religious rite or rule
desbodramyento overflowing; flood
desbodrar overflow; flood (v)
desbokado bad mouth; insulting
desbolsar make a payment; cover the expense
desbolver amuse; distract; entertain
desbolvido capable; skillful; alert
desbotonar unbutton
desbragado (lit) without (his) underwear; fig for: without money
desbragar denude; take away someone's clothes or underwear
desbrochar undo buttons and hooks; open a hole to allow excess
      liquid or gas to come out (v)
desbrolyar disentangle; unravel; clear up
desbuelvez alertness; skillfulness
descendemos we go down; let us go down
descendio went down
desconfiado distrustful; suspicious
descubriosse su tienda entre was discovered in the middle of his tent
descuverto uncovered
descuvierta bare
descuvijô revealed Himself; **descuvijô sovre eyos Rey de Reyes delos**
      Reyes the supreme King of Kings revealed Himself unto them
      (Passover's Haggadah)
descuvrimiento appearance
desde since
desden disdain; scorn (n)

desdeñador disdain, scorn (n)
desdeño disdain (n)
desdeñozo disdainful
desdevanado emptied; uncoiled
desdoganar clear at the customs (Ital *sdogana* customs)
desdorar remove the glitter (v)
desdublado unfolded
desdyempos/(a) destyempos at unusual moments; at the wrong time
desdyentado toothless
desembro December
desendensya descent; lineage
desendyente descendant
desentralizar decentralize
deseo wish; desire (n); desirable; **deseo cumplido** wish-come-true
desesperar despair (v)
desfacharse to become insolent
desfamasyon defamation
desfashar untie the swaddling clothes of a newborn baby; untie a bandage
desfavoravle unfavorable
desfazedero continuous squandering; tendency to waste
desfazer undo; destroy
desfazyendar make someone lose his fortune
desfecha defeat; failure
desfeuzia suspicion; defiance; lack of trust
desfiar defy (v)
desfilachar unravel the threads of a tissue or of women's stockings; to be taken by nostalgia
desfinkar pluck; tear off (Port *fincar*)
desfio defiance; provocation
desflorar deflower
desformasyon deformation
desfuersas lack of strength
desgañar make someone lose the desire
desgarrado ragged
desgraciado disgraceful; unfortunate
desgrasya catastrophe; misfortune
desguarnir strip furniture or curtains of all garnish, adornment or ornament
desgustar disgust

deshado left; abandoned; divorced; **deshado es pedrido** (lit: abandoned is lost) you should not act with proud and refuse what is offered to you, under the pretext that it is not enough—because if you refuse it, you risk to lose it, so accept it now!

deshadura divorce; repudiation

deshar let; abandon; bestow

deshifrar decipher

desido (se) decided

desierto desert

desinko old Turkish money, equivalent to five paras; **no vale un desinko** something without any value

desiño drawing

desjachado flattened; crushed

desjarrapado badly dressed

desjarretado extremely weakened; extenuated

desjayirsiz someone who does not help anybody (T *hayirsiz*)

desjen harmony; order (H)

desjenado disgraceful; clumsy

desjuersado without strength; not on the go, suffering from lumbago; overpowered by extreme lassitude

deskadenar remove the chains

deskadensya maturation; expiration; due date for payment of a bond

deskaer expire; to become due

deskaeser decline; sink; forfeit; lose all esteem and consideration

deskaido expired; having come to term; ruined; abandoned (building, furniture); in bad shape

deskalavro wound at the forehead; mental exhaustion resulting from a sustained effort to resolve a problem

deskalso shoeless

deskamado covered with scales; fish ready to be grilled

deskaminado having lost one's way

deskansar rest; relax

deskanso rest (n)

deskantarse regain all abilities and senses

deskarada women leading an immoral life

deskarado insolent; shameless (masc)

deskargar discharge (v)

deskariñar feel nostalgia

deskariño nostalgia of a person or country

deskarnado with torn skin

deskaro insolence
deskarrankar uproot violently
deskartar choose; sort
deskasharetado made lean; downcast; salient, emaciated face bones
deskavesado headless; tired from struggling with a tough problem
deskerensya disaffection; hostility
deskojido specially selected; chosen; elected
deskolgar unhook
deskolorado discolored
deskonfiado distrustful
deskonoser ignore
deskonsejar advise against
deskonsiderar disregard (v)
deskonsolado inconsolable
deskontente discontent
deskontinuar discontinue
deskonto discount (n)
deskorajar discourage
deskorchar pull off the skin
deskornado with the horns sawed off
deskoronar remove the crown; dismiss a royal authority (v)
deskorosonar act in a way that all affection by other people is stiffled
deskorrer run (fluid); drip (v)
deskorsar deliver a speech (v)
deskorsoz speeches; deskorsoz de Bar Mitzvah Bar Mitzvah speeches
deskovijar remove the bed covers
deskozir/deskuzir undo the sewing
deskreditar stop a credit
deskredito discredited
deskripsyon description
deskrivir describe
deskulpa excuse (n)
deskuvridor discoverer
deskuvyerta discovery
deskuydo negligence
deslendrar remove lice from the hair
deslustar make unvarnished
desluytar remove the symbols of mourning such as veil, armband, etc.
desmagajar reduce to very small, unusable bits (v)
desmañetizar dehypnotize; demagnetize

desmantekar remove the butter
desmarañar free somebody from an obsession
desmayado fainted
desmayar faint (v)
desmazalado unfortunate (from H *mazal* luck)
desmelar disentangle
desmembrar dismember
desmenguado reduced; diminished
desmenguar reduce; diminish (v)
desmentir deny
desmenuzar crumble; cut into pieces (v)
desmodrado someone who acts strangely or atypically
desmodrar act in a strange or unusual way
desmoladera sharpening stone
desmolar sharpen
desmoludara deterioration; decay
desmonetizar demonetize; make someone lose social prestige
desmontar dismount; undo piece by piece
desmoralizar demoralize
desmoronar disrupt; make fall in ruin
desnaturar denature
desñegarse deny oneself (v)
desnudar undress
desñudar untie
desnudez nudity
desnudo naked; destitute
desolar desolate (v); sadden
despajamyento removal of the hay
despaldado someone with a displaced shoulder; tension on the
    shoulder
despapar wring (v)
desparecer disappear
desparisyon disappearance
desparte (en) (prep) in particular; besides
desparte in addition to
despartimyento separation; departure; repartition
desparzido dispersed; scattered
despasensyado made impatient
despasensyar make lose patience
despasyenado without zeal; disaffected

despecharse provoke jealousy by pompously displaying goods that
    others cannot afford
despechugado disheveled
despedasado torn into pieces
despedrar remove the stones of a camp or a field
despedrer squander (v)
despegar unglue
despeñado someone who has ceased suffering; death after prolonged
    suffering
despeñar clear a pledge or a pawn; pay a debt
despensada pregnant woman nearing term
despensero intendant
desperdrer squander; dilapidate
despertar wake up; awaken
despertez vivacity; alertness
desperto woke up; awaken
despeynar undo the hair
despies - (y tambien) despies (and this) after that
desplantar uproot a plant; extirpate
desplazer displease
despligar deploy
desplumar take the feathers away; dispossess
despojar plunder; take as booty; dispossess
despolvorear season with salt, pepper. etc; cover with flour, sugar, etc.
desponible available
desposivle deprived of goods; ruined
despot Greek orthodox bishop
despota despot
despovlar depopulate; ravage (v)
despozado fiancé
despozarse get engaged
despozoryo engagement
despreçiada - (fue) despreçiada su señora en sus ojos his wife (was)
    downgraded in his eyes
despreokupado not preoccupied; free of worries
despresyasyon depreciation
despues after; afterwards
despuevlado not populated
despulgar remove the fleas
despuntar appear; appear at the horizon

despyojar remove the lice
desque once
desraigar uproot (v)
desrazonivle unreasonable
desregulado deregulated
desreinar exhaust; to have pain in the kidneys
desrepozado indisposed; uneasy
desrepozar molest; incommodate (v)
dessatento impoliteness
dessear wish; desire (v)
desseo desire (n); y a ti su desseo and his desires will be carried on
    to you
dessiyado remove the seal
destabafar remove from the brazier or the flame substances that could
    extinguish it
destakar detach; remove the tie (v)
destejar remove the tiles of the roof
destemodo in this way
destenir detain (v)
desterràdos thrust (n)
desterrar exhume; ha desterraste you have chased me
desterro hunted
destilasyon distillation
destinasyon destination
destino destiny
destrenzar let down
destronamuento dethroning
destronar dethrone
destronkar cut the trunk of a tree; amputate a limb
destrueser cause fear
destruir destroy
destruktiva woman who wastes money, provisions, linen, etc.
destruktivo destructive
desturbar disturb
desuaynado pulling the sword from its sheath
desvaneser tire (v); annoy by continuous blabber
desvanesido (adj) someone who talks nonsense; someone who has fan-
    tastic ideas
desvaporado evaporated
desvareo delirium

desvayanada drawn (sword)
desvaynado unsheathed
desvaynar undo a hem; unsheath
desvedar lift a ban (v)
desvelado someone who suddenly awakens from sleep
desvelopar develop
desventura misfortune; adversity; reversal of fortune
desverguensa absence of shame
desverguensado bold-faced; brazen-faced
desvestir take away the clothes
desviar deviate (v)
desvidar unscrew
desvio deviation
desyelar thaw (v)
desyelo thawing
desyervar weed out (grass)
detadràrse tarry (v)
detalyar detail; expose in detail (v)
detalyo detail
detardaussé was late
detektiv detective
detenedor holder of an object (pin, pincer)
detenensya delay (n)
detener hold; hold to oneself; detain (v); que detener detuuo lu por to
    do valua a casa de Abimelech he has made totally sterile the
    entire house of Abimelech (Fer Bib Gen)
detente no me tokes conceited person who gets offended by any act of
    familiarity coming from "inferior" people. This is an ironical
    allusion to the New Testament, Saint John XX, 17: *no me tangere*
    do not touch me
detras on the back
deueler experience pain; feel guilty; to be afraid
devañar roll a thread, a rope or a ribbon to a ball-shaped skein
devda debt
devenir to become
devente ancient Turkish money
dever must; owe
devian azer they should have done
deviar deviate
devino he guessed

devisa debt
devizar see
devlet state; government (T kanunn)
devletdje from the of the government (T *devletçe*, kanunn)
devorar devour
devoreo sudden and and pressing hunger
devre change of position (of a bale, sack, or package) (T)
devuado devoted
dexar leave (v)
dexara varon a su padre y madre the young man will abandon (leave)
    his father and mother (Fer Bib Gen)
dexe - (no te) dexe I did not let you; I did not allow you
dexis me let me
deydad deity (Ferrara Siddur)
deyo kon eyo (prep) (lit: managing the goat and the cabbage) fig for:
    handling blame and praise at the same time
dezabonar cancel a subscription
dezaeyo wish (n)
dezafeksyonarse detach oneself; cease to be affectionate
dezafektar disaffect
dezafogarse to be set free; open one's heart; let go feelings
dezagradavle disagreeable; unpleasant
dezagradecer pay back with ingratitude
dezagradensya ingratitude
dezagradesido not welcome; undesirable
dezagradesimiento ingratitude
dezagrado discontent; displeasure
dezakomodado situation of someone who is disturbed in his habits
    and comfort; discomfort (n)
dezakomodar produce discomfort (v)
dezakordado not tuned (instrument)
dezakostumdrado not accustomed; having lost the habit
dezarinar free from quicksand (v)
dezarmamyento disarmament
dezarmar disarm
dezarrijar unfold clothes, tissues, etc.; unwrinkle
dezatado untied
dezatar detach; untie; free from bond (v)
dezaunado disunited
dezavantajado disadvantaged

dezavrigar deprive of shelter, of foothold; remove from protection
dezayunar to have breakfast
dezayuno breakfast
dezazer undo
dezazimyento squandering (more formal: *desfazimiento*)
dezeado wanted; desired
dezeavle desirable
dezecha defeat; failure
dezechado refused; rejected; excluded; eliminated; discarded
dezembrolyas disentangle; help to get out of a confusing situation
dezempeñar lift a pledge; pay the due to stop a pledge; remove a commitment; cancel an appointment
dezeñador drawer; someone who draws
dezenfadado exorcised; freed from bad influences; magical ceremony by which a newborn is liberated from bad sprits
dezenfadar franchise (v); free from bad influence
dezeno tenth
dezenredado disinherited
dezenredar free from a net; liberate from a difficult situation
dezenteressar lose interest; pay off someone's share in a company
dezenterrar exhume
dezenvainar undo the hem
dezeo (de alkavo) last wish
dezeo desire; aspiration; envy; will
dezéôzo desirous; needy
dezeredar disinherit
dezermandado being denied by brothers
dezermandarse get involved in a conflict with brothers
dezesperado despairing; hopeless
dezesperansa despair (n)
dezesperar despair (v)
dezesperare despair (v)
dezespero despair; hopelessness
dezgrasya disgrace
dezidera words which should not be taken literally
dezidero blabber (n)
dezierto desert (n)
deziluzyon disillusion (n)
deziluzyonado disillusioned
deziluzyonar disillusion (v)

deziocho eighteen
dezir say; express in oral or written form
dezisiete seventeen
dezistimyento desist; stop (n)
dezistir desist
dezkonsejar dissuade
dezmayo fainting; dezmayo fuerte strong fainting
dezmudar take clothes off
dezokupado idle; without work
dezokupar free from work (v)
dezokupasyon idleness; leisure
dezolar get desolated
dezonestedad dishonesty
dezonesto dishonest
dezonor dishonor (n)
dezonor dishonor (v)
dezonorado dishonored
dezonoravle dishonorable
dezonra injury; insult; offense
dezorado someone with a bad time management
dezoras/a dezoras at irregular and unusual hours
dezorden disorder
dezorganizado disorganized
dezoryentado disoriented
dezotorizar revoke mandate or power
dezovedeser disobey
dezraygar uproot (v)
dezreynarse hurt one's lumbar; to have a renal stone crisis; to have a
    lumbago
dezunido disunited
dezuzado uninhabited
dezyerto desert
dezyertor deserter
di - (a mi Arco) di en la nuue (I shall put) my Ark in the clouds (Fer
    Bib Gen)
di agora mi hermana bien a mi por ti thus tell that you are my sister,
    so that I shall be well treated because of you (Abraham to his
    wife Sara when he is with the Pharaoh) (Fer Bib Gen)
di I gave

dia day; en el dia on the day; en el dia el este this day (Salonica Pesach
  Siddur); dia bueno happy day; happiness; good day; dias negros
  black (bad) days
diabet diabetes
diabetiko diabetic
diaboliko diabolic
dialekto dialect
diametro diameter
diarea diarrhea
diaspora diaspora
diavleria devilish acts
diavlez reprehensible ingenuity; skillful but dishonest maneuvers
diavlo devil
dibuk imaginative creature which causes havoc, destruction and devastation (H)
dibur de merkader merchant's promise; promise made by a trustful
  person (H)
dibur promise; commitment
dicát attention (T *dikkat*)
dich straight; rigid; vertical (T *dinç*)
dicha order; command (n)
dichas sayings
dicheron they said
dictovka dictation (Bulg)
dido ek dido person whom someone does not want to designate by
  name in order not to attract attention, because the other person is
  standing nearby and should not know that the conversation is
  about him/her
didyez old Turkish coin of little value
dientadura false teeth, denture
diente tooth
dies ten
diestra right (adj f)
dieta diet
diez ten
diezen tenth
diez mil ten thousand
diezinueve nineteen
diezinueven nineteenth

dieziocho eighteen
diezmo dime
difasmasyon defamation
diferencia difference
diferenciar differentiate
diferente different
difetozo defective (Ital *difettoso*)
difeza defense
difinder prohibit (v, Monastir dialect)
difirenti different
difísil difficult
difteria diphtheria
difuncto defunct
digestivle digestible
digi digi dialect of Jews from the interior provinces of the Balkans. It
    is characterized by a slightly Portuguese pronunciation: the d and
    the g sound hard; the names which terminate in -o in Judeo-
    Spanish are pronunced with a -u instead (see words from the
    Monastir dialogue in this dictionary), for example: *dishu* instead
    of *dicho*. Such peculiarities in pronunciation have resulted in the
    city Israelites (Istanbul, Salonica) to ironically use the term for all
    Jews living in the interior provinces
dignidear cane, especially the one used by the blind (T *deynek*)
dijerir digest (v)
dijestivo digestible (n)
dijestyon digestion
dikat attention! take care! (T *dikkat*)
dikduk grammar; syntax (H)
dikotes tranquilizer
diktador dictator
diktadura dictatorship
dikte dictation(n)
dil of the
dilbaza charming, graceful woman (T)
dilenji beggar (T *dilenci*)
dilenjilik status of the beggar (T *dilencilik*)
dilettante amateur (Ital)
dilinjear ask for alms
diluuio flood (n)

diluvyo great flood
dimalo veil of a Jewish woman
dimandar ask; request (v, Monastir dialect)
dimensyon dimension
diminituvo diminutive
diminusyon diminution
dimyon resemblance (H)
din justice; jurisprudence; judgment; the law (H)
dinamiko dynamic
dinamita dynamite
dinar monetary unit in a number of countries
dinastia dynasty
dinero money
dingun no one
dinguno no one
diñidad dignity
dinim norms (H)
diñitaryo dignitary
diñitozo someone who has a reserved, slightly haughty attitude
diño worthy; deserving
dinsiz without religion; atheist (T); dinsiz imansiz with no religion and
    no faith (T)
dinyo deserving
dio - (lo) dio gave it
Dio God; Dio de Yaacov God of Jacob; dios gods
dip bottom; depth; abyss (T)
dipla antipathy; animosity
diploma diploma
diplomado graduate; diplomat
diplomasia diplomacy
diplomatiko diplomatic
dipsiz uneducated, insolent person (T)
diputado deputy
dirà will say
diran they will say
dirdir (onomatopoeia) irritating chatter (T)
direk pole; mast; pillar; column; stand (T)
direksyon direction
direktiva directive

direkto direct (adj)
direktor director
direktoryal directorial
diri I shall say
dirijente director
dirijir direct (v)
dirito law; right to dispose of something; right to claim something
    from another person (Ital *diritto*)
dirush speech; sermon; homily (H)
disfamar defame
disgustar disgust; discontent (v)
disgusto disgust; discontent (n)
dish parasi (lit: tooth money) (T) payment claimed by the Janissaries
    after they were served food and drink at a Jewish house, because
    they pretended that the food was hard to masticate. Idiomatic
    expression for a paradoxical claim of someone who, instead of
    being thankful for what he has received, complains and
    revendiates.
disharelik apartment reserved to men in a Turkish residence (T *dishari*
    outside)
dishi I told
dishipla apprentice; servant
dishiplika young female servant; very young apprentice
dishiplina discipline (n)
dishiplinado disciplined
dishiplinar discipline (v)
dishiplo disciple
dishiplo student; disciple
dishli person with missing teeth (T *dish* tooth)
disho he said
disimulado dissimulated
disimular dissimulate
disimulasyon dissimulation
disipado dissipated
disko disk
diskordante discordant
diskordya discord
diskorsar make a speech
diskorso speech
diskreto discrete

diskulpa excuse (n)
diskulpado proven not guilty; excused
diskulpar prove somebody's innocence; excuse
diskusion discussion
diskusyon discussion
diskutavle discussible
diskutidero mania of holding endless discussions
diskutir discuss (v)
disminuir diminish
disolusyon dissolution
disosyar dissociate
disosyasyon dissociation
dispartir (si) say good-bye; see off
dispensa dispense (n)
dispensar dispense (v)
dispensaryo dispensary
dispersar disperse
dispersyon dispersion
displazer a unu resent
disponer dispose
disponilbidad availability
disponivle available
disposto disposed; inclined
dispozar dispose
disproporsyon disproportion
disproporsyonado disproportionate (adj)
disproporsyonar disproportionate (v)
distansya distance (n)
diste (a mi nome) diste semen you have given no child to me (Fer
    Bib Gen)
distengar distinguish
distingido distinguished
distingir distinguish
distinksyon distinction
distraer distract
distraksyon distraction
distribuidor distributor
distribuir distribute
distribusyon distribution
disturbar trouble; impede; importune

disturbo trouble; importunity
dita social logo; insignia (Ital *ditta*)
dite fishing nets (Gr)
diunidad divinity (Ferrara Siddur)
divagasyon divagation
divan the Ottoman Sultan's Council of Vizirs (ministers). The Sultan used to listen the Council's sessions from behind a curtain. It is said that at one time, the Grand Rabbi, the Patriach of the Greek Orthodox Church, and the Patriach of the Gregorian Armenians held a ministerial rank and participated in the Council's sessions
divan divan; Turkish-style sofa (T)
divane crazy (T)
diversidad diversity
diverso diverse
divertimyento entertainment
divertyente entertaining
divia di ser must be
divinidad divinity
divino divine
divizar divide
divizyon division
divorsado divorced
divorsar divorce (v)
divorsyo divorce (n)
diximos we tell (Ferrara Siddur)
dixo said
diya day
diz knee (T)
dizazer undo (v)
dizenyo design
dizesej sixteen
dizesyete seventeen
dizesyeten seventeenth
dizinueve nineteen
diziocho eighteen
dizir say
dizisyete seventeen
dizisyeten seventeenth
dizyertir desert (v)
dizyerto desert (n)

djente people
djephane ammunition (T *cebhane* kanunn)
djerah surgeon (T *cerrah* kanunn)
djerahlik surgery (T *cerrahlik* kanunn)
djereme penalty; fine (T *cereme* kanunn)
djesaret courage (T *cesaret* kanunn)
djeza penalty (T *ceza* kanunn)
djeza penalty; fine (T *ceza*)
djinganá Gypsy
djinoyu knee (Monastir dialect)
djis kind; species; race (T *cins*)
djis de perro bad person
djodru thick (Monastir dialect)
djordu thick (Monastir dialect)
djube robe with long sleeves and long shirt worn by men in the
    Ottoman Empire (T *cübbe*)
djuderia Jewish quarters
djudio Jew
djugo game
djunto together
djuntos vos fuitech you went together
djusgar judge (v)
djusgo judge (n)
djustamente justly
djusticia justice
djusto just
djustu correct (adj) (Monastir dialect)
djuzdju court; tribunal (Monastir dialect)
djuzgar judge (v)
dobla doubloon (old Spanish gold coin)
doblado doubled; folded
dobladura fold; inner layer of tissue in a jacket or coat
doblar fold (v)
dobre loyal
doctor de matasano lit: doctor who kills the healthy
docuneár tease; tease by touching (from T *dokunmak*)
dodo word said to make children sleep
dogana customs
dogañero customs officer (Ital *doganiere*)
dogma dogma

dogmatiko dogmatic
dogmatismo dogmatism
doje twelve
doktor doctor
doktoresa female doctor
dokumentado documented
dokumentar document (v)
dokumento document (n)
dokunear hurt; damage by tightening; cause harm; disturb
    (T *dokunmak*)
doladizo idol
dolanderear swindle; fraud; cheat (v, T *dolandirmak*)
dolandirji swindler; impostor (T *dolandirici*)
dolandirjilik fraud; swindle; imposture (T, *dolandiricilik*)
dolap cupboard (T)
dolar dollar
dolash surveillance; round of the guards (T *dolashmak* make a round)
dolashear return to the same place several times; turn around the sur-
    roundings (T *dolashmak*)
doleansas painfulness; complaints; recriminations
dolensya indisposition; complaint about pain
dolente dolent; someone who feels a pain and complains about it
dolma eggplant, tomato, pepper, squash or cabbage stuffed with a mix
    of ground meat, rice and spices (T)
dolma rice balls steamed in wine leaves, cabbage or lettuce
dolma variety of squash or pumpkin used as a vegetable. The pulp is
    used for stuffing pastries and pies or to make preserved fruit (T)
dolor pain (of childbirth); **dolor de kavesa** headache; **dolor de tripa**
    bellyache; **dolor de tripa le vino** he got scared
dolorido painful
dolorio painfulness; lamentations
dolorozo painful
dolorsiko light pain
doloryozo painful
dolse sweets; desert
dolyente (adj) suffering; painful; uneasy; moaning out of pain
dolyente ill
domeno domain
dominador dominator
dominar dominate (v)

dominasyon domination
domingo Sunday
domino society game popular among Sephardim
domuz pork; pig (T) used as an insult
doña lady
donador donor
donannma illumination; fire work; bright, shining light; navy (T)
donar make a donation
donasyon donation
donde de aqui vienes y adonde andas where do you come from and
   where are you going? (Fer Bib Gen)
donde from where; thereby
dondurma popular oriental ice cream consisting of milk, julep and
   sugar (T)
dondurmadji ice cream vendor (T)
donme member of a Judeo-Muslim sect, follower of the Smyrniot Messiah Sabbatai Sevi. The sect was started by the pompous conversion
   of 300 families in Salonica (1683); following schisms resulted in the
   formation of three sub-sects. While fervent Muslims on the exterior,
   it is believed that the Donmes practiced a kind of crypto-Judaism.
   It was reported that during the time of the Varlik Vergisi (wealth
   tax, capital tax) imposed primarily on Jewish, Greek and Armenian
   minorities, the Donmes were treated as a category in between these
   religious minorities and the Muslims. After the Turkish War of
   Independence and the Treaty of Lausanne (1922), at the time of the
   Turkish-Greek population exchange, the Donmes moved from
   Salonica to Turkey. Ataturk, himself a native of Salonica (but not a
   Donme, according to his family roots) felt sympathetic to the
   Donmes. He thought that they would enthusiastically integrate
   themselves into the new Republic of Turkey and become productive
   and prosperous citizens. The Salonician Judeo-Spanish historian
   Joseph Nehama extensively described crypto-Judaic practices
   among the Donmes. His Istanbul counterpart Avraham Galante
   had to be more cautious.
dono gift; present; talent; aptitude; natural gift
donum ancient Turkish agricultural measure of variable value, which
   went from 562 to 1600 square meters and sometimes far more
   (for practical purpose 1,000 square meters)
donzel young man
donzeya very beautiful young woman

dor century; generation; era
dorada dorado
dorador - (al) **dorador** around
dorar make shine like gold (v)
dormid stay (sleep) there for this night (imp) (Fer Bib Gen)
dormidera poppy seed
dormidero persistent somnolence; estar kon **dormidero** to have a persistent envy to sleep
dormido (adj and n) sleeping; slow, sleepy individual
dormidor sleeper
dormir sleep (v); **dormiremos** we shall sleep
dormirse fall asleep
dormisina somnolence; untimely sleepiness
dormitorio dormitory; sleeping pill; narcotic
dormyente sleeping; motionless
dos los mundos from the worlds (Ferrara Siddur)
dos two
doskel teacher
dota dowry
dotar give a generation
dotor doctor
dotrina doctrine
dotrinado disciplined; straightforward person
dotrinar teach; indoctrinate; reprimand
dotrino teaching; education; moral counselling
dover duty; moral obligation; moral law (opposed to Ital *dirito* civic law)
dovlet state; government; governmental power; public good; wealth; power; independence (T *devlet*)
doz two
doza dose
dozaje dosage; measuring a dose
dozar measure a dose
doze twelve
dozen twelfth
dozena dozen
dozientas (tos) two hundred
dozmil two thousand
dozudear arrange (from T *dizmek*)
dozyentos two hundred

draga female monster eating children or men and causing devastation;
loud, ill-tempered, scolding woman; very active woman; se fizo
una draga (lit: she became a *draga*) she assumed all the task by
herself; she put up with an enormous task
drago/dragon dragon
dragona woman of exuberant activity
drajme/drama drachm (Greek monetary unit)
drama city in Thrace
drama drama
drama weight measure worth 3,205 grams (400 dramas = 1 oke)
(okka); an ancient Turkish weight equaling 1,282 grams
(T *dirhem*); ya se kuantos dramas peza (lit: I know how
many *dramas* he weighs) I know him very well, I know
his morality
dramali an inhabitant of Drama
dramatiko dramatic
dramatizar dramatize
dranear drain (v)
drapero merchant of drapes
dravear drive (v, Eng)
dreno drain; tube; catheter
drezina small wagon circulating on railroad tracks, for control and
surveillance
droga drug; fizo la droga (arch) (lit: he did the drug) the advice/the
suggestion has had an effect
drogeria drugstore
drogerio exaggerated accumulation of medicines and drugs
drogista drugist
duana customs
duanera customs officer
dubara loud noise; unsound maneuvers; trick; fraud (T)
dubaradji trickster; turbulent person; swindler
dubarina tumult; disturbance; confusion
dublado doubled; folded
duble fold; folding
dubyar doubt (v)
dubyo doubt; uncertainty
dubyozo doubtful; suspicious; problematical
ducados ducats (gold coins)
ducha interminable discussion

duda doubt (n)
dudozo doubtful; suspicious
dueledor someone who worries, who is in pain, who keeps himself in
    state of alertness in order to avoid disorder
dueler hurt; cause pain (v)
duelista fighter in a duel
duelo pain; worry; anxiety
dueños de firmamiento people who have entered in an alliance
duerme (arch) third person indicative of verb *dormir* sleep
dukado ducat (ancient gold coin)
duke Duke
dukeza duchess
duko cash payment; ruby on the nail; pagar duko pay cash
dukunear touch; indispose (T *dokunmak*)
dula prosperity; grandeur
dulanderear swindle (v, T *dolandirmak*)
dulanderji swindler (T *dolandirici*)
dulandiridjilik swindling (T *dolandiricilik*)
dulce sweet
dulci di rozas marmalade made of rose petals
dulgyer carpenter (T *dülger*)
dulse - (agua) dulse potable water; tyempo dulse sweet, nice tempera-
    ture
dulse marmalade; preserves; dulse blanco (lit: white sweet) white and
    thick sweet paste, a favorite Passover dessert, spread on bread or
    served in a glass of very cold water
dulsera plate on which the sweets are served
dulsor sweetness
dulsura marmalade; preserves; sweets; espartir la dulsura distribute
    sweets at the occasion of a happy event
dulsurias all kinds of sweets and desserts
dulyer carpenter (T *dülger*)
dumalan celery; radish; fig for: narrow-minded individual
dúman smoke (n, T)
duna (contraction of *dünya güzeli*) extremely pretty woman; beauty
duna badly managed
dunamna see *donanma*
dunke (conj) therefore; thus; by consequence (Ital *dunque*)
duo duo; music for two voices, for two instruments
dupyar double (v)

126

dupyo double (adj)
dupyode doubled
duralma see *donanma*
durama oakwood paneling; wooden carpentry (T)
duramadji carpenter (T *dogramaci, doghramaci*)
durante during
durar last (v)
duravle durable
durbin binocular (T *dürbün*)
durera constipation; **mal por durera, peor por shushunera** idiomatic
    expression used for someone who always finds something to com-
    plain about and who is never satisfied
dureza hardness
durmido sleepy, slow person
durmiendo sleeping
durmir sleep (v)
duro hard; firm; solid; painful; disagreeable
duro hardly; with rudeness
dusekchi carpenter; mattress maker (T *döshekçi*)
dush shower-bath
dushar shower (v)
dusharse take a shower
dusheme wooden floor; wardrobe; cupboard
dushman enemy; harmful person (T *düshman*)
duspues after
du'uzu July (Bab)
duvdar doubt (v)
duvdo doubt; suspicion (n)
duvdozo doubtful; uncertain; suspicious
duyulear notice (v); perceive; resent (T *duyulmak*)
duz uniform; smooth; straight (T *düz*)
duzen order; arrangement (T *düzen*)
duzena dozen
duzudeado in order; arranged; uniform; flat; straight
dyense third person of subjective present of verb *dar*
dyentadura denture
dyente tooth
dyenteziko small tooth; teeth of the first denture
dyentista dentist
dyentozo toothed; equipped of teeth like spines

dyentudo someone with long teeth
dyezen tenth
dyezena lot of ten
dyezicho eighteen
dyezimueve nineteen
dyezmo dime; tenth part of the year's benefits or revenues. Sephardic
   families used to give on tenth of their revenues for philanthropic,
   pious, cultural causes or any other public interest institution.
Dyo God
dyoza goddess; female idol

E

ebdomaderyo weekly (n, from F *hebdomadaire*)
ebraismo characteristic feature of Hebrew occurring in another
   language
ebrayko Hebraic
ebrazyante Hebraist
ebreo Hebrew language; **los ebreos** the Hebrews; the Jews
echa action; act
echada allusion; insinuation; **una echada y una estopada** a series of
   hurting and malevolent insinuations
echado chased; expelled; discharged
echadura allusion; insinuation
echar chizos bewitch
echar de lado throw to the side
echar la jhavela try to seduce a man into marriage
echar throw; lay on the bed (v)
echarse kon go to bed with
echas good and bad actions
echizera sorceress
echizeria sorcery
echizo sorcery
echo job
echos business
echosse Abraham sobre sus façes Abraham threw himself on his face
   (Fer Bib Gen)
ecizero magician; sorcerer
ed witness

edad age (n)
edepsiz individual without education (T)
edepsizlik effrontery; impudence (T)
ederneli inhabitant of Edirne (Adrianopolis) in Thrace
edifikar build; construct (v)
edifisyo edifice; building
edisyon edition
editor editor
editoryal editorial
edukado educated
edukar educate
edukasyon education
edukativo educational
edukatrice educator (fem)
edut witness; testimony; attestation (H)
een gueko in suspense; without precise instructions
efendi gentleman
effektivo effective
effektuar effect (v)
effeto effect (n)
efikache efficient
efikasidad efficiency
efod ceremonial garb of the High Priest, Kohen ha Gadol when he
    officiated in the Temple of Jerusalem. The garb was scarlet,
    embroidered with gold and garnished with precious stones (H)
eg (prep) here it is
Egisyano Egyptian (Ital *Egiziano*)
Egito Egypt (Ital *Egitto*)
eglenje distraction; entertainment (T *eglence, eghlence*)
eglisia church (from F *église*)
egoismo egoism
egoista egoist
eguardo regard; respect
egzajerar exaggerate
egzajerasyon exaggeration
egzaktamente exactly
egzakto exact
egzamen examination
egzaminar examine (v)
egzarko Eastern bishop; head, leader of an independent church

egzasperado exasperated
egzejete exegete
egzekusyon execution
egzekutante executive
egzekutar execute (v)
egzekutivo executive
egzema eczema
egzemplar (adj) exemplary
egzemplar sample (n)
egzemplo example
egzempyo example
egzensyon exemption
egzentado exempt (n)
egzentar exempt (v)
egzersar exercise; exert (v)
egzersido exercised
egzersisyo exercise (n)
egzibisyon exhibition
egzijensya exigency
egzijente exigent
egzijible something that can be demanded
egzijir demand (v)
egzilado exiled
egzilar exile (v)
egzilo exile (n)
egzistensya existence
egzistir exist
egzistyente existent
egzodyo exodus
egzonerado exonerated
egzorbitante exorbitant
egzortasyon exhortation; prepping
egzotiko exotic
egzotismo exotism
egzuberante exuberant
ejal cabinet where the Pentateuch is kept (H)
ejipsjano Egyptian
Ejipto Egypt
ejrea necessity; need (H)
ek (prep) behold; here it is

ekdes bequest; gift by will; donation (H)
ekilibro equilibrium
ekivalente equivalent
eklezyastiko ecclesiastic
eklipsa eclipse
eko echo
ekonomia thriftiness; keeping track of expenses
ekonomikamente economically
ekonomiko economical
ekonomista economist
ekonomizar save; spare (v)
ekonomo accountant
ekonomyozo economical person
ekselensya excellency (title)
eksentriko eccentric
eksepsyon exception
eksesivo excessive
ekseso excess
eksik olsun something that is not essential or important
eksitado excited
eksitar excite (v)
eksitasyon excitation
ekskluido excluded
ekskluzivamente exclusively
ekskluzividad exclusivity
ekskluzyon exclusion
ekspatriasyon expatriating
ekspektiva expectation
eksperimentador experiment (n)
eksperimental experimental
eksperimentalmente experimentally
eksperimentar experiment (v)
eksperto expert
eksplikador someone who clarifies and explains
eksplikar explain
eksplikasiones explanations
eksplorador explorer
eksplorar explore (v)
eksplorasyon exploration
eksplozivo explosive

eksplozyon explosion
eksponer expose (v)
eksportador exporter
eksportasyon exportation
ekspozar expose
ekspozisyon exposition
ekspressamente expressly
ekspression expression
eksprimir express (v)
ekspropriar expropriate
ekspropriasyon expropriation
eksterminado exterminated
eksterminador exterminator
eksterminar exterminate (v)
eksterminasyon extermination
eksterno extern
eksteryoramente on the exterior
eksteryorizasyon exteriorization
ekstra (adj and n) extraordinary
ekstraordinaryo extraordinary
ekstravagante extravagant
ekstremista extremist
ekstremo extreme
ekzema eczema
ekzematozo eczematous
El Criador the Creator
El enaltiessen por estar He who dwelleth on high
El God
el he; he who
El ke no es nombrar the One of whose Name is not allowed to be
    pronounced
El nora alila first words of the final prayer of Kippur. This prayer is
    recited with extreme fervor. It is a call for prayer.
elaborar elaborate (v)
elastiko elastic (n)
elastisidad elasticity
elefante elephant
elegantantamente elegantly
elegante elegant
eleksyon election

elektivo elective
elektor elector
elektoral electoral
elektrichita electricity
elektriko electrical
elektrisidad electricity
elektrisyen electrician
eleme kimur (lit: coal which is selected with care) people of the worst
    category, dangerous individual (T *eleme kömür*)
elementaryo elementary
elenguito a little too long
elenguo long (cloth)
elenguor length
elengura length
elenismo Hellenism
eleno Hellenic
elevado elevated
elevo student; disciple
elevu student; disciple (Monastir dialect)
elezido elected
elezir elect (v)
eliminasyon elimination
ella - (con) ella with her
ellos them; themselves; ambos ellos both of them
eloquencia eloquence
eluenga tongue (organ)
elul September. twelfth month of the Jewish calendar, at the end of
    year and the beginning of the autumn season. Among Sephardic
    families, this was a popular time for moving.
elyamo yalesa! call of the firemen to encourage each other when
    pumping water. It is a humorous expression for people who are
    energetically fulfilling a heavy task.
emanar emanate
emanasyon emanation
emansipasyon emancipation
embabukado seduced; lured; cheated
embabukár deceive
embabuko illusion; chimerical hope
embafado impregnated; penetrated by sadness, suffering, rancor,
    humiliation, or suppressed rebellion

embalaje packing in bales
embalar pack in bales (v)
embalsamado mummified; stuffed with aromatics to prevent rotting
embañado drenched; wet until the bones
embañador member of a pious group who washes a dead person, performs the last grooming and enshrouds the corpse
embañadura last grooming of the dead
embandyerar decorate with flags
embarasada pregnant
embarasado embarrassed
embarateser to become cheaper
embargo embargo
embarko embarkation; departure
embarrador eraser
embarrar erase
embas bet (n, T *bahis*)
embasada embassy
embasador ambassador
embasho - (de) embasho sly; perfidious
embaso on the floor
embastador craftsman; worker who makes cotton more flaky and removes dust from woolen mattresses cotton
embatakado excrement; fig for: acting like a busybody; hairsplitting person
embatakado soiled; dirty; covered with excrement; morally soiled; damaged reputation
embatakar soil; stain (v); go to the bathroom (vulg)
embate wind coming from the sea
embelekado person who worries without reason about health and security
embelekar cheat; lure (v)
emberrar bell (v)
embevar absorb like a sponge; imbibe
embevido impregnated
embezado accustomed; trained
embezar learn
embiado emissary
embiamiento sending
embiar send
embiava en eyos (He) brought (sent) upon them

embidar increase the stake; raise the bet
embidya envy; jealousy
embio dispatch; remission
embio lo chased him (Fer Bib Gen)
embio nos por destruir lo por dañar lo he has sent us to destroy him,
    to harm him (Fer Bib Gen)
embirlantado covered with diamonds; very precious; endowed with
    goodness, activity, intelligence, beauty, patience; presented in a
    good light
embit new bet added to original pledge in a game
embivdada widow
embivdado widower
emblankesido whitened; very clean
embodado bride, groom or relatives who are busy with the
    preparation of the wedding. The festivities used to last eight days.
embolada/vaka embolada stupid-looking individual. This is an allusion
    to the bull in the arena whose horns were decorated with leather
    balls and who has very slow reactions.
embolsado wrinkled (fabric, paper)
embolsar put in the purse (v)
embolver wrap rapidly without care; involve somebody in an occupa-
    tion which makes him/her forget
emborachar make drunk; exalt
emborra chases
embovar render stupid
emboveser render stupid
emboveserse to become stupid; lose one's vivacity
embra female
embragar/embralgar tie the cords of drawers or the shoelaces; get
    ready to go on the road
embrolyar set in confusion (v)
embrolyon person who creates confusion
embroyo confusion; imbroglio
embrujar wrap; cover entirely (v)
embrujo envelope
embruneser darken
embruteser make ugly
embudo funnel
embuelto wrapped
embuelvido involved

embultura face; traits; aspect
embutido fully stuffed; person who is deeply immersed in an idea
embutir fill tripes to make sausages
emen emen at the point of; at the critical moment; just at that moment
    (T *hemen hemen*)
emigrado emigrant
emigrante emigrant
emigrar emigrate
emigrasyon emigration
eminensya eminence
emir name written command (n, T *emirname* kanunn)
emir order (n, T kanunn)
emisfero hemisphere
emisyon emission
emmedrado (lit: soiled with excrement) compromised in a
    dishonorable business; extremely obsequious
emmelado sticky person
emosion emotion
empajada large narrow-necked bottle enclosed in wickerwork
empajador taxidermist
empaketido packed
empalar impale
empaldar swaddle a baby
empalukado clumsy
empañado having lost its shine; misty
empapado imbibed
empapelado wrapped in paper
empapushar stuffed with food
empatronyamento appropriation
empecho beginning
empedidor someone who forbids something
empedimyento prevention; obstacle
empedrar pave with stone blocks
empegar coat; cover with a protective layer
empeñado pawned
empeorear worsen
empepinarse stiffen after being offended (v)
emperador emperor
emperatvo imperative
empereteser darken (v)

emperial imperial
emperiko empirical
emperio empire
emperlado covered or adorned with pearls
emperlo but; nonetheless; however
empesar/empessar begin; start (v)
empesuñado stubborn
empido crying; spasm; halting one's breath
empiojado covered with lice
empiojarse to be covered with lice (v)
emplantar create; found
emplaster plaster (v)
emplasto plaster (n)
empleado employee
empleador employer
emplombado plumbed; sealed
empoderar take possession
empokeser diminish the quantity
emponente imposing
emportador importer
emportansa importance
emportante important
emportasyon import (n)
emposante impressive
emposesyamento taking possession
emposibilidad impossibility
emposivle impossible
empostemado exasperated; enervated
empozisyon imposition; contribution; taxation
empregado employee
emprendar give as a pawn
emprender learn
empression impression
emprestado loaned
emprestar loan (v)
emprestimo loan (n)
empresto loan (n)
emprezaryo impresario
emprezo in jail
emprimaro at the beginning; in the first place

emprimeria printing house
emprimidor printer; typesetter
emprimir print (v)
emprovesido impoverished
empues after
empues de su engendrar after she had given birth
empushar push; incite; engage in something (v)
emreanearse to be transported by joy
emrenear rejoice (T *imrenmek*)
emulasyon emulation
en bon ora in a propitious time
en bunora in good fortune
en in; **mi (en) mi** I myself
en sima on top
en tiempo at the time; during
enadado soaked; inundated
enadar swim (v)
enafeyte adorned
enaltésse (He) lifteth
enaltesser exalt
enamorado in love
enano dwarf
enarenar cover with sand (v)
enarkar shaped like an ark
enbeneyar ride (v, T *binmek*)
enbonora Good-bye
enbreve in summary; suddenly; impromptu
encafissiar die (v)
encarnada ingrown nail
encastenada built of stone
encendido flaming
encerrado jailed
enchachar pay reverence to (v)
enchadizo goiter; ganglion
enchikeser reduce in size
enchikesimyento reduction in size
enchorrear inundate
enchusa pie (with spinach, eggplant, squash)
encintamiento giving birth

encintaronse de hijos de Loth su padre they (the daughters of Loth) became pregnant of the sons of Loth from their father (Fer Bib Gen)

encintoçe/encintosse/ençintosse she became pregnant

enclavar nail (v)

encomenta recommendation; command

enconado in a state of impurity

encontrar encounter (v)

encorçado pouty, sulky person

encoruosse a tierra he prostrated himself; he bowed down (Fer Bib Gen)

encorvar bow oneself; worship (v)

encorvàronse they bowed themselves; worshipped

encubierta covered; hidden (fem) (Ferrara Siddur)

encubierto - (y delante de ti sere) encubierto (and I shall be) hidden from before your face

encubrién - (si) encubrién de Abraham lo que vo haziente shall I hide from Abraham what I shall do (Fer Bib Gen)

encuentro encounter (n)

endagora (adv) now; it has been an instant; in one moment

ende (adv) within

endecha de tesabea endecha solemn tune recited on the of the ninth day of the Jewish month Av, as a remembrance of the destruction of the Temple of Jerusalem

endecha dirge, funeral song; solemn, mournful tune

endechár eulogize

endechiso undecided; hesitant (Ital *indeciso*)

endechizyon indecision (Ital *indecizione*)

endeflado full of bitterness

endek ditch (n, T *hendek*, kanunn)

endelantre (de agora, de oy en delantre) (adv) from now on; starting from now

endeñarse condescend; humiliate oneself by accepting an invitation from an inferior

enderechamyento reparation; retribution; correction

enderechar redress; arrange correctly

enderecharse redress oneself; enter the good path; correct one's posture; straighten one's back

enderechura as usual; as always

endevanar spin a hem around a spool
endevdado in debt
endevina fortuneteller (fem)
endevinar find out; divine (v)
endevino (vido que se) ençinto (she saw that) she was pregnant
endevino fortuneteller (masc)
endiferensya indifference
endiferente indifferent
endikar indicate
endikasyon indication
endispensavle indispensable
endispozisyon indisposition
endivina riddle
endivya endive
endjidar hurt; give pain
endjuntos together
endoloryado painful; person with a great sorrow
endomajar cause harm; damage (v)
endonar dress elegantly
endono adornment
endorada dorado (fish)
endorar cover with gold; decorate
endorarse to become loaded with gold; to adorn in a very rich
      manner (v)
endormecer get sleepy; calm down; turn away someone's attention in
      order to laugh at him/her
endormesimyento numbing
endulkadera female magician who practices exorcism and prepares
      herbal mixtures
endulkador male magician
endulko incantation; charm; magical practice to treat a mental diseases
      or a mysterious disease
endulsar sweeten
endurar harden
endureserse to become hardened, cruel, or inflexible; se le
enduresyo el korason (lit: his heart hardened) he has become incapable
      of sweetness and pity
enduresido hardened; someone who has become cruel, inflexible, or
      stubborn
enduresimyento hardening; stubbornness; obstination

endurmeser make numb
endyamantar cover with diamonds or jewels
endyavlar pervert; render malevolent (v)
endyentar get the first teeth
endyozar deify
eneglear entertain (T *eglenmek, eghlenmek*)
enella in her; from her
enemigo enemy; en kaer tu enemigo no alegres do not rejoice when
   your enemy falls; a tus enemigos! ni a tus enemigos! ni a mis enemigos, a los enemigos de lost jidyos! (lit: to your enemies! Not
   even to your enemies, not to my enemies nor to the enemies of
   Israel!) this is so abominable that it should not be wished to
   anyone
enemistad enmity; hatred
enemistozo unfriendly
enerjia energy
enerjiko energetic
enfadado newborn who has just received a name and is consequently
   sheltered from the bad spirits
enfamante infamous
enfarinado covered with flour; hypocritical person
enfarinar cover with flour; hide the true natures of a thing
enfashado swaddled infant; swaddling a baby
enfashadura swaddle (n)
enfastyado bored
enfastyar bore (v)
enfastyo boredom
enfastyozo boring; fastidious; disgusting; disturbing
enfavoreser favor (v)
enfechizar bewitch; seduce; fascinate
enfedeser to become rotten; spread a fetid smell
enfedesimyento putrefaction
enfermedad/enfermidad infirmity; disease; ailment
enfermeria infirmary
enfermo sick
enfeuzyar give the faith; reinforce a belief
enfiilar string a thread; hold together by a thread
enfilada deceitfulness; action aimed at causing trouble for someone but
   having only little effect
enfilandrar inflict great sorrow; afflict (v)

enfilandrarse ruminate on black memories; grind the black, swallow
    bilious saliva (v)
enfilendrado stuffed with bitterness; strongly afflicted
enfiltrar infiltrate; inoculate (v)
enfiltrasyon infiltration
enfinkar plunge a pointed object(v)
enfirmeriya infirmary
enfirmyer paramedic (n)
enfirmyera nurse (n)
enfistolado having a fistula or a pustule
enfistolarse to be affected with fistulae; to have a purulent
    inflammation of the skin
enflakeser lose weight; weaken
enflamado inflamed
enflamar inflame
enflamasyon inflammation
enflamavle inflammable
enflechar kill with arrows; pierce with arrows; stare with furious eyes
enflorado flowered; with flower designs (cloth, paper, carpentry)
enflorar flower (v); decorate with flowers; flourish
enfloreser produce flowers; prosper; vivas y enfloreskas, komo el
    peshiko en el agua freska, el peshiko para komer y el chikitiko
    para engrandeser may you live, grow and flourish, like the little
    fish in fresh water, the little fish to be eaten and the small fish to
    grow (said when a child sneezes)
enfloresido flowered; in full state of prosperity
enfloresyente florescent
enfluensa influenza; flu
enfluensar influence (v)
enfluente influent
enfluir influence (v)
enfodrar double the inner face of clothes with lining (v)
enforcar hang (v)
enforkado hanged; aser enforkado to be hanged
enforkar hang (v, Port)
enfornado something that is put in the oven
enfornador worker in charge of putting bread, pastry etc. in the oven
enforrar put lining in a jacket, coat, etc. (v, Port); enclose in horse-
    cloth or saddle-cloth; wrap oneself; cover oneself warmly
enforro lining

enfortecer strengthen; reinforce
enfortecido reinforced
enfortesimyento reinforcement
enforticier strengthen
enfrankeadas - en favlado le agrada emplear palavras enfrankeadas he takes pleasure in using frenchified words
enfrankeado frenchified; Europeanized, westernized. Among all European nations who influenced the Turks and the Sephardic Jews in Turkey, the French (T *Frenk* or *alafranga*) influence was the strongest. The reason for this is that the first friendly contact with a European nation was made between the King of France, François the First and Soliman (Süleyman) the Magnificent, followed by a grant of extraterritorial privileges for Frenchmen, mainly merchants in Istanbul, the so-called Capitulations. The rabbinate strongly opposed the frenchifying of the Jews, especially after the opening of schools by the Paris-headquartered Alliance Israélite. Because of the French education in these schools, French started to replace Judeo-Spanish as the family language among the Sephardic elite.
enfregoneado rumpled; crumpled; ruffled
enfrenar put a break; refrain; moderate; slow down
enfrente in front of
enfronar cover with horse-cloth (v)
enfruteser give or produce fruits (trees)
enfuliñado covered with soot
enfureser make furious; irritate
enfushkar give blisters
enfyelar load with gall; embitter; sadden
enfyestado (adj) celebrating a feast
engañador someone who deceives or cheats
enganates you have misled
enganchado crooked; cunning; sly; malevolent
enganchar catch with a hook; shape as a hook (v)
engancharse hang on; to be caught by a grappling; make faces, gesticulate; twist, wring; to become cunning or artful; get immobilized
engangrenarse to become gangrenous; worsen
enganiar/enganyár fool; cheat; mislead (v)
engaño deception
engendra - empues de su engendra after his birth
engendrar give birth

engendro fathered; gave birth; engendered; generated
engeniero engineer
engfloresimyento flowering; prosperity
englenear entertain; distract (T *eglenmek, eghlenmek*)
englenje entertainment (T *eglence, eghlence*)
englobar unite; put together (v)
engloreserse glorify oneself
englutir gulp; engulf; swallow (v)
engodrar gain weight
engodreser swell tremendously
engomar coat with gum; glue (v)
engormado (adj) exasperated by suffering, irritation, or exhaustion
engoznar place hinges (v)
engrandecer grow; enlarge
engrandissir grow; enlarge
engrasyado someone who has received a divine gift; someone who is loved by everyone
engrasyar grant the gift of being loved and successful
engratitud ingratitude
engrato unthankful
engreñar surround; cover with cloudiness (in the eyes)
engreshado soiled; covered with grease
engroso wholesale
engroviñado rumpled; ruffled
engrutir swallow; gobble (v)
enguantado wearing gloves; strained; forced; unnatural; obsequious
enguayar lament about a dead person; moan; cry loudly (v)
enguente ointment
enguentiko (lit: small ointment) ointment prepared by an old woman in the Jewish neighborhood of La Kula (the Tower), around the Galata Tower in Istanbul. She prepared and sold ointments in little cosmetic boxes, which were very popular among women of the Sephardic high society.
enguerkado alert; vivacious; resourceful
enguyos nausea (Port)
enharemado excommunicated
enheremar excommunicate (from H *herem* excommunication)
eniadido allied with; joined with
eniadir add to what exists
enigma enigma

enigmatiko enigmatic
enimigo enemy
enjaminado - guevo enjaminado hard boiled egg. The preparation of
   the *guevo enhaminado* was quite a tradition among Sephardic
   Jews who splurged on hard boiled eggs. The eggs were placed in
   a recipient of terra cotta, together with water, onion peels, salt,
   pepper, and some olive oil. The recipient was then put into the
   hot cinders of the bread oven, which could be found in every
   Sephardic household, and remained there all night. *Guevos
   enhaminados* were a very popular dish during Saturday and holiday morning visits between males.
enjandrazonar rumple; crumple; tumble; ruffle (v)
enjaraganearse to be idle; to be lazy; remain sluggish
enjaremado excommunicated
enjaremar excommunicate
enjarrado cheese covered with a thick layer of fat and kept in a clay
   pot to ferment and harden
enjaryentado worm-eaten
enjazineado person of sickly condition
enjazinearse to become ill
enjeñar improvise
enjendura ingenious procedure
enjenera artichoke
enjeño ingeniosity
enjeñoyado kneeling
enjeñozidad ingeniosity
enjentrado engender; give birth
enjermeste (contraction of *en jerem este*) may he be cursed, may he be
   excommunicated, may he be discarded like dirt
enjeúozo ingenious
enjidear harm; offend; shock; impede; cause pain (T *incitmek*)
enjoviyado put together as a hem
enjoyado covered with jewelry
enjunto/enjuntos together
enjurya injury
enjuryar injure (v)
enjustedad injustice
enjustisya injustice
enjusto unjust
enkadenado chained

enkadrar frame (v)
enkafurearse get angry (from T *küfür* insult)
enkaladoe wall painter
enkalkado pressed; heaped up; piled up; stuffed, well filled; convinced; fanatical; very fervent oriental Jew deeply rooted in tradition
enkalko feeding to the extreme; forced feeding; intense, persisting indigestion
enkalo smearing; debasement; disparagement
enkamburado hunchback
enkaminado put on the way; guided; wise, reasonable person
enkañado soiled; someone whose honor was afflicted by a reprehensible act
enkandeleado candled
enkaneser to become gray; whiten (of the hair); age (v)
enkangayamento mingle in a business
enkangrenar get gangrene or corrupt; worsen
enkaño malpractice
enkantador enchanter
enkantamyento enchantment
enkantar enchant; fascinate
enkante/enkanto enchantment
enkapado resentment; waiting for an occasion to take revenge; waiting to teach someone a lesson
enkapricheado to become stubborn
enkaresido made increasingly expensive
enkargar load merchandise on a ship, train, or truck; confide a task or a mission
enkargarse assume; load (v); get drunk (coll)
enkargo charge (n)
enkarnado incarnated; penetrated in the flesh
enkarnesido someone who has gained weight
enkarselar incarcerate; imprison
enkarselasyon incarceration
enkashada copulation (vulg); pouting; sulking of which the surrounding does not take any account; act which is meant to be hostile, but which provokes by its inefficacy, resulting in laughter of the person who was supposed to be the target
enkashador cashier
enkashar stick in (v); play a trick on somebody (vulg)
enkasharse introduce oneself; sneak in without invitation

enkaso cash (n); incoming money
enkastañado chestnut-colored hair
enkavesar attempt to persuade; bring back to reason
enkaza at home; at the heart
enkishevdo Turkish dance. A man and a woman are dancing in front
    of each other, with raised arms and bent fingers, turning slowly
    and harmoniously around each other, without ever touching each
    other
enklavadijo nailing; something that is nailed; manner of nailing some-
    thing; inextricable belief; fanaticism; superstition; ardent observa-
    tion of religious practices
enklavado (n) very pious person; fanatic; superstitious person
enklavado nailed; pato enklavado (lit: nailed duck) person who does
    not like to move. Allusion to the goose raised for goose liver paté
    whose feet are nailed on a plank to prevent it from moving
    during force-feeding
enklavadura nailing; fanaticism; superstition
enklavar nail (v)
enklinado tilted; inclined
enklinar incline; penetrate
enklinasyon tendency; inclination
enkochar cook; to become mature; reach the peak
enkojer tighten; narrow; wrinkle; rumple (v)
enkolado starched
enkolar starch (v)
enkolgador coat hanger
enkolgar hang (v)
enkomedansa order; recommendation
enkomenda purchase order; command
enkomendado recommended; ordered
enkomendar recommend
enkomendaria would recommend; would trust
enkonado polluted; profaned; soiled; someone who has become
    untouchable; taboo; someone who did not perform his ablutions
    after getting up in the morning; despues de fazer sus menesteres e
    mesmo de urinar kale lavarse lass manos pot no kedar enkonado
    after going to the bathroom or after urinating, you must wash
    your hands in order to avoid impurity
enkonar profanate; pollute; soil
enkono soiling; (religious) impurity

enkonshada pouting; sulking; sulkiness
enkontradijo undesirable encounter, for example a meeting which
    aggravates a disagreement between two people; encounter
    between a young girl and a young which fails to end in an
    engagement
enkontrar encounter (v)
enkonyamyento profanation; soiling; loss of ritual purity
enkorachar encourage
enkorachar put in a saddle-bag, a case or an envelope. Especially used
    when speaking about the *talet* (veil in which the practicing Jew
    wraps himself during the prayer), the *tephilim* (the phylacteries)
    and the prayer book
enkorado scarred
enkorajar encourage
enkorar scar (v)
enkorcharse pout (v)
enkorkovarse to become a hunchback; incline oneself; bow; degrade
    oneself; humiliate oneself
enkorladear redden
enkoronado crowned
enkoronamyento crowning
enkoronar crown (v); give someone a very big satisfaction
enkortado cut into pieces; put in pieces (v)
enkorvamyento bowings and reverences in sign of devotion, fear,
    humility, or great respect
enkoshar make lame
enkreivle incredible
enkrostar form a crust; cover with a crust; scar (v)
enkuadrado framed
enkuadrar frame; hang out tapestry; lay (v)
enkuentrar encounter (v)
enkuentro encounter (n)
enkuernado horned
enkueskado hardened
enkulevrado contorted like a snake; twisted; artful; crafty; hostile;
    malevolent
enkulkar inculcate
enkulpar inculpate
enkuvyerta hidden thing; secret (n)
enkyanarse pout (v)

enkyeto anxious
enkyifurearse get angry (from T *küfür* rap, swearing)
enkyusa pie with a thick layer of cheese
enladinar translate into Ladino
enlashar enlace
enlodar cover with dirt or mud
enlokosido maddened
enloryedo someone who feels satisfaction or joy. Also used as an
    antiphrase: soaked in bitterness
enluytar mourn
enmalecedos - no enmalecedos do not mistreat them; do not harm
    them (Fer Bib Gen)
enmalesimyento perversion; perversity
enmaliciér ill-treat
enmaskarse mask oneself (v)
enmateryado purulent
enmelado (y) sticky and soiled (with)
enmelado honeyed; flattering; sticky like honey; sticky person;
    obsequious
enmeladura trace of honey on clothes or utensils; obsequiosity; partici-
    pation in doubtful business
enmelamyento being involved in a business or a quarrel (neg)
enmelar sweeten with honey; flatter with honeyed words
enmentar cite a name; mention a name (v)
enmoleskar mix (v)
enmudeser become mute; keep the silence; refuse to speak; lose the
    ability to speak
ennadado bathed; soaked in water; inundated
ennegar deny
ennegreser blacken; turn beige or yellowish
ennnudar tie a knot
ennoceser to become night
ennovleser ennoble; to be ennobled; to be exalted; to be dignified; to
    be raised
ennudo knot (n)
ennuvlado cloudy; downcast
enorme enormous
enozo pouting
enpies - (kedo) enpies he stood up

149

enpostar put at the post (v)
enprimero printer
enquesta inquiry
enradar catch in the net
enradijo disorder; disagreement; embroiling; intricacy; confusion; per-
    plexity
enraigado rooted
enraigar root (v)
enramar hook on; hook up; snatch (v)
enrareser rarefy
enrarsmarse get hoarse; to have a frog in the throat
enrasmado hoarse; frayed; fretted; bloodshot (eyes)
enrasmo hoarseness
enredijo confusion; disorder
enrekeser enrich; get rich
enrekesido enriched
enriqueci I enriched; they got enriched
enriva above; over
enriva de el upon himself
enriva up; above
enrokeserse render one's throat hoarse
enrokesido hoarse; someone who has a hoarse voice
enroskar roll in a round shape; roll in a spiral
ensalsar conserve in salt (v)
ensammararse wrap oneself in fur
ensanche let him attract with sweetness; let him lure
ensangrentado blood stained; soaked with blood
ensavanado cunning; sly
ensembrar sow (v)
ensenante teacher
ensendyo fire (n)
ensensyo incense; aromatic oil obtained through distillation
ensenyamento teaching
enserado covered with wax; statue of wax; person who stands immo-
    bile like a statue of wax
enserklado surrounded
enserrado shut in; relegated to a closed place; put away; enclosed
enserrar put away; enclose; shut in; encompass; surround; include;
    contain; confine; introduce the newlywed couple to the nuptial
    chamber at the wedding night

enshaguar rinse
ensharopado syrupy; tasty
ensharopar soak in syrup; sweeten
enshashar praise (v)
enshavonada rubbing with soap
enshavonado little laundry
enshavonar wash with soap; cover with soap
enshudyado very fat; pato enshundyado (lit: fattened goose) lazy person. Allusion to the goose raised for goose liver paté whose feet are nailed on a plank to prevent it from moving during force-feeding
enshugadura bath linen
enshugante bloat paper
enshugar dry; rub with a towel
enshundya fowl fat; goose fat
enshuto dry (adj); dried
ensidente incident
ensiklopedya encyclopedia
ensima (adv and prep) above; on; moreover; in addition
ensistensya insistence
ensistir insist
ensiyar seal (with the official stamp) (v)
ensodreser deafen
ensodresimyento deafening
ensoma (adv) in sum; in the whole; in summary; at last
enspektor inspector
enspirar inspire
enspirasyon inspiration
enstituir establish in a position or office (v)
enstitusyon institution
ensultar insult (v)
ensulto insult; injury
ensuña grudge; resentment; animosity
ensupeto suddenly
ensupito suddenly
ensuportavle insupportable
ensuzyado dirty; soiled
ensuzyadura dirt; soiling
ensuzyar soil (v)
ensuzyarse soil oneself

ensyerro shutting in; locking in; keeping in
entachonado stained
entanto however; in spite of; anyway
entapetar cover with carpet
entarnado interned
entassar pile up; accumulate
entavlado immobilized; put in a cast
entavladura setting of a cast on a fractured limb
entavlar immobilize a fractured limb in a cast (v)
entejado frozen with cold; very cold
entejar inflict a very cold temperature
entekiado tubercular
entekiar cause tuberculosis; inflict suffering or exasperation
entekiarse to become tuberculous; to be continuously exposed to
    suffering, humiliation, or anxieties
enteligensa intelligence
entelijensya intelligence
entelijente intelligent
entenado adoptive son
entenar adopt a child
enteñavlado darkened; in mourning
entendedor individual with quick understanding
entender understand
entendidos knowledgeable (Salonica Pesach Siddur)
entendimiento understanding; mal entendimiento misunderstanding
entendimyento comprehension
enteñevlar darken; mourn (v)
enteñido very drunk
enteñir dye; impregnate with paint
entensyonado resolved; intentioned
ententar intend
enteramente wholly
enteres interest (n)
enteres judios between Jews
enteresado interested
enteresamyento particular interest
enteresar (se) be interested in
enteresar interest (v)
enternar intern; keep away
enternato boarding school

entero whole
enterpesido stultified; stupefied; besotted
enterpreta interpret
enterpretar interpret
enterpretasyon interpretation
enterrado buried
enterrador undertaker's man
enterramyento burial
enterrar bury
enterromper interrupt (v)
enterrupsyon interruption
entersante interesting
entervalo interval
entervenir intervene
entervensyon intervention
enteryor interior
enteshe filigree
entestinal intestinal
entestino intestine
entezado stiff; strained; forced; unnatural
entiender understand (v)
entikiado someone with a hang-up; someone who has constant
    anxieties; tubercular
entinienter dip (v)
entisyon intention
entisyonarse make a resolution; put something in one's head
entitolar give a title to somebody
entivyar get lukewarm
entizmadura covered with soot
entiznado sooted; darkened; exasperated; someone who has gone
    through a lot of sorrows and grief
entolerensya intolerance
entolondrado someone who has received a stroke on the head
entonces/entonches then; at that time
entonteser stupefy; beset (v)
entonteserse to become stultified; to be besotted
entornar surround
entorno surroundings
entorpeser stultify; stupefy
entosegado poisoned

entosegamyento poisoning
entosegar poison (v)
entraña entrails; insides
entrañas entrails
entrar enter
entre among; between; from the midst; **entre su tienta** in the middle of
his tent
entrecote con sivoya entrecote with onion
entregada delivery
entregador telltale
entregar confide; deliver
entrelashar intertwine; twist; interweave
entremetedor matchmaker
entremetedura mediation; intervention; interference; interposition
entremetor someone who puts himself between two parties;
matchmaker
entressar weave; plait; braid hair
entretenimyento maintenance; support
entretenlo distract him; entertain him
entrevista interview; also first encounter between prospective bride and
prospective fiancé in a matchmaking proposal
entri medius in between
entrimos came in
entudresido stultified; stupefied
enturavan they surrounded
enueheçer get old (Fer Bib Gen)
enuolente bravery; daring
envaneser render vain
envanesyimento vanity; pride; boasting
envelóp envelope
enverano summer
envitar invite (v)
envitasion invitation
envitasyon invitation
enxalçanse access; reach (n, Ferrara Siddur)
enxeremar excommunicate
enzinas plains
epistola letter; request; memoir; long text (Gr)
epitafya epitaph (Gr)
epizodyo episode

era was; consisted of
eran were
eredador inherit
eredar inherit (v)
eredensya heritage
ereditaryo hereditary
ereje heretic
eresça - (no agora) eresça (do not) get angry (now)
eresçio was very angry; was very irritated; porque eresçio a ti? why are
    you angry, irritated?
eressimiento fierceness
ergat unskilled worker (Gr)
ergulír ache (v)
erigir erect (v)
erir strike to wound or kill (v, more elaborate form of *ferir*)
ermana sister
ermano brother
Ermeni Armenian
ermósyo/ermoyo growth of the field; fresh grass
ermoveser germinate
ermoyissiér grow
ermozo beautiful
ermozura beauty
eroe hero
eroiko heroic
eroina heroin
eroismo heroism
errante wandering; nomad
errar err
erremo sad; abandoned; miserable; unfortunate; with bad intention;
    fatal; ruinous; satanic
erudisyon erudition
erudito erudite (adj)
eruv imaginary line marking the border of the residence. For observant
    Jews, it is not allowed to cross this border on Sabbath.
es is
esbelar make aware; act or react in a quick and reckless way; break
    the back; get tired; feel pain (T *bel* waist, place of the belt)
esbivlamyento violation; transgression of a religious commandment or
    sacred rite

esbivlár violate

esboro flow of words; volubility (neg)

escalera stairway; escalera de Camondo famous stairway in Istanbul, built by the Italian-Jewish count Camondo.

escallentar heat (v, Ferrara Siddur); y el estén a la puerta de la tienta como escalentarse el dia and he was sitting at the door of the tent during the heat of the day (Fer Bib Gen)

escapadizo fugitive (Fer Bib Gen)

escapar end (v); la visita no se escapa the visit does not end; fue como escarnación en ojos de sus yernos it seemed to his son-in-laws that he was making fun (Fer Bib Gen); nuestras casas escapô He spared our houses (from Passover Haggadah)

escapar/eskapar escape (v)

esclamaciión complaint; cry; scream

esclamaçion complain; cry; scream (n)

esclamaciôn exclamation

esclamantes complaints; exclamations

esclamar exclaim (v)

esclamar/esclamir sigh; cry (v)

esclaressar light up

esclaresse el sol the sun rises

esclavedad slavery

esclavo slave

escoger choose (v)

escogieron they chose; de todo lo que escogieron of all the things they have chosen

escogio he chose

esconder hide (v)

escondido - en escondido in secret

escondiosse he hid

escóva broom

escribo I write (Moroccan Sephardic ballad)

escrouchir a sus dientes grind one's teeth

escrouchir retort (v)

escuchad me di dicha hear me say; listen to me

escuchar hear; listen

escudo shield (n)

escuentra - como escuentra el who resembles to him

escureser darken

escuridad darkness

escuridad darkness; obscurity
escuro dark
esfondar crumble; crash (v)
esfondar stave; beat in; break up
esfongato fallen in; giving way to
esfongato omelette with cheese and eggs
esfongos Sephardic dish of baked spinach, topped a mix of cheese,
    mashed potatoes and eggs
esforsar (se) force (oneself)
esforso effort
esfriado having a cold or a flu
esfriado someone who has a cold or a flu
esfriar chill (v); give a cold or the flu
esfriarse catch a cold or a flu
esfuegra mother-in-law
esfuegro father-in-law
esfuenyo sleep (n); esfuenyo no le esta entrando (lit: sleep does not
    enter him) he cannot sleep
esfuliñar sweep chimneys; clean up from the basement to the attic
eshek jasina (adv) (lit: like a donkey would do); stupidly
eshek yebi (adv) (lit) like a donkey; (fig) without any regard to one's
    self-awareness (T eshek gibi)
eshemplar (adj) exemplary
eshemplaryo (n) sample (of a book, a medal, a furniture)
eshemplaryo exemplary
eshemplo example
eshjuela short-handled ax; mason's ax
eshjuelada stroke of an ax
eshjuelo house carpentry using an ax
eshper expert
eshpiomluk spying
eshpion spy (n)
eshpionaje spying
eshpionar spy (v)
eshpital hospital
eshtajera furniture stand (n)
eshuegra mother-in-law
eshuegro father-in-law
esjueko wooden shoe
eskadansya expiration term; maturation of bills

eskaldado boiled down; scalded
eskaldado scalded; suffering from a light irritation of the skin; frugal
   dish made of bread, usually crumbs, boiled in water and
   sprinkled with oil, grated cheese or sugar; someone who has lost
   a lot of money in gambling or speculations; someone who has
   paid an excessive price for a purchase or service
eskama fish scale
eskambil thump on the head or neck with the flat hand (T)
eskandalo scandal
eskapado delivered
eskapadura term; achievement; deliverance
eskapar finish; terminate; achieve
eskapasyon end; achievement
eskara grill (n, T *iskara*)
eskarado insolent; cynical
eskaramyento insolence; cynicism; impudence; shamelessness
eskaravajamentikos word without any meaning, used humorously for
   something undescribable
eskaravajo cockroach
eskaravato cockroach
eskargar discharge (v)
eskarinyo longing; nostalgia
eskarvador digger; searcher; rummaging
eskaso avaricious; stingy
eskeletiko skeletal
eskeleto skeleton
eskidji secondhand dealer
eskifozo disgusting; repugnant
eskiler alayim let me take the old things (T) (shout of the secondhand
   dealer in the street)
eskino spine
eskitarse to be exhausted; to be excessively tired
esklamar exclaim (v)
esklamasyon exclamation
esklareser clarify; dawn (sun)
esklaresimyento clarification; commentary; attenuation of darkness;
   progression of the morning light
esklavaje slavery; servitude
esklavarse enslave oneself; assume a task which does not leave any
   free time

esklavedad servitude; salir d'esklavedad to become free
esklavo slave
eskojedor sorter; someone who is specialized in sorting a special kind
    of merchandise
eskojer choose; sort
eskola school
eskolado dripped; someone who has lost his fortune or strength
eskolamento gonorrhea
eskolaryo student
eskonde (se) hide oneself
eskonder hide (v)
eskondidas hiding
eskondimiento hiding; hideout; inaccessibility
eskontro unpleasant encounter
eskopetada stroke with a broom
eskopo aim; intention; design (Ital scopo)
eskorchador person who flays animals at the butchery; profiteer
    (lawyer, physician)
eskorchadura excoriation; flaying; asking for an exorbitant price
eskorchar excoriate; flay
eskoryado (adj) slightly flayed skin
eskova broom (n)
eskovada rapid and superficial sweeping of the floor with a broom
eskovatea rapid and superficial sweeping of the floor with a broom,
    followed by rinsing with water
eskrito written
eskrivir write
eskruchir gnash; produce a strident noise
eskruteador scrutinizer; someone who does profound research
eskuchar hear
eskudiyar pour soup; serve food; confess; reveal; divulge a secret
eskudiyar serve a meal
eskudo shield (n)
eskuentrar go in front of; confront (Ferrara Siddur)
eskulterear save oneself; escape from a danger, an unwanted task or
    companion (T kurtulmak)
eskupidijo spit; spitting (n)
eskupido someone who is the spitting image of somebody else
eskupidor spittoon
eskupir spit (v)

eskurantismo obscurantism
eskureo darkening; obscurity
eskuridad darkness
eskwéntrar go in front; confront; encounter something unpleasant
    (Jud-Sp Dict Madrid)
esmolar sharpen the utensils
esmolarse gain experience by going through trials; refine oneself; to
    become better aware; acquire good manners
esmouido vagabond (n)
esnaf tradesman; artisan (T kanunn)
esnafche keeping with the needs of a tradesman (T *esnafçe*, kanunn)
espada sword
espalda shoulder (n)
espandedura expanse; extent
espandidura expanse; extent; extension; area
espantar - espantar (se) to be afraid
espantar scare (v)
espantar se to be afraid
espantaso scary person; coward
espanto fear (n); que espanto something scary
espantoso fearful; someone who scares easily
Espanyol Ladino
espartete separate from (imp)
espartia divided; y destez se esparzio toda la tierra and from these)
    was populated all the earth (Fer Bib Gen)
espartieronse they separated (Fer Bib Gen)
espartimientoa separations; separated groups; distributions;
    subdivisions (Salonica Pesah Siddur)
espartimyénto covenant; partition; distribution
espartir set on the table (v)
espeça species
espejo mirror (n)
esper expert
esperansa hope (n)
esperar wait
espertar (se) wake up
espeso very meticulous
espesor thickness; stickiness; fig for: being boring and sticky
espesura muncho very thick; sticky
espesura thickness; sticky, bothering person; very meticulous person

espina spine; fishbone
espinaka spinach
espinga dart; impetigo; herpes
espinika en medio small-size mackerel
espino spine
espinosa spiny; spicy
espinota a sort of fish
espionar spy (v)
espirito spirit; que en el espirito de baxo de los cielos whoever has)
    spirit of life under the skies (Fer Bib Gen)
espital hospital
espojado stripped; ravaged
esponde expands
esponja sponge (n)
esponjado washing and rinsing of the floor
esponjar thorough cleaning of the floor
espontaneo spontaneous
espor sport
esportivo sportive
espoza spouse; wife
espozada bride-to-be; spouse
espozado fiancé
espozarse get engaged
espozo husband
esprimidor lemon squeezer
esprimir squeeze (v)
esprito spirit
espulgado cleaned (especially used for meat free of nerves and tendons
    and thus declared proper for consumption according to Jewish
    ritual law)
espulgador Jewish butcher skilled in the art of stripping the meat off
    the slightest nerves to make it ritually clean for the Jewish kitchen
espuma foam (n, also: eskuma)
espumante foamy; vino espumante sparkling wine
espumozo foaming
espuntar emerge at the horizon (sun, moon, celestial object or other);
    come from a very far and undetermined place
espurgar expurgate; free from all that is unnecessary; reduce to the
    necessary
espyegasyon explanation

essencia essence
esta this (fem)
esta/estas it is; you are; this; these (fem)
estaba was
estabilimyento establishment
estabilir establish
estabilizar stabilize (v)
establecer establish
estableserse settle down; establish oneself
estada sojourn; duration of residence
estadia short sojourn; difficult situation; period of life full of suffering
    and misery
estado state (n)
estafeta mounted courier; rapid messenger
estajar separate; put an interval between two things (v)
estajo separation; interval; interstice
estaka stake (n)
Estambolli inhabitant of Istanbul
estamos we are
estampa printing house; typography; printed matter
estampadir printer; typesetter
estampado printed; reproduced by the image
estampadura printed; price paid for printing
estampadura printing workshop
estampar print (v); typeset
estamperear de gritos deafen by screaming
estampilla stamp; stamp mark
estampiya imprimatur; mark of authenticity
estampiyar authentify
estañado tinned (kitchen utensils); someone who has been subject to
    harsh reproaches, or who has received very severe punishments;
    powerful; resounding
estañador craftsman who tins kitchen utensils
Estanbol Istanbul
Estanbolli inhabitant of Istanbul
estancia residence
estankar stop the running of a liquid
estanko stop; arrest; suspension of an effort or a march
estansya sojourn (n)
estante subsisting

estar to be; y no pudieron por estar a uno (and they could not) remain
  (stay) one with the other (Fer Bib Gen)
estas these (fem pl)
estasyon station
estasyonaryo stationary
estatistika statistics
estatua statue
estatutos statutes
este this (masc)
estempereado shaken; stupefied
estemperear shake (violently); unsettle; disturb; esta purga estamperea
  this laxative is very strong
estenografo stenographer
estenso extent; extension; length (Ferrara Siddur)
ester estemez whether wanted or not (T)
estera mat; straw mat; mat made of esparto, a grass growing in
  southern Europe or North Africa
esterero manufacturer and vendor of mats
esterilidad sterility
esterilizar sterilize
esterilo sterile
esterlina - lira esterlina British pound sterling
estia splinter (n)
estifa bags; packages; cases; bales of cloth (Gr)
estifado dish made of sour prunes, meat and onions cooked for a long
  time
estifador worker who piles up merchandise in a storehouses or ships;
  trimmer
estigmatizar stigmatize
estilar get exhausted by a long reverence
estilo stomach pangs due to hunger
estima esteem (n)
estimasyon estimate (n)
estindatchí investigator (from T istinbat bringing a hidden matter to
  light, or istinbatçi someone who brings a hidden matter to light)
estinkak interrogation (T)
estio been
estipular stipulate
estirar extend, stretch out
estiva merchandise; things in good order

esto I am
estofa silk
estomagal pad impregnated with alcohol and sprinkled with pepper,
    applied to the stomach to relieve indigestion
estomago stomach
estonses then; in this case
estopado inappropriate language
estopar block up with tow or oakum; stuff a running tap; delicately
    weave a cloth to repair a tear
estoryador historian
estoryano historian
estos these (masc pl)
estovieron they were (Salonica Pesach Siddur)
estoy - que estoy (that) I am (Moroccan Sephardic ballad)
estrafutarse do not give any importance to something; do not pay
    attention; do not take into account (Ital *strafuttarse*)
estrañar intrigue (v)
estrañedad strangeness
estrapajado treated with the greatest disdain
estrapajo disdain; disparagement (Ital *strappazzo*)
estrashado ravaged; ruined
estrashador someone who causes ravages, destroys, ruins; someone
    who does not care about the things he uses
estrashar cause ravages; act like a vandal
estraúero stranger
estréa star (n)
estrechar (lit: get narrow) fig for: get disturbed
estrechar (se) get worried
estrechiko very little; rather insufficient; just right; barely sufficient
estrecho narrow (adj)
estrechura narrowness; misery; constraint; danger
estrellas stars
estremeser terrify; cause great fear
estremeserse shake with fear; to be terrified
estremesido someone who shakes with fear; terrified
estremesivle terrifying
estremisyon terror; panic
estrena good news
estrenamyento inauguration
estrenar use for the first time

estreno inauguration
estreya star; **saltar a las estreyas** eat something very spicy; see the
    thirty six candles; to be unable to master oneself
estreyado sky full of stars; illumination of the sky
estreyeria astronomy; astrology
estreyero astronomer; astrologer
estriktamente strictly
estrikto strict
estrinjado squeezed; tight
estrinjar squeeze; tighten; stretch; hold tight; tighten; cause anxiety,
    cause a feeling of deep worry
estripar remove the tripes
estropyado crippled
estropyar mutilate; cripple
estruidor destroy
estruir destroy; put out of service
estruirse to be lost irremediably; to be exhausted; to be destroyed; to
    be worn
estruisyon destruction; damage; ruin
estruktura structure
estrupidez stupidity
estruyir destroy
estu this
estuary history
estubi tow (rope, flax, hemp or jute); oakum (Gr)
estudeser stun; make giddy
estudiar study (v)
estudio study (n)
estudrir stun; make giddy
estudyante student
estudyar study (v)
estudyo study (n)
estudyos studies
estudyozo studious
estufa sweating room, stove room; incubator
estufado trenched; deeply wet
estufar impregnate; imbibe
estukador plasterer; stucco worker
estukar stucco
estupendo admirable; marvelous (Ital)

estupidita/estupidad stupidity
estupido stupid
estuuieron alli they were there
estuuo resided; had residence
estuvites you were
estuweerser inspire great fear (v)
estyedra the left side; the left hand
estyedrear use the left hand
estyedreo left-handed
estyedro left (as contrary to right)
estyerkero garbage box
estyerko/estyerkol household garbage
esvachear give up (T *vazgeçmek*)
esvaneser disappear
esvarear express oneself without constraint
esvaynado remove from the sheath
esveltez sveltness
esvelto svelte
esventrar tear open
esveranero estival
esverano summer
etaj floor (F *étage*)
etchaderérdech - (lo) etchaderérdech you will throw (the boy in the
    river) Pharaoh's command in the Haggadah, from the Passover
    Haggadah)
etchando throwing
etchar throw (v); etchar con fuersa throw with strength
etcho job; business
eter ether
eternal eternal
eternidad eternity
etiketa label (n)
etiko ethical
etniko ethnic
etrog fruit of the citrus tree; large lemon. The forty nine days from the
    second day of Passover till the Pentecost are called *omer*. Every
    morning during this time, a beadle or a member of the Sephardic
    community used to go from house to house with an *etrog* and a
    lulav (branch of a palm tree) which everyone holds during the

brief instants required to recite the benediction of that particular day of the omer period.

evakuar evacuate
evakuasyon evacuation
evaluasyon evaluation
Evanjil New Testament
evaporasyon evaporation
evazivo evasive
eventual eventual
eventualidad eventuality
eventualmente eventually
evitar avoid
evokar evoke
exaktitud exactitude
exgzemplaryo exemplary
experyensa experience (n)
exportar export (v)
expulgar remove lice or fleas; clean off all impurities; prepare meat according to Jewish ritual law
exteryorizar exteriorize
extra help hired for an exceptional occasion
eya her
eyos themselves
ezá medicine
ezadji pharmacist (T *eczaci*)
ezitante hesitating
ezitar hesitate
ezitasyon hesitation
eziyet ill-treatment (T *eziyet*, kanunn)
Ezmirna Izmir (Smyrna)
ezvacheo giving up; diversion; renunciation; forgetting

F

faba bean; el fablán a ella (he who) was speaking to her (Fer Bib Gen)
fablo he spoke
fabrika factory
fabrikante manufacturer

fabrikar manufacture (v)
fabrikasyon manufacturing
fabula fable
fabulista fabulist
fabulozo fabulous
facer make; do
faces faces
facha face (n, Ital *faccia*)
facha luzya beautiful face
fachata facade
faches faces; surface; ha recebi tus faches tambien por cosa esta here I
    have received well your prosternations; I grant you one more
    grace; I still grant you this grace (Fer Bib Gen); sobre façes de
    todos sus hermanosc moraro he set his tents in front of the eyes
    of all his brothers (Fer Bib Gen)
fachika face thinned by suffering, pain, or deprivation
facil easy
facilita facility; easiness
facilitar make easy
fada fairy
fadado bewitched person; person with a bewitching charm
fadamyento family feast of ritual character during which a newborn
    daughter is given a name
fadar give a name to a newborn girl (to the newborn boy the name is
    given during the ceremony of circumcision)
fadarju fate, luck (Port *fadario*)
fadaryo fate; luck; destiny; bad luck; difficult life (Port)
fadika little fairy; mysterious individual who can evoke spirits, obtain
    their help and fight against bad spirits
fado destiny; sort; sorcery; enchantment
fagamos let us do
fagan - que le fagan that they should make him
fagfur porcelain
Fahrettin Kerim bottle filled with the Turkish alcoholic beverage raki,
    a humoristic allusion to the mayor and governor of Istanbul,
    Fahrettin Kerim, a teetotaller
fakir fakir; ascetic of India living from alms; poor man (Arabic)
fakiriko individual who inspires compassion because of his misfortune
faktor factor
faktura bill (n)
fakturar bill (v)

fakuldad faculty, ability; freedom of action; faculty of a university
fakultativo facultative
falaja omen; prediction
falaja soothsayer; female fortuneteller (usually a Gypsy); echarse a la
    falaja consult the female seer
falaka punishment commonly practiced in Turkey, consisting of
    beating the soles of the feet with a stick. It was not only executed
    on suspect criminals in police stations, but also in schools at the
    end of the school day, as a public event with the terrified school-
    mates watching. The moaning of the punished was accompanied
    by prayers of the audience. (T)
falceta shoe knife used by the shoemaker
falda flap of a cloth; front of an apron or a robe; part of the body
    going from the belt to the knees of a sitting person
faldar petticoat
faldas - sakudirse las faldas shake the flaps of a skirt, laplets of the
    clothes; get rid of breadcrumbs or dust; decline all responsibility;
    wash one's hands (an allusion to the religious ceremony of taslij,
    when the clothes are shaken on the waterfront as a symbolic gesture
    to get rid of sins. It has been reported that in small, isolated Jewish
    communities such as the tiny Jewish community of Bursa, the per-
    formance on a riverfront was omitted and the ritual was performed
    in private, in order to avoid a public display of a ritual which might
    have seemed strange to the local Turkish population and provoke a
    hostile reaction (From: Ida Cowen, Jews in remote corners of the
    world, p. 276, Prentice-Hall, Englewood Cliffs, NJ, 1971).
faldji fortuneteller (masc)
faldjia fortuneteller (fem)
faldukuera pocket; small sack; paras para la faldakuera pocket money;
    petty cash
falduquere purse (Monastir dialect)
falimento bankruptcy (Ital *fallimento*)
falkon falcon
fallar find; discover; encounter (Ferrara Siddur)
falsamyento breaking of word; denial of a promise; lie; cheating
falsar lie; betray; break one's word
falsaryo forger
falseador counterfeiter; forger
falsifikador counterfeiter; forger
falsifikasyon falsification
falso false

falson (in card games) card which is not used, which is discarded
falta lack; absence; deficit; fault
faltar lack; to be in shortage
faltava lacked
fama fame; reputation
fambre hunger
fambrero starvation
fameliko starving
famia family
familia family
familiar family member; relative
familiararse familiarize oneself
familyar familial; habitual
familyaridad familiarity
famiyozo someone who is in charge of a big family
famozo famous
fanal signal light of a ship; beacon
fanar lantern; lighthouse
fanatiko fanatic
fanatizar fanaticize
fanatizmo fanaticism
fandagmeno boaster; braggart
fanela (woolen) undershirt
fanéla sweater
fanella undershirt
fanfaron blusterer; fallow; swaggerer
fañozo snuffler; person speaking through his nose
fantastiko fantastic
fantazia fantasy
fante the jack in card game; card game where jack is the master card
fara - quien fara (who) will make
farash shovel used to collect the sweepings when cleaning the floor
fardate apply make-up (from F *se farder*)
farfuyar sputter; jaber
farina flour
farinozo farinaceous; white with flour
farmasia pharmacy
farmasien pharmacist
farmasista pharmacist
farmasiya pharmacy

farmason freemason
farsa farce; party; theater entertainment
farsi Persian language
farto satiated; filled; nourished; fed
fasafiso nonsense; meaningless talk or undertaking; dealing with petty, meaningless details and thereby creating the impression of doing something important
fasaria, fasarias agitation; embarrassment; getting busy; big gestures to make believe that the work undertaken is very difficult
fashismo fascism
fashista fascist
fasil easy (F *facile*)
fasilidad ease (n); easiness
fasta till
fasulya (haricot/runner) bean (T *fasulye*)
fat fact
fatal fatal
fatalista fatalist
fatiga fatigue
fatigante tiring; fastidious; importune
fatigar make tired; cause importunity
fatigozo tiring
fava broad bean
favladero blabber mouthing; tendency to speak non stop (especially of someone who has high fever or is in delirium)
favlar mintiras lie (v, Monastir dialect)
favlatina babbling; endless chatter
favlistan bad mouth; slanderer
favor favor
favorizar favor (v)
fayadura action of finding
fayár find; discover; encounter (Jud-Sp Dict Madrid)
faze did
fázemos o nos fama let us acquire a reputation
fazer di mismo imitate (Monastir dialect)
fazer make
fazer relámpagu flash; lighten (Monastir dialect)
fea ugly (fem)
fealdad ugliness; filth; obscenity; indignity
fecha fact; act; action

fechiko modest business; bread earner
fechizeo sorcerer
fechizeria art; sorcery; magic practices
fechizo charm; sorcery; enchantment; bewitching
fecho business; commerce; occupation; work; task
fechu matter; topic (Monastir dialect); mature; ripe (Monastir dialect);
    office (Monastir dialect); profession (Monastir dialect)
fechura way; form; design; money paid confectioning
fechuria pharmaceutical preparation; medicine; home remedy
fedán market place; plaza (Haketia)
fedayi martyr or person ready to become one; enterprising man serving
    a leader (T *fedai*)
feder stink; aggravate; importune; embarrass; **de la kavesa fede el
    peshe** it is the head of the fish that rots first; it is the chief who
    gives the bad example (proverb)
federse rot; spoil; to become corrupted; to become fetid; demonstrate
    self-sufficiency and arrogance
fedór bad smell
fedorento stinking; full of self-sufficiency and arrogance
fedorina persistent smell; lasting arrogance and haughtiness
fedyendo stinking
fegado liver
fekondar fecundate
felek sort; destiny (T); **aharvado por el felek** struck by destiny; impov-
    erished by bad luck
feliche happy
felichidad happiness
felichitar congratulate (Ital *felicitare*)
felís happy (Ital *felice*)
felisidad happiness
felisitar congratulate
fellah Egyptian peasant; uneducated, poor, badly dressed person
fendir ruin one's health
fener signal; beacon; lantern; street lamp (T *fener*)
feo ugly (masc)
feouzia faith; confidence (Salonica Pesach Siddur)
feradje wide, usually dark clothes in which Turkish Muslim women
    used to wrap themselves when going out.
feraj broad; ample; spacious; wide (clothes, lodging); generous
    (T *ferah*)

ferajlanearse rest comfortably; enjoy rest; being at ease

feraklik ease; facility; comfort; tranquillity; relief; generosity; breadth of view, broad-mindedness (T *ferahlik*)

ferida de mayores slaying of the first-born—one of the Ten Plagues of Egypt (Exodus)

ferida wound

feridas plagues

ferido smitten; wounded; por me ferido (if I) am wounded

ferir smite; wound

fermoso beautiful (Ferrara Siddur)

fermózo beautiful (Jud-Sp Dict Madrid)

fermozure syn of *eremozxura* beauty

fernet drunk; estar fernet talk senselessly

ferose ferocious; wild; animales feroces wild animals

ferramenta pike of the grave digger; tools used by an undertaker

ferroja rust (n)

ferrojenteado rusty; aged without vigor, without alertness

fertil fertile

fertlidad fertility

fervor fervor

ferya fair (n)

fesad intrigue; sedition (T kanunn)

fesad strange event; riots (T *fesad*)

fesaddji intrigant; seditious

fesadji agitator

fesfese hypochondriac; someone who has secret fears, unfounded scruples (T *vesvese*)

feshusedad aggravation; setting on edge; irritation of the nerves

feston festoon

fetva Muslim religious decision, usually pronounced by the Sultan in his capacity as caliph, or by any other religious authority. A fetva from the Sultan, addressed to the kadi (the local judge exerting jurisdiction according to the Muslim code of law, the sharia) was required for the construction of a synagogue. Such fetvas written in the usual Ottoman flowery style have been preserved and were translated by the renowned historian of Turkish Sephardic history, Professor Avraham Galante, who was also a deputy in the Turkish National Assembly, the Büyük Millet Meclisi.

feúzya/féouzia faith; confidence

fevereo February

fevereyro February

fevrie (F *février*)

fey faith

fez Turkish headgear in the Ottoman empire until the vestimentary reform of Kemal Ataturk, who prohibited the wearing of the fez. Originally a simple cap without a shade, the fez took the shape of the gibus (from the name of the French manufacturer), a hat without brim. When visiting Paris in 1841, Sultan Abdul Aziz admired this headgear of the French bourgoisie so much that he introduced it in Turkey. All subjects of the Sultan, Jews included, adopted the fez, particularly the high classes. For Muslims the fez acquired a religious connotation because the absence of a brim allowed the forehead to touch the earth or the floor during the ritual prosternation in prayer. This religious connotation was the reason for Ataturk's prohibition of fez and turbans and the adoption of European-style hats.

fiador travelling vendor of cloth, bedcovers, tablecloths, baby-linen, and trousseau who went from door to door, giving credit to housewives and getting paid by installments

fiaka showing off; ostentation (T *fiyaka*)

fiansa bail; bond; security; surety; pledge

fiansa warrantor

fiasko complete failure; *fazer fiasko* fail completely

fidalgez sobriety; someone who eats very little, has a weak health; reserved, discrete person

fidan young plant; planted tree; root; young, innocent man or woman

fideldad fidelity; constant attachment

fideo noodle; vermicelli; angel's hair; popular pastry formed like a comma or a teardrop that Sephardic women used to prepare at home, by rolling bits of oiled, well-kneaded flour paste between the thumb and the index. The Sephardic women tried to keep themselves busy during the days of ritual fasting, by minutely preparing the *fideos*; sebaceous matter which can be removed by rubbing the wet skin; (fig) very thin, weak person; *fazer fideo* beat his feet in impatience; do not stand in place; to be on ardent amber; *fideos con domates* vermicelli with fresh tomatoes; *fideos con ceso* oven-baked noodles with cheese and cream

fiduz enraged; bitten by a wild dog; furious (T *kuduz*); *perro fiduz* dog with rabies; furious-looking individual; someone subject to his/her rage

fiede (it) stinks
fiel bile
fiel faithful
fieldad fidelity
fierro iron (n)
fiesta feast (n)
fiestar celebrate
figado liver
figas mockery
figito small fig
figo fig
figura figure; face; form (n)
figurar figure (v)
figurin fashionable; engraving; dandy
figúzia trust (n)
fijá daughter
fijastro son of the first (or other) spouse; son-in-law; son with whom
     one has a bad relationship; son who is little loved by his parents
fijera/fijero fig tree
fijiko small boy; small child
fijo son
fijon amariyo yellow wax bean
fijón bean (Gal *feijo*, *feixoo*; Port *feijào*)
fijon blanco white bean
fijon verde green string bean
fijonada stew of dried beans with roasted brown onions
fiksar fix (v)
fiksasyon fixation
fiksidad fixation
fikso fixed
fil elephant (T)
fila thin pastry, usually triangular dough filled with cheese and parsley
     (from Gr *phylla*, *phyllo*)
fila fur fideos noodle dough
fila rank, file (n)
filacha lint used for surgery; linen formerly used to dress wounds; tow
     (of hemp, flax or jute); oakum
filacheador spinner or cord manufacturer; craftsman who cords wool
     or cotton for mattresses or pillows
filachear reduce to threads or fibers

175

filachozo cloth or woman's stocking losing threads
filadero merchant of weaving threads
filador manufacturer of threads; spinner; wire drawer
filan and so forth (T)
filandrozo full of long threads; cordy
filantropia philantrophic
filantropo philantrophist
filar spin (v)
filatelista philatelist
filatura spinning factory
fildishi ivory (T)
fildjan cup
fildján cup; coffee cup; tea cup (Monastir dialect)
filero small stream; brook
filete tool used by shoemaker to cut leather
fileto meat from the back, tenderloin used to make filet mignon
filial filial
filigranado filigree
filigranar filigreeing; manufacture jewelry with delicate gold and silver
  threads
filikas triangular shaped pie or pastry wrapped in phyllo (see *fila*) and
  filled with cheese, egg, parsley or cinnamon and clove
filin exhausted; ruined; insolvent
filindrozo impregnated with bitter saliva
filinera bitter saliva
filo thread
filozofia philosophy
filtrar filter (v)
filvan tacking; basting
filvanar tack; baste (v)
fin end (n)
fin till; de fin de dias at the end of (after) a certain time
fina squandering; waste
final final
finalidad finality
finalmente finally
finansya finance (n)
finansyar finance (v)
finansyaryo/finensyaryo financier
findiriz crack; cleft; slit; rip

findirizero philander; womanizer; homosexual
findjan coffee cup
findjaniko small coffee cup
finga very small thing; bread crumb; little bite of a delicacy; no dar ni
    finga refuse to give even a very small bite
fiñidura prolonged and minute mashing
finio kneaded; shaped; formed
fiñir mash for a long time
finjan coffee cup
finkes token in a game
fino fine, delicate
finojo/finozo fennel
finta feint; pretense; disguise; trap; ambush (n)
fira waste; loss of weight; leakage
firma signature
firmamiento covenant; alliance
firman imperial decree; document with the imperial signature (the
    Sultan's monogram
firmar sign (v)
firme firm
fisfishli (onomatopeia) simulates the "froufrou" sound of bubbling;
    tinsel; something which has a false shine; sparkling; foil
fishek firecracker; bullet, rocket; cartridge; broiled corn seed;
    cylindrical stack of gold or silver coins
fishu scarf; piece of silk or lace cloth folded in triangle and used to
    cover a woman's neck and shoulders
fishugado irritated; put on edge; to be obsessed by one's assiduities
fishugar put on edge; irritate the nerves; importune; torment; animate;
    tease; excite; lure (v)
fista till
fistikyi pistachio (adj)
fistura fistula
fit (adv) compensation of losses and gains in games (T)
fita (conj) acronym of *fista* (until that) and *tina* (till) m'akompaño
    fita'n casa he has accompanied me back till home
fitero the most elevated degree; peak hour
fitijas, fitijos daughters, sons (said with disdain about children misbe-
    having towards their parents)
fitil wick; quick match
fitildji troublemaker

fiyaka showing off; arrogance
flaca skinny (fem)
flaco/flako skinny (masc)
flacu skinny; underweight; weak (Monastir dialect)
flakeza state of being skinny or weak
flama flame
flambada flambé
flambante flamboyant
flamur linden tea (T *ihlamur*)
flanela flannel; flannel underwear
flebit phlebitis
flecha arrow
flechear throw arrows; throw piercing glances; overwhelm; harass with
    offensive remarks
flechero archer
flochura looseness; poorly tied; state of a person lacking energy or
    will; weakness; softness
flor flower (n)
flosho relaxed; not tight; poorly tied
flotar float
fob acronym for *franco bord* free on board. Term used for the price
    including all freight costs until boarding a ship.
foburgo neighborhood at the outskirts of a town
fodra fabric for lining
fodre lining (Port *forra*)
fogarero brazier (Port *fogareiro*); en vyerno toda la famiya biviyw al
    derredor del fogarero during the winter, the entire family lived
    around the brazier
fogatina the hottest period of the year; choking heat; accumulation of
    work
foja leaf
fojera fern
folin soot
folklor folklore
folor anger
folyeton fly sheet; feuilleton
folyo brochure
fondador founder
fondo deep
fondo fund (n)

fonsado army; legion; multitude
fonsádo army
fonsario grave
forastero stranger; alien
forchina hairpin (Ital *forcina*)
forfanteri bragging
forka gallows
forma shape (n)
formalidad formality
formar shape (v)
formasyon formation
formidable formidable
formidavle formidable
formiga ant
formigeo accumulation of ants
formigero anthill; swarm of ants
formigo very rich cake with honey and almonds; se kyere formigo
   something very substantial is required
formozo beautiful
formozura beauty
formula formula
formular formulate
fornada batch; baking; breads and dishes cooking in the oven
fornaza furnace
fornikasyon fornication
forno oven
forro free; liberated
forsa energetic, vigorous effort
forsado compelled; forced
forsar oblige; constrain; force (v)
forsel suitcase with a solid lock
forseliko trunk
fortaleza fortress; strength
fortaleza de poder mighty hand
fortaleza strength; vigor; intensity; fortress
fortifikar fortify
fortifikasyon fortification
fortuna good luck; riches; patrimony, goods and possessions
fortuna storm (n, T *firtina*)
fortunadamente fortunately

fortunojo stormy; tempestuous; agitated; restless
fosforo phosphorous
fostan skirt; dress; woman's shirt
fostana woman's robe
fostanella/fustanella skirt with multiple folds which is part of the traditional Greek man's costume; kilt
fota peak (n)
fóya grave; ditch
foya leaf
foyika small ditch; dimple
fragua building
fraguár build; **nos fraguava** had built for (us)
fraguemos let us guilty
fragulo strawberry
fraguo built
fragwála strawberry (from Ital *fragola*)
frajlanear set on a seat; reside in a spacious home (T *ferahlamak*)
franga fringe (n)
frangolato clumsy individual
frangula strawberry
franjola loaf of bread
frankamente in all truth; frankly
frankear frenchify; westernize (iron). Some Sephardic families changed from Judeo-Spanish to French, after studying at the Alliance Israélite, which had schools all over the Ottoman Empire. In some Sephardic families who considered themselves part of the social elite, the imitation of French (or Western) manners was pushed to the extreme, to the point of being ridiculous. Imitation of the West and rejection of the traditional habits and values was not only fashionable among the Jewish elite, but among Turkish Muslims as well. People imitating the West were called *Frenkleshmish Türkler* (Frenchified Turks). The frenchification or westernization was strongly opposed by the conservative rabbinical class.
frankedad ridiculous imitation of European manners
frankeria excessive and grotesque imitation of Western manners and habits
frankeza franchise; sincerity; loyalty
Frankia France. Also a synonym for the countries of the Occident, because the first European merchants in Turkey were French, and the first commercial (and later extraterritoriality) privileges, the

so-called Capitulations, were granted to the French as a result of the alliance between Soliman (Süleyman) the Magnificent and Francis I, King of France. The alliance between Francis and Soliman was primarily forged against the Habsburg Emperor Carlos Quintus.

frankito drawing; decoupage (the art of decorating surfaces by applying cutouts of paper, lineoleum, plastic) and then coating with several layers of finish (varnish or lacquer). The cutouts often showed the outlines of a man or a child.

frankito young European living in Istanbul

franmason freemason

franzola baguette (French bread) (F *franzole*)

frasa sentence; phrase (n)

fraternal fraternal

frauar build

fraza phrase (n)

fregado dishes ready to be washed

fregar rub (v); lit: rub somebody with nonsense; try to make worthless statements or merchandise appear worthy; **me lo frego** cheated me, gave me worthless merchandise

fregata fleet

fregatina obstinate rubbing; scratching of an itchy body part; stuffing of a skull

fregón piece of cloth used to rub

fregóna dirty; badly dressed woman (Jud-Sp Dict Madrid)

freido fried

freir fry (v)

freirse worry; get anxious about; **no se frie por ningunos** (lit: he does not care about other people's worries) he is an egoist

frente forehead

freole forehead

fresa strawberry

fria - **sangre fria** cold blood

frigalda di muez nut-filled pastry

friir fry (v)

frijalda di ceso cheese-filled pastry

frio cold

frio frio chills

fritada fried cheeseball, meat ball, spinach ball; fried mixture of eggs and flour; **fritadas di gayna** patties in which matzohs soaked in water replace the bread (eaten during Passover); **fritadas di karne blanka** chicken breast patties

fritas de kartof kon kezo potato patties with cheese

fritas di espinaka spinach and meat patties

fritas di kartof potato and beef patties

fritas di mirindjenas con sos di vinagre eggplant fritters in vinegar sauce

fritas di mirindjenas stewed eggplant fritters

fritas di miyoyo brain fritters

fritas di prasa leek and beef patties

frito fried

froña horsecloth; cover; pillowcase; saddlecloth

frontera/fronyera frontier

frontiera boundary; frontier

fruchigen let them grow; let them fructify

fruchigudad fruitfulness

fru-fru (onomatopoeia) noise of a piece of silk

frutchiguar fructify; multiply (a divine benediction to the people of Israel "fructify and multiply")

fuchigarer I shall make grow

fué became

fue was; became; **fue fraguán** was built; **fue como uno de nos para saber bien y mal** (he) was like one of us to know the difference between good and bad; **fue tomada** was taken; **fue demoudada** was moved; **y fue** and it (so) happened; **y fue a el onjeva** so that he had sheep (Fer Bib Gen); **y fueron todos dias de Mahalel** (and) they were all the days in the life of Mahalel

fuego fire (n)

fuemos we were (Salonica Pesach Siddur)

fuente fountain; **fuente de las aguas** source of the water

fuentes sources

fuera would be; **de fuera** outside; **antes ke se fuera** before he goes

fuero privilege of a city or collective recognized by law, by royal decree or custom (in former Spain)

fueron - **si lo fueron** if they were

fuersa strength (noble form of *huersa*)

fuerte strong

fuesa ditch; sepulcher

fuessa ditch (Ferrara Siddur)

fuesse was
fui I have been
fuistes you have been
fuitech - vos fuitech you went
fuitina running away
fukara poor; unfortunate; pityful
fukarako person deserving pity or compassion
fulano somebody; unknown person; somebody of whom the name is
    unknown
fular scarf (F *foulard*)
fulin covered with soot; dirty; badly taken care of
fulus pennyless; without any money (T)
fumada puff of smoke
fumador smoker
fumar smoke (v); esta fumando is smoking
fumasina very dense smoke
fumear release a small stream of smoke; exhale smoke in little blows
fumigasyon fumigation
fumo smoke (n)
fumozo smoky
fundasyon foundation
fundido lost at sea; drowned; shipwrecked
fundidor destroyer; person who causes shipwreck
funebro somber; melancholic; mournful
funerales (pl) funeral
funksyon function
funtana fountain
fuórame I went to
fúrcha brush (n, Monastir dialect)
furcha brush for clothes (T, Gr)
furcha de dyentes toothbrush
furchada brushing; brush to beat off the dust
furchear brush (v)
furchino/forcina hairpin (Ital *forcina*)
furgon van; carriage; wagon
furon frustrated individual
furroje rust (Gal *furruje*)
furtuna tempest; storm
furyente violent; carried away by fury; having an expression of fury
furyozo furious; carried away by anger

fushka small blister
fusil gun (F *fusil*)
fusilyar/fuziyar shoot with a musket; shoot by firing squad
fuskin muck; dung; manure
fusta skirt
fustuk pistachio
fustukes peanuts; roasted peanuts
fustuki (adj) pistachio color
futbal football; socker
futuro future (n)
fuyír flee; run away
fuyir run away; te **fuyes** thou didst flee; **fuyeron** they fled; they ran
    away
fuyô fled
fuzo spindle; sheath; case; hollow cylinder which serves as a recipient
    for a pen; box in which are saved silver or gold coins
fyaka despairing slowness; nonchalance; nonchalant show-off; **favlar**
    kon fiyaka go, walk, or talk very slowly
fyakedad slowness; dawdling; creeping; quibbling
fyasko fiasco; **fazer fyasko** fail
fyel bile
fyelozo very bitter; surly; crabbed; currish; dogged; crusty
fyero iron (n)
fyerreria foundry
fyerrerio iron store; accumulation of iron objects
fyerrero ironsmith; blacksmith
fyerreziko small object made of iron; small piece of iron
fyerro iron (n); **rezyo komo el fyerro** solid like iron
fyerros (slang) money; dough
fyesta feast (n)
fyestar celebrate
fyongo ribbon in the form of a knot (for the head, a dress, curtains)
fyuba clasp or buckle holding the hair of a toupee

G

gaava arrogance; pride (H)
gabardina raincoat; overcoat
gabay president, administrator or treasurer of a synagogue or community

gabineto room reserved for intellectual work and special conversations
(Ital *gabinetto*)
gadol/el gadol lit: (the) big one; (the) chief; (the) commander (H)
gafa gaff; awkward, unskillful, clumsy action
gaina abafada braised capon
gaina chicken
gaina con aroz chicken with rice
gaina con kartof chicken with potatoes
gaina con zarzavat chicken with vegetables
gala gala; festivity with an official character
galana virgin
galanteria gallantry
galera jail (n)
galeria gallery
galeta hard biscuit
galgal wheel (H)
galileano (adj) from Galilea
Galili (adj) from Galilea
gallina chicken
galnte gallant
galut exile; captivity (H)
gam sorrow; pain; anxiety (T)
gamancia sus bien profit; gain one's property
gamba red pepper
gámba thigh
gambas in vinagre peppers in vinegar
gambas inchidos con karne stuffed red peppers
gamelio camel
gaméo camel
gameyo camel
gamsíz careless (T)
gana appetite, envy (n); tener gana envy (v)
ganàdo cattle
ganado herd; shepherd; pastor
ganancia gain; richness (n); ganancia que ganaron profit they made
ganandon someone who is successful in business but may be unable to
keep the profit
ganansya gain; benefit
ganar gain; win (v)
gancho hook; cramp; clamp (n)

185

ganeden paradise
gangliyon ganglion
gangozo speaking from the nose
gangrena gangrene
gangrenarse to become gangrenous (v)
gangrenozo gangrenous
gante glove
garansia warranty
garante guarantor
garantizir guarantee
garato salted tuna
garez grudge; resentment; hatred (T)
garezli grudging, striving for revenge (T)
garganta throat
garon throat
gaznéte windpipe
gazoz bubbling lemonade, soda
gazozo (lit) gaseous; fig for: joyously satisfied
gazyera small portable petroleum stove
gebirim gentlemen
geçmish olsun (lit: let it be passed) expression used when somebody
      recuperates from a disease or has had an accident (T)
Gemara Gemara commentary part of the Talmud (as opposed to
      Mishna, being the law part)
gemido groaning
generaçiones generations; **generaçios nascidos de casa** all those that
      were born in the house (Fer Bib Gen)
geniza archives, storeroom with old books, old papers, usually in the
      basement of a synagogue; closet which loose pages of holy books
      or Hebrew manuscripts (H)
gente nation; people; **gentes** nations; **si gentio tambien justo mataras**
      will you as well destroy the just people/the just nation (Abraham
      to God in relation to the threatened destruction of Sodom and
      Gomorrah) (Fer Bib Gen)
gerra war
gerush exile (n); mass expulsion from a country (H)
gesto temper (n); **buen gesto** good temper; good gesture
geto ghetto
getres cover made of leather or fabric for lower legs and top of shoes

gewetch di peshkado stewed fish (striped bass, turbot or hake)
geyna hen
gezera sentence; condemnation; calamity; public misfortune; divine
    chastisement (H)
gia guide (n)
gigante giant
gigantes giants
gilgul transmigration of souls; reincarnation; metempsychosis (H)
gimoteo whimpering; wining
girilali insinuating, fishing in troubled water
gitara guitar
givir rich, notable person (T)
giyer (T) liver
giyotina guillotine
gizado ragout; stew; cooked dish
gizandera cook (n, fem)
gizandona cook (n, fem)
gizar cook (v)
gizbar treasurer of the synagogue (H)
globo globe
gloria glory
glorifikasyon glorification
gobernador governor
godriko the little fat one
godro fat (adj)
godron (adj) corpulent; pot-bellied; stocky
godrura fat (n)
gol lake (T *göl* kanunn)
goler smell (v)
golondrina swallow (n)
golór odor
golpe stroke
gomitar vomit (v)
gomma gum
gondola gondola
goralji fortuneteller (from T *görücü*)
gostoso tasty
gota drop; gout
goulash con hrandajo di masas goulash with eggs
governador governor

governar govern
gozar enjoy; exult; **y gozôzos** that we may exult (Haggadah Passover)
gracia grace
grája crow
grajerio flock of crows
grajon young crow
Gran Rabbino Grand Rabbi
grand great
grande big
grande big; **el Grande de la komunita** notable; leader
grandes big people; giants
grandeza greatness
grandure size (Monastir dialect)
graniko small grain
granizo hail (n)
grano grain
graváta necktie
graves grave; **hazinura graves** grave disease
graviyina carnation; **no tokar, no aharvar ni kon palos de graviyina** treat a person with the greatest care and caution; **seras graviyina enriva de mi kavesa** (lit: you will be a carnation on the top of my head) you will be received and treated with the greatest affection
gregaya Greek neighborhood
Gregos Greeks
gritalon someone who screams a lot
gritalona woman who screams a lot
gritar scream (v)
gritaron/gritalon bawling; grumbling; yelling; howling
grito scream; shout; cry (n)
gritos de dolor scream of pain
griyo cricket
grosh piaster, Turkish money (one hundredth of a Turkish pound). Its value dropped considerably during the Sultan's reign. One grosh (T *kurush*) was divided into forty *paras*; **estar trenta i mueve para'l grosh** (lit: one more para will be needed to make a piaster) to be at the edge of (health, bankruptcy); **un gameyo, un grosh, onde esta el grosh** they are offering a camel for one piaster only, but everybody is so poor, where to find the piaster?
grua crane; stork
guadràda guarded; hidden

guadrador guardian
guardarades you will guard; you will keep
guardarla guard her
guardaroba closet for cloth
guardelo 24 oras keep him/safe keep him for 24 hours
guay de su madre poor dear of one's mother
guebirim gentlemen
gueinam hell
guelindón penis (Haketia)
guerfano orphan
guerkeriyas the works of the devil
guerko/guerku devil
guerta garden; door
guertelano gardener; farmer
gueso bone
güestro your
guesudo someone with thick, large bones
guevo egg; **guevo limon** mixture of eggs, olive oil and lemon usually
    served with fish; **guevos con ceso blanco** eggs with white cheese;
    guevos con domates, pipiritzas i ceso blanco eggs sauteed with
    tomatoes, peppers and white cheese; **guevos con kashkaval** eggs
    and katchkaval cheese; **guevos con sivoya** eggs sauteed with
    onions; **guevos inhaminados** hard-oiled eggs; **huevos ruvyos**
    russet eggs
guezmo smell (n)
guf body (H kanunn)
guizandona cook (fem)
guizar cook (v)
gullabi (T) warden in a lunatic asylum
gupa light salted raw small fish, a Sephardic delicacy
Gurdji Georgian Jew, synonym for rich, but illiterate and bad-
    mannered
gurlia adder (according to popular belief, the apparition of an adder in
    a residence is a good omen)
gursuz inauspicious; bad omen; bringing bad luck; devoid of any amia-
    bility (T *ughursuz*)
gustar taste (v)
guste taste (n)
gusto taste (n)
guvetch vegetable casserole; **guvetch con karne blakan** beef stew

guzanento covered with vermin
guzaniko small worm
guzano de Yerushalayim bug
guzano worm; caterpillar
gwadiar keep; guard (v)
gweso bone
si guardan mi hermano yo am I my brother's keeper (Cain about Abel)
(Fer Bib Gen)

H

haber news (T)
hablo he spoke
hachgaha communal religious district (H)
hademe servant (T kanunn)
hadji Muslim who has done the Pilgrimage to Mecca, one of the five
basic requirements of Islam (T *haci*)
hadrikas small gestures to give one oneself an air of importance
hadroso posturing
hafiye detective
hafiyelik spying; investigation
haftear steal (v)
hafteo he stole (Haketia)
haftona spanking; beating; slapping
hagades - a los varones estes no hagades cosa so that you do not harm
these young men
haha clumsy; crazy, disheveled woman; uncoordinated woman
haham rabbi (Sephardic rabbi); haham de mezikas rabbi who used to
move from table to table, from a Bar Mitzva or wedding banquet
to a family memorial banquet, receiving food everywhere
haham Sephardic rabbi
Hahamim doctors of the religious law; religious scholars; rabbis;
knowledgeable people
hahán rabbi
haketia Moroccan Judeo-Spanish
hakim judge; magistrate (n, T kanunn)
haksíz unfair (T)
hal state; situation; condition (T); en ke hal in what state; vuestro hal
your condition

halavro rundown; dilapidated neighborhood
hali carpet
halila ve hal God forbid
halis authentic (T)
halisa the right to repudiate a deceased brother's widow, in case the
brother died without leaving a male heir. The idea of this is to
liberate the childless widow from marrying the brother of the
deceased. If a man dies without leaving a child, his brother is
supposed to marry the widow. It is only after having being repu-
diated that the widow can remarry someone else.
halladas who find themselves there
hallán - y sera todo hallán a mi me matara and so it will be that
anyone who finds me will kill me
hallar find (v)
hallare - si hallare if I shall find there
hallaron vega they found the countryside
hallo gracia found grace
hallo tu siervo gracias en tu ojos he has found your servant grace in
your eyes
hallola he found her
haluka millenary Jewish Palestinian institution that collected alms and
donations for rabbis and other Jewish people in the Holy Land,
particularly Jerusalem and Tiberias, through special commissaries
(*shaliah*) in Jewish communities of the Diaspora.
halva Turkish sweet made of sesame; **halvah di gris** semolina halvah
hamal errand boy; porter
hamarat hardworking; industrious. Term used among Sephardim to
describe the praiseworthy qualities (good housewife, good
hostess) of a new bride or a young girl proposed for engagement.
hambre hunger; starvation
hambrera hunger
hamear heat up
hamets leavened bread
hamin dulci veal with fruit
hamor donkey
hamora female donkey
hamoriko small donkey; affectionate word used in Sephardic
households for the donkey which was used for running daily
errands
han inn; office or commercial building (T kanunn)

Hanalel (name) Hanalel el papel (iron) document which is alleged to be important and looks important, but which in reality is worth no more than paper

handji innkeeper (T *hanci* kanunn)

handrajero rag dealer

handrajo kon paras (lit: rags with money!) shout of the rag dealer, used to describe stupidity and ignorance or empty words

handrajo rag; gag; shred of cloth; tatter; strip

handrajon vendor who goes door to door to buy and sell rags

handrajonero someone who gives useless advice, who has projects that make no sense

hanef hypocrite; sly (H)

haneziko small building containing shops, businesses, offices and workshops

hanino person with very white skin

hanum Turkish lady; an affectionate and caressing name given to little girls, young girls, or women; hanum durmyendo, el mazal despyerto (proverb) the damsel does not even suspect the beautiful destiny which life is keeping in store for her (said about a young girl who ignores everything of life, and whose future is solidly insured)

hanumeler honey-suckle (flower)

hap pill

harab decaying; falling in ruins; in state of destruction; destroyed; old (T)

haragán lazy person

haraj tax paid by the non-Muslims (*reaya*) in the Ottoman Empire (T)

haram interdicted by religion; a thing that is enjoyed without entitlement (T); pan haram person who eats a bread that he/she has not earned; haram yiyeji parasite

haramaji someone who uses a thing without paying for it; someone who unjustly gets advantages; blind passenger

haras - asi haras como hablaste do as you have said

harem female members of a family (T, kanunn)

harif smart, sly person

harina flour

harjelik/harchlik pocket-money (T *harclik*)

harlo do it

harose/harosseth/harosi dish eaten during the Passover Seder ritual. Mixture of mashed potatoes, almonds, walnuts, raisins, dates, cinnamon and wine, wrapped into a lettuce leaf

harrova carob
harta map (T *harita*, kanunn)
harvador spanker (kanunn)
harvar beat (v)
harvo beat; strike; spank (kanunn)
haryeno worm-eaten
has excellent; of very good quality; pure
hasbon account; calculation
hase calico
hashabi kaghidi (T) (lit: with all due respect) allegedly important but
     in reality absolutely worthless paper or document
hashabi worthless, deprived of any validity and authenticity
hashfurro shoeless, unimportant person
hasid pious; devout; deeply religious
hasta until
hatan fiancé; someone who celebrates his wedding; "fiancé of the
     Torah": faithful who receives the privilege to read in the
     synagogue at the morning prayer, on the last day of Sukkoth,
     the first passage of Genesis from the Torah scroll. At the exit
     from the temple, the *hatan* is solemnly escorted by the crowd to
     his house.
hatir favor; thought; idea; memory; mind; influence (T); azer hatir do
     a favor; por hatir influence; consideration (T *hatir* kanunn)
Haua Eve (Fer Bib Gen)
havajiji plant which grows near the water with edible rhizome
have bird
haver companion (H)
haver friend; associate (H)
havra synagogue; used in Turkish in a rather negative connotation, in
     expressions such as havra patirdisi noise coming from the prayer
     place of the Jews (Jews were considered irreverently noisy people)
havuz artificial basin; pond (T kanunn)
havyar caviar; (fig) doing nothing (at work)
hayal soldier (H)
haydut bandit (T kanunn)
haydutluk banditry (T kanunn)
hayim - le hayim! to your health! (toast); hayim tovim wish addressed
     to a person who has just sneezed: may you enjoy a happy and
     healthy life! According to popular belief, sneezing was a sign of a
     nearing death

hayra person in rags
hayrat pious foundation (T kanunn)
hayre goodness; benefit (n, T *hayir*)
hayvan animal (T); also used to scold someone to scold a misbehaving person
hayya animal (H kanunn)
haz a ti does to you
hazak baruh benediction; wish; vow; congratulations to a person who has just accomplished a pious work or a meritorious action (H)
hazan cantor
hazan officiating at the synagogue
hazanear recite the prayers or lamentations at a funeral
hazara return of a purchased object; restitution of a borrowed; counter-script in accounting
hazer make; do
hazerlosan servir she will serve the inhabitants of the premises
hazertee por gente grande I shall make you a great nation (Fer Bib Gen)
hazián llower they made it rain
hazimyento disease (kanunn)
hazine treasure; treasury (T)
hazino ill; sick
hazinu sick (Monastir dialect)
hazinura illness; sickness
hazinura sickness
hazir pork (H)
hazira return, refund (n, kanunn)
hazne public treasury (T *hazine* kanunn)
he here is; that is; there is; here is; **he mi firmamiento contigo** here is my covenant (alliance) with you (Fer Bib Gen); (i agora) **He tu mujer** (and now) there is your wife
Hebreo Hebrew
hecha made up (fem)
hechos doings; actions (Ferrara Sidddur)
Heden Eden
heder local school
helal lawful; legitimate
hembra female
hendiasse la tierra con su bos the earth resounded with his voice (Ladino Bible of Ferrara)

henoso (jenozo) gracious

heredar inherit; take possession of; en que sabre que lo) heredare how who (by what) shall I know that I will inherit it (Fer Bib Gen); en que sabre que la heredare by what shall I know that I will inherit it (Fer Bib Gen)

heredaria country; inherited land; heirloom (Fer Bib Gen)

heredera will inherit

herém ban; excommunication

herir kill (v); no herir a el todo hallán so that anyone who would find him does not kill him

herira cabeça will crush head

hermana sister

hermano brother

hermoleo he made it germinate

hermolesco he made it germinate

hermollecera will produce

hermolleciesse it grew

hermollo germ (n)

hermoza beautiful (fem)

hermozo beautiful (masc)

hevrá club; fraternity (H)

Hevron Hebron

heziste - (que) heziste? (what) did you do?

hianetlik treason; malicious act (T hiyanetlik kanunn)

hiba affection; zeal

hiel poison (n)

hierba grass

higo fig

higuera fig tree; vine; vineyard (Ladino Ferrara Bible)

higuiero fig tree

hija daughter

hijo son

hijo de oveja lamb

hijo de vaca veal (Fer Bib Gen)

hijos foros freemen

hilo thread (n)

hinchidad fullness; plenitude

hinzir pig; pork; perfidious, perverse; cruel; heartless (T hinzir)

hipócrita hypocrite

hirbo marionette

hirieron they vanquished them; they beat them; hirierion con
    çiuedumbre they struck with dazzling force
hiriolos vanquished them; beat them
historia history
historico historical
hiyanet treason; treachery
hizieron guerra con Berah rey de Sodom they made war with Berah
    the King of Sodom; desciendere agora y verri si como su
    esclamaçion la veniente a mi hizieron fin y si no sabre I shall go
    down now, and I shall see if they have entirely done all the things
    (of which the rumor has come until me) and if this is not so I
    shall know it (Fer Bib Gen)
hizmét help, serve (v, T)
hizmet service; duty (T kanunn)
hizo he did
hizoles vestir he made them wear
hodja teacher; Muslim cleric (T hoca)
hodjalik teacher's job (T hocalik kanunn)
hoja leaf
hokabaz juggler; conjurer; mountebank; buffoon
hokabazlik juggling; conjuring; fraud
holento sickly person
holera cholera
holgo he rested
homaz Pentateuch (H humash)
hombre man
homre man
honra glory
honrra glory (Ferrara Siddur)
hopo brainless, superficial individual (T hoppa)
hora hour; hora buena (lit: good hour) exclamation expressing a
    happy wish, or expressing the fear that something unpleasant
    may have happened; hora mala (lit: bad hour) exclamation to
    wish bad to someone who said or did unpleasant of offensive
    things
horhor aga contemptible, clumsy and ridiculous individual
horhor fistula
hormet respect; overpayment(T hürmet); de hormet (adv) more; in
    excess; in supplement

hormigua ant
horno de fuego fuming oven
hosha hot drink made of boiled dried figs and raisins; fruit in syrup;
    also fig: mixture of various things (T *hoshaf*); hoshaf ister misin?
    (lit: do you want a *hoshaf?*) The story goes that while climbing
    the stairs to his apartment, the Sephardic journalist B. saw a bur-
    glar coming out of his apartment, and without losing his
    coolness, he offered him a drink; eshek hoshaftan ne anlar! (lit:
    what does a donkey understand from *hoshaf*) it is like throwing
    pearls before a swine
hostaleraz debauched women (Ladino Ferrara Bible)
hotel hotel
hotelji hotel keeper
hová obligation
hovarda (lit: spendthrift or running after women of low virtue) in
    Judeo-Spanish: generous benefactor
hrandajo wiping clothe; rag; cheap, worthless person or thing
hristiar (si) sanctify oneself (Monastir dialect)
hristu cross (Monastir dialect)
huente fountain; faucet
huentezika medical practice much in use until the end of the
    nineteenth century. A wound produced in the arm was
    maintained by placing in a grilled and salted chick-pea (*leblebi*)
huerco hangman
huerto garden
huessos bones
huir run away
hukumat government (T *hükümet*, kanunn)
hukyum sentence (T *hüküm*)
hulasa summary (T *hulâsa* kanunn)
humiyar lower, bow oneself
humiyôsse they bowed themselves
humo smoke (n)
hundiar drown (Ferrara Siddur)
hutz outside (H)
huyendo running away (Moroccan Sephardic Ballad)
huyo - y huyo delantre de ele and he fled in front of him (Fer Bib Gen)
huz latrine
hwersa strength

I

i and
ibé bag (from T *hibe*)
ibra freeing from claim (T kanunn)
ibrik ewer; vase with handle and beak used to prepare and serve coffee
idad age (n)
ideya idea
idioma language
idjra execution (T *icra* from Kanun Name)
ifade statement (T from Kanun Name)
iftira slander; calumny (T kanunn)
igado liver
ihtisali neccesary (T *iktizali* kanunn)
ihtizá necessity (T)
ihzar summons (T kanunn)
ija daughter
ijada urinary infection
ijastro son of a spouse in a previous marriage (noble language for *hijo*)
ijo son; ijo de un judio son of a Jew; ijo de un mamzer son of a
    bastard; ijo de un perro son of a dog
ijon (noble language for *hijon*) iron used to ridicule the use of *ijon*
    instead of *fijon*
ijos foros freemen
ilaka interest; concern; connection; relationship (T *alaka*)
ilam judicial decree in writing (T *ilâm* kanunn)
illa at all cost; to be done with undue insistence; to de done beyond
    any consideration (T *ille*)
ilmuera daughter-in-law
ilo thread (n)
imaginar/imajinar imagine
imaje image; statue; idol
imajinador someone who creates or imagines
imajinasyon imagination
imajinavle imaginable
imam Muslim cleric
imambayildi (lit: the imam fainted) Turkish dish (stuffed eggplant with
    meat) which is supposed to be so good that it made the imam
    faint (T)
imán belief (T)

imansiz faithless; atheist (T)
imateryal immaterial
imbat southwest wind, sea breeze (T)
imediatamente immediately
Imperio Otomano Ottoman Empire
impisidju beginning
importar matter (v)
impuesto tax
inat stubbornness
incantar catch by surprise (v, Monastir dialect)
inchidos filled
inchir fill (v); inchir la kavesa fill the head
inchusa pie; inchusa di apricot apricot pie; inchusa di ceso con otra
    masa afrijaldada cheese pie; inchusa di leche milk pie; inchusa di
    prasa con masa fina leek pie; inchusa di spinaka con masa mal
    tomada spinach pie; inchusa di vishna sour cherry pie
inde agora this very minute
inde still; as yet (Port *inda*)
indemás still more; besides (Port *ainda mais*)
ine despite this; all the same nonetheless (T *gene*)
ingenuo naive
inieta granddaughter
inieto grandson
inkizisyon inquisition
inmientris while (Port)
innát obstinacy (from T *inad*)
inquisidor/inkizidor inquisitor
inshala God willing! (T *inshallah*)
intelijensia intelligence
intrimentis while (Port)
intusedju poison (n, Monastir dialect)
inuerno winter
invierno winter
invitasion invitation
inyegar deny
inyervar (se) get irritated (v)
inyervo nerve
inyervos nerves
inyervozo nervous
inyeto grandson

inyetos grandchildren
inyeve snow (n)
inyúdo knot (n)
ipoteka mortgage
ir go (v)
ira indignation
irade imperial decree (T kanunn)
irmanu brother
irtikâb committing a dishonest act (T *irtikâp*)
iscapar exhaust (v, Monastir dialect)
iscapar finish; terminate (v, Monastir dialect)
iscolje college (Monastir dialect)
iscujer chose (v, Monastir dialect)
iscunder hide (v)
iscuntrar encounter, find (Monastir dialect)
iscuvar sweep the floor (v, Monastir dialect))
ishala! God willing!
ishbitirici agent who takes care of administrative issues for a fee, like
     getting passports, permits, certification of military compliance
ishbozan individual intervening in a disturbing, inappropriate way in a
     promising business (T)
ishlear function well (tool, a machine, a key) (T *ishlemek*)
ishportaci peddler (usually a Sephardic Jewish trade in Istanbul) (T)
iskendje torture (T *ishkence*)
ispantar (si) to be afraid of
ispantar scare
ispantu fear; terror (n, Monastir dialect)
ispidje corn; maize (Monastir dialect)
ispicieru shopkeeper; grocer (Monastir dialect)
ispinu thorn (Port *espinho*)
istorya story
itaat obedience (T, from Kanun Name)
iussanos secundos y terceros second and third floors
ivan were
iyyar May (H)
iziyét difficulty (from *eziyet* ill-treatment)
izla island
izlas islands
Izmirli person from Izmir

izo did
izo did
izquierda left (fem)

J

jaba gratis; todo esta jaba everything is exceptionally cheap
jabadji someone who tries to get things for free; blind passenger; parasite
jabón soap
jajik appetizer made of chilled yogurt seasoned with oil, vinegar, sliced or grated cucumber, garlic and fennel
jaketa jacket; vest
jam window-glass; pane of glass
jam/jan honorary title preceding the name of middle-class, aged persons
jamas never
jamay never. Used only in the proverb kyen negro nase jamay se enderecha who is born bad, never rectifies oneself; the defects with which one is afflicted at birth never correct themselves
jambaz acrobat; dancer on cord; very skillful but dishonest person; someone who fishes in troubled waters
jamdji dealer of window-glass; glazier
jan beindim the defiant and dandy-like way in which young, elegant people used to wear their fez, inclined to one side instead of straight on the head to express their carefree style (T *can beghendin*)
jandarmá police officer; gendarme
januario January
janvie January (F *janvier*)
jarope syrup
jarpear plant (v)
jarpeo (he) planted (Haketia)
jelatina di peshado jellyfish; jellied whiting
jenabet impertinent; bad-mouthed; a state of impurity; foul brute (T *cenabet*)
jenayo January
jeneral (military) general

jeneral general (adj)
jeneralidad/jeneralita generality
jeneransyo generation
jenero gender
jenerozo generous
jengel hook
jenitor father; mother; progenitor; los jenitores the parents, the
    progenitors
jenjibre ginger
jenjivre gum
jenne/jennem hell (T *cehennem*)
jenneme! (exclamation) go to hell!
jennemebudjanina lost corner in hell; lost place in the middle of
    nowhere (T *cehenneme bucaghina*)
jennét heaven, paradise (T *cennet*)
jenoso gracious
Jesús Jesus
jijifranko/jijifrango little master; dandy
jiles (pl. of *jil*) little bells of a Basque tambourine; cymbal (T *zil*)
jilveli lackadaisical; mincing; seducing
jilves being lackadaisical; mincing manners; grace; charm; flattering
    words (T *cilve*)
jimír cry (v)
jinganelik ignoble; vile, sordid (T *çingenelik*)
jinganeria suburban zone where gypsies camp
jingano Gypsy (T *çingene*)
jinoyo knee
jins gender; kind; nature; origin
jiradas affected grimaces
jitano Gypsy
jonk junk
jornal newspaper
joya jewel
joyero jeweler
Juderia Jewish quarter
Judesmo/Judezmo Ladino; Judaism
Judio Jew; Judio bendicho blessed Jew; Judio santo meleh aolam holy
    Jew king of the world
juevez Thursday
jugador actor

jugar kartas play cards
jugar play (v); **solo puedes jugar** you can only play
jugares you will play
jugete toy
jugón jacket
juissios judgments
juizos judgements (Ladino Bible of Ferrara)
julio July
junio June
juntos together
jurar to swear
jurnal journal, newspaper, periodical (Port *jornal*, F *journal*)
jurô (He) swore
justedad justice
justicia justice
justo just
juzdám/juzdan wallet (from Turkish *cüzdan*)
juzgador judge (n)
juzgar judge (v); **no juzgara mi espirito en el ombre sempre** my spirit
     will not always be in contest with man (Fer Bib Gen)
jyovintud youth (Ital *gioventu*)

K

kaba rude; vulgar
kabadayi swashbuckler; bully, tough guy; guy having guts; the best of
     anything (T)
kabahat fault
kabala Kabbala
kabesa head (n)
kabinet cabinet; toilet
kablenim liable (H kanunn)
kachakchi smuggler (T *kaçakçi*)
kachar hunt (v)
kachavida screwdriver (Ital *cacciavite*)
kache kache paying what is asked without bargaining (T *kaç?* how
     much?)
kacher haval yellow Turkish-Greek-Bulgarian cheese
kacher kosher (Sephardic)

kacherear make escape; juggle away; subtract to control or attention; make disappear furtively (v, T *kaçirmak*)

kacherearse escape; slip away (v)

kacheta very visible redness; blushing; **le suvyo kachetas pretas** he became all crimson

kada every

kadar until; till; up to (T)

kadayif oriental pastry made of fine shreds of flour paste, honey, butter, seasoned with cinnamon; **ekmek kadayif** bread kadayif, a dessert served with thick cream (kaymak) on the side; **te l kadayif** shredded kadayif

kadém luck (T)

kadena chain (n)

kadenado lock (n)

kadin Turkish lady; Muslim lady

kadish Jewish prayer for the peace of the soul of a dead person. It requires the presence of a minyan, i.e. ten male adults.

kadun woman (T *kadin*)

kaer fall (v)

kafé coffee

kafedji café owner; coffee maker

kafetyera cafeteria

kafrô transgression of religious principles and rites; blasphemy (from T *küfür* insult, blasphemy; also from Judeo-Spanish *kifur*, insult)

kaftan caftan

kafurear blaspheme; growl; get angry (from T *kâfir* miscreant, unbeliever)

kagada (vulg) mass of excrement; cowardice coming from fear

kagadero (vulg) diarrhea; cowardice

kagadijo (vulg) going to the bathroom

kagado (vulg) someone who has soiled his underpants; someone who is the object of public disdain because of his shameful conduct

kagador (vulg) someone who is defecating; the posterior part of the body

kagadura (vulg) excrement; dirt; **kagadura de moshka** excrement of a fly; **kagadura de raton** excrement of a mouse

kagajon (vulg) dirt, filth; insignificant and ridiculously pretentious person

kagajoneria (vulg) hollow; futile; inconsistent projects exposed in a flux of confused explanations

kagajoniko (vulg) ridiculous and pretentious person
kagalon (vulg) one who defecates too often; coward; pusillanimous
kaganera (vulg) diarrhea; cowardice because of danger
kagar (vulg) defecate (v)
kagarse (vulg) do it in his underpants (v)
kagatina (vulg) violent diarrhea; cowardice, pusillanimity; blabbering;
   flow of lamentable, pitiful words
kagon (vulg) one who usually defecates in his underpants; falsely
   brave. Sephardim used to tell the story about a Turk, a Greek, an
   Armenian and a Jew standing in line. Suddenly and unexpectedly
   a canon is fired with thundering noise. The Turk, the Greek and
   the Armenian run away in terror. The Jew stands undauntedly
   firm in his place, apparently without losing his calm. They come
   to congratulate him. He simply says: "Bring me clean pants."
kahal synagogue
kahpe (vulg) prostitute; person lending him-/herself to sly and
   infamous practices (T)
kaida fall (n)
kaido fallen
kaidura fall; surrender of a fortified place
kaik launch; departure for leisure rides along the shore or the harbor;
   rowing boat (T kayik)
kaikdji boatman (T kayikçi)
kaji almost
kaki brown-yellow
kakuleta hood; head covering
kal temple; synagogue; Kal de los Frankos Frankish synagogue in the
   Jewish quarters of Istanbul
kalavasa squash
kalavasada sweet dish consisting of squash and pumpkin, garnished
   with grilled almonds
kalavasikas al orno baked zucchini with cheese; kalavasikas con ajo
   zucchini with garlic; kalavasikas con domates al orno baked
   zucchini with cheese and tomatoes; kalavasikas con domates y
   sevoya zucchini with tomatoes and onion; kalavasikas con mirrind-
   jena i kartofeles stewed zucchini with eggplant and potatoes;
   kalavasikas in sos di domates small zucchini in tomato sauce;
   kalavasikas inchidos con karne in sos stuffed zucchini in French
   tomato sauce; kalavasikas inchidos con karne stuffed zucchini;
   kalavasikas lenas con ceso zucchini stuffed with white cheese

kalavasita small squash
kalay tin (T)
kalaydji tinsmith (T)
kalayladear cover copper plates and other copper kitchenware with
    a tin layer; solder two pieces tin covered steel with melted tin
    (T *kalaylamak*)
kalb fake, falsified; moneda kalb fake money, counterfeit money
kalbazanlik counterfeiting (T *kalpazan* kanunn)
kaldeano/kaldeo Chaldean
kaldirim parasi sidewalk surcharge (T)
kaldo boiling; broth
kaldudo aqueous; juicy; containing an excess of broth
kale fortress (T kanunn)
kale must be (word of Catalan and Aragon origin); kale ke (arch) it is
    necessary. This expression goes back to the Castilian language of
    the sixteenth century; it is conserved today in Catalan and
    Aragonese. The modern Spanish equivalent is *hay que/es
    necessario ke*; kale ke ayga must be; kale ke venga it is necessary
    that he comes (Judeo-Spanish, Catalan, Aragonese) The modern
    Spanish form is *es necessario que venga; tiene que vinir*; kale vivir
    a la moda one must live according to custom (Judeo-Spanish,
    Catalan, Aragonese; modern Spanish form *hay ke vivir a la
    moda*)
kalebend confined to a fortress (T kanunn)
kalem pencil
kalizones con ceso wrinkled phyllo dough with cheese
kalkadosh the holy synagogue. Title by which the name of every syna-
    gogue is preceded (H *kal kadosh* holy synagogue)
kalkan turbot, a very appreciated fish in the Sephardic kitchen,
    specially when served fried (T)
kalkanal heel
kalkomani decalcomania (the art or process of transferring figures and
    designs from specially prepared paper to wood, metal, glass;
    decal)
kalma calm; lull
kalmar (se) quiet down (v); (se) kalmo he quieted down
kalomnia calumny; slander
kalomnyador slanderer
kalomnyar slander (v)
kalor heat (n)

kalosh rubber shoe
kalsa sock
kalsado shoe; (fig) drunkard
kalso drawers; breeches; underpants
kaltaban lazy; good for nothing
kaltak horse saddle; prostitute
kaltchonet elastic band holding underwear
kalup mold; shape; model, shoemaker's mold; two bronze molds in the shape of truncated cones, fitting into each other, with a wood fire heated from below and between which the fez was inserted to iron it, straighten it in such a way that it would take the shape of a brimless cylindrical scullcap (T *kalip cap*); **dar la fez al kalup** iron the fez in the mold to make it look elegant
kalvasara court of Bedlam broke loose; place of disorder and confusion
kama bed
kama dagger (T); **travar kama** draw a dagger; threaten with a dagger
kama de parida decorated bed of a woman after childbirth
kamada hay spread out to make it look like a bed
kamareta room. Expression used by the Archipreste de Talavera in *El corbacho in Estrugo* (*Los Sefardis*, p. 91, Editorial Lex, Havana, 1958) Modern Spanish form *habitación/cuarto*; **kamareta d'echar** bedroom
kambur hunchback (T)
kambura hump
kamdjik whip (n, from T *kamçi*)
kaminando walking
kaminar walk (v)
kamino road
kamiza de yenso shirt worn by Sephardic women in Salonika
kamiza larga long shirt, like a baby dress, considered as amulet
kamiza shirt
kamizeria place where shirts are manufactured or sold
kamizika small baby shirt
kampaña countryside; fields in the outskirts of a city; vacation spot. For wealthy Sephardim, the most favored summer vacation spots were in the Prince Islands in the Sea of Marmara, southeast from the Bosporus. The most popular ones were Burgaz (Greek-Byzantine name Antigoni) and Büyükada (Greek name Prinkipo), the largest of the Prince Islands. The Judeo-Spanish preference for

these islands was so strong that towards the end of World War II, when the Americans invaded the Solomon Islands in the South Pacific, a cartoon appeared in the most famous Turkish comics magazine, the *Akbaba* (The Vulture). The left side of the cartoon shows the Americans invading the Solomon Islands, the right side shows the Jews invading the Prince Islands. The humorist nickname for Jews in Turkey is Salamon, the Turkish word for Solomon.

kampania/kampanya bell

kampo camp

kamyo foreign exchange

kanal canal

kanalizasyon canalization

kanalya rabble; rascal; scoundrel; despicable person capable of the worst actions

kanamo hemp

kanape couch (F *canapé*)

kanarino small canary

kanarya canary

kanata jar; flask; recipient of terra-cotta

kañavola hemp seeds. In former times, roasted hemp seeds were a popular treat, especially for children. During the wintertime, the street vendor stood on the right side of his circular flat container, in the middle of which stood a chafing-dish where the hemp seeds were roasted, and while turning the hemp seeds, he called: "Bruya, bruya la kanamola frita!" (Hot! Hot are the roasted hemp seeds).

kande - asukar kande candied crystallized sugar

kandela candle; tener la kandela lit: hold the candle (for the wife's lover), meaning: to be a cuckold.

kandelar candelabra; candlestick

kanderear convince; persuade; to be seduced; trick, defraud (T *kandirmak*)

kandidato candidate (n)

kandidatura candidacy

kandil wick; ancient oil or petroleum lamp

kanela cinnamon

kanesa head

kanfanfana bootmaker's section in the Balat, the Jewish neighborhood in the southern shore of the Golden horn, which later became famous for its fez (from *kavhahana* boot maker)

kangaraviya/kankara viyas common things presented as marvels; naïve
and ridiculous juggling tricks
kanja boat-hook, long hook, pole (perch) ending in a hook
kansado tired
kansar (se) get tired (v)
kanser cancer
kanserozo cancerous
kanserya fatigue
kantadera female singer
kantadero tendency for uninterrupted singing which exasperates other
people
kantador singer
kantar ancient Turkish weight measure worth 40 okes (about 123
pounds)
kantar sing (v)
kantara pitcher; jar; jug
kantaro urn; jar; terra-cotta pot
kantiga popular song
kantikas little chansons
kantor cantor at the synagogue
kantorero; maker of terra-cotta pots
kantos songs
kanun law (T kanunn)
kanunname legal code, penal code (T). The Ottoman penal code was
translated into Judeo-Spanish around 1860 by Yehezkel Gabbay,
with Hayyim Nissim Piperno as the typesetter
kapache able; capable (Ital *capace*)
kapak kayido lit: the cooking pot with a fallen top. Exclamation com-
parable to the English "Oh my gosh" (combination of T *kapak*
cover and Judeo-Spanish *kayido* fallen)
kapara expiatory sacrifice; expiation, atonement; consolation used if
an object breaks or gets damaged; an injunction not to worry,
though something unpleasant may have happened, it will bring
good fortune in the future
kaparra caper
kapasidad capacity
kapatchita ability (Ital *capacità*)
kapidji concierge; doorman
kapikomshu communication between two apartments (T *kapi komshu*
door neighbor)

kapital capital (adj); very important
kapital capital (n)
kapitala capital city (n)
kapitalismo capitalism
kapitana women's jacket with fur lining worn by Jewish women from Salonika
kapitulo chapter
kapkana catch what you may
kapladear coat (v)
kapo chief; director; guard (Ital *capo*)
kara face; en la kara on the face; kara preta black face; dark face; kara de luna lit: face of the moon. Judeo-Spanish paraphrase to describe a beautiful woman; kara de pokos amigos lit: face of few friends; Judeo-Spanish paraphrase for an unfriendly person
karafa carafe
karahaber dark news; bad news (T)
karahaberdji messenger of bad news
karakol police headquarters (T)
karantina quarantine
karapikado/el karapikado person with a wrinkled face
karar decision; decree; right quantity; dar karar decide (v); el karar de gregos the number of Greeks
karavides crayfish (T)
Karay Karaite. A Jewish sect which rejects the Talmud and rabbinical writings, recognizing only the Ancient Testament. The Istanbul Karaites were either Turkish-speaking Crimean Karaites (and possible descendants of Khazar Turks, i.e. Arthur Koestler's Thirteenth Tribe, converted to Judaism), or Byzantine Khazars speaking Greek. The Karaites did not speak Judeo-Spanish.
karaylan dark; unfriendly; unpleasant; disagreeable; sullen (T *karaoghlan*)
karayoz figure of Turkish folklore (T *karagöz*)
kardyako cardiac
kardyografiya cardiography
kardyologo cardiologist
kardyolojiya cardiology
kare in card games, four of the same cards
kargamyento loading of merchandise or packages
kargar pack or expedite packages
kargo cargo; obligation; responsibility; commitment

karia cavity
karides shrimp (T)
karikatura caricature
karishiklik disorder; confusion; agitation (T *karishiklik* kanunn)
karkino cancer
karmador sorcerer
karmadora sorceress
karmakarishik very disorderly
karnabit cauliflower (T)
karne meat
karo dear; expensive
karotsa carriage
karpuze/karpuz watermelon (from T *karpuz*)
karraya glass lamp with large borders which are filled with oil and a
    wick dipped into it. Hanging from the ceiling, it was part of
    every Jewish home, on top of the family's table. During the
    Ottoman era, the karraya was lit on Fridays before sundown to
    keep the Sabbath table illuminated. In synagogues and oratorios,
    the karraya was kept permanently alight.
karrucha tire
kart hard; dry (fruit, vegetable, meat)
karta cards; playing cards
karta letter
kartofis con sivoya yellow potatoes with onions
kartofis inchidos con ceso potatoes stuffed with white cheese
karu car
karvonis rascals
kasaba small town, borough (T kanunn)
kasamiento/kazamiento marriage
kasap butcher
kasha chest; coffin
kasha de jeves chest; box made of walnut wood
kashika small box (with the -*ika* diminutive which is used in the
    Aragon dialect; the -*ito* suffix which is mostly used in modern
    Spanish is rare in Judeo-Spanish)
kashkarikas lit: Sephardic dish made of squash peel, minced into small
    cubes; fig: acts of a person who tries to play tricks
kashkaval/katchkaval Turkish-Greek hard yellow cheese; kashkaval
    asado grilled katchkaval; kashkaval pane batter-fried katchkaval
kashkita orange peel in syrup

kashko skull
kashon drawer
kashterar mix up; interfere unnecessarily (T *karishtirmak*)
kastanya chestnut
kastigar punish; chastise
kastigo punishment
kastiyo castle
kastor beaver; beaver's fur
kastrado castrated
kat layer; stratum; floor in a building
katalan/katalona Catalan (from Span Catalogna)
katálogo catalogue
katife velvet
katorze fourteen
katorzen fourteen
katran tar
katrepengle/a katrepengle with refined care (from F *tiré à quatre épin-gles*); meterse a katrepengle dress with refined care
kav(x)ane set for serving coffee; coffee-house (T *kahvehane*)
kavakador someone who digs too much into things, ending up bringing in the open things which would better stay dormant or forgotten
kavas doorman; guard in an embassy or consulate. In the Ottoman empire, he was generally of Albanian origin.
kave coffee (Turkish coffee)
kaveos/kaveyos hair
kaver fit; be able to fit in a container (v)
kaverengi color of coffee; brown; yellow-brown (T *kahverengi*)
kavesa head; kavesa de apio de Odesa lit: head of celery of Odessa; fig: big head but no intelligence; kavesa de chifalo lit: head of gray mullet; fig: empty headed; know-nothing; kavesa de lenyo head of wood; stupid person; kavesa de piedra stone-headed; kavesa ke no entra klavo lit: head that no nail can enter; stubborn
kavesal cushion; pillow; head of bed
kavesera head of the bed; set of luxurious bed-cover and pillows for wedding and childbirth bed, decorated with embroidery of fine metal threads
kavo - al kavo in the end
kavod honor (H)

kavra goat
kavrika small goat
kavza cause (modern Spanish *causa*; the second element of the *au*-
    diphtong has become *v* in Judeo-Spanish)
kavzo case; legal case
kaxya/kehaya Jew nominated to be the mediator between the Jewish
    community and the Turkish authorities (T *kâhya*)
kaya/kayabalik goby a fish very appreciated by the Sephardim.
    Because of excessive and uncontrolled fishing, it has almost disap-
    peared (T)
kayada hush
kayades silence
kayadez silence
kayado being silent; silent
kayar shut up; to be silent
kayd register (v, T kanunn)
kaye street
kayentar heat (v)
kayente hot; warm
kayer fall (v)
kayesi (large) apricot; peach-apricot (T *kayisi*)
kayesi apricot (T *kayisi*)
kayezika small street
kayida fall (n)
kayik rowing boat (T)
kayiktchi boatman (T)
kayma banknote; bill (T *kayme* kanunn)
kaymak very thick cream highly appreciated in Turkey, from the
    milk of the female buffalo kept in a dark stable. The kaymak is
    usually served on top of Turkish coffee. Also the cream layer on
    top of yogurt.
kaymakam, administrative officer at the head of kaza, i.e. subdivision
    of a vilayet, a Turkish province (T kanunn)
kayme ancient Turkish money, worth five pounds
kayo - se kayo he fell
kaza accident (T kanunn)
kazadas di ouva grape tartlets
kazaka cloak; cassock; garment with broad sleeves
kazaka undershirt with wide sleeves
kazakita undershirt for a baby

213

kazal places outside of Istanbul
kazalina woman from a place outside of Istanbul
kazamentero matchmaker
kazan caldron
kazandibi residue which remains at the bottom of the caldron in
  which mahallebi (Turkish custard) or sütlaç (Turkish rice
  pudding) is cooked
kazar marry
kaze house
kazik - echar un kazik lit: throw a stake, meaning cheat (From T *kazik*
  stake and Judeo-Spanish *echar* throw)
kazmir cashmere; woolen drape
ke fue what was it?
ke haber? how are you?
ke mal mos tenga let wickedness befall us. For superstitious or
  humorist reasons, euphemisms or expressions were used contrary
  to their intended meaning. The sentence really means *ke mal no
  mos tenga* let wickedness not befall us.
ke which; than
ke? what?
keaya miyo nno sos tu I do not
kebap kebab-grilled, roasted meat
kebaptchi vendor of kebab; **shish kebap** kebab on spit
kechar/keshar complain
kechida complaint
kedar stay (v); **uno ke kedaria** somone who would stay
kedate azno stop the donkey
kef relaxation (T *keyif*)
kefte/köfte meat patty, meatball (T *köfte*)
kefur insult (T *küfür*)
kehila community
kelepur worthless or cheap object; worthless person (T *kelepir*)
kemado burned
kemaltekere lit: that (one) who wishes you bad. Practically an expression of sympathy used towards a person who has suffered the
  loss of a close one. It could also be used ironically.
kemar burn (v); **i ya se esta kemando** and he is burning; **kemar (se)**
  burn oneself (v)
kemha compound weave; polychrome silk; silver and gilt silver threads,
  which used to be produced by the imperial Ottoman workshops

ken who; whom (Port *quem*, modern Spanish equivalent: *quien*)
kenef (vulg) toilet
kere wishes
kerensia/kerensya affection
kerer love; wish (v)
kereste timber; lumber (T kanunn)
keriath reading (H)
kerida dear (fem)
kerido dear (masc)
kerméz oriental bug living on oak trees, from which a crimson dye is
     extracted for wool coloring
kesha/keshada complaint
keshar complain
keshf discovery; inquest (T kanunn)
keshke expression of regret that things have not come out the way
     they should have
kesion - te aplano la kesion I settle your matter; I resolve your
     problem
kestyon question (n)
kestyonar interrogate (v)
kestyonaryo questionnaire
Ketana/la Ketana the Valley of the Sweet Waters of Europe, at the
     mouth of the Golden Horn, a favorite picnic place at the turn of
     the century for the Sephardim of Istanbul, especially from the
     neighborhood of Haskoy and Balat. It was reported that a zebra
     was living there, the only zebra in Istanbul at that the time.
ketuba marriage contract. Illuminated, beautifully decorated ketubas
     were part of the Sephardic art in the Ottoman Empire.
ketubot marriage contracts
keyadura silence
kezada di merendjenas con masa little eggplant pies
kezada marzipan cake
kezadas di ceso con masa afrijaldada cheese tartlets
kezo blanko feta cheese
kezo cheese
kezo kasher Turkish-Greek hard yellow cheese
ki no moz vemos that we have not seen each other
ki sea should be; will be
ki that
kibir vain (T)

kibrites matches (T *kibrit*)

kidush benediction of wine, accompanied by an oblation at the beginning of Sabbath or high Jewish holidays; **fazer kidush** fill his wine glass to the top (H)

kidushim nuptial blessings; **dar kidushim** solemnly marry a woman; **aniyo de kidushim** wedding ring

kijo - **el kijo** he wanted

kilipur ciego worthless sample

kindi time between noon and sunset

kindime lace ribbon inserted (T *kedime*)

kira rent (n, T kanunn)

kirida dear; darling (fem)

kirim long, fur-lined overcoat for man or woman

kirlangitch swallow (n)

kirugio surgeon

kiꞥada jaw

kishla military barracks (T *kishla*)

kislev (H) December

kislimu (Bab) December

kita las paras take out the money

kitadera godmother

kitador godfather of the child to be circumcised

kitadura ceremony in which the godfather holds the newborn submitted to circumcision in his arms, on top of a pillow; present given for the newborn by the godfather or godmother

kitamanchas craftsman taking fat stains out of garments

kitar get; draw; separate from; take out (v)

kitarse pasaporte get a passport

kitate de tu mujer separate from your wife (imp)

kite - **se kite la djube** take out your robe

kitô - **(nos) kitô** He brought us from

kiyamet great abundance; exaggeration; great suffering; extreme difficulties; too much (adv); enormously (T)

kjoftes di karne in sos di domates meatballs in tomato sauce

kjoftes di karne meat patties

klal general rule, category (H kanunn)

klareza clarity

klaro clear (adj)

klavidon metal thread used for embroidery; metal wire around silk core (T *kilaptan*)

klima climate
klimatizisyon air-conditioning
klinika clinic (n)
klisa church
klub club
knas fine; penalty (H kanunn)
knesset Israeli Parliament
kobardo coward
kocha lame; limping (fem)
kocho lame; limping (masc)
kodiche code (n, Ital *codice*)
kodja yemish/kudja yemish wild strawberry-like fruit growing on a
     tree (*T koca yemish*)
kodrero con ajo fresco lamb with French onions and garlic
kodrero con arroz lamb and rice
kodrero con spinaka lamb chops with spinach
kodrero in papel al orno baked leg or shoulder of lamb
kodrero mutton; lamb
kofya ancient headgear of married Sephardic women, consisting of a
     small oblong pillow covering the head and descending towards
     the back of the neck, on which are fixed an arrangement of mul-
     ticolored ribbons and tulles. Married Sephardic woman were sup-
     posed to wear the kofya when going out, receiving guests or
     attending solemn ceremonies. Otherwise, they would wear a
     simple *bambala* (head handkerchief) at home.
Kohen priest officiating at the Temple of Jerusalem; descendant of the
     clergy at the Temple of Jerusalem. The descendants of Aaron,
     brother of Moses, form a class which is submitted to certain mat-
     rimonial restrictions and to the avoidance of impurity, such as
     contact with a dead body. They have a special role in solemn syn-
     agogue functions, and when attending a circumcision, they are to
     receive a symbolic piece of silver; **Kohen ha Gadol** high priest at
     the Temple of Jerusalem; **birra de Kohen** Kohen's anger. Kohen
     had a reputation for a bad temper.
kojembral field planted with cucumbers (Ladino)
koket coquette
koketeria coquettish behavior
kokona mistress of the house; well-dressed woman; woman with loose
     morals (vulg). Also used by a wife for the spoiled mistress of her
     husband, when she herself is neglected or even mistreated (Gr).

kokoz very poor; penniless; destitute; financially wiped out

kokteyl cocktail

kol cabbage; **kol con arroz** cabbage with rice; **kol dulce con karne** sauteed cabbage with beef

kol guard unit; patrol; night patrol in the streets. In Ottoman times, nightly pedestrians had to fear the night patrol, as much as the marauders, which the patrols were supposed to chase (T *kol* arm, military or watchmen patrol); **fuy ke viene el kol** run away! danger! the kol is coming!

kol nidre/kal nidre prayer at the beginning of the Kippur liturgy asking for forgiveness for all the vows and promises that may have been infringed over the past year or those which might be infringed during the new year. This prayer is thought to have been introduced into the ritual for the Jews who were forcefully converted during the Inquisition, because they externally practiced the rites of the imposed religion, but secretly persevered in the practice of Judaism.

kola tail; **tomar por la kola** (lit: catch from the tail) attach too much importance to something; exaggerate

kolado filtered

kolana chain (n)

kolay easy (T)

kolayladear facilitate (from T *kolaylamak*)

kolaylik easiness (T kanunn)

kolcha wadded; padded bedcover; coverlet; **kolcha de parida** coverlet for a woman after childbirth

kolchon mattress; woman who neglects her personal care

kolomba pigeon; dove

kolondrina king's oil; scrofula

kolondrina saliva

kolor color

kolorado red

koltuk armchair. In the Judeo-Spanish language of Salonika, a square cloth to cover Elijah's chair in the brit milah ceremony (T *koltuk*)

kolyos mackerel

komadre midwife

komadrear tell meaningless stories; chatter

komadrón obstetrician

komanda purchase order; being in command of a team

komanya supply (n, T)

komar gambling; dice game (T *kumar*)
komardji passionate gambler; breakneck; rough rider
komarka habits; customs; traditions
komash tissue; quality of a tissue; **es buen komash** it is of good quality
    (for an object); he is of good morality; he/she is a person easy to
    live with; he/she is a person of good character
kombate combat; struggle (n)
kombibado invitee; guest
kombibador someone who extends an invitation; emissary in charge of
    the invitations
kombibar invite; convoke a reunion (v)
kombite feast; invitation
komca rose; bud (T)
komedero overeating; eating too much
komedura deterioration coming from excessive use
komemorar commemorate
komer eat (v); **kedar sin komer** fast; **komer i eskupir** lit: eat and spit.
    Said about hard or dry vegetables and fruits, which are hard to
    chew; **komi** I ate; **komimos** we ate
komerchante tradesman; merchant
komerchar make commerce
komerchear do the customs clearance; dispatch
komerchero customs agent; dispatcher
komercho commerce; customs administration
komeriko small meal for two persons
komersyal commercial
komersyalizar coerce
komesina itching
komida food; meal; banquet
komisaryo commissar; official in a communist government
komo how; **komo le paso** how did it go; how did you pass; **komo te**
    yamas what is your name
komodine night table
komodo commode
kompedron buttocks. Each time this part of the body was mentioned,
    it was customary to add the apology *pudor kon pardon*, which
    rhymes with the word *kompedron*
kompla rhymed verse
komportar comport (v)
komportarse behave (v)

komporto behavior
komposto compost (n)
kompozado composed
kompozantes elements; components; constituents
kompozar compose (v)
kompozisyon composition
kompozitor composer
kompra buy; acquisition (n)
komprado bought
komprador buyer of foreign exports. In Turkish the word has a conno-
    tation of excessive profit making and of profiteering.
komprar buy (v)
komprimado compress (n)
komprime pastille; troche; pill
kompromiso compromise; act by which a litigation is submitted to an
    arbiter
kompromisyon compromising act
komun common
komunismo communism
komunisto communist
komunita community
komunitá community
komur charcoal (from T *kömür*)
kon il tiempo in time
kon with
konak halting place; government house (T kanunn)
kondanar condemn (v)
kondanasyon condemnation; no te kondano I do not condemn you
konde count (title of nobility)
konduktor driver of public transportation
kondurya shoe (T *kundura*)
kondurya shoe (from T *kundura*)
kondúrya shoe
konduzir conduct; drive (v)
konfeksyon ready-to-wear clothes; elaborate but not very practical gar-
    ment
konferensya conference
konfesar confess
konfit candy; comfit distributed at weddings and other festivities
konfitera candy bowl; candy box

konfites candies, sugared almonds
konfitura preserve (n)
konfonder confuse (v)
konhugar bring together; conjugate (Port *conchigar*)
konosido known (adj); acquaintance (n)
konsagrar tie two families together by the bonds of marriage
konseja story
konsejas folk tale
konsejika small story; anecdote
konsejo advice; counsel (n); konsejo de un viejo perro advice of an old
    dog; (no bueno) konsejo not a good advice
konsiderar consider
konsiderasyon consideration
konsigo with oneself
konsiltable conciliatory
konsilyante conciliatory
konsilyar reconcile (v)
konsilyo council; committee
konsiña consignment
konsiñar consign; hand over or deliver officially
konsizo concise
konsizyon concision
kontado/kontante money that the bride's father gives to the
    bridegroom as part of the marriage agreement
kontame una konseja tell me a story
kontar tell a story (v)
kontornar give a proper contour to; pass around (v)
kontra against
konvenido convened; arranged
konvenir arrange; convene; to be convenient
konvenser convince
konvensido convinced
konya rose (From T *konca* bud, rosebud)
kopri/kupri bridge (T *köprü* kanunn)
koracha in the Judeo-Spanish of Salonika, a bag for phylacteries and
    prayer-shawl. See also *talega*
koraje courage (From F *courage*)
korason heart; korason de judio heart of a Jew (a good person);
    korason de oro golden heart
korban sacrifice (from T *kurban*)

korbán sacrifice
Korbàn Pessah Passover Lamb
kordon cord; chain (n)
korijar correct (v)
korkova hump
korkovado hunchback
kortadura cut (n); wound made with a cutting instrument
kortakavesas (lit: one who cuts heads) grotesque individual trying to
    terrify people by grotesque and ridiculous threats
kortaleña woodcutter
kortamiento cutting; kortamiento del achugar cutting; inauguration,
    presentation of the dowry before a wedding
kortar cut (v); kortar fashadura ceremony marking the starting of the
    cutting of the baby's clothes, held in the early months of
    pregnancy.
kortijo interior courtyard; patio
kortina curtain; curtain for closing off the bed
kortinaj canopy surrounding the upper part of the bed
koru small wood; grove (T kanunn)
kosfuegros remote relatives like cousins or uncles on the spouse side or
    the relations between in-laws on both sides
kosho lame; limping
kösk villa, summerhouse; small building typical of Ottoman
    architecture (T köshk)
koskiyas tickling
Kosta Istanbul (H for Constantinople, kanunn)
kostek watch chain worn under the jacket (T köstek); kostek de oro
    gold watch chain
kostiya rib (n)
kostura sewing
kosuegro relative
kovdo elbow
kovét power
kovre copper
kovrero coppersmith
koyon naive person who can be easily fooled (Ital coglione)
koza thing; koza fea the ugly thing. Euphemism for male genitals;
    koza negra the bad thing. Euphemism for male genitals or other
    taboo words.
kozido cooked

kozir/kozer cook (v)
kreendome believing me
kreyer believe
kriar raise (v)
kriatura creature
kriminal criminal
Kristiano Christian
kriza crisis; relapse of disease with fever
kroitor tailor (Romanian Judeo-Spanish)
krosta crust
kuadra - (no le) kuadra muncho (lit: much understanding does not
    reach him) unintelligent
kualo what; kualo se paso what happened
kualunke whatever (Ital *qualunque*)
kuandu when
kuaranten fortieth
kuarenta forty
kuartikos di mirindgena kon karne beef and eggplant stew
kuarto fourth
kuartos/kuartikos Sephardic dish made of quartered eggplant
kuatro four
kubar(a) godfather, godmother
kubara godmother
kuchara spoon
kuchiyo knife
kudurear (lit: become enraged) amuse oneself crazily with a bedeviling
    zest and no concern for good manner (T)
kudureo indecent entertainment (*kudurmak*)
kuedra cord; rope
kuedra del lavado clothesline
kuerpo body
kueshko pit
kufa large basket (T *küfe* kanunn)
kufyo spoiled; rotten
kúkla doll
kukulitra striped crêpe cotton used for shirts and undershirts. In Izmir
    also the undershirt made from this material
kukuretch barbecued mutton intestines served in slices. Also small
    sausages garnished with pulp, small pieces of meat, liver, etc.,
    heavily spiced and served very hot (T *kukureç*).

kukuyero breeder of silkworm
kukuyiko little cocoon
kukuyo cocoon of silkworm
kula tower; La Kula Old Genovese Tower of Galata at the center of
    the Jewish quarter uphill over the Istanbul harbor, where
    Sephardic specialties such as salt cured tuna (*garato*, *lakerda*) or
    dried fish with bulging egg sacks (*liparidas*) were sold.
kuladear watch; keep under surveillance; spy on (T *kollamak*)
kuladeo spying; keeping under surveillance
kulaksiz (lit: without ears) district of Hasköy on northern side of the
    Golden Horn
kulanbey rowdy; urchin; young scamp; merry fellow (T *külhanbeyi*)
kulanear use; utilize; employ habitually (T *kullanmak*)
kulebro serpent
kulero active pedophile
kuléro type of diaper
kuliba hut; sentry box (T *külübe* kanunn)
kulibera virago
kulibero individual with no education (n); bad-mouthed; poorly
    educated (adj)
kuliko small rear-end
kulina saliva (Ital *aquolina*); traer la kulina a boka bring the saliva to
    the mouth
kulo rear; anal region (vulg); kulo de pipino (lit) rear-end of cucumber
    (vulg) a matter about which a lot of noise is made but which has
    no results
kulpa fault
kumar gamble (T)
kumarbazlik gambling (T kanunn)
kumash chicken coop (T *kümes*)
kumbaro godfather (Salonika Judeo-Spanish, from Gr *koumbaros*)
kumiendo itching; eating
kumpania/kumpanya company
kuna crib
kundak arson (T kanunn)
kunduryero shoemaker
kunusheár chat (v, from T *konushmak*)
kupa drinking glass; cup
kura remedy (n)

kurabiye cake made with almonds or nuts
kuramaña soldier's bread in the shape of a crown
kürk fur; fur coat (T)
kürkdji fur dealer; fur merchant
kursos classes; errands
kurto short
kuru muabet conversation in the course of which no refreshments or
    drinks are taken; conversation with no results (T *kuru muhabbet*)
kuryendo/koryendo running
kuryente/koryente stream; river; current; air current; draft
kushak belt; sash used as a belt (from T *kushak*)
kusur failure to do one's duty (T kanunn)
kuti box (from T *kutu*)
kutiko small box
kuydado! attention!; be careful!
kuydadozo careful; cautious
kuyumji goldsmith; jeweler (T *kuyumcu*)
kvartikos di mirindjenas cubed eggplant
kwenta story
kwero skin
kyase bowl; cup in which broth or Turkish coffee is served
kyatib Turkish functionary; clerk; secretary; accountant
kyeaya/kyehaya village chief; chief of a residential quarter;
    intermediary between residents and the authorities; improvised
    defender (T *kâhya*)
kyebab grilled meat; spit-roasted meat; meat cut into small pieces
    mixed with lamb kidneys, fragments of liver, brain, or bone
    marrow which is grilled on a spit (T *kebab*); ni shish ni kebab
    (lit: nor spit-broiled nor kebab) said about anything undecided,
    undetermined; uncertain words, hesitant orders, fleeting words
    one does not know how to interpret
kyefal mullet
kyefsizlik indisposition; temporary illness (T *keyifsizlik*)
kyelipur bargain; good occasion; despicable person of bad faith
kyeman/keman violin (T *keman*)
kyemanji/kemandji violinist (T *kemanci*)
kyemer arcade
Kyemeralti/Kemeralti (lit: under the arcade) famous red light street in
    the Karakeuy district of Istanbul, between the harbor and the
    Galata tower

kyen who (prep and interrogation); the one who; those who
kyendi beyenmez (lit he does not like himself) pretentious individual of
    little importance; eternally dissatisfied person
kyepaze/kyepaze blackguard; blubber; sorry fellow (T *kepaze*)
kyepazelik/kepazelik scandal; open dishonor
kyeradji - (no ay) kyeradji (lit: there is no tenant) brainless person
kyeradji tenant; someone who rents horses; member of a caravan
kyerash offering of a drink, a meal, a cake (Gr)
kyerata knave; rascal; scoundrel. Sometimes the word kyerata is used
    in an affectionate and admiring way to designate a very clever,
    very skillful person (T *kerata*)
kyereste construction wood; plank, timber; lumber
kyerestedji dealer in construction wood
kyesat dead season in business; period of no sale (T *kesad*)
kyeshke would God have liked it!; would have been better; would
    have been preferred (T *keshke*)
kyezap/kesab acid; vitriol
kyibrit/kibrit matches
kyima/kiyma ground meat (T *kiyma*)
kyimali/kiymali containing ground meat (T); liparida kiymali dried
    fish full of eggs, full of caviar. A Sephardic delicacy sold around
    the Jewish neighborhood of La Kula
kyimur heating coal; charcoal (T *kömür*)
kyofte oblong meat patty grilled on charcoal
kyohne apathetic; indolent; sleepy; languishing; old-fashioned person
kyok root (T *kök*)
kyosele thick and hard leather used for shoe soles; hard, uneatable
    meat or steak (T *kösele*)
kyoshe/kyushe corner (T *köshe*)
kyosk/kyoshk kiosk; pavilion (T *köshk*)
kyula long; pointed cap (T *külah*)
kyurdi Kurdish (T *kürt*)
kyurdi long overcoat with fur lining (Gr *gourdi*)
kyuspa residue of ground seeds; old bread, cake or tart
kyutuk log (T *kütük*)

L

la the (fem)
la'az any foreign language
labar/lavar wash (v)
labarse/lavarse wash oneself
labio lip; language
laboratoryo laboratory
laboryozo hard working; arduous
labrador de tierra cultivator
labrar cultivate
ladino medieval Castilian used for a primitive translation of the Bible
    and Hebrew prayers; Ladino has been used for biblical, liturgical
    or rabbinical texts and some historical texts. Ladino is a literal
    word by word translation of Hebrew into Spanish keeping the
    Hebrew syntax in contrast to Judeo-Spanish which is the spoken
    language of the Sephardim.
ladio corner in which one rests
lado - a su lado at his side
ladron thief
ladu side (Monastir dialect)
lafazan blabbermouth; a mill to produce unceasing words; a true
    word-mill
lagarta/lagarto lizard
lagen de sangre (lit) basin full of blood; it is said that when the
    Scythian Amazons defeated and killed Cyrus, King of the
    Persians, they dipped his head in a basin full of his blood, which
    became the theme of a famous painting
lagen pan; basin (T *leghen*)
lagna cabbage (T *lahana*, Gr *lahano, lahanon*); kapama de lagna cab-
    bage in the pot prepared with sautéed onions, butter, ground
    meat, rice and pinola nuts; salata de lagna cabbage salad with
    parsley, decorated with olives and peppers
lago lasso
lagrima tear (n)
lagrimear shed tears; let the tears drop from sickly eyes
lagrimozo soaked in tears (speaking of sick eyes)
lagum underground passage; tunnel; sewers (T *laghim*)
laguna lagoon

lahay roi the living one who sees me (name of Agar's well)

laico laic; worldly person

lakerda salted tuna; in a derogatory meaning, all that was given or offered is *lakerda*, meaning something after all not very valuable or meaningful (T)

lakirdi conversation; words exchanged in the course of conversation (T); **echar lakirdi** talk; devise; **es lakirdi!** it is only talk with no substance, with no base; **dar lakirdi** maintain the small talk; **pasar el tyempo kon lakirdi** spend the time chatting

laksativ laxative

lamber lick (v)

lambriskon someone who licks; someone who by habit of gluttony licks the utensils which have contained food or sweets; someone who pampers oneself in caresses and cajolery

lambriskona female gourmand; a glutton who avidly tastes all the dishes; who scratches all the utensils in which food has been cooked, or in which food has been deposed, particularly sweets and preserves. According to popular belief the wedding of a *lambriskona* is accompanied by torrential rains.

lambrusko ear (of corn); handful of corn gleaned; bunch of grapes neglected at the time of the harvest or the vintage, and which is the lot of the poor according to biblical tradition (see the story of Ruth and Booz in the book of Judges)

lamentarse lament; complain; despair (v)

lamentasyon lamentation

lamentavle pitiful; mediocre; bad

lampa lamp

lampara lamp

lampe lamp (Monastir dialect)

lampero manufacturer or vendor of lamps

lamya tapeworm; tenia; **tener lamya** to be continuously hungry; bulimic

lana wool; **abasha la lana, suve el algodon** when the price of wool falls, the price of cotton rises (meaning there is always a natural compensation, a spontaneous equilibrium of things in this world; you cannot lose and win all)

landra pest; budding ulcers; malignant pustulae in the neck, in the groin; the sixth plague of Egypt

landre mite

langosta locust; individual who devours and makes ravages

lanozo woolen; sheep well-furnished with wool
lapa - arroz lapa rice boiled without any fatty substance
lapa cataplasm; in old medicine it was common to apply on the back
    warm catapalasms of hemp seeds
largo long
largura length
lashon akodesh/lashon hakodesh (lit) sacred language; Hebrew
    language; language of the Bible; biblical Hebrew
lashon language; tongue (H)
lastikli (adj) elastic; equivocal; that can be interpreted in many ways
lastimoso pitiful; lamentable
lauad vuestros pies wash your feet
lavado laundry
lavandera laundry woman
lavar wash; se lavaràn las manos they will wash their hands (Passover
    Haggadah)
lavorante worker
lavorár work (v)
lavoro work (n, Ital)
lavrar embroider
lavurador worker (Monastir dialect)
lavyo lip
lazaret hospice
lazdrada miserable (fem)
lazdrar do burdensome, hard work; labor; struggle at work; work
    assiduously; strive (v)
lazéria burden
lazerio work; task (n)
lazim necessary (T); ne me lazim what for?; why should it be done?; I
    prefer not to interfere, not to get mixed with, not to get involved
    (words of the egoist, of the apathetic who stands aside from
    involvement); es de los ne me lazim he is an egoist
lebantar get up; se lebanto he got up
leche milk; leche papeada milk custard; leche con arroz milk-stewed
    rice, similar to baked rice pudding, made quite simply by cooking
    rice in milk favored with vanilla and adding sugar, plenty of
    grated lemon rind, cream and cinnamon in the appropriate order.
    The lemon rind is what gives this preparation its special perk.
lecheria dairy
lechero milkman

lechos de la civilization affairs; doings of civilization
lechos de la sivdad city business
lechuga lettuce
legriniado grouchy; complaining all the time
legrinyada wretched, grouchy woman
leguentina watch chain
lehli interchangeably Polish or German (Ashkenazi) Jew living in
  Istanbul. Intermarriage between Sephardim and Ashkenazim was
  a taboo or at least a rare occurrence.
lehlia woman of bad mores; woman of ill repute (because of intercommunal strife the *lehlis*) (Polish newcomers) had a bad reputation
  among the Sephardim, which explains the negative connotation of
  the word *lehlia, lehli* woman.
lei law
leil ha-shamira vigil night; the night before the *brith milah*
  (circumcision ceremony), is dedicated to prayer and study of the
  Torah, viewed as a means to protect the mother and newborn
  during these difficult and traditionally risky hours. Rabbis and
  scholars were invited to the house of the mother and child, where
  they prayed and studied the Torah the whole night through. Over
  the generations the night took a more festive turn, with romances
  (especially those dealing with birth) being sung. Throughout the
  night it was forbidden to leave the infant unattended in his
  cradle. It was customary for the grandmother or another close
  relative to hold the infant in her arms until the time of the
  ceremony.
lej le shalom go in peace
leka nosht good night (Bulgarian Judeo-Spanish)
leksiko lexicon
lektor reader
lemaan ashem for the love of god; I beg you abstain; refrain from this;
  it is dangerous; do not do it at any cost!
lemli wet (adj, from T *nemli*)
leña wood
leñador wood cutter
lenantarse get up; raise oneself
leñata beating; a volley of blows of strokes; a thrashing
lendra nit, eggs of a parasitic insect, esp. louse attached to the hair
  (search for nits was common in Sephardic and Turkish schools)
lengua vulgar Ladino

lenguada sole (fish)
lenguage language
lenk lame (Persian)
lentejas lentils
lenya piece of wood; heating wood for stove; komer lenya (lit) to eat
    wood; (fig) to receive blows, beatings (this expression has its
    equivalent in various Balkan languages, but not in the Romance)
leolam effectively; the fact is; nonetheless; nevertheless it is certain that
    (H)
león lion
leon ogre
leoncillo lion cub
leprozo leper
leshana aba the year to come (from H next year in Jerusalem)
leshano remade
lesho far
leshos/lexos far away; de leshos from far; from far away
leshura remoteness; very large distance
letra letter
levadura leaven; yeast; ferment
levantaduos get up; rise (imp, Fer Bib Gen)
levantara oriental
levantaronse they rose; they got up
levantate (imp) get up! rise!
levantime I arose
levantosse a he raised against
levdado fermented
levdarse to become leavened (v)
levyatan gigantic and fearsome monster (cited in the Bible, in the Book
    of Job)
Ley Law; Ley de Moche Law of Moses; at times it could have an ironical
    undertone if it is meant to denote that somebody is making an
    emphatic statement on a matter or rule that is not that important
lezet taste; flavor; what makes the taste; enjoyment; pleasure (T)
lezetli tasty
lezetsiz tasteless (T)
libade waistcoast worn over the entari (loose robe); it was generally
    made of the same fabric as the *entari*, although at times its back
    part was made of a simpler material. Also called *fermele,
    mechere, yelek.*

liberan - (lo) liberan they free him
liberar deliver; free (v)
libra mi alma del malo con tu espada deliver my soul from evil with
    thy sword
librar deliver; free (v)
libro/livro book
ligado liver
lijera (fem) lighthearted; carefree; light-brained; superficial; not very
    seriously minded; frivolous; oriented towards not very deep
    concerns
likidar/llkuidar liquidate (v)
likor liquor
likorino smoked mullet
likuanda restaurant (T *lokanta*)
likuidasyon liquidation
lila lily
lima file (n)
liman seaport (T)
limpia clean (fem)
limpieza cleanliness
limpio clean (adj)
limunio mourning
linaje family; lineage
lindo pretty
lingwa judia Ladino
lingwa tongue
lión lion
lira Turkish pound; Turkish gold pound; in Ottoman times one lira
    corresponded to one hundred piasters and one piaster was worth
    forty *paras*; the smallest monetary unit was the *mangir*, an obso-
    lete copper coin
lishisten nishasta starch (n, T *nishasta*)
lisyon lesson
litchouga lettuce
lívre free (adj)
livriko little book
livro book
livyanez taking something lightly; paying superficial attention;
    disregard; absence of serious concern. Antonym: *pezgadia*

livyano someone who does not take thing seriously; who does not concentrate on things; who only takes a casual interest in matters
llagas sores
llago hit
llamar call; name (v)
llamela call it; name it (Ferrara Siddur)
llamo called; **llamo nombre Henoc** He called the name Enoch
llanura - **no estes en toda la llanura** do not settle on the entire plain
llave key
llegar arrive
llegate adelante withdraw from there; retire from there
llegosse he approached himself; he arrived; he came close to; he reached
llena full
llorar cry (v)
llouver rain (v)
llover rain (v); **hyzo llover** he made it rain
lo suyo his own
lo that
loap sort of home made quince jelly
loar give thanks
lobo/lovo wolf
loco crazy
lodero great accumulation of mud
lodo mortar; mud
lograr succeed; obtain what is desired (v)
lojika logic
lokanda/locánta restaurant (T *lokanta*)
lokantadji restaurant keeper (T *lokantaci*)
loko atavanado extremely crazy to the point of jumping to the ceiling (also tautology because both *loko* and *atavanado* mean crazy, but in the Judeo-Spanish language one likes to overstress, overemphasize a point by such tautologies)
loko crazy; mad
lokura madness
lombo back (body part) or thigh; loin
longi far (Port *longe*)
longu long; far (adj, Monastir dialect)
longura length

lonja wharf in Balat; in later years the population living near lonja had a bad reputation and the people of the Lonja (Lonca) district were labeled as low class.

lonje - dii lonje (from) far

lonje port

lonso/lónso bear; figurative stupid; boor (Aragonese); individual deprived of good manners; coarse; bad-mannered; lonso baila the bear is dancing; fig: the idiot, the graceless, the klutz is dancing

lonson stupid; gross (but with a somewhat affectionate undertone, like speaking to a young person who may accidentally have committed a blunder)

loor praise (n)

loque the one; the thing

loryas period of great prosperity, when everything goes one's way

los lyebo he brought them

lotaria lottery

loumar veil of a Jewish woman

lu ki what

luar place (n)

luego de mano by hand

luego immediately; instantly; on the spot

luenga tongue; luenga con ajo tongue with garlic; luenga con azeitunas tongue with black olives

lugar place (n)

lugare place (n, Moroccan Sephardic Ballad)

lukso luxury; luksos luxuries; deseo de luksos desire of luxuries

lulav bundle in which are associated branches of palm, myrtle and willow, accompanied by an etrog. At a synagogue it is agitated as a joyful sign in the course of the morning prayers during the first seven days of Succoth, except the Sabbath; it is blessed even at the residence, when the beadle moves from door to door, presents it to the devotion of the women which announce the corresponding day of the omer period.

lumbre fire for cooking and heat

luminarios luminaries

luminozo lighted

luna moon; abashado de la luna (lit.: come down from the moon) very simple and out-of-touch person

lunes/lunez Monday

lungor length (Monastir dialect)
lungure distance (Monastir dialect)
lus the (pl)
lustraji shoe shiner (T *lustraci*)
lustre luster; brilliance; shine
lustro varnish (n)
luvya rain (n)
luyto mourning; mourning apparel
luz light (n); luz grande great light
luz the (pl)
luzero shining celestial body
luzillo little light
luzyo brilliant young man endowed with many qualities
lyamado called; named
lyamar call; name (v); komo te lyamas? what is your name ?
lyero error; estar en el lyero to be in error; to be wrong
lyevado taken together; taken away; a ser lyevados to be taken away;
      taken together
lyevar bring together; take away; take together
lyo I; lyo so I am

M

ma but
maasé story
machador someone who defiles, destroys, crushes
Machiah Messiah
macho matrix; vagina; female organ of reproduction (vulg). Decent
      word: *madre*.
macho/matcho male
madeira wood
madera wood
madero de boxes fir-tree wood (Ladino Bible of Ferrara, Kings)
madero wood
mâdrasta stepmother
madre con hijos mother with children
madre mother
madri mother

madrugada sunrise

madrugador someone who gets up with sunrise; someone who gets up early

madrugares, andades a vuestra carrer you will rise early in the morning and you will go on your way, pursue your road (Fer Bib Gen)

maestra teacher; tutor (fem)

maestranut good neighborly relationship

maestro master (masc); maestro alastri a master, but a comic personage who would be master of the clods or fools

magazen large store (archaism; F *magazin*, modern Spanish *almacén*)

magazin shop (F *magazin*)

magefa epidemic; mortality

maghna/manna manna

mahal(l) quarter, neighborhood (T *mahalle*)

mahalles Jewish quarter

mahkeme/majkyeme court of justice (T)

mahona/maona freight boat for loading and unloading of merchandise to and from a merchant ship (Gr)

mahsul crop (T kanunn)

maimimim see *Deunmes, Dönmes*. Jew from Salonika who converted to Islam

maish salary; pay (from T *maash* literally)

majado ground; crushed; azaite majado very pure oil (Ladino Bible of Ferrara, Kings)

majasava idea; intention; project; imagination; advice; opinion

majorgar dominate; extend over; subjugate

majpul appreciated (T *makbul*); accepted; acceptable; liked (T *makbul*)

majsos on purpose; deliberately (T *mahsus*)

majsus special (T *mahsus*)

makabiada periodical concentration of Makabi sports groups to organize sportive competitions, games

makara pulley; bobbin (T)

makare formula of wish: may the sky will; may it be so!

makarron macaroni

makarronado macaroni dish

makatli fabric of rough cotton bearing squares in color

makbul acceptable (T kanunn)

makina machine

mal bad

mal mudiri head of the finance office (in a district) (T *mal müdürü,*
   kanunn)
maladares dunghill
malah angel (H)
malaño bad year; unlucky year
malarronero manufacturer and merchant of macaroni; individual who
   makes furious threats which turn out to be futile and vain
malasuerte misfortune; bad fortune
malatia disease; illness
malato invalid
malavida bad life; unlucky life
maldad meanness; malice; badness
maldicha cursed; wicked (fem)
maldicho wicked (archaism, modern Spanish equivalent is *maldito*; the
   modern Spanish forms ending in *-ito* show the influence of
   Church Latin which was not shared by Sephardic Spanish)
maldisyon curse (n)
maldito/maldicho/maldixo cursed
male neighborhood (from T *mahalle*)
male residential quarter (T *mahalle*)
malebi chodjughu (lit) child of *mahallebi*, softie. In the military there
   was a story that the young draftees of Istanbul do not make
   tough soldiers like the traditional Turkish *Mehmetcik* (Turkish
   equivalent of the American GI, British Tommie, French poilu or
   Russian Ivan); the draftees from Istanbul have been softened by
   too good a life and they are not for the Spartan conditions of
   military life as much as the hardened young boys of solid Anato-
   lian stock.
malebi cream of farina with milk, usually served with cinnamon and a
   sprinkling of rose water from a special folkloric silver-colored
   elongated (with narrow neck) sprinkler
malebidji maker and vendor of *mahallebi*
malefisyo maleficence
alefisyozo malefic
malelevado badly educated; badly groomed; impolite
maleli resident of a *mahalle* (quarter); ruler of a quarter; fellow
   member of the community; Djoha no kyere a la mala, ni los
   malelis lo kyeren a Djoha (ironical) Djoha (a folkloric character)
   does not like his quarter and the residents of the quarter do not
   like Djoha; Djoha is disgusted with his quarter and goes to live

elsewhere; this is the last drop which makes the glass spill, the residents of the quarter cannot tolerate his eccentricities anymore, the blues of Djoha; Djoha carries his penates elsewhere and the residents of the quarter can now relax, they are satisfied.

malentendido misunderstanding

malezador wrongdoer (Judeo-Spanish creation from the base word *maldad*, by adding *-dor*, the noun agent; the modern Spanish word is *malechor*)

malfavlado bad-mouthed; individual who speaks badly about others and intentionally distorts the facts and reality

malicioso malicious

maliñidad malignancy; slyness; perfidy

maliño malignant

malisya malice

maliye tax office (T *maliye*)

mallah angel who interferes providentially to help one out of danger or a big worry

Mallah Amaveth the angel of death; the devil (H)

malo bad

malograr die in the prime of age; destroy; damage (v)

malor misfortune; unhappiness (F *malheur*)

malorozo unhappy (F *malheureux*)

malquerencia enmity; ill-feeling; hostility

malsin/malshin bastard (H)

maltez inhabitant of the island of Malta (in Oriental tales, in popular legends, the Maltese always appear as audacious and fearsome pirates)

maltrato ill treatment

mama mother; grandmother (Gr *mame*)

mamá mother

mamika affectionate name given to the mother

mamuasele young lady (F *mademoiselle*)

mamzér bastard (H)

man mano immediately, following one after the other

maná Mrs.

manadero source, origin; primary cause

mañana morning

mañane the next morning (Port *amanhà*)

manansyozo from which abundant waters are coming out; rich in fecund sources

manar emanate (v)
Manastir Monastir, a previously Ottoman city and nowadays a town
in Yugoslavia
mancar to be short of, to be in lack of, lack of
mancar miss (v)
mancha spot, blemish, stain (n)
manchado stained
manchar stain (v)
manda command; order; shipment
mandadiko menial service rendered by a child or an unimportant
person
mandado commission, service (such as delivering a message or running
an errand); El Mandado, El Mandado del Dyo One Who is sent,
One Who is Sent by God, the Messiah; per mandado de
(locution, adv) by order of
mandador sender, expedient
mandamiento word of God; divine command
mandar send; send for; expedite; bequeath (v)
mandarina tangerine
mandato mandate; power of attorney (Ital)
mandolina/mandolino mandoline
mandolinista mandolin player
mandra park for flock, sheep, or live-stock; sheepfold; open area surrounded by walls which serves as a storage space for construction
materials; storage place where materials coming from demolition
are thrown pell-mell. It is alleged that before the riotous events of
Edirne and Thrace around 1934, Thracian Jews who later moved
to Istanbul were prosperous owners of mandras and dairy farms.
The word *mandra* has a Greek origin. In Turkish it means sheep-
pen, cheese dairy (also called *mandira*).
maneadero/meneadero moving mania, being in motion all the time
maneado stirred, agitated
manear/menear agitate, shake, move, make move (v)
maneken mannequin
manera manner; de manera ke in such way that
maneras de mandjares dessert
manere gender, kind (Monastir dialect)
maneser sunrise; wish to see dilapidated
manga sleeve
mangada boasting; bragging; rodomontade

mangrana pomegranate
mangu sharpshooter (Monastir dialect)
maniéra barren woman
manikomyo madhouse, insane asylum (Ital *manicomio*)
manjares desserts
mankansa lack of
mankar miss, lack (v); (no) mankaron de they did not miss to; (no)
   mankavan they did not miss, they were not in need of; ke no le
   manke may you not miss him (her); may he (she) remain with
   you, be with you
mankeza lack of respect; impoliteness; act of showing disrespect;
   unevenness; oddness; uneven behavior; lopsided behavior
manko (adj) defective
manko (adv) less; a lo manko at least; en manko de nada in less than
   nothing, in less than no time
mano hand; (su) mano en todos e mano de todos en el His hand will
   be risen against everybody and everybody's hand will be upon
   him (Fer Bib Gen)
mansana apple
mansanal apple tree
mansanilla/mansanilla chamomile
mansarda granary, loft, lumber-room
mansevedumre show, manifestation of courage, spectacular of the kind
   inherent to youth; youthful boasting
mansevez youth
manseviko attractive young man
mansevo young
Mansevo! way to address a young man, as an injunction
mansevu bachelor; young man (Monastir dialect)
mansub rank, position (T kanunn)
manta blanket
manta carpet, bedcover made of rough tissue
mantar cork; fungus (T)
mantardji bragger, boaster who tries to blanket, to deride the others
manteca/manteka butter
mantekero maker/vendor of butter
mantekozo unctuous, buttered
mantel tablecloth
mantenedor provider, purveyor
mantener maintain, provide, purvey to the needs of a family (v)

mantenerse maintain oneself, subsist
mantenisyon maintenance, subsistence
mantenuta kept woman; mistress
mantenuto gigolo
manteque butter (Monastir dialect)
mantero manufacturer of coats
manto coat, mantle, woman's coat; cloak (F). Also a popular
    expression among women, a craving for fashionable clothing.
manual manual
manula handle (of a door)
manus hands
manyana morning
manyanada morning; early morning
manzebo young man (Moroccan Sephardic Ballad)
maonadji operator of a *maona*; man that loads and unloads freight to
    and from boats; boatman who works on barges
mar de sal sea full of salt
mar sea
marachudos baked almond cookies (a baked version of marzipan)
maramán napkin, serviette (Monastir dialect)
marauilla marvel (Ferrara Siddur)
marauilloso marvelous (Ferrara Siddur)
maravia wonder (n)
maraviya (maravia) marvel, marvelous
maraza controversy, quarrel in bad faith, pestering, shuffling
mare de atra associate grand rabbi
marear confused
marear get dizzy (v); los ojos me se mareyan my eyes get dizzy
maredo idiot, stupid, confused
mareo confusion, vertigo
marfil ivory
marfil mother-of-pearl (Monastir dialect)
marido husband
maridu husband (Monastir dialect)
marinero mariner, sailor
marino marine
markadura action of marking
markar mark (v)
marksismo Marxism
marksista Marxist

marmelada jam; **marmelada di prunas negras** prune jam
marmerusa: **vyeja marmerusa** hideous woman whose ruffled hair gives
   her the appearance of an old mad shrew
marmol/marmor marble
marmolero monumental mason
marmulear murmur (v)
marmurerar protest in murmuring; mutter; grumble (v)
mars March
marheshvan November (H *heshvan, heshbon*)
marsik imperfectly burnt charcoal giving off poisonous fumes; figuratively ugly (T)
martez Tuesday
martiyo hammer
maryoneta puppet; frivolous person without character
más more; **(avle) mas apoko** speak slower; **(de la) mas mueva** of the
   newest (fem)
mas more; **de mas en mas** more and more
masa afrijaldad flaky dough, semi- or not-so-very puffy puff pastry
   (especially good for cheese pies) made of flour, salt, margarine or
   butter softened to room temperature, sour cream and egg; **masa
   fina** fine dough made with flour, salt, margarine or butter
   softened to room temperature, safflower oil, vinegar, soda water;
   masa mal tomada a simple pastry dough made with flour, salt,
   margarine or butter, vinegar and water
masa dough
masa paste; unleavened bread; matzo
masaci/masaji/masadji/masa (matza) baker (the Turkish derived Judeo-
   Spanish morpheme *-ji* comes from Turkish *-ci/cu* which was
   added to words of Latin or other origins to indicate profession,
   maker, seller or habitual actions)
masapan marzipan, unbaked almond cookies. It was the traditionally
   served sweet at births, circumcisions, weddings and bar mitzvahs,
   to the point that when its preparation was seen in a kitchen, it
   was a good sign that a celebration was on the way. This soft
   almond confection comes from Spain. To prepare a marzipan,
   shelled almonds and lemon juice are added to a water-sugar mixture boiling in a heavy saucepan, cooked while stirring vigorously,
   removed from heat, allowed to chill. Marzipan balls are shaped
   with rose-water moistened hands and placed on paper
   manchettes. Compared to its current Spanish version, the

Sephardic marzipan has a more granular texture and more natural appearance, round and topped with a single blanched almond.

masedonyano Macedonian

masero massager

mashallah (lit) what God hath willed!; wonderful! (used to express admiration or wonder; to admire a child without saying he would incur the risk of the evil eye; charm worn by children, also placed by Turkish taxi drivers near the front window of the car to avert the evil eye)

mashallah inshallah what has God willed! God willing! a matter which is not in human hands, which depends on God's will

maska mask

maskanta mortgage

maskantardji someone who gives loans with a mortgage

maskara mask, someone who does a masquerade, a ridiculous person; a cartoon; individual who shamelessly fails to keep his word; individual who betrays his own folk, his party and who is publicly banished, proscribed (It, T); fazerse maskara become the object of public shame, disdain

maskaralik shameful behavior which brings public disdain

maslahat business, affair (T kanunn)

maslat case, event of which a detailed account is given, which is exposed with care, without omitting

masraf expense (T)

massa dough

matador killer

mataluva tiny silver-colored candies

matan sperm; semen (H)

matança killing

matapyozos (lit) kills lice; (fig) avaricious, penny-grabber

matar slain

matasano doctor who kills healthy people

matava had slain

matmazel miss, young girl, mademoiselle (F mademoiselle, Monastir dialect, also used in Turkish)

matolo he killed him

matrapaz intermediate who directly purchases agricultural products and resells them to wholesalers (T madrabaz)

matsà - (dela) media matsà the matzoh which is in the middle (Passover Haggadah)

maullar/maulyar meow; bark; howl

mauya someone who cries and complains all the time

mavi blue (T); **mira este syelo mavi** look at this blue sky (Said to give hope, to help regain confidence); **las mavis** women with blue eyes; **por las mavis me muero** I die for women with blue eyes

mavlacha rosebug, beetle; children in the Jewish quarter would buy a beetle, tie a string to it and let it buzz and in between keep it in a match box

maya ferment, yeast

maymon monkey (T *maymun*)

maymona/maymuna monkey; in this case the Turkish word has been given a Spanish suffix: the Spanish feminine ending -*a* is used to indicate gender

maymondjuluk object of laughter or irony (T *maymunculuk*)

maymoneria buffoonery; practical joke

mayo May

mayoneza mayonnaise

mayor first-born

mayoral master; leader; team leader; **mayoral compañero** principal officer and favorite of the king Yoab (Ladino Bible of Ferrara, Kings) **mayoral del fonsado** Joab commander of the army

mayorales the principals; the main notables at the court; the courtiers; the princes (Fer Bib Gen); **mayorales de petcha** taskmasters

mayorganse they maintained themselves

mayorgaronse reinforced themselves (the waters in the Flood, Fer Bib Gen)

mayoriya majority

maytap irony; **(tomar al) maytap** make fun of

mayyor larger, older

mazal luck; fortune (H); **mazal bueno** good luck

mazalozo/mazaloza fortunate, lucky (Monastir dialect)

Mazaltó good fortune (woman's name, from fem *Mazal tov*)

mazbata official report; minutes; protocol; long memorandum; tiring memo; interminable letter (T)

mazo mallet

mazura measure taken at the tailor (Romanian Judeo-Spanish)

mazurka sort of dance

Me'am Loez [lit translation "from a foreign place" (taken from Psalm 114:1)]. The masterpiece of Sephardim literature, an extensive

detailed commentary of the Bible. It is an encyclopedia that
includes all the treasured knowledge accumulated over centuries
by the great authorities of Judaism. It was written to bring to the
people all the knowledge of the Law and biblical exegesis, translating the Hebrew into Judeo-Spanish. The word *lo'ez* alludes to
la'az (foreign language) in opposition to the *lashon hakodesh*
(Holy language, i.e. Hebrew) in which it originally had been
written. The work was initiated by Ya'acob Meir Juli who began
the Me'am Loez with a commentary on the Genesis
(Constantinople 1738). Other Jewish scholars continued his
work. The classic Me'am Lo'ez, consisting of the entire
Pentateuch was completed in 1773.

meana tavern (T *meyhane*)
meana/meane/meyane tavern (T *meyhane*)
meanadji tavern keeper
meara grotto; cave (H *meara*, T *maghara*)
mechara/chirki/chepken long sleeved jacket usually made of velvet or
    from similar fabrics as the *entari* (loose robe), with the addition
    of squirrel or weasel for lining. The jacket worn by the Sephardi
    women of Izmir was decorated with chain stitch or metal thread
    embroidery and with silk or metal thread ribbons.
media/medio half (fem, masc); un medio one half; (kon) media boz at
    low voice
medíco/mediko doctor
medida measure (n)
medikeria (popular language) faculty of medicine; medical school
medikeria medicine (science of medicine, profession of medicine)
medina city, capital
medjid/medjidie silver coin of 20 piasters
medjidie de oro, Ottoman gold lira (T *mecidiye*, kanunn)
medjlis ruhani spiritual (religious) religious council of the Jewish Com-
    munity (tautology)
medjlis umumi jeneral general council of the Jewish Community in
    Istanbul (characteristic tautology of the Judeo-Spanish which
    repeats the same adjective in Turkish and Spanish
medjlis/midjlis assembly (T *meclis*)
medyo/medio middle; half
mégo mage magician
mejor, mehor better
mejoria/mehoria amelioration, betterment of an illness

mektep school (T kanunn)

melamedim school teachers

Melc(h)izedech, rey de Salem Melchizedek, King of Salem (Fer Bib
Gen)

meldado annual religious ceremony for the peace of the soul of the
dead; it is an occasion for a family gathering, usually concluded
by a dinner or banquet.

meldahon learned, erudite, scholar (n)

meldar read (v); (from Gr. *meletan*; the Spanish verb for read is *leer*)

meldar reading of memorial prayer for the dead, usually accompanied
by a family dinner or banquet that brings together even distant
relatives who often do not see each other more than once a
year (n)

melezina remedy (n)

melezinar treat with remedies; cure; heal (v)

melsa spleen

membrár remember; commemorate; (por) membrar so that I remember
(I recall)

membro remembered; member; (no) menguauan cosa they did not
miss anything; they did not lack anything; they were not in want
of anything (Lad Bible Ferrara Kings)

memguaron diminished; withdrew (the waters of the Flood, Fer Bib Gen)

memoro remembered

memorya memory

memuarayo may I be dead! expression of distress, slightly on the
humoristic side, used when something wrong is heard or happens;
could be also an expression of real distress

memur official employee (T kanunn)

memuriet official duty (T kanunn)

menear/meneyar stir (v)

menekshe violet (flower, T)

meñene press; clamp; mangle; fetters, shackles, irons; torture
instrument, torture boot which squeezes and crushes the foot
(T *mengene*)

menester need (n); u menester need to go to toilet; azer su menester go
to the bathroom

menesterozo needy; needed

mengene press; clamp; mangle (n, T)

mengua less

menguar diminish

menora lamp, menorah, candelaber (H)
menteshe hinge (T *menteshe*)
mentira lie
mentirozo/minterozo/mintirozo liar
meoyera skull
meoyero skull
meoyo brain; (no le bolta el) meoyo (lit) his brain does not turn; it
    does not turn the brains (Judeo-Spanish paraphrase to say he is
    not intelligent); (ya le vino el) meoyo he got his good senses; he
    finally knew what to do; he finally understood the situation; he
    finally became conscious that someone is trying to fool him
meoyudo someone who has brains; someone who is wise
merakli fond of; interested in (from T *merakli*)
mercador merchant
mercar buy
merced benevolence; grace; mercy (Ferrara Siddur)
merçed mercy, grace, benevolence (H)
merceria haberdashery, retail dealership in men's furnishings, as shirts,
    ties, gloves, socks, and ties (British meaning)
mercô - (lo) mercô he bought it
merdjan coral (T *mercan*)
merekiá melancholy; worry (from T *merak*)
merenjena/merendjena eggplant; in Istanbul Sephardic families,
    eggplant was rather called *berendjena*; merendjenas inchidos con
    karne stuffed eggplant
mereser deserve, merit (v); lyo no lo meresko I do not deserve it
meresido merited, deserved
meresimyento merit (n); reward or punishment which follows an act of
    conduct which is either meritorious or blamable, according to the
    case.
meresyente meritorious, sign of esteem, deserving of reward
meridion south
meridyonal meridional
meringa meringue; pastry made of egg whites and sugar
merito merit (n)
merkader merchant
merkado market
merkador buyer; merkador de ropas viejas buyer of old clothes, old rags
merkame buy me, buy for me
merkar buy (n, archaism; Modern Spanish *comprar*)

merkida buying, purchasing (Judeo-Spanish creation by adding -ida,
    the noun suffix to *merkar*; modern Spanish word *compra*)
merko (se) he bought himself
merrekiya melancholy; worry
meruba square Hebrew script; angular script generally reserved to
    headings and titles, or for religious texts printed with masoretic
    vowels
mes month
mesad auction (T *mezat*, kanunn)
mesadder typesetter (H kanunn)
mesdjid Muslim place of prayer which has no minaret (T *mescit*)
meshe oak (T); meshe odunu oak wood; figuratively head as hard as
    the oak wood; stupid, idiot; coarse fellow to mean a stubborn,
    pig-headed person (T)
meshguliyet occupation, job (T)
meshquita mosque
mesibera benediction (H)
mesmo/mezmo same; si mesmo/si mezmo himself
mesquino poor (n)
messagero messenger
messageros messengers
mestura flies
metad/mitad half
metalik/metelik obsolete coin of ten paras (forty paras make a piaster;
    hundred piasters make a Turkish pound); coin of little value;
    metelik no tyene he does not have even one metelik, he is very
    poor
metan - (ke lo) metan en preso put him in jail; jail him
mete put (imp)
metelo put it; metelo en basho put it down
meten (se) a jugar kartas they play cards; they start playing cards
meter (se) put oneself in; te la metere (vulg) let me put it into you
    (vulgar manner to proposition for sex); meter ala meñene drive
    up against the wall; squeeze tightly; meter nombre name, give a
    name (v); ke nombre le meteras which name will you give him
metér place, put (v)
meterse en medio put oneself in the middle; intervene (a typical Judeo-
    Spanish periphrasic expression instead of the Spanish *intervenir*
    or *interponerse*)
metikulozo meticulous

metio (se) a baylar he started to dance
metitech you put
metodiko methodical
metodo method
metres mistress (a somewhat derogatory word placing emphasis on the
    fact that the woman is not a real wife)
metro subway
metropolito dignitary of the orthodox church, intermediary between
    the patriarch and the archbishops
metyo - (ke los) metyo en buena humor which put them in good
    humor, in good mood
mevleane (lit) local, monastery of the order of Dervishes founded by
    Mevlana Jelaluddin-i Rumi, esp. the order of "Whirling
    Dervishes"; (in popular language) café, place where Turkish
    coffee is served
meydan public square (T kanunn); (el puevlo se arokoje en el) meydan
    the people, the crowd gathers in the public place
meyina paté of puff dough garnished with a stuffing of cheese and
    eggs
meyo brain
meza desk; table
mezada monthly pay
mezarana cemetery; place left in neglect, in abandonment; desolate
    place; (kavayo de) mezarana aged horse, unable to perform
    services, which is left to itself, goes pasturing wherever it can find
    grass, even entering the tombs of the cemetery
meze/mezet Turkish hors d'oeuvres, Turkish delicatessen (T)
mezedakya broiled inner organs (ensemble formed by the heart, lungs,
    liver, and spleen) of lamb served as an hors d'oeuvre
mezetikos various and abundant Turkish hors d'oeuvres
mezmo same
mezos ways, means
mezurado measured; composed; moderate
mezurar measure, evaluate (v); me lo mezurare I shall measure it
mezuras measures; mezuras seriosas serious measures
mezuza parchment carrying verses 4 to 9 of chapter VI and the verses
    12 to 20 of chapter XI of Deuteronomy, which is contained in an
    usually cylindrical metal case, and which is fixed at a man's
    height to the downstroke of the door.
mi me; a mi señor el rey to my lord the King (Lad Bible Ferrara Kings)

mia my (fem)
midrash oratory which also serves of study room for the rabbi (H)
miedo fear (n); (he) miedo he was seized by fear
miel honey
mientris during; in the mean time (Monastir dialect)
miercolez Wednesday
miga/miga de pan bread crumb
migero plie accumulation of bread crumbs
migita quite small bread crumb
migitero avaricious individual, who would not lose even a bread
     crumb, who does not give away, or who does not allow to be lost
     even the smallest thing that can serve him; who preserves the
     most insignificant things
migo konmigo with me
migrante migrant
mijor - (de la) mijor of the best
mijorear/mehorar improve
mil thousand
mil(l)et religious community, group defined by religion and language,
     nation (T millet, kanunn)
mila circumcision
milagro miracle
milagrozo miraculous
miles - por miles by thousands
miles thousands
milesimo thousandth
militar military; (servisio) militar military service
millarias numerous
milyon million; milyones millions
mimosa mimosa
mina di miyoyo brain-filled pastry loaves, an exotic sophisticated dish
minister need (n, Monastir dialect)
minoria minority (age)
minoridad minority in numbers
minorita minority in numbers (Ital)
minsa ancient Austrian gold coin worth 12.36 gold franks (very much
     sought by money hoarders)
mintir lie (v)
minuskulo tiny

minusyozo minute (adj)
minuto minute (n)
minutos - unos kuantos minutos a few minutes
minyan required presence of at least ten men at religious ceremonies
     and prayers
mira! look! (lo) mira looks at him
mirada gaze, glance (n)
mirada sight
miradas kalmas quiet sights, quiet scenes
miralay (T) lit: colonel; as a pun from Judeo-Spanish *mirar* a man who
     looks too much at women
mirandera housekeeper
mirando - en mirando a los sielos while looking at the skies
mirar look at; check; observe; (la) mirarà will check it; will look at it
mircader trader, dealer (Monastir dialect)
mircansie trade (Monastir dialect)
mircar buy (Monastir dialect)
miri belonging to the state, public (T *mirî*, kanunn)
mirindjena eggplant; mirindjena gizada stewed eggplant
misericordias mercy (n)
mishmara night guard (H)
Mishna Law part of the Talmud, in contrast to the Gemara which has
     the commentaries and traditions
Misir Charshisi spice market on the south side of the Galata bridge
     famous for its enormous variety of spices
Misir Egypt (T)
misir maize (T)
miπiricar tell a secret (v, Port *mexericar*)
misirli Egyptian (T)
mismo same
mitad half
mitap - kitap mitap a quantity of books (*mitap* is a nonsensical work
     rhyming with *kitap* book, the Turkish practice of nonsensical
     rhyming is being imitated in Judeo-Spanish)
mitersi (para) put oneself at; put himself to the task (Monastir dialect)
mitpahat binder for the Torah (also called *fasha*), made of an
     expensive fabric but without writing on it, given to the synagogue
     for good luck before or after birth. In the book Orhot Yosher
     wrote in Salonika (eighteenth century) it is written: "After the
     woman who has given birth has purified herself and goes to the

251

synagogue, something should be contributed to the synagogue, in place of the sacrifice offered by the woman after childbirth...a mitpahat...is not the best way to observe the commandment, since every synagogue has several of the mitpahot stored away in a box. It would be better to donate a tallit to the synagogue, or a book to the beit midrash, or to have a book repaired...contribute something so that an orphaned woman can be married...donate a pair of tefillin to the poor."

mitzva/mitzve good action

miyatá middle

miyoyo brains; **miyoyo con agristada** brains with boiled mayonnaise; **miyoyo con domates** brains in tomato sauce; **miyoyo falso** mock brains dish traditionally made with green plums and chicken balls instead of brains; (*miyoyo*), of course if there were enough green plums (a favorite with children) left, because the children greedily consumed the uncooked fruit before it had a chance to reach its destination. If green plums are not available, lemon juice makes a good substitute. Cooked in citric juices, the chicken balls acquire the soft texture of brains.

mizdrah east

mizerikordya mercy

mizerikordyozo merciful

mizerya misery

mizeryozo poverty-stricken; who lives in misery; down-and-out

mizitra skimmed white cheese

mizmiz pusillanimous, miser; avaricious; someone who does the most petty savings (T)

mizmizlik sordid avarice (T)

mizurar measure (v, Monastir dialect)

mizure measurement

Moab Moab

moabet familiar conversation, in which one speaks about anything, with the passing hours, conversation where one reminisces or tells anecdotes; (echar) **moabet tal**, devise without precise object

moabetchi person who has the talent to entertain long conversations nourishing these with tales and anecdotes

moadim big Jewish holidays of the year; **moadim le simha** may the holiday be for joy

moare silk fabric with shimmering reflections

moayar temporary, provisional, tentative, optional (T *muhayyer*)

mobil mobile
mobilidad mobility
mobilizar mobilize (v)
mobilizasyon mobilization
mobilya ensemble of furniture assorted for the regular use of a house-
    hold, an office, an administration (T)
mobilyadji furniture dealer, furniture vendor
moble object which serves the usage or the decoration of an
    apartment; furniture
moblerio considerable assembly of furniture, for the most part
    superfluous and encumbering
moblero furniture merchant
mobliko ensemble of furniture which decorates an apartment, a room,
    an office
moblista manufacturer and vendor of furniture
moça virgin, virgin young girl (Ladino Bible of Ferrara, Kings)
moco/moko mucus from the nose
moços criados servants
mocoso/molozo one with mucus especially of the nose; (fig) a
    worthless person; a repulsive person; a nothing
moda fashion
modernizar modernize (v)
moderno modern
modista modist
modo mode, way; de ke modo? in which way?
modoz modes, ways
modrear bite gently (v)
modredura bite (n)
modrefuy/modrefuz scorpion; person who perfidiously insinuates
    calumny; who plants the seeds of suspicion, sows discord all of
    this with an air of innocence
Modrehay/Mordehay Mordechai, uncle of Esther in the Bible (Book of
    Esther); allusion to a reversal of chance, a turn of fortune. Aman
    (Haman) the enemy of the people of Israel had obtained the royal
    authorization from the king of Persia Ahasverus to slaughter all
    the Jews of Persia. Upon the intervention of Queen Esther (herself
    Jewish), the roles were reversed. Mardochee dressed in a
    sumptuous apparel was gloriously paraded through the streets of
    the Persian capital, while the cruel Aman ended in the gallows;
    (coll) play the stupid one to avoid reaching for his wallet; feign

not to understand that one is asked to contribute to an expense, a
charity and thus let somebody else pay instead.

modrer bite (v)

modrio - la modrio, la morio bit her

modu gender, class (Monastir dialect)

moed Jewish feast treated as a holiday (H)

moel operator of circumcision (H)

moendiz/muendiz engineer (T *mühendis*)

moer mohair; fleece of the long and silky angora cloth; tissue made
from mohair

mófo rot; state of being molded

mofozo invaded by mold

mofto runt

moftu abortion (Port *movito*)

mogados/maronchinos, marzipan cakes

mojado wet (adj)

mojar/amojar wet (v)

mojo wetting; immersion (in water or in other liquid)

moko mucus from the nose; **moko de trenta y loko** (lit) nasal mucus
of thirty-one lunatics (fantasy and burlesque remedy which was
ironically intended to be against an imaginative disease); **(kedar
kon sus) mokos enkolgando** (lit) stay with his nose mucus hanging,
stay all humiliated, lose his countenance when one has ridiculously
failed while bragging to succeed fully; be totally ashamed

mokozo someone who lets mucus run without blowing his nose; idiot,
sot and blabbermouth, bragger

mola! halt!

moldear to have the means, procure the resources (v)

móleja thymus

moleskina fabric serving as a lining for clothes; varnished fabric
imitating the Moroccan leather used for seat covers

molestar molest, derange, annoy (v)

molestya molesting, derangement

moleta crutch; (kaminarcon) **moletas** walk with crutches

molido ground, minced, reduced to powder (adj)

molinero miller

molino mill (n); **de onde vyenes? - del molino?** (lit) from where are
you coming? from the mill? (said about somebody who is
exhausted after an harassing, extenuating work, who stumbles
into sleep

molo mall; quay

Monastir city lying in the southwestern part of what was Yugoslavia
some 180 kilometers northwest of Salonika and about 650 km
west of Constantinople, 65 km to the southeast of Ochrida. The
geographical situation of Monastir in relation to other cities is
such that it was completely isolated insofar as Jewish and
linguistic contacts are concerned (this explains the existence of a
special Monastir dialect of Judeo-Spanish).

Monastirli inhabitant or native of Monastir [the use of the -*li*
ending from T -*li/lu* denotes nationality or origin, as in
Amerikali (American), Parisli (Parisian) to which -*s* is added
to form the plural in Judeo-Spanish (Monastirlis, Izmirli,
Saloniklis, Istanbulis).

monotonia monotony

montaña/montania mountain

montañero/montañez mountaineer

monte mount

montefuskpo person who is difficult to approach; somber character

montes hills

monton de sal mount of salt

mora mulberry

morada residence; dwelling; moradas lodges; dwellings

morador resident

morán - (el) morán who dwelt; who resided

morár sojourn; reside (v)

morare - (hizo) morare he lodged him; he made him reside; he made
him establish residence

morena dark-skinned (fem)

morenika young attractive brunette

morenura state of what is brown

morfina morphine

morhunear/morjunear dawdle; stroll; hang around, lounge (v)

morir die (v)

moro - (Abraham) moro en tierra de Canaan (Abraham) dwelled in
the land of Canaan (Fer Bib Gen)

Moro Moor; Muslim

morsyegano - (ir komo) morsyegano go blindly

morsyegano bat

mortal mortal

mortaldad mortality

mortaldàd murrain; plague, pestilence; any of the cattle diseases, such as anthrax, foot-and-mouth, Texas fever

moruk old man; (slang) father envisioned as the absolute master of the family

moruna cod; azeyte de moruna cod liver oil

morvet delay, adjournment (T *mürvet*)

mos us

mosafir/musafir guest (T *misafir*)

mosafirhane/musafirhane guest house

mosafirlik/musafirlik being a guest

moshka young woman, servant (humorous or slightly malicious deformation of the word *mosca*) (fly, insect in Spanish), a prevalent practice among the Sephardim)

Moshka/moxka fly (n)

moshkero abundance of flies

moshkito fruit fly

moshkon mosquito

moshkonerio affluence of mosquitoes, of little flies; (fig) affluence of cousins

Moshon Moses; humorist personage of folk stories

moso del saray servant of the harem

moso young man; male servant

mosotros we

mostacho/mustacho mustache

mostra sample

mostrar show (v)

mostroso someone who presents well (from Judeo-Spanish *mostrar* to show)

mosu male servant (Monastir dialect)

mota frog in the throat; filament which sticks to the tip of a pen or a feather used as a pen when one attempts to write on a paper that is not entirely smooth; bit of hay which sticks to a broom; black filaments emitted by a fuming petroleum lamp which float in the air and go to form a deposit of soot

mouer move from; (en su) mouerse del Oriente (as they) moved from the Orient (left the Orient) (Fer Bib Gen)

mouido fugitive (Fer Bib Gen)

moussaka baked dish made with eggplant, tomato paste diluted in bouillon, fresh tomatoes, chopped lean beef, finely chopped large yellow onion, eggs, egg, fresh bread crumbs, chopped parsley, coarse salt, pepper, garlic and frying oil; **moussaka di kalavsika** zucchini moussaka; **moussaka di kartofel** potato moussaka; **moussaka di macarones** macaroni moussaka

movia aborted; **(se) movia** he moved himself

moxca fly (n)

mozaismo Mosaism, religion given to the Jews by Moses

mozayika mosaic (decoration)

mozayiko mosaic, which relates to the Jewish religion

mozotros we, us

muaf excempted (T kanunn)

muamele procedures, formalities required by the authorities

muameledji officious intermediary who, for a fee, proceeds to follow the formalities next to authorities, equivalent to dispatcher, *despachante* (T *muamele*)

mucha pena great agony

muchacha abierta loose woman (some idioms in Spanish form reflect Balkan ways of thinking and are common to all areas of the Balkans or translations of Balkan expressions); *abierta* (lit) open coincides with the Turkish word *açik* which means not only "open", but also "free in manner, licentious, brazen".

muchacha young woman

muchachez period in which one is considered not to have attained yet the maturity given by age, childhood, adolescence, youth; (word created from the Judeo-Spanish base *muchacho* by adding the noun suffix *-ez*, by analogy with the word *mansevez*; the Modern Spanish equivalent is *juventud*; in this case the Judeo-Spanish and Modern Spanish languages have gone their separate ways)

muchidumbre - (no sera contado de) **muchidumbre** multitude that one will not be able to count

muchigar multiply; increase the population very much (v)

muchigare I shall multiply (increase tremendously) the population (Fer Bib Gen)

muchigaronse (the waters) multiplied

muchiguar multiply (v); the Judeo-Spanish has kept the fifteenth century Spanish word, while in Modern Spanish *multiplikar* is used instead

muchiguen they multiply

mucho much (Ferrara Siddur); **muchoo myel da dolor de vyentro** excess of honey gives colic; too much of a good thing is not a

good thing; also said about excessive, exuberant demonstrations
of amiability, affection which do not presage anything good.

muchus various (pl, Monastir dialect)

mudança change (n, Ferrara Siddur)

mudar (se) move away

mudar move, change lodging (v)

mudaron (se) they moved away

mudir director (T *müdür*, kanunn)

mudo mute person

mudriô bit

muela molar; (dolor de) muela toothache

mueler grind, mill (v)

muerte death

muestra our (fem)

muestra sample

muestro our (masc)

Muestros - Los Muestros Our People, name of a Sephardic review in
Brussels, Belgium

mueva new (fem)

mueve nine

muevo jedit new (made up of the Judeo-Spanish word muevo 'new'
followed by the Turkish word *jedit* '*cedit*, new) having the same
meaning; reduplication is used to intensify the meaning by
coupling Judeo-Spanish and Turkish words with the same
meaning.

muevo kazado newlywed

muevo new (masc)

muevo riko nouveau riche; newly enriched; someone who went from
rags to riches

muez walnut

muezozjal/muezezero walnut tree

muezzin the Muslim cleric who from the balcony of the minaret tower
calls the faithful to prayer (the cry of the muezzin is so beautiful
that he evokes nostalgia for people who are no longer living in
Turkey anymore, or for foreigners who have visited Turkey)

muflus bankrupt; someone who cannot acquit his debts, who has lost
all (T *müflis*)

mufti mufti, Muslim ecclesiastic in charge of supervising the
maintenance of religious practices and traditions; Muslim
spiritual guide

muhayyev inculpate (v, H kanunn)
müheme Turkish practice of nonsensical rhyming
mujde good news (T *müjde*)
mujerika small woman, familiar word for little young woman or
    young married woman
Mujullu - Janna detras de Mujullu one after the other, in single file
mukabele reciprocation (T kanunn)
mukata rent paid to the Evkaf, the authority running religious
    charitable foundations and properties and pious foundations. The
    government department in control of these estates) for cultivated
    land turned into a building land or garden (T *mukataa*, kanunn)
mulino mill (n)
mulk property, real estate (T *mülk*, kanunn)
mulkiye civil service (T *mülkiye*, kanunn)
mulkye real estate, building (T *mülk*, mülkiye)
mulkyiziko small building
mulo mule
multa fine (adj, Ital)
multasim contractor or farmer of any branch of the public revenue
    (T *mültesim*, kanunn)
muncho much; (no le kuadra) muncho (lit) much understanding does
    not reach him; he is not intelligent (Judeo-Spanish paraphrase)
mundadura decorticating fruits
mundar decorticate fruits (v)
mundo world
mungrina - Ashkenzi mungrina individual who is always of a somber
    humor, grumbler, grouchy; whining
mungrinozo melancholic; who discourages all approach by a scowling
    look
muñi muñi skinflint, penny grabber, a rat; a person who goes on the
    head lowered, shaving the walls, sweating misery, but who in
    reality is a false beggar, a very rich person
muntaña mountain
muntañe mountain (Monastir dialect)
muntañique hill (Monastir dialect)
mupak kitchen (T *mutfak*)
murador resident (Monastir dialect)
muraya city wall
muriendo dying; (se esta) muriendo he is dying

murio died
murir die (v)
murledea stamp with a seal (T *mühürleme*, kanunn)
musade permission (T *müsaade*, kanunn)
musafir guest, visitor (T)
musafires espesos sticky guests, guests who do not leave easily
mushama linoleum (T *mushamba*)
mushcón mosquito (Monastir dialect)
mushmula medlar, fruit of the Eurasian tree Mespilus germanica that
   resembles a crab apple and is used in preserves (T); cara de mushmula face of mushmula, wrinkled face
mushteri customer (T *müshteri*, kanunn)
mushudo someone who has thick lips
musiu gentleman (F *monsieur*)
mustaço mustache
musteri client (T *müshteri*)
musyu, el musyu the monsieur, the master, the patron, the master of
   the house (in the language of the domesticity, the master upstairs
   for the people downstairs)
mutalik dependent upon, related to (T *müteallik*, kanunn)
mutasarif governor of a sandjak (subdistrict of a province, T kanunn)
mutbak/mutpak kitchen (from T *mutfak*)
mutchacha - las mutchachas de la reji (lit) the young girls of the Régie
   (a foreign concession which used to control the tobacco manufacturing in Istanbul, until the Turkish Republic nationalized it into
   a state-controlled monopoly); the young girls working at the
   Régie were popular in Istanbul as the French midinettes (girls
   working in Paris' large department stores like La Samaritaine, etc,
   the object of many romantic stories) in Paris. It happened that
   because they did not have enough money for the *dota* (dowry)
   Jewish girls working at the reji (cigarette factory) ended up marrying a non-Jew who had no such requirement.
mutchatchas young girls; mutchatchas ermozas beautiful young girls
mutchigàr multiply (v)
mutcho (muncho) too much
muteber(r)i property relinquished for a pious motive (T *müteberri*,
   kanunn)
mutlak (adj) absolute, irrevocable, unconditional (T)
muto grumbler, mutterer
mutra scowling face, sulking, shunning look, expression

muur seal (T *mühür*, kanunn)
muvashir usher (in court); bailiff (T *mübashir*, kanunn)
muvimiento/muvimyento movement
muzeum museum
myel honey
myelozo honeyed; obsequious; someone who has exaggerated polite
    manners
myentres during; in the meantime; in the time or space that a thing
    lasts; meanwhile; nevertheless; however
myerkolez Wednesday

N

na so; so it is; hey there; this is; here is
na! behold (T)
nacçimiento birth
nacido born
nada mas nothing more; de nada from nothing; de nada vide hayre I
    saw no benefit, cure from nothing; hitch nada nothing [used in
    Salonica, made of T *hiç* (nothing) followed by Spanish *nada*
    (nothing); reduplication was used to intensify the meaning; this
    occurred with the combination of a Turkish word preceded or
    followed by a Spanish or Greek translation)
nada nothing; nothingness
nadador swimmer; nadando en su sangre swimming (drowning) in his
    blood
nadar swim
naftalina naphtalene
nagüita shirt
nahalá inheritance (H)
nakra mother-of-pearl
nal horseshoe (T)
nalga buttock
nalgado someone who has big buttocks
nallo! here he is! there he is! ecce homo!
nam surname; fame; reputation; tomar buen nam have a good reputa-
    tion, gain fame
namaz prayer of the Muslim
namaz - fazer namaz pray in the Muslim way

namorada woman who is the object of love with whom one has intimate relations without being bound to her by the ties of marriage

namorado (adj) caught by, who admires the qualities of someone; in love, caught by love, lover, one with whom intimate relations are being had without the ties of marriage

namorarse fall in love, be caught by love; take pleasure in watching something, someone, let oneself be fascinated, admire for his (her) qualities, charm, beauty (v)

namorikos small not so serious love, flirtation, passing sentiment of love

namosia mosquito net

namuzli honorable, who has an honorable reputation, honest (T *namuslu*)

nána grandmother

nañas/kastañas chestnuts

nankyor ungrateful (T *nankör*)

nanniko dwarf (coll)

nano/nanno dwarf

nanuz honor, respectability (T *namus*)

naranja orange, bitter orange (T *turunç*)

naranjero orange tree, bitter orange tree

naranjon wild orange

nargile/nargyile Turkish water pipe (T *nargile*)

naris nose

nariz nose; nostrils

nark officially fixed price (T *narh*, kanunn)

narkotiko narcotic

nascio is born; fue nascido (was) born

naser to be born

nasi prince

nasido born; newborn; nasido kon mazal marked by destiny to be always surrounded by happiness

nasilisa (adv) one way or another; whatever it is (T *nasilsa*); nasilise ya pasimos l'añada somehow or other, we have been able to cover the expenses of the year

nasimiento/nasimyento birth

nasional national

nasional sosialismo national socialism

Nasraddin Hodja legendary and folkloric personage who is full of
wisdom, at times grave, at times ironical (To him are attributed
all kinds of adventures, full of lessons, common sense and logic.)
Its Sephardic equivalent is Djoha who impersonates several of
Nasraddin (Nasreddin) Hodja's stories.

nasyente in the process of being born; **el sol nasyente** the sun which
appears at the horizon; **un fecho nasyente** a new business

nasyon nation

nasyonal national

nasyonalidad nationality

nasyonalizar nationalize (v)

nasyonalizasyon nationalization

natal natal

natasyon swimming

natura nature

natural natural

naturalizar naturalize

naturalizasyon naturalization

nature character; temper (Monastir dialect)

navaja pocket-knife

navajada stroke by pocket-knife; wound made by pocket-knife

navajero manufacturer of pocket-knives

nave ship (n)

navι prophet (H)

navi ship (n, Monastir dialect)

navio ship; boat

naz coquetry; coyness; whims; disdain; smirking; endearment

nazar evil eye; (echar) **nazar** cast a bad spell; strike by evil eye

nazar no! evil eye no! Expression used to conjure the evil eye: may he
be (she, it) be preserved from the mischief of an evil eye (said
about a person exuberant of health or a very beautiful object)

nazarlik amulet to protect against an evil eye, usually a blue stone of
varying size with a rather raw drawing of an eye

nazi Nazi

nazismo nazism

nazli disdainful; someone who plays at being difficult to please;
someone who pretends not to be keen; coquette; spoiled; coy
(T *nazli*)

nazudo someone who has a large nose

neeman honest; faithful; conscientious (H)
nefer private soldier (T kanunn)
neft (brut) petroleum
nefus/nufus birth certificate, identity card (T *nüfus*)
negasyon negation
negativa denial; refusal
negativo negative
neglijé dressing gown; women's lingerie
nego denied
negociante/negosyante merchant, tradesman, businessman
negociar negotiate (v)
negosyar negotiate (v)
negosyasyon negotiation
negosyo business, trade
negra a bad women; a prostitute
negra golor bad smell
negras manners deprived of amiability, brusque, severe
negregon bruise (n)
negregura perversity; badness
negrina badness; bad mood; tendency to groan, to grumble; be in a
    dark mood; somber
negrito/negreziko (adj) slightly bad; not satisfying
negro wicked
negror darkness
negru black (person) (Monastir dialect)
nekamá vengeance, revenge
neme lazim what good does it do! (T)
neseçita/necsessita necessity
neshama soul (H)
nesim miracles
netila ablution
nevla fog
nevouá prophecy
nevuá prophecy
nezaret supervision (T kanunn)
nezik fragile (from T *nazik*)
niduy anathema, excommunication (H)
niembrô remembered
nieve snow (n)
nikâh marriage (T kanunn)

nikurina dirt of the body, of the underwear
nin nor
niña girl
ningun none
ninguno/denguno no one (archaism, one of the most salient character-
    istics of Judeo-Spanish; the Modern Spanish equivalent is *nadie*)
ningunos nobody
ningunu none (Monastir dialect)
ninia/niña young girl
niño young man; lad
nisan (H) April
nisannu (Bab) April
nishan mark, decoration (T kanunn)
niyet intention; good luck (T)
nizam order, law (T kanunn)
no no; not; (y) no el, que tomo a el Dio (and) he did not appear any-
    more, was not to be seen anymore, as God took him (Fer Bib
    Gen); no sale de avondo de su obliga does not come out of his
    obligation; has not done his duty (from Passover's Haggada)
no se I do not know
no seer not being; nothingness
no vamos olvidarmos we shall not forget
nobet surveillance, guard; guard duty; also return of feverish or crisis
    condition in an illness (T *nöbet*)
nobetchi sentry, watchman (T *nöbetçi*, kanunn)
noce/noche/notche night
nochada night
nochadia bad news
noche de shemira night of vigil before the circumcision, which was
    dedicated to prayer and study of the Torah. In recent times the
    noche de shemira started to take a more festive turn with
    romances being sung and occasionally musicians being hired. As
    early as the mid-seventeenth century R. Hayyim Palacci, Grand-
    Rabbi of Izmir, pointed to the changing nature of this practice
    and found its new turn to be objectionable.
noche night
nombra shadow; la nombra de tus alas the shadow of your wings
nombradiya surname
nombrar speak of somebody, recollect the name and memory of that
    person with devotion

nombre name (n); y fue su nombre en todas las gentes derredor and
   his name went (was known to) all the people (the nations)
   around
non not
nóna grandmother (Ital *nonne*)
nóno grandfather
nos us; nos abastava would have been sufficient for us (from the
   Dayenu chant in the Passover Haggadah); como vno de nos por
   saber bien e mal (like one of) us to know good from bad (Fer Bib
   Gen)
nosion notion
nosotros ourselves
notche night
nouedades news (Ferrara Siddur)
nouenta ninety (Fer Bib Gen)
nouio groom (n, Ferrara Siddur)
novembre November
novela novel
noventa ninety
novia bride
novio bridegroom
novyadika sweet which has the form of a human body (prepared for
   the celebration of Purim)
novyo groom (n)
nozotros ourselves
nudez nakedness
nudo naked
nueba/nueva de nuebo again; one more time
nuebo/nuevo new; (fem)
nuera daughter-in-law
nuestro our
nueue nine (Ferrara Siddur)
nueuecientos nine hundred (Fer Bib Gen)
nueve nine
nueven ninth
nuevezimo ninth
nuevo new
nuevo - de nuevo again
nuevos - (de los) nuevos new
nula zero (Monastir dialect)

nulo null
numerozo numerous
nunca never
nunka never
nuue cloud (Ferrara Siddur); clouds
nwestra our
nyervo nerve
nyeta granddaughter
nyeto grandson

Ñ

ñañato fetus
ñaúas kastañas badly pronounced word, which by its consonance
    comes close to the word that one wants to use, but which has
    been forgotten or which is not known, but which the interlocutor
    can guess
ñegar deny
ñegasyon denial, negation
ñervezikos over excitation, febrile behavior
ñervozidad nervousness
ñeve snow
ñome (contraction of *entendyome*) do you understand?
ñovetina (long) snowstorm
ñudo knot (n)
ñudo syego blind knot, very complicated knot impossible to
    disentangle like the Gordian knot cut by Alexander the Great

O

o or
oazis oasis
obligado obliged
obligar oblige (v)
obligo obliged; **obligo santo de natura** a holy obligation of nature
obra work; production; opus
obras humanas human works
obrero worker

observador observer
observar observe (v)
observasyon observation
obskurantiste obscurantist
obstaculo obstacle
obtener obtain (v)
ochaua eighth (Ferrara Siddur)
ochavo eighth, octave
ochen eighth
ochenta eighty
ochentena ensemble of objects or persons of about eighty
ocho eight
ochosientos eight hundred
ochosyentos eight hundred
octobre October
oculto occult
oda room (T kanunn)
odabashi man in charge of the rooms in an inn (T *odabashi*, kanunn)
odjak furnace for kitchen (T *ocak*, kanunn); odjak de pyedra quarry,
    (T kanunn)
odre leather bottle; odre de azaite leather bottle of oil
odrenar/ordenar put in order, prepare, organize, give an opportunity to
offender offend
oficial del etcho official of a particular job or business
oficial/ofisyel official
ofisier officer
ofisyante person who recites the prayers for a religious congregation,
    who accomplishes the rites of the cult (usually the word *hazan* is
    used instead)
ofisyer officer; military on a rank equal or superior to second
    lieutenant
ofisyo job, function, office
ogar home; hearth; habitation in which all the family lives in intimacy
    (somewhat forgotten expression); domestic sojourn; brazier
ograshar struggle with; try to accomplish; get busy (T *ughrashmak*)
ogúr luck (from T *ugur*, good luck)
oherayehudi enemy of the Jew (H)
oido audition; ear
oidor auditor
oir hear (v)

oja term used by high class people for *foja* leaf
ojada glance
ojal buttonhole
ojankos wide-open eyes
ojeado harmed by the evil eye; **pan ojedeado** bread ruined by the evil eye
ojear look at with a sentiment of envy, jealousy, covetousness; cast an inauspicious spell by means of evil eye (v)
ojento envious, jealous
ojero dark circles under the eyes
ojetada concupiscent look
ojetear devour with the eyes; look at something with concupiscence
ojetero someone who looks at women in a perverse, shameless way
ojido ear
ojo eye
ojo eye; **mi ojo ve mi oreja oye** my eye sees, my ear hears
ojos eyes; **ojos a ojos** eyes to eyes; (fig) anxiously awaiting
ojra ocher variety of red clay utilized to scour copper utensils, for wall painting
oka oriental weight measure corresponding to 1282 grams (the oka is divided in 400 drams) (dirhem)
okazion occasion; bargain (F *occasion*)
okulista oculist
okupar occupy (v)
okuparse get busy; take care of (v)
okupasyon occupation
olam aba future world, world to come, the other world; the paradise where siege the just people, those of Israel and those of the Nations
olám world (H)
ole immigrant to Israel (H)
ole-hadash new immigrant to Israel
olim immigrants to Israel
olio oil
oliva olive
olival/olivar olive tree
olla pot
olmak da var this appears improbable, but after all, nothing is impossible
olor, golor odor

oluk pipe, tube, gutter (T)

olvidadijo voluntary, intentional forgetting; fazer olvidadijo feign forgetting

olvidado forgotten

olvidador someone who forgets, someone who has an unfaithful memory

olvidadozo forgetful; who remembers little; whose memory is belated; who has little memory

olvidar forget (v)

olvido forgetting; omission; oversight

ombiligo umbilicus

ombre/ombri man

omeleta omelet

omer period which goes from the second day of Passover to Pentacost. These 49 days are counted day by day by the faithful. Over the centuries this period has been marked by calamities which fell upon the Jews living in Palestine, particularly in the course of the insurrection by Bar Kochba against the Romans (132-135 AD). In that period Jewish fighters fell in masses and a cruel epidemic brought death to many of Rabbi Akiba's (a fervent supporter of Bar Kochba) disciples. The period of Omer is considered inauspicious, ill-omened and all manifestations of rejoicing are banned, except on the thirty-ninth day when there was a lull in the ravages of the epidemic. This day is consecrated to festivities and entertainment. Among others, what is celebrated is the memory of Rabbi Simon ben Yohai to whom is attributed the authorship of the Zohar.

omezillo insults

on gyolou/on gyolu member of a Sabbatean (followers of the pseudo-Messiah Sabbatai Sevi) subsect which passed for receiving in its midst the adepts of various races, on the sides of an originally Sephardi majority, (T); on yolu (also called *Jonozo*, snuffler, person that speaks through his nose)

onda wave (n)

onde Sham, onde Bagdad? where is Damascus, where is Bagdad? (you are confusing two cities which are far away); these are things which have no relation between themselves

onde where; whereby

ondo deep

ondozo wavy; agitated by waves

ondular curl (v)
ondura depth
onesto honest
ongaresko/ungaresko Hungarian language
ongarez/ungarez Hungarian
Ongaria/Ungaria Hungary
onor honor
onorado honored, respected
onorar to honor
onoravle honorable
onze eleven
onzien eleventh
opa cassock; tunic
opera opera
operador operator; surgeon
operasion/opersayon operation; surgery
opereta operetta
opinion opinion
opinion publika public opinion
oponente opponent
oponer oppose (v)
opozisyon opposition
oppa/oppala special expression used when someone makes an effort to
     get up, to lift oneself or to lift a heavy object; cry of
     encouragement to somebody else to make an effort to get up or
     lift an object
optado appropriated, be accepted
or light (H)
ora hour; watch; ora buena! good hour! (expression wishing that
     something good is happening, when one is suddenly faced with
     rather unexpected news or visit); ora de biuente hour of the
     living; at this same time; at the present time (Fer Bib Gen); ora
     konvenida hour agreed upon, time agreed
oración de David prayer of David
oracion prayer
oraçion prayer; oration
Or-Ahayyim (lit) Light of Life; name of the Jewish Hospital in Balat
     (Golden Horn)
oraje thunderstorm

orajozo stormy
oral oral
orar pronounce; formulate; wish (v)
orario timetable
orasa ground tile used to polish copper kitchenware (T *horasan*)
orasiones prayers
orasyon prayer, oration
orasyonar pray (v); Judeo-Spanish creation from the Judeo-Spanish
    base *orasyon* by adding *-ar* to the infinitive ending; Modern
    Spanish equivalent is *rezar, orar*)
oratoryo oratory
orden order
ordenadas con cedro beams of cedar wood (Ladino Bible of Ferrara,
    Kings)
ordenar order, command (v)
ordinaryo ordinary
ordona orders, commands
ordono ordered, commended
ordu army (T kanunn)
ore clock (Monastir dialect)
oregano que sale e pared hyssop any of the several aromatic herbs of
    the genus Hyssopus, of the mint family, esp. Hyssopus officinalis,
    native to Europe, which grows small blue flowers which grows
    on the wall (Ladino Bible of Ferrara, Kings)
oreja de Aman ear of Haman (villain from the Book of Esther), a spe-
    cial sweet prepared for the festivities of Purim commemorating
    the story of Esther
oreja ear
orejal earring
orejales earrings (archaism; modern Spanish *aretes*)
organdi organza
organizar organize (v)
organizasyon organization
organo organ (anatomy, music instrument)
orgolyozo arrogant; excessively proud; vain
orgóyo arrogance
oriente orient
origano oregano
orijinario originally

orijinario/orijinaryo native of
orilla de la mar seashore (Ladino Bible of Ferrara, Kings)
orina/urina urine
orinadero irresistible tendency to urinate all the time
orinar/urinar urinate (v)
orman forest (T kanunn)
ornero baker
orno oven; stove
Ornos de la Masa de Haskoy The masa bakeries of Haskoy (the
    Passover masa prepared in these bakeries was quite famous and
    would reach the smallest Jewish agglomerations)
oro gold; oro batido gold in leaflets; oro fino pure gold; (kostar su
    pezo de) oro (lit) to be worth its weight in gold; to be very
    expensive; (onde se mete el) oro arrelumbra (lit) where gold is
    placed it shines. Said about a person of quality who reveals his
    (her) value whatever the position in which (he, she) is placed or
    whatever the task confided; (se van el) oro y elaver, keda el lodo
    a la paré (lit) the gold and the appearance go away, and what is
    left is the woman with her defects (meaning the high dowry
    meant to make one forget the defects, ugliness and physical
    defects); once the dowry is used up, what is left is the woman
    with her defects.
orozo happy (F heureux)
ortiga nettle
ortodokso orthodox
oso/orso/lonso bear
osul/usul method (T usul)
osurma (vulg) passing gas; fart (n)
osurukchu/osurmadji (vulg) someone who passes gas too often
otomatikamente automatically
otomatiko automatic
otomobil automobile, car
otoridades authorities
otorita authority
otoritaryo authoritarian
otra masa afrijaldad sour cream dough
otra other (fem)
otra vez another time
otri someone else

otro charshi (lit) another market (from T *çarshi* market, bazaar); (fig)
that's another story, thing, affair
otro other (masc)
otrun other
otruna vez another time
otruna/otruno another (fem, masc)
ouejas flocks of sheep
ouva grape
ovadecer/obedecer obey (v); (azares) ovedecer make it to be obeyed;
achieve to be obeyed; succeed in being obeyed
ovejas (ovézas) flocks of sheep
ovistes plazer took pleasure
ovligado bound to; obliged; obligated
ovligar/obligar oblige (v)
ovligo/obligo duty; obligation
ovra work; opus (n)
ovrar labor, work (v)
oxéo he chased
óya kettle; pot
oyada content of a pot
oyd mi boz listen to my voice
oyda de oreja ear's hearing (Ferrara Siddur)
oyda hearing (Ferrara Siddur)
oydo - no fue oydo it was not heard (Ladino Bible of Ferrara, Kings)
Oydurear/uydurear invent; fabricate, make unfounded allegations (v, T
uydurmak)
Oydurma/uydurma invention; fabrication; non-sustained allegation
(T *uydurma*)
oyeme a mi listen to me
oyeme! oyime! hear me!
oyer/oy/oyir hear (v); lo ke oyeron what they heard
oyga! (imp) listen!
oyir hear (v); demandaste a ti ynteligencia para oyr juizo you asked
your intelligence to hear the judgment (Ladino Bible of Ferrara,
Kings)
ozadia reprehensible daring; tener ozadia have a cheek; have the boldness
ozadiar dare to do something; daring

P

pa pa pa! interjection used to express a big damage, an excess of
disgust, of indignation in front of a revolting spectacle; has one
seen a thing so disagreeable, so scandalous!

pachá leg (from T *paça*); fatty Turkish dish which is prepared by
boiling the feet of butchered animals. The resulting broth was
believed to alleviate the effects of drunkenness (one would be a
likely consumer of such broth at dawn after a night of partying
and heavy drinking at the tavern). Appropriately there were in
Istanbul and other places cheap restaurants open at wee hours
where such broth would be served.

Pacharo/pasharo bird

pachás legs

pachavra miserable rag, vile thing/individual (Gr, T); **estar una
pachavra** be all in, be rundown, without any drive; to be
disgusted by everything; bet without will; let himself go down;
fazerse pachavra humiliate oneself, demean oneself by begging,
imploring

pachekas beautiful legs of a young girl

padeser suffer the consequence, endure, support (v)

padrasto/padrastro second husband of a widowed mother; stepfather;
denatured father who treats his children with cruelty

padre father; (el) **padre i la madre** the parents (archaism; modern
Spanish *los padres*)

padregàl flint

Padres Lazaristas Lazarist Fathers (Dominican Fathers) who used to
run the College Saint Benoit, an excellent French Lyceum
providing high-quality education both for humanities and mathe-
matics in preparation for further university studies

padreziko quite young father full of grace and beauty (also used sometimes with a bit of derision, irony)

paga pay (n)

pagamiento payment

paganos pagans

pagar pay (v)

page pay, wage (n, Monastir dialect); **à la page** up to date (F)

paja straw, (drinking) straw; food deprived of any taste; insipid;
thing without value; hay; **paja no kome** (lit) he does not eat hay;
said to remind that the good graces of a public functionary, of a

controller must be paid with a bribe (Ottoman style of doing official business)

pájaro bird

paje page, page-boy (Monastir dialect)

pajero merchant of hay, of forage

palabra word (Moroccan Sephardic Ballads)

palacio/palazio palace

paladar palate

palamida frita fried tuna

palamida tuna

palasyo palace

palavra word, vocabulary; gift of the word; language; also unconfirmed rumor, empty word (T); **tomo la palavra** took the word, meaning started to speak; **suas amargas palavras** his bitter words

palavraci/palavradji boasting; person who talks a lot and says nothing; person who is boastful; a braggart; a blabbermouth (T)

palavrada a nasty word

palavradear insult (v)

palavradero interminable blabbering

palavras meaningless, empty words or promises

palavrota bad word, four letter word spoken without reflection

Palestina Palestine

palestinyano Palestinian

paleta shovel

paletada blow with a shovel (n)

palikar well built, vigorous, courageous, sturdy young man (Gr)

paliko small stick

palma palm of the hand

palmas applause (n)

palmo measure of length represented by the distance from the extremity of the thumb to the tip of the little finger when the hand is well extended overstretched (22 to 24 cm)

palo stick; rod; **kara de palo** (lit) wooden face; (fig) impassive face which is not moved by emotion, fear or shame; **tener la boka un palo** have a dry mouth (after a fast or prolonged sleep)

paloma/palomba dove; pigeon

palomino pigeon

palpadura palpation, touching

palpar palpate (v)
palpavle palpable
palpitasyon palpitation
pálto jacket; overcoat (F *paletot*)
palyadji secondhand clothes dealer (Gr *paleos* old)
pambuk cotton (T *pamuk*)
pan bread; pan con azeite bread with olive oil (a Judeo-Spanish
    specialty used as a starter with fried bread to break the fast of
    Kippur; also used at times as a snack for hungry children); pan y
    manteca bread and butter; kitar su pan earn his bread
panaderia baker's shop, bakery
panadero baker
panair fair, market (T, Gr *panayir, panayiri*, kanunn)
pañal diaper; linen for intimate feminine usage; linen used to cover the
    baby for swaddling
Panayia/Panaya image of Mary, mother of Jesus, Holy Virgin (Gr)
pancha fat belly
pandero tambourine
pandja/pandjar red beet (T *pancar*)
pandjeka small red beet
pandjermanista pan-Germanist
panelenismo pan-Hellenism
panezikoi small bread
panfleto pamphlet
panislamismo pan-Islamism
paño de buz compress of ice
paños kayntes hot compresses
panpan (children's language) corporal punishment
pansyon fee paid in a boarding house; boarding school
pantalon pants
pantera panther
pantufla slipper
pantuflada blow with a slipper
pantuflear drag around in slippers (v); run after ancillary adventures
pantuflero slipper manufacturer; bawdy person, libidinous individual
    who roams around at night in his slippers, silently in between
    feminine beds; individual who runs after the servant girls in the
    household
panturkismo pan-Turkism

panush afflicted by strabismus

panyo/paño drape; woolen tissue; clothes; garments; overcoat; compress

papa baby food; puree

papa de linasa cataplasm of hemp seed applied hot usually to the back

papa nickname for father

Papa Pope

papada double chin due to obesity

papagayo parrot; figuratively person who speaks stupidly repeating words not really understood; (avlar com un) papagayo to speak nonstop like a parrot

paparra grande a lot of fuss, a lot of noise about something which after all may not be that important

paparra soup made of bread; frugal dish made of boiled bread sprinkled with oil and crated cheese

paparron obese, corpulent and disgraceful individual

papas y allasharas fraud; criminal procedures; suspicious, obscene manners; doubtful promiscuity; intrigues, conspiracies, machinations; absurd news; ridiculous, nonsensical inventions which are spread with great reinforcement of squawking

papas, papaz Greek Orthodox priest

papasyega bat, also called *mursyegano*; a la papasyega (adv) in the darkness; blindly

papaz priest; papaz efendi Mister priest, Your Honor priest, Your Gentleman Priest

papaz yahnisi lit: the priest's meat, Stew with onions; fish or meat stewed with vegetables.

papaziko young Greek ecclesiastic; Greek Orthodox seminarian

papel paper; Turkish lira (pound) from the time it was in paper bank notes

papelada usually food content of a large cornet (cone) of paper

papelaria accumulation of official papers and documents. A Turkish name for such "paper bureaucracy" was *kirtasiyecilik*

papelera brown paper bag

papeleras paper sheet covered with signs, drawings, Kabbalistic magical formulae applied to the ears to treat mumps (folklorist medicine, it was considered to be a highly used, sovereign remedy). The papeleras were prepared by rabbis renowned for their erudition of practical (applied) cabbala (Kabbala), an abundant source of magical, miraculous remedies

papelerio pile of useless papers
papelero merchant of papers
papeliko small bit of paper; in folklorist medicine, powdered remedy
    enclosed in a conveniently folded paper
papeteria paper shop
papika soaked with water (adj and adv); fazerse papika be soaked
    with water to the bone
papis feast (n)
papiyon necktie knot; bow tie
papo bird's crop
paprikas di vitella veal stew with peppers
papú grandfather (Gr *papu*)
papu padre familiar way of saying ancestor; herensia del papu padre
    inheritance from the ancestor
papuch roasted chickpeas, mixed with sugar and reduced to a very
    fine powder
papuchu shoe, slipper; worn out slipper, worn out shoe (T *papuç*)
papupadre old man
par pair
para for; so that
parabever tip (n)
parachukli surname, nickname
paradear parade (v)
parar remedy; ward off (v)
paras money, currency (from T *para*); na estas paras here is this
    money; here this money; yol parasi road money; travel allowance
    (T)
parazita parasite
pardon pardon (n); si aboniguares pardon if forgiveness is denied; if
    the request for forgiveness is not well received
pardon! excuse me
pardonar pardon, forgive (v)
pare/pared wall; side
pareka money recently acquired by nouveau riche; money which con-
    fers power and prestige (ironical)
parentera parenthood; kinship
pareser look like, seem, appear (v); parese ke it seems that; parese
    komo it seems like
paresido similar
paresiendo seeming

paresiendole seeming to him
pareziko well-matched young couple
parfumado perfumed
parfumar perfume (v)
parfumeria perfume shop; ensemble of various perfumes
Parhó Pharaoh (Lad Bib Ferrara, Moroccan Sephardic Ballad)
parida a woman who has just given birth
parido husband of the woman giving birth
paridura parturition; giving birth
pariente relative; parientes parents; relatives (archaism instead of the
    Modern Spanish *padres*)
parientis parents (Monastir dialect)
pario gave birth to
parir birth (n)
parir give birth (v)
parlak brilliant (T)
parmaceto white of whale; oily substance which is present in the head
    of the sperm whale
parmak flattery
parmaktchi vile flatterer, sycophant
parnas unpaid, benevolent administrator of a synagogue, or a commu-
    nity, brought to this honorable position by a vote of the faithful
parnasa nourishment, subsistance, means required to sustain oneself;
    revenue allowing one to live
Parô Pharaoh
parpar bearing, impressive stature
párparo eyelid
parsanata parsandata in Nehama's Judeo Spanish-French dictionary,
    very long interminable list of objects or names; verbose writing
    deprived of interest; thick letter in which one extends himself ad
    infinitum on a mass of futile details; **parsanata grande** long list or
    mass of meaningless, superfluous, worthless papers and
    documents requested by bureaucratic officialdom (a bit of
    tautology since the word *parsanata* itself would have sufficed to
    say the same thing)
partal package of clothes or linen poorly tied together; bundle
partaliko poor man's bundle
parte - de su parte from his side, from his part
parte part

parti party (entertainment)
participante participant
partida part; political party; (una grande) partida a large part, a big
    part, a big portion
partido political party
partiduras estas the things that had been partaken, divided
partiosse he divided (his troops) (Fer Bib Gen)
partir go; depart, start going, make dispositions to leave a place, get
    going, leave on a trip; break; ruin; shatter (v); partir kueshkos
    crack the shell of walnuts, almonds, apricots; partir leña break
    wood for heating or the oven; partir melon cut the melon; partir
    pan cut the bread
partirà will partake; will separate
partisipar participate (v)
partisipasyon participation
parto childbirth
partyo en koryendo departed running; left running
parvenir reach; to be able to; accomplish; manage to do; to succeed
    (v, F parvenir)
parvinir reach, arrive to, achieve (v)
parvino reached
pas peace
pasa raisin
pasado past
pasajero passenger
pasajes passages, ways; episodes
pasamano ramp, balustrade, guard rail of a stairway
pasandu walking by
pasaporte passport
pasar pass, experience, go through; lo que pasaron los judios what the
    Jews had to go through
pasaro bird
pasas raisins
pasatempo (lit) what helps to pass the time (Ital, Gr); grilled pumpkin
    or melon seeds which are untiringly crunched at the hours of
    leisure, while chatting
pasatyempo agreeable use of leisure time
paseante stroller; strolling person
pasear leisure travel

pasensia patience

pasha Pasha, formerly the highest title of Turkish civil or military offi-
cials, lord, now reserved for generals. Affectionate name given in
Sephardic families to the son of the family or to a young man;
with some pretense word of affection used by the mother-in-law
for the son-in-law.

pasha Sephardic dish, calves' trotter soup, for those who relish a
robust, glutinous and flavorful soup (the dish is also called
patcha, calves' feet), It is prepared with calves' feet chopped into
slices, water, onion, celery, carrot, parsley, bay leaf, peppercorns,
allspice kernels, crushed garlic cloves, lightly beaten eggs, vinegar
and salt.

pashanna wife of a pasha

pashariko small bird, sparrow

pasharo bird; pasharos large birds and prey birds as opposed to
pasharikos, used to designate singing birds in general (the
majority of Sephardic immigrants had lived predominantly in
Spanish cities, and they did not have vocabulary related to rural
life; thus they had no names to designate particular birds; they
only had names for the general classes of birds, and as to the particular birds, names were taken from Turkish, Bulgarian, or
Serbo-Croatian, depending on where the Sephardim resided).

pashayiko literally small pasha, affectionate name given to a young
boy; another word of affection for son, preferred nephew, son-in-
law

pasiente patient (adj)

pasifiar pacify

pasifiko pacific

pasika raisin; small grain of dry raisin; raisin without seed, raisin of
Corinth; person afflicted by a defect of the tongue preventing the
pronunciation of the whistling *s* which is then substituted by the
Castilian *z*, the Greek *q*, the English *th* (thus the word pasika
itself is rendered as the Castilian paziza).

pasivita passivity

paskual pascal (reserved exclusively for the period of Passover)

paso step (n); paso rezyo firm step

paso un ano a year passed; (lo ke) paso what came to pass; what
happened

pasquar celebrate the Passover (v)

pasra a popular family game of cards

passar entre pass through
passar pass; hizo passar he let pass
passouk (H) pasuk, verse of the Bible or from a prayer
pastár pasture (v)
pastel meat pie, pastry; pastel di karne con masa fina ground beef pie
pasteliko small pie or pastry
pastor shepherd; pastor de ovejas shepherd of sheep
pastoral pastoral
pasyon passion
pata duckling; penis (vulg); pata con kol agra duckling with
    sauerkraut
pataka ancient Turkish money which was initially worth as much as a
    Venetian ducat (seven gold franks) and which gradually got deval-
    uated
patladear de yorar burst into tears
patladear explode, burst (from T *patlamak*). The Turkish verb ending -
    mak has been transformed to the Spanish infinitive ending -*dear*
    most frequently used for verbs of Turkish origin).
patlasyon explosion (T *patlamak*)
pato duck
patriarkal patriarchal
patriarkato patriarchate; dignity of the Patriarch who represented the
    Jewish Nation next to the Roman Authority; dignity of the Patri-
    arch of the Greek Orthodox Church; the siege of the Greek
    Orthodox Patriarch in the Phanar district of the Golden Horn in
    Istanbul
Patriarko Greek Orthodox Patriarch; supreme authority of the Greek
    Orthodox Church with siege in Istanbul
patriarko patriarch
patriota patriot
patriotismo patriotism
patron/patrón owner of business; boss; master
patrulya patrol (n)
patrulyar patrol (v)
patudo person with large hands, large feet, large paws
pausa pause (n)
pava female peacock
pavil bee wax; candle; wick of an oil, alcohol or petroleum lamp
    which flickers continuously and is on the way to extinction
paviyon pavilion

pavo peacock
pavona female peacock
pavor fear (n)
paxaro bird
payiz country
paylacho/pagliacho clown
paz peace
pazar market; fair (T)
pazari quality of merchandise such as fabrics, pottery, furniture and
    others of common manufacturing not involving special care or
    refinement
pazarlik bargaining, Grand Bazaar style bargaining
pazdan night guard who walked non-stop through the isolated streets
    watching the tranquillity and silence (T *pazvant*). He would mark
    the hours by strokes of his iron club hitting the slabs of the pave-
    ment. On Friday night and also the Saturday night he would
    come in Jewish homes at sundown to light or extinguish the
    lamps, to cover with cinders the fire of the brazier. For his good
    offices, he would receive a small piece of sesame bread or a
    handful of dry raisins.
pazi in salsa di limon Swiss chard in lemon sauce
paziar stroll; walk (n, Moroccan Sephardic Ballad)
pealino very pious Jew who lets the hairs of his temples grow in long
    curls which descend on both his cheeks (is said in derision about
    Jews of a piety scrupulous and exaggerated); also a name given
    without amenity by the Sephardim to the Ashkenazim
pecador sinner; pecadores sinners
pecar sin (v)
peccado iniquity; sin
pecdo - a la puerta pecdo yazien the pain of the sin is at your door
pechkire ornament (from T *peshkir* napkin)
pecho chest
pechudo someone who has a much developed chest
pechuga chest of a butchery animal, of a fowl
pechugal plaster, compress placed over the chest; pectoral; pectoral
    ornamental set that the High Priest would put on his chest when
    officiating in the Temple of Jerusalem
pedadera jail (n)
pedadero tendency to emit gas often, to fart often (vulg)
pedador buttocks (vulg)

pedagogia pedagogy
pedagogo pedagogue
pedagojiko pedagogic
pedankyon quite young boy, pretentious, who gives his opinion on everything in front of persons of age and experience
pedar fart (v, vulg)
pedasiko small piece
pedaso piece; (en) pedasos in pieces
pedir request; need (v)
pedo fart (n)
pedo kick (n)
pedorro someone who farts often (vulg); person who spends himself in terrible treats, in fabulous promises, always empty; person who boasts about his power, his means, his high relations, all imaginary
pedrada blow with a stone
pedredio pile of stones and marbles
pedregina rocky place improper for cultivation
pedregozo full of stones
pedrer lose (v) Transformation of letters in a word, of consonant clusters with *r* is frequent in Judeo-Spanish, especially with the *rd* combination instead of *dr*)
pedrika pebble
pedrikeador predicator, preacher, orator, speaker
pedrikear preach, make a sermon, give a speech, make a conference (v)
pedrimyento act of loss, loss, perdition
pedrisko hail (n)
pedron absolution, pardon (transformation of *rd* such as in *pardon* into *dr*)
pedronado absolved
pedronavle pardonable, excusable
pegadozo sticky; contagious; sickly sweet, smooth, suave, caressing to the point of exasperation, obsequious
pegima lesion, malformation, physical defect (H)
peizaje landscape
peka red spot on the face, on the skin of the hands, spots of redness, bud on the skin; tyene la kara yena de pekas has the face full of red spots
pekado sin (n); ke pekado what a pity
pekar sin (v)

peketas/pekates you sinned
peki - (yo) peki I sinned
pekunario financial
pelàgo pool; lake
pelagos sea, high sea
peléa fight (n)
peleador fighter
pelear fight (v)
pelegrino stranger; pilgrim
pelejo tendon; very hardened, tough meat; sinew
pelerina preta black tippet
pelerina tippet; a scarf of fur or wool, for covering the neck or the
    neck and shoulders, and usually having ends hanging down in
    front (F *pélerine*)
peligro peril; danger
peligrozo perilous, dangerous
pelikudi scrap of wood, wood shaving
pelit (lit) tassel of oak, fruit of the oak tree encased in a cupula; (fig)
    vigorous, resistant, solid (by allusion to the hardness of the
    cupula of the oak) T *pelit*
pelivan wrestler, boxer, gladiator; tall individual and of very vigorous
    appearance (T *pehlivan*)
pelo hair
pelota ball
peltek stutterer (T)
peludo hairy
peluka/peruka wig
pena effort; (vale la) pena it is worth; it is worth the effort
pena pain, agony; pen
penaba worked hard
penalidad penalty
penar work hard; strive (v)
penbe pink (T *pembe*)
penchembe/pershembe Thursday (T)
pendara piece of five cents, money of very low value
pendevish small lumps of fat fried in olive oil
penia rock (n)
penina small pen or feather to write
peninsula peninsula
penitensya penitence

pensaba he was thinking
pensada thought
pensamiento thought
pensar think (v)
penseryozo worried, concerned, preoccupied
penso he (she) thought
pensyonaryo resident of a boarding house; student of a boarding
    school
peñuar robe that the women where in the interior of the house as a
    French *peignoir; deshabillé, robe-de-chambre*, bathrobe, dressing
    gown
peor worse, worst
peoria state of what by comparison is worst; the fact of getting worst,
    worsening, aggravation
pepinal/pepinar field planted with cucumbers
pepinero vendor of grilled pips of squash, pumpkin
pepiniko/pipiniko small cucumber, gherkin
pepino, pipino cucumber; tasteless, insipid thing to eat; object without
    attraction; kulo de pepino bitter tip of cucumber (vulg)
pepita film that forms at the tip of the tongue of birds or fowl and
    prevents them from eating; grilled seed of cucumber, melon or
    watermelon, which is pushed between the teeth and of which an
    enormous consumption is made in the Orient to help spending
    the time
pepitada drink prepared with grilled and crushed pips of squash or
    pumpkin, mixed to water or milk, with sugar added
pepitear reveal a secret bit by bit, by little words
pepiteo continuous consumption of broiled pips; revelation of a secret
    bit by bit, by furtive indiscretions
pepitozo rich, abundant in pips (cucumber, squash, pumpkin, melon)
peque - que peque a ty in what had I offended you (Fer Bib Gen)
pequeño small; little
pera pear
perche tuft of hair on the forehead (T *perçe*)
perde curtain; screen; Turkish puppet theater; reserve, consideration
    that one has for the others; for someone towards whom one must
    observe a proper demeanor (T)
perder lose (v)
perdicion perdition
perdon pardon remission of a penalty (n)

perdonansa forgiving
perdonar pardon (v); forgive
perdonaras you will forgive
peregrino migrant, immigrant
peregrino sera tu semen your posterity will inhabit as a stranger a land
  which it does not own
perejil parsley
pereza laziness (Ladino)
perezozo lazy (Ladino)
perfeksioniata/perfeksyonista perfectionist
perfeksyon perfection
perfeksyonamento/perfeksionamento making perfect, further
  improving
perfeksyonar make perfect, improve (v)
perfekto perfect
perfil profile; the thin cutting edge of a knife, a penknife, a sword
perforador perforator
perforar perforate (v)
perforasyon perforation
pergamnino parchment
periemos we lose; periemos la ermozura we lose our beauty; periemos
  la siluet we lose our figure
perigrino stranger (Fer Bib Gen)
perikolo danger
perikulozo dangerous (Ital *pericoloso*)
perio - (se le) perio he lost it
periperiposar/mosa de periperiposa said in derision about a
    pretentious young girl who dresses in an attire too loud, too
    gaudy, and who at the same time is clumsy
perishan (adj) dispersed; disorganized; helpless; desolate; lamentable
perkalina light, fine cotton fabric, used as lining; percale
perkurador provider of a family
perla pearl
perlado adorned with pearls
permisyon permission
pernil tie, fastening which fixes the drawers on top of the knee
pero but
perpetual perpetual
perra female dog; perra mala (vulg) bitch
perrada group of dogs

perro dog; perro ijo dotro (insult) dog son of another
persegido pursued by his enemies, by his creditors; who goes in all
    haste as if he had the police on his track
persegidor someone who runs after; pursuer
persegimyento pursuit (n)
persegir pursue (v)
persiguio he ran after (the kings); he gave pursuit to the kings
persiguolos he ran after them (Fer Bib Gen)
persil parsley
persistante persistent
persistir persist (v)
persona person
personal personal
personalidad personality
pertenesido deserving, pertinent, convenient
pertinente pertinent, appropriate
pertukal/portokal orange, orange color (T *portokal*)
pertukalera/portolalera orangeade, orange drink
pertukareo/portokalero orange tree
perturbar perturb (v)
perush commentary of the Bible or Talmud (H)
perversidad perversity
perverso pervert (n)
pervertesimyento perversion
peryel compasses (T *pergel*)
peryita loss
pesagdez heaviness; reprehensible obstination; insistence; exaggerated
    scruple
Pesah Passover
pesame condolence; expression of sympathy
pesgadia heaviness; heavy charge or task; meticulous application of
    laws, rites, usage
pesgado heavy; very meticulous; importune; unbearable by dint of
    being too meticulous
peshcado al orno baked red snapper; peshcado con agristada fish with
    boiled mayonnaise; peshkado llado con mayonaisa cold bass with
    mayonnaise sauce; peshkado llado in sos di limon i dereotu cold
    bass in lemon and dill sauce; peshkado plaki stewed fish (halibut
    or other not too bony fish); hake, mackerel, halibut or other
    firm-fleshed fish in tomato and wine sauce

peshkadito small fish (used in the familiar Judeo-Spanish way of miniaturizing names in an affectionate or humorist tone)

peshkado/peshcado fish (n)

peshkar fish (v)

peshkera fishery

peshkero sudden affluence of fish

peshkes gift, present given to the masons and construction workers in the process of completing a building when the roof is laid on top. The presents consisted of tissues, clothes, shoes all exposed on ropes stretched above the roof in between pickets. By analogy for the wedding banquet only those who had given a present to the bride were invited to stay. When the tables were being made ready for the dinner, after the ball which followed the nuptial blessing, a herald would proclaim, quite blandly and in a loud voice: *kyen echo peshkesh ke se kede, kyen no ke se vaya* "whoever has made a donation let him stay, and whoever has not let him go" (T *peskes*).

peshkir bath linen, ensemble of hand towels, towels which serve for the bath (T)

peshkuezo godro well nourished individual, robust

peshkuezo neck, nape

peshtamal large bath-towel (T)

peshutudo coarse individual, blunderer

pesimismo pessimism

pesimista pessimist

pestaña eyebrows

pestañozo who has the eyebrows very long (archaic); who has the eyes bulging out of their sockets; sickly, visibly overwhelmed by deprivations and worries

peste plague

petcho chest

petimetre young snob with pretentious manners (F *petit-maître*)

petisyon petition

petrisifon boastful, braggart; sophisticated, convoluted, complicated, mannered young man (F *qui pétrit des chiffons*)

petrolyo petroleum

peynada rapid styling of the hair; a stroke of the comb

peynadero uninterrupted strokes of the comb; mania of combing the hair

peynar comb, style one's hair

peyne comb (n)
peyniziko pocket comb
pez bitumen
pezár weigh (v)
pezgado heavy
pi a simple word, a syllable; a lip movement coming from a chief and
  constituting an imperious order which immediately triggers a
  drastic action from the part of the one of those to whom it is
  addressed; **pi dishites muerte meresez** you said only one word and
  you already deserve death, you should not have said anything,
  you should not have made even the smallest comment; **(un) pi si**
  dishe al punto to deve se azer I only need to give an
  imperceptible order for everything to be marvelously executed; I
  am slavishly obeyed; **(sin dizir ni un) pi** without uttering even one
  word
piadad/piyadad mercy; compassion; pity
picadu compassion, sympathy, pity, shame (Monastir dialect)
pichar urinate (v)
pichava en kada punto he urinated at every moment
pichkado fish (n)
pidar break wind (v, vulg, Port *peidar*)
pidyon haben redemption of the first-born son. If the firstborn of a
  woman is a son the father has to redeem him from a Kohen
  (priest) for five shekels (silver or gold coins equivalent to five
  shekels, or with silver objects). The ceremony (*rexmido, rexmir*)
  is held thirty days after birth. The Kohens, the Levis (levites) and
  mothers who are daughters of Kohens and Levites are exempt. To
  the Kohen's questions, the father replies that he chooses to
  redeem his son, and hands him the coins. After the ceremony,
  however, the Kohen returns the payment to the father, and
  receives a gift in return. In Ankara, Istanbul, and Thrace the
  mother wore her wedding dress and veil at the ceremony; but by
  mid-twentieth century, only the veil continued to be born
piedra rock; stone; **piedra de molino** millstone
piedrada wound caused by a stone
piedras presyozas precious stones
piedrer lose (v)
piedrisco hail (n)
piedrisica pebble
pies de teatro theater play

pies feet
pilaf rice dish with butter, oil seasoned with pepper (T)
pilotar pilot, drive a boat or a vehicle in a difficult pass; serve as guide
    for a traveler
piloto pilot (n)
pilpilanjarifa subtle argumentative person; someone who splits a hair
    in four (is said in derision about somebody who thinks he is very
    shrewd) (H)
pilpul very subtle and shrewd method of dialectic, to the point of
    being paradoxical, which is used in the exegesis of the Bible and
    Talmud; subtle argumentation (H)
pimienta/pimyenta pepper condiment, pepper powder
pimienton/pimyenton pepper; (dolma de) pimienton stuffed pepper
pimyentero vendor of pepper
pindola pill
pineta oblong porcelain dish to serve salad
pino pine tree; summit
pintado painted
pintador painter
pintar paint (v)
pinti avaricious; who tries to manage or avoid even the smallest
    contributions; picky; finicky; meticulous; petty; who pays
    attention to insignificant details, to trivialities in order to
    criticize these
pinti miserly; somebody who is very meticulous on unimportant mat-
    ters or issues; picayune (T)
pinzela pea' green pea (Gr pizeli, T bezelye)
piojo louse; vermin; amatar piojo (lit) kill a louse; (fig) live in misery
    and idleness, live as a miser
piójo louse
pipa pipe; (se beber) pipa (lit) smoke a pipe (Port vs. Spanish se fuma
    en pipa)
pipino cucumber; fig: a person or thing of little value
pipiritza green pepper; pipiritzas asadas grilled whole peppers; grilled
    pepper salad; pipiritzas com ceso casserole of green pepper and
    feta cheese; cheese-stuffed green peppers; pipiritzas llenas con
    arroz stuffed pepper; pipiritzas in mirindjena con ceso baled egg-
    plant and pepper with cheese sauce
pipitas dried and salted watermelon seeds
pipitika pumpkin seed; pipitikas salted watermelon seeds

pir the highest point, the maximum, the zenith; the peak
piramida pyramid
pirata pirate
pirateria piracy
pirina powder from crushed olive pits, used as a fuel
pirlanta diamond; fig: a person of very high value (T)
piroga dugout canoe
piron fork
pirón fork (Gr *pirun*)
pironear peck into the small dishes, into the plates exposed on the
    table for the meal without installing oneself squarely for the
    dinner (v)
pirux comment (n)
piryan lover, person in love, man who lives with a woman without
    being tied to her by the bonds of marriage (used in a negative
    sense)
pisar step on
pishabaylande (lit) someone who urinates while dancing; (fig)
    individual who does not have the spirit to follow through with
    his ideas, his projects, his work; individual without any program;
    individual who goes from one task to another without achieving
    anything; individual who lacks perseverance and on whom one
    cannot count.
pishada urine evacuated in one time; echar una pishada urinate; echare
    una pishada let me urinate
pishadera chamber pot (vulg); public urinal; (vulg) organ through
    which one urinates
pishadero mania to urinate frequently
pishado infected by urine; ropa pishada linen with urine stains
pishador someone who urinates, who is in the process of urinating
pishadura fee paid in a public urinal; urine stain
pishalon someone who urinates all the time
pishana public urinal
pishar urinate (v)
pishin immediately; on the spot cash payment; requirement for on the
    spot payment with no credit (*peshin*)
pishkado fish (n)
pishkul tassel which hangs down from the top of the brimless
    Ottoman cap, the fez (T *püskül*); tuft; (fig) difficulties
pisho piss; urine

pishon child with enuresis; child who urinates in bed
pishtamal large towel used when leaving Turkish bath
pishtol pistol, gun, rifle
pishtolada gun shot; wound caused by gun
pishutero debauched, libertine
pisma teasing
pismozo stubborn person
pison (female) breast
pisotear demean, humiliate, treat with great disdain
pista trail, track, trace left by a living being; narrow path on the slope
    of a mountain
pistil/pestil dish made of apricot pulp or green prunes, mixed with a
    light amount of sugar (T *pestil*); fazer a uno pestil (pistil) preto
    abuse someone; submit someone to reproaches; beat someone
    without pity
pistola long, interminable, fastidious writing
piston (lit) piston; (fig) string-pulling; friend or support in the right
    place
pita Oriental bread, usually stuffed with beans, etc.
pitirína dandruff
piu piu at most; at the most; at the maximum (Ital)
piyasa marketplace
piyut psalm, liturgical chant; poem; poetry
pizada strong pressure exerted by the foot inadvertently or on purpose
    on the foot of someone else, or any part of the body, or an object
pizar reduce to powder with a mortar; crush, grind (v)
pizmon popular song; chorus; refrain (H)
placa - en la plaça dormiran (in the) street they will sleep
plañida lamented
plano plain; flat (adj)
plano plan (n)
plasa place; marketplace
plata silver; money
platera cupboard; shelf
platicar converse (v)
plato dish (co-exists in the Judeo-Spanish language with its T
    originated synonym *çini*, which in Turkish means porcelain,
    crockery, china)
platonik platonic (adj)
plazer pleasure; koria detras de plazeres run after pleasures

plazo solemn feast; (al) plazo el que te hablo such (so) as he had
    spoken about
plazos seasons; (a) plazo (in this) season
pleito/pleto fight, quarrel; kaza de pleitos house of fight; house in
    which people fight with each other
plenismedad integrity (Fer Bib Gen)
plenismo integrity; full of integrity
plomo lead; bullet
pluguiere - (en lo) pluguiere en tus ojos where it will please your eyes;
    such as will please your eyes (Fer Bib Gen); faz a ella lo que
    plugiera a tus ojos do unto her (Agar) as will be pleasing to your
    eyes; do to her as you like
poco little; (un) poco (a) little
poder can (v)
poder power (n)
poderoso/poderozo powerful
podesta dominion; domination; sovereignty
podestad dominion; domination
podestania dominion; high power, royal power, imperial power
podestares en el he will be under your power; you will dominate him;
    you will have power upon him (Fer Bib Gen)
podesten let them dominate
podia - si podia if I could
podjiko/pozi ko small well
podon podon showing up in a leisurely, careless way
pojo con arpadjik chicken with glazed baby onions; pojo con azeitunas
    chicken with olives; pojo con bambya chicken with okra; pojo
    con binbriyo chicken with quince; pojo con bizelias chicken with
    garden peas
poka gente few people
poka little, few (fem)
poko little, few (masc); un poko a little; un poko manko a little less;
    un poko preniadika a little pregnant; azer un poko vida have
    some fun; go out
polilla mite
politica/politika politics
politico/politiko political
poliya mite; entrar poliya (lit) be invaded by mites; (fig) someone who
    harasses with siege with his solicitations, who importunes by
    repeating non-stop his revendications, desires and prayers;

meterse una poliya, una poliya negra becoming obsessing by the
perpetual repetition of the same solicitation, recommendation,
warning, litany; worry about the care that one is obliged to give to
something, to someone; worry which obsesses, which eats away at;
repetitious and whining to the point of becoming bothersome

poliyado invaded by mites

polk regiment (Bulgarian Judeo-Spanish)

polkovnic/polkovnik colonel (Bulgarian)

polliya mite

polpa pulp

poluo powder; dust

polvo dust; powder; farina; akeyos polvos trusheron estos lodos (lit)
these dusts have brought this mud; (fig) nothing has changed
(example of an expression which is a translation from Turkish or
another Balkan language; the Judeo-Spanish expression here is the
translation of the Turkish o toz bu çamurdur, literally 'the dirt of
the past is the mud of today.')

poner put (v); poner se go down; settle upon (v)

ponian were putting

ponte bridge (also called from T köprü)

popularida popularity

popularyo popular

populasion/populasyon population

por by; to; into

por cavsa for the cause; por cavsa que because; por cavsa deque for
what reason

por dezir in saying, for saying

por ditcho by the word, by reason

por esto for this; therefore

por que because

por tanto nonetheless; nevertheless; consequently

porfiaron they pushed too hard, they made violence

porfio con elles mucho he pressed them too much; pressured them
too much

porloseco on dry land (from the Passover Haggadah)

pornas you will put

porne I shall put

porque why, because; porque no denunciaste a mi why didn't you
warn me (that she was your wife) (about Abraham not telling the
Pharaoh that Sara was his wife) (Fer Bib Gen)

porselena porcelain
porsyon portion
portal gate
porto port, harbor (Ital)
portokal/portukal orange (fruit); orange (color) (from T)
posession possession
posessor de cielos y mare possessor (owner; master) of the skies
    and sea (Fer Bib Gen)
posesyon possession
    position by a vote of the faithful
poso he stopped on, stopped upon
possessor owner
possuydo possessed (Ferrara Siddur)
posta mail; post office
postají/postadji mailman (T)
poste mail (n)
posto position, high position, government position
postos se vendian con paras government positions were sold for
    money
posula note, list, ticket (T *pussula*)
pot kirmak commit a faux pas
potrivita well-adjusted (Romanian Judeo-Spanish)
poyo chicken
pozar put down (v)
pozarse land (v)
pozision/pozisyon position (n)
pozo well (n); pozos wells
pranga fetters attached to the legs of a criminal (T, kanunn); jail, labor
    camp
prasa leek
prasfucho leek and meat pie
pratika practice (n)
pratiko practical
praza con azeitunas leek with olives
preçio - tu preçio micho mucho I appreciate you very much (Fer Bib
    Gen)
precioso precious
predispozisyon predisposition
prefikso prefix
pregunta question (n)

preguntar ask, question (v)
preniada pregnant
prenismo simple-minded
prenyades pregnancy
prestes speed; kon prestes with speed
presto fast, quickly
prestozo rapid, fast
prestu quickly
presyado precious; appreciated
presyozo precious
preteksto pretext
pretender pretend (v)
pretensyon pretention (n)
preto black (Port vs. modern Spanish *negro*); (ojos) pretos black eyes
pretu black (person) (Monastir dialect)
préva trial
previz cornice, any prominent, continuous, horizontally projecting feature surmounting a wall or other construction, or dividing it horizontally for constructional purposes; painting frame
prevô tried
prexil parsley
prezentar present (v)
prezentasyon presentation
prezente present, gift
prezidente president
prezion jail (v)
prezo jailed
pricurar di deal with (v, Monastir dialect)
primavera spring
primer first
primera(o) first (fem, masc)
primeramente primarily
primero first (masc)
primo cousin; first cousin; (fem) prima
primogenito first-born
princesa princess
principe prince
principio beginning (Monastir dialect)
prinçipio beginning

printchipesa princess
prisipiar start, commence (v)
privalersi (di) avail oneself of (Monastir dialect)
probabelmente/provabelmente probably
probabilita probability
probabo - tu has probado mi corazón you have probed, you have put
    my hear on trial
probar probe, put on trial
probecho benefit; improvement; profit
problema problem
profesor professor
profeta prophet
progresar progress (v)
progreso progress (n)
prohibido forbidden (adj)
proksimo near, close, proximate
proksimo tyempo near future
prometa promise (n)
prometer promise (v)
pronto ready (arch)
prontu ready (Monastir dialect)
pronuncyar pronounce (v)
pronunsyando - en pronunsyando while pronouncing
propaganda propaganda
propagandista propagandist
propajador propagator
propajar propagate (v)
propajasyon propagation
proponedor proponent; someone who makes a proposition
proponer propose (v)
propozar propose (v)
propozisyon proposition
propozito proposal; a propozito by the way
propuesta proposition
propuesto proposed
propyo own (adj); kon sus propyas manos with his own hands
prostéla apron
protejado protected; someone who enjoyed the consular protection
    under the regime of capitulations (capitulations which granted to

foreign powers commercial, consular and extraterritorial
privileges were abolished at the time of Atatürk, founder of the
Turkish Republic)
protestar protest (v)
protestasyon protest (n)
protokolaryo protocolar
protokolo protocol
prova proof, trial, attempt
provaya poor population of a quarter, a village, a country; quarter
inhabited by poor people, slum
prove/probe poor
provécho profit (n)
provedad poverty (Judeo-Spanish creation by adding to the Judeo-
Spanish base *prove*. *-dad*, the noun suffix; the Modern Spanish
equivalent is *pobreza*)
prozelitismo proselytism
prudensya precaution
prupuzar suggest (v, Monastir dialect)
publikar publish (v)
publikasyon publication
pude - no los pude suportar I couldn't support them
pudo - yo no pudo acceptar I could not accept
pudrir rot, putrefy, to become corrupted (v)
pudrisyon passionate concern about health, wellbeing, commodities,
etc.
puede ser maybe
pueder to be able to; can; may
puedeser perhaps, maybe
puercu pork (Monastir dialect)
puerkito small pork
puerko pork
puerpo body
puerpudo corpulent
puerro leek; idiot, stupid, ignoramus
puerta door; tener entrada de puerta (lit) to have entrance to the door;
well equivalent (this expression follows the equivalent expression
in various Balkan languages)
puerto de salidura exit port
puerto port

pues since
puevlo people; puevlo aladinàn people of barbarous language
puja augmentation, increase of quantity, weight, value
pujado accrued, augmented; being heavier, more voluminous
pujamiento action of increasing, accruing
pujansa augmentation
pujar/pujier augment, increase (v)
pujita surplus, regain, recrudescence, augmentation
pul postage stamp (T)
pulga flea
pulgador butcher who is charged to strip the meat from fat and
     tendons to make it proper for the Jewish kitchen
pulgerio/pulgero affluence, invasion of fleas
pulgita very small flea; tiny and insignificant individual
puliya someone who whines and complains continuously
pulso pulse (n)
pulsu wrist (Monastir dialect)
pulverizador pulverizer
pulverizar pulverize (v)
pumada ointment
punchada sting (n)
punchadika little, but quite sharp sting or bite like a bedbug sting
punchadika small sting
punchar sting (v); (bisba) puncha bee stings
punchon/púnchon stiletto, puncheon, sting; (fig: a little stinging suspi-
     cion, doubt or concern)
punta de pie kick, kick with the foot (n); (de) punta a pie a from the
     tip of the foot to the head
punta tip
punto - kavesa punto point; moment; stitching made on the cloth to
     pass the thread, to sew; en kada punto at every moment
puntos en la espalda kicks on the shoulder
puntoso very meticulous person; person putting the dots on the i's
puntózo picky
puntu minute (Monastir dialect); a puntu immediately (Monastir
     dialect)
puñu punch (n, Monastir dialect)
punyo fist; punch in the face; apretar su punyo tighten his fist; punyo
     serrado closed fist, tight fist

purgatorio purgatory
Purim festival of Purim
purimlikes Purim gifts (with the T noun forming -*lik* suffix added to
    the Hebrew word)
puro cigar
puro pure
pusat arm, equipment (T, kanunn)
pusela put it; lay it (Ferrara Siddur)
pusht vile, of shameful mores, depraved (T)
pushtluk vilification, depravation
puso he put
pusso he put (Haketia; Moroccan Judeo-Spanish)
pusula small scribbled note (T)
puta whore
putana prostitute
puúo/punyo punch (n)
puvlikasyon publication
puvliko public (adj)
puvlisiadad publicity
puvlisita publicity
pyango/piyango lottery; winning at the lottery; le salio pyango he had
    something very good, like a lottery win, happening to him
pyano piano
pyanto scream of the screech owl, of the owl; complaint, crying,
    reproach
pyas/piyas bean salad
pyasa/piyasa marketplace, market value
pyato dolce sweet plate served at the end of a meal (Ital)
pye foot
pyedestal pedestal
pyedra stone
pyedregina loose stones; place covered with irregular stones which
    make walking difficult
pyedrogozo full of stones, of rocks
pyerna leg, thigh
pyesa piece
pyezes - los pyezes the feet

Q

qixada jaw
quadrupéa quadruped; animal
quando when
quantitdad amount
quanto how much; por quanto by; for; of
quarenta forty
quarto fourth
quatregua chariot (Fer Bib Gen Kings)
quatro four
quatrocientos four hundred
quatropea animals of the earth
que that; who; passouk que eran nuestros padres coumientes which
    our ancestors ate (from the Passover Haggadah)
que a ti what aileth thee
que ansi dize el passouk so it is said in the Scriptures
qué esto heziste what have you done
que fue which was
que troucho that (He) brought
qué to
quebrantar break; damage; shutter (v)
quebrar break; shutter (v)
quejarse complain
quemar burn (v)
quemô burned
querer want
querida dear (fem)
querido dear (masc)
queso cheese
quiça should watch; should be careful; should fear; by fear of
quidar di leave, let stay from (Monastir dialect)
quién who; quién como Adonay nuestro Dio who is like unto the
    Eternal, our God
quienzen fifteenth
quinientos five hundred
quinto fifth
quinze fifteen
quizensje affection, love (Monastir dialect)
qusharse complain

R

ráash earthquake

rabano - (el) rabano rabbi from *rábano*, radish (a predominant
    Sephardic practice of word corruption with humorous or
    malicious intent)

Rabbi Akida dizien Rabbi Akiba said

rabinato rabbinate; **Gran Rabinato** Grand Rabbinate

rabino rabbi; **Gran Rabino** Grand Rabbi

racismo racism

racontar tell, retell (Passover Haggadah, Salonica)

rafraganar relax, be tranquil, lounge after hard work (v, T *rahatlama*)

rafreskamyento refreshment; refreshing drink

rafreskar refresh

Rahman piyadoso merciful God

raiz root

rajamana/rajamana letsila all that there is of worst, of wholly
    detestable; extremely pitiful, like Job's afflictions (H)

raki Middle-Eastern brandy obtained by the distillation of raisins.
    While the Muslim religion prohibits the drinking of alcohol, raki
    is still in a way the national drink of the Turkish bon-vivant. A
    sizable quantity of raki is openly consumed in the open air joints
    of Istanbul called *açik hava gazinosu* (open air gazino, café)
    where traditionally men sit at the tables with no female escort
    and they joyously, at times exuberantly, sip raki while listening to
    the notes of female oriental music singers. This kind of lurid
    entertainment is called *raki sefasi* (pleasant entertainment with
    raki). The beverage is consumed from one liter bottles comically
    called *Fahrettin Kerim* by allusion to the teetotaler mayor of
    Istanbul, a leader of *Yeshil Ay* (The Green Crescent) a militant
    organization of teetotalers. While listening to the singers, or to
    the *çalgici* (players of oriental music instruments) the happy rev-
    elers will say *gel keyfim gel* [come my *kyef* (leisurely
    entertainment, enjoyment) come]; **el raki arrebive al peshe**
    (popular adage of bon-vivant: every cooked fish becomes salutary
    and vivifying when accompanied by a shot of raki).

rakidji merchant of raki, tavern keeper

rama/ramo branch

ramatizmo/romatisma rheumatism

ramayu ulterior motive, afterthought

ramazan/ramadan ninth month of the Muslim calendar dedicated to daily fasting; during Ramadan all feuds are expected to be suspended; solemn Muslim holiday which follows the fasting period

ramifikar ramify

ramifikasyon ramification

ramo derivation, section of an enterprise; trait of infirmity or mental deficiency

rana frog

ránda band of lace in European style attached to the hem of a garment or bed linen

randebú meeting place (F *rendezvous*)

rañu mucous (Port *ranho*)

rápa cloth

raporto report

rapoza/rapoze fox

rasa race, kind

rasgar/razgar tear (v)

rasgava - si no rasgava a nos a la mar if he had not divided the sea for us (from the Passover Haggadah)

rashá wicked (H)

rashaj nasty, wicked individual; criminally hardened person; inveterate, confirmed bachelor

rashi commentaries of the Bible and the Talmud due to the famous doctor of the Law Salomon Itshaki, of Troyes (France, eleventh century) and to his school; special Hebrew alphabet used for the publication of Rashi's commentaries; manuscript alphabet in cursive used by the Sephardim (this cursive alphabet is distinct from the one of the Ashkenazim, the use of which has been generalized in Israel. The word Rashi itself originates from the initials of Rav Shelomo Yitzhak).

rasyonalista(o) rationalist (fem, masc)

ratón mouse

ratonado eaten, gnawed by rats or mice

ratonera mousetrap

rav Ashkenazim rabbi

ravano radish; person deprived of culture and intelligence; a lifetime stupid and worthless person

ravdon torrent

ravya/ravia anger

ravyozo fiery; quick-tempered; raging; furious

raya lightning, thunder; rails (of railroad)

raya/reaya non-Muslim subject of the Ottoman Empire

rayada jam made of grated and grilled gourd and/or pumpkin
    immersed in a syrup of sugar aromatized by cinnamon

rayar radiate; spread the rays all around; grate, grind (v)

ra'yet conformity, obedience (T *riayet*, kanunn)

rayiz/raiz root

rayo ray

razimo bunch of grapes

razimozo which gives grapes abundantly

razon reason

razonador someone who enjoys entering into an unending discussion

razonamiento reasoning

razonavle reasonable

reaksyon reaction

reayet respect, consideration (T *riayet*)

rebellaron they revolted

rebi title given to the rabbi; rabbi (H); impassive individual that
    nothing upsets, who persists obstinately in his resolution, in spite
    all the solicitations, all the interventions

rebolteado revolted

rebolton turbulent person prone to make noise, to speak in a noisy
    tone, to create derangement, to disturb the tranquillity and
    routine of habitual occupations

reboluio labio de toda la tierra he confused the languages of all the
    earth (at the time of the attempt to construct the tower of
    Babel—Fer Bib Gen)

rebozuamos let us confuse

recamar embroider

recamado (adj) embroidered (masc, fem); **tunicas recamadas**
    embroidered tunics

reçebible receive them (imp)

recem nascido newborn

rechina/rezina resin; viscous and inflammable matter which flows out
    of some trees (pine, fir tree, larch)

rechinato resinous; vino rechinato wine with a small percentage of
    resin (*retsina*)

reciente recent

recitar recite (v)

recompensa reward
recontantes those who speak of
recontar speak of (v)
recuerda reminds of (archaic Castilian)
recuerdar remind of (v)
recuerdo memory, remembrance; keepsake, souvenir; commemoration
redaksyon editorial office
redaktor editor
redaktor in kapo editor-in-chief
redingot redingote; men's garment, ample and going down till the
    knees; ceremonial cloth
redja/ridja request (n), supplication (T *rica*)
redjadji supplicant; one who implores pity and indulgence
redondo round (adj); el top es redondo the ball (T *top*) is round
    (expression heard among Jewish fans of soccer games, meaning
    that the outcome of a soccer game is often unpredictable;
    anything may happen, in soccer all options are fair game, even a
    team which is not first league can win on its lucky day)
reflane proverb
refran proverb
refranro book of proverbs, collection of proverbs
refregadero unfortunate tendency to friction, rub uninterruptedly a
    part of the body, as if one was suffering from continuous itching
refregador specialist who cures fractures; masseur
refreksyon reflection
refutar refute (v)
refuzar refuse (v)
regaalador someone who gives presents
regadiza was irrigated
regadúra irrigation
regalada - ija regalada dearest daughter; su regalada a mother's dearest
    daughter (*ijo*);
regalado dearest son
regalo present; gift
reganchon one who acts in an affected way to give himself undue
    importance instead of acting straightforwardly; one who purpose-
    fully complicates things
regimento regiment
regla rule; las reglas the rules
regmición redemption; joy

regmido redeemed, bought again
Regmidôr Redeemer
regmir pay a ransom to deliver a Jewish captive, a Jewish slave
regmissiôn deliverance
regmisyon redeeming of a Jewish prisoner, a captive, a slave (a very
    revered custom and a traditional obligation of Jewish
    communities, no Jew should be allowed to remain a slave; it is a
    blessed action to redeem Jewish slaves, and communal funds are
    kept in reserve for the accomplishment of this blessed duty and
    task).
regoldar burp; regurgitate (v)
regoldo burp; regurgitation (n)
regrayamento thankful acknowledgment
regretado regretted, deceased, late
regretar regret (v, F *regretter*)
regreto muncho I am very sorry
regular/regularyo regular
regularmente regularly
reid laugh (imp)
reina queen
reinado kingdom
reir laugh
reis head, chief (T kanunn)
reitina burst of laughter
rejim diet; special diet to cure an illness or to lose weight; azer rejim
    make a diet (v)
rejion region
rejisa washing of a corpse and covering it with a shroud; brotherhood
    of pious volunteers who wash the dead
rejistrado registered
rejistrar register (v)
rejistro register (n)
rejmidor redeemer
rejyonal regional
rekaer fall again
rekavdar cash; reenter credits; recuperate (v)
rekavdarse take his (her) revenge (v)
reklam advertising (F *réclame*)
reklamar reclaim (v)
rekluzo recluse

rekojer assemble, collect, harvest, pick what is spread out and concentrate it, catch, nab (v)
rekojimyento meditation
rekolta harvest
rekomandasyon recommendation
rekomendar recommend
rekompensa recompense (n)
rekompensar recompensate (v)
rekonkuesta conquest (n)
rekonkuestar conquer (v)
rekonoser recognize (v)
rekonosiente thankful
rekonstituir reconstitute (v)
rekonstitusyon reconstitution
rekonstruir reconstruct
rekonstruksyon reconstruction
rekorso recourse
rekovrar recover; recuperate (v)
rektifiar rectify (v)
relampageo successive flashes, bursts of lightning
relampago - El Relampago popular Judeo-Spanish newspaper run and published in Istanbul by Eli Kohen, strongly opposed to Grand Rabbi Nahum (early twentieth century)
relampago lightning; flash of lightning; **geurra relampago** blitzkrieg
relato narration, relation
relijion/relijyon religion
relijioso religious
relijioza nun
reloj clock; el balansiin del reloj the play, the dance of the pendulum of the clock
remada stroke of the oar
remamsarse become stagnant; settle (archaic Castilian)
remanesçio de çierto remained certainly
remaniscedos those remaining from; the remaining who were escaping from the battle of the kings of Sodom (Fer Bib Gen)
remanso - se remanso settled; el tiempo se reamanso the weather turned well after all (archaic Castilian)
remar handle the oar
remarka remark (n)
remarkar remark (v)

rematare I shall exterminate
remayar remake the stitches of a sock, a knitting, a tissue
rembolsar reimburse (v)
rembolso reimbursement
remedio remedy (n); topo remedio found remedy
remendar patch up; vamp up; revamp (v)
remendo piece added, patch added to mend a cloth; repair
remendon shoe repairman
remesa remission, dispatch, transfer of money by the intermediary of
    a bank
remitimos we leave it up
remitir remit, give to, deliver to; leave it up to (v)
remojado wet, dipped in; remojeran la oja de apio they will dip the
    leaf of celery (Salonica Sephardic Haggadah)
remorso remorse
remouién - la remouién sobre la tierra those that crawl on earth;
    reptiles
remouilla crawling like a reptile; reptile
removiente moving
renaser be born again
renasyensya rebirth, renaissance
renasyimento rebirth
renda rent (Port)
rendida fixed revenue
rendikonto account, report of a financial transaction, of the activity of
    a society, a corporation or a charitable foundation
rendyer render (v)
rendyeron kuento (se) they noticed
rene kidney
renegar deny (v)
rengrasyar thank (v); rengrasyo te I thank you
renkontrar meet, encounter (v); renkontrar (se) meet each other (v);
    renkontran (se) they meet each other
renovado renewed
renovar renew (v)
rensenyamento information
rensenyar give information; inform (v)
reompieron (se) they broke
reparasyones reparations

repartir divide up

repentido one who vividly regrets his reprehensible actions, his religious failings, his sins and makes the firm resolution not to relapse again; one who mortifies himself to be pardoned; one who feels regret to have engaged himself in a business, a question he considers after the fact to be prejudicial to his interests and good name.

repentimyento repenting, regret (n)

repentir regret

repetar repeat (v, modern Spanish *repetir*; F *répéter*)

replika replica

replikar replicate

reportar carry a sum, an addition from the end of a page to the next page

reporter accountant

reporto carry-over of a sum

reposo rest (n)

repotreo life of pleasure, of perpetual feasting

repotron one who enjoys, who likes to enjoy, bon vivant (F *jouisseur*); puerpo repotron person who only thinks to have fun, to enjoy life, to draw pleasure from everything, the life of a party who knows how to put cheerfulness in a reunion and who is the first to have fun.

repozado rested

repozar rest (v)

repozo rest (n)

reprezentasyon representation

reprezentato representative

republika republic

Republika Turka Turkish Republic

repudyar repudiate (v)

repudyasyon repudiation

repuesta response, answer

repueston one who is argumentative, who retorts with vivaciousness to all the observations which are made to him; insolent, irreverent

repulgo hem (n)

reputado reputed, renowned

reputasyon reputation

requerire I shall demand, require, ask

resefta prescription (F *recette*)

resepsyon reception
reserva reserve (n)
resfolgado who is in a state of relaxation, of détente, of well being, being carefree
resgatado redeemed slave, captive
resgatar redeem a slave, a captive (v)
resim official ceremony (T kanunn)
resivida receipt; kontra resivida against receipt
resjodes i saba neomeniae expression used to design the menial benefits, gratifications, bonuses which are added to the gross pay of a servant or an employee. The first day of each month (*rosh hodesh*) is considered as a half-holiday. *Resjodes* are minor holidays added to the days that are squarely holidays.
reskaldada hot cinders under a fireplace or a portable stove
reskapado escapee, one who has escaped an accident, a mortal danger
reskayentor heat which comes from a fire sitting under the cinders
reskuñar scratch (v)
reskuño scratch (n)
resmirar (se) gaze (v)
respectimos we respected
respektar respect (v)
respekto respect (n)
respirar respire, breathe (v)
respirasyon respiration
resplandeciente shining; full of splendor
resplandor splendor
responder answer (v)
responsabilidad responsibility
responsavle person in charge (n); **responsavle de las komidas** person in charge of food, of meals
responsavle responsible (adj)
responsavlo person with responsible authority (n)
responsavlo responsible (adj)
résta de dukados gold coin necklace
reste string of beads (Port *reste*)
restos remains
retardataryo latecomer
retener retain (v)
retirada retreat; backing up

retirar retire, take away (v)
retirarse withdraw; retire from business; distance himself from an
    activity, a club, an enterprise; disinterest oneself from a question,
    a crush on somebody, a flirt (v)
retomar retake (v)
retornar return; come back; come back to one's senses after fainting (v)
reunamonos let us gather, let us assemble (archaic Castilian)
reunir assemble, gather (v)
reushir be successful (v)
reushita/reuchita success (F *réussite*)
reusho succeeded
revani a kind of sweet made with semolina
revelar reveal
revelasyon revelation
revendikar revendicate (v)
revendikasyon revendication
reverencia salute; bow (n)
reverendo reverent
reverensya reverence
reveyar make an insurrection, rebel, deny, renounce one's faith (v)
revinido revenue
revista review
revizar revise, control, examine with attention (v)
revizyon revision
revokasyon revocation
revoltar revolt, rebel (v)
revoltozo rebellious
revolucion/revolusyon revolution (Ferrara Siddur)
revolusyonaryo revolutionary
revuelta revolt
Rey del Mundo King of the Universe
rey king
reye king (Moroccan Sephardic Ballad)
reyenado dish of vegetables stuffed with rice and ground meat or
    chicken (with tomatoes, eggplants, squashes, green peppers);
    azeitunas reyenadas olives stuffed with anchovies
reyete - (que) reyete someone who smiled
reynante one who reigns; reigning; one who is at the head of the state
reynar reign (v)

reyne kidney; las reynes the lumbar regions, the kidneys
reynon kingdom
reyosse he smiled
rezalet meanness, despicable act, villainy, humiliation inflicted, experienced in public (T); salir a rezalet become a public laughing stock
rezalitlik state of what has become the object of scandal, of what provokes general disgust, which produces revulsion in public opinion (T *rezaletlik*)
reze prayer
rezerva reserve; provision of food supplies, money preserved for times of shortage
rézico danger
reziduo residue, deposit, dregs, sediment
rezil vile, dishonored, disgraced, ridiculous (T)
rezin kazado newlywed
rezio solid
rezistensya resistance
rezistente resistant
rezistir resist (v)
reziu solid (Monastir dialect)
rezmido/rezmir redemption of the first son (H *pidyon haben*)
rezolver resolve (v)
rezultado result (n); el tenia el tino en el rezultado his mind was in the result; he had his mind concerned with the result
rezyane cumin, sort of umbillifera the grains of which are aromatic, reminding the taste of brandy; these are used to aromatize brioches and cakes
rezyo solid
rhumatizmo/rhumatizmo rheumatism
ribon olamin Master of the worlds, the Master of the world (name given to God in prayers). It is also at times an interjection, refering to a surprising spectacle or conduct
ribuy recrudescence, affluence (H)
ridja request (T *rica*, kanunn)
ridome bottle (n, Monastir dialect)
rifa lottery (kanunn)
riflo breath
riga line traced with a pencil or a pen

rigado striped, on which lines are drawn

rigano oregano aromatic plant from which a spice and an estimated perfume are drawn; *organno* is also used as an aromatic herb to remove the unpleasant aroma of certain dishes

righalu gift

rigmiô luégo redeemed (Passover Haggadah)

rigrasjar thank (v, Port *regraciar*)

rigritar feel; hear (v, Monastir dialect)

riir laugh

rijo festive meal

rikeza wealth

riko rich

rikon super rich, very rich person; moneybag

rikota ricotta cheese

rima rhyme (n)

rimador mediocre poet

rimon/rimonim metal ornament (often made of precious metal such as gold or silver) in the shape of a pomegranate set with precious stones and adorned with little bells that top the superior extremities of the rods on which the manuscripts of the Torah parchment are rolled

rincon corner; retreat (n); private quarter

riñon kidney, lamb kidney

rio river

ripueste contest, answer (n, Monastir dialect)

riqueza wealth

risumat dues, taxes (T *rüsumet*, kanunn)

riu lake (Monastir dialect)

riuxir/riushir/reushir succeed (v)

riza handkerchief

riza laughter, burst of laughter; rizas - las rizas laughter

rize smile (n, Monastir dialect)

rizeka small handkerchief

rizikador one who risks willingly, who exposes himself to danger without hesitation

rizikar risk, endanger (v)

riziko risk, peril, danger; meterse en riziko expose himself to danger

rizo administration; way of administering, governing, conducting an enterprise, a household

rizon person always ready to laugh, to take life from the good side
without any malice; person who creates drive and good humor in
his (her) entourage

rizoto rice; rizoto a la milaneza, rice with tomato sauce, sprinkled with
parmesan cheese

rodear roll, march around, turn in circle, surround; roam (v)

rodias - de rodias on the knees, kneeling

rodondo round (adj)

roendando corroded; consumed; gnawed

roendar corrode; consume; gnaw; nibble (v)

roendarse to be consumed by anxiety

rofidan - guevo rofidan soft-boiled egg (T *rafadan*)

rofit trade guilds; tradesman; artisan (T *esnaf, hirfet, taife*)

rogador one who prays, who prays to God,

rogar pray (v)

rogativa intense prayer, instant supplication; **kon rogativas** by dint of
supplication

rogo he begged

roido/ruido/bruido noise

roka plant used for salad; plant of which the leaves with a strong
smell are eaten as a salad (Gypsy women used to go through the
streets of Istanbul with the cry *roka, roka salad*); roka salad a
tasty salad of *roka* with a special flavor

roke dress (n, Romanian Judeo-Spanish)

rollo de papel paper roll

rolo roll (n)

romancillo song

romanesido leftover

Romaniotes Greek speaking Jews who lived in territories of the Byzantine Empire conquered by the Ottomans. The name is derived
from "Rome" as in "Eastern Roman Empire."

romansa ballad

romanse Ladino

romansero collected romances; collection of romances; book of
romances

romanso novel

romansyero novelist

romantico romantic

romantismo romanticism

romastismos rheumatism

rompedero unceasing chatter which causes the exasperation of those
     present

rompedor impenitent chatterbox

romper break (v); **rompe (se) todo** everything gets broken; **rompe-
     kavesas** (lit) breaks heads; (fig) person who chats noisily and non-
     stop; **romper la monotonia** break the monotony; **rompi** I broke

ronda round (n), security round

rondjar chase away

ronkador someone who snores

ronkar snore; sleep deeply (v)

ronkear speak with a hoarse voice (v)

ronkedad hoarseness

ronkera persisting hoarseness

ronkerio noisy and continuous snoring

ronkido lasting snoring

ropa cloth, tissue; undergarments

roscas di alhashu walnut filled crescents

rosjodes neomenia the first day of each lunar month is celebrated by
     the Jews as a semi-holiday

roske ring-shaped cookie, ring shaped yeast cake

rosto roasted meat; roast

roto broken-down, broken; **vidro roto** broken glass

rovar rob (v)

rovina/ruvina/ruina ruin (n)

rovinador person who causes ruin

rovo theft

royo/ruvyo russet; red-haired. According to popular belief, red-haired
     people have a difficult, not very accommodating character. The
     children used to shout at the passage of such a person *royo mal
     pelo, kavesa de kodredo* (lit: redhead with the bad hair, head
     of mutton).

roz pink color

roza rose

rozado perfume with rose; **agua rozada** rose water, rose scented water
     which it was customary to spray the visitors at the ceremonies of
     engagement, marriage and circumcision

rozal, rozero rose bush

rozeta ring of which the setting carries a diamond cut in the shape of
     a rose, on one side; rose-shaped diamond ring; hairpin worn by
     Sephardic women of Izmir

rozolyo liquor, very lightly alcoholic brandy scented with rose
rregalado dearest
rremeldar read again
rrenunsya renunciation
rrepresentante representative
rresivir receive (v)
rresivyeron they received
rriirse laugh at (v); (se) rriien de mi they laugh at me
rropa merchandise
ruah wind blow; soul; roaming soul which according to popular
     credence enters a living body creating a second personality, a dou-
     bling of personality (the intruder speaks, orders, demands and
     substitutes its will for that of the possessed; this psychopathic
     phenomenon was common among Oriental populations,
     especially Jewish, till the beginning of the twentieth century. Pow-
     erful exorcism by an old magician woman, a Muslim enchanter, a
     cabalistic, a master of the words, was required in order to
     convince the intruder of the soul to leave).
rubí ruby, precious stone of a vivid, transparent red; raggie (a groove
     cut in masonry to receive flashing; a manufactured masonry unit
     usually of terra cotta, grooved to receive flashing, also called
     raggie-block)
rubisa wife of a rabbi (H)
rubisika young girl who is very pious, very devoted, with her mouth
     full of benedictions, preoccupied with doing good, always ready
     to offer her help to anyone, to prodigate herself in advises of
     good behavior.
rubla ruble (Russian currency)
ruda raw; coarse (adj, fem, masc)
rùda the rue plant, believed to be effective against the evil eye
rufyan pimp; mediator, intermediary to offer and bring in prostitutes;
     procurer of prostitutes (Ital, T *pezevenk*)
rugozo ruguous; covered with rugosities, with bumps; of irregular sur-
     face
ruido noise; unusual noise
ruidos rumors
ruidozo noisy
ruja/rija wrinkle (n)
rulo roll (n, F *rouleau*)
rum/rhum brandy

rumano Romanian
rumatismal rheumatic
rumor rumor
rumorozo noisy
rupo measure of length for tissues, carpets, paper, thread, ropes (one
    eighth of a *pic*, an old measure corresponding to 65 cm)
rushfeldji/rushvetchi one who allows himself to be corrupted by bribes
    (a very common practice in the Ottoman empire where
    government officials where poorly paid; in fact bribes were a *sine
    qua non* to get any official business moving, to obtain any neces-
    sary permit, document or certification); the one who buys the
    conscience of functionaries by means of bribes (T *rüshvetçi*).
rushvet bribe (n, T *rüshvet*)
ruso/rusesko Russian language
rutbe degree, grade, rank (n, T *rütbe*, kanunn)
rutina routine
rutinyero (adj) routine; one who always follows the same procedure,
    without thinking of changing or improving it
ruvio russet
ryo he smiled; he laughed

S

saát clock; hour (T)
saatchi watchmaker, watch repairman, watch dealer
saba Sabbath
sábana/savana bed sheet
saber (n) knowledge
saber (v) know; saber saberas know with certainty
sabiduria knowledge
sabientes knowledgeable persons
sabikali recidivist (T kanunn)
sabir patience (T); kon sabir with patience
sabirli patient (adj, T)
saboerear savor, enjoy
sabotador saboteur; bungler
sabotar sabotage; bungle (v)
sabursiz/sabursuz impatient (T *sabirsiz*)
saca make come out (imp)

sacalos throw them out

sacar (arch) take out of; bring from; bring forth; saçerdo al dio alto
  sacrificator to the God high and sovereign (Fer Bib Gen)

sach kitchen utensil with raised borders made of a metal sheet, zinc or
  tin and on which are placed bread, paste, pastries to be baked in
  the oven

sachliran baldness

sachma nonsense; allusion, insinuation, pointed talk (T saçma); echar
  sachmas make allusions in view of indirectly recalling something;
  make malevolent, malignant insinuations

sacô (se) sacô withdrew

saco produced his (its) jet; saco - (se) saco a si mesmo took himself
  out of; delivered himself out of (Salonica Pessach Siddur); saco a
  el fuera he made him go out; saco pan i vino brought out bread
  and wine

sacomos delivered us from; brought us forth (Salonica Pessach Siddur)

sadik faithful, devoted, trustworthy (T)

sadik saint; person of a scrupulous loyalty, attentive to observe all recommendations of the Law, very pious, very virtuous, a just
  person (H tsadik)

sadikero very charitable, one who gives alms discretely with a great
  sense of justice and discernment (in Jewish charity the giver, the
  donor should remain unknown, he should avoid to identify himself, not to humiliate or offend the recipient of charity; such
  requirement of discretion is also a tenet of the other religions)

sadrazam/sadirazim Grand Vizir, prime minister of the Ottoman
  empire (T sadrazam, kanunn)

sadrela/sardela sardines; estar komo (lit) sadrelas en kuti be like
  sardines in a box; (fig) be very tightly seated, placed one against
  the other

sadrelero vendor of sardines

saéta arrow

saetero archer

safañon chilblain; strong itching due to winter cold, specially in the
  feet; las aguas de Nisan son la mijor melezina para los safañones
  (lit) the waters of April are a sovereign remedy against chilblain;
  (fig) chilblain disappears when the good weather comes

safanorya carrot

safek doubt, scruple (H)

safi pure (T)

safir sapphire
saframan leather with very fine hair, downy, silky
safran saffron
safumeryo incense
sah official seal on a document to show that it has been examined and
    registered (T kanunn)
sajakol (adv) all in all, overall, in the sum, in the sum of all; in
    summary; in conclusion; in reserve (H)
saka water carrier, water porter (T)
πaká/shaka joke (n, T)
sakar take out; remove; sakar el pye del lodo (lit) take foot out of the
    mud; (fig) extricate oneself from a bad move; win a large amount
    of money which ensures well being for a long time, for life; los
    katalanes de la pyedras sakan panes (lit) the Catalans are able to
    take out bread from stones; the Sephardim who originated from
    Catalonia are very hard working.
sakarado sacred
sakarina saccharine
sakat defective; cripple; infirm (T sakat)
sakatlik infirmity, blemish (T kanunn)
sakeador looter
sakeamyento sacking; looting
sakear sack; loot; destroy (v)
sakiz mastic, an aromatic resin used as chewing gum in Turkey
sako bag; sako de juta bag of jute; sack of jute
sakrifikador someone who makes sacrifices
sakrifikar sacrifice (v)
sakrifisyo sacrifice (n)
sakrilejyo sacrilege; a deficiency, a wanting, a crime, a delict, a breach
    against the veneration owed to the divinity; grave infraction of
    the cult
sakrosankto sacrosanct; very holy; doubly holy
sakudida shaking
sakudidero tendency of a housewife, eager as she is to maintain clean-
    liness, to proceed excessive housecleaning
sakudido very thorough cleaning of the house, of any premises; very
    meticulous revision (inventory) of a pocket's contents, of a furniture,
    for the purpose of cleanliness, removing the rubbish, rearrangement;
    drastic purging of the digestive system; fazer sakudido to do
    thorough housecleaning to get rid of everything that is cumbersome

sakudidor duster; feather duster; fascicle, bundle of feathers, rush, horsehair used to beat on furniture, carpets or clothes in order to dislodge the dust

sakudir shake (v)

sakula pouch, wallet

sal de la arca come out of the Ark (imp)

sal go forth

sal salt (n); **sal i pimienta** salt and pepper

sala hall; living room; sitting room; lounge

salada/salata salad

saladado paid, acquitted

saladiko a little too salty; a little too expensive, of a price overblown; what leads to excess expenses; **kuento saladiko** note, addition, invoice presenting an amount deliberately exaggerated; an outrageous price

saladura action of salting, of adding salt

salam whole, without any break or crack, in good condition, healthy; out of danger; safe, wholly secure; honest, one in whom trust can be placed without reservation (T *saghlam*)

salamalek excessive compliments, exaggerated demonstrations of politeness and the currency with the afterthought of leading astray, of obsequious but insincere courtesy (Arabic *selam aleyk*)

salamalikero obsequious person who spends himself on compliments, attentions and demonstrations of courtesy

salamandra stove with continuous fire

salameria retail shop of salami

salamerias cuddling, exaggerated demonstrations of respect, consideration,, affection; obsequiousness

salamero flatterer; cuddler; one who bows and scrapes, obsequious; trader in meat products

salami/salama salami; sausage of coarsely ground meat seasoned with garlic

Salamon adalari the Salamon Islands, a jocular name given to the Prince Island, in the northern Sea of Marmara, southeast of Istanbul, primarily the second Burgaz and the fourth Büyükada, because they are a favorite resort of Jewish summer vacationers

Salamon Bicerano modern Sephardic writer and poet in Judeo-Spanish

Salamon popular designation of the Jew in Turkish language and cartoons, its female counterpart is Rashel

salamura marinade

salana salana (adv); in all good faith; without any afterthought;
     without the slightest shadow of malice; **fazer salana salana** speak
     candidly, without any ambiguities
salaná slaughterhouse (from T *salhane*)
salaryo salary
salata salad; aki va salir salata (lit) here the salad will come out; (fig)
     the things will degenerate in quarrel, in fight, brawl, scuffle,
     bloody riot; **salata amestechada** mixed salad; **salata di gijon
     blanco** white bean salad; **salata di fijon vedre** green bean salad;
     salata di mirindjgena eggplant salad; **salata di pipino** cucumber
     salad; **salata di tchukundur** beet salad
salatyera set to prepare a salad (oil, vinegar, salt, pepper)
salchicha/salsicha sausage
salchicheria butcher, shop of meat products
salchichero butcher, dealer in meat products
saldar pay; acquit (v)
saldran - (y reyes de ti) saldran and kings will come from you (Fer Bib
     Gen)
salep a starchy, demulcent drug or foodstuff consisting of the dry
     tubers of certain orchids, particularly from the root of *Orchis
     mascula* (the word entered the English language around 1730-
     1749 from its Turkish origin); hot drink made from the product
     of this root; (vulg) sperm, a spot of dried sperm
saleptchi merchant of salep
salgan - (ke) salgan afuera let them go out; **salgas** may you go out
salid come out (imp)
salida diarrhea
salida exit (n)
salidura going out; exit (Salonica Pessach Siddur)
saliente going out
salieron they went out
salio went out; (le) **salio piyango** one who has won the lottery; (el que)
     salira the one who will leave, who will come out
salir go out
salisudo the three substantial meals which are taken to honor the Sab-
     bath, particularly the third one which takes place between noon
     and the closing of the holy day, before sunset and the apparition
     of the first star (ordinarily this meal consisted of an abundant
     salad embellished with salted fish and hard boiled eggs)
salmo psalm

salon drawing room, parlor (F)
Salonik/Saloniko Salonica
salonisyano Salonician
saltabico grasshopper; satirically one who is jumpy like a grasshopper
saltàdech skipped
saltampyes grasshopper, cricket also called *langosta*; very mobile
person who moves at any moment, who does not stay in place,
superficial person, inconstant who has no continuity in his
actions, talks and tasks he undertakes
saltanat ostentation; pomp, spectacular demonstration of riches,
opulence and power; sovereignty, authority, dominion, rule and
magnificence; rule and power of the sultanate (T)
saltar jump; pass over
saltimbanki acrobat, circus-rider
saltô passed over
salud health
saludar salute (v)
saludas you salute
saludavyendo if health permits
saluo but; except
salvador savior
salvaje savage
salvajeria savagery
salvar save (v); salvar (se) save oneself (v)
salvo only; except
salvu except (Monastir dialect)
salyera - (para ke) salyera so that it would come out
salyo just came out; went out on the road
sam ha-navet poison (n, H kanunn)
samán hay (Monastir dialect)
saman straw (T kanunn)
samanalti (lit from T under the hay); perfidious; sneaky
samára/samarra/samárra fur, fur coat, also called *kürk* (from T *semer*
pack-saddle)
samas(s)/samaz/sammaz/sammas de la Keila synagogue beadle
sammasa surplus light in the lamp holder of Hanukkah, in the
menorah of Hanukkah; the eighth flame is kept alight all the
seven days that the holiday lasts, while the seven other regular
luminaries burn one the first day, two the second day, three the
third day and so forth...

samovar samovar

samsada sort of fritter stuffed with crushed almonds kneaded in honey and aromatized with cinnamon

samsadikas small pies covered with phylo dough

samur fur of sable; ornamental garnish of the mantle of very Oriental citizen (Muslim or Jewish)

sanabukata take this, take this thrashing (T *al sana bu kadar:* take for you so much); dar a sanabukata administer a thrashing; hit without pity

sanador healer

sanane? interrogation marked with disdain: what does it have to do with you, why do you care about it, what is it to you? (T)

sanar heal, cure (v)

sanatoryo sanatorium

sandal sandal

sandareta disorderly young girl, in perpetual aimless motion, moving for futile motives or even no motive; superficial and impulsive girl

sanduka sarcophag; tomb in the shape of a crate, made of tiles or in stone and covered by a slab bearing funeral inscriptions; coffin with artistic moldings

sandvich/sanvich sandwich (Engl)

sanedrin/sanhedrin sanhedrin; superior court which previously resided in Jerusalem; assembly of notables and spiritual luminaries holding exceptional authority to render decisions on the religious, juridical and moral tenets of Judaism

sanfason without any mannerism, done without any special preparation, as it comes, without ceremony, in all familiarity; unpretentiously; informally; without any ceremony (F *sans façon*)

sanginaryo violent; bloodthirsty

sangluo hiccup

sangradura action of bloodletting

sangrar draw blood by opening the veins, a kind of ancient therapy (v)

sangre blood

sangreficio/sakrifisyo sacrifice

sangre-fria mastery of oneself; calm in front of danger; cold-blooded; cool

sangres bloods

sangrudo sympathetic; beautiful; seductive

sangruto/sangluto hick up

sania wreath; anger

sankyi (adv) as if, as if one would say (T *sanki*)

sanmaz beadle, caretaker of synagogue

sano healthy; sano i bivo healthy and alive

sansasyon sensation

Santa Kavza Holy Cause

santed sanctuary

santo saintly; El Santo Benditcho (The) Most Holy, blessed be He

Santral Telephone Central, operator in charge

Santuvario temple, sanctuary

sapateta shoe down at heel, to be discarded as scrap, worn out

sapato(s) shoe(s); slippers

sapiacho person, specially woman, ragged, straggling, without character and dignity

sapyo (adj) rotten; with cavities; hollow, dried out object; un fruto sapyo a fruit rotten from the interior

saque produced; que to saque de Ur who made you leave Ur (Fer Bib Gen)

sar fear (n); tener sar to be afraid

sar(r)af money-changer (T *sarraf*, kanunn)

sar(r)aflik profession of a money-changer (T *sarraflik*, kanunn)

Sara Sarah (Abraham's wife); Afligio la Sara Sarah therefore mistreated her (Agar thus mistreated her)

saradear la toka wrap on the head, around the *toka* (headgear of high ranking rabbis) along band of tissue

saradear surround; ring; wrap around the body or the head (T *sarmak*)

saragosi related to Saragossa, inhabitant of Saragossa (The inhabitants of Syracuse (Sicily) are also called *saragosi* instead of *sarakuzanos*.) The families originating from both Saragossa and Syracuse had all the *alcuna/alcunia* (last name) of Saragossi throughout the Orient.

saraguellos breeches, flap of trousers crudely held in position (ironically said about drawers, underpants poorly fixed in place on the back); (drawers and breeches poorly held or falling were a matter of good-hearted humor and a common joke among the Sephardim); la kaza de saraguellos this person is so miserable to the point of not being able to hold his drawers in place; he is deprived of all know-how, of all experience. The expression *no se save atar las bragas* meaning he does not know how to tie his breeches is used in the same sense.

Sarampion/sarampyon measles

saranda le demando penenda le dio he was asked forty for a merchandise, and, he stupidly offered fifty (said about a naive person who lets himself be fooled)

saray/sarray/seraglio, palace (T)

sardela sardine; very thin person, lean, slender giving the impression of not being able to hold on his/her legs

sare wood, forest (Monastir dialect)

sarear surround, envelop (v, T *sarmak*)

sarikli turbaned; Muslim ecclesiastic (cleric) wearing a turban

sarilik jaundice (T)

sarjado scratched, grazed, scraped to the point of bleeding

sarlâr go forth (v); (ansi) **sarlan con grande ganancia** thus they will go forth with great gain

sarna mange; boils; obsessed, demanding individual with acrimony and rapacity

sarnozo afflicted by mange; a poor wretch, a nothing who deserves no consideration

sarnudadero persistent continuous sneezing

sarnudar sneeze (v)

sarnudo sneeze (n)

sarpicár sprinkle (v)

sarsiça sausage

sartén frying pan

saserdote priest, minister of a cult

satán satan; the devil

sataneria diabolic action

satí kordón chain with watch (T *saat* watch)

satisfaksyon satisfaction

satisfazer satisfy (v)

sava testament; last will; advice given, recommendation given to his close ones by a dying person, by a person advanced in age (H *tzava*); dar sava leave to his close ones, before dying, certain principles, certain recommendations to which they owe to conform themselves with devotion

savaná sheet; bed sheet

save knows

saveduria knowledge

saver savras know you will know (Salonica Pessach Siddur)

saver know

saverisyo knowledge used in a tricky way, like in order to create misin-
     formation
savesh - no savesh you don't know
savientes knowledgeable
savio/savyo wise son; knowledgeable; scientist
savor flavor, taste(n)
savoreador wine sampler, tester
savroziko (adj) charming, gracious, seductive (speaking of a person); es
     morenika savrozika she is a beautiful, charming brunette
savrózo/savrozo tasty
sáyo men's costume robe, also called *entari*; outer coat dress in
     costume of married Sephardic women of Salonika (Gr *saias*)
sayóla inner skirt
sayran animated scene; altercation, dispute; risible spectacle; subject of
     entertainment for the mocking witness in the case of those who
     become the prey of gawders (T *seyran*); dar sayran give oneself
     in spectacle
sayrandji person who takes malicious pleasure in watching quarrels,
     brawls, the making of hair fly out, the tearing of hair out
schlemelach innard pilaf, a sumptuous and variegated pilaf with
     baby lamb or veal sweetbreads, hearts, lungs, kidneys
     and liver
se him; it; itself
sea let it be; sea Talmud agar pooch de agues please take a little water
     (Fer Bib Gen)
sebax morning; the morning after the wedding night (T *sabah*)
sebeb/sebep determinant cause, motive (T)
seca drought
secarse dry oneself (v)
secento sixth
seco dry; (por lo seco) on dry land (from Passover Haggadah)
secreto secret (n)
sectaryo sectarian
sed be (imperative)
sed thirst; amatar la sed quench the thirst
seda silk
sedaka alm, charity (H,T)
sede thirst
sedef mother-of-pearl (T)

seder symbolic commemorative ceremony of the deliverance from slavery in Egypt, celebrated before the meal on the first and second nights of Passover

sediente thirsty

Sedom Sodom

sedro cedar

seduta session, reunion of a committee, of a council (Ital)

seer being

Sefarad Spain

Sefaradi/Sefardi Sephardic

sefardiso Jews coming from Iberian countries, dispersed in the Middle East, in Europe and America; demography, history and customs relating to Jews from Spain and Portugal.

sefte first stroke of business; first sale of a commodity; good luck wish related to (from T *siftah*) such first stroke

seguinte following; next; (el dia) seguinte next day

seguita continuity, consequence, succession of; retinue, trail of

segundo second (adj)

segurador insurer

seguramente surely, for sure, without any doubt

seguransa safety, reliability, surety; firmness; certitude

seguridad security, confidence, peace of mind of one who knows that he is sheltered from any attack, from any surprise

segurita/sigorta security, ensemble of precautions taken to avoid an unfortunate surprise; insurance company

seguritadji/sigortadji insurance man, insurance agent

seguro secure, sure, safe, certain, firm

séhel intelligence

sehiyanu/shehiyanu word of benediction pronounced when for the first time of life or the first time of a season an early produce, the first of something is tasted. The same benediction is pronounced when something exceptionally admirable is contemplated. The wording of the benediction is such: "Lord, blessed is Thy name to have allowed us to assist at this happy moment."

sehora sadness, sorrow

seicentos six hundred

seja eyebrow

sejade prayer rug; small carpet (T *seccade*)

sejen six

seka drought; **seka la kabesa** dry head; **la seka** (lit) the one who is dried up, whithered, fem.; (fig) mother-in-law instead of *suegra* (a common Sephardic practice of word transformation with humorous or malicious intent).

sekana danger, peril, distress (H)

sekar dry (v)

sekera drought

seko dry (adj)

sekondo second (adj)

sekreto secret

sekso sex

seksto sixth

sekstuple sextuple

seksual sexual

sekta sect

sektarismo sectarianism, fanatism

sektor sector

sekuestrador sequesterer

sekuestrar sequester (v)

sekuestrasyon sequestration

sekura dryness

selamet deliverance; salute (T); **salir a selamet** escape a desperate situation

selamlik in Muslim houses, the apartment reserved to men, by opposition to *haremlik*, the apartments reserved to women; imperial Ottoman ceremony of Friday (Muslim day of rest) in which the Sultan in great pomp would go to the mosque to make his devotions.

selar (se) to be jealous

selarse be jealous of

selebrado celebrated

selebrar celebrate (v)

selebrasyon celebration

selévro/serebro brain

selimiye a kind of brocade characterized by stripes and intertwined flowering branches; woven in Selimiye (site of the famous military barracks on the Asiatic shore of Istanbul); used for women's *entaris* (dresses, skirts)

sello seal (n)

selo jealousy

seloza jealous (woman) (adj)
selozo jealous, envious; characteristic of fiancé, husband or lover who
    jealously watches his woman, keeps an eye on her
selula cell; selula familial cell; selula humana human cell
semana week; semana buena (greeting) good week
semanada duration of a week
semanadika duration of a week passed in trance or anxiety; benevolent
    salary, gift, weekly pocket money appreciated as a good deed, a
    privilege by the person receiving it and envied by others.
semanal weekly
semanero person on a weekly pay, beneficiary of a weekly salary
sembrado sowing, sowing season, sowed field
sembrador someone who sows
sembradura action of sowing; sowing
sembrar sow, plant (v)
sembultura general aspect of a person, appearance, vision one has of a
    person
semeja similar
semejança similarity
semejante similar
semen race
sémen semen; seed; posterity
semiente seed
semiha ordination of a rabbi (H)
semita Semite
semitiko Semitic; referring to the Semitic race
semitismo ensemble of people speaking a Semitic language; everything
    that relates to the populations of Semitic race (abusively,
    everything that relates to Jews)
semola flour; flour of wheat, generally millet; flour of quality wheat
    preserved from all fermentation with which the pancakes of
    semura (pascal bread) are prepared.
sempatika(o) sympathetic (fem, masc)
sempiterno eternal; everlasting
sempleza simplicity
sémplice simple, plain (Monastir dialect)
semplice simple, uncomplicated; with no mixture; with no affectation,
    with no excess mannerism; natural (Ital)
semplifikasyon simplification
semplifilar simplify

semplisita simplicity

semura - espartir la semura partake a piece of good fortune among the privileged, the favorites, in disregard of all justice, by abuse, by prevarication

semura pascal bread prepared with flour preserved from all humidity; boyo de semura compact cake, pancake, made of semolina without leavening, with which the three *bokados* (mouthfuls, made of a lettuce leaf surrounding a piece of kneaded bread without leavening) are prepared at the symbolic ceremony of the first Passover night. The *boyos de semura* represent the bricks and the rubble stones handled by the Israelites when they were slave labors building the fortresses of the Pharaohs.

seña gesture

sena meal; (El Gran Rabino de Edirne Becerano y Atatürk) senaron encuntos The Grand Rabbi of Edirne Becerano and Atatürk shared a meal together (from Avraham Galante, *Türkler ve Yahudiler*, annex) (The Turks and the Jews) section on Atatürk and the Jews).

señal sign

señales signals

señas signs; motions of the hands, the fingers, the face, the lips to which is attributed a more or less conventional meaning

sencia/syensya science

sencillamente plainly; simply

sene adarim double month of Adar on certain years, as determined by the Hebrew calendar, which thereby counts thirteen months instead of twelve (Hebrew months are based on the phases of the moon which start again every twenty nine and a half days, thus twelve lunar months correspond to 354 days; to establish a coincidence between the lunar and solar years, with a nineteen-year cycle, seven months of a second Adar are intercalated).

senectud senescence; old age

sened procuration (T *senet*, kanunn)

seniza ash

senizero ashtray

seno breast

señor senior

señoron Grand Senior

sensasyon sensation

sensasyonal sensational

sensen tiny pastille of licorice which is sucked to freshen the breath
senserita sincerity
sensia science; sensia de la vida life sciences
sensio sense; buen sensio common sense; sensios artistikos artistic
     sense
sensivilidad sensibility
sensivle sensitive
senso sense; significance; el senso de un byervo the meaning of a word;
     goal, reason, motive
sensor censor
sensura censure (n)
sensurar censure (v)
sensya science; sensyas sciences
sensyudo scientist
sentenciár sentence (v)
senteya sparkle (n)
sentimiento sentiment
sentir feel (v)
sentir hear; feel (v)
sentirse feel oneself (v); sentirse obligado feel oneself obliged
sentro center
sepet basket; trunk; dowry trunk (also called *baul, forsel, kasha*) usu-
     ally wickerwork (T *sepet*)
sepet havasi last music played to signal to the guests the end of a party
     or a dance
sepetlemek get rid of a person or a request; get rid of a tiresome
     person; to sack, dismiss
septembro September
septentrionon septentrion
ser be
sera will be
serado closed
seraser compound weave, gold and silver cloth product of the imperial
     Ottoman workshops in Istanbul (T)
serbest free (adj, T)
serbestlik freedom (T)
sereal cereal
seréis you will be
seremonia ceremony; seremonia de uzo customary ceremony
seremonya ceremony

seremonyozo ceremonial, obsequious
sereza cherry
sergerde chief (T kanunn)
sergi order for payment of money from a public office (T kanunn)
sergun banishment; exile (T *sürgün*)
seria would be
serioso/seryozo serious; to whom importance must be given
serka close (adj)
serkano close one; relative
serkano close to, near (adv)
serklo circle
serme/sermaye capital (financial, T)
serpid grow and multiply in all abundance (imp, Fer Bib Gen)
serpiente producer
serpieron they produced (Fer Bib Gen)
serrado closed
serradura closing; lock; (ora de la) serradura closing time
serrar close (v)
serro- (ke) serro who closed
serseri vagabond, drifter, bum (T)
servicio bondage; service
servidor servant
serviente servant
servir serve (v)
servis service; neck; nape of the neck; (anatomy and gynecology)
    female cervix
servisio service; servisio del laboratuar de la polisia service of the
    police laboratory
seryo seriousness
seryozo serious
sesenta sixty
sesentaiyeh sixtieth
sesh six; a la sesh at six o'clock; a la sesh i media at six and a half
sessenia unleavened bread (from Salonica's Passover Haggadah)
setenta seventy
setentaiyen seventh
sevai patterned silk material used for women's clothes (T *sevayi*)
sevoya onion
sexomania sexomania
sexo sex

sey bendiçion you will be blessed

seya be it

séyida - (fue) séyida en being upon something

seyido - para ke seyas séyido so that you may be

seys six (Ferrara Siddur)

sezo brain

sezudo person with very dense, bushy eyebrows

sezudo sensible, reasonable, cautious

sfacato shameless, wild; deprived of any feeling of shame; agitated, disturbing, tumultuous; insolent (Ital *sfacciato*)

sfongo spinach with cheese

sfongos Judeo-Spanish Passover dish, baked spinach topped with flattened hemispheres of mashed potato-egg mix with grated cheese

sfueñiziko a short moment of sweet sleep; **fazer un sfueñiziko** furtively doze, surreptitiously doze

sha apocope let us see, let me see (the last letter of the word *desha* is contracted)

shabatu February (Bab)

sha vere let us see a little, let me see

shaare door of light; reason for hope, the light at the end of the tunnel; (H); **shaare or ve shaare beraha** altercation; reprimand; uninterrupted series of violent reproaches; **avre la boka i disho shaare/veshaare beraha** he opened the mouth and erupted into a volcano of accusations and insults

shabat Saturday; weekly day of rest

shabsal stunned, dazed, scatterbrained, idiot, moron, stupefied

shaday good, powerful; six pointed star; King Solomon's seal; jewelry (pendant), primarily in gold, shaped as a six-pointed star and holding the name of God (H)

shadrivan water reservoir, water depot, water fountain; tank of water with a jet in the middle; fountain from which come out water jets which rise in the air; tank attached to mosques for ablutions (T *shadirvan*)

shaed witness (T *shahit*)

shaedlik witnessing

shairit morning prayer (H)

shaka chronic migraine

shaka joke; light pleasantry; practical joke, prank (from T *shaka*)

shakadji joker, prankster

shakera trick, hoax; hazing; bullying

shakikera headband which is tightened on the forehead in an attempt to calm the migraine

shakular- (azer) shakular-makulas joke, tell a joke from T *shaka* (joke); an imitation of the Turkish practice of nonsensical rhyming known as *mühleme*, literally 'meaningless words')

shakureko vague, uncertain

shal/shali shawl, especially a cashmere shawl, homespun woolen cloth made of cashmere goat wool, camlet, alpaca (T *shal/shali*)

shaliah messenger, collector of alms for the Holy Land; delegate sent to countries worldwide to collect money for the religious community in Jerusalem; somebody dressed like a *shaliah* with too broad sleeves and ill-fitting winged toga or clothes (ironical)

shalom peace; **shalom beraha ve tova** peace upon you; benediction and abundance; **shalom el aguador** legendary personage whose profession was to supply households with water drawn from public fountains or mountain springs (This personage was imagined to be a poor devil of a guy, with miserable aspect, always dripping sweat and water).

shalvar(es) Turkish baggy trousers (T)

shalvarliya woman wearing a *shalvar* (Turkish baggy pants); the *liparidas* (a highly praised small dry fish eaten by the dozens, a highly appreciated delicacy of the Sephardim) when they are swollen with eggbags are called *havyarliya* (full of caviar) *shalvarliya*.

sham alaca satin from Damascus, striped silk and cotton material used for men's robes

shamalaga embroidered tissue manufactured originally in Damascus; tissue with embroideries in vibrant colors

shamandura buoy which is suspended to the external edge of a boat to dampen an eventual shock (T *shamandira*); many purpose word corresponding to a thing, thingamajig, what is his (her) name, what did you call it (a word used to call an object of which the name escapes).

shamar slap in the face, box in the ear (from T *shamar*); whip

shamata great noise, uproar, din, racket, row, commotion, hubbub, tumult. hurly-burly, turmoil (T)

shamatadji a noisy, uproarious person

shamatali noisy, loud, spectacular; impressive with loudly dazzling rags; individual who asserts himself with bad tasting luxury, a great reinforcement of publicity, loud tam-tam noises; flashy, showy; loud

shambabasi a kind of sweet pastry originally from Damascus (T)
shambaklavasi small dry (with no honey syrup) baklava pastry
    originally from Damascus (T)
shambashuga leech
shameziko pastry
shamizikos di fila con cezo puffed cheese triangles; shamizikos di fila
    con carne di picadura di pujo chicken-filled pastry triangles
shamos ver de los ojos let us get pleasure, let us enjoy the occasion of
    rejoicing which has presented itself to us
shamosver apotope, contraction of *deshamosver* let us see, explain
    yourself, defend yourself, show what you know how to do
shantaj blackmail (F *chantage*; francisized T *shantaj*)
shantör blackmailer; (maestro) shantör master blackmail
shanu traka traka fantasy world, fantasy date, very remote period
shap alum, aluminium potassium sulfate used in medicine as an astrin-
    gent and styptic, *i.e.* serving to contract organic tissue, to stop
    bleeding (at the Turkish officer's schools there was a rumor some-
    what jokingly circulated, that *shap* (alum) was added as an anti-
    aphrodisiac to reduce the sexual drive).
sharada charade
sharki song; Oriental melody on a slow tone; travar sharki take a nos-
    talgic pleasure in passionately singing an Oriental song
sharkidji singer
sharlatan charlatan
sharope syrup; kind of sweet made of sugar boiled in water, lightly
    sprinkled with lemon juice, which softens at cooling (very appre-
    ciated in the Orient); (adj) very sweet to the point of becoming
    sickening; person with benevolent manners and a language
    impinged with sweetness; es un sharope de ombre, es sharope he
    is a *sharope* of a man, a sharope, he is a person full of goodness;
    sharope blanco white thick sweet paste, sometimes mastic-
    flavored, often served to guests with a spoon during Passover hol-
    idays; sharope de vishna syrup of griotte (morello) cherry
shasheado confused
shashear confuse; astonish
shashkin taken aback; staggered; astounded; bewildered; confused;
    stupid; hallucinated; disconcerted; dazed
shashut/shashuto cross-eyed, squint-eyed
shashutear squint (v)
shâstre tailor

shavda tasteless, in figurative a boring girl (*e.g. una blonda shavda*, a
     not so glamorous blond)
shavdear render bland, tasteless (a dish, a witty remark, an anecdote)
shavdo bland; insipid; without salt; person with no attraction, no
     charm, no spirits, unappealing
shavdura blandness, tastelessness, insipidity
Shavod Pentacost
shavon soap
shedaka almsgiving (H kanunn)
sheela question asked a Talmud scholar to get a clarification on, to
     resolve a problem of rite, cult, jurisprudence, or a matter of con-
     science (the response to a *sheala* is called a *teshuva*)
shef chief (F *chef*)
Shef de Protokol Chief of Protocol
shehina divina presence, glorious return of the divine presence
     wherever a good action is accomplished, presence which places an
     aura over the saints, the persons of very high virtue, which
     lightens their way and guides their steps; serene rejoicing which
     reigns within a group of saints who accomplish with piety and
     meditation an act of common life, a ritual meal, a family
     gathering in which the ancestor blesses his offspring while they
     stand full of respect, with fervor and emotion.
shehita ritual slaughter
shekel contribution to be paid by every Jew; Israeli currency
sheker sugar (T)
shekerdjilik sweet shop, candy shop, pastry shop; confectioner
shekerleme candied fruit; sugar-plum; doze, nap, a sweet and quick
     nap
shekerli sweetened with sugar; a well sweetened coffee; a gift given in
     supplement to the agreed price
sheliha personage wearing extremely ample and disgraceful clothes (by
     allusion to the very large and long sleeved toga, simulating the
     wings of a pious messenger, which was solemnly worn by him;
     shelihut mission, mandate to be accomplished); round of money
     collection by the *shaliah* throughout the Diaspora (H)
Shelomo Ameleh King Solomon
Shelomo hameleh Solomon the King
shelte/chilte mattress (T *çilte*)
shem name (n); magic name of occult powers; abracadabra; **dezir un
     shem** articulate a fateful word capable of producing a miracle;

execute a task with the magic dexterity of a Houdini, of a conjurer (H); **shem ameforas** name of the Divine Power (H); **Hashem** the Name, God (H); **baruch hashem** blessed be God's name (H)

shema/shemah first word of the Jewish faith creed which solemnly asserts the divine unity, which also serves to designate this creed itself (H); **saver komo la shemah** know perfectly; **dezir la shemah** recite the creed which is enunciated as: listen (shemah) Israel, the Lord our God is the only God (Deuter, V-6)

shemata excommunication, major anathema (H)

shemen de fer/shimen di fer railway, ensemble of vehicles which travel over the railways (T adapted from F *chemin de fer*)

shemura flour conserved away from humidity since the harvest, from which are made the three biscuits without leavening which will serve in the celebration of the Passover ceremony to represent the bricks that the Israelites had to manipulate when they were constructing fortifications of the Pharaohs as slaves in Egypt.

shena scene of a theater play; entertaining spectacle; **asistir a uns shena** watch an incident with a curious eye (quarrel, accident); **fazer shena a uno** look for a fight with someone, make a scene; theater scene where the action takes place

shenaryo scenario

Sherez Serrez, town in Macedonia

Sherezli inhabitant or native of Serrez; what is related to Serrez

sherilop person without character, versatile, whimsical; person which changes opinion all the time; person who has no fixity in conduct, in relations; person with no *esprit de suite* (continuity in following up a thought or a task)

sheringa syringe (T *shiringa*)

sherit ribbon, very narrow ribbon, strip, cordonnet, shoelace; tape, belt, film; tapeworm (T)

shesenta sixty

shesentos six hundred

shesh besh dice game; very hazardous enterprise; **echar shesh besh** adventure oneself in a very hazardous enterprise; be very anxious about the outcome of a certain matter

shesherear disturb; give vertigo; make one go off the deep end; make one lose his marbles (from T *shashmak*)

sheshereo vertigo (from T *shashirmak* get confused)

sheshereos dizziness; dizzy spells (F *suvieron*); **sheshereos** he felt dizzy

sheshit variety, assortment (T *çeshit*)

shete lashon (lit) seven tongues; (fig) person who by calculation presents a fact sometimes in one way sometimes in another way according to his interest of the moment; opportunist

shevat (H) February

sheytan devil, Satan; crafty man; sharp little devil (from T *sheytan* devil)

sheytaneria craftiness, skill; cunning (synonymous *guerkeria*)

shifro number

shilvane attic, loft, loge (masonry) garret, gallet, spall (a chip or splinter as of stone or ore); a hole, miserable lodging; (from T *shirvane* miserable lodging, Gypsy's lodging)

shimata uproar (T *shamata*, kanunn)

shimén di fer train (Monastir dialect, T *shimendifer*)

shinana ostentatious, noisy luxury; tralala (affectation to look for great pomp); aim to strike someone's fancy; décor, decoration of facade to the effect of creating a sensation, astonishment, amazement, to provoke the admiration of people with a superficial mind

shinanali spectacular, flashy, of noisy luxury

shiñon bun

shirit tape, ribbon, trimming (T *sherit*)

shirito superficial, impulsive young girl who continuously changes her mind; featherbrain

shirma gold thread

shirta ferta so-so; jogging along; **shirta firta ya pasamos el dia** so-so, we have been able to provide for our needs of the day

shish skewers, spit

shisko fat, obese (T, implies a kind of benign irony)

shkola school (Serbo-Croatian Judeo-Spanish)

Shoa Holocaust (H)

shofar ram horn used at the synagogue in the course of certain solemn services: Kippur, Roshashana, public prayers (Primitively it was used as a call for gathering in case of war, for a grave proclamation, in the year of the jubilee to call for the restoration to the original owners of sold property, for the liberation of slaves.) The walls of Jericho crumbled at the resounding of the shofar.

shohad bribe (n, H kanunn)

shohet ritual slaughterer

shojad bribe (n)

shomer guard
shonda urinary catheter
shop Albanian; synomym for: very stubborn person
shorbet/shurbet sherbet (T *sherbet*)
shoret errant (downright, thorough, notorious, utter, confirmed,
     flagrant) liar; mythomaniac
shube branch of an office (T *shube*); dordundju shube Turkish political
     police, Turkish bureau of political investigation with its notorious
     office at a location in the Eminönü district part the south end of
     the Galata Bridge and the famous New Mosque (Yenicami),
     equivalent to the British intelligence service, American CIA,
     French Deuxième Bureau (T *dördüncü* Shube)
shube doubt, suspicion; dar shube/meter en shube give cause, motive
     to suspicion (T *shüphe*)
shubeleado taken by doubt, disturbed by doubt
shubelear doubt, suspect; inspire suspicion (v)
shubeli doubtful, suspicious (T *shüpheli*)
shubesiz devoid of doubt; certain; without any doubt; well understood;
     certainly (T *shüphesiz*)
shubu (adv) immediately; *illico e presto* (right away, instantly, pronto);
     without any delay; as said as done
shueelika small axe, hatchet; exclamation which expresses that one
     interminably persists in demanding a thing in spite of all common
     sense
shueliko- mos kansimos a darle a entender ke no ay lo ke demanda.
     Shueliko! no matter how we explain to him that what he
     demands cannot be done, does not exist. Wasted effort, waste of
     time!
shuki- (tomar al) shuki make fun of
shukyur (adv) Thank God! God be blessed!
shunniko e munniko any people who do not interest us at all;
     unknown people; any kind of uninteresting guy or chap
shunrada resounding failure
shunrra (vulg) male organ
shurut conditions, articles of an agreement (T *kanunn*)
shushika strongly spiced small sausage which is broiled on a spit
shushunera - dar shushunera provoke an urgent and pressing need to
     go to the bathroom; evoke a sudden feeling of fear; le tomo
     shushunera he was ceased by terror
shushunera/shushurella diarrhea

shushurrear blabber tirelessly (v)

shushushu onomatopoeia; **estar shushushu** speak very longly and at
loud voice; blabber untiringly; **azer shushushu mushushu** to
whisper [heard in Bulgaria; this expression uses an onomatopoetic
form probably coming from the Turkish *Sus!* (Be quiet!), or from
the Bulgarian *susna* (to whisper, to murmur); it is an example of
imitation in Judeo-Spanish of the Turkish nonsensical rhyming].

shwenjiziko nap (n)

si him; they

si if; **si (mos quitava) de Ayifto** if He had brought us forth from Egypt
(from the Passover Haggadah); **si no azia en eyos justicia** if he
had not inflicted judgment upon them (the Egyptians), from the
Haggadah

sia chair; **sia para sirkunsir** circumcision chair

siar saw (v)

siaset (azerlo) punish, put to death (T *siyaset*, kanunn)

siaset ashikâri place of public execution (T kanunn)

siatranu thing (Port *sicrano*)

sibdad city

sidjil very intense cold which obstructs the nostrils and hinders the respiration

siedra left, left side

siedra saw (n)

siega blind (fem)

siego blind (masc)

sielo sky; **(los) sielos** the skies

siempre forever; always

sien hundred

siendo asi being it so

sienpre/siempre always

sientar listen (v); **(se) siente** one hears; **sienten un ruido** they hear a
noise; **(no se) sienten engajados** they do not feel themselves
engaged

sientezimo - **un sientezimo** one hundredth

sierpan let them produce, let them multiply

sierpe reptile

sierpén who crawl like serpents

sierpid grow in all abundance (imp)

sierta - **(una) sierta kuantita** a certain quantity; **siertas kozas** certain
things, some things; **siertas mesuras** certain measures

sierto certain, some; **fin un sierto grado** until a certain degree
sieruo slave (Ferrara Siddur)
siervo slave
siete seven
siglo century
signal sign (n)
signo sign (n)
Signor Lord
sigorita insurance company
sigorta insurance (T)
sigortadji insurance agent (T *sigortaci*)
sigun according to
sigunda(o) second (fem, masc)
siguramente certainly; surely
sigurita insurance
siguritad security; **medidas de siguridad** security measures
siguro certain; sure
siim sign, symbol (T *sim*, kanunn)
sikatriz/sikatriza scar (n)
sikinti tension; boredom; oppressive feeling (T)
sikishear (vulg) copulate; abandon oneself to sexual excess; run after
    the skirt (T *sikishmek*)
siklear tighten; grab tightly; **siklear la cintura** tighten the belt
    (T *sikmak*)
siklearse experience boredom in isolation, idleness, in the absence of
    agreeable occupation, of any entertainment, any diversion; get
    vividly preoccupied with a hitch, a mishap, a disturbing problem;
    get worried
siksheo (vulg) life of debauchery; past time devoted to licentious
    practices
siktir! (vulg) go to hell!
siktirear (T, vulgar, Judeo-Spanishized verb) repel with disgust, send
    to hell
sikyime! (inter, very vulg) I do not give a darn about it! I do not care!
    I don't give a rap! I don't give a hoot! (T *sikimi ye* eat my penis)
silensyo silence
silensyozo silent
silla seat; chair (Ferrara Siddur)
silla throne (Ladino Bible of Ferrara, Kings)
silueta silhouette; outline

sim wire, tinsel used in embroidery
sima top; summit; en sima over, on top
siman sign; mark; symptom; omen; prognostic (H)
simánu June (Bab)
simantov good sign; good omen (H)
simbultura appearance, aspect of a person (usually negative); confuse
    appearance, fleeting shadow, furtive, phantastic apparition; se le
    ve la simbultura at long last we see the face of this ungrateful,
    forgetful person who obstinately neglects to show up, to make an
    apparition, to pay a visit
simeteryo cemetery; simeteryo de Hasköy historical cemetery of
    Hasköy near the similarly named old Jewish quarter in the
    Golden Horn. The experience of Jewish inhabitants of that
    neighborhood were often very contradictory: on one hand,
    Jewish visitors to the cemetery were greeted at the little café
    near the Golden Horn ferry by old-fashioned, kind-hearted
    Turkish gentlemen, who were ready to offer them Turkish coffee
    with a piece of Turkish delight *(lokum)*; on the other hand, the
    cemetery with its old, often overturned tombstones was a favorite
    hangout of children and teenagers from nearby neighborhoods,
    who threatened to throw stones at visitors—mostly Jewish
    women with their children—who had come to the cemetery to
    pay tribute to their ancestors' graves. There were no guards;
    occasionally a cemetery guide would help visitors identify
    the tombs.
Simhat Torat ninth day of the feast of Succoth
simit sort of donut covered with sesame, circular or in the shape of a
    crown which is baked on a metal tray. While the original *simit*
    was eaten hot with halva, currently in Istanbul it is a circular
    sesame covered pastry, sold unheated by street vendors.
simpatia sympathy
simpatiko sympathetic
simpliche simple
simplifikar simplify (v)
simsar broker
simyente seed; semen; grain
sin without
siñal signal
sini tinned copper tray which used to serve as an eating table; it
    was laid on the floor or on top of a low wood support a few

centimeters high around which family members and guests would
sit in a squatting position (T)
sinistre sinister; of bad omen; which causes mourning, affliction; fright
sinistro catastrophe; huge damage resulting from fire, flood, grave
accident, ship sinking, earthquake
siniza ash
sinjap squirrel, squirrel fur (T *sincap*)
sinken fifth
sinkeno fifth of a series
sinko five
sinkuenta fifty
sinkuenten fiftieth
sinkuentena an ensemble of fifty
sino if not without this, if not without that
siñor mister, gentleman, lord (Monastir dialect)
siñoron person who enjoys financial well-being, independence and
who is free of any worry; person who has an affluent lifestyle,
who is comfortably well off
sinserita sincerity (from Latin *sin sera,* without wax, pure like filtered
honey)
sinsero sincere
sinta ribbon
sintir hear, listen (v); la sinti I heard; sintio el kavzo listened to the
case; heard the case; sintio frio frio he felt cold, cold; his all body
was shivering; no te va sintir I will not hear you
sintir/sentir feel (v)
sintura belt
sinuzit sinusitis
sinvervuensa (lit) without shame; shameless; chalky; brazen; insolent
sinyifikasyon signification
sinyor mister; gentleman
sira rank, order, sequence, following, line (of writing) (T *sira* kanunn)
sirade/serrado closed
sircanu close, near (Monastir dialect)
sircuzír circumcise
sirena siren
sirkolar/sirkukar circulate (v)
sirkonstensya circumstance; (una) sirkonstensya mueva a new
circumstance
sirkülasyon circulation

sirma gold wire, brass wire, iron wire, glittering, gleaming, brightly shining metal wire used to adorn a wedding dress and embroideries; lace or embroidery with silver and/or gilt silver thread (T)

sirpier increase abundantly

sirta ferta (adv) so-so; equivalent to the French *comme-ci comme-ça;* it is as good as it is bad; a little more a little less; to be jogging along; so-so (Gr)

siruiente servant (Ferrara Siddur)

siryako Syriac, a Semitic language close to Aramaic, previously spoken in Syria (still spoken in rare villages). All the knowledge of the ancient Greek authors has been summarized in multiple epitomies (abridged version of a book, particularly a history book) written in the Syriac language.

siryo candle; (religious) church candle

sisit woven the twenty six knots of which represent the name of God; the *sisit* is fixed to the four corners of the *talet* (liturgical masculine veil-shaped garment from which one never separates), as an affirmation of the constant presence of God, witness of all actions accomplished during the day (See Numbers XI, 36; Deuteronomy XXII, 12).

sistema system, morality, procedure

sisterna cistern

sistrano (used alone or together with *fulano* somebody) someone, an unidentified, unnamed person; *sistrano* itself means one such person, any person, the first come; **fulano i sistrano se meten de akodro para echar el sako a un mercader** two chaps come to an agreement to take a buyer in, to dupe a buyer

sita satire

situado located, residing; **es situado** resides

situar situate, locate (v)

situasyon situation; **situasyon de** of today's situation

siva rishona the seven fundamental principles of the Jewish religion: 1. Believe in One Unique God; 2. Hold God' Name in great respect, stay away from blasphemy; 3. Do not commit adultery or incest; 4. Do not commit homicide; 5. Do not steal; 6. Do not eat shreds of meat from a beast still fluttering, quivering; 7. Establish laws to govern the relations between humans living in a society, courts to apply these laws; respects these laws and the decisions rendered by the courts

siva the seven days of mourning observed at the death of a close (H)
sivan June (H)
sivdad city
sivdadano citizen
sivdadika small city
sivilizasyon civilization
sivoikas agras dulces sweet and sour onions
siya chair
siyar sit on a chair (v)
siye di cunar stirrer (Monastir dialect)
siyero treasure
skala dock, landing stage, quay, wharf; skala de la lenya dock for dis-
     charging of heating wood; skala de los vapores ship dock; skala
     del estyerkero dock for removing and loading garbage
skapadishu end
skaravajo cockroach
skarlatina scarlet fever
skekerdji vendor, merchant of sugar; vendor of candies
skifo disgust (n); skifozo disgusting
skotura worry, embarrassment, mishap, hitch, trouble (Gr)
skulkarichia/(e)skularichas earring (Gr *skoulariki*; also called *arojales*)
slanchyo run up, boost, momentum, acquired speed, good start made
     with drive, decisively (Ital *slancio*); tomar slanchyo develop
     oneself, be successful, make an useful extension
slavo Slavic
Smirne/Smirna/Izmir Smyrna
smoking tuxedo
Smyrnyote Smirniote, Izmirli inhabitant of Smyrna (Izmir)
snob snob
snobismo snobism
snoga/anoah sort of balcony at the second floor reserved for women
     (this word is a deformation of *synagogue*)
so i mo i Patarich sarcastic proverb to designate a very scattered audi-
     ence, group composed of insignificant persons
soare social gathering in the evening (from F *soirée*)
soba stove (T)
soberrana sovereign
sobrar be in excess (v)
sobre above; on
sobrina niece

sobrino nephew
sobriyedad sobriety
socheta society (Ital *societá*)
soda soda; sodium bicarbonate; seltzer water; seltzer
sodjeftar subjugate, make subject to the rule of, drive into submission
sodjefto submitted, subjugated, enslaved
sodjeto matter which people talk about, on which a study is made (Ital
    sogetto)
sodredad deafness
sodriko a familiar way to say deaf
sodro deaf; (el) Sodro private nickname used between Istanbul
    Sephardim refering to Inonu, the Turkish President of the
    Republic who was reputedly deaf (Muslim Turks were not
    supposed to know)
sof sof finally (H kanunn)
sofa sofa, large couch
sofayfas olive-shaped dry fruit with a brown skin and a powdered
    content around the pit (children's nibbling)
soffle di ceso blanco soufflé of white cheese
sofiguado submitted, dominated, deprived of liberty
soflama ardor of flames; light fever; abatir la soflama make the
    temperature come down by mean of cold compresses
soflamado with congested face; all disturbed and anxious as expressed
    by the congestion of his face
sofra dining table (T)
sofreir fry lightly (v)
sofrito di bitella con limon veal scallopini with lemon
sofrito lighly fried; aliment which has been lightly fried
softa student of Muslim theological school, Muslim seminarian; fanat-
    ical Muslim; blind partisan (supporter) of old, backward customs,
    adversary of any kind of reform and ready to start agitating and
    rioting at the slightest attempt of innovation. At the sadly
    notorious *31 Mart Vakasi* (Event of March 31) in 1909, the
    Softas at the delight of the so-named Red Sultan Abdulhamid II
    were aroused into rioting for the overthrow of the *meshrutiyetçi*
    (Constitutionalist) Young Turk government. They nearly
    succeeded until the constitutionalist army's lightning march from
    Salonica to Istanbul, under the command of Mahmut Shevket
    Pasha which brought the downfall of Sultan Hamid II and his
    exile to Salonica.

sofu devout; very pious; very religious; fanatically religious; minute and rigorous observant of the rites and practices of Islam; fundamentalist

sogeftos sorrow

sograna comb consisting of fine teeth on one side and large teeth on the other

sojet/shohet ritual slaughterer

sojuzgalda subjugated

sokestrar sequester (v)

sokorrer help, rescue (v)

sol sun; (y el) sol se puso (and the) sun set down; (y fue el) sol para ponerse (and as) the sun was setting down (Fer Bib Gen)

solacerse find solace (v)

solamente solely

solar floor

soldado soldier

soledad loneliness

solenidad solemnity

soleta sole

soletina long period of loneliness

solevantado overexcited, brazen, fiery

solevantamyento puffing up, swelling; uprising, revolt

solevantar uplift, heighten, enhance, elevate higher, push to rebellion, riot (v)

solevar uplift (v)

soleziko sun which heats moderately and under which one takes pleasure to expose himself (herself) in winter

solidumbre solitary place, desert; painful feeling of loneliness, anxiety felt in loneliness

solo only; alone; (y) andán solo y hijo (and) I shall go alone without child, I shall remain without child (Fer Bib Gen) solómbra shade, shadow,

soltar abandon (v); (la) solta en bacho he throws her on the floor

solup breath, respiration (T *soluk*)

solüsyon/solusyon solution

sombra shade

someter submit; expose to (v)

somos we are

somportar stand (v); (no puedo mas) somportar mi pasadia I cannot stand my life anymore

son ring (v)
son they are
son voice; (buen) son good voice
soñador dreamer, one who sees dreams, one who imagines, considers,
    imagines that, considers that, reflects, reflects upon, thinks over
soñar (se)/soniar (se) dream (v)
sonar ring (v)
sonase bell, little bell, hawk's bell
sonaza accompaniment
sonbayo has seduced me
sonda probe; sounding line; borer; drill; catheter; feeding tube
sondar probe (v)
soño (se) dreamed
soño dream (n)
sonova doce was ringing twelve o'clock
sonriza smile (n)
sonrizo smile
sontraér to be the cause; generate
sontramiento products generated
sontrayér continue
sopliko supplication
soplo breath
soportar support; tolerate (Ferrara Siddur)
soportar/somportar stand; tolerate (v)
sorear consume with more or less usefulness, spend, make it disappear
    by utilization; waste away (v, T sürmek)
sorer ayehudim persecutor of the Jews, tormentor of the Jews, fierce,
    unremitting enemy of the Jews; fierce Antisemite (H)
sorer persecutor, one who inflicts suffering, torture, hard humiliation
    (H)
soro large quantity, pile, heap, mass of, cluster, pack, bunch, collection
    of; jumble of doctrines, of objects (Gr soros)
sorretar roam, wonder; turn into a farce, into a light comedy (v)
sorretero vagabond, who walks aimlessly and endlessly
sortir go to the bathroom (especially in school language, leave the
    classroom to go to the toilet); (F sortir go out)
sortirse do it in one's pants; wet/soil one's pants
soruntluk scrap, worthless objects which only create clutter; kitar
    soruntluk get rid of scraps which create clutter
sorver swallow, guzzle (v)
sorvetina sniffing, snuffing

sorvido exhausted, tired out, worn out, consumed; slimmed,
   downtrodden; reduced; having lost weight because of deprivations
   or sexual abuses
sorvidor snorer; one who sucks, who draws in liquid with his lips
   while making a light whistle; sniffer; one who hisses, wheezes,
   whistles
sorviko a mouthful, a sip; dar un sorviko take a sip
sospezo suspense (n); what is not achieved, what is not concluded
sospiro sigh (n)
sostansya substance
sosyeta society
sosyolog sociologist
sosyologia sociology
sota/aguas de la sota magical preparation inflicted to the woman sus-
   pected of adultery; death follows if inculpated is guilty; survival
   proves innocence (H); bever las aguas de la sota be submitted to
   perpetual tortures, undergo, suffer a barbaric treatment, be drunk
   of bitterness
sotener support (v)
sotlach rice pudding (T *sütlaç*)
soto (preposition) under (indicates subordination, Ital *sóto*); estar soto
   las ordenes be submitted to the orders; estar soto komando be
   under the command
soto thicket (a thick or dense growth of shrubs, bushes, trees)
soto-director assistant director
sotometer submit, take under his domination (v)
sotoskrito underwritten
sova/siva roughcast, roughcast by overuse; covered by a layer of
   plaster on the wall (T *siva*)
sovadji/sivadji plasterer (T *sivaci*)
soverenedad sovereignty
sovrado unused, leftover which is not needed, in excess
sovralsado magnified, praised to the skies
sovrar to be in excess (v)
sovrar to be in surplus, in excess, surpass the needs (v); ya abasta y
   sovra there is more than needed; there is enough and in excess;
   no me sovra I will have nothing leftover; I need the totality; I
   cannot keep any part for other use
sovre above; on; on top; over; sovre el signo over the sign; sovre los
   cielos above the skies; above the heavens; sovre nos upon us

sovredicho as said before
sovrefaz surface
sovreksitado overexcited
sovrenombre nickname
sovri close to (Monastir dialect)
sovrinado cousin
sovriniko young cousin, little cousin
sovrino (a) nephew, niece
sovrino cousin
soy race, familial extraction (T); **ser de buen soy** born to a good
     family, have good parentage; **es de soy** he is of a good race, he is
     well raced, of a good lineage; **soy de perro/soy de azno/soy negro**
     (insults) race of dog, race of donkey, dirty race; **soy - no dechar**
     soy, no dechar soy sano base insult in booing all the race, by
     going as high as possible in the genealogical tree
soydear ransack, rob, strip bare; sack (v, T *soymak*, kanunn)
soyli of good race, of good extraction
soyma air dried mullet (or other fish) from which the skin is detached
     easily
soysuz individual who is badly born; of bad extraction
soysuza vixen, shrew
soytari buffoon, clown, acrobat (T)
soyzade (lit) in Turkish son of good extraction; of noble lineage; of
     nobility; of great height; one whose high birth is recognized by
     his conduct, retinue, distinguished manners
sozde allegedly, pretending, assumed, so to say, as the others say
     (T *sözde*)
spalda shoulder; back
spanyol Ladino
spanyol/spanyol Spanish, Judeo-Spanish
spanyolit Ladino
sparanga asparagus
spektador spectator
spektakolo spectacle
spektator/spektatör spectator
spetene kamot suffering inflicted to someone (H); **fazer sovre el puerpo**
     de uno spetene kamot make someone sustain the most barbaric ill
     treatments
spina/espina spine; fishbone

spinaka spinach; spinaka con arroz spinach and rice; spinaka con ceso
   al orno baked spinach au gratin
spiritu match (n, Monastir dialect)
spiritu(s) match(es) (Gr *spirto*)
spongdja/espondja sponge
sport sport
sportivo sportive
stá is
stabilidad stability
stabilizado stabilized
stabilizar stabilize (v)
stabilizasyon stabilization
stankar stop water from coming, stop a stream; stem; make
   watertight, waterproof; stop, cease (v)
stanko arrest, suspension
stanlar de favlar stop talking; stankar de riir stop laughing; stankar de
   yorar stop crying
stasjon del shemen de fer railroad station
statistica statistics
stavamos/stavamus we were
stavle stable (n)
steso same (Ital)
stifa row (n)
stifadon (navigational expression) one who stows
stifadura stowing
stifar stow; secure (v)
stilo fountain pen
stilo stomach cramps due to hunger, hunger pangs
stivaleta kick with a boot (n)
stopachada coarse insult; incongruity (Ital *stopacio*)
stosekretaryo undersecretary
stridor/destruidor destroyer
stringar hug; embrace tightly; grip; clutch; tighten; tie while tightening (v)
struimyento/destruimyento de mundo (lit) destruction of the world;
   despair mixed with anger in the face of a disturbing event the
   importance of which is exaggerated
su his; es su bien it is a thing which is his, belongs to him; su solas
   himself alone; (a su) solas from himself alone

su water (T); su parasi water money; charge for water; water fee (T)
subia was going up
subieron they came to know; (he agora a mi dos hijas que no)
   subieron baron (I have two daughters here who still) have not
   known men (Lot about his daughters—Fer Bib Gen)
subir go up; rise
sublime corrosive; very toxic mercury chloride
subordinasyon subordination
subsistenya subsistance
subsistir subsist (v)
subtraksyon subtraction
subvenir meet, cover the needs
sudadero tendency to sweat continuosly
sudado soaked with sweat
sudadura action of sweating; exhaustion resulting from hard work
sudante remedy, potion which provokes sweating
sudar sweat (v)
sudario shroud
sudeste southwest
su-director assistant director
su-direksyon assistant directorship
suditansa subjects; citizenship
sudito subject of a state; citizen
sudjeftos subjects (Salonica Pesach Siddur)
sudor sweat (n)
sudores jelas/yeladas cold sweats
suedyano inhabitant of Sweden
suegra mother-in-law
suelto free of conjugal ties
sueño/suenyo dream
suerte fate, destiny, lot
suetar wish (v, F souhaiter)
suetavle desirable
sueto wish, vow (n)
sufizensya quantity which suffices for a given purpose
sufiziente sufficient
suflo breath, breathing; se el korto el suflo her breathing stopped
sufreir/sofreir fry lightly
sufriensa suffering

sufriente suffering; indisposed, sick
sufrir suffer (v)
sufrito/sofrito lightly fried
sugdjerar suggest (v)
sugdjestyon/sugjestion suggestion
suidji water vendor; vendor who delivers the water jars at home
suisidarse commit suicide (v)
suisidyo suicide
sujesion suggestion
sujetos subjects
suka cabana, hut elevated for the duration of the holiday of Succoth
    and in which family meals are taken. The *suka* is tastefully,
    joyfully and even luxuriously fitted. The walls are decorated with
    tissues, carpets; the make-up of the hut is made of reeds. Every
    part is strewn with foliage and flowers. Within the *suka* reigns an
    air of serenity and joy.
suko, sukot Feast of the Booths
sultan sultan, emperor, ruler of the Ottoman Empire
sultana wife of the sultan
sulu bamya (lit) watery okra; (fig) person who is not serious, person
    who makes statements which are not serious (T)
sulúk breath (from T *soluk*)
suluk leech (T *sülük*)
Sulukule (lit Watery Tower) a neighborhood of Istanbul where one
    can expect to see Gypsy dance shows or even dancing bear
    shows (T)
sulup/soluk breath, respiration (T *soluk*); me se toma el sulup my
    breath gets caught, I cannot breathe
sulvider forget (v); (para ke no te se) sulvide nada so that you don't
    forget anything
suma sum; (grande) suma large sum
sumar add up; totalize (v)
sumetido submitted
sumetir submit (v)
sumisyon submission
sumo juice, sap; sumo no le sale no juice, not even one drop of juice
    comes out of him; extremely stingy
sumozo juicy
sunido sound, noise (Port)

sunned circumcision according to the Muslim rite (T *sünnet*); sunned
   dughunu marriage of a *sunned* person, celebrated in great pomp
   at the occasion of the circumcision of a young Muslim boy
   (T *sünnet düghünü*)
suntansyozo/sostansyozo substantial
supa soup
superfisia surface
supieron que desnudos ellos they knew that they were nude (Adam
   and Eve in the garden of Eden after eaten the forbidden fruit, Fer
   Bib Gen)
supito - (en) supito suddenly
supo he knew; he came to know
suportar support (v)
suporto support
supozar suppose (v)
supozisyon supposition
supplicio torture, agony, torment
supremir/suprimir suppress (v)
supresyon suppression
suprimido suppressed
supuesto assumed, supposed; (en) supuesto assumedly, supposedly
supyera soup bowl
supyerada the full content of a soup bowl
suret form, figure (n, T kanunn)
surgun exile, deportation (T *sürgün* kanunn); forced deportation of
   population by the Ottoman government in the time of Mehmed
   the Conqueror
surgunli someone who goes into exile (T *sürgünlü*, kanunn)
surgunlik place of exile (T, *sürgünlük*, kanunn)
surme lock which closes hermetically (T *sürme*)
surpreza surprise (n)
suruntluk scrap, garbage, sweeping
sus diozes their gods
sus their
sus! hush (T)
susám sesame seeds (T); tajikos de susam sweet, nougat, paté of fruits
   in honey, sprinkled with sesame or ground with sesame and then
   cut in lozenges after baking in the oven
suspirar sigh; gasp (v)

susta notch; security catch
sustansya/sostansya substance
sustentador supporter; sustain
sustentár sustain; support; hold
sustrar subtract (v)
sutliman (lit) milky harbor (T *sütliman*); (fig) situation smoothed; for-
    malities made all easy for one who presents a petition; very
    friendly attitude towards petitioner, dead calm
suvenir souvenir; memory of; object offered as a gift destined to
    remind the recipient person a loved one or a memorable event
suveremos let us go up
suvidero repeated ascension of a stairway untiringly to the great
    annoyance of those witnessing it
suvidiko de color pretty high in color
suvidiko overcooked
suvido al reverso riding backwards (*e.g.* a donkey, like the Turkish
    folkloric hero Nasreddin Hoca, from whom the Sephardim
    invented the legendary Coha)
suvido rising, riding
suvidura augmentation, the part of a salary consisting of the raise; the
    improvement of wages, of remuneration
suvio rode; went up
suvio syetes he blew his stack
suvir go up; rise; gain altitude; rise to depart (v)
suvrindad kinship
suvriniko very young cousin
suvyente riding on horseback; ascending a slope
suvyeron a poko a poko they got up slowly
suyo his; also yours in a polite way instead of *tuyo*, addressing some-
    body in the third person; (este es lo) suyo this is his, this is yours
suyudji water carrier, water porter
suzeni chain stitch embroidery; needle (T)
suziedad dirt; (la) suziedad used for society (a transformation of word
    from *suzio* dirty, a prevalent practice among Sephardim with
    humorous and sometimes malicious intent)
suzio/suzyo dirty, unclean
suzyedad dirt, dirtiness
suzyo dirty
svelto slender

sviserano Swiss

syegamente blindly; the eyes closed; without thinking; without reflection

syegar make blind (v)

syegetina deep darkness; the absolute darkness in which there is no
    landmark, no point of reference to guide one's steps

syego blind (n)

syekolo century

syelo sky

syete seven

syemore/siemore always

syemprebive always lives; immortal (flower; various plants of which
    the little leaves which surround the flower last very long, vine)

syen one hundred

syerpa bad-mouthed, slanderous, scandalmonger, intriguing woman, a
    shrew

syerpa de sete kavesaz shrew with seven heads; bad-tempered, cantan-
    kerous woman, looking for a fight, ready for unfriendly retort,
    full of gall, rancor, spleen, malice (allusion to the hydra of Lerne
    exterminated by Hercules who chopped its seven heads with a
    single stroke)

syerpe i guzano es todo lo ke keda de un puerpo muerto a swarming
    of snakes and worms in a dead body

syerpe snake, serpent, reptile; malicious being

syerpes - estar arrodeado de syerpes be surrounded by fierce, unremit-
    ting enemies

syerrada sharp cut with a saw

syerva hind, doe

syervo deer

syete kandelas (lit) seven candles; the name used by the Jew of Izmir
    for the ceremony of giving a name to a girl; also called *fadas
    tadamyento*

syete seven

sylvestre in the likeness of a savage; like a savage; similar to a savage

T

ta(r)buradji mischief maker; evil culture, bad manners (contracted
    Hebrew phrase *tarbut ra'a.* to which the Turkish-derived Judeo-
    Spanish suffix -*dji*, from T *ci/cu* was added)

taahud obligation (T *taahhüd*, kanunn)

taanid ritual fast

tabaka layer; story, floor of building; level (T); shelf of a cupboard; layer of dust or dirt; kaza de tres tabakas three-floor house

tabako/tobako tobacco (synonymous *tutun*, T *tütün*); snuff tobacco; bragas de tabako puffy drawers made of very coarse drapes which stop at the knees

tabaña tannery, leather-dressing (alum treatment for dressing results in conversion of coarse hides obtained from ship, lamb or kid into a very fine quality leather), tanning workshop or retailer where such leather is sold

tabatyera tobacco case; cigarette case; snuff tobacco case; snuffbox

tabela sign; sign plate

tabernaklo tabernacle; tent under which the Holy Ark of the Alliance was guarded; precious chest in which were enclosed the Tables of the Law brought by Moses from Mount Sinai; sanctuary

tabetu January (Bab)

tabiet/tabiat habit; nature; character of a person (T)

tabietli person who observes good manners without ostentation; ser tabietli maintain oneself in a honorable social rank

tabla - pasear a uno en tabla indiscretely expose someone's intimate things to the malevolent comments of the public; disseminate bad rumors about somebody

tabla tray, large plate in metal, elaborately adorned wood, glass or crystal used to serve tea, coffee, pastries or jam; large tray of the ambulant vendor (ordinarily carried over the head in delicate equilibrium, as a crown on top of a pillow)

tablada contents of a tray

tabladji merchant, vendor in open air

tabur battalion; huge crowd

taburra aberration; lack of reason; deviation; confusion, distraction; madness; being distraught with grief; to go off the deep end; lose his marbles

tachon large spot; stain; estar a tachoness wear clothes visibly covered with stains

tachonor clumsy and negligent person

tadrada de Pesah Passover evening

tadrada evening

tadransa delay, diversion, procrastination, postponement

tadrar to be late (v); venir tadre come late

tadre (adj) late

tadre (n) evening; afternoon

tadrizo late

tafanaryo buttocks, bottom (Ital *tafanario*)

tafaruk eminently opportune; that comes unexpectedly and causes an agreeable surprise

taflan laurel

tafta (adj) of or resembling taffeta (originated from Persian *taftah*, silken or linen cloth)

tafta (n) very thin silk tissue; taffeta (a medium-weight or light-weight fabric of acetate, nylon, rayon or silk, usually smooth, crisp and lustrous, plain-woven and with a fine crosswise rib effect; any other fabrics of silk, wool, linen in use at different periods)

tahin sesame residue from which the sesame oil is extracted to make halva; tahin i pekmez tahini and thick grape syrup mixture which is used as a dessert

tahsa part of a job assigned to a worker; task

tahtaliman (lit) wood port; harbor; burlesque name of body part on which one sits

tahvil security, commercial bill (T kanunn)

taifa group of men working together on the same task; team

taife trade guilds; tradesman; artisan (also *esnaf, hirfet, rofit*)

tajada entrenched; withdrawn from (fem); seras tajados lest you not perish; (por quanto seras) tajados por delicto de la villa by fear that you do not perish in the punishment that I shall inflict to the city (Fer Bib Gen)

tajador one who massacres, slaughterer; one who slaughters, cuts the cadavers into pieces

tajamyento action of murdering, of committing carnage

tajar slice; cut, prune, sharpen, cut out, cut into pieces; (tambien) tajaras will you make perish as well...

tajiko small piece of fruit, dough, cake; homemade delicacy prepared with almond paste, walnut, all sorts of ground dry fruits, honey, sugar, aromatized with mint, sprinkled with sesame, baked on a fire and then cut into squares

tajikos de almendra/de menta nougat made of almonds and sesame aromatized with mint

tajlij - fazer tajlij repent

tajlij religious ceremony celebrated in a group on the first day of Shavot (Pentacost), on the second if the first day is a Saturday;

the ceremony is held near water (sea, lake, river, water stream).
Among prayers recited, the most special for the ceremony are the
last three verses of the last and seventh chapter of Micah, where
God grants forgiveness for all of the sins which are supposed to
be thrown in the water. At the end of the ceremony the faithful
shake their clothes, by this symbolic gesture letting the sins fall
heavily into the water where they disappear.

tajo fruit slice (melon, watermelon)

tajo treated, made an alliance (*Ladino*)

tajon large slice of cake or fruit

takat various particularities which characterize a person, his physical
aspect (is used only in the expression *no deshar takat sano a
uno*), insult somebody by passing in review all his particularities;
address directly to him or spread on him all kinds of acerbic criti-
cism, invectives, denigrate all the particularities which
characterize him, without allowing him any grace or respite (T).

takatuka unceasing repeated blow enervating for those who listen at
these; hail of blows; (adv) work furiously, without interruption,
with zeal and celerity

takla somersault; tumble; fall; cartwheel (n)

taklear tease; mock; criticize ironically (T *takilmak*)

taklit (adj) fake; (n) imitation; mock someone by imitating, caricaturing
his behavior or attitude; imitation or copy of a valuable object
which it is tried to have pass as the original; counterfeiting (T)

tako heel of a shoe

takos wooden clogs (also called *galechas*)

takrir statement, deposition (T kanunn)

taksa tax

taksador member of a communal commission whose task was to fix
the amount of tax on wealth or capital revenue that had to be
paid by each taxpayer of the community

taksasyon/taksadura taxation

taksi taxi

taksirat damage due to negligence; damage caused by mistake,
inadvertently, by involuntary act

taktika tactic

takto tactfulness; delicacy; knowledge of how to resolve a matter tact-
fully

takum gang, squad of men (T *takim* kanunn); ensemble of effects necessary to clothe someone completely; complete set of clothes;

complete set of jewelry or decorations; couple or pair; **un takum de kamizas** a couple of shirts

takya/takye cap, bonnet; **echar la takya** renounce Judaism by throwing down in a precipitous movement the *takya* used as a Jewish headgear; (in popular language) renounce as the pursuit of non-fruitful effort; admit to having lost, to having been vanquished; cease to persevere in a task that one recognizes is impossible to bring to a satisfactory conclusion; **kitar la takya de uno i meterla a otro** acquit oneself of a debt by borrowing from somebody else; live off of expedients

tal such

talamo/tálamo (Salonican spelling) wedding dais, Jewish weddding canopy

talaro thaler, Austrian gold coin worth a florin which for a long time was a common currency in countries of the Middle East; five drachmas

talash wood scrapings

talega usually for *tefillin* (phylacteries) and *talit* (prayer shawl)

talento talent

talentuozo talented

talet Jewish prayer shawl

talika stagecoach for long displacements

talko talc powder

talmidim disciples; students (H)

talmud tora school of religious teaching maintained in every Jewish community

talmudista scholar studying the Talmud, versed in the knowledge of the Talmud; doctor of Jewish Law, doctor of the Torah, rabbi

talum military exercise; well aligned rank; well disciplined (T *talim*)

tam honest, person of integrity, just, perfect; full of innocence; devoid of any kind of afterthought (T)

tam (n) cream which floats on an alimentary substance and which is allowed to settle down after boiling; oily residue of sesame from which oil was extracted by pressure (from Ottoman T *ta'am/t'am*, food, meal)

tam complete; that is missing nothing; **venir tam a la ora** come to an appointment exactly in time (T)

tamahkyar stingy, avaricious (T)

tamahkyarlik stinginess; avarice (T)

tamam (adj) complete, ready, entirely in order; signal given to indicate that everything is order and that departure can be relied on (for ship, train, car)

tamarino tamarind (fruit known for its' laxative properties)

tambien as well; also; more; equally; too; in surplus; moreover; furthermore

tamburin - fazerse la kavesa un tamburin a scatterbrained person momentarily unable to pursue a reasoning following intense and prolonged intellectual work, abstruse calculations, meticulous research; person deafened by a persistant noise, by interminable volubility and blabber; the buttocks

tamburin drum; large chest; tambourine

tamid oil lamp lit permanently

tammuz July (H)

tan serka so close

tan so much; that much; also

tanda reunion which took place in an annex of the synagogue the Saturday after the morning prayer, to which ordinarily participated the members of the fraternity of inhumation who gave to the dead their last toilet

tandada a round of the cabarets, of the taverns; a round of drinks offered by someone paying for the others

tandu lamb meat roasted over a small fire (T *tandir*)

tane distinct from mass; piece; grain; seed; pip (T)

tane tan in separate grains; one by one (T)

tañedera woman who exerts the profession of musician and sings at family events or ceremonies accompanied by a Basque drum (leather drum equipped with little bells) or a tambourine

tañer play a musical instrument (v)

tango dance, tango

tani/tanid ritual fast

tank tank

tansyon arterial blood pressure

tantasyon/tentasyon temptation

tantativa/tentativa attempt (n)

tantaz oras so many hours

tantéla lace (n, F *dentelle*)

tanti familiar, affectionate word for aunt

tantiko a little bit

tanto/tanta (adj, adv, masc, fem) as much; quantity of same importance as another one to which it is compared; (de) **tanto en kuando** from time to time; (entre) **tantas** among so many talks; (entre) **tantos** among so many; (uno entre) **tantos** one among so many

tanyedor/tañedor tambourine player, drummer, professional musician

Tanzimat the political reforms in the Ottoman Empire in the XIXth century, starting from the *Gülhane Hatti* Charter (Bill of Rights for all subjects Muslims and non-Muslims as well) delivered by the Grand Vizir Reshid Pasha in the reign of Sultan Abdul Medjid).

tapadeo cork

tapadura action of occluding, covering wth a cork, wrapping; bottling

tapar/tapárto occlude; put a stopper; cover (v)

tapet rug

tapete carpet, rug; **tapete alaja** rug from Alaca

tapete trukmen Turkish rug

tapetero weaver who makes carpets; carpet maker; carpet merchant

tapetiko small carpet

tapo real estate property deed; title-deed (T *tapu*)

tapon cover, cork; person so ugly that nobody can stand it; **tapon de redoma** top, cap, cork of a bottle; cover of pitcher; **tapon de kuti** box cover; **tapon de oya** earthen pot cover; **tapon de tendjere** cover of metal cooking pot, of caldron; **tapon de pila** (lit) sink cover, sink stopper; (fig) person for which one has little consideration, who is invited as the fourteenth person to a table (not to have thirteen is considered unlucky) or fourth at a bridge game and who is invited only because of the need to cover a hole; **tapon de garon** gag; obligation to keep silence; **tapon de vista** very ugly person, unpleasant object the sight of which is disagreeable; **tapon ke se le meta an la boka del alma!** (curse, malediction) may he have in his throat a gag which chokes him!

tara weight of a merchandise's wrapping; tara, defect, imperfection, physical or moral failing; **echar la tara abasho** (lit) subtract the weight of the *tara* from the total weight; make the part of exaggeration in a story

tarabispapu father of great grandfather, great great grandfather

tarabisvava mother of great grandmother, great great grandmother tarabulu Tripoli of Asia, Tripoli of Syria (T *Trabus*); kusuk (kushak) de tarabulu large belt of coarse serge (a twilled worsted or woolen fabric used especially for clothing), dyed in various colors, which made several times the turn of the belt and used by men of the popular class (originally belts of this kind were made in Tripoli).

taraka firecracker (from Castilian *traca*); rir kon tarakas laugh one's head off, roar with laughter

taral crown-shaped cookie

taralito crown-shaped small cookie

tarama fish (carp) red caviar (synonymous *havyar korelado*) roe caviar salad (goes well with a stiff drink, esp. raki (arak) or Pernod). The caviar salad is prepared well diluted in olive oil and lemon and strongly reinforced with the inside soft part of bread.

tarañeto great grandson

taranja/turunch special kind of Turkish bitter orange from which preserves and a refreshing soft drink are made (from T *turunç*)

tarapana/tarapane mint house where the money is minted

tarapapú great grandfather

tarator yogurt soup

taratur sauce made of vinegar and ground walnuts; yogurt mixed with vinegar, garlic and cucumber slices

taraza balcony (F *terrasse*)

tarde evening

tardjuman translator; interpreter (T *tercüman*)

taref any aliment improper for the Jewish kitchen (opposite *kasher* kosher)

tarefa task, determined work that must be done

tarentella very animated sort of dance

targum Aramaic language belonging to the family of Semitic languages, spoken by the people of the ancient Palestine; translation of the Bible in this language

tarkiza dark, somber mood, gloomy, dismal humor

tarla arable field, garden bed (T kanunn); cultivated field

tarpush voluminous turban worn only by the Muslim faithful who had accomplished the pilgrimage to Mecca

Tarragano native of Tarragona or originating from there. Patronym of many Sephardic families

tarrasa terrace, balcony of a house; pergola

tarrasino large balcony usually decorated with flowers

tartuga turtle

tarze attire; clothing; way of being dressed, appearance, allure (T *tarz*); (tener buen) **tarze jave** an elegant stature, a good and slender bearing

tas - eski tas eski hamam (lit) old cup old Turkish bath; (fig) the same old story

tas bowl or cup with rounded bottom

tas kebab/taskyebab Turkish beef stew; dish of meat cut into small pieces and roasted

tasa bowl; **tasa de banyo** metal bowl for washing one's body in the *hamam* (Turkish public bath)

tashak testicle (T)

tashakli (lit) having testicles; (vulg) having balls; (fig) bold, virile

tashirear carry (T *tashimak*, kanunn)

tashretu October (Bab)

tatarañeto great great grandson

tate hold on (imperative)

tatruador tattoo maker

tatuaje tattoo (n)

tatuar tattoo (v)

tauk chicken

taukdji vendor of chicken

tavan (T) ceiling; (v) Tavan, name of God to avoid designating Him by one of His consecrated names in agreement with one of the ten commandments, Exodus XX, 7; Deuteronomy V, 11); **El Tavan ke meta su mano** May the Divine Hand be upon it; May God will to help (said when undertaking the realization of a project); **El Tavan ke nos guarde!** (lit) let the roof guard us!; (fig) Heaven Protect us! **(El) Tavan ke nos perdone!** (lit) May the Ceiling forgive us!; (fig) May God forgive us!; **Bendicho el Tavan!** (lit) Blessed be the Ceiling!; (fig) Blessed be God!

tavanarasi (lit) in between the ceiling; sneaky (a somewhat negative name given to Armenians at a time when intercommunal prejudice was common, due to poor intercommunal exchanges)

tavatur public rumor which creates scandal, hubbub

taverna tavern

tavernero tavern keeper

tavla de dulse tray for serving sweets; set for serving sweets

távla tray; board, plank

tavlada floor, flooring, platform
tavlada soil (n, Monastir dialect)
tavli/tavla backgammon
tawshan hare; hare fur (T *tavshan*)
tayarine noodle, homemade lasagna
ta'yin appointment, designation (T *tâyin*, kanunn); soldier's ration;
    daily ration to which one is entitled at the canteen (for a worker,
    a student at a boarding school, or a prisoner)
taze fresh (T)
tchalgi band (musical) (from T *çalgi* musical instrument)
tchapeyo hat
tchapinas shoes
tcharchi market (n, from T *çarshi market*)
tchat onomatopoeia; Dr. Tchat a character in the Istanbul of the late
    forties and early fifties who pretended to be a doctor (or could
    indeed have been a doctor gone mad according to certain rumors)
    and had adopted the onomatopoeia "tchat" which he would con-
    stantly repeat and tell to people walking by. Dr. Tchat used to
    circulate in municipal parks and streets with a benevolent happy
    face and a pile of newspapers under the armpit at times followed
    by a trail of mocking children, clicking his fingers and saying
    "Tchat" which would be vociferously repeated by bemused
    children. Dr. Tchat was often the topic of conversation in
    Sephardic families.
tchibuk stick, cigarette holder (from T *çubuk*)
tchop garbage (T *çöp*)
te you (singular); te dishos i me dishos (proverb) lit: you said I said;
    (fig) quibbling, squabbling, bickering, contesting, disagreement;
    small quarrel; te vaz azer bueno you will get healthy
tebet January (H)
tedesco/tudesko German
tefila prayer
tefilin phylacteries consisting of tiny cubic leather cases held in
    position by leather strips, one on the forehead between the two
    eyes, the other on the left arm (the phylacteries contain,
    transcribed on parchment, passages from the Pentateuch affirming
    the unity of God and the deliverance from Egypt). Phylacteries
    must be worn by male adults, starting from after the Bar Mitzvah
    at the age of thirteen, when one starts becoming responsible for
    his actions.

tefter notebook, register, (from T *defter*)

tefteriko small notebook

teftish inspection; municipal agent who checks for cleanliness and the maintenance of good order in the city (T)

teilim Psalms of David (very pious Jews had the custom to recite daily all the 150 psalms of David, taking advantage of their moments of liberty)

teja tile from the roof; **aresevir una teja** receive a tile; be victim of an accident

tejada blow (n) with a tile

tejado/tejo roof

tejar cover with tiles

tejer knit (v)

tejor rigidity, stiffness, absence of flexibility

tek one only, without pair (T); **un orejal tek** only one earring; **venir tek a una fyesta** come alone to a festival without being accompanied by his wife

tekana/takana rabbinical ordinance with bearing on a rule, an order, a prescription

tekaut/tekaud retired person (T *tekaüd*)

tekia consumption, tuberculosis; **azno no muere de tekia** (lit) a donkey does not die of consumption; the imbecile, the sot let themselves live; they are neither worried nor killed by an application to duty, concern of doing well, preoccupation for tomorrow; **es una tekia** he is importune at all moments, a disturber who never ceases to harass; importunity, obsession

tekka/tekke dervish monastery (prohibited at the time of Atatürk). In former times Jews were welcome at the *tekkes* of the Bektashi dervishes (the most open-minded among the dervishes) for philosophical discussions

teklif ceremonial manner, etiquette observed with regard to respectable persons with whom one is not familiar; formal behavior; proposal, offer (T); **no tenemos teklif entre mozotros** we mutually treat ourselves without ceremony; we have no formality between ourselves; we let small misdemeanors go by between ourselves without these causing the least friction.

teklifsiz without ceremony (T)

tekmil (adv) entirely, without omitting anything

teknika technical

tekniko technician

tekstil textile
tekstualmente textually, word by word
tekyir mullet (fish)
tel tinsel for embroidery (T)
tel wire (T kanunn)
tela cloth; canvas
telada cream on a liquid; dandruff
telar weaver's loom; weaver's workshop
telefon telephone
telefoneo telephoned
telegrama telegram
telegraphista telegrapher
telek/tellek Turkish bathhouse attendant (T)
telepatia telepathy
teleskopo telescope
televizyon television
telex telex
telkadayif sweet dish of thin shreds of batter baked with butter and
    syrup
tellal town crier; public herald (T); kitar tellal announce something
    publicly, with hue and cry; talk indiscretely something that should
    have remained secret
telve coffee on the bottom of the coffee cup. The Turkish coffee is a
    decoction, not an infusion which explains the sediment of
    grounds. The sediment at the bottom of coffee cups gave rise in
    the Orient, among Sephardic as well as Turkish families, to an
    entire art of reading the future from the coffee. It was common in
    family gatherings that an old aunt with a typical name such as *la
    tia Fortune* would look at the coffee cups and read the future
    from there.
tema theme
temas fear (imp)
tembel/tendel lazy (T)
tembellik laziness
temblante trembling
temblar tremble (v)
temblor tremor; trembling; shivering
temblores chills; (le tomo una) temblor his entire body was shivering;
    temblores de la muerte mortal fear; invincible chills caused by
    cold, by panic fear

temedor who fears, who fears the chastising and respectfully conforms himself to superior orders, to laws and prescriptions

temel base, foundation (T)

temenna Oriental salute, bringing the fingers of the right hand to the lips and then to the forehead (T)

temer fear (v)

temerozo fearsome; who inspires great fear; violent; very intense

temi I feared

temiente fearful (of God) (Ferrara Siddur)

temieron they were stopped by fear

temio he feared

temor fear

temour respect mixed with fear inspired by one who holds authority and has the power to chastise

temouridàd/temeridad terror; violent fear (Ladino)

temperamento temperament

temperansya temperance, moderation

temperatura temperature; (a alta) temperatura at high temperature; (a basha) temperatura at low temperature

tempesta storm

templadera gold jewel for women after childbirth, similar to the *lelál* (head decoration of silver, gold or pearls), (T *hilal*, crescent)

templear use economically (v)

templo temple; sanctuary; synagogue; el Primer Templo First Temple of Jerusalem built by King Solomon and destroyed by Nabukadnezar in the year 586 BC; el Segundo Templo Second Temple of Jerusalem built by Ezra and Nehemi in the Vth century BC and destroyed in the year 70 AD.

tempranero premature, hasty

temprano (de) early; temprano de dia early in the day (Salonica Pesach Siddur)

temyente faithful who observes the religious prescriptions with piety and punctuality

tenaylik tranquillity, serenity, absence of any noise, calm

tenda tent

tendensya tendency, inclination

tendensyozo tending to only one sight

tender to have a tendency to; be disposed to; be predisposed to; extend (v); tendera su mano will extend his hand

370

tendido over-stretched; extended (Salonica Pesach Siddur)

tendio su tienta he set his tent

tendjere pot, cooking pot, caldron, saucepan (T *tencere*)

tendjere yuvarlandi kapaghini buldu (lit) the saucepan rolled and
found its lid; (fig) birds of a feather flock together

tenebrozo dark, shadowy, mysterious; inspiring suspicion and fear

teneke tin; tin plate; tin container; person without a penny (T); teneke
de agua tin container of water

tenekedji seller or vendor of tin plates, tin containers

tenemos - (lo) tenemos en muestro korason we have it in our heart;
tenemos debasho de mano we have under the hand

tener have, hold, possess, maintain (v); tener asukar have sugar in the
urine (diabetes); tener gana have the wish (v); di tenerti to have
you; tener te dishos i me dishos kon uno have a bone to pick
with somebody

tenevlia darkness

tengas may you have

tenghere/tendjere saucepan (Haketia) (T *tencere*)

tengo memester de I have the need of, I need to; tengo menester de
vervos I need to see you; (non) tengo I have (nothing)

tenida session; reunion

teniendosen abrasados holding each other embraced

tenikyel tin can; tenikyel de gaz petroleum tin; tenikyel d'azeyte oil tin;
kaza de tenikyel slum house made of old tin cans

tenis tennis

tenk old measure of weight, the quarter of a drachma, the 1600th part
of an oke (the tenk also represented the eight tenth of a gram)

tenor tenor

tentativa tentative, attempt

tentenometokes very susceptible person who gets disturbed by
everything (person who should not be detached)

tentura liquid which dyes; tincture; tentura de yodyo tincture of iodine

teologo theologian

teoria theory

tepdil transvestite, disguised; (adv) incognito (T *tebdil*)

tepe summit (T)

tepe/tepelúk cap, in the costume of Jewish women of Bosnia

tepsi large circular copper tray, with little elevated borders which
serves as a dinner table

ter sweat (T)
terakki progress (T); Ittihad ve Terakki Union and Progress Party of
    the Young Turks
terbie/terbiye correctness (T *terbiye* kanunn)
terçero third
terdjuman translator, dragoman (T *tercüman*)
terdjume translation (T *tercüme*)
terivle terrible
terlik slipper (T)
termal thermal
terminal terminal
terminar end; terminate (v)
termino term, end, ending, extremity
termometro thermometer
ternar - no ternar basharisiz there won't be any trouble
terno tender, affectionate
terregina cloud of dust
terrero earth
terretemblo earthquake
territoryal territorial
territoryo territory
terror terror
terrorismo terrorism
terrorista terrorist
terrorizar terrorize (v)
tersane dockyard (T *tersâne*, kanunn)
tersenas paludean fevers which return every forty-eight hours
tersene the wrong way, the wrong way around; back to front; upside
    down; against the grain; in reverse sense; in an annoying contrary
    manner; contrary to what one expected (T *tersine*)
tersyo third
tertip arrangement (T kanunn)
tertir/tertil caterpillar (T *tirtil*)
teryaka remedy prepared in mixing powders in honey; *teryaka*
    consisted of a more or less large number of mineral, vegetable,
    animal substances and mainly opium amalgamated with
    honey and wine and to which were attributed miraculous
    virtues; in former times there was great consumption of *teryaka*
    in the Orient to induce euphoria, beautiful dreams and fantasy
    visions

teryaki/teryakyi/tiryaki person accustomed to *teryaka* mixtures, to alcoholic beverages, to opium in its diverse forms, who cannot deprive himself from these substances without enduring atrocious sufferings; opium addict, drunkard, or impenitent smoker (more recently the addiction of the *teryaki* called *teryakilik* was primarily focused on smoking)

tesahublik becoming a protector (T *tesahüblük*, kanunn)

tesedor weaver; person who knows how to combine businesses, who is skillful in creating enterprises and productive collaborations

teshabeav the 9th of the month av of the Hebrew calendar. A day of sorrow in which the destruction of the first and second temples are commemorated, as well as the fall of Betar at the end of the Bar Kochba rebellion, and various other catastrophies which have affected the people of Israel

tesidero spleen of someone who spends his time darning old, torn tissues

tesido tissue, textile; **merkador de tesido** buyer of textiles, dealer in textiles

testamentario executor of a will

testamento testament

testarudo stubborn

testiguo witness

testireada unique effort of great effectiveness; serve, put to disposition with great promptness (T *yetishmek, yetishtirmek*)

testirear provide in all speed

testreada - una testreada in a single stroke

teta breast, teat; **(dar) teta** breast feed

tetadera teat, pacifier

tetadura action of nursing

tetanos ashisi vaccination against tetanus

tetanos tetanus

tetár nurse (v)

tetona women with prominent breasts

teva chair in a synagogue; podium on which the official at the synagogue stands to read to the assembly of the faithful a section of the Torah, to pronounce a sermon, to make a declaration

tezkere memorandum (T kanunn)

tezya workshop (T *tezgâh*, kanunn)

tezyahtar shop assistant; merchant who himself serves the clients, skillful merchant who knows how to persuade the buyers

thalamo nuptial; marriage bed (Ferrara Siddur)

ti you; your (delantre) ti in front of you; face to you; **ti mismo** yourself

tibio uncle (from *tibio, tivio* lukewarm; transformation of word with a humorous or malicious intent, a prevalent practice among Sephardim)

tidjaret trade, commerce (T *ticaret,* kanunn)

tiempo time; weather; **bien tiempo** good weather

tienda tent

tiene has; holds; **tiene paras** has money; **(no) tiene ganas de komer** he does not have the wish to eat

tierno tender; affectionate; of a tender age

tierra earth; **tierra de Ayifto** land of Egypt; **tierra que no a elles** land which does not belong to them

tijeras scissors

tiketa etiquette; ceremonial manners' **a resevir a uno kon tiketa** receive someone with demonstrations of courtesy

tikiya tuberculosis

tikum first prayer of the day at sunrise by the very pious

tikyir-tikyir (adv) falling one by one, very distinctly, and making a light chiming, jingling noise (T *teker teker*); **echar lagrimas tikyer tikyer** pour big tears

tilyo tilia linden tea; sudorific infusion prepared with tilia flowers

timarana/timbarana/timarhane insane asylum (T *timarhane*); **estar en un timbarana** be, sojourn, live at a place, within a surrounding where the greatest disorder is the rule, with screams, noises, perpetual squabbling and agitation

timbrado stamped

timbro postal stamp; tax stamp (n)

timidez timidity

timido timid

timon helm, rudder bar

timonero helmsman

timuridad terror, fear (Monastir dialect)

tinaja jug; barrel; **tinaja en pedasos** jug in pieces

tinajon large tank; large wine vat

tindjire/tendjere pot, casserole, saucepan (T *tencere*)

tiñevla darkness; shadows

tinia/tinya ringworm

tino complexion; color of the face

tino memory, discernment, attention; judgment, sense; care shown to observe an act, a movement, to conform oneself to

recommendations, to execute a task; (le vino al) tino it came to
his (her) memory

tinta ink

tintero inkwell

tintura tincture, tincture of iodine

tintureria dry cleaner; dyer's workshop

tinyozo afflicted with ringworm

tipki exactly the same, completely conform (T)

tipo type

tipografia typography

tiraj circulation (e.g. of a newspaper)

tirania tyranny

tiraniko tyrannical

tirano tyrant

tirar draw, throw (v)

tirbushon corkscrew (F *tirbouchon*)

tirilo scatterbrained, brainless person, of an inconstant character,
impulsive

tirinello very nervous young person who agitates oneself with no purpose, who does not stay in place and who is unable to
accomplish assiduous and regular work; featherbrained; crank

tiro bullet, projectile always in motion in stone or metal, which was
used in former times to load a canon; no le pasa tiro nothing
moves him, he is like a pachyderm; he is supremely apathetic

tiryaki addicted; one in a state of restlessness before getting a first cigarette; smoker

tiryakilik addiction; state of one who is restless before getting his first
cigarette

tishpishti almond cakes

tishri October (H)

tisji misji one way or another, whatever it be; after a fashion;
somehow or other

titereo trembling from cold; chill (n)

titireár tremble (T *titremek*)

tito very credulous but stupid person, easy to fool

titulo title

tivyar be lukewarm, tepid, mild; attenuate the heat

tivyeza mildness; being lukewarm

tivyo lukewarm, tepid, mild; person who is deficient in demonstrations
of friendship; with little zeal; poorly attentive; almost indifferent

(by antiphrase, when it is a question of the weather, of the temperature *tivyo* means the opposite, it signifies very hot: *el tyempo esta tivyo*, there is an intense heat); **resivo tivyo** reception, greeting with little warmth; **kedar tivyo delantre un prodjeto** appear little disposed to accept a project

tiya aunt

tiyo uncle

tizana herbal tea

tizia consumption, tuberculosis

tizna/tizón soot

tizon de fuego bramble of fire

toaleta toilet (F *toilette*)

tobillo ankle

tocar touch (v); **(por) tocar a ella** of touching her

todavia nonetheless

todo all; everything; **todas all of them (fem); toda la gente** all nations; **todo quien que no dize, tres cosas estas en Pessah** whoever does not make mention of three things at the Passover Feast (from Passover Haggadah); **todos** all of them; **todos los dias de la tierra** as long as the earth will last (Fer Bib Gen); **todos in une** both (Monastir dialect)

tok within (H kanunn)

toka turban of Muslim clerics; also of the spiritual leader of a Jewish community

tokadera woman who touches everything

tokado hat, headgear of Sephardic women mainly in Izmir, Rhodes and Bosnia

tokador scarf; **tokador de parida** scarf with embroidered amuletic inscription for women after childbirth; **tokador de banyo** square scarf to cover the hair in the bath

tokar touch, palpate, feel with the hand; play a musical instrument; deal with, bless (v); **tokar el pulso** take the pulse; try to guess the dispositions, the intentions, the project of someone; **tokar pyano** play the piano; **tokar mandolina** play mandoline

toke way to play a musical instrument; the touch in playing a music instrument; **(tener el) toke livyano** have a light touch; **(tener el) toke pezgado** have a heavy touch

tokmak large wooden hammer, mallet

tolerar tolerate (v)

toleravle tolerable
tolerensya tolerance
tolerente/tolerante tolerant
tolondrado who has contusions, bruises and bumps on the forehead,
    on the head
tolondro bruise (n)
tolondron large bump on the forehead, on the head
toma action of taking, of taking a sample; epilepsy; (le) toma he has
    epileptic seizures
tomada taken (fem); (que fue) tomado dalli from which it had been
    taken
tomador who takes, who monopolizes; skillful but otherwise egoistic
    person who likes to take presents, assure advantages for himself,
    but who manages not to give anything in exchange; es de los
    tomadores he is of those who willingly receives, but never offers
    anything to anyone (It is laughingly said that the lineage of
    Aaron, ha Kohen (brother of Moses, first priest of Israel, ancestor
    of the sacerdotal class and of the members of the Kohen families)
    belongs to this category of people); it is an allusion to numerous
    passages of the Pentateuch where it is said, the Kohen will
    attribute to himself (es de Koen, es de los) tomadores, de los ke
    toman i no dan, he is one of the Kohens, of those who take and
    who do not give
tomadura epilepsy
tomamos esta okazyon we take this occasion, we take this opportunity
tomantes those who were due to take his daughters
tomar take (v); have a drink; tomar a el take him; tomar al pelo (lit)
    take to the skin; (fig) make fun of; tomar al shuki make fun of;
    tomar aver aerate oneself; get fresh air; tomar - (un) tomar de
    paras a bundle of money (from T tomar bundle)
tomaste you took
tomat tomato
tomatada abundant dish of tomatoes (in salad or stew); blow given
    with a tomato
tomba tomb sepulcher; por la tomba de mi padre (sermon, oath) I
    swear it by taking as witness the tomb of my father
tombekyi tobacco in leaves for the water pipe; water pipe (T tömbeki)
tombola tombola (family game, like bingo, raffle)
tomo volume, tome

tomo este echo enriva de el he took this task, this job, this business
   upon himself; (me) tomo la mazura he took my measurements
   (Romanian Judeo-Spanish)
tonelada one thousand kilos, one ton, ton
tongas robes
tontedad stupidity
tonto stupid
top cannon; ball, soccer ball (T); (el) top es redondo (lit) the soccer
   ball is round, (fig) the soccer game can go either way
topacho disgraceful, badly built, badly dressed individual (n, T topaç)
topachudo (adj) disgraceful, clumsy, puffy, swollen, obese
topada ingenious discovery which makes it possible to come out of
   embarassment; skillful retort, riposte; clever pretext, excuse; way
   out
topadijo simulated find; fazer topadijo de una koza pretend to have
   found something while its place had been well known by the supposed finder
topador finder; someone who finds a lost object or a solution to face a
   difficulty
topar find (v)
topar remedio find a remedy
topeshir chalk (T tebeshir)
tophane/topane storehouse of artillery and ammunition (T)
Tophane/Tophane district of Istanbul to the east of the harbor district
   of Karakeuy known for its ill-reputed dens and houses; (las
   keranas de) Tophane the houses of ill repute, the brothels of
   Tophane
topishilada mark perfectly traced with chalk; sign of control and
   thankfulness
topo - (lo ke) topo what he found
toptan wholesale
toptandji wholesale dealer
topuz ball, sphere
Tora the first books of Law in the Bible, the Pentateuch
torba bag (T kanunn)
torcha torch
tore tower
torerios exploits; acts denoting much skillfulness
torlak uncouth individual prone to violence, who is out of control,
   who does not obey to any discipline; wild youth (T)

tornar turn; return; turn over; come back (v); (tu) tornara you will
   return; torno he returned; he brought back; (se) tornô atras was
   driven back; torno de los estudios returned from his studies;
   tornar tornare I shall not fail to return
tornaranse - (y) tornaranse las aguas de la tierra andar y tornar (and)
   the waters of the earth will withdraw more and more from the
   earth (The Great Flood, Fer Bib Gen)
torobolos troublesome and uncontrollably, brazenly turbulent to the
   point of madness
torpedad stupidity, awkwardness, dull-wit
torrar toast, grill (v, Monastir dialect)
torrente torrent
torta cake
tortol dove
tortola turtledove (archaic Castilian)
torturar torture (v)
tos cough (n)
toser cough (v)
tósigo poison (n)
tostada toast (n)
tostado grilled
tostar broil, grill (v)
tosto - (se) tosto bueno it is well toasted; (y eya) me tosto a mi en
   suvida and her she toasted me (she made me suffer, she
   persecuted me) in her lifetime
Totonya old and notorious German club in the Jewish section of
   Istanbul, in the previously stepped street of Istanbul going from
   the tunnel at the south end of the European quarter (embassy
   row) of Pera, to the district of Karakeuy leading to the harbor
   and Galata bridge. The Totonya was located not very far from
   the Sephardic quarter of La Kula around the Galata tower, and it
   was in or near the area occupied now by a karakol (police
   station). It also seems that it was not very far from the Shiite
   tekke where self-flagellation was customary on the day of
   Muharrem commemorating the bloody murder of Hüseyin, son of
   the fourth caliph Ali at Kerbela (Mesopotamia).
tou thou; you; tou dizien thou canst assert
tous your
tovaja/tuvaja towel
trabajar work (v)

trabajo work (n)
trabulus in Salonika, a wide sash for men's costume
tradision/tradisyon tradition
tradisionel traditional (F *traditionnel*)
traer bring (v)
trahana sort of noodles made of wheat floor, yogurt, milk and eggs
(T *tarhana*)
traidor traitor
traigan - (lo) traigan bring (him)
traisyon betrayal, treason
trak apprehension; stage fright (from F *trac*)
traka - shanattraka traka (burlesque expression to indicate an
underdetermined but very old period, the usage and lifetimes are
outdated since a long time)
trampeár to cheat
tramusu lupine (Port *tremoço*)
tramvay tram
transcurridar run its course, be finished, pass (v, arch Castilian); han
transcurrido have passed
transferar transfer (v)
transira he will expire; he will die
transmeter transfer, transmit (v)
transtorñanse (who) which was turning here and there
transtornàr convert (v); (el azien) transtornàr who converteth (from
Passover Haggadah)
trasbuyendo being boiled
trasseraron have brought me, conducted me out of
trastornar destroy (v)
tratamiento treatment
tratar treat (v)
trauán they touch; trauaron los varones por varones por la mano these
man took him, caught him by the hand (Fer Bib Gen)
travado (text) extracted
Travajos Publikos Public Works
travar pull, pull off (v); quando travo when he pulled off
travestido/travestito transvestite
trayer bring (v); trayer mazal bring luck
trayermela to bring this (fem) to me
traymiento bringing (n); actualization (Ferrara Siddur)
trazera rear end (more vulgar than *boron*)

trefa non-kosher food, impure
treinta thirty
treje thirteen
trejen thirteenth
tremblar tremble (v); (las manos estavan) tremblando the hands were
    trembling
Trenidad Trinity
treno train
trenta thirty
tres three
tresalir to be ecstatically happy (v)
tresientos three hundred
tresmil three thousand
treynta thirty (Ferrara Siddur)
treze thirteen
trezen thirteenth
trezientos three hundred
triandafila rose (Gr *triandafilo*)
tribunal court
triestino from Trieste
trigo wheat
trinar trill, sing (bird), (v)
tringa crumb; drop; infinitesimal quantity; extremely stingy
tripa stomach; abdomen; belly; tripas intestines; entrails
tripika potbelly, plump belly
triplado tripled
triplar triple (v)
triple triple (adj)
triplo triple (n)
tripudo paunchy, obese, pot-bellied
trishar cheat (v, F *tricher*)
triste sad
tristeza sadness
triumvirato triumvirate
triyaki grouch (from T *tiryaki*)
troakadura action of transforming, transformation
troka exchange (n)
trokadijo transformation in evil
trokador who operates a change, a reform; who barters one object
    against another

trokamyento change, transformation, reform

trokar change (v); **trokar modadura** change linen; **trokar de kaza** change house

trokido exchange, barter (n)

trompa sort of curved trumpet; trump; **no se desperta ni a son de trompa** he does not wake up, even at the sound of a trumpet; he has a very heavy sleep, he does not wake up easily

trompesador who causes to stumble, to run up into, to come up against; one who opposes an obstacle, who collides with, who causes to stumble

trompesar collide with, form an obstacle (v)

trompeson obstacle, slip, collision, jerk experienced when colliding with an obstacle

trompeta trumpet, bugle

tronchedad stupidity

troúchér bring (v); (me) **troucho** he brought me

trukando changing

trushi pickles, (T *turshu*)

trushi/turshi marinade of vegetables: redbeets, green peppers, cabbage, cauliflower, eggplant, tomato, squash, cucumber; **meter en trushi** conserve in a marinade reinforced by aromatic plants, or in vinegar; **azer trushi** (lit) make *trushi*; what ought to be done with a thing or a document presented as valuable, but which in reality is of no use, no importance; **valer para meter en trushi** (lit) worth of being put in *trushi*; worth very little (speaking of an incapable person who cannot be employed usefully for the accomplishment of any task); **fazerse trushi** get wet from head to toe (get wet all over); get soaked in the rain or in an unexpected, accidental dipping into water; **trushi di domates korelados** pickled half-ripe tomatoes; **trushi di karfiol** pickled cauliflower; **trushi di karpuz** pickled watermelon; **trushi di kol** pickled cabbage; pickled cabbage with vegetables; **trushi di pipinos** pickled cucumbers; **trushi di pipiritzas inchidas con kol** pickled cabbage-stuffed green peppers

truxo brought

tsadik person renowned for his probity, his spirit of fairness and clarity; just, pious, virtuous and charitable, all at the same time

tsedaka alms, charity

tu all (from F *tout*); (estar a) **tu** be ready to acquit oneself of all cares with vigilance, exactitude and clarity; keep an eye on everything;

arrange oneself for rendering all kinds of services at any time; do not let anything miss; be of a faultless devotion

tu/Tu thy; **tu** you; (estar konuno ke) **tu ke yo** be with someone on an equal foot

tuberkuloza tuberculosis

tubiko small tube, catheter

tubishva the fifteenth day of the month of Chevat in the Hebrew calendar when the rebirth of plants is celebrated by eating a lot of fruits

tudro who learns and understands with great difficulty

tufenk gun, rifle (T *tüfenk/tüfek,* kanunn)

tuferada foul smelling whiff emanating from a humid place which has remained closed for a long time

tugra seal, arabesque which appeared in the official Ottoman documents and which contained the signature of the Ottoman Sultan (as an example the document issued by the Sultanate to authorize the building of a new synagogue would be affixed with the *tugra*). The *tugra* appeared also in relief in Ottoman coinage.

tuguerto crooked

tul/tulle very light cotton or silk tissue which originated in the city of Tulle, France

tula/tughla brick (T)

tuluat kind of improvised drama (T)

tulumba parasi fireman's fee (in former times the city had no firemen, and the firemen were volunteers, but were paid a fee by the residents of the quarter which they serviced; traditionally there were often rival legions of Armenian, Jewish, Greek and Muslim Turkish who often fought folklorist battles until they could grab the lantern of the opposing faction; then they made up and retired in a friendly way)

tulumba pump (T)

tulumba tatlisi a sweetmeat made of dough soaked in syrup

tulumbadji old style firemen until the modern Turkish Republic of Atatürk started to set the City's firemen squads

tumbana drum, tambourine

Tünel sector at the southern end of the Frankish district of Pera in Istanbul, just before reaching Yüksekkaldirim the street which descends towards the harbor district of Karaköy. (A tunnel was built by the French, from the top of Yüksekkaldirim to Karaköy)

tunel tunnel

tupe insolent daring, cheek (F *toupet*)
tupir block, stop (v)
tura duration
tura the Sultan's monogram, usually on documents
turali/tughrali ornamented with the imperial monogram (T kanunn)
turban turban (F, originally from Persian *tübend*)
turbin binoculars (from T *dürbün*)
turfanda/trifanda primer of fruits and vegetable
turk/a la turka in the Turkish manner, in the Oriental way; **muzika a la turka** Oriental music; **vestirse a la turka** dress in the old Turkish way; **kabine a la turka** Turkish toilet consisting of a hole flanked on both sides by platforms to step on while standing on the rump, squatting, in contrast to *alafranga*, the sitting type European toilet; **gizar a la turka** cook the Turkish way
turkandre quarter inhabited by Turks
turkesko the Turkish language
Turkia Turkey
turlu variety, kind, sort (T *türlü*); **turlu turlu marifet** all kinds of tricks, of stratagems; **turlu/türlü** (T) cooked mixed vegetables, ratatouille
turnat molded to fit (Romanian Judeo-Spanish)
turnu cushion or pad that the ladies of old times would put under the skirt over the buttocks, the fashion of these times requiring that feminine figure should have a prominent derrière; **el turnu** burlesque name of the posterior part
tus your
tutaniko lightly broiled piece of bone marrow which is gulped down as an hors-d'oeuvre
tútano marrow
tutleado disturbed, disoriented, discountenanced, disconcerted
tutor tutor
tutris female tutor
tutulear make one lose his means of action, astound him, intimidate him by violent reproaches and shouting (v, T *tutulmak*)
tutuleo stupor, dazing, astounding
tutun tobacco (T *tütün*)
tutundji tobacco dealer (T *tütüncü*)
tutush a thing which is concrete, palpable; a thing which can be grasped (T) one cannot grasp what he says; (**en lo ke dize no s'aferra**) **tutush tutsheár** kindle (v, from T *tutushmak* catch fire, be on fire)

tutushearse quarrel, attack verbally; discuss with bitterness; come to
offending words, acts of violence (v, T *tutushmak*)

tuuersedor one who bends, who has the strength to bend or twist a
very hard body; one who draws people to evil, who makes people
drift away from the right path; tuuersedor de braso arm twister;
energetic, authoritarian person who knows how to repress, abuse,
disorder; who knows how to impose his will on the most
audacious; who knows how to command the respect of the
boldest, of the hotheads

tuuersido distorted, crooked, curved, folded by application of force;
dishonest individual

tuuerta - la tuuerta young girl afflicted of strabismus, dejected,
counterfeited

tuuertedad crookedness, inequity

tuuertez state of what does not go in a straight line

tuuerto crooked, distorted, contorted, going in zigzag; not just, which
infringes the principles of morality; (adv) slanted, at angle; acting
with cunning and dishonesty; lo tuuerto injustice, what goes
against probity and equity

tuuo ser got to be (Ferrara Siddur)

tuve zahuth had compassion; act of goodness (Salonica Pesach Siddur)

tuviense ambre are hungry (have hunger, from Passover song A
Lahmania); tuviense de menester are needy (have need, from
Passover song A Lahmania)

tuvieron (ke) tuvimos they had what we had

tuvimos la fortuna we were fortunate enough to have; we had the
happy opportunity to have

tuvimoz la okazyon we had the occasion, we had the opportunity

tuvir have (v)

tuviteis mazal you were lucky (phrase combined of Judeo-Spanish and
Hebrew words)

tuvla brick

tuvo lugar took place

tuvyeron poka eskola they had little schooling

tuyidura paralysis, impotence, crippling (with rheumatism)

tuyimento action of paralyzing

tuyir paralyze; cause the loss of a limb's (or limbs') motion (v)
tuyisyon paralysis; forced mobility

tuyisyon! order imparted angrily not to touch anything; Keep your
hands up! Hands up! Stick'em up!

tuyo your, yours; (es) tuyo it is yours; (lo mio) tuyo i le tuyo mio mine
   is yours and yours is mine; you can dispose of my goods and I
   can dispose of yours; everything we own is shared in common; lo
   yuyo yuyo y lo mio tuyo yours is yours and mine is yours; you
   can dispose of my goods with no need for reciprocity
tuyos yours
tuzla salt marsh
tuzladji worker in salt marsh
ty you
tyempeziko very humid, rainy and windy weather
tyempo time; weather
tyerra earth; mal de la tyerra bien de los sielos (lit) bad from earth
   good from skies (about a person who does not appreciate his
   good luck and acts or complains badly); yerro de mediko la
   tyerra lo kovido physician's mistake, the earth covered it; the
   earth hides the errors of the inexperienced physician
tyerrezika small lot of land; small island; (ironically) dust which accu-
   mulates on parquet floor or badly kept furniture
tyesto earthen jar in which ornamental plants and flowers are kept;
   insignificant, despicable individual
tyranizar tyrannize (v)

U

ubiquidad/ubikuidad ubiquity
ubtiner obtain (Monastir dialect)
uch etek (lit) three skirts, *entari* (loose robe) with slits along the sides
uchker chikur (draw-string belt-sash for holding up pants or drawers
   (T *chikur*)
uda/oda room (T *oda*)
uedado a ti hacer como la he no cosa esta this will not be said about
   you (Fer Bib Gen)
uentana endow
uertido will be spilled
uertión sangre del ombre en el ombre who will spread the blood of
   man in man (Fer Bib Gen)
uevo egg; uevo limon egg lemon mix to cook fish
ugurli good luck, bringing good luck (from T *ugur*)

ugursuz bad luck bringing; mean, malicious; **(un) ugursuz** emphatically malicious
uidu ear
uiuo alive
ulan! My good fellow!; **bre ulan!** Hi, you! My good fellow!; Now then! My good fellow!
uldurear accommodate (v, T *uydurmak* fit)
ulema doctors of Muslim theology; learned men
ulser ulcer; sore
ulserar ulcerate (v)
ulserozo ulcerous
ultimatum ultimatum
ultimo last, ultimate
ultraviyolet ultraviolet
ululu September (Bab)
ulvidadoso forgetful
ulvidar forget (v)
umá nation
umanidad humanity
umidad humidity
umido humid
umildad humility
umilde humble
umiliar humiliate
umilyasyon humiliation
umo smoke (n)
umoreskas humorous stories
umoresko humorous
un a, an
unde (se) sinks
undo deep
unia nail (n)
unidad unity
unido joined; united; **mantenerse unido** keep united
unifikador unifying
unifikar unite (v)
unifikasyon unification
uniforma uniform
uniformamente uniformly

uniforme uniform
uniformidad uniformity
uniko unique
unikornyo unicorn
unir unite (v)
unita unit (n)
universal universal
universalidad universality
universalmente universally
universidad university
universitario academic, scholarly; nivel universitario academic level,
    scholarly level
universo universe
uno one
unos some (pl)
untadura smearing, dipping, greasing, oiling
untar dip in a sauce or soup; anoint
untarà will dip
unya nail (n)
unyada nail mark; nail scratch
unyon union; Unyon i Progresso Union and Progress, the Party of
    the Young Turks who overthrew the absolutist Red Sultan Abdul-
    hamid II and instituted a constitutional monarchy under Sultan
    Reshad Mehmed V. The final march to overthrow the Sultan
    started in Salonica and there were Jews among the Unionists.
Unyonista Unionist; member of the Union and Progress Party; Young
    Turk
uranyo uranium
urbanidad urbanity; politeness, good manners
urbanismo urbanism; town-planning
urbanista urbanist; town-planner
urbanizar urbanize (v)
urbanizasyon urbanization
urbano urbane
urea urea
uremiya uremia
uretra urethra
urgensa/urjensiya urgency
urgente/urjente urgent
urgentemente/urjentamente urgently

urina urine
urinar urinate
urinaryo urinary
uriye coast (Monastir dialect)
urologiya/urolojiya urology
urologo urologist
ursa bear
urti cover (n, T *örtü*)
usul method, procedure (T *kanunn*)
ut lute (T)
utanmáz shameless (T)
uterino uterine
utero uterus
util useful
utilita/utilitad utility
utilitaryo utilitarian
utilizar utilize (v)
utilizasyon utilization
utilizavle/utilizable usable
utilmente usefully
utopiko utopian
utopiya utopia
uvular ovulate
uvulasyon ovulation
uydurear adapt, adjust; make similar (Judeo-Spanishized verb of T
  uydurmak invent) of truth, to skillfully mask the contradictions
  by the stroke of a thumb, to make an ill-founded story or supposition look plausible
uydurmasion/uydurmasyon lie; fabrication (T from the verb *uydurmak*
  cause to conform or agree; make to fit; adapt; invent; make up;
  find a way of getting or doing); the Turkish meaning of the word
  uydurmasyon is invention, fable, made-up, concocted; it is used
  in Turkish slang and jokingly as an "invented word". The *-syon*
  or *-sion* ending is not a Turkish one, it is derived from the Judeo-
  Spanish *-sion* or the Modern Spanish *-ción*.
uzado used, deteriorated by usage
uzadu usual (Monastir dialect)
uzar (si) get accustomed to (Monastir dialect)
uzo usage, habit, custom
uzu custom (Monastir dialect)

uzualmente usually
uzura usury
uzuraryo usurer
uzurpador usurper
uzurpar usurpate (v)
uzurpasyon usurpation

V

va will come
va! go!
vaca cow
vadáy surely (H *bevaday*)
vagon railway car
vaka cow; (fig) good person
vale mas has more value; (no) vale has no value
valen are worth
valer to have value; to be worth (v)
vali governor of a province (T)
valian - (no) valian la pena they were not worth the effort
valija suitcase
valije suitcase (Monastir dialect)
valle valley; valle de lagrimas valley of tears
valor value (n)
valorizar give value
valorozo valuable
vamos a Balat let us go to Balat, district of the Golden Horn (from an
    often repeated quatrain); (mos) vamos we go
vampiresa female vampire
vampiro vampire, bloodsucker; malignant spirit; exploiter
van - (junto ke se) van let them go together; (si) van (they) leave
vana shapeless; vain
vanaglorya/vanagloria vainglory
vandalismo vandalism
vandalo vandal, brute
vanidad vanity
vanilla/vaniya vanilla
vano vain, useless
vapor/vapora vapor, steam

vapor/vapur ship; steamboat (T *vapur*); (subir al) vapor board a ship
vaporozo vaporous, steamy
vaquero/vakero cowhand; cowboy
vara/vàra rod
varadero dry dock; skid
varadura running aground
varak thin metal used for decoration (T *varak*, Gr *varaki*)
vardat revenue (T *vâridat*, kannunn)
variabilidad/varyabilidad variability
variable/varyable variable
variar vary (v)
variasyon/varyasyon variation
variedad/varyedad variety
variete/varyete variety show
varikozidad varicosity
varis varice, abnormal dilatation of vein
varises varicose veins
Varlik Vergisi exorbitant Tax on Property which was imposed to non-
    Muslim elements of Turkey in the winter of 1942-43 (during
    World War II) under penalty of being sent to labor in the
    hardship region of Eastern Turkey for non-compliance (the law
    was later repelled).
varón young man of virile age
varones de la fama people of fame, renowned people, famous people,
    celebrities (Fer Bib Gen)
varyeta variety
vaso cup
vate go (imp); vate al diavlo go to the devil; go to hell
vava/bava grandmother (Gr *yaya*)
váyase go away (imp); may you go
vaza vase
vazia empty (fem)
vaziar empty (v)
vazio/vaziyo empty; (fig) one who speaks emptily, who is vain
vazyar empty (v)
vedaronse they ceased
vede I prevented; I stopped; (y) vede yo tambien a ti pecar a mi (and) I
    prevented you to sin against me; vedesse por ser a Sarah
    costumbre como las mujeres Sara was prevented from having
    children; she was barren, sterile

vedrá truth
vedre green
vedrura greenery
veer see (v)
vega fertile plain
vejes/vejez old age; peevishness
vekalet being an agent, a proxy (T *vekâlet*, kanunn)
vekayosse/vekayotze and the like (H kanunn)
vekialet ministry (T *vekâlet*); authorization to act for another person, to be an agent for another person
vekil cabinet minister; delegate with representative power; agent; proxy (T kanunn)
vekialetname document authorizing a person to act for another one; power-of-attorney to act for another one; proxy
vektor vector
vektoryal vectorial
vela sail; candle
velado veiled, covered; blurred, fogged
velo veil (n)
velodromo cycle track; bicycle track; **velodromo de Paris** in reference to the night in which the Nazis rounded the French Jews in the *vélodrome de Paris* for deportation to the concentration camps
velosidad velocity; speed
velosita velocity, speed
veluntàd acceptance
velur velvet
ven come (imp)
vena vein
vencedor victorious
vendedor vendor
vender sell (v)
vendidad sale; **vendidad del dia** day's sale
vendra will come
venemos - (a todo lugar que) **venemos ay** (at all places that) we come (we arrive) there are
veneno poison (n)
veneravle/venerable venerable
venereo veneral
Venezia Venice
Veneziano Venetian

venga may you come; (le rogo ke) venga he begged him to come
vengado - (sera) vengado will be vindicated; will be avenged
vengador avenger
vengan please come to
vengansa/vingansa revenge
vengar (se) take revenge; to avenge oneself (v)
vengar avenge (v)
venialidad venality
venid come (imp)
venir come
Venisiano Venetian
ventana window
vente twenty
venteisinko twenty-five
ventilador ventilator
ventilar ventilate (v)
ventilasyon ventilation
ventura fortune
ver see; (se) verá will be seen
vera edge, side
veramente truly, really
verano summer
verasidad truthfulness
verboso/verbozo verbose
verdad truth
verdadero truthful; authentic
verde green; with capital a code word among Turkish Jews to
    designate Muslim Turks; it refers to the green flag of Islam, the
    Sandjaki-Sherif, the Holy Flag of the Prophet
verdugo executioner
veredikto verdict
veremos let us see
vergi tax
verguensas - (las) verguensas the shameful ones, the genital organs
    (euphemisms were used for taboo or dirty words; in the same
    way as the "private parts" is used in English to designate the gen-
    itals. The Sephardim were a very religious and superstitious
    people who used euphemisms for taboo and dirty words)
verguensozo ashamed
verguenza shame

verifikar verify, check on (v)
verifikasyon verification
vernan they will enter
vernas you will enter (Fer Bib Gen)
vernas you will go to your fathers in peace (blessing at the moment of
    death, Fer Bib Gen)
versado versed in
versatil versatile
versifikasyon versification
version version
verso towards; verso la tadre towards the evening
verso verse
versu towards, in the direction of (Monastir dialect)
vertikal vertical
vervuensa shame
vestido garment, suit; Torah-mantle
vestimienta clothes, clothing
vestir wear; dress (v)
veygan - (sin ke lo) veygan without being seen
veynte twenty (Ferrara Siddur)
vez time; vezes times; (siete) vezes (seven) times; (en) vezes from time
    to time
vezino neighbor
viajador traveler; travel agent
viajar travel (v)
viaje travel; journey (n)
vianda provision
vibrar vibrate (v)
vibrasyon vibration
vida life; screw (n, T); vidas lives
vidéla calf
vidjuh prominent personality, notable (T vücuh)
vido beheld it; saw it
vidrad truth
vidreria glass shop
vidrero glass shop owner; glass vendor
vidro glass
vieho - (de moço hasta) vieho from young to older
viejizika little old woman; affectionate expression for little old woman

viejo old; viejos entrados en sus dias old people entered in their days
      (old people entered in the days of advanced age) (Fer Bib Gen)
viene y coma come and eat (an invitation to passerbies to come and
      share in the Passover banquet)
viento wind
vierbo word (vs. *verbo* in modern Spanish)
vierj virgin
viernez Friday
viga roof
vihuela harp
vijilansia vigilence, mastery of the situation, valorization of the
      situation, appreciation of the situation, estimate of the situation
vijilentes guards; police guards
vijita visit; doctor's fee
vijitador visitor
viktima victim
vila villa; cottage
villa town
villano villain
vimos we noticed
vinagre vinegar
vinagreta/viunegreta vinaigrette
vinagrozo vinegary, tart; bad-tempered, sour
vindikar vindicate (v)
vindikasyon vindication; vengeance, revenge
vinideru next, proximate (Monastir dialect)
vinienti next (Monastir dialect); (las) vinientes the coming ones,
      (which) approach us, meaning feasts and sacred seasons which
      approach (from Passover Haggadah)
vinieron they came
vinir come (v)
vinkular link (v)
vinkulasyon linkage
vinkulo link (n)
vino came; vino el punto the time came
vino wine
vinya/viña (lit) vine; life instead of *vida*, transformation of word, a
      humorous Sephardic practice
violar violate (v)

violasyon violation (n)
violensya violence
violente violent
violeta violet (n, flower); violet (adj)
virdure greens, vegetables (Monastir dialect)
virolojia virology
virolojista virologist
virrey viceroy
virtuoso/virtuozo virtuoso
virtuozidad virtuosity
virus virus
visibilidad/vizibilidad visibility
visible/visivle visible
viskozidad viscosity
viskozo viscous
vista view; sight
vistido cloth
vistir wear (v)
vistosidad/vistozidad being colorful, flashiness
vistozamente/vistozamente showily, attractively, colorfully
vistozo colorful; flashy; showy
vistozo lit: having sight; the blind one (for superstitious reasons,
     euphemisms or expressions were used contrary to their intended
     meanings)
visual/vizual visual
vital vital
vitalidad vitality
vitalita vitality
vitalizar vitalize (v)
vitamina vitamin
vitaminado vitamin-supplemented, vitamin-added
vitikultura viticulture
vitrina glass showcase; shop window, store window
vituperar vituperate; censure; condemn
viuda widow
vivaracho jaunty; lively; vivacious
vivasidad vivacity
vivido vivid; graphic
viviente living; los vivientes the living
vivir live (v)

vivo live (adj)
viyamus - ki (lu) viyamus may we see (the)
viza visa
vizino neighbor
vizir minister who sits in the Sultan's Council the *divan* (T); in the
    Ottoman Empire the Grand Mufti, the Grand Rabbi, the
    Patriarchs of the Greek Orthodox and the Armenian Orthodox
    Church held the privilege to sit in sessions of the Divan
vizita doctor's fee; doctor's honorarium
vizita visit (n)
vizon mink
vno one (Ferrara Siddur)
vocal vowel
vodka vodka
voilette veil worn in front of a woman's hat (F)
vokabulario vocabulary
vokal vocal
vokalizasyon vocalization
vokasyon vocation
vokasyonal vocational
volador flyer
volanes flounces of dress
volante flying
volar/vuelar fly (v)
volatil volatile
volatilla a flight of birds
volframo wolfram
volkan volcano
volkaniko volcanic
volontad/voluntad will; willingness
voltaje voltage
voltimetro voltmeter
voluminozo voluminous
voluntad/veluntad will; volition; willpower
voluntaryamento voluntarily
voluntaryo voluntary
voluptuozidad voluptuousness; sensuality
voluptuozo voluptuous; sensual
volver return, go back (v)
vomitat/gomitar vomit (v)

vomito/gomito vomit (n)
vomitona/gomitona access of vomiting; bad sick turn
vorasidad voraciousness
voraz voracious, ravenous, greedy
vos you
vosiferar vociferate (v)
vosiferasyon vociferation
votar vote (v)
voto vote (n)
vozotros/vosotros yourselves
vuelar go back; return; revolve; (se) **vuelvio para** he came back for
vuelo flight
vuelta turn; walk, stroll
vuesos bones
vuestro your
vuestros yours; **vuestros padres** your fathers
vulgaridad vulgarity; triviality
vulgarizar vulgarize; popularize; extend, diffuse (v)
vulnerar injure, wound
vulneravle vulnerable
vulva vulva
vulvar vulval
vyóla - (la) vyóla night of vigilance, before the circumcision (word
      used in Istanbul, Thrace and Salonika, also called *nóche de
      shmirá*)

W

waliyúsa chorus of rural musicians or Gypsies going through the street
      with rustic flutes and bask drums
washer washing-machine (Engl)
wata wadding, padding
wéko vague; indeterminate; lacking precision; **(en) wéko** (adv) in the
      gray line; imprecise; **(kedar en) wéko** to lack instructions; to lack
      clear orders; to lack direction; remain in the dark
wélla young girl or woman sloppily dressed; female with coarse man-
      ners (or using incoherent language)
widi clumsy young man; a bizarre person, grotesque or ridiculous (the
      Judeo-Spanish equivalent of *schlemiel* in Yiddish)

winc winch (Engl, also from T *vinç* with similar meaning)
wuerko devil

X

X - rayos X X rays
Xaber - (Ke) Xaber? What's New? a newsletter which used to be pub-
    lished irregularly (last issue in the late 1970s) which contained
    news about activities, publications, recordings and institutions of
    Sephardic interest in the USA and abroad
xalebi headgear in the shape of a ball, worn by Sephardic women in
    Istanbul, Bursa and Jerusalem until the mid-19th century (like the
    T *hotoz*, ball or egg-shaped headgear for women)
xámsa pattern of a hand with five fingers, according to Muslim belief,
    it drives away evil spirits (T *hamsa*)
xasé cotton, usually white without any pattern (T *hasa/hase*)
xenofobia xenophobia
xenofobo xenophobe, xenophobic
xenon xenon
Xerez old name of the town of Jerez
xeroderma (dermatology) a disease in which the skin becomes hard,
    dry and scaly
xerofilia (botany, zoology) ability to survive, grow and flourish in a
    dry environment
xeroftalmiya (ophtalmology) abnormal dryness of the eyeball
xerografiya electrostatic printing process for copying texts, figures or
    graphics
xilofono xylophone

Y

y and; or; (y por) Ysmael te oy, lo bendixe el (and for) Ismael I have
    listened to your prayer, I blessed him; y diredech Ye shall say
    (from the Passover Haggadah); y estas eyas namely; namely these;
    y fué it happened
ya indeed did
yaban rustic, clodhopper, person without education, intelligence,
    knowledge nor experience (T)

yabana - a la yabana - without thinking, stupidly; kaminar a la yabana
    take action without program, go as it comes, go to the adventure
yabandji stranger, foreigner; person deprived on any information on
    the milieu where he (she) finds oneself, alien; new in country,
    without expertise, novice (T)
yabani person without education and manners
yachni di fijon amariyo stewed yellow beans; yachni di fijon blanco
    stewed white beans; yachni di fijon verde stewed green beans;
    yachni di kol kolorada stewed red cabbage; yachni di kartofis
    stewed potatoes
yades (yadis) word said in starting a game in which the two partners
    each take one end of the V-shaped chicken bone holding the
    winglet; the partners pull on their end of the bone and say
    "yades" when the bone is broken, thus undertaking as a bet not
    to say a selected word of common use; the one who says it first
    loses the bet.
yadran necklace (T *gerdan*); yadran de perlas pearl necklace; yadran
    fino necklace of real pearls; yadran falso necklace of artificial
    pearls
yafta placard (T kanunn)
yàga hand; yoke
yága wound
yaghli greasy; oily, dripping oil (T *yaghli)*
yaghli mushteri (lit) greasy, oily client; (fig) client who buys almost
    nothing, yet acts as if he is a major buyer (from T *yaghli*
    müshteri)
yaghma loot (n, T kanunn)
yaghmadji looter (T *yaghmaci*, kanunn)
yagladear oil, grease; facilitate, make easy (v)
yagum jug (T *gügüm)*
yagur yogurt, buttermilk (Bulgarian)
yahni di champignones button mushroom stew
yaka collar
yakishear agree with, look well, look elegant; (este vestido no te) yak-
    ishea this outfit does not look well on you (T *yakishmak)*
yakisheo harmonization; judicious rapprochement; what is agreeable
    to see; befitting honorable conduct
Yakovatchi honorific form that the name Yako takes when it is
    question of a rich personage, enjoying great prestige; also
    affectionate name given to a small child called Yako

yaldiz glitter; gilding (T)

yaldizear give the appearance of gold to a painting by sprinkling it with filings of brass (v)

yaldizli glittering with the appearance of gold

yalla move forward, let us go (T)

yallear attack with enthusiasm, throw oneself into something

yama (he/she) calls

yama patch (n T); patch to repair a cloth

yamada call-up, invitation

yamado (adj) invited, convoked; male person with first name of, person called

yamar call (v); name (v); (komo te) **yamas?** what is your name?

yambole bed cover of high wool roughly woven, commonly used in the Orient, in former times a specialty of Bulgaria

yamin yedaberu (proverb) let time take its course (the regular course of things will show us the path to follow); the facts will tell who is right (H)

yan/ghan window

yaneza quality of what is flat, smooth, non-accidental, non-hollow, with no bumpy protrusions

yangaz importune, individual who is impossible to tolerate because of his fastidious moods (n)

yangazlik fastidious moods

yanginvar (inter) fire! alarm cry to call for help in case of fire (T)

Yangola high way bandit who in former times terrorized the Balkans, pilfering, ransoming, massacring; fearsome individual, of a cynicism supremely offending

yanishear accost, approach, get a feeling of, sound ground, sound the territory (T *yanashmak)*

yankesidji (T) pickpocket; dangerous individual, capable of any kind of action

yano flat, uniform, plane

yantar/yentar eat (rare)

yapi building, construction, building in way of construction; construction yard (T)

yapidji construction worker, mason

yaprakes dish made of grape leaves stuffed with rice and pineseeds with or without chopped meat, and cooked in olive oil; meatball or cheese ball wrapped in grape leaves, in celery, cabbage leaves or lettuce (from T *yaprak* leaf). Grape leaves filled with rice and cooked in a piquant dill and lemon sauce, with salt, pepper and a pinch of sugar (lighter than the version with meat, can also be eaten cold with yogurt; fresh mint may be substituted for the dill); **yaprakes di kol agra** stuffed pickled cabbage leaves; **yaprakes di kol dulse** stuffed sweet cabbage leaves; **yaprakes di pazi** stuffed chard leaves

yaprakitos (another version of *yaprakes*) meat-stuffed grape leaves in a sauce of honey, fresh-tasting dill, tangy lemon and tomato puree; the sauce gives this traditional Greek dish its specifically Sephardic flavor)

yara wound, lesion

yarabi (aman) (inter) My God! God of the Sky! (exclamation after receiving bad news)

yaradeador person who inflicts a wound (T kanunn)

yaradeadura act of wounding (T kanunn)

yarda yard, English length measure worth 914 millimeter

yardán necklace (from T *gerdan* neck and *gerdanlik* necklace)

Yarden Jordan river (H)

yardim/yardum help, assistance (T)

yaredear/yaraladear wound, make a wound (v)

yarma kind of peach very highly appreciated in Turkey which splits into halves by applying gentle pressure

yarseat anniversary day of a death, religious ceremony performed in the memory of the dead at the anniversary of death (German and Yiddish, *Jahrzeit*)

yarum hodo His Majesty (H kanunn)

yasak prohibited, forbidden; (inter) One cannot pass! (T)

Yasakchi sign interdicting the crossing of a road, the entrance of a place. A *yasak* (no penetration) zone for foreigners is marked by warning signs at the locality of Kavak in the northern Bosphorus.

yasemi jasmine, acacia

yashmak veil composed of two kerchiefs worn by Turkish women; veil of the Turkish/Oriental woman (T)

yastik cushion, pillow (T)

yatak receiving stolen goods (T kanunn)

yaur ghiaour non-Muslim, infidel (for the Jews the term *chifut* is used)

yave key

yaver aid-de-camp, aid de camp; lord in waiting; lieutenant colonel (T)

yaveyenes indeed you come

yazeromos we will lay in bed with

yaziessen let them lay down
yazio con el laid on bed with him
yazma cotton kerchief printed mainly with flowers (T also called
    yemeni, muni, mendil)
yegar reach, arrive (v); (avian) yegao had arrived; yegar a la verdad
    reach the truth
Yehuda Judah
yelado cold
yeléc waistcoat, vest (T *yelek*, Monastir dialect)
yelek inner coat; sleeveless waistcoat, long or short, worn by men or
    women over the *entari* (T)
yem fodder (T kanunn)
yemeni printed cotton scarf, daily headcover for women
yenar fill (v)
yeniceri Janissary force in the Ottoman army, dismantled after the
    Massacre of the Janissaries in Okmeydan (Istanbul) by command
    of Sultan Mahmud II (1826); the massacre was followed by the
    execution of the Jewish bankers Aciman and Karmona who
    among other things may have had Janissary connections
yeno full
yenso chemise, shirt worn under the dress by the Sephardic women of
    Salonika (*kamiza de yenso*)
yerarse to be wrong
yerneziko (affectionately) young son-in-law that the in-laws consider a
    particularly good catch for their daughter
yerno son-in-law
yerrar make a mistake; (se esta) yerrando he is making a mistake
yerro/yérro/yero mistake, error
yerua/yerva grass; herb
yeshiva talmudic school
yevar en prezo take with; take away, put into jail
ygñorar ignore (v)
yidek head decoration made of pearls; chain of precious metal with a
    charm (T *yedek*)
yilade ice (Monastir dialect)
yilar get cold
yiro de kama sheet covering the foot of the bed (Gr, *yiro*; also called
    pye de kama)
yirrar (si) err, make a mistake (v, Monastir dialect)
Yitró Jethro (Moses' father-in law, Moroccan Sepheradic Ballad)

ymam bayalda/ymam bayildi/imam-bayildi a dish of aubergines with oil; stuffed baby eggplants. The dish is said to come directly from the court of the Turkish Imam (leader in Muslim public worship; Muslim religious leader). The literal translation means the Imam fainted (the dish was so good that when the Imam ate it, he fainted from delight). Tiny baby eggplants (a small grayish variety available in Greek and other Mediterranean vegetable stores) are stuffed with a sweetish mixture of onions, raisins and parsley, individually topped with a clove of garlic, lightly sauteed and baked in olive oil.

yntelecto intellect (Ferrara Siddur)

yntincion intention (Ferrara Siddur)

yo I

yol parasi road money; travel allowance

yol road (T kanunn)

yol teskeresi pass, passport (T *yol tezkeresi*, kanunn)

yoldji traveler (T *yolcu*, kanunn)

yolyero jeweler

yoradera professional female criers at funerals

yorar cry (v)

yorshim heirs (H kanunn)

yra anger (Ferrara Siddur)

ysança custom

Yshac Isaac

yslas islands

ysquierda left

ysquierdare I shall go left

yudyo Jewish

yugular jugular

yuláf oat (Monastir dialect)

yuldji/yoldji traveler (T *yolcu*); (estar) yuldji go on a trip; be on the verge of traveling

yuntos together

yurultu noise (T *gürültü*, kanunn)

yute jute

yuzleme sugar-coated fritter (from T *gözleme*)

yzquierda left side

Z

zabit Turkish officer (T)

zabt taking possession, seizure (T kanunn)

zabtie ministry of public security, police (T *zabtiye*, kanunn)

zabtiedje under the authority of the police (T *zaptiyece*, kanunn)

zade noble; of noble birth; born into a family which has distinguished itself by military exploits or outstanding services to the state (T); es de los zades son of noble birth, he belongs to a family heritage which is famous or opulent

zafir sapphire

zaharina saccharine

zahut good works, charity; charitable act which can bring divine favor upon the person who accomplishes it, either in this life or beyond (H)

zaif weak (from T *zayif*)

zampara womanizer, ladies' man (T)

zapatero shoemaker

zapateta slipper

zarzamora wild mulberry

zarzavá/zarzavat vegetable (T)

zarzavatchi vendor of vegetables (T *zerzevatçi*); greengrocer

zarzawá vegetable

zavalli unfortunate, poor (T)

zayre storage of grain and other provisions (T *zahire*, kanunn)

zehut merit, good deed

zejut honor; integrity (H Haketia)

zelo zeal

zeloso zealous, ambitious

zengin rich (T)

zepelin zeppelin

zero zero, nullity

zerzuvi/zorzovi bright blue

zevzek silly; giddy; talkative; blabbermouth; chatter box

zilkade very poor; totally depleted (T)

zimbul hyacinth (T *sümbül*; in the Judeo-Spanish word *i* and *u* have replaced the Turkish *ü*)

zimpara sandpaper

zindandji prison/dungeon guard (T *zindanci*, kanunn)
zingana Gypsy
ziyara/ziyaret pilgrimage to the Holy Places (T)
zodiako zodiac
zona prostitute (H)
zona zone, area, belt; section, district
zoolojia/zoolojiya zoology
zoolojista zoologist
zorbalik use of force, violence (T kanunn)
zorlan by force (T kanunn)
Zudeo-espanyol Judeo-Spanish; Ladino
zumo que salió de las uvas juice that came out of the grapes (archaic
    Castlian)
zumo/sumo juice, sap
zurna clarinet

ENGLISH-LADINO DICTIONARY

A

a, an un
Aaron Arón
abandon (v) soltar, deshar; abandoned deshado, erremo
abdomen tripa
aberration taburra
abhorrent aborriciente
ability fakuldad, kapatchita (Ital *capacità*)
able capache (Monastir dialect), kapache (Ital *capace*); to be able to
    parvenir (F *parvenir*), pueder
ablution ablusyon, netila
abnormal anormal
abolish baldar
abominable abominavle
aborted movia
abortion moftu (Port *movito*)
about çatra patra; çirka (Ital *circa*)
above (adv and prep) ensima, enriva, sobre, sovre
Abraham Avraám, Avrám
abrogation baldadúra
absence absencia, falta
absolute absoluto; mutlak (adj)
absolution absolusyon, pedron
absolved pedronado
abundance brerekyét (T *bereket*)
abuse (n) abuzo; (v) abuzar
abyss abysmo, avismo, dip (T)
Abyssinia Abisinya
academic universitario
accept achetar (Ital *accettare*), akseptar; accepted majpul (T *makbul*)
acceptable majpul (T *makbul*), makbul (T kanunn)
acceptance veluntàd
access enxalçanse (Ferrara Siddur)
accessory aksesoryo
accident aksidente, kaza (T kanunn)

407

accidental aksidental
acclimatize aklimatar
accommodate akomodar, uldurear (v, T *uydurmak* fit)
accommodating avenivle
accompaniment sonaza
accompany acompañar; accompanied akompanyado
accomplish parvenir (F *parvenir*)
accord avenimyento
according to asegñn, sigun
accordion akordeon
accost yanishear (T *yanashmak*)
account (n) rendikonto, cuento, hasbon
accountant contador, ekonomo, reporter
accrued pujado
accruing pujamiento
accumulate entassar
accusation akuzasyon
accuser afeador
accustom akostumbrar; akostumbrado, embezado
ace (in card and dice games) azo
ache (v) ergulír
achieve parvinir; atemorense (Fer Bib Gen); achievement eskapadura,
    eskapasyon
acid kyezap, kesab
acquaintance (n) konosido; acquaintances alishik (T *ilishik* connection)
acquire adquirir
acquisition kompra
acquit saldar; acquitted saldado
acrobat jambaz, saltimbanki
acrobat soytari (T)
across averé
act echa; act in a brisk way bruskár
action echa; action of nursing tetadura; actions hechos (Ferrara
    Sidddur)
actor jugador
actualization traymiento (Ferrara Siddur)
adapt amoldar, akomodar, uydurear; adaptation adaptasyon
add ajustar, añader; add up sumar; addition adisyon
adder gurlia

addicted tiryaki
addiction tiryakilik
address (n) adres; address oneself adresar (se)
adept adepto
adjournment morvet (T *mürvet*)
adjust adjustar, uydurear
administer administrar
administration rizo
administrator administrador
admirable estupendo (Ital)
admiral amiral
admiration admirasion
admire admirar
admission admisyon
admit admeter
admonish bastereár (T *bastirmak*)
adolescent bajúr (H *bahur*)
adopt a child aporfizar, entenar; adoption adopsyon
adoptive adoptivo; adoptive son entenado
adored adorado
adorn adornar; adorn in a very rich manner (v) endorarse; adorned
    enafeyte; adornment aféyto, endono
Adrianopolis Andrinopoli
adulterer adúltero
adulteress adúltera
advance avansar; advanced avansado; advanced in age babayamin
advantage aprovechamyento
advantageous avantajozo
adventure azar
adventurer aventurero
adverb adverbo
adversity adversidad, desventura
advertising reklam (F *réclame*)
advice konsejo, majasava, sava (H *tzava*)
advise acavidar (Port *cavidar*), akonsejar, consejer; advise against
    deskonsejar
adviser consejero
advocate (n) abogador
aeration ayreasyon

affair maslahat (T kanunn)
affection byenkyerénsya, byenkyérer, hiba, kerensia, kerensya,
    quizensje; affectionate terno, tierno
afflict enfilandrar, afrii, affriyar; afflicted by mange sarnozo; affliction
    afliçion
affluence ribuy (H)
after (prep) dempues, despues, duspues, empues; afternoon tadre;
    afterthought ramayu; afterwards despues
again de nuevo, nueba, nueva de nuebo
against kontra, against receipt kontra resivida
age (v) enkaneser; age (n) edad, idad
agency agencia
agenda agenda
agent agente, vekil (T kanunn)
aggravate apezgár, feder
aggravation apezadumbre, apezadúmbre, feshusedad, peoria
agitate ajitar, arremanear, manear, menear; agitated maneado, sfacato
    (Ital sfacciato); agitated by waves ondozo
agitation fasaria, fasarias
agitator ajitador, fesadji
agony agonia, mucha pena, supplicio
agree with yakishear
ailment enfermedad, enfermidad
aim búto, eskopo (Ital scopo)
air aire, airi (Monastir dialect), aver (Monastir dialect), ayrada, ayre;
    air hole abaca (from T baca chimney); air-conditioning
    klimatizisyon
airplane avyon
alarm alerta (n); alarmed alarmado
alas barmimam (H), ai! Ah!, aman, ay ay ay
Albania Albania
Albanian Albanez, Arvanit
alchemist alkímiko
alcoholic alkoóliko, bekei (n, T)
alert (adj) enguerkado
alertness desbuelvez, despertez
alga alga
Algeria Algeria
alien ajeno, forastero
alive biua (fem), bivientes (pl, Salonica Siddur), uiuo

all todo, tu (from F *tout*); all at once dentrada; all in all sajakol (H);
    all present abastado; all that aun
Allah Alá
allay amortízir
allegation oydurma, uydurma (T *uydurma*)
allegedly sozde (T *sözde*)
allegory alegoria
alliance aliansa, firmamiento
allure tarze (T *tarz*)
allusion echada, echadura, sachma (T *saçma*)
ally (n) aliado; ally (v) aliar; allied with eniadido
almanac almanak
almond almendra; almond tree almendro, almendral, almendrero
almost ayno, çirka (Ital *circa*), kaji
alms sedaka (H, T), tsedaka; almsgiving shedaka (H kanunn)
aloe asivar
alone solo
alpaca alpáka
alphabet alef bet, alfabé, alfabeta, alibé
also atán, tambien
altar altar, àra
alter (v) alterear
altercation sayran (T *seyran*)
alternate alternar
altruist altruista
aluminum aluminyo
always siempre, sienpre, syemore, siemore
Amalecite Amalék
amalgam amalgama
amalgamate amalgamar
amateur amadór, amator (Monastir dialect), dilettante (Ital)
ambassador embasador
amber ambára, ambér
ambient ambyente
ambit ámbito
ambition ambisyon
ambitious ambicioso, zeloso
ambulance ambulansya
ambush aselada
ameliorate amelyorar

amelioration mejoria, mehoria
amen amen
America Amerika
American Amerikano
amicable agradavli (Monastir dialect)
ammunition djephane (T *cebhane* kanunn)
among entre
amorous afera
amount quantitdad
ample feraj (T *ferah*)
amuse desbolver
analogy analogia
analysis analiz; blood analysis analiz de sangre; urine analysis analiz
    de urina
analyze analizar
anarchy anarchia
anathema niduy (H)
anatomical anatomiko
anatomist anatomista
anatomy anatomia
anchor ankora
anchovy anchúya
and i, y; and so forth filan (T); and still more aindamas
Andalusian Andalúz
anecdote konsejika
angel angel; angels angeles, angel malah (H)
anger folor, ravya, ravia, sania, yra (Ferrara Siddur)
angry aksi (T)
anguish angustia
animal animal, beemá (H), béstya, hayvan (T), hayya (H kanunn); ani-
    mals of the earth quatropea
animate fishugar; animated animado
animosity dipla
ankle tobillo
annals análes
annihilate atermar
anniversary aniversaryo
announce anunsyar
annoy anujar (Port), molestar; annoyed by arraviar (se) (Monastir
    dialect)

annunciation anunsyasyon
anoint untar
anomaly anomalia
anonymous anonimo
another otruna, otruno (fem, masc); **another time** otra vez, otruna vez
answer (n) repuesta, ripueste (Monastir dialect); (v) responder
ant formiga, hormigua
antecedent antesedénte
antedate (v) antedatar
antenna antena
anterior anteryor
anthill formigero
anticipate antisipar
antipathy antipatia, dipla
antique (adj) antiuo
antique (n) antika; **antique** (adj) antigo; **antique dealer** antikadji
antiquity antiguedad (Ferrara Siddur)
anti-Semite antisemita
anxiety ansia, ansya, apretamyento, apreto, apuro, duelo
anxious ansyozo, enkyeto
any alguno; **anyone** alguno; **anyway** altrónde (Ital), andjak (T *ancak*)
apartment apartamento (F *appartement*)
apathetic akedado, kyohne
apoplexy damla (T)
apostolate apostolato
apparent aparente
apparition aparesimyento, aparisyon
appeal (n) apélo
appear aparescer, despuntar, pareser
appearance aparensya, ayrada, descuvrimiento, sembultura, simbultura
appetite gana
appetizing apetitózo
applaud aplaudir
applause palmas
apple mansana; **apple tree** mansanal
apply make-up fardate (from F *se farder*)
appointment apuntamyento, ta'yin (T *tâyin*, kanunn)
appreciate apresyar; **appreciated** apresyado, majpul (T *makbul*),
     presyado
apprehension trak

apprentice aprendista, chirak (T), çirak, dishipla
apprenticeship aprendisaje
approach (n) ayegamyento, ayego; (v) yanishear (T *yanashmak)*,
    aproprincar, aserkar
appropriate apropriar, pertinente; **appropriated** optado
appropriation empatronyamento
approval aprobasyon, aprovasyon
approximate (v) aproprincar
approximately ayno, çatra patra
approximation aproksimasyon
apricot abrikok (Port *albricoque)*, kayesi (T *kayisi)*
April avril, nisan (H), nisannu (Bab)
apron prostéla
aqueous kaldudo
Arab Arap
Arabia Arabia
Arabic language arabi
arable aravle
Aragon Aragón
arbiter arbito
arbitrate arbitrar
arboriculture arbolikoltúra
arc arko; arkol
arcade arkada, kyemer
arch arka
archeologist arkeologo
archeology arkeolojia
archer flechero, saetero
architect arkitekto
architecture arkitektura
archives geniza (H)
arctic arktiko
ardent ardyente
ardor ardor; **ardor (of flames)** soflama
arduous laboryozo
area zona
aristocracy aristokrasya
aristocrat aristokrata
aristocratic arostokratiko
arithmetic aritmetika

ark arca
arm (n) armo (weapon), pusat (T, kanunn); brasso, brazo, **arm in arm**
    a la brachéta (Ital *a braccetto*); (v) armar; **armed** armado
armament armamyento
armchair koltuk
Armenia Armenia
Armenian Armeno, Ermeni
armistice armistisyo
army armada, fonsado, fonsádo,ordu (T kanunn)
aroma bar (T *bahar*)
around (al) dorador, alderedór
arrange adjustar, adobar, akomodar, aranjar, arresentar, dozudear
    (from T *dizmek*), konvenir; **arranged** duzudeado, konvenido;
    arrangement aranjamiyento, arranjamiento, arreglamyento,
    arréglo, arresentyamento, tertip (T kanunn)
arrest (n) stanko
arrive arivar, arrivar, asodesér, llegar, yegar; **arrived** arrivo, ayego
    ayego
arrogance arrogansya, brio, çalum (T *çalim*), fiyaka, gaava (H),
    orgóyo
arrogant arrogante, orgolyozo
arrow flecha, saéta
arsenal arsenal
arson kundak (T kanunn)
art arte
arterial blood pressure tansyon
arthritis artritismo
artichoke anginara, articho, enjenera
article in a newspaper artikolo
articulate artikular
artificial artifisyal
artillery artiyeria
artisan artezáno, esnaf (T kanunn), rofit (T *esnaf, hirfet, taife*), taife
artist artista
artistic artistiko
as a; **as always** enderechura; **as if** (adv) sankyi (T *sanki*), como; **as if**
    one would say sankyi (T *sanki*); **as much** altretánto (Ital), atán,
    tanto, tanta; **as soon as** apenas; **as usual** enderechura; **as well**
    altretánto (Ital), tambien; **as yet** ainde (Port *ainda*, Monastir
    dialect), inde inde

ascending a slope suvyente
ash seniza, siniza
ashamed verguensozo
ashtray senizero
ask demandar, dimandar, dimandar, preguntar; **ask for alms** dilinjear
asparagus sparanga
aspect aspekto, ayrada, embultura
asphalt asfalt
asphyxiate asfiksyar
aspiration dezeo
ass asno
assassin asasino
assassinate asasinar
assault (n) asalto; **assault** (v) asaltar
assemble rekojer, reunir
assembly adjunta, medjlis, midjlis (T *meclis*)
assimilate asimilar; **assimilated** asemejado
assimilation asimilasyon
assist asistir; **assisted** arremedyado
assistance yardim, yardum (T)
assistant asistyente, ayudante; **assistant director** soto-director,
    su-director, su-direksyon
associate (v) asosyar; (n) haver (H); **associated** asosyado
assorted asortido
assortment assortimento, sheshit (T *çeshit*)
assume asumir, enkargarse; **assumed** sozde (T *sözde*), supuesto
assumedly (en) supuesto
assure asegurar, asigurar
Assyria Asiria
Assyriology asiryolojia
asthma asma
astonish shashear; **astonishing** adjaib (T *acaib*)
astounded shashkin
astounding tutuleo
astrologer estreyero
astrology estreyeria
astronomer estreyero
astronomy estreyeria
asymmetry asimetria
at all cost illa (T *ille*)

at home enkaza
at least a lo manko, almenos, bari (T)
at midnight amedia noche
at most piu piu (Ital)
at six and a half a la sesh i media
at six o'clock a la sesh
at that time entonces, entonches
at the beginning emprimaro
at the most (adv) dale dale
at the point of emen emen (T *hemen hemen*)
at the time en tiempo
atavism atavismo
atheist dinsiz (T), imansiz (T)
Athenian Ateneo
Athens Atena
athlete atléta
athleticism atletismo
atlas atlas
atmosphere atmosfero
atmospheric atmosferiko
atonement kapara
atrocious atróche (Ital)
attachment apégo, atamyento
attack (v) atakar; attacked attakado
attempt (n) prova, tantativa, tentativa, tentativa; attempt to persuade
    enkavesar
attention atansion, atansyon, atension, dicát (T *dikkat*), tino;
    attention! dikat (T *dikkat*), kuydado!
attentive aplikado, atentivo
attenuated atenuado
attest (v) atestiguar; atestar
attic shilvane (from T *shirvane*)
attire tarze (T *tarz*)
attract atirar, atraer; attraction atraksyon
attractively vistozamente, vistozamente
attribute (v) atribuir
attribution atribusyon
auction almoneda, mesad (T *mezat*, kanunn)
audacious atrivido, aventurado
audience audencia

audition oido
auditor oidor
augment aumentar, pujar, pujier; augmented pujado; augmentation
    puja, pujansa, pujita, suvidura
augur (v) agorar
August agosto, av (H), abu (Bab)
aunt tiya
auscultate askultar
auscultation askultasyon
Australia Australia
Austria Austriya
Austrian Austriako
authentic halis (T), verdadero
authenticate estampiyar
author autór
authoritarian autoritaryo, otoritaryo
authority autoridad, otorita, saltanat (T); authorities otoridades
automatic otomatiko; automatically otomatikamente
automobile auto, automobil, otomobil
autumn autúño
avail oneself of privalersi (di) (Monastir dialect)
availability disponilbidad
available desponible, disponivle
avarice (T) tamahkyarlik, mizmizlik (T)
avaricious eskaso, matança (fig), mizmiz (T), pinti, tamahkyar (T)
avenge (v) vengar; avenger vengador
aviation aviasyon
avoid evitar
awaken despertar, desperto
awkward gafa
awkwardness torpedad
ax balta

B

babbling favlatina
baby bebé
Babylon Babilóna, Bavél
bachelor bekar, bekyár (T *bekâr*), mansevu (Monastir dialect)

back (n, body part) lombo; spalda; **backing up** (n) retirada; **backward** atrás, atrazado
backgammon tavli, tavla
background ambientación
bad mal, malo; **bad conscience** apezadumbre, apezadúmbre; **bad manners** ta(r)buradji; **bad mood** negrina; **bad news** karahaber (T); **bad news** nochadia; **bad omen** gursuz (T *ughursuz*) gweso; **bad person** djis de perro; **bad smell** fedór; **badly built** topacho (T *topaç*); **badly dressed** desjarrapado; **badly dressed individual** topacho (T *topaç*); **badly groomed** abdal (T *aptal*); **bad-mannered** depsiz (T); **bad-mouthed** malfavlado, syerpa; **bad-tempered** vinagrozo
badness maldad, negregura, negrina
bag çanta (T), ibé (from T *hibe*), sako, torba (T kanunn); **bag of gold** bolsa de oro; **jute bag** sako de juta; **bags** estifa (Gr)
Baghdad Bagdad
baguette franzola (French bread) (F *franzole*)
bail fiansa
bailiff muvashir (T *mübashir*, kanunn)
baker masaci, masaji, masadji, masa (matza), ornero, panadero
bakery panaderia
baklava baklava
balance (n) balansa; (v) balansar
balcony balkone, taraza (F *terrasse*), tarrasa
baldachin baldakino
baldness sachliran
bale bala, balo
ball bala, pelota, top (T), topuz
ballad romansa
ballast balasto
balloon balón
balsam bálsamo
balustrade pasamano
ban herém
banana banana
band (musical) tchalgi (from T *çalgi* musical instrument), banda
bandage bandaje (F)
bandit bandido, brigante, haydut (T kanunn); **banditry** haydutluk (T kanunn)
banished arrepudyado

banishment sergun
bank banka
banknote kayma
bankrupt muflus (T *müflis*); bankruptcy falimento (Ital *fallimento*)
banquet banketo, komida
baptize bautizar
bar bar
bar mitzvah barmitzva; Bar Mitzvah speeches deskorsoz de Bar
    Mitzvah
barbarism barbaria
barber arrapador (Monastir dialect), berber (T)
bare descuvierta
barely apena
bargain kyelipur, okazion (F *occasion*); bargaining bazarlik
    (T *Pazarlik*), pazarlik
bark maullar, maulyar
barometer barometro
barracks baraka
barrel barril, bóta, tinaja; barrel maker barriléro
barren (woman) maniéra
barrow arabeka
barter (n) trokido
base (n) temel (T); base (v) bazár
basement basaménto
bashful arrezistado
basil aljavaka
basin lagen (T *leghen*)
basket sepet
bastard bastádro, malsin, malshin (H), mamzér (H); bastardize
    abastadrear
baste (v) filvanar
basting filvan
bat morsyegano, papasyega
batch fornada
bath banyo, banyu; bathed ennadado; bath linen enshugadura, peshkir
    (T); bathtub bañéro
battalion tabur
battle batálya
be ser, estar; to be afraid tener sar; espantar (se); be afraid of ispantar
    (si); to be ashamed averguensar (se); to be born again renaser; be

careful! kuydado!; to be delayed atrazarse; to be destroyed
estruirse; to be enough bastár; to be exhausted; skitarse; to be
exhausted estruirse; to be full artar; to be hanged aser enforkado;
to be idle enjaraganearse; to be in distress asararse; to be in
shortage faltar; to be interested in enteresar (se); to be late
atrazarse; to be set free; dezafogarse; to be silent kayar; to be successful reushir; to be terrified estremeserse
beacon fanal, fener (T *fener*)
beadle sanmaz
bean (haricot/runner beans) fasulya (T *fasulye*), ava, faba
bean fijón (Gal *feijo, feixoo*; Port *feijào*); green string bean fijon verde;
white bean fijon blanco; yellow wax bean fijon amariyo
bear lonso, lónso, oso, orso, lonso, ursa
beard barva; short beard barvika; bearded barvúdo
beast beemá, behema (H)
beat (v) harvar, batir (Port), harvo (kanunn); beat ajarvar(from H
herev short sword); beat up aharvar (from Arabic *harb* strike,
war); beating haftona
beatitude beáta
beautiful hermozo, ermozo, fermoso (Ferrara Siddur), fermózo (Jud-
Sp Dict Madrid), formozo, sangrudo; beautiful face facha luzya
beauty ermozura, formozura
beaver kastor; beaver's fur kastor
because por cavsa que, por que, porque; because of al lugar
become devenir; become cheaper embarateser; become free salir
d'esklavedad; become gangrenous (v) gangrenarse; become gray
(hair) enkaneser; become hardened endureserse; become ill
enjazinearse; become insolent desfacharse; become night
ennoceser; become pale demudarse; become rotten enfedeser;
become sad atrisrarse; become stubborn enkapricheado; become
stultified entonteserse; become stupid emboveserse; become tubercular entekiarse
bed cama, kama; bed sheet sábana, savana, savaná; bedbug chincha
(Gal *chincha*), çinça; bedfellow çalik
Bedouin beduino
bee bezbe (Monastir dialect); bee sting bizbon; bee wax pavil
beef buey; small beef bueyeziko; beef stew guvetch con karne
beetle mavlacha
before adelantre, ántes, asta
beggar dilenji (T *dilenci*)

begin (v) empesar, empessar; **beginner** adjami (T *acemi*); **beginning**
    empecho, impisidju, principio (Monastir dialect), prinçipio
behave (v) davranear (T *davranmak*), komportarse
behavior komporto
behold (prep) ek; **behold na!** (T)
being seer; **being a guest** mosafirlik, musafirlik; **being upon something**
    (fue) séyida en
belief imán (T)
believe creer, kreyer
bell (v) emberrar; **bell** (n) chingirák (from T *çingirak*), kampania,
    kampanya, sonase
bellow brameár
belly tripa; **bellyache** dolor de tripa
below (de) baxo, debasho
belt çentura; çintura, kushak (from T *kushak*), sherit (T), sintura,
    zona; **belts** cinturas
bench banco, banko
bend (v) abokar
benediction hazak baruh (H), mesibera (H)
benefactor byenazedór, dador
benefit (n) probecho, hayre (T *hayir*); (v) aprouechar (se) (from
    Ferrara Siddur)
benevolence byenkyerénsya, merced (Ferrara Siddur), merçed (H)
bequeath mandar
bequest ekdes (H)
beret baréto
besides (prep) desparte (en), indemás (Port *ainda mais*)
besiege asedyar
best - of the best (de la) mijor
bet (n) apuesto, bás (T *bahis*), embas (T *bahis*); (v) apuestar
betray falsar; traisyon
better mejor, mehor; **betterment** (of an illness) mejoria, mehoria
between entre; **between Jews** enteres judios
bewildered shashkin
bewitch echar chizos, enfechizar; **bewitched person** fadado
bicycle track velodromo
bidet - portable bidet badéla
big grande; **big-boned** guesudo
bile adéfla, fiel, fyel
bill (n) faktura, kayma (T *kayme* kanunn); **bill** (v) fakturar

billion bilyon
binocular durbin (T *dürbün*), derbil (T *dürbün*); binoculars turbin
    (from T *dürbün*)
bird ave, have, pacharo, pasharo, pájaro,pasaro, pasharo, paxaro;
    bird's crop papo
birth parir, nacçimiento; giving birth paridura; birth certificate nefus,
    nufus (T *nüfus*); birth nasimiento, nasimyento
biscuit biscocho
bit mudriô; a little bit tantiko
bitch perra (vulg)
bite (n) modredura; (v) modrer; bite gently modrear
bitterness amargór, amargura
bitumen cal, pez
bizarre demudamyento
blabber (n) dezidero; favladero; blabber tirelessly (v) shushurrear;
    blabbering palavradero; blabbermouth lafazan, palavraci (T),
    rompe-kavesas (lit: breaks heads)
black (person) negru (Monastir dialect), (person) pretu (Monastir
    dialect), preto (Port vs. modern Spanish *negro*); blacken
    ennegreser; blackguard kyepaze, kyepaze (T *kepaze*); blackmail
    shantaj (F *chantage*; francisized T *shantaj*); shantör; blacksmith
    fyerrero
bland shavdo; shavdura
blanket manta
blaspheme kafurear (from T *kâfir* miscreant, unbeliever)
blasphemy kafrô (from T *küfür* insult, blasphemy; also from Judeo-
    Spanish *kifur*, insult)
blast (v) auflár
blemish (n) mancha, sakatlik (T kanunn)
bless (v) bendigar, tokar; blessing amosi (H), bendision, berahà
blessed benditcho, byenaventurádo; blessed Jew Judio bendicho
blind (n) syego; (adj) ciego, çiego, siego; blindly syegamente; go blindly
    ir komo morsyegano
blister- small blister fushka
blitzkrieg geurra relampago
block (v) tupir; (n) blóko
blond byóndo
blood sangre; action of bloodletting sangradura; blood-stained
    ensangrentado
blow (v) çuflar, çuflet

blow çaketon; blow on asoplar; blow with a tile tejada
blue azúl, blu (Monastir dialect), mavi (T); bright blue zerzuvi,
    zorzovi; blue sky çadir mavi
blunderer peshutudo
blurred velado
blushing kacheta
board távla; board the ship subir al vapor; boarding school enternato
boaster çakon
boastful petrisifon (F *qui pétrit des chiffons*)
boasting mangada, palavraci, palavradji (T)
boat navio; boat-hook kanja; boatman (T) kayiktchi, kaikdji
    (T *kayikçi*)
bobbin makara (T)
body guf (H kanunn), kuerpo, puerpo
boil (v) buyir; boiled buyído, boiled down eskaldado; boiling buyéndo,
    buyór, buyitína, buyór, kaldo
boils sarna
bold-faced desverguensado
boldness ozadia
bond atadero, bond fiansa
bondage servicio
bone gueso, gweso; bones huessos, vuesos
book libro, vro, livro
boor arbánte
boost (n) slanchyo
boot bota
borax borása
border bodre
bore (v) enfastyar; enfastyado
boredom enfastyo, sikinti (T); experience boredom siklearse
boring alenguaziko, enfastyozo
born nacido, nasido; to be born naser
borough kasaba (T kanunn)
Bosnian boshnák
boss ámo
boss patron, patrón
both ambos; both of them ambos ellos
bother baderear
bottle bokal, botcha, ridome (Monastir dialect)
bottom dip (T); (buttocks) tafanaryo (Ital *tafanario*)

boulevard bulevár
bound to ovligado
boundary frontiera
bouquet bukéto
bow (n) reverencia; bow tie papiyon
bowl chanaka, kyase, tasa
box cásha, kuti (from T *kutu*); small box kutiko, kashika
boxer pelivan (T *pehlivan*)
boy hijo, fijo; small boy fijiko
boycott (n) boykót; (v) boykotár; boycotting boykotáje
boyfriend amigito
brace armatura
braggart asoltador, fandagmeno
bragger mantardji
bragging forfanteri, mangada
brain meoyo, meyo, selévro, serebro, sezo; brains miyoyo
braised abafado
branch (of an office) shube (T *shube*), rama, ramo
brandy rum
brass alárze, brónzo
brave brávo
bravery bravúra, enuolente
bravo ashkulsun (T *ashkolsun*), askolsun! (T), bravo
brawler çiçaron
brawling çiyon
brazen solevantado; brazen-faced desverguensado
brazier brazéro; fogarero (Port *fogareiro*); ogar
bread pan, çuspa, casole (Port *cassoula, caçoula*); bread crumb finga,
    miga, miga; bread earner fechiko
break (v) quebrantar, quebrar, romper; break the monotony romper la
    monotonia; break up esfondar
breakfast dezayuno
breast pison, seno, teta; breast feed dar teta
breath bafo (Port), riflo, solup (T *soluk*), soplo, suflo, sulúk, sulup,
    soluk (T *soluk*)
breathe respirar
breathing suflo
breeches brága, kalso, saraguellos
breeder of silkworm kukuyero
brevity breuedad (Ferrara Siddur)

bribe (n) rushvet (T *rüshvet*), shohad (H kanunn); (v) shojad
brick tula, tughla (T), tuvla; bricks adôves
bride calá, novia; bride-to-be espozada
bridegroom novio
bridge bridj, kopri, kupri (T *köprü* kanunn), ponte
brigade brigáda
brigand brigante, brigánte (Ital)
brilliance lustre
brilliant çil, parlak (T)
bring traer, trayer, troúchér; bring luck trayer mazal; bring back to life
    arrebivir; bring together konhugar (Port *conchigar*), lyevar;
    bringing traymiento (Ferrara Siddur)
brioche boyo
brisk (adj) brúsko, búzdro
British pound sterling lira esterlina
broad feraj (T *ferah*), ancho; broad bean fava
broaden anachar
brocade brokádo
brochure broshúra, folyo
broil (v) tostar; broiled asada
broken roto; broken-down roto; broken glass vidro roto
broker simsar
bronze brónzo; bronzed bronzádo
brooch bróce
brood çokada (n); brood over eggs çokar
brook filero
broom escóva, eskova
broth kaldo
brothel bordélo (It *bordello*)
brother ermano, hermano, irmanu; brother-in-law badjanak
    (T *bacanak*), cuñado
brown hair brúno
brownish brunácho
bruise (n) negregon, tolondro
brush (v) furchear; (n) fúrcha (Monastir dialect); brushing furchada
brutal brutál
brutality brutalidád
brutalize (v) brutalizár; ajarvar (from H *herev* short sword)
brute vandalo
bucket cuvá (Monastir dialect)

bud komca (T)
budget bujéto
buffalo búfalo, búfano
buffet bufé
buffoon bufón, soytari (T)
buffoonery bufonáda, bufonería, maymoneria
bug guzano de Yerushalayim
bugle trompeta
build edifikar, fraguár, frauar; building yapi (T) edifisyo, fragua,
    mulkye (T *mülk*, mülkiye); small building mulkyiziko; built of
    stone encastenada
Bulgarian bulgarésko, búlgaro
bulimic tener lamya
bull bic
bullet (n) plomo, fishek, tiro
bully kabadayi (T)
bullying shakera
bum serseri (T)
bun shiñon
bunch of grapes razimo
bundle (n) partal; poor man's bundle partaliko
bungle (v) sabotar
bungler sabotador
burden lazéria
bureaucracy burokrásya
bureaucratic burokrátiko
burial enterramyento
buried enterrado
burlesque burlésko; burlesques burleskas
burn (v) kemar, quemar; burned kemado, quemô
burp (n) regoldo; burp (v) regoldar
burst arrevantar, patledear (from T *patlamak*); burst into tears
    patladear de yorar; burst of laughter reitina, riza
bury enterrar
business echos, etcho, fecho, maslahat (T kanunn), negosyo; business
    deal alichverich (T *alishverish*); businessman negociante,
    negosyante
busybody demudadiko
but ama (T), andjak (T *ancak*), emperlo, ma, pero, saluo
butcher degoyador, kasap, salchichero; butcher shop salchicheria

butter manteca, manteka, manteque (Monastir dialect); **buttered**
    mantekozo
buttermilk yagur
buttock nalga, asentadera; **buttocks** asentador, kompedron, pedador
    (vulg), tafanaryo (Ital *tafanario*)
buttonhole butuñere (Monastir dialect), ojal
buy (n) kompra; komprar, mircar (Monastir dialect), mercar, merkar
    (archaism; modern Spanish *comprar*); **buyer** alidji (T *alici*),
    merkador; **buying** merkida
by por; **by hand** luego de mano; **by necessity** demenester; **by reason**
    por ditcho; **by the way** a propozito

C

cabaret çentro (Ital *centro*)
cabbage kol, lagna (T *lahano*, Gr *lahano, lahanon*)
cabin chosa
cabinet kabinet; **cabinet minister** vekil (T *kanunn*)
café owner kafedji
cafeteria kafetyera
caftan kaftan
cajole arregaladór
cake torta
calamity bela (T)
calculation hasbon
caldron kazan
calf vidéla
calico hase
call (v) llamar, lyamar, yamar; **call-up** yamada
calm (n) tenaylik, aserenado; (adj) calma, kalma; **calm down**
    endormecer
calumny alilá (H), iftira (T *kanunn*), kalomnia
camel gamelio, gameyo; **camels** camellos
camp kampo
camphor alkanfór
can (v) poder, (v) pueder
Canaan Chenaan (Fer Bib Gen); **Canaanites** Chenaani
canal kanal
canalization kanalizasyon

canary kanarya; **small canary** kanarino
cancel a subscription dezabonar
cancellation anulamyento, anulasyon
cancer kanser, karkino
cancerous kanserozo
candelabra almenara, kandelar
candid bovankyón, bovarrón
candidacy kandidatura
candidate (n) kandidato
candies konfites
candle (n) vela, kandela, pavil, siryo
candled enkandeleado
candlestick candelabre, kandelar
candy konfit; **candy shop** shekerdjilik; **candy bowl** konfitera; **candy box** konfitera
cane baston, dignidear (T *deynek*); **cane strokes** bastonáda
cannon top (T)
canoe piroga dugout
canticle chantika
cantor (at the synagogue) kantor, hazan
canvas tela
cap baréto, boneka
cap takya, takye
capable akadir (T *kadir* capable), capache (Monastir dialect)
capable desbolvido, kapache (Ital *capace*)
capacity kapasidad
caper alkaparra, kaparra
capital (adj) kapital; (n, financial) serme (T *sermaye*); (n) kapital; **capital city** (n) kapitala
capitalism kapitalismo
captive cautiva cavayo, resgatado
captivity galut (H)
car auto, karu, otomobil; **car driver** chofer (F *chauffeur*)
carafe karafa
caramel balgamún
card carte; **card game** bridj
cardiac kardyako
cardiography kardyografiya
cardiologist kardyologo
cardiology kardyolojiya

carefree lijera (fem)
careful kuydadozo
careless gamsíz (T)
caressing arregaladór
caretaker of a synagogue sanmaz
cargo kargo
caricature karikatura
carnation graviyina
carob harrova
carpenter carpintero, dulgyer (T *dülger*), dulyer (T *dülger*), duramadji
        (T *dogramaci, doghramaci*), dusekchi (T *döshekçi*);
carpentry - wookwork carpentry durama (T)
carpet hali, manta, tapete; small carpet tapetiko
carriage carrose (Monastir dialect), furgon, karotsa
carrot safanorya
carry tashirear (T *tashimak*, kanunn); carry out complir; carry-over of
        a sum reporto
cartel boréo
cartwheel takla
case (n) maslat, caso, kavzo
cash (v) arrekavdár, rekavdar; (n) enkaso; cash payment duko
cashier arrekavdadór, enkashador
cashmere kazmir
cassock kazaka, opa
castle castillo, kastiyo
castor oil azeyte de rizino
castrated kastrado
Catalan katalan, katalona (from Span Catalogna)
catalogue katálogo
cataplasm lapa
catastrophe desgrasya, sinistro
catch (n) bonansa; (v) aferar; catch a cold or a flu esfriarse; catch by
        surprise incantar (Monastir dialect); catch in the net enradar;
        catch with a hook enganchar
category klal (H kanunn)
caterpillar bavóza, guzano, tertir, tertil (T *tirtil*)
catheter (urinary) shonda, dreno, tubiko
cattle ganàdo
cauliflower karnabit (T)

cause (n) kavza (modern Spanish *causa*; the second element of the au-
diphtong has become *v* in Judeo-Spanish), cavso; **cause deafness**
asodreser; **cause disgust** askear; **cause fear** (v) destrueser; **cause
great fear** estremeser; **cause harm** endomajar; **cause pain** dueler
(v); **cause the formation of an abscess** (v) empostemar; **cause
trouble** bulanear **nauseate** (from T *bulanmak*); **cause tuberculosis**
entekiar
caution akavido
cautious kuydadozo, sezudo
cavalcade caualgadura (Ferrara Siddur)
cave meara (H *meara*, T *maghara*
caviar havyar
cavity karia; **with cavities** sapyo
cease (v) apuçar (Monastir dialect), stankar
cedar sedro; **cedars** çedros
ceiling tavan (T)
celebrate fiestar, fyestar, selebrar; **celebrated** selebrado
celebration selebrasyon
celery apio, apyo, dumalan
celestial body luzero
celibate bekyarlik
cell selula; **human cell** selula humana
cement çimento, cimiento
cemetery bedajayim (H *beth ahayim*, lit: house of the living),
mezarana, simeteryo
censor sensor
censure (n) sensura; (v) sensurar, vituperar
centenary centenaryo
center çentro (Ital *centro*), sentro
century dor, siglo, syekolo
cereal sereal
ceremonial seremonyozo
ceremony seremonia, seremonya; **without ceremony** teklifsiz (T)
certain cierto, seguro, shubesiz (T *shüphesiz*), sierto, sierta, siguro;
certainly (de) cierto, de cierto, decierto, shubesiz (T *shüphesiz*),
siguramente
certificate çertifikato
certification asiguransa
certify asegurar, asigurar, asyertar, constar

certitude seguransa
chain (n) kadena, kolana, kordon; chain with watch satí kordón
    (T *saat* watch); chained enkadenado
chair sia, silla (Ferrara Siddur), siya; circumcision chair sia para
    sirkunsir; chair (in a synagogue) teva; sit on a chair siyar (v)
Chaldean kaldeano, kaldeo
chalk topeshir (T *tebeshir*)
chamber pot basin, çata, chukal, çokal, pishadera (vulg)
chamomile mansanilla, mansanilla
chance azlaha (H), bajtina (T *baht*), mudança (Ferrara Siddur)
change (v) trokar; change linen trokar modadura; change house trokar
    de kaza; (n) trokamyento; changing trukando
chapter kapitulo
character nature (Monastir dialect); character of a person tabiet, tabiat (T)
charade sharada
charcoal komur (from T *kömür*), kyimur (T *kömür*)
charge (n) enkargo
chariot quatregua (Fer Bib Gen Kings)
charitable caritativa; very charitable sadikero
charity byenfezénsya, caridad, sedaka (H, T), tsedaka, zahut (H)
charlatan çarlatan, sharlatan
charm endulko, fechizo; charming savroziko (adj); charming, graceful
    woman dilbaza (T)
chase away rondjar
chased echado
chastise kastigar
chat (v) kunusheár (from T *konushmak*)
chatter çarlar, çarlear, komadrear
chatterbox rompedor
cheap barato
cheat (v) dolanderear (T *dolandirmak*), embelekar, enganiar, enganyár,
    trampeár, trishar (v, F *tricher*); cheated embabukado; cheating fal-
    samyento
check (n) çek; (v) mirar; check on verifikar
cheek care
cheese ceso, kezo, 'queso
chemise yenso
cherry sereza
cherubs cherubim

chest arca, kasha, pecho, petcho; chest (furniture) almaryo; small chest
(furniture) almaryiko
chestnut castania, kastanya; chestnuts nañas, kastañas; chestnut-
colored hair enkastañado
chicken poyo, tauk, gaina, gallina; chicken coop kumash (T *kümes*)
chief capu (Monastir dialect), gadol, el gadol, kapo (Ital *capo*), reis (T
kanunn), sergerde (T kanunn), shef (F *chef*); Chief of Protocol
Shef de Protokol
chilblain safañon
child criatúra; small child fijiko; childbearing criar; childbirth parto;
childhood çikez; childishness buchukchulúkes (T *buçuk*)
chill (v) esfriar; (n) titereo; chills frio frio, chills temblores
chimney badja (T *baca*), chimney çemimea
chin - double chin papada
china (dish) çini
Chinese çines
Chinese language çinesko
chocolate çikolata, çokolata; chocolate factory çokolateria
choke aogar
cholera holera
choose (v) escoger, deskartar, eskojer
chorus pizmon (H)
chosen deskojido
Christian christiano, Kristiano
Christianity christiandat
Christians Cristianos
chronic migraine shaka
chronicler artikolista
church eglisia (from F *église*), klisa
cicada çiçigaya
cigar puro
cigarette çigaro; cigarette case tabatyera; cigarette holder çibuk;
cigarette holder tchibuk (from T *çubuk*)
cilantro culantro
cinder çispa
cinnamon kanela
circle arcu (Monastir dialect), serklo
circular (letter) çirkolar
circulate sirkolar, sirkukar

circulation (e.g. of a newspaper) tiraj, sirkülasyon
circumcise bautizar, cercucir, circuçir, sircuzír; circumcised cercucido,
    circuncidado; circumcised penis birit; circumcision berit
    milá, mila
circumstance sirkonstensya
circus çirko (Ital)
cistern sisterna
cite a name enmentar (v)
citizen sivdadano, sudito; citizenship suditansa
city ciudá; ciudad, medina, sibdad, sivdad; city wall muraya
civil service mulkiye (T *mülkiye*, kanunn)
civilization sivilizasyon
claimant demandador
clamp (n) gancho, meñene (T *mengene*)
clap (v) dar palmadas
clarification esklaresimyento
clarify esklareser
clarinet zurna
clarity klareza
class modu (Monastir dialect)
classes kursos
clay barro
clean (v) alimpiar; (adj) limpio; cleaned espulgado; cleanliness
    limpieza
clear (adj) klaro, clear off desbarasar
clearly ashikyare (T *ashikâr*)
cleave (v) çatladear (T *çatlatmak*)
cleft findiriz
client alidji (T *alici*), musteri (T *müshteri*); serious client agir mushteri
    (T *agir mushteri, aghir mushteri*)
climate aver (Monastir dialect), klima
clinic klinika
cloak kazaka, manto (F)
clock ore (Monastir dialect), reloj, saát (T)
close (adj) proksimo; (v) serrar
close (adj) serka, sircanu (Monastir dialect); close one serkano; close
    to serkano, sovri (Monastir dialect)
closed cerro, cerrado, serado, serrado, sirade
closet armáryo

closing serradura; **closing time** (ora de la) serradura
cloth rápa, ropa, tela, vistido
clothes panyo, paño, vestimienta
clothesline kuedra del lavado
cloud(s) nuue (Ferrara Siddur)
cloudy brumózo, ennuvlado; **cloudy sky** (syelo) bulanik
clown paylacho, pagliacho, soytari (T)
club hevrá, klub
clumsy barbuzáen, desjenado, empalukado, topachudo
coach carrose (Monastir dialect)
coachman arabadji (T *arabaci*), carruseru
coarse ruda; **coarse insult** stopachada (Ital *stopacio*)
coast uriye (Monastir dialect)
coat (v) kapladear, manto; **coat hanger** enkolgador
cockroach eskaravajo, eskaravato, skaravajo
cocktail kokteyl
cocoon of silkworm kukuyo
cod bagaláu, moruna; **cod liver oil** azeyte de moruna
code kodiche (Ital *codice*)
coerce komersyalizar
coffee kafé, (Turkish coffee) kave; **coffee cup** findjan, finjan; **small
     coffee cup** findjaniko
coffin arón, kasha
coin cornado
coincide by chance (v) arrasladéar (T *rastlamak*)
cold (adj) calade (Monastir dialect), frio, yelado; **very cold** entejado;
     cold blood sangre fria; **cold-blooded** sangre-fria
collar yaka
collect arekojer, arrekojer, rekojer
college iscolje (Monastir dialect)
collide with trompesar
collision trompeson
colonel polkovnic, polkovnik (Bulgarian)
color bóya, kolor; **colored** boyadeádo; **being colorful** vistosidad,
     vistozidad; **colorful** vistozo; **colorfully** vistozamente, vistozamente
comb (n) peyne; (v) peynar
combat (n) kombate
come venir, vinir; **come back** retornar, tornar; **coming together**
     adjuntamyento

command (n) dicha, manda, enkomenda; **to be under the command**
   estar soto komando; (v) ordenar; **commands** ordona; **commander**
   gadol, el gadol (H)
commemorate komemorar, **commemorate** membrár
commemoration recuerdo
commence (v) prisipiar
commended ordono
comment (n) pirux
commentary esklaresimyento
commerce fecho, komercho, tidjaret (T *ticaret*, kanunn)
commercial komersyal
commissar komisaryo
commission (n) mandado
commitment dibur
committee konsilyo
commode komodo
common komun; **common cold** abashada
communal religious district hachgaha (H)
communism komunismo
communist komunisto
community cahale, concluission, kehila, komunita, komunitá, mil(l)et
   (T *millet*, kanunn)
companion (lit: foot companion) ayaktash (T *ayaktash*), compañero,
   haver (H)
company (military) bulluk (T *bölük*), compañia, kumpania, kumpanya
compare (to a model or standard) apariguar; **compared** asemejado
compasses peryel (T *pergel*)
compassion piadad, piyadad, picadu (Monastir dialect); **to have com-**
   passion agidear (T *acimak*)
compelled forsado
complain kechar, keshar, keshar, quejarse, qusharse, lamentarse
complaint esclamaciiôn, esclamaçion, kechida, kesha, keshada, pyanto;
   complaints doleansas
complete (adj) tam, (adj) tamam, complido, atemo (Fer Bib Gen), complido; **complete failure** fiasko
complexion tino
comply cumplir
components kompozado
comport (v) komportar
compose (v) kompozar, cumpuzar

composed cumpuzadu (Monastir dialect), kompozado, mezurado
composer kompozitor
composition kompozisyon
compost (n) komposto
compound weave seraser; compound weave kemha
comprehension entendimyento
compress (n) komprimado; compress of ice paño de buz; hot
    compresses paños kayntes
compression apretamyento
compromise kompromiso
compromising act kompromisyon
comrade (lit: foot companion) ayaktash (T *ayaktash*)
concentration arrekojimyento
concern ilaka (T *alaka*); concerned penseryozo
concierge kapidji
conciliatory avenivle, konsiltable, konsilyante
concise konsizo
concision konsizyon
concupiscent look ojetada
condemn kondanar, asetensyar, vituperar
condemnation gezera (H), kondanasyon
condense apurar
condescend (v) deñar, endeñarse
condition hal (T); conditions shurut (T kanunn)
condolence pesame
conduct (v) agyar, konduzir
conference konferensya
confess atorgár, confesar, konfesar
confide entregar
confidence avtajá (H), feouzia (Salonica Pesach Siddur), feúzya,
    féouzia, seguridad
conform (adj) tipki (T)
conformity ra'yet (T *riayet*, kanunn)
confront eskuentrar (Ferrara Siddur), eskwéntrar (Jud-Sp Dict Madrid)
confuse (v) konfonder, shashear; confused arraviado, avanado, marear,
    maredo, shasheado, shashkin
confusion dubarina, embroyo, enredijo, karishiklik (T *karishiklik*
    kanunn), mareo, taburra
congratulate felichitar (Ital *felicitare*), felisitar; Congratulations!
    aferin (T)

conjugate konhugar (Port *conchigar*)
conjurer hokabaz (T *hürmet*)
conjuring hokabazlik
conquer (v) rekonkuestar
conquest (n) rekonkuesta
conscientious neeman (H)
consecrate dedikar (It *dedicare*)
consequence seguita
consequently por tanto
conserve abiguar, abiuiguar; conserve in salt (v) ensalsar
consider konsiderar
consideration konsiderasyon, por hatir (T *hatir* kanunn), reayet
    (T *riayet*)
consign konsiñar
consignment konsiña
console afalagár
constipate afatigar, afitar
constipation durera
constrain (v) forsar
construct (v) edifikar
construction worker yapidji, yapi (T)
consult (v) danishear (T *danishmak*)
consume roendar; roendando, sorvido; consumed by anxiety roendarse
contagious pegadozo
contemptible alchak (T *alçak*)
contest (n) ripueste (Monastir dialect)
continue sontrayér
continuity seguita
contorted tuuerto
contribution empozisyon
control (v) revizar, averdadear
controversy maraza
convene konvenir; convened konvenido
convenient pertenesido
convent convente
conversation çarla, lakirdi
converse platicar
convert (v) transtornàr, bautizar
convince kanderear (T *kandirmak*), konvenser; convinced enkalkado,
    konvensido

cook (n) ajtchi (T *ashçi*), (fem) gizandera; gizandona, (fem)
    guizandona; (v) cuiziér, gizar, guizar, kozir, kozer, enkochar; cook
    with saffron asafranar; cooked kozido; cooked with saffron
    asafranado; cooking pot çanaka (T *çanak*), tendjere (T *tencere*)
cookie biskuchiku
copper alárze, bakir (T), kovre
coppersmith kovrero
copulate sikishear (vulg)
copulation (vulg) enkashada
coquetry naz
coquette çijifyongo, koket
coquettish behavior koketeria
coral merdjan (T *mercan*)
cord kordon, kuedra
coriander culantro
cork (n) tapon, mantar (T), tapadeo
corkscrew tirbushon (F *tirbouchon*)
corn ispidje (Monastir dialect)
corner kyoshe, kyushe (T *köshe*), rincon, (corner in which one rests)
    ladio
cornice previz
corporal punishment panpan (children's language)
corporation boréo
corpulent godron, paparron, puerpudo
correct (adj) djustu (Monastir dialect); (v) korijar
correctness terbie, terbiye (T *terbiye* kanunn)
corrode roendar; corroded roendando
corrosive sublime
corrupt (v) abastdrear; (adj) corrupto; to become corrupted pudrir
cost (n) custo
cottage vila
cotton algodon, pambuk (T *pamuk*)
couch kanape (F *canapé*)
cough (n) tos; (v) toser
council konsilyo
counsel (n) consejo, konsejo
count (title of nobility) konde; (v) contar
counterfeit money moneda kalb; counterfeiter falseador, falsifikador;
    counterfeiting kalbazanlik (T *kalpazan* kanunn); counterfeiting
    taklit (T)

country campo, heredaria (Fer Bib Gen), payiz; **countryside** kampaña
courage ánimo, djesaret (T *cesaret* kanunn), koraje (from F *courage*)
court djuzdju (Monastir dialect), tribunal; **court of justice** mahkeme,
  majkyeme (T)
courtesy cortesia
cousin primo/a, sovrino, sovrinado; **young cousin** sovriniko
covenant espartimyénto, firmamiento
cover (n) tapon, (n) urti (T *örtü*); (v) cubrir, occlude, (cover with a
  protective layer) empegar, çokar; **cover with carpet** entapetar;
  cover with diamonds or jewels endyamantar; **cover with dirt or
  mud** enlodar; **cover with sand** (v) enarenar; **cover with sand**
  arenar; **cover with tiles** tejar; **covered** cubiertos, encubierta
  (Ferrara Siddur), velado; **covered with lice** empiojado, empiojarse;
  covered with soot enfuliñado; **covered with wax** enserado
coverlet kolcha
cow vaca, vaka
coward espantaso, kobardo
cowardice (vulg) kagadero, kagatina
cowboy vaquero, vakero
crabbiness dañadoriko
crack (n) çatla (T *çatlak*), çatleadura, findiriz; **cracked** çatleado
craftiness sheytaneria
craftsman embastador; **craftsman's workshop** atelyé; **craftsmanship**
  artezaneria
crafty enkulevrado
crane grua
crash (v) esfondar
crayfish karavides (T)
crazy budalá (T), divane (T), loco, loko
create emplantar
Creator (the) El Criador, Criador
creature criado, kriatura
crêpe bumuelo
crib kuna
cricket griyo
crime delicto
criminal kriminal
criminality criminalidad
cripple (v) estropyar; (n) sakat (T *sakat*); **crippled** estropyado
crippling tuyidura

crisis crize (Port *crise, crize*), kriza
criticize (with irony) taklear (T *takilmak*)
crooked enganchado, tuguerto, tuuersido, tuuerto
crookedly averé
crookedness tuuertedad
crop mahsul (T kanunn)
cross (n) cruz, hristu (Monastir dialect); cross- eyed shashut, shashuto
crow cueruo, cuervo, grája; flock of crows grajerio; young crow grajon
crowd - huge crowd tabur; crowds ahali
crown (v) enkoronar, corona; crowned enkoronado; crowning
   enkoronamyento
crumb tringa
crumble desmenuzar, esfondar
crumple enjandrazonar; crumpled enfregoneado
crusade cruzada
crush (v) pizar
crushed desjachado
crushed majado
crust krosta
crutch moleta
cry (v) esclamar, esclamir, jimír, llorar, yorar; crying empido, pyanto
cucumber pepino, pipino
cuddler salamero
cuddling salamerias
cultivate labrar
cultivator labrador de tierra
cumin rezyane
cunning ensavanado, sheytaneria
cup copo, copu (Port *cup*), kupa, vaso, fildjan, fildján (Monastir
   dialect); cup holder áza; cupboard dolap (T), platera
cure (v) melezinar, sanar, ondular
currency paras (from T *para*)
curse (n) maldisyon
cursed maldicho/a (archaism, modern Spanish equivalent is *maldito*),
   maldito, maldicho, maldixo
curtain kortina, perde (T)
curved tuuersido
cushion almohadal, kavesal, yastik (T)
custom adet (T), custumbre, uzo, uzu (Monastir dialect), ysança
customary ceremony seremonia de uzo

customer mushteri (T *müshteri*, kanunn)
customs cumerchu (Monastir dialect), dogana, duana, komarka;
customs officer duanera, dogañero (Ital *doganiere*); customs agent
komerchero
cut (n) kortadura; cut (v) kortar; cut into pieces enkortado; cutting
kortamiento
cutlet brizóla (T *pirzola*)
cymbal jiles (T *zil*)
cynical azpan, eskarado
cynicism arsizlik (T), eskaramyento

D

dagger kama (T)
dairy lecheria
damage (n) daño, estruisyon; (v) dañar, endomajar, malograr,
quebrantar; damaged dañado; damaging dañozo, danyozo
dame damma, dama
dance (n) bayle, tango; (v) baylar; dancer bailador; female dancer bayladéra
dandruff pitirína
dandy jijifranko, jijifrango
danger (n) riziko, estrechura, peligro, perikolo, rézico, sekana (H);
dangerous peligrozo, perikulozo (Ital *pericoloso*); dangerous individual eleme kimur (T *eleme kömür*)
dare atriviar, ozadiar; daring atrivido, enuolente, ozadiar
dark aleskuro, escuro, karaylan (T *karaoghlan*), tenebrozo; dark blue
azúl; dark hair brúno; dark, somber mood tarkiza; darken
empereteser, embruneser, enteñevlar, escureser; darkened
enteñavlado; darkening eskureo; darkness (deep darkness)
syegetina, escuridad, eskuridad, negror, tenevlia, tiñevla; dark-
skinned morena (fem)
darling (fem) kirida
darn (v) arrekuxir
dart espinga
date (time) data; (v) datar; date (fruit) datle, datli (Port *datile*); date
tree datlanal, datlanar
daughter fijá, hija, ija; daughter-in-law ilmuera, nuera
dawdle morhunear, morjunear

dawn (v) alborear; (n) alvoráda
day dia, diya; **the next day** (el dia) seguinte; **the day before yesterday**
    antiyer
dazed shabsal
dazing tutuleo
dead season in business kyesat (T *kesad*)
dead-end street çikma sokak (T *çikmaz sokak*)
deaf sodro; **deafen** ensodreser
deafening ensodresimyento
deafness sodredad
deal with tokar, pricurar di (v, Monastir dialect); **deal wisely**
    assaventér; **dealer** mircader (Monastir dialect)
dear kerido; querido; **dearest** rregalado
death muerte
debasement aperreamyento, enkalo
debate debate
debauched pishutero; **debauched women** hostaleraz (Ladino Ferrara
    Bible)
debauchee çalik
debt devda, devisa
decagram dekagramo
decalcomania kalkomani
decay desmoludara; **decaying** harab (T)
deceased regretado
deceitful person dalaveraci (T); **deceitfulness** enfilada
deceive embabukár
December desembro (It *dicembre*), kislev (H), kislimu (Bab)
decentralize desentralizar
deception bulmá, engaño
decide (v) dar karar, decidir; **decided** decidido, desido (se)
decipher deshifrar
decision askama (H), decizyon (Ital *decisione*), karar
declaim (v) deklamar
declaration deklarasyon
declare (v) deklarar
decline deskaeser
decompression desbafo
decorate adornar, endorar; **decorate with flags** embandyerar
decoration (T kanunn), dekorasyon
decorator dekorador

decorticate fruits mundar; decorticating fruits mundadura
decree karar
dedicate dedikar (It *dedicare*); dedicated aplikado
dedication dedikas
deep undo, fondo, ondo; deep sleep adormeçimiento; deep voice
  bozarrún; deepen aprofondar
deer syervo
defamation desfamasyon, difasmasyon
defame disfamar
defeat (n) desfecha; (v) dezecha
defecate (vulg) kagar
defect defekto, defeto, tara
defective difetozo (Ital *difettoso*), manko, sakat (T *sakat*)
defend (v) defender; defender abogador, defendedor
defense difeza, defensa, defeza (Ital *difesa*)
defiance desfeuzia
defiance desfio
definite definitivo
definition definisyon
deflower desflorar
deformation desformasyon
defunct difuncto
defy (v) desfiar
degenerate (v) dejenerar, abastadrear; degenerated dejenerado
degrade oneself enkorkovarse
degree rutbe (T *rütbe*, kanunn)
dehypnotize desmañetizar
deify endyozar
deity deydad (Ferrara Siddur)
delay (n) detenensya, (n) morvet (T *mürvet*), tadransa, alikudear
  (T *alikoymak*); (v) atadrar, atrazar, adyar (Port); delayed
  atardado; delaying atardamyento
delegate delegado
delegation delegasyon
deliberately majsos (T *mahsus*), dando i tomando
deliberation deliberasyon
delicate delikado, fino
delicious delisyozo
delight deleyte (Ferrara Siddur), deliryo
delirium deliryo, desvareo

deliver entregar, dar, liberar, librar (v); deliver to remitir; deliver a
   speech (v) deskorsar; deliverance delivransa, regmissiôn, selamet;
   delivered eskapado; delivery entregada
demagnetize desmañetizar
demagogue demagogo
demand (v) demandar, egzijir
demarcate demarkar
demean pisotear
dementia avanamyénto
democracy demokrasia
democrat demokrata; democratic demokratiko; democratize (v)
   demokratizar
demolish dererokado, derrokar
demolition demolisyon, derrokiyo
demon demonio
demonetize desmonetizar
demonstrate (v) demostrar
demonstration demostrasyon
demonstrative demonstrativo
demoralize desmoralizar
denature desnaturar
denial ñegasyon, negativa
denied nego
denounced denunçio
dentist dyentista
denture dyentadura
denude desbragar
denunciation denuncia
deny desmentir, ennegar, inyegar, ñegar, renegar; deny one's faith
   reveyar; deny oneself desñegarse
depart partir; department departamento
departure despartimyento, embarko
depend depender; dependency dependensya
dependent dependyente; dependent upon mutalik (T *müteallik*,
   kanunn)
depleted zilkade
deplorable deploravle
deploy despligar
depopulate despovlar
deport deportar

deportation deportasyon, deportation surgun (T *sürgün* kanunn)
deported deportado
deposit (v) depozitar, rezidu, depozito
deposition takrir (T kanunn)
depository depozitaryo
depravation pushtluk
depraved pusht (T)
depreciation despresyasyon
depression desbafo
deprivation afriisyón, afriission, affrisyón
deprived of liberty sofiguado
depth ondura
deputation deputasyon
deputy deputado, diputado
derange molestar; deranged bozúk (T)
derangement bozeadúra, molestya
deregulated bozúk (T), desregulado
deregulation bozeadúra
derivation ramo
derive (v) derivar; derived derivado
dermatology dermatolojia
dervish dervish (T *dervish*)
desalinization desaladura
desalinize (v) desalar
descend (v) decindir
descent desendensya, abashada
descendant desendyente
describe deskrivir
description deskripsyon
desert desierto, dezyerto, dezierto, dizyerto; uninhabited desert
    asolapado; desert (v) dizyertir
deserter dezyertor
deserve mereser; deserved meresido
deserving diño, dinyo, pertenesido
design dizenyo
designation ta'yin (T *tâyin*, kanunn)
desirable dezeavle, suetavle
desire (n) deseo, desseo, dezeo; (v) dessear; desired dezeado
desirous dezéôzo
desist dezistimyento, dezistir

desk meza
desolate (v) desolar, perishan (adj)
despair (n) dezesperansa, dezespero; (v) desesperar, dezesperar,
    dezesperare, lamentarse; despairing dezesperado
despite this ine (T gene)
despot despota
dessert dolse, maneras de mandjares
destination destinasyon
destiny destino, fado, felek (T), suerte
destitute desnudo, kokoz
destroy arrematar, arrematar, derrokar, desfazer, destruir, estruidor,
    estruir, estruyir, malograr, sakear, trastornar; destroyed
    arrematado, bozeádo, bozúk, harab (T); destroyer derrokador,
    fundidor, stridor, destruidor
destruction derrokiyo, estruisyon
destructive destruktivo
detach dezatar; detach oneself dezafeksyonarse
detail detalyo
detain (v) destenir, alikodear (T alikoymak kanunn), detener
detective detektiv, hafiye
deteriorate (v) amurchár (Port murchaer-se, Monastir dialect); deterio-
    rated bozeádo, (deteriorated by usage) uzado
deterioration desmoludara
determinant cause sebeb (T)
dethrone destronar; dethroning destronamuento
devastated asoládo
develop desvelopar; development desarrollo
deviate (v) desviar, deviate deviar
deviation desvio, deviation taburra
devil demonio, diavlo, guerko, guerku, satán, sheytan (from T sheytan
    devil), wuerko; devilish acts diavleria
devoted devuado, sadik (T)
devour devorar; devour with the eyes ojetear
devout hasid, sofu
dew derusha (H)
diabetes diabet
diabetic diabetiko
diabolic diaboliko; diabolic action sataneria
dialect dialekto
diameter diametro

diamond brilánte, briyánte, pirlanta (T)
diaper pañal
diarrhea (vulg) kagadero, kaganera, kagatina, bozéo, diarea, salida,
   shushunera, shushurella
diaspora diaspora
dice dado; dice game komar (T *kumar*)
dictation (n) dikte, dictovka (Bulg)
dictator diktador; dictatorship diktadura
did izo
die (v) arresvalarse, encafissiar, morir, murir; die in the prime of age
   malograr; died murio
diet dieta
difference deferensya, diferencia
different diferente, difirenti
differentiate diferenciar
difficult difísil; difficult situation estadia; difficulty iziyét (from *eziyet*
   ill-treatment)
diffuse vulgarizar
digest (v) dijerir; digestible (n) dijestivo, digestvle
digestion dijestyon
digger eskarvador
dignitary diñitaryo
dignity diñidad
dilapidate desperdrer
dilapidation çurukluk (T *çürüklük*)
dime diezmo, dyezmo
dimension dimensyon
diminish (v) desmenguar, abatir, amenguar, disminuir, menguar;
   diminish the quantity empokeser; diminished desmenguado,
   memguaron
diminution diminusyon
diminutive diminituvo
dimple foyika
dining table sofra (T)
dip (v) entinienter; (in a sauce or soup) untar; dipped in remojado;
   dipping untadura
diphtheria difteria
diploma diploma
diplomacy diplomasia
diplomat dipkomado; diplomatic diplomatiko

direct (v) agyar, dirijir; (adj) direkto; direction direksyon
directive direktiva
director direktor, dirijente, mudir (T *müdür*, kanunn)
directorial direktoryal
dirge endecha
dirt ensuzyadura, suziedad, suzyedad, (vulg) kagadura, kagajon; dirti-
    ness suzyedad; dirty askeozo, çurro, embatakado, ensuzyado,
    fulin, suzio, suzyo
disadvantaged dezavantajado
disaffect dezafektar; despasyenado
disaffection deskerensya
disagreeable dezagradavle
disagreement enradijo
disappear deperdar (se), desparecer, esvaneser; disappearance
    desparisyon
disarm dezarmar; disarmament dezarmamyento
discernment tino
discharge (v) deskargar, eskargar
disciple dishiplo, dishiplo, elevo, elevu (Monastir dialect)
disciples talmidim (H)
discipline (n) dishiplina; (v) dishiplinar
disciplined dishiplinado, disciplined person dotrinado
discolored deskolorado
disconcerted shashkin, tutleado
discontent (n) disgusto, eskontente, dezagrado; (v) disgustar
discontinue deskontinuar
discord diskordya; discordant diskordante
discount (n) deskonto
discourage deskorajar
discover fallar (Ferrara Siddur), fayár (Jud-Sp Dict Madrid); discoverer
    deskuvridor; discovery deskuvyerta, keshf (T kanunn)
discredited deskredito
discrete diskreto; discretely baséter
discuss (v) diskutir; discussion dando i tomando, debate, diskusion,
    diskusyon
discussible diskutavle
disdain (n) desde, desdeño, desdeñador, estrapajo (Ital *strappazzo*),
    naz; disdainful desdeñozo, nazli (T *nazli*)
disease enfermedad, enfermidad, hazimyento (kanunn), malatia

449

disentangle desbrolyar, desmelar, dezembrolyas
disgrace dezgrasya; disgraced rezil (T); disgraceful desgraciado,
    desjenado, topacho (T *topaç*), topachudo, topachudo
disguise (n) finta; disguised tepdil (T *tebdil*)
disgust (n) disgusto, angustia, skifo; disgust (v) disgustar, desgustar;
    disgusting skifozo, eskifozo
dish plato
disheveled bragil, despechugado
dishonest dezonesto; dishonesty dezonestedad
dishonor (n) dezonor; (v) dezonor; dishonorable dezonoravle; dishon-
    ored dezonorado, rezil (T)
disillusion (n) deziluzyon; (v) deziluzyonar; disillusioned deziluzyonado
disinherit dezeredar; disinherited dezenredado
disk disko
dismal humor tarkiza
dismember desmembrar
dismount desmontar
disobey dezovedeser
disorder dezordem, enradijo, enredijo, karishiklik (T *karishiklik*
    kanunn)
disorganized dezorganizado, perishan (adj)
disoriented dezoryentado, tutleado
dispatch (n) remesa, embio
dispensary dispensaryo
dispense (n) dispensa; dispense (v) dispensar
disperse dispersar; dispersed desparzido, perishan (adj)
dispersion dispersyon
displease desplazer
displeasure dezagrado
dispose disponer, dispozar
disposed disposto; to be disposed to tender
dispossess desplumar, despojar
disproportion disproporsyon
disproportionate (v) disproporsyonar; (adj) disproporsyonado
dispute sayran (T *seyran*)
disregard (v) deskonsiderar
disrupt desmoronar
dissatisfying negrito, negreziko
dissimulate disimular, disimulado
dissimulation disimulasyon

dissipated disipado
dissociate disosyar
dissociation disosyasyon
dissolution disolusyon
dissolve derritir
dissuade dezkonsejar
distance (n) distansya, lungure (Monastir dialect)
distillation destilasyon
distinct apartadu (Monastir dialect); distinction distinksyon
distinguish démoudar, distengar, distingir; distinguished distingido
distorted tuuersido; distorted tuuerto
distract distraer, desbolver
distraction distraksyon, eglenje (T *eglence, eghlence*), taburra
distress (n) demenester, apreto, sekana (H)
distribute distribuir
distribution distribusyon, espartimyénto; distributions espartimientoa
    (Salonica Pesah Siddur)
distributor distribuidor
district zona
distrustful desconfiado, deskonfiado
disturb deranjar, desturbar, dokunear (T *dokunmak*), estemperear,
    shesherear (from T *shashmak*); disturbance dubarina; disturbed
    bulandereádo, tutleado; disturbing sfacato (adj) (Ital *sfacciato*)
disunited dezaunado, dezunido
ditch (n) endek (T *hendek*, kanunn), fóya, fuesa, fuessa (Ferrara
    Siddur); small ditch foyika
divagation divagasyon
divan divan (T)
diver dalgitch (T *dalgiç*)
diverse diverso
diversion ezvacheo, tadransa
diversity diversidad
divide divizar; divide up repartir; divided espartia
divine (v) endevina; divine command mandamiento; divino
divinity diunidad (Ferrara Siddur); divinidad
division divizyon
divorce (v) divorsar; (n) divorsyo, deshadura; divorced divorsado
dizziness sheshereos
do azer, facer, hazer; do a favor azer hatir; do nothing (asentarse)
    batal; do the customs clearance komerchear

dock skala   .
dockyard tersane (T *tersâne*, kanunn)
doctor doktor, dotor, Medíco, mediko; **female doctor** doktoresa;
    doctor's fee vijita; **doctor's fee** vizita
doctrine dotrina
document (v) dokumentar; **document** (n) dokumento; **documented**
    dokumentado
doe syerva
dog perro
dogma dogma; **dogmatic** dogmatiko; **dogmatism** dogmatismo
doll kúkla
dollar dolar
dolphin delphin
domain domeno
domestic animal behema
dominate (v) dominar, majorgar; **dominated** sofiguado
domination dominasyon, podesta, podestad
dominator dominador
dominion podesta, podestad, podestania
donation donasyon, ekdes (H)
donkey asno, azno, hamor; **donkeys** asnos; **female donkey** hamora;
    small donkey hamoriko; **female donkeys** asnas
donor donador
door guerta, puerta; **door of light** shaare; **doorman** kapidji, kavas
dorado (fish) endorada, dorado
dormer abaca (from T *baca* chimney); **dormer-window** abaca (from T
    baca chimney)
dormitory dormitorio
dosage dozaje
dose doza
double (v) dupyar; **double** (adj) dupyo; **double chin** barviáácho
doubled doblado, dublado, dupyode
doubt (n) shube (T *shüphe*), dubyo, duda, duvdo, safek (H); **taken by**
    doubt shubeleado; **without any doubt** shubesiz (T *shüphesiz*); (v)
    dubyar, duvdar, shubelear; **doubtful** dubyozo, dudozo, duvdozo,
    shubeli (T *shüpheli*)
dough masa, massa
dove kolomba, paloma, palomba, tortol
down (de) baxo, abacho, abaxo, debacho; **down here** aki abasho;
    downcast ennuvlado; **downtrodden** sorvido

dowry ajugar, ashugar, dota
doze (n) sfueñiziko; doze for a little while fazer un sfueñiziko furtively
 doze, surreptitiously doze
dozen dozena, duzena
drachma (Greek monetary unit) drajme, drama
drag (v) arastar, arrastár (Port), arrastrar; dragged arastado
dragon drago, dragon
drain (v) dranear, caño, dreno, drama
dramatic dramatiko
dramatize dramatizar
drape (v) panyo, paño
draw tirar
drawer kashon
drawers brága, kalso
drawing desiño, frankito; drawing room salon (F)
drawn (sword) desvayanada
dream (v) soñar (se), soniar (se); (n) soño, dream sueño, suenyo;
 dreamer soñador
drenched embañado, estufado
dress (v) vestir, roke (n) (Romanian Judeo-Spanish); dress elegantly
 endonar, fostan; dressed arrekojido; dressing gown neglijé
dried arresekado, enshuto
drifter serseri (T)
drink (n) breváje; drink (v) bivier; bivir; drinking glass kupa
drip (v) çorrear, deskorrer
drip damladear (v); dripping çorredero, çorreo, çorreteo, çorretero
 (Haketia); dripping oil yaghli (T yaghli)
drive (v) agyar, dravear (Eng), konduzir; driver (of public
 transportation) konduktor
drop tringa
drought seca, seka (H), sekera
drown affincar (from Salonician Passover Haggadah), aogar (se), hundiar (Ferrara Siddur); drowned fundido; drowning aogando
drug droga
druggist drogista
drugstore drogeria
drum (n) tumbana, dau, davul (T davul), tamburin; drums daules
drummer tanyedor, tañedor
drunk fernet; (very) enteñido; drunkard (fig) kalsado, borracho, bekei
 (T); drunkenness borrachéz

dry (adj) seko, enshuto, seco, (fruit, vegetable, meat) kart; (v) sekar, (with a towel) enshugar; dry oneself secarse; dry cleaner tintureria; dryness sekura
ducats (gold coins) ducados
duchess dukeza
duck baba, pato
duckling pata
duct alkadrúz (Port)
dues risumat (T *rüsumet*, kanunn)
duke duke
dull-wit torpedad
dung fuskin
dunghill maladares
duo duo
durable duravle
duration tura
during durante, en tiempo, mientris, myentres; during this time enmyentres
dust (n) poluo, polvo; cloud of dust terregina; duster sakudidor
duty dover, hizmet (T kanunn), ovligo, obligo
dwarf enano, nanniko, nano, nanno
dwelling morada; dwellings moradas
dye (v) enteñir
dying muriendo
dynamic dinamiko
dynamite dinamita
dynasty dinastia

E

each cada
eagle aguila
ear (of corn) lambrusko, oido, ojido, oreja, uidu
early temprano (de); early in the day temprano de dia; early bird madrugador; early morning demanyanika
earring orejal, skulkarichia, (e)skularichas (Gr *skoulariki*); earrings orejales
earth terrero, tierra, tyerra; earthenware pot çomlek (T *çömlek*); earthquake ráash, terretemblo

ease (n) fasilidad, feraklik (T *ferahlik*); easiness facilita, fasilidad,
     kolaylik (T kanunn)
east mizdrah; Eastern bishop egzarko
easy facil, sil (F *facile*), kolay (T); easy to fool person tito
eat (v) cumier, komer, comer, ahlat (from H *ahal*), yantar, yentar; eat
     as a glutton arresvalar; catcn by rats or mice ratonado; eating
     kumiendo
eccentric eksentriko
ecclesiastic eklezyastiko
echo badkol (H), eko
eclipse eklipsa
economical ekonomiko; economical person ekonomyozo; economically
     ekonomikamente
economist ekonomista
economize avansar
eczema egzema, ekzema
eczematous ekzematozo
Eden Heden
edge bodre, bordúra, vera
edifice edifisyo
edition edisyon
editor editor, redaktor; editor-in-chief redaktor in kapo; editorial edito-
     ryal; editorial office redaksyon
educate edukar; educated edukado
education dotrino, edukasyon
educational edukativo
educator (fem) edukatrice
effect (n) effeto; (v) effektuar
effective effektivo; effectively leolam (H)
efficiency efikasidad
efficient efikache
effort esforso, pena; worth the effort vale la pena
effrontery edepsizlik (T)
egg guevo, uevo; eggs besim (H); soft-boiled egg guevo rofidan
     (T *rafadan*)
eggplant berenjena, merenjena, merendjena, mirindjena
egoism egoismo
egoist egoista
Egypt Ayifto, Egito (Ital *Egitto*), Ejipto, Misir (T); Egyptian Ayissiano,
     Ayisyano, Egisyano (Ital *Egiziano*), ejipsjano, misirli (T)

eight ocho
eighteen deziocho, dieziocho, dyezicho, diziocho
eight hundred ochosientos, ochosyentos
eighth ochaua (Ferrara Siddur), ochavo, ochen
eighty ochenta
elaborate (v) elaborar
elastic (n) elastiko, lastikli (adj)
elasticity elastisidad
elbow kovdo
elect (v) elezir; elected deskojido, elezido
election eleksyon
elective elektivo
elector elektor; electoral elektoral
electrical elektriko
electrician elektrisyen
electricity elektrichita, elektrisidad
elegant elegante; elegantly elegantantamente
elementary elementaryo
elements kompozantes
elephant elefante, fil (T)
elevate (v) alsar; elevated altiuo (Ferrara Siddur), elevado
elevator asensor
eleven onzien
elimination eliminasyon
eloquence eloquencia
emanate emanar, manar
emanation emanasyon
emancipate (v) achilear (from T açilmak open oneself)
emancipation emansipasyon
embargo embargo
embarkation embarko
embarrass feder; embarrassed embarasado; embarrassment fasaria,
    fasarias, skotura (Gr)
embassy embasada
ember bráza; small piece of ember brazika
embitter amargar, enfyelar
embrace (v) abrasar, stringar
embroider brodár, lavrar, recamar; embroidered arrekamádo,
    recamado; chain stitch embroidery suzeni (T)
emigrant emigrado, emigrante

emigrate emigrar
emigration emigrasyon
eminence eminensya
emissary embiado
emission emisyon
emotion emosion
emperor emperador
empire emperio
empirical emperiko
employee empleado, empregado
employer empleador
emptied desdevanado
empty (v) vaziar, vazyar; (adj) vazio, vaziyo
emulation emulasyon
enchant enkantar; enchanter enkantador; enchantment enkantamyento,
enkante, enkanto
enclose enserrar; enclosed enserrado
encounter (n) encuentro, enkuentro; (v) encontrar, (v) enkontrar,
enkuentrar, renkontrar, fallar (Ferrara Siddur), iscuntrar
(Monastir dialect)
encourage enkorachar, enkorajar
encyclopedia ensiklopedya
end (n) fin, termino, acabamiento, eskapasyon, skapadishu; (v) acabár,
escapar, terminar; ending termino; endless chatter favlatina
endanger rizikar
endearment naz
endive endivya
endow uentana
endure padeser
enemy dushman (T düshman), enemigo, enimigo; enemies
angustiadores (Fer Bib Gen); enemy of the Jew oherayehudi (H)
energetic enerjiko, forsa, enerjia
enervated empostemado
engagement despozoryo
engender enjentrado
engineer engeniero, moendiz, muendiz (T mühendis)
engraving figurin
engulf englutir
enhance solevantar
enigma enigma; enigmatic enigmatiko

enjoy asaborar, gozar, saboerear; enjoy oneself arrepotrear
enlace enlashar
enlarge engrandecer, engrandissir
enmity enemistad, malquerencia
ennoble ennovleser
enormous enorme; enormously kiyamet (T)
enough bastánte; enough! básta
enraged fiduz (T *kuduz*)
enrich enrekeser; enriched arrekolmádo, enrekesido
enslave oneself esklavarse; enslaved sodjefto
enter entrar
entertain desbolver, eneglear (T *eglenmek, eghlenmek*), englenear
    (T *eglenmek, eghlenmek*); entertaining divertyente; entertainment
    divertimyento, eglenje (T *eglence, eghlence*), englenje (T *eglence,
    eghlence*)
entirely tekmil
entrails entraña, entrañas, tripas
entrenched tajada
envelop sarear (v, T *sarmak*); envelope embrujo, envelóp
envious ojento, selozo
environment ambiente
envy (n) gana, embidya; envy (v) tener gana
epicurean apikorós
epidemic magefa
epilepsy tomadura
epileptic fit toma
episode epizodyo; episodes pasajes
epitaph epitafya (Gr)
equally tambien
equilibrium ekilibro
equipment pusat (T, kanunn)
equivalent ekivalente
equivocal lastikli (adj)
era dor
eradicate arrematar, arrematar
erase embarrar; eraser embarrador
erect (v) erigir
err errar, yirrar (si) (v, Monastir dialect)
errands kursos
errant shoret

error lyero, yerro, yérro, yero
erudite (adj) erudito, meldahon
erudition erudisyon
escape (v) escapar, eskapar, kacherearse; **escape a desperate situation**
    salir a selamet; **escape from danger** eskulterear (T *kurtulmak*);
    escapee reskapado
essence essencia
establish (in a position or office) enstituir, estabilir, establecer; **establish**
    oneself estableserse; **establishment** estabilimyento
esteem (n) estima
estimate (n) estimasyon; **estimated** byenkyísto
eternal eternal, sempiterno
eternity eternidad
ether eter
ethical etiko
ethnic etniko
etiquette tiketa
eulogize endechár
Europeanized enfrankeado
evacuate evakuar
evacuation evakuasyon
evaluate mezurar
evaluation evaluasyon
evaporated desvaporado
evaporation evaporasyon
evasive evazivo
Eve Haua (Fer Bib Gen)
even afilou, aun, afilu (H), ainde (Port *ainda*, Monastir dialect); **even if**
    afillu, aunque; **even though** ainde (Port *ainda*, Monastir dialect)
evening tadrada, tadre, tarde, akontesimyento; **evening party** soare
    (from F *soirée*); **evening entertainment** almusama (T *müsamere*)
eventual eventual; **eventuality** eventualidad; **eventually** eventualmente
everlasting sempiterno
every kada; **everything** todo
evil eye (ojo) burakador, aynara (H *ayin ara*), nazar
evoke evokar
exact egzakto
exactitude exaktitud
exactly egzaktamente; **exactly the same** tipki (T)

exaggerate egzajerar
exaggeration (adv) kiyamet (T), egzajerasyon
exalt emborachar, enaltesser
examination egzamen
examine (v) egzaminar; examine in depth badkár (H); examine in full
aprofondir; examine with attention revizar
example egzemplo, egzempyo, eshemplo
exasperated egzasperado, empostemado
excellency (title) ekselensya
excellent buenissimo (It *buonissimo*), has
except afueras, saluo, salvo, salvu (Monastir dialect); excepted muaf
(T kanunn); exception eksepsyon
excess demazya, ekseso; to be in excess sovrar, sobrar
excessive demazyado, eksesivo
exchange (n) troka, trokido
excitation eksitasyon
excite (v) eksitar; excited eksitado
exclaim esclamar, esklamar
exclamation esclamación, esklamasyon; exclamations esclamantes
excluded dezechado, ekskluido
exclusion ekskluzyon
exclusively ekskluzivamente
exclusivity ekskluzividad
excommunicate enheremar (from H *herem* excommunication),
enjaremar, enxeremar; excommunicated enharemado, enjaremado
excommunication herém, niduy (H), shemata (H)
excoriate eskorchar
excoriation eskorchadura
excrement (vulg) kagadura, embatakado
excusable pedronavle
excuse (n) deskulpa, diskulpa, çikma (T); (v) diskulpar; excuse me af-
edersin, pardon!; excused diskulpado
execute (v) egzekutar; execution egzekusyon, idjra (T *icra* from Kanun
Name); place of public execution siaset ashikâri (T kanunn); executioner verdugo
executive egzekutante, egzekutivo
executor of a will testamentario
exegete egzejete
exemplary (adj) egzemplar, eshemplar, eshemplaryo, exgzemplaryo

exempt (n) egzentado; exempt (v) egzentar; exemption egzensyon
exercise (v) egzersar; exercise (n) egzersisyo; exercised egzersido
exhaust (v) iscapar (Monastir dialect), desreinar; exhausted sorvido
exhibition egzibisyon
exhortation egzortasyon
exhume desterrar, dezenterrar
exigency egzijensya
exigent egzijente
exile (n) sergun (T *sürgün*), surgun (T *sürgün* kanunn), galut (H),
    gerush (H); (v) egzilar; exile (n) egzilo; someone who goes into
    exile surgunli (T *sürgünlü*, kanunn); place of exile surgunlik
    (T, *sürgünlük*, kanunn); exiled egzilado
exist egzistir; existence egzistensya; existent egzistyente
exit (n) salida, salidura (Salonica Pessach Siddur)
exodus egzodyo
exonerated egzonerado
exorbitant egzorbitante
exorcise aprekantar; exorcised aprekantado, dezenfadado
exotic egzotiko
exotism egzotismo
expanse espandedura, espandidura
expatriating ekspatriasyon
expectation ekspektiva
expedient mandador
expedite mandar
expelled echado
expense masraf (T)
expensive karo; a little too expensive saladiko
experience (n) experyensa; (v) pasar
experiment (v) eksperimentar; (n) eksperimentador; experimental
    eksperimental; experimentally eksperimentalmente
expert eksperto, eshper, esper
expiration deskadensya; expiration term eskadansya
expire deskaer; expired deskaido
explain eksplikar; explanation espyegasyon; explanations
    eksplikasiones
explode patladear (from T *patlamak*)
exploiter vampiro
exploits torerios

exploration eksplorasyon
explore (v) eksplorar; explorer eksplorador
explosion eksplozyon, patlasyon (T *patlamak*)
explosive barút (from T *barut* gunpowder,cannon powder), explosive
    eksplozivo
export (v) exportar; exportation eksportasyon; exporter eksportador
expose (v) eksponer, ekspozar; expose in detail (v) detalyar; expose
    oneself to danger meterse en riziko; expose to someter
exposition ekspozisyon
express (v) eksprimir
expression asikomansi, ekspression
expressly ekspressamente
expropriate ekspropriar
expropriation ekspropriasyon
expurgate espurgar
extend tender, estirar, vulgarizar; extended tendido (Salonica Pesach
    Siddur)
extension estenso (Ferrara Siddur)
extent espandedura, espandidura
extenuated desjarretado
exterior (di) afuere (Monastir dialect)
exterminate (v) eksterminar; exterminated eksterminado
extermination eksterminasyon
exterminator eksterminador
extern eksterno
extinguish abafar, amatar; extinguished amatô
extirpate arrankar, arrankar, desplantar
extracted (text) travado
extraction - of good extraction soyli
extraordinary (adj and n) ekstra, ekstraordinaryo
extravagant ekstravagante
extreme ekstremo
extremist ekstremista
extremity termino
exuberant egzuberante
exult gozar
eye ojo; eye of a needle (el) burakito de l'aguja; eyebrow seja; person
    with very dense, bushy eyebrows sezudo; eyeglasses antojos, baté
    enayim (H, ironically used); eyelid párparo

F

fable fabula
fabricate oydurear, uydurear (v, T *uydurmak*)
fabrication oydurma, uydurma (T *uydurma*), uydurmasion,
    uydurmasyon
fabulist fabulista
fabulous fabulozo
façade fachata
face (n) figura, kara, cara, care (Monastir dialect), embultura, facha,
    faches (Ital *faccia*); faces faces
facilitate alivyanar, kolayladear (from T *kolaylamak*), yagladear
facility facilita, feraklik (T *ferahlik*)
fact fat, fecha
factor faktor
factory fabrika
facultative fakultativo
faculty fakuldad
fade (v) amurchár (Port *murchaer-se*, Monastir dialect), demudar
fail fazer fyasko; fail completely fazer fiasko; failure desfecha, dezecha,
    shunrada
faint (v) desmayar; fainted desmayado; fainting dezmayo
fair (n) ferya, panair (T, Gr *panayir, panayiri*, kanunn), pazar (T)
fairy fada; little fairy fadika
faith feúzya, féouzia, feouzia (Salonica Pesach Siddur), fey, in all good
    faith salana salana (adv); faithful fiel, neeman (H), sadik (T);
    faithless imansiz (T)
fake (adj) taklit (T), kalb; fake money moneda kalb
fakir fakir (Arabic)
falcon falkon
fall (n) kaida, kaidura, kayida, takla; (v) cayer, kaer, kayer; fall again
    rekaer; fall asleep dormirse; fall in love namorarse; fallen kaido;
    fallen in esfongato
false falso; false intent dientadura
falsification falsifikasyon
falsified kalb
fame fama, nam
familial familyar; to become too familiar with a subordinate abarabar
    (T *beraber* together)

familiarity familyaridad
familiarize oneself familiararse
family derredor, famia, familia, linaje; **family member** familiar
famished ambriyénto
famous afamado, famozo; **famous people** varones de la fama (Fer Bib
  Gen)
fan aventador
fanatic enklavado, fanatiko
fanatical enkalkado
fanaticism eklavadura, fanatizmo
fanaticize fanatizar
fanatism sektarismo
fantastic fantastiko
fantasy fantazia
far longi (Port *longe*), lesho, longu (adj, Monastir dialect); **from far** dii
  lonje; **far away** aleshado, leshos, lexos
farce farsa
farm çiflik (T *çiftlik*); **farmer** çifçi (T *çiftçi*), guertelano
fart (n) osurma (vulg), pedo; (v) pedar (vulg)
fascicle sakudidor
fascinate enkantar
fascism fashismo
fascist fashista
fashion moda; **fashionable** figurin
fast (adj) presto, prestozo
fast (n) ayuno; (v) ayunar
fastidious enfastyozo, fatigante; **fastidious moods** yangazlik
fat (adj) godro, (adj) shisko (T); **very fat** enshudyado; (n) godrura; **fat
  person** barril
fatal fatal; **fatalist** fatalista
fate fadarju, fadaryo (Port *fadario*), suerte
father padre, baba (T), jenitor, (in the language of children and adolescents) bábu; **father-in-law** esfuegro, eshuegro; **father of great
  grandfather** tarabispapu; **fathered** engendro; **fathers** abot
  (Haketia)
fatigue fatiga, kanserya
faucet huente
fault kabahat, kulpa
favor (n) favor, hatir (T); **favors** buenos; **big favors** grandes buenos; (v)
  enfavoreser, favorizar

fear (n) espanto, ispantu, miedo, pavor, sar, temor; by fear of quiça
    timuridad (Monastir dialect); (v) temer; fearful (of God) temiente
    (Ferrara Siddur), espantoso; fearsome temerozo
feast (n) fyesta, papis, fiesta, kombite; (v) arrepotrear
February fevereo, fevereyro, fevrie (F *février*), shevat (H), shabatu (Bab)
fecundate fekondar
fecundity brerekyét (T *bereket*)
fed farto
fee avait
feel sentir, sintir, rigritar (v, Monastir dialect); feel oneself (v) sentirse;
    feel obliged sentirse obligado; feel guilty deueler; feel nauseous
    bulanayar; feel nostalgia deskariñar; feel pain (v) degueler, esbelar
    (T *bel* waist, place of the belt)
feet pies
felicity beáta
fell asleep adormeciose
female embra, hembra; female idol dyoza
fenced cercado
fennel finojo, finozo
ferment (n) levadura; fermented alevdado, levdado
fern fojera
ferocious ferose
ferret (v) arremoshkar
ferryman barkero
fertile fertil; fertile plain vega
fertility fertlidad
fervor fervor
festival esveranero
festive meal rijo
festivity allegria
fetters pranga (T, kanunn)
fetus ñañato
feverish (slightly feverish) asoflamado
few poka; few people poka gente
fez fez
fiancé aprometido, despozado, espozado, hatan
fiasco fyasko
fidelity fideldad, fieldad
field (cultivated) tarla (T kanunn), ámbito, campo
fierceness eressimiento

fiery ravyozo, solevantado
fifteen quinze
fifteenth quienzen
fifth quinto, sinken; fifth of a series sinkeno
fifty çincuenta, cinquenta, sinkuenta; an ensemble of fifty
    sinkuentena
fiftieth sinkuenten
fig figo, higo; small fig figito; fig tree fijera, fijero; fig tree higuera
    (Ladino Ferrara Bible), higuiero
fight (n) peléa, pleito, pleto; fight (v) pelear; fighter peleador; fighter in
    a duel duelista;
figure (n) figura, (n) suret (T kanunn); figure (v) figurar
file (n) lima, fila
filial filial
filigree enteshe, filigranado
fill (v) inchir, yenar; filled farto, inchidos
filter (v) filtrar; filtered kolado
filth fealdad
final final
finality finalidad
finally finalmente, sof sof (H kanunn)
finance (n) finansya; finance (v) finansyar
financial pekunario
financier finansyaryo, finensyaryo
find (v) hallar, fallar (Ferrara Siddur), fayár (Jud-Sp Dict Madrid),
    iscuntrar (Monastir dialect), topar; find out endevina; find solace
    solacerse; find a remedy topar remedio; finder topador; finding
    fayadura
fine (n) knas (H kanunn), djereme (T cereme kanunn); djeza
    (T ceza)
fine (adj) fino, multa (Ital); finest artero
finger dado, dedo
finicky pinti
finish (v) iscapar (Monastir dialect), bitire(y)e, bitirear (T bitirmek,
    kanunn), eskapar
fire ensendyo, fuego; fire! Yanginvar! (T); firecracker taraka (from
    Castilian traca), fishek; fire work donannma (T)
firm (adj) seguro, bábachko, duro, firme; firmness seguransa
first primer, primera(o) (fem, masc); first-born primogenito, mayor

fish (n) peshkado, peshcado, pishkado, pichkado; (v) peshkar; fish
    scale eskama; fishbone espina, spina, espina; fishery peshkera;
    fishing nets dite (Gr)
fist punyo
fistula fistura, horhor
fit (v) kaver
five cinco, çinco, sinko
five sinko
five hundred quinientos
fix (v) fiksar; fixed fikso; fixed price nark (T *narh*, kanunn); fixed rev-
    enue rendida
fixation fiksasyon, fiksidad
flag bandiera
flambé flambada
flamboyant flambante
flame flama
flaming encendido
flannel flanela
flashiness vistosidad, vistozidad
flashy shinanali, vistozo
flask kanata
flat (adj) plano, (adj) yano
flattened desjachado
flatter with honeyed words enmelar
flatterer salamero
flattery dalkaukluk, dalkavuk (T), parmak
flavor lezet lezet (T), savor
flay eskorchar; flaying eskorchadura
flea pulga; flea market (lit: lice market) bitpazar (T)
flee fuyír
fleet fregata
flies mestura
flight vuelo
flint padregàl
flirtation namorikos
float flotar
flocks of sheep ouejas, ovejas (ovézas)
flood (n) desbodramyento, diluuio; flood (v) desbodrar
floor (in a building) kat, etaj (F *étage*), solar. tavlada

florescent enfloresyente
flour arina, farina, harina
flow çorrear; çorreo; flow of words esboro
flower (n) flor, chichek (from Turkish *çiçek*), çiçek (T); (v) enflorar;
     flower shop buketyéra; flowered enflorado, enfloresido
flu enfluensa
fly (n) moshka, moxka, moxca; abundance of flies moshkero; fruit fly
     moshkito; fly sheet folyeton; (v) bolar, volar, vuelar; flyer volador;
     flying bolante, volante
foam espuma, eskuma; foaming espumozo; foamy espumante
fodder yem (T kanunn)
fog derusha (H), nevla; fogged velado
fold (n) dobladura, duble; fold (v) doblar; folded doblado, dublado
folk tale konsejas
folklore folklor
following seguinte; following without interruption man mano
fond of merakli (from T *merakli*)
food comida, komida
fool (v) enganiar, enganyár
foot pye
football futbal
for para; for free (adv) debaldajon debaldes; for goodness sake! aman;
     for sure seguramente; for what reason por cavsa deque
forbidden defendido, prohibido, yasak
force (v) forsar; force (oneself) esforsar (se); forced enguantado,
     forsado; forced feeding enkalko; forced labor angarya (T); use of
     force zorbalik (T kanunn); by force zorlan (T kanunn)
forehead frente, freole
foreign exchange kamyo
foreign language la'az
foreigner yabandji
foreskin çerradura
forest orman (T kanunn), fare (Monastir dialect)
forever siempre
foreword akdama (H)
forged açecalan
forger falsaryo, falseador, falsifikador
forget olvidar, sulvider, ulvidar; forgetful olvidadozo, ulvidadoso; for-
     getting ezvacheo, olvido
forgive pardonar, perdonar; forgiving perdonansa

forgotten olvidado
fork piron, pirón(Gr *pirun*)
form (n) suret (T kanunn), fechura; **form a crust** enkrostar
formality formalidad
formation formasyon
formidable formidable, formidavle
formula formula
formulate formular, orar
fornication fornikasyon
fortification fortifikasyon
fortieth kuarenten
fortify fortifikar
fortress fortaleza, kale (T kanunn)
fortunate mazalozu (Monastir dialect), mazalozo; **fortunately**
    fortunadamente
fortune (H) mazal, azyenda, ventura; **fortuneteller** goralji (from T
    görücü), (fem) endevina; (masc) endevino, (fem, usually a gypsy)
    falaja, faldjia; (masc) faldji
forty quarenta, kuarenta
forward adelantre
found (adj) achadu (Port *achado*)
found (v) emplantar
foundation basaménto, fundasyon, temel (T)
founder fondador
foundry fyerreria
fountain cheshme (T *çeshme*), fuente, funtana, huente; **fountain pen**
    stilo
four quatro, kuatro
four hundred quatrocientos
fourteen katorze
fourteenth katorzen
fourth quarto, kuarto
fox rapoza, rapoze
fragile nezik (from T *nazik*)
frame (v) enkadrar, enkuadrar; (n) armatura, çerçeve; **framed**
    enkuadrado; **framework** çati (T), çerçeve
France Frankia
franchise (n) frankeza; (v) dezenfadar
frankly frankamente
fraternal fraternal

fraternity hevrá (H)
fraud bulmá, dolandirjilik (T, *dolandiricilik*), papas y allasharas
freak arrojada, bót
free (adj) lívre, forro, serbest (T) (adj and adv) azat (T *azat*); (v)
  delivrar, liberar, librar; free from work (v) dezokupar; free of
  worries despreokupado; freedom alforria, serbestlik (T)
freemason farmason, franmason
freemen hijos foros, ijos foros
freight boat mahona, maona (Gr)
frenchified enfrankeado
frenchify frankear
fresh taze (T)
friction (n) arrefreggádo
Friday viernez
fried freido, frito
friend amigo, arkadash (T *arkadash*), haver (H); friendliness
  amabilidad; friendly afavle, amavle; friendship amistad,
  byenkyerénsya, byenkyérer
frighten atorvar
fringe (n) franga
fritters bumuelo
frivolous lijera (fem)
frog rana; frog in the throat mota
frolic arrojada
from de, de onde; from her enella; from here de aki; from inside de
  dentro; from nothing de nada; from the (fem) dela; from the
  (masc) del; from whence de adonde; from where dende; from
  where donde
frontier frontera, fronyera, frontiera
frontyard corte
frosted ashlama (T)
fructify frutchiguar
fruitfulness fruchigudad
frustrated individual furon
fry (v) freir, friir; fry lightly sofreir, sufreir; frying pan sartén
fugitive escapadizo (Fer Bib Gen), mouido (Fer Bib Gen)
fulfill cumplir; fulfilled cumplió
full llena, yeno; full of bitterness endeflado; fullness artadura,
  hinchidad
fumigation fumigasyon

fuming oven horno de fuego
fun - make fun of (tomar al) shuki
function funksyon, ofisyo; (v) **function well** (tool, a machine, a key)
    ishlear (T *ishlemek*)
fund (n) fondo; (v) asementar
fundamentalist sofu
funerals funerales; **funeral song** endecha
fungus mantar (T)
funnel embudo
fur (coat) samára, samarra, samárra, kürk; **fur coat** kürk (T); **fur**
    dealer kürkdji
furious fiduz (T *kuduz*), furyozo, ravyozo
furnace fornaza, **furnace for kitchen** odjak (T *ocak*, kanunn)
furniture mobilya; **furniture manufacturer/vendor** moblista; **furniture**
    merchant moblero; **furniture stand** (n) eshtajera; **furniture vendor**
    mobilyadji
furthermore tambien
fuss - a lot of fuss paparra grande
futile (vulg) kagajoneria, abes
future (n) avenir (F), futuro

G

gain (n) ganancia, ganansya; **gain** (v) ganar; **gain altitude** suvir; **gain**
    weight engodrar
gala gala
gallant galnte; **gallantry** galanteria
gallery galeria
gallows forka
galosh (rubber shoe) kalosh
gamble kumar (T); **gambler** komardji; **gambling** komar (T *kumar*),
    kumarbazlik (T kanunn)
game djugo
gang takum (T *takim* kanunn)
ganglion anchadizo, enchadizo, gangliyon
gangrene gangrena; **gangrenous** gangrenozo
garbage chop (T *çöp*), çop (T), suruntluk, tchop (T *çöp*), **garbage box**
    estyerkero

garden guerta, huerto; gardener bagshaván (from Turkish *bahçivan*), guertelano

garlic ajo

garment vestido

garret-window abaca (from T *baca* chimney)

gas - natural gas avagazi (T *havagazi*)

gaseous gazozo

gasp (v) suspirar

gate portal

gather arrekojer, reunir

gaze (n) mirada; gaze (v) resmirar (se)

gender jenero, jins, manere (Monastir dialect), modu (Monastir dialect)

general (n) jeneral, general (adj) jeneral; general rule klal (H kanunn); generality jeneralidad, jeneralita

generate sontraér

generation arnánsyo, arnancio, arnásyo, dor, jeneransyo; generations generaçiones

generous jenerozo

gentile arel

gentleman benadam (lit: son of a man), bey, chilibi (from T *celebi* a royal prince), efendi, musiu (F *monsieur*), siñor (Monastir dialect); gentlemen gebirim, guebirim

germ (n) hermollo

German Aleman, tedesco, tudesko

germinate ermoveser

gesture seña

get kitar; get a passport kitarse pasaporte; get accustomed to uzar (si) (Monastir dialect); get angry arrayyarse; get angry enkafurearse (from T *küfür* insult); get angry enkyifurearse (from T *küfür* rap, swearing); get angry with arraviar (se) (Monastir dialect), arraviar, arravyar, arraviado; get busy (T *ughrashmak*); get busy okuparse; get cold yilar; get desolated dezolar; get dizzy marear; get engaged despozarse; get engaged espozarse; get irritated (v) inyervar (se); get lukewarm entivyar; get old enueheçer (Fer Bib Gen); get ready aparejar; get rid of (a person or a request) sepetlemek; get sleepy endormecer; get the first teeth endyentar; get tired (v) kansar (se); get tired cansar (se); get tired esbelar (T *bel* waist, place of the belt); get up alevantar(se); get up lebantar;

get up lenantarse; get worried estrechar (se); get wrinkled arrujarse

gherkin pepiniko, pipiniko

ghetto geto

ghost aparisyon, dañador

giant gigante; giants gigantes, grandes

giddy zevzek

gift dadiva, dono, regalo, rezente, righalu

gigolo mantenuto

gilding yaldiz (T)

ginger jenjibre

girl niña

give dar; give a cold or the flu esfriar; give a kiss çupar; give a slight fever asoflamar; give a speech pedrikear; give a title to somebody (v) entitolar; give an opportunity odrenar, ordenar; give birth engendrar; give birth enjentrado; give birth parir; give blisters enfushkar; give information rensenyar; give notice avizar; give presents arregalar; give thanks loar; give to remitir; give up arrepentirse; give up esvachear (T *vazgeçmek*); give value valorizar; giving birth encintamiento

gladiator pelivan (T *pehlivan*)

glance (n) mirada, ojada

glass vidro; glass shop vidreria; glass shop owner vidrero

glass showcase vitrina

glitter yaldiz (T); glittering with the appearance of gold yaldizli

globe globo

gloomy tarkiza

glorification glorifikasyon

glorify afermoziguar; glorify oneself engloreserse

glory gloria, honra, honrra (Ferrara Siddur)

glove gante

glue (v) apegar, engomar

glutton arrevanador

gnash eskruchir

gnaw roendar; gnawed roendando

go (v) ir, andar, partir; Go! Ade; Va!; go away from alezar de; go back volver, vuelar; go down abashár; go down poner se; go forth sal, sarlár (v); Go forward! ade; go in front of eskuentrar (Ferrara Siddur), eskwéntrar (Jud-Sp Dict Madrid); go in peace lej le

shalom; go on a trip estar yuldji go on a trip; go out salir; go
through pasar; go to bed with echarse kon; go to hell! (exclamation) jenneme!; go to hell! siktir! (vulg); Go to hell! Vate!; go to
the bathroom (vulg) embatakar; go to the bathroom sortir,
sostinar (F *sortir* go out); go up subir; go up suvir
goal búto
goat cabra, kavra; small goat cavretico; cavrito, kavrika
God Adonay, Alá, Dio, Dyo, El; gods dios; God forbid halila ve hal;
God knows Aláh bilir; God the Almighty Alláh kyerim (T); God
willing! inshala (T *inshallah*); God willing! ishala!
goddess dyoza
godfather (of the child to be circumcised) kitador, kubar(a), kumbaro
(Salonika Judeo-Spanish, from Gr *koumbaros*)
godmother kitadera, kubar(a), kubara
going out salidura (Salonica Pessach Siddur), saliente
goiter anchadizo, enchadizo
gold oro; gold thread bríl, shirma; gold wire sirma; golden heart
korason de oro; goldsmith kuyumji (T *kuyumcu*)
gondola gondola
gonorrhea eskolamento
good bien, bjen, bueno, byén, shaday; good action mitzva, mitzve;
good enough bueniko; good faith befá (T *vefa*); good luck
fortuna; good luck niyet (T); good manners derej eres (H); good
manners urbanidad; good news estrena; good news mujde
(T *müjde*); good night leka nosht (Bulgarian Judeo-Spanish);
good occasion kyelipur; good sense buen senso; good temper·
buen gesto
Good-bye enbonora
goodness buendad, hayre (T *hayir*)
goose fat enshundya
gout gota
govern governar; government hukumat (T *hükümet*, kanunn)
devlet (T kanunn), dovlet (T *devlet*); government house konak
(T kanunn)
governor gobernador, governador
grace gracia, merced (Ferrara Siddur), merçed (H); graceful cuellu
gracious henoso (jenozo), jenoso, savroziko (adj)
grade (n) rutbe (T *rütbe*, kanunn)
gradually apoko apoko
graduate diplomado

graft ashlama (T *ashilamak*); **grafted tree** ashlama (T kanunn)
grain grano, simyente, tane (T); **small grain** graniko
grammar dikduk (H)
granary ambar (T), anbar (T), mansarda
Grand Rabbi Gran Rabbino
grandchildren inyetos
granddaughter inieta, nyeta
grandeur dula
grandfather agüelo, nóno, papú (Gr *papu*)
grandmother mama (Gr *mame*), nána, nóna (Ital *nonne*), vava, bava
    (Gr *yaya*)
grandson inieto, inyeto, nyeto
grape ouva; **green grape** agraz
graphic vivido
grass hierba, yerua, yerva; **grasshopper** çiçigaya, saltabico, saltampyes
grate (v) rayar
gratis (adv) baldajón, badyavá, baldes, debaldajon, debaldes, jaba
grave fonsario, fóya, graves
grazed sarjado
grease (n) yagladear
greasing untadura
greasy yaghli
great grand; **great flood** diluvyo; **great grandfather** tarapapú; **great**
    grandson tarañeto; **great great grandfather** tarabispapu; **great**
    great grandmother tarabisvava; **great great grandson** tatarañeto;
    greatness grandeza
greedy voraz
Greeks Gregos
green vedre, verde; **green bean** ayshe; **green pea** bizelia (T); **green pea**
    pinzela (Gr *pizeli*, T *bezelye*); **green pepper** pipiritza; **greenery**
    vedrura; **greengrocer** zarzavachi; **greens** virdure (Monastir dialect)
greeting akolyo (Ital *accogliere, accoglienza*)
grill (n) eskara (T *iskara*); (v) asar, torrar (Monastir dialect), tostar;
    grilled asada, tostado; **grilled meat** kyebab
grind (v) mueler, pizar, rayar; **grind one's teeth** escrouchir a sus dientes
grocer bacál, bakal, ispicieru (Monastir dialect)
groom (n) nouio (Ferrara Siddur), (n) novyo
grope (v) apalpar (Monastir dialect), apalpar
groping apalpadura
gross lonson

grotto meara (H *meara*, T *maghara*)
grouch triyaki (from T *tiryaki*); grouchy aksi (T), batiriko, legriniado;
    grouchy woman legrinyada
ground (adj) majado, (adj) molido, ámbito; ground meat kyima, kiyma
    (T *kiyma*)
grove koru (T kanunn)
grow engrandecer, engrandissir, ermoyissiér
growl kafurear (from T *kâfir* miscreant, unbeliever)
grudge ensuña, garez (T)
grudging garezli (T)
grumble (v) marmurerar; grumbler muto
grumbling gritaron, gritalon
guarantee garantizir
guarantor garante
guard (n) kapo (Ital *capo*), nobet (T *nöbet*), shomer; (v) gwadiar,
    bekleár, bektchi (T *beklemek*); guard unit kol; guarded guadràda;
    guardian apotropos (kanunn), guadrador; guards vijilentes
guest kombibado, mosafir, musafir (T *misafir*), musafir (T); guest
    house mosafirhane, musafirhane
guide (n) gia
guillotine giyotina
guitar gitara
gum gomma, jenjivre
gun fusil (F *fusil*), pishtol, tufenk (n, T *tüfenk, tüfek,* kanunn); gun
    shot pishtolada
gutter caño, oluk (T)
guzzle sorver
gypsy çingene; çingane (T), djinganá, jingano (T *çingene*), jitano;
    zingana

H

haberdashery merceria
habit adet (T), tabiet, tabiat (T), uzo; habits komarka
habitual familyar
habituate akostumbrar
hail (n) granizo, (n) pedrisko, piedrisco
hair kaveos, kaveyos, pelo; hairpin forchina (Ital *forcina*), furchino,
    forcina (Ital *forcina*); hairy peludo

half medio, medyo, medio, metad, mitad, mitad; **one half** un medio
hall sala
Hallelujah Alavàd; Alavàd a Adonay
halt! mola!
halvah halva (Turkish sweet made of sesame); **semolina halvah** halvah
    di gris
hamlet cazal (Monastir dialect)
hammer martiyo
hand mano
hand yàga; **hands** manus; **Hands up!** tuyisyon!
handkerchief riza
handle (of a door) manula; **handle the oar** remar
handshake apreton de mano
handyman argat (Gr)
hang enforcar, enforkar (Port), enkolgar; **hang around** morhunear,
    morjunear; **hang on** engancharse; **hanged** enforkado; **hangman**
    huerco
happen acontesser, afitar, akonteser, asodesér; **happened** acontissio,
    akontesimyento
happiness azlaha (H), felichidad, felisidad
happy alegri, beáto, byenaventurádo, cuntenti (Port *contente*, Monastir
    dialect), feliche, felís (Ital *felice*), orozo(F *heureux*); **to be ecstati-
    cally happy** tresalir
harass asigiyir
harbor porto (Ital), tahtaliman
hard duro, kart; **hard biscuit** galeta; **hard boiled egg** guevo
    enjaminado; **hard work** ammalik; **harden** endurar; **hardened**
    enduresido, enkueskado; **hardening** enduresimyento; **hardness**
    dureza; **hardworking** çalishkan (T *çalishkan*), hamarat, laboryozo
hardy aventurado
hare (fur) tawshan (T *tavshan*)
harem harem (female members of a family) (T, kanunn)
harm (n) daño; (v) dañar, enjidear (T *incitmek*); **harmful** dañozo,
    danyozo
harmonica armonika
harmoniously armonyozaménte
harmonization yakisheo
harmonize akishear (T *yakishmak*), armonizar
harmony armonia, desjen (H)
harp árpa, vihuela; **harpist** arpista

harsh búzdro
harvest rekojer, rekolta
has; has performed a
haste adjile (T *acele*); hasten (imp) apresura
hasty tempranero
hat çapeo, chapeyo, chapeyu (Monastir dialect), tchapeyo; hat box
çapeyera
hated aborresido
hatred enemistad, garez (T)
have tener, tuvir; have breakfast dezayunar; have compassion apiadar;
have enough abastissiar; have enough time abastissiar; have lunch
almorzar; have pity apiadar; having a cold or a flu esfriado;
having abiendo
hay çop (T), samán (Monastir dialect)
hazard (v) azardar; hazard (n) azar; hazardous azardózo
hazelnut alviyána; hazelnut tree alviyanéro
hazing shakera
he el; he who el
head (n) kabesa, reis, cabeça, cavesa, kanesa, kavesa; (heads of)
flowers cabeças; head covering kakuleta; head of the bed
kavesera; head of the state reynante; headache basharisi
(T *bashagrisi, bashaghrisi*), dolor de kavesa
heal (v) melezinar, sanar
healer sanador
health salud; healthy sano; healthy and alive sano i bivo
hear escuchar, eskuchar, oir, oyer, oy, oyir, oyir, rigritar (Monastir
dialect), sentir, sintir; hear me! oyeme! oyime!; hearing oyda
(Ferrara Siddur)
heart coraçon, corazón, korason; heart beats batidos
hearth ogar
heat (n) calor, kalor; (v) escallentar (Ferrara Siddur), kayentar; heat up
hamear
heaven jennét (T *cennet*)
heaviness apezadumbre, apezadúmbre, pesagdez, pesgadia
heavy pesgado, pezgado; heavy drinker çupador
Hebraic ebrayko
Hebraist ebrazyante
Hebrew Hebreo; Hebrew language ebreo; Hebrews (the) los ebreos
heel calcañar, kalkanal, tako
heifer bezerra

height alteza, altura
heighten alsar, solevantar
heirloom heredaria (Fer Bib Gen)
heirs yorshim (H kanunn)
hell gueinam, jenne, jennem (T *cehennem*)
Hellenic eleno
Hellenism elenismo
helm timon
helmsman timonero
help (n) amparo, ayuda; (v) ayudar, hizmét (T), sokorrer, yardim,
    yardum; helped arremedyado; helper ayudante; helpless
    desamparado, perishan (adj)
hem (v) avaynár; hem (n) repulgo
hemisphere emisfero
hemorrhoids almorrána
hemp kanamo; hemp seeds kañavola
hen choque (Port *gallinha choca*), geyna
henna aljeña
her eya
herb yerua, yerva; herbal tea tizana (F *tisane*)
herd ganado
here aka, aki, aqui; here he is! nallo!; here is na
hereditary ereditaryo
heretic çatlak (T), ereje
heritage eredensya
hero barragan (H), eroe; heroic eroiko
heroin eroina
heroism barragania, eroismo
herpes espinga
herring aringa
hesitant endechiso (Ital *indeciso*)
hesitate çekinearse, dehiyár, ezitar
hesitating ezitante,
hesitation ezitasyon
hey there na
hiccup sangluo
hick up sangluto, sangruto
hidden (fem) encubierta (Ferrara Siddur), guadràda
hide (v) esconder, eskonder, iscunder; hide oneself eskonde (se)
hideout eskondimiento, eskondidas; hiding eskondimiento

high alto
hill cuesta, muntañique (Monastir dialect); hills montes
him a quien, se, si; himself si mesmo, si mezmo
hind syerva
hinge menteshe (T *menteshe*)
His Majesty yarum hodo (H kanunn)
his su, suyo
historian analysta, estoryador, estoryano
historical historico
history estuary, historia
hit ajarvar (from H *herev* short sword), bater
hitch skotura (Gr)
hoarse enrasmado, enrokesido; speak with a hoarse voice ronkear;
    hoarseness enrasmo, ronkedad; persisting hoarseness ronkera
hoax shakera
hold (v) detener, sustentár, tener; hold together by a thread enfiilar
hole (miserable lodging) shilvane (from T *shirvane*), abujero, burako
hollow (vulg) kagajoneria; hollow out ahuecar (v); hollowed ahuecada
holocaust alsayon, Shoa (H)
home ogar; home remedy fechuria; homemaker balabaya; homeowners
    balebatim
homily dirush (H)
honest brávo, namuzli (T *namuslu*), neeman (H), onesto, salam
    (T *saghlam*), tam (T)
honey miel, myel; honeyed enmelado, myelozo; honey-suckle (flower)
    hanumeler
honor (n) kavod (H), nanuz, onor, zejut (H Haketia), honorar; honor
    (v) akatar; honorable namuzli (T *namuslu*), onoravle; honorarium
    aspaka (H); honored onorado
hood kakuleta
hook (n) gancho, çengel; çingel (T *çengel*), jengel; hook on enramar
hope (n) esperansa, avtajá (H); hopeless dezesperado; hopelessness
    dezespero
horned enkuernado
horse saddle kaltak
horsecloth froña
horseshoe nal (T)
hospice lazaret
hospital (lit: house of health) beit ahayim (H), eshpital, espital

hostility deskerensya, malquerencia
hot kayente; hot thermal springs banios; hot water pad buyót
hotel hotel; hotel keeper hotelji
hour hora, ora, saát (T)
house casa, caza, kaze; household garbage estyerko, estyerkol; house-
    keeper mirandera
how cómo, komo; how are you? ke haber?; how did it go? komo le
    paso?; how much por quanto; how much quanto; however (de)
    cierto, andjak (T *ancak*), emperlo, entanto, myentres
howl maullar, maulyar
hug (v) stringar
human binadán; human being criado
humanity umanidad
humble annáv, umilde
humid tyempeziko, umido; humidity umidad
humiliate arebachar, pisotear, umiliar; humiliate in front of others
    arrepudyar; humiliate oneself enkorkovarse
humiliation umilyasyon
humility umildad
humorous umoresko; humorous stories umoreskas
hump corcova, kambura, korkova
hunchback enkamburado, kambur (T), korkovado
hundred cien, ciento, çient, sien; hundreds cientos
hundreth - one hundreth un sientezimo
Hungarian ongarez, ungarez; Hungarian language ongaresko,
    ungaresko
Hungary Ongaria, Ungaria Hungary
hunger ambre, fambre, hambre, hambrera; hunger pangs stilo
hungry ambierto
hunt (n) caça; (v) depistar, kachar; hunted desterro
hurt (v) dañar, dokunear (T *dokunmak*), dueler (v), endjidar
husband espozo, marido, maridu (Monastir dialect); husbandman
    arador
hush kayada; sus! (T)
hut chosa, çosa, kuliba (T *külübe* kanunn)
hyacinth zimbul (T *sümbül*)
hymn cantàr
hypochondriac fesfese (T *vesvese*)
hypocrite debasho en basho, hanef (H), hipócrita

I

I lyo, yo; I myself mi (en) mi
ice booz (from T *buz*), buz (T), yilade (Monastir dialect); ice cream
  vendor dondurmadji (T); ice cube kalip de buz; iced ashlama (T)
idea hatir (T), ideya, majasava
identity card nefus, nufus (T *nüfus*)
idiot bovo, maredo, puerro, shabsal
idle aylak (T), batál, dezokupado; idle talk brazón; idleness
  dezokupasyon
idol doladizo
if si; if not without this sino
ignoble jinganelik (T *çingenelik*)
ignoramus puerro
ignorant amaáres (H *am aaretz*), desavido
ignore deskonoser, ygñorar
ill dolyente; ill-feeling malquerencia
illiterate amaáres (H *am aaretz*)
illness malatia
ill-treat enmaliciér; ill-treatment eziyet (T *eziyet*, kanunn), maltrato
illuminate alumbrar, arrelumbrar
illumination donannma (T)
illusion afanamyento, embabuko
image imaje
imaginable imajinavle
imagination imajinasyon, majasava
imagine imaginar, imajinar; imagine oneself asímijar (se) (Monastir
  dialect)
imbecile abdal (T *aptal*)
imbibe embevar, estufar; imbibed empapado
imbroglio embroyo
imitate fazer di mismo (Monastir dialect)
imitation taklit (T)
immaterial imateryal
immediately a puntu (Monastir dialect), imediatamente, luego, man
  mano, pishin, shubu (adv)
immersion (in water or other liquid) mojo
immigrant peregrino; immigrant to Israel ole (H); new immigrant to
  Israel ole-hadash
immobilized entavlado

impale empalar
impatient saburiz (T *sabirsiz*), sabursuz (T *sabirsiz*)
impede disturbar
impediment dejiya
imperative emperatvo
imperfection tara
imperial emperial; imperial decree irade (T kanunn)
impertinence arsizlik (T)
impertinent jenabet (T *cenabet*)
impetigo espinga
impolite malelevado; impoliteness dessatento, mankeza
import (n) emportasyon
importance emportansa
important emportante
importer emportador
importune yangaz
importunity disturbo, tekia
imposing emponente
imposition empozisyon
impossibility emposibilidad
impossible emposivle
impostor dolandirji (T *dolandirici*)
impotence tuyidura
impoverished emprovesido
impregnate estufar; impregnated embevido
impresario emprezaryo
impression empression
impressive emposante
imprint damgua (Turkish *damga*)
imprison enkarselar; imprisonment aprezamyento
improve mijorear, mehorar, perfeksyonar; improvement probecho
improvise enjeñar
impudence edepsizlik (T)
impure trefa
impurity (religious) enkono; in a state of impurity enconado
in en; in addition demas; in addition to desparte; in all truth
    frankamente; in any case ainde (Port *ainda*, Monastir dialect); in
    between entri medius; in case a caso; in conclusion sajakol (H); in
    debt endevdado; in effect (de) cierto; in excess (adv) de hormet; in
    excess demasia; in front of delante, delante, delantre; in front of

enfrente; **in front of you** delantre ti **in front of you; in good fortune** en bunora; **in her** enella; **in jail** emprezo; **in love** enamorado; **in mourning** enteñavlado; **in order** duzudeado; **in particular** (prep) desparte (en); **in saying** por dezir; **in secret** en escondido; **in spite of** entanto; **in sum** (adv) ensoma; **in summary** (prep) bréve, en breve; **in summary** enbreve; **in summary** sajakol (H); **in surplus** tambien; **in suspense** een gueko; **in that way** de assi; **in the air** (adv) avaya (T *havaya*); **in the direction of** versu (Monastir dialect); **in the end** al kavo, alkavo; **in the first place** emprimaro; **in the meantime** myentres; **in the past** antanyus; **in this case** estonses; **in this way** ansina; **in this way** destemodo; **in time** kon il tiempo; **in vain** badyavá (T *bedava*); **in vain** en baldez

inauguration estrenamyento, estreno
inauspicious gursuz (T *ughursuz*)
incantation endulko
incarcerate enkarselar
incarceration enkarselasyon
incarnated enkarnado
incense ensensyo, safumeryo
incident ensidente
incite empushar
inclination enklinasyon, tendensya
incline enklinar; inclined disposto, enklinado
incognito tepdil (T *tebdil*)
incongruity stopachada (Ital *stopacio*)
inconsolable deskonsolado
increase (v) pujar, pujier; increase abundantly sirpier; increase the stake embidar
incredible enkreivle
incubation çoka
incubator estufa
inculcate enkulkar
inculpate akulpar, enkulpar, muhayyev (H kanunn)
indecision endechizyon (Ital *indecizione*)
indeterminate wéko
indicate amustrar (v, Monastir dialect), endikar
indication endikasyon
indifference endiferensya
indifferent endiferente

indignation ira
indigo añir, azúl, çivit (T)
indispensable endispensavle
indisposed deranjado, desrepozado, sufriente
indisposition dolensya, endispozisyon, kyefsizlik (T *keyifsizlik*)
indoctrinate adotrinar, dotrinar
indolent kyohne
industrious çalishkan (T *çalishkan*), hamarat
inequity tuuertedad
inexperience adjamilik (T *acemilik*)
infamous enfamante
infiltrate enfiltrar
infiltration enfiltrasyon
infirm sakat (T *sakat*); infirmity enfermedad, enfermidad, sakatlik
   (T kanunn); infirmary enfermeria, enfirmeriya
inflame enflamar; inflamed enflamado
inflammable enflamavle
inflammation enflamasyon
influence (v) enfluensar, enfluir, por hatir (T *hatir* kanunn)
influent enfluente
influenza enfluensa
inform asaventár, avizar, rensenyar
informally sanfason (F *sans façon*)
information rensenyamento
infringing tuuerto
ingenious enjeúozo; ingeniousity enjeño, enjeñozidad
ingratitude dezagradensya, dezagradesimiento, engratitud
inhabit abitar; inhabitant abitante
inherit eredador, eredar, heredar; inheritance nahalá (H)
iniquity peccado
initiate asementar
injure enjuryar, vulnerar
injury dezonra, enjurya, ensulto
injustice enjustedad, enjustisya
ink tinta
inn albergo (Ital), brisko, han (T kanunn)
innkeeper handji (T *hanci* kanunn)
innocent bovankyón, bovarrón, buenivle
inoculate (v) enfiltrar
inquire (v, archaic) deprendér, averiguar

inquiry enquesta
inquisition inkizisyon
inquisitor inquisidor, inkizidor
insane asylum timarana, timbarana, timarhane (T *timarhane*)
inside adyentro, arientro, aryénto, aryentro, dedyentro
insignia dita (Ital *ditta*)
insinuating girilali
insinuation echada, echadura, sachma (T *saçma*)
insipid shavdo; insipidity shavdura
insist ensistir; insistence ensistensya
insolence deskaro, eskaramyento
insolent arsiz (T), azpan, depsiz (T), deskarado, eskarado, repueston,
    sfacato (adj) (Ital *sfacciato*), sinvervuensa; insolent person
    dipsiz (T)
inspection teftish (T)
inspector enspektor
inspiration enspirasyon
inspire enspirar; inspire great fear (v) estuweerser
instantly luego
instead of al lugar
institution enstitusyon
insufficient az (T)
insult (v) ensultar, palavradear; (n) dezonra, ensulto; kefur (T *küfür*);
    insulting desbokado; insults omezillo
insupportable ensuportavle
insurance sigorta (T), sigurita; insurance agent seguritadji, sigortadji,
    sigortadji (T *sigortaci*); insurance company sigorita
insurer asigurador, segurador
integrity plenismedad (Fer Bib Gen), plenismo, zejut (H Haketia)
intellect yntelecto (Ferrara Siddur)
intelligence dáath (H), enteligensa, entelijensya, intelijensia, séhel
intelligent entelijente
intend ententar
intention entisyon, eskopo (Ital *scopo*), majasava, niyet, yntincion
    (Ferrara Siddur); intentioned entensyonado
interest (n) enteres, ilaka (T *alaka*); interest (v) enteresar; interested
    enteresado, interested in merekli (from T *merakli*); interesting
    entersante
interior enteryor; interior courtyard kortijo
intermission antrakto

intern enternar; interned entarnado
interpret enterpreta, enterpretar; interpretation enterpretasyon;
    interpreter tardjuman (T *tercüman*)
interrogate (v) kestyonar
interrogation demanda, estinkak (T)
interrupt (v) enterromper, curtar; interruption enterrupsyon
intertwine entrelashar
interval aralik (T), entervalo
intervene entervenir, meterse en medio; intervention entervensyon,
    entremetedura
interview entrevista
intestinal entestinal
intestine barsak (T), entestino
into por
intolerance entolerensya
intrigue (v) estrañar; (n) fesad (T kanunn), dalavera; someone who ini-
    tiates intrigues fesaddji
introduce oneself enkasharse
introduction akdama (H)
inundate enchorrear, ennadado; inundated enadado
invalid malato
invent oydurear, uydurear (v, T *uydurmak*)
invention oydurma, uydurma (T *uydurma*)
investigation búshkita, hafiyelik
investigator bushkadór, estindatchí (from T *istinbat* bringing a hidden
    matter to light, or *istinbatçi* someone who brings a hidden matter
    to light)
invitation convite, envitasion, envitasyon, invitasion, kombite, yamada
invite (v) envitar, kombibar; invitee kombibado
involved embuelvido
irascible asobrevyado
iron (n) fyero, fyerro, fierro; iron store fyerrerio; ironsmith fyerrero
irony alay (T), maytap
irregular - of irregular surface rugozo
irreverent repueston
irrevocable mutlak
irrigate abreuar (Fer Bib Gen), arregár; irrigated arremojado
irrigation arregadúra, regadúra
irritable airado
irritate agrear, enfureser, asobrevyado, fishugado

is stá; **Is it so?** acaba
island izla; islands izlas, yslas
Istanbul Estanbol, Kosta (H for Constantinople, kanunn)
it se
itching buyitína, komesina, kumiendo
ivory fildishi, marfil
Izmir Ezmirna (Smyrna)

J

jabber farfuyar
jackal çakal (T)
jacket jaketa, jugón
jail (n) galera; (v) aprezar; jailed aprezado; encerrado
January jenayo, januario, janvie (F *janvier*), tevet (H), tabetu (Bab)
jar kanata, kantaro, kantara
jaundice sarilik (T)
jaw kixada, qixada
jealous selozo; to be jealous selar (se); to be jealous of selarse; jealous
    women seloza; jealousy embidya, selo
jellyfish jelatina di peshado
Jesus Jesús
Jew djudio, Judio; Jews (the) los ebreos; Jewish quarter Juderia,
    djuderia
jewel joya; jeweler joyero, kuyumji (T *kuyumcu*)
job echo, etcho
joined unido; joined with eniadido
joke (n) shaká, shakalish (from T *shaka*); (v) (azer) shakular-makulas
    (from T *shaka*)
joker burlón, shakadji
journal jurnal (Port *jornal*, F *journal*); journalist artikolista
joy allegria, regmición; joyful alegre, babadján (T *babacan*)
Judaism Judesmo, Judezmo
judge (n) juzgador, hakim (T kanunn), djusgo; (v) djusgar, djuzgar,
    juzgar
judgment tino, din (H); judgments juissios
jug tinaja, kantara
juggler hokabaz
juggling hokabazlik

juice sumo
juicy kaldudo, sumozo
jujube asofayfa; asofafya
July julio, tammuz (H), du'uzu (Bab)
jump saltar
June junio, sivan (H), simanu (Bab)
junk jonk
jurisprudence din (H)
just djusto, justo
justice adalet (T), din (H), djusticia, justedad, justicia
justly djustamente

K

Kabbala kabala
Kaddish kadish
kebab çevirme; kebab-grilled kebap
keep (v) gwadiar;, alikodear (T *alikoymak* kanunn); keep away
     enternar; keep informed asaventár
keepsake recuerdo
khaki (brown-yellow) kaki
kid cabrito
kidney (lamb) riñon, rene, reyne
kill (v) herir
kind (n) turlu (T *türlü*), djis (T *cins*), jins, rasa
kindling wood çira (T)
king rey, reye (Moroccan Sephardic Ballad)
kingdom reinado, reynon
kinship suvrindad
kiosk kyosk, kyoshk (T *köshk*)
kiss (n) bezo, beso; kiss (v) bezar; kissing with the lips bezadura
kite balón
knave kyerata
knead (imp) amasa; kneaded finio
knee diz (T), djinoyu (Monastir dialect), jinoyo
kneel arrodiyarse; kneeling de rodias, enjeñoyado
knife kuchiyo
knit tejer
knock (v) chafteyar (T *çarpmak*), bater

knot (n) ennudo, inyúdo
know conocer, saber, saver; know with certainty saber saberas; knowledge cunisensje (Monastir dialect), saber, sabiduria, saveduria;
  knowledgeable savyo
known (adj) konosido
Koran Alcorán
kosher kacher (Sephardic)
Kurdish kyurdi (T *kürt*)

L

label (n) etiketa
labor ovrar; labor camp pranga (T, kanunn)
laboratory laboratoryo
lace dantela, tantéla (n, F *dentelle*)
lack (v) miss, faltar, mancar; (n) falta; lack of mankansa; lack of self-confidence (v) arrezistado
lackadaisical jilveli
lacked faltava
lad delikanli (T), niño
Ladino Espanyol, Judesmo, Judezmo, lingwa judia, romanse, spanyol, spanyolit, Zudeo-espanyol
lady damma, dama, doña
lagoon laguna
laic laico
lake gol (T *göl* kanunn), pelàgo, riu (Monastir dialect)
lamb cordero, hijo de oveja, kodrero, kocho, kosho
lame lenk (Persian)
lament lamentarse; lamentable lastimoso, perishan (adj); lamentation alguaya, lamentasyon; lamentations dolorio; lamented plañida
lamp lampa, lampara, lampe (Monastir dialect), menora (H); manufacturer or vendor of lamps lampero; lampshade abazur
  (F *abat-jour*)
land (v) pozarse; landing stage skala; landscape peizaje
language (H) lashon, idioma, labio, lenguage; sacred language
  (Hebrew language) lashon akodesh, lashon hakodesh
lantern fanar
larger mayyor; large basket kufa (T *küfe* kanunn)
lasagna tayarine

lasso atadijo, lago
last (v) durar; (adj) ultimo; last name alcuñe (from T *künye*), alkunya
     (from Turkish *künye* register of names); last will sava; last wish
     dezeo (de alkavo); last years of life anos de alkavos
late atardado, atrazado, tadrizo, tadre, (deceased) regretado; to be late
     tadrar; come late venir tadre; latecomer retardataryo
latrine huz
lattice bagdadi
laud avantar
laugh reir, riir; laugh at rriirse; laugh one's head off rir kon tarakas;
     laughter riza
laundry çamashir (T), lavado; laundry woman lavandera
laurel taflan
law din (H), dirito (Ital *diritto*), kanun (T kanunn), lei, Ley, nizam
     (T kanunn); law practice avokateria; lawful helal; lawsuit dava
     (T); lawyer avokado, avokato
laxative laksativ
lay on apozar; lay on the bed (v) echar; lay the foundation (v)
     acimentar (Fer Bib Kings I); layer kat, layer tabaka (T)
laziness pereza (Ladino), tembellik
lazy tembel, tendel (T), perezozo (Ladino), kaltaban; lazy person
     haragán
lead (n) plomo
leader mayoral
leaf foja, foya, hoja
leakage fira
learn (v, archaic) deprendér, ambezar, aprender, embezar, emprender;
     learned ambezado, meldahon; leather bottle odre
leave (v) dexar, quidar di (Monastir dialect); leave it up to remitir
leaven levadura; to become leavened levdarse; leavened bread hamets
leech shambashuga, suluk (T *sülük*)
leek prasa, puerro
left (as contrary to right) estyedro, (fem) izquierda, siedra, ysquierda;
     left hand estyedra; left side estyedra; left side yzquierda; left-
     handed estyedreo; leftover romanesido, sovrado
leg pachá (from T *paça*), leg pyerna; legs pachás; leg of mutton but
     (T *bud*)
legal case kavzo
legal code kanunname (T)
legal sciences derito (Ital *diritto*)

legitimate helal
leisure dezokupasyon
lemon squeezer esprimidor
length elenguor, elengura, estenso (Ferrara Siddur), largura, longura,
    lungor (Monastir dialect)
lentils lentejas
leper leprozo
lesion pegima, yara
less manko, mengua
lesson lisyon
lest (adv) asér (from H *aser* misappropriation, taking away)
let (v) dechar, deshar; let yourself (te) dechar; let down destrenzar; let
    it be sea; let it shine arrelumbre; let stay from quidar di; (Mona-
    stir dialect); let us go yalla (T); let us see veremos
letter carta, epistola (Gr), karta, letra
lettuce alechuga, lechuga, litchouga
level (of building) tabaka (T); academic level nivel universitario
lexicon leksiko
liable kablenim (H kanunn)
liar mentirozo, minterozo, mintirozo
liberate (v) delivrar, (from a difficult situation) dezenredar; liberated
    forro
liberation alforria
libertine deryade (T), pishutero
library biblioteka
licentious alchak (T *alçak*)
lick (v) lamber
licorice byambali (T *meyan bali*)
lie (n) falsamyento, mentira, uydurmasion, uydurmasyon; (v) favlar
    mintiras (Monastir dialect), mintir, falsar
lieutenant colonel yaver (T)
life vida; life of debauchery siksheo (vulg); life of pleasure repotreo
lift alevantar (v); lift a ban (v) desvedar
light (n) luz; lighten alumbrar, arrelumbrar, fazer relámpagu (Monastir
    dialect); lighten up asender, esclaressar; lighted luminozo; lighter
    çakmak; lightbulb ampula; lighthouse fanar; lightning raya,
    relampago; flash of lightning relampago; light fever soflama;
    light rain arregáda; lighthearted lijera (fem); bursts of lightning
    relampageo

like (adv) como, asegun; **and the like** vekayosse, vekayotze
    (H kanunn); **like this** asi, de assi; **likewise** altretánto (Ital)
lily (flower) lila
limping kosho
linden tea tilyo tilia
line (of writing) sira (T *sira*, kanunn)
lineage desendensya, linaje
lining enforro, fodre (Port *forra*)
link (n) vinkulo; **link** (v) vinkular
linkage vinkulasyon
linoleum mushama (T *mushamba*)
lion león, lión; **lion cub** leoncillo
lip labio, lavyo
liquidate (v) likidar, kuidar
liquidation likuidasyon
liquor likor
list posula (n) (T *pussula*)
listen escuchar, sientar, sintir
litigant baal adavár; baal aftaja (H)
little chico, pequeño, poco, poko; **a little** un poco, un poko; **a little less**
    un poko manko
liturgical chant piyut
live (n) vivir, biuir (Ferrara Siddur); (adj) vivo; **lived** biuio; **lively**
    vivaracho
liver fegado, figado, giyer (T), igado, ligado
living viviente, biuo (Ferrara Siddur), bivientes (pl, Salonica Siddur);
    living room sala
lizard lagarta, lagarto
load (n) denk; (v) enkargarse
loaf of bread franjola
loan (v) emprestar; (n) emprestimo, empresto; **loaned** emprestado
local school heder
locate situar; **located** situado
lock (n) kadenado, cavenádo, chapa, serradura
locust langosta
lodges moradas
loft mansarda, shilvane (from T *shirvane*)
log kyutuk (T *kütük*)
logic lojika

loin lombo
loneliness soledad, soletina
long (cloth) elenguo, largo, longu
longing eskarinyo
look at (v) mirar; look like pareser; look well yakishear; this outfit
    does not look well on you este vestido no te yakishea
    (T yakishmak); look! mira!
loosen arrafganeár (T)
looseness flochura
loot (n) yaghma (T kanunn); (v) sakear
looter sakeador, yaghmadji (T yaghmaci, kanunn)
looting sakeamyento
lord bey, siñor (Monastir dialect), Lord Signor
lose (v) pedrer, perder, piedrer; lose interest dezenteressar; lose weight
    aflakar; lose weight enflakeser
loss pedrimyento, peryita
lot suerte
lottery lotaria, pyango, piyango, rifa (kanunn)
loud shamatali; loud noise dubara (T)
lounge (n) sala; (v) morhunear, morjunear; lounge after work
    rafraganar (T rahatlama)
louse piojo, piójo
love - for the love of God lemaan ashem
love (n) amor; (v) amar, kerer, (v) quizensje (Monastir dialect); lover
    amánte, namorado, piryan
lower (v) abashár, humiyar
lowliness bashéa
loyal brávo, dobre
loyalty derechitud
luck mazal (H), kadém (T); good luck mazal bueno, ogúr (from T
    ugur, good luck), fadarju, fadaryo (Port fadario); good luck ugurli
    (from T ugur); lucky mazalozu (Monastir dialect), mazalozo
luggage bagaje
lukewarm tivyo; being lukewarm tivyeza
lull kalma
lumber kereste (T kanunn), kyereste; lumber dealer kyerestedji;
    lumber-room mansarda
luminaries luminarios
lump búlto
lunatic delifesfes (T)

lupine altramúz, tramusu (Port *tremoço*); lupine bean atramuz; lupine
    seed atramuz
lure (v) embelekar
luster lustre
lute ut (T)
luxury lukso; luxuries luksos; desire of luxuries deseo de luksos

M

macaroni makarron; macaroni dish makarronado
Macedonian masedonyano
machine makina
mackerel kolyos
mad loko
maddened alokado, enlokosido
made of compuesto
made increasingly expensive enkaresido
made sweet adulsado
made up (fem) hecha
madhouse manikomyo (Ital *manicomio*), avanamyénto, lokura, taburra
magician (fem) endulkadera; (masc) endulkador, ecizero, mégo
magistrate (v) hakim (T kanunn)
magnified sovralsado
magnifying glass derbil (T *dürbün*)
maiden demuazel (F *demoiselle*)
mail (n) posta, poste; mailman postadji, postají
maintain mantener, tener; maintain oneself mantener
maintenance entretenimyento, mantenisyon
maize misir (T)
majority mayoriya
make azer, fazer; make a diet azer rejim; make a donation donar;
    make a hole (v) burakar; make a mistake yerrar; make a mistake
    yirrar (si) (Monastir dialect); make a payment desbolsar; make a
    resolution entisyonarse; make a speech diskorsar; make blind
    syegar; make commerce komerchar; make easy facilitar; make
    escape kacherear (v, T *kaçirmak*); make facer; make fun of burlar;
    make fun of tomar al alay; make hazer; make heavy apesgar;
    make lame enkoshar; make numb adurmeser; make numb atudrir;
    make numb endurmeser; make perfect perfeksyonar; make ready

approntar; **make rich** arrekolmar; **make round** arredondear; **make
shine like gold** (v) dorar; **make similar** uydurear (Judeo-
Spanishized verb of T *uydurmak* invent); **make stay** azer estàr;
make strange desmodrar; **make thirsty** (v) asedár; **make tired**
fatigar; **make ugly** embruteser; **make watertight** stankar
make-up bóya
male macho, matcho; **male organ** shunrra (vulg)
malformation pegima (H)
malice maldad, malisya
malicious malicioso; **malicious being** syerpe
malignancy maliñidad
malignant maliño
mall molo
mallet mazo
malpractice enkaño
Maltese maltez
man hombre, homre, ombre, ombri
manage to do parvenir (F *parvenir*)
mandate buyurultu (T kanunn), mandato
mandolin mandolina, mandolino; **mandolin player** mandolinista
mange sarna
manna maghna, manna
mannequin maneken
manner manera
mantle manto
manual manual
manufacture (v) fabrikar; **manufacturer** fabrikante; **manufacturer of
coats** mantero; **manufacturing** fabrikasyon
manure fuskin
map harta (T *harita*, kanunn)
marble marmol, marmor
March mars, adar (H), addaru (Bab)
march around rodear
marinade salamura
marine marino; **mariner** marinero
marionette hirbo
mark (n) nishan (T kanunn), siman (H), damgua (Turkish *damga*);
damua; (v) markar
market bazar (T *pazar*), charshi, charsí (T *çarshi*), tcharchi (from T
çarshi market), merkado, panair (T, Gr *panayir, panayiri*,

kanunn), pazar (T); **marketplace** fedán (Haketia), charshi (T),
  piyasa, plasa, pyasa, piyasa; **market value** pyasa, piyasa
marking markadura
marmalade dulse, dulsura
marriage casamiento, kasamiento, kazamiento; **marriage contract**
  ketuba; **marriage contracts** ketubot
marrow tútano
marry kazar
martyr fedayi (T *fedai*)
marvel marauilla (Ferrara Siddur)
marvelous estupendo (Ital), marauilloso (Ferrara Siddur), maraviya,
  maravia
Marxism marksismo
Marxist marksista
marzipan masapan
mash (for a long time) fiñir
mask maska, maskara; **mask oneself** (v) enmaskarse
mason yapidji
massager masero
masseur refregador
master (n) (masc) maestro, musyu, el musyu, adón, mayoral, patron,
  patrón; **master of the house** balabay (H); **mastery of oneself**
  sangre-fria
mastic almasiga, sakiz
mat (straw) estera
match (n) spiritu (Monastir dialect); **match(es)** (Gr *spirto*) spiritu(s);
  matches kibrites (T *kibrit*), kyibrit, kibrit
matchmaker entremetedor, entremetor, kazamentero
matrix macho
matter (n) fechu (Monastir dialect); (v) importar
mattress almadraque, chilte (T *çilte*), kolchon, shelte (T *çilte*)
maturation deskadensya
matzo (unleavened Passover bread) masa
May mayo, iyyar (H), ayaru (Bab)
may pueder; **may it be so!** Makare; **maybe** puede ser, puedeser
mayonnaise mayoneza
meal komida
meal sena
mean (adj) aksi (T); **mean** (v) aconsejar (Fer Bib Kings I); **meaning**
  (adv) çioe (Ital *cioe*)

meanness maldad, rezalet
means mezos; to have the means moldear
meanwhile myentres
measles sarampion, sarampyon
measure (n) medida; measure (v) amezurar, mezurar, mizurar
    (Monastir dialect); measure a dose dozar; measured mezurado;
    measurement mizure; measures mezuras
meat basár (H), carne, karne; meat patty kefte, köfte (T köfte); meat
    pie pastel; meatball albondiga, kefte, köfte (T köfte)
mechanic artezáno
medal dekorasyon
meddler demudadiko
mediation entremetedura
mediator rufyan
medical school medikeria
medicine fechuria, medikeria, ezá; medicine bottle botcha de kura
mediocre lamentavle; mediocre poet rimador
meditation rekojimyento
meet renkontrar; meet each other renkontrar (se); meet the needs sub-
    venir; meeting place randebú (F rendezvous)
melancholic funebro, mungrinozo
melancholy merekiá (from T merak), merrekiya
melon çapeo
melt derritir
member membro
memorandum tezkere (T kanunn)
memory hatir (T), memorya, recuerdo, tino
menorah menora (H)
mention (v) amintar (Monastir dialect)
meow maullar, maulyar
merchandise estiva, rropa
merchant baziryán (T bazirgân), komerchante, mercador, merkader,
    negociante, negosyante
merciful mizerikordyozo
mercury azógre
mercy merced (Ferrara Siddur), merçed (H), misericordias,
    mizerikordya, piadad, piyadad; Mercy! aman
meridional meridyonal
meringue meringa
merit (n) meresimyento, merito, zehut; (v) mereser; merited meresido

meritorious meresyente
messenger messagero, shaliah; **messenger of bad news** karahaberdji
Messiah Almashiah, Machiah
method metodo, osul, usul (T *usul*)
methodical metodiko
meticulous metikulozo, pinti
middle medyo, medio, miyatá
midwife komadre
migrant migrante, peregrino
mild tivyar, tivyo; **mildness** tivyeza
miles - **by miles** por miles
military militar; **military service** (servisio) militar; **military barracks**
      kishla (T *kishla*); **military service** askerlik, askyerlik (T *askerlik*)
milk leche; **milk custard** leche papeada; **milkman** lechero
mill (n) molino, mulino; **mill** (v) mueler; **mill stone** piedra de molino;
      miller molinero
million milyon
millions milyones
mimosa mimosa
minced molido
mineral deposit almadén
minister of a cult saserdote
ministry vekialet (T *vekâlet*); **ministry of public security** zabtie
      (T *zabtiye*, kanunn)
mink vizon
minority (age) minoria, (in numbers) minoridad, minorita (Ital)
minute (adj) minusyozo, puntu (Monastir dialect); **minute** (n) minuto;
      a few minutes unos kuantos minutos; **minutes** mazbata (T)
miracle milagro; **miracles** nesim
miraculous milagrozo
mirror (n) espejo
mischief maker ta(r)buradji
miser mizmiz (T)
miserable lazdrada (fem)
miserly pinti, apretura
misery mizerya
misfortune desgrasya, desventura, malasuerte, malor
mishap skotura (Gr)
miss (v) mancar, mankar
Miss matmazel (F *mademoiselle*, Monastir dialect, also used in Turkish)

mist derusha (H)
mistake yerro, yérro, yero
mister siñor (Monastir dialect)
mistreat ajarvar (from H *herev* short sword)
mistress mantenuta, metres
misunderstanding mal entendimiento, malentendido
mite landre, polilla, polliya
mix (v) enmoleskar; mix up (v) kashterear (T *karishtirmak*)
moan (v) enguayar; moaning alguaya
mobile mobil
mobility mobilidad
mobilization mobilizasyon
mobilize mobilizar
mock taklear (T *takilmak*); mock someone by imitating taklit (T);
     mockery burla, figas
mode modo
moderate (adj) mezurado, arreglado
moderation temperansya
modern moderno; modernize modernizar
modes modoz
modest annáv
mohair moer
molar muela
mold kalup; molded to fit turnat (Romanian Judeo-Spanish)
molest (v) desrepozar, molestar; molesting molestya
momentum slanchyo
Monday lunes, lunez
money (slang) dekaras, (slang: dough) fyerros, dinero, paras (from T
     para), plata; moneybag rikon; money-changer sar(r)af (T *sarraf*,
     kanunn); profession of a money-changer sar(r)aflik (T *sarraflik*,
     kanunn)
monkey maymon, maymona, maymuna (T *maymun*)
monotony monotonia
monsignor beyefendi
month mes; monthly pay aylik (T), mezada
moody (coll) batiriko
moon luna
moral law dover (opposed to Ital *dirito* civic law)
morality sistema

more (adv) de hormet, demas, mas, más, tambien; **more and more** de
  mas en mas; **moreover** altrónde (Ital), andjak (T *ancak*), ensima,
  tambien
morning demañana, demaniana, mañana, manyana, manyanada, sebax
  (T *sabah*); **the next morning** mañane (Port *amanhà*); **morning**
  prayer shairit (H)
moron shabsal
morphine morfina
mortal mortal; **mortality** magefa, mortaldad
mortar almirez, barro, lodo
mortgage ipoteka, maskanta
mosaic (n) mozayika, (rel) mozayiko
Moses Moshon
mosque meshquita
mosquito moshkon, mushcón (Monastir dialect); **mosquito net**
  namosia
mother madre, madri, mama (Gr *mame*), mamá, jenitor; **mother of**
  great grandmother tarabisvava; **mother with children** madre con
  hijos; **mother-in-law** esfuegra, eshuegra, suegra; **mother-of-pearl**
  marfil (Monastir dialect), nakra, sedef (T)
motionless dormyente
motive sebeb (T) sebep
mount monte
mountain montaña, montania, muntaña, muntañe (Monastir dialect);
  mountaineer montañero, montañez
mourn (v) enteñevlar, enluytar; **mourning** ansia, luyto; **mournful** funebro
mouse ratón; **mousetrap** ratonera
mouth boka
move (v) manear, mudar; **move away** mudar (se); **move forward**
  adelantar, avansar; **move from** mouer; **movement** muvimiento,
  muvimyento; **moving** removiente
Mrs. maná
much mucho (Ferrara Siddur), muncho
mucous rañu (Port *ranho*)
mucus (rom the nose) moco, moko, moko
mud lodo
mulberry amóra, mora; **mulberry tree** amoréro
mule mulo
mullet (fish) tekyir, kyefal

multiply frutchiguar, muchigar, muchiguar, mutchigàr
mummified embalsamado
municipality belediye (T)
murdering tajamyento
murmur (v) marmulear
murrain mortaldàd
muscular strength barragania
musculature adalet (T)
museum muzeum
must dever; must be divia di ser
mustache mostacho, mustacho, mustaço
mute (person) mudo; become mute (v) enmudeser
mutter marmurerar; mutterer muto
mutton kodrero
my mia (fem)
mysterious tenebrozo

N

nail (n) unia, unya; (v) enclavar, enklavar; nail mark unyada; nail
    scratch unyada; nailed enklavado; nailing enklavadijo
naïve ingenuo
naked desnudo, nudo; nakedness nudez
name (n) nombre, shem, alcuñe (from T künye); (v) llamar, lyamar,
    yamar; what is your name? komo te yamas?
nanny çaça, dada
nap (n) shwenjiziko
nape peshkuezo
napkin maramán (Monastir dialect)
narcotic narkotiko
narration relato
narrow (v) enkojer; (adj) estrecho; narrowness estrechura
nasty rashaj
natal natal
nation gente, nasyon, umá; nations gentes; national nasional,
    nasyonal; national socialism nasional sosialismo; nationality
    nasyonalidad; nationalization nasyonalizasyon; nationalize (v)
    nasyonalizar
native of orijinario, orijinaryo

natural natural, semplice (Ital); **naturalization** naturalizasyon;
   naturalize naturalizar
nature natura
nausea (Port) enguyos
nauseous bulandereádo
nazism nazismo
near (adj) proksimo, sircanu (Monastir dialect); **near** (adv) serkano;
   near future proksimo tyempo
necessary ihtisali (T *iktizali* kanunn), lazim (T)
necessity dejrea (H), ejrea (H), ihtizá (T), neseçita, necsessita
neck peshkuezo, servis; **necklace** yadran (T *gerdan*), yardán (from T
   gerdan (neck) and *gerdanlik* (necklace); **necktie** graváta; **necktie
   knot** papiyon
need (n) dejrea (H), ejrea (H), menester, minister (Monastir dialect);
   need (v) pedir; **needy** dezéôzo, menesterozo
needle aguja, alguja, suzeni (T)
negation negasyon, ñegasyon
negative negativo
negligence deskuydo
negotiate negociar, negosyar
negotiation negosyasyon
neighbor vezino, vizino; **neighborhood** cortíjo, mahal(l) (T *mahalle*);
   neighborly relationship maestranut
neophyte adjami (T *acemi*)
nephew sobrino, sovrino
nerve inyervo, nyervo; **nerves** inyervos
nervous asabi (T), inyervozo; **nervousness** ñervozidad
nettle ortiga
never jamas, jamay, nunca, nunka; **nevertheless** myentres, por tanto
new nuebo, nuevo, nuevo, de los nuevos, muevo, jedit; **New Testament**
   Evanjil; **newborn** nasido; **newborn** recem nascido; **newlywed** rezin
   kazado, muevo kazado
news haber (T), nouedades (Ferrara Siddur)
newspaper jornal, jurnal (Port *jornal*, F *journal*)
next seguinte, vinideru (Monastir dialect); **next to** a cerca, allado; **next
   year** anio el vinien (from Passover song A Lahmania)
nibble (v) roendar
nickname parachukli, sovrenombre
niece sobrina, sovrina; **night before** antinotche; **night guard**
   mishmara (H)

night noce, noche, notche, nochada, noche; **night table** komodine;
   night guard bekdji, bektchi (T *bekçi*)
nightingale berbil, bilbil; **little nightingale** berbeliko (T *bülbül*)
nine mueve, nueue (Ferrara Siddur), nueve
nine hundred nueuecientos (Fer Bib Gen)
nineteen dyezimueve, dizinueve, diezinueve
nineteenth dizinueven
nineth nueven
ninety nouenta (Fer Bib Gen), noventa
ninth un nuevezimo
no no; **no one** dingun, dinguno, ninguno, denguno (arch)
noble zade
nobody ningunos
noise bruido, roido, ruido, shamata (T), sunido (Port), yurultu
   (T *gürültü*, kanunn); **noisy person** shamatadji
noisy ruidozo, rumorozo, shamatali
nomad errante
non not; **non-kosher food** trefa; **non-Muslim** yaur ghiaour
nonchalance fyaka
none ningun, ningunu (Monastir dialect)
nonetheless emperlo, leolam (H), por tanto, todavia
nonsense fasafiso, sachma (T *saçma*)
noodle fideo, tayarine
nor nin
norms dinim (H)
nose naris, nariz
nostalgia (of a person or country) deskariño, eskarinyo
nostril burako, nariz
not no; **not tuned (instrument)** dezakordado
notable vidjuh (T *vücuh*); **notable person** givir (T)
notch susta
note posula (n) (T *pussula*)
notebook defter (T), tefter (from T *defter*); **small notebook** tefteriko
nothing nada; **nothing more** nada mas; **nothingness** nada, no seer
notice avizo; (v) duyulear
notify (v) ambizar (Monastic dialect)
notion nosion
nourishment parnasa
nouveau riche muevo riko
novel novela, romanso; **novelist** romansyero

November novembre, marheshvan (H), arakshamma (Bab)
now (adv) endagora, agóra, ahora, aora; Now then! bre
nudity desnudez
null nulo; nullity zero
number shifro
numbing endormesimyento
numbness atudrimyénto
numerous millarias, numerozo; numerous years añóryos
nun relijioza
nuptial bed thalamo (Ferrara Siddur)
nuptial blessings kidushim
nurse (v) tetár
nurse (n) enfirmyera; nursemaid alechadera
nurtured akerensyado

O

oak meshe (T)
oasis oazis
oat avena, yuláf (Monastir dialect)
obedience itaat (T, from Kanun Name), ra'yet (T riayet, kanunn)
obese paparron, shisko (T), topachudo, tripudo
obey ovadecer, obedecer
object buto, butu
obligated ovligado
obligation hová, kargo, ovligo, obligo, taahud (T taahhüd, kanunn)
oblige forsar, obligar, ovligar, obligar; obliged obligado, obligo,
    ovligado
obscurantism eskurantismo
obscurantist obskurantiste
obscurity escuridad, eskureo
obsequious enmelado, myelozo, pegadozo, seremonyozo;
    obsequiousness salamerias
observation observasyon
observe mirar, observar; observer observador
obsessed sarna
obsession tekia
obstacle empedimyento, obstaculo, trompeson
obstetrician komadrón

obstinacy innát (from T *inad*)
obtain obtener, ubtiner (Monastir dialect)
occasion okazion (F *occasion*)
occlude tapar, tapárto
occult oculto
occupation meshguliyet (T), okupasyon
occupy okupar
octave ochavo
October oktobre, tishri (H), tashretu (Bab)
oculist okulista
odor golór, olor
of de; of the del, dil
offend enjidear (T *incitmek*), offender
office buro, ofisyo
officer ofisier, ofisyer, zabit (T)
official (n) oficial del etcho, oficial, ofisyel
ogre leon
oh ajay (Haketia); Oh! (interj) aniyá (T *haniya*)
oil (n) azéyte, azzeite, azeite, olio, (v) azeytar, yagladear; oiling
    untadura; oily yaghli
ointment enguente, pumada, bamia (Turkish *bamya*)
old aidado, harab (T), viejo; old age senectud, vejes, vejez; older
    mayyor; oldest son behor; bojor
olive aceytùna, azeytuna, olive; olives azeitunas; olive grove azytunal;
    olive oil aezyte de oliva; olive tree azeytunero, olival, olivar
omelet omeleta
omen falaja, siman; good omen simantov (H)
omission olvido
on sobre; on purpose majsos (T *mahsus*); on the back detras; on the
    back of atras; on the contrary altro ke (adv) (Ital); on the exterior
    eksteryoramente; on the floor embaso; on the knees de rodias; on
    the side al lado; on the spot luego; on top ariva; on top arriba;
    on top en sima
once desqueone by one tane tan (T)
one uno; one hundred syen; one more time nueba, nueva de nuebo;
    one only tek (T); one vno Ferrara Siddur); one way or another
    nasilisa (T *nasilsa*); one way or another tisji misji; one who (prep
    and interrogation) kyen; one year duration añada
onion sevoya

only salvo, solo
onomatopoeia shushushu
open (v) abrir, avrir; open one's heart dezafogarse; (adj) avyerdo;
    opening avyertura; openly ashikyar (T kanunn), avyertamento
opera opera
operation operasion, opersayon
operator operador
operetta opereta
opinion majasava, opinion
opponent oponente
opportunist shete lashon (lit: seven tongues)
oppose oponer
opposition opozisyon
oppress appretar, aprimir; oppression appréto
oppression apuro
oppressor angustiador
optimist baal aftaja (H); optimistic avtajali
optional moayar (T *muhayyer*)
opus obra, ovra
or o
oral oral
orange naranja (T *turunç*) pertukal, portokal (T *portokal*), portukal
    (from T); wild orange naranjon; orange peel marmelade antiko di
    portokal; orange tree naranjero, pertulareo, portokalero;
    orangeade pertukalera, portokalera
oration oraçion, orasyon
orator darsan (H), pedrikeador; oratory oratoryo
order (n) desjen (H), duzen (T *düzen*), enkomedansa, nizam (T
    kanunn), orden, sira (T) dicha, emir (T kanunn), manda; (v)
    ordenar; ordered arresentado, atakanádo, enkomendado, ordono;
    orders ordona
ordinary ordinaryo
ordination of a rabbi semiha (H)
oregano origano, rigano
organ organo
organization organizasyon
organize odrenar, ordenar, organizar
organza organdi
Orient oriente; oriental levantara; Oriental music muzika a la turka

origin jins, manadero; **originally** orijinario
ornament aféyto, pechkire (from T *peshkir* napkin); **ornamental**
    dekorozo
orphan guerfano
orthodox ortodokso
ostentation fiaka (T *fiyaka*), saltanat (T); **ostentatious luxury** shinana
ostracized arrematado
ostrich abestruz
other otro, otrun
Ottoman Empire Imperio Otomano
our muestro, nuestro, nwestra; **ourselves** nosotros, nozotros
outline (n) silueta
outside afera, afuera, de fuera, hutz (H), **outside of** afueras
oven forno, orno
over excitation ñervezikos
overall sajakol (H)
overcoat gabardina, pálto (F *paletot*), panyo, paño
overcooked suvidiko
overeating komedero
overexcited solevantado, sovreksitado
overflow (v) desbodrar; **overflowing** desbodramyento
overpayment hormet (T *hürmet*);
oversight olvido
over-stretched tendido (Salonica Pesach Siddur)
overwhelm flechear
ovulate uvular
ovulation uvulasyon
owe dever
own (adj) propyo; **owner** possessor; **owner of business** patron, patrón

P

pacific pasifiko
pacifier çupon, tetadera
pacify pasifiar
package bala, denk; **packages** estifa (Gr)
packed empaketido
padding wata
paddle (n) balsa

pagans paganos
page paje (Monastir dialect)
pageantry dandana (T *tantana*)
paid saladado
pain duelo, gam (T), pen, pena, (of childbirth) dolor; **light pain** dolor-
    siko; **painful** dolente, dolorido; dolorozo; doloryozo,
    endoloryado; **painfulness** doleansas, dolorio
paint (v) pintar, boyadear (v, from T *boyamak*); **painted** boyadeádo,
    pintado; **painter** boyadji (T), pintador; **painting** bóya
pair par
palace palacio, palazio, palasyo, saray (T), sarray (T), seraglio (T)
palate paladar
pale demudado
Palestine Palestina
Palestinian palestinyano
palm of the hand palma
palpable palpavle
palpate palpar, tokar
palpation palpadura, palpitasyon; **palpitations** batidos
pamphlet broshúra, panfleto
pan lagen (T *leghen*)
pane of glass jam
panic estremisyon
panther pantera
pants chakshir, pantalon
paper papel; **brown paper bag** papelera; **pile of useless papers**
    papelerio; **paper merchant** papelero; **paper shop** papeteria
paper roll rollo de papel
paprika çuska (Gr)
parade (v) paradear
paradise ganeden, jennét (T *cennet*)
paralysis tuyidura, tuyisyon
paralyze tuyir
paralyzing tuyimento
paramedic (n) enfirmyer
parasite dalkauk (T *dalkavuk*), parazita
parchment pergamnino
pardon (n) pardon, pedron, perdon; (v) pardonar, perdonar
pardonable pedronavle
parenthood aparyentamento, parentera

parents derredor, los jenitores, parientes (arch), parientis (Monastir
    dialect)
parlor salon (F)
parrot papagayo
parsley perejil, persil, prexil
part (n) parte, partida; a large part una grande partida
participant participante
participate partisipar
participation partisipasyon
particular interest enteresamyento
parturition paridura
party (n) parti, farsa, (political) partida, partido
pass (v) pasar, passar; pass around (v) kontornar; pass over ashirear
    (T ashirmak, kanunn), saltar; pass through passar entre
passages pasajes
passenger pasajero
passion pasyon
passivity pasivita
Passover Pesah
passport pasaporte, yol teskeresi (T yol tezkeresi, kanunn)
past pasado
paste masa
pastille komprime
pastoral pastoral
pastry pastel; pastry shop shekerdjilik
pasture (v) pastár, apasénto
patch (n) yama (T); patch up (v) arrekuxir, remendar; patched up
    arremendado
patent leather shoes çapin (Port chapin)
path caminu (Monastir dialect)
patience pasensia, sabir (T); with patience kon sabir
patient (adj) sabirli (T), pasiente
patio cortijo, kortijo
patriarch patriarko
patriarchal patriarkal; patriarchate patriarkato
patriarchs abot (Haketia)
patriot patriota; patriotism patriotismo
patrol (n) patrulya, kol; (v) patrulyar

paunchy tripudo
pause (n) pausa
pavilion kyosk, kyoshk (T *köshk*)
pavilion paviyon
pawn emprendar; pawned empeñado
pay (n) maish (from T *maash*), pay paga, page; (v) pagar, saldar; pay a
    debt despeñar; pay cash pagar duko; pay off amortízir; pay rever-
    ence to (v) enchachar; payment pagamiento
peace pas, paz, shalom; peace of mind seguridad
peach brisko; peach tree briskéro
peacock pavo
peak (n) fota, pir; peak hour fitero
peanuts fustukes
pear pera
pearl perla; adorned with pearls perlado
pebble pedrika, piedrisica
pedagogic pedagojiko
pedagogue pedagogo
pedagogy pedagogia
peddler (usually a Sephardic Jewish trade in Istanbul) ishportaci (T)
pedestal pyedestal
pedophile kulero
peel (n) cáscara, cashque (Monastir dialect)
peevishness vejes, vejez
penal code kanunname (T)
penalty djereme (T *cereme* kanunn); djeza (T *ceza* kanunn), klisa
    (H kanunn), penalidad
pencil kalem; pencil sharpener aparadór (Port)
pendant (of watch, necklace, etc.) brelók
peninsula peninsula
penis guelindón (Haketia), pata (vulg)
penitence penitensya
penitent baal teshuva (H)
penniless fulus (T), kokoz
Pentateuch homaz (H *humash*)
people djente, gente, puevlo
pepper (spice) pimienta, pimyenta; (vegetable) pimienton, pimyenton;
    pepper vendor pimyentero
perceive duyulear (T *duyulmak*)

perdition pedrimyento, perdicion
perfect perfekto; **making perfect** perfeksyonamento/perfeksionamento;
    perfection perfeksyon; **perfectionist** perfeksioniata, perfeksyonista
perfidious (de) embasho, den basho enbasho, samanalti (lit from T
    under the hay)
perfidy maliñidad
perforate perforar; **perforated** burakádo
perforation perforasyon
perforator perforador
perfume (n) bar (T *bahar*); (v) parfumar; **perfume shop** parfumeria;
    perfumed parfumado
pergola tarrasa
perhaps puedeser
peril (n) riziko, peligro, sekana; **perilous** peligrozo
periodical jurnal (Port *jornal*, F *journal*)
permission musade (T *müsaade*, kanunn), permisyon
perpetual perpetual
persecutor sorer (H)
Persian Adjem (T *acem*); **Persian language** farsi
persist persistir
persistent persistante; **persistent somnolence** dormidero
person alma, persona; **person in charge** responsavle; **personal** personal;
    personality personalidad
persuade kanderear (T *kandirmak*)
pertain apartenér
pertinence apartenénsya
pertinent pertenesido, pertinente
perturb arreboltear, perturbar; **perturbation** deranjamyento
perversion enmalesimyento, pervertesimyento
perversity enmalesimyento, negregura, perversidad
pervert (n) perverso; **pervert** (v) endyavlar
pessimism pesimismo
pessimist pesimista
pest landra; **pestering** maraze
pestilence mortaldàd
petition arzoal (T *arzuhal*), arzuhal (T kanunn), petisyon
petroleum (brut) neft, petrolyo
petticoat faldar
petty pinti; **petty cash** paras para la faldakuera
phantom aparisyon, dañador

Pharaoh Parhó (Ladino Bib Ferrara, Moroccan Sephardic Ballad), Parô
pharmacist ezadji (T *eczaci*), farmasien, farmasista
pharmacy farmasia, farmasiya
philander findirizero
philantrophic filantropia
philantrophist filantropo
philatelist filatelista
philosophy filozofia
phlebitis flebit
phosphorous fosforo
photographer arretratador
phrase frasa, fraza
phylacteries tefilin
physical defect pegima (H)
piano pyano
pick up arekojer
pickles trushi (T *turshu*)
pickpocket yankesidji (T)
picky pinti, puntózo
pie (with spinach, eggplant, squash) enchusa, inchusa
piece pedaso, pyesa, tane (T); **small piece** pedasiko; **in pieces** (en)
     pedasos
pierce (v) afinkar, affinkar; **pierce with arrows** enflechar; **pierced**
     burakádo
pig (derogatory) domuz (T), hinzir (T *hinzir*)
pigeon kolomba, paloma, palomba, palomino
pile (n) soro (Gr *soros*); **pile up** amontonar, entassar
pilgrim pelegrino; **pilgrimage** (to the Holy Places) ziyara, ziyaret (T)
pill hap, komprime, pindola
pillar direk (T); **pillars** atamarales
pillow almoáda, kavesal, yastik (T); **pillowcase** froña
pilot (n) piloto; **pilot** (v) pilotar
pimp rufyan
pin alfinete; alfineti (Gal *alfinete*)
pine tree pino
pink color roz, penbe (T *pembe*)
pious hasid, sofu; **pious foundation** hayrat (T kanunn)
pip tane (T)
pipe alkadrúz (Port), çibuk, oluk (T), pipa; **smoke a pipe** se beber pipa
piracy pirateria

pirate pirata
pistachio (n) fustuk; (adj) fistikyi; pistachio color (adj) fustuki
pistol pishtol
pit kueshko
pitcher bokal, ibrik, kantara
pitiful lamentavle, lastimoso
pity piadad, piyadad, picadu (Monastir dialect); have pity adjidear
    (T acimak), agidear (T acimak); what a pity ke pekado; pityful
    fukara
placard yafta (T kanunn)
place (n) luar, lugar, lugare (Moroccan Sephardic Ballad), plasa; place
    (v) metér; place on apozar
plague mortaldàd, peste; plagues feridas
plain plano, sémplice (Monastir dialect); plains enzinas; plainly sencil-
    lamente
plaintiff davadji (T davaci, kanunn)
plait entressar
plan (n) plano
plane yano
plane-tree çinar
plank távla
plant (v) jarpear, sembrar
plantation of trees bósko
plaster (n) emplasto, alchin (T alçi), pechugal; (v) emplaster; plasterer
    estukador, sovadji, sivadji (T sivaci)
platform tavlada
platonic platonik; platonic love amor platonik
play (v) jugar; play a musical instrument asunar (Monastir dialect),
    tañer, tokar; play cards jugar kartas; play the piano tokar pyano
plaza fedán (Haketia)
pleasure plazer
plenitude hinchidad
ploughman arador
pluck desfinkar (Port fincar)
plug (n) aradera
plunder (v) arrevatar, despojar
plunge (v) dalear; plunge oneself dalearse
pocket aldikera, faldukuera; pocket comb peyniziko; pocket money
    ashlik (T ayyashlik), paras para la faldakuera, harjelik, harchlik
    (T harclik); pocket-knife navaja

poem piyut
poetry piyut
point to apuntar
pointed agudo
pointless abes
poison (n) hiel, intusedju (Monastir dialect), veneno, sam ha-navet
     (H kanunn), tósigo; (v) avenenar, entosegar; poisoned entosegado;
     poisoning entosegamyento
pole direk (T)
police headquarters karakol (T)
police officer jandarmá
polish (v) alisar, aplaynár (Port)
politeness derej eres (H), urbanidad
political politico, politiko
politics politica, politika
pollute enkonar; polluted enkonado
pomegranate mangrana
pomp dandana (T *tantana*), saltanat (T)
pompous dekorozo
pond havuz (T kanunn)
pool pelàgo
poor (n) mesquino, (very poor) zilkade (T), ani (H), fukara, rove,
     probe, zavalli (T); poorly educated kulibero
poppy seed dormidera
popular popularyo; popular song kantiga; popularity popularida
popularize vulgarizar
population ahali, populasion, populasyon
porcelain fagfur, porselena
pork (derogatory) domuz (T)
pork hazir (H), hinzir (T *hinzir*), puerko, puercu (Monastir dialect);
     small pork puerkito
port lonje, porto (Ital), puerto
porter ammal (T *hammal*), ammaliko, hamal
portion porsyon
portraitist arretratador
position (n) posto, pozision, pozisyon, mansub (T kanunn)
possess tener; possessed possuydo (Ferrara Siddur); possession
     posession, posesyon
post office posta
postage stamp damgua (Turkish *damga*), pul (T), timbro

poster avizo
posterity sémen
postpone adyar (Port); postponement tadransa
posturing hadroso
pot chanaka, olla, óya, tendjere (T *tencere*), tindjire, tendjere
     (T *tencere*); content of a pot oyada
potable water (agua) dulse
pot-bellied tripudo
potbelly pancha, tripika
pouch buchicha (Port *bochicha* cheek), sakula
pout (v) enkyanarse, enkorcharse; pouting enkonshada, enozo
poverty aniyut (H *ani* poor), apretura, provedad; poverty-stricken
     mizeryozo
powder poluo, polvo, poder
power kovét; power of attorney mandato; powerful poderoso,
     poderozo, shaday, barragan; powerful men barraganes
practical pratiko
practice (n) pratika
prairie çair (T *çayir*)
praise (n) loor; praise (v) alavàr, avantar, enshashar; praiseworthy
     alavádo
prank arrojada
prankster arrojador, burlón, shakadji
pray (v) arrogar, rogar; prayer oracion, oraçion, orasyon, reze; prayers
     orasiones; prayer for the soul of a deceased askava (H); prayer
     rug sejade (T *seccade*) (Jewish) prayer shawl talet
preach darsar (from T *ders* lesson), pedrikear; preacher darsan (H),
     pedrikeador
precaution prudensya
precious precioso, presyado, presyozo
predication derush (H)
predicator pedrikeador
prediction falaja
predisposed - to be predisposed to tender predisposado/predispozado
predisposition predispozisyon
preface akdama (H)
prefix prefikso
pregnancy prenyades
pregnant embarasada, preniada; pregnant woman (nearing term)
     despensada

premature tempranero
preoccupied penseryozo
preparation aparejo, aprontamyento
prepare aparejar, aparijar (v, Monastir dialect), approntar, odrenar,
    ordenar
prescription resefta (F *recette*)
present (n) dadiva, dono. prezente, regalo; (v) prezentar
presentation prezentasyon
preserve (n) konfitura; preserves dulse, dulsura
president prezidente; president of a synagogue gabay
press (n) meñene (T *mengene*); (v) bastereár (T *bastirmak*)
pressure apretamyento, apretón
pretend contenér, pretender; pretending sozde (T *sözde*)
pretense finta
pretension pretensyon
pretext çikma (T), dejiya, preteksto
pretty lindo
prevention empedimyento
pride envanesyimento, gaava (H)
priest papaz, saserdote
primarily primeramente
primer of fruits and vegetable turfanda, trifanda
prince charif, nasi, principe
princess princesa, printchipesa
print (v) emprimir, estampar; printed estampado, estampadura; printer
    emprimidor, enprimero, estampadir; printing house emprimeria,
    estampa; printing workshop estampadura
prison guard zindandji (T *zindanci*, kanunn)
probability probabilita
probably probabelmente, provabelmente
probe (n) sonda; (v) probar, sondar
problem problema
procedure sistema, usul (T kanunn); procedures muamele
proclaim denunciar
procrastination tadransa
procuration sened (T *senet*, kanunn)
produced saque
producer serpiente
production obra
profanate enkonar

profanation enkonyamyento
professor profesor
profile perfil
profit (n) aprovechamyento, probecho, provécho, gamancia sus bien;
    (v) aprovechar
progress (n) adelantamiento, terakki (T), progreso; (v) adelantar,
    avansar, progresar
prohibit (v) difinder (Monastir dialect); prohibited defendido, yasak;
    prohibition asur (H)
project majasava
prologue akdama (H)
prolong (v) alongar (Fer Bib Kings I)
promise (n) prometa, dibur; promise (v) prometer
promptly alesta
pronounce orar, pronuncyar
proof (n) prova
propaganda propaganda
propagandist propagandista
propagate propajar
propagation propajasyon
propagator propajador
property mulk (T *mülk*, kanunn)
prophecy nevouá, nevuá
prophet navi (H), profeta
proponent proponedor
proposal propozito
propose proponer, propozar; proposed propuesto
proposition propozisyon, propuesta
proselytism prozelitismo
prosper enfloreser
prosperity azlaha (H), dula, engfloresimyento
prostitute (vulg) kahpe (T), kaltak, negra, putana, zona (H)
protected protejado
protest (n) protestasyon; protest (v) protestar
protocol mazbata (T), protokolo
protocolar protokolaryo
proverb reflane, refran; book of proverbs, collection of proverbs
    refranro
provide mantener

provider mantenedor
provision vianda; **provisional** moayar (T *muhayyer*)
provocation desfio
proximate (adj) proksimo
proximity approprinquidad (Ferrara Siddur)
proxy vekil (T kanunn)
prudence akavido
pruritus arraskatina, buyitína
psalm piyut, salmo
public (adj) miri (T *mirî*, kanunn), puvliko; **public disdain**
    aperreamyento; **public herald** tellal (T); **public opinion** opinion
    publika; **public rumor** tavatur; **public square** meydan (T kanunn);
    public treasury hazne (T *hazine* kanunn); **public urinal** pishana;
    Public Works Travajos Publikos
publication publikasyon; puvlikasyon
publicity puvlisiadad, puvlisita
publicly ashikyar (T kanunn)
publish publikar
puff (n) baforada; (v) auflár; **puff of smoke** fumada; **puffing up**
    solevantamyento; **puffy** topachudo
pull travar; **pull off** travar; **pull off the skin** deskorchar
pulley makara (T)
pulp polpa
pulse (n) pulso
pulverize pulverizar
pulverizer pulverizador
pumpkin seed pipitika
punch (n) puúo, punyo, puñu (Monastir dialect)
puncheon punchon/púnchon
punish apeñar, kastigar, siaset (azerlo) (T *siyaset*, kanunn); **punishment**
    castigo, kastigo
puppet maryoneta
purchase order enkomenda, komanda
purchasing merkida
pure has, puro, safi (T)
puree papa
purgatory purgatorio
purpose buto
purse bolsa, falduquere (Monastir dialect)
pursue persegir, asegiyir, asigiyir; **pursuer** persegidor

pursuit (n) persegimyento
purulent enmateryado
purveyor mantenedor
push (v) arondjar, empushar; push on arrimar; push violently
    arrempushar
pusillanimous mizmiz (T)
put metér, poner; put aside apartamyénto; put aside apartar; put asleep
adurmeser; put down pozar; put in jail yevar en prezo; put in
order arresentar; put in order odrenar, ordenar; put on apozar;
put on trial probar; put oneself in meter (se); put oneself to a
task mitersi (para) (Monastir dialect); put to death siaset (azerlo)
(T siyaset, kanunn); put together englobar
putrefaction enfedesimyento
putrefy pudrir
pyramid piramida

Q

quadruped quadrupéa
quagmire batakaná (T batakhane)
quagmire çamurluk
quarantine karantina
quarrel (n) pleito, pleto
quarrel (v) tutushearse (T tutushmak)
quarrel baraja
quarrelsome bushkapléytos
quarry odjak de pyedra (T kanunn)
quarter çirek (T çeyrek)
quay molo
quay skala
queen reina
quench the thirst amatar la sed
question (n) kestyon
question (n) pregunta
question (v) preguntar
questionnaire kestyonaryo
quickly presto
quickly prestu
quick-tempered ravyozo

quiet arrepozadiko; **stay quiet** kedate arrepozado
quiet calma (Port *calmo*)
quiet down (v) kalmar (se)
quince bembriyo
quince binbriyo

R

rabbi (el) rabano; Ashkenazim rabbi rav, haham (Sephardic rabbi),
    hahán, abino
rabbinate rabinato
rabbinical court bed din (H)
rabble kanalya
race djis (T *cins*), rasa, semen, soy (T)
racism racismo
radiate rayar
radish dumalan, ravano
rag handrajo
rage birra
ragged desgarrado
raging ravyozo
ragout gizado
railroad station stasjon del shemen de fer
rails (of railroad) raya
railway shemen de fer, shimen di fer (T adapted from F *chemin de fer*);
    railway car vagon
rain (n) luvya; **rain** (v) llouver, llover; **rain shower** arregáda; **rainbow**
    arko, arkol; **raincoat** gabardina; **rainy** (weather) tyempeziko
raise (v) kriar; **raise oneself** lenantarse; **raise the bet** embidar
raisin pasa, pasika; **raisins** pasas
ram baruez, barvéze
Ramadan ramazan, ramadan
ramification ramifikasyon
ramify (v)ramifikar
ramp pasamano
ran corrio
rancid bayát (T)
rank (n) mansub (T kanunn), rutbe (T *rütbe*, kanunn), sira (T), fila
ransack soydear

rapid prestozo; rapid messenger estafeta
rarefy enrareser
rascal kanalya, kyerata; rascals karvonis
rat ahbár
ration ta'yin (T *tâyin*, kanunn)
rationalist (fem, masc) rasyonalista(o)
rattan çunko
ravage (v) despovlar, estrashar; ravaged espojado, estrashado
ravenous voraz
ravine dere (T)
raw ruda
ray rayo
reach (v) alkansar, ayegar, parvenir, parvinir (F *parvenir*), yegar;
    reached ayego (Fer Bib Gen), parvino
reaction reaksyon
read (v) meldar (from Gr. *Meletan*); read again rremeldar; reader
    lektor; reading keriath (H)
readiness aprontamyento
ready (adj) tamam, pronto (arch), prontu (Monastir dialect); ready-to-
    wear clothes konfeksyon
real estate mulk (T *mülk*, kanunn), mulkye (T *mülk*, mülkiye), real
    estate property deed tapo (T *tapu*)
really veramente
rear (vulg) kulo; rear end trazera (vulg)
reason (n) razon; reason for hope shaare
reasonable razonavle, reasonable sezudo; reasoning razonamiento
rebel (n) asi (T kanunn); (v) reveyar, revoltar
rebellion asilik (T, kanunn)
rebellious revoltozo
rebirth renasyensya, rebirth renasyimento
receipt resivida
receive arresevir, rresivir
recent reciente
reception resepsyon
recidivist sabikali (T kanunn)
reciprocation mukabele (T kanunn)
recite recitar (v)
reclaim (v) reklamar
reclined areskovdado, arrescovdado, arreskovdades
recluse rekluzo

recognize rekonoser
recommend enkomendar, rekomendar; **recommendation** encomenta,
    enkomedansa, rekomandasyon; **recommended** enkomendado
recompensate (v) rekompensar
recompense (n) rekompensa
reconcile (v) konsilyar
reconciliation avenimyento
reconstitute (v) rekonstituir
reconstitution rekonstitusyon
reconstruct rekonstruir; **reconstruction** rekonstruksyon
recount (v) contar
recourse rekorso
recover arrekavdár, rekovrar
recriminations doleansas
recrudescence pujita, ribuy (H)
rectify rektifiar
rectitude derechura
recuperate arrekavdár, rekavdar, rekovrar
red kolorado; **red beet** pandja, pandjar (T *pancar*); **small red beet**
    pandjeka; **red caviar** tarama; **red pepper** gamba
redden çamushkar, enkorladear
redeem (a slave or a captive) resgatar; **redeemed** regmido, rigmiô luégo
    (Passover Haggadah); **redeemed slave** resgatado; **Redeemer**
    Regmidôr, rejmidor
redemption regmiciôn
red-haired ruvyo, royo
redingote redingot
redress arriftar, enderechar; **redress oneself** enderecharse
reduce desmenguar, apurar; **reduce in size** enchikeser; **reduced** desmen-
    guado, sorvido
reduction in size enchikesimyento
reenter credits rekavdar
refine arrefinar
reflection refreksyon
reform (n) trokamyento
refrain (v) pizmon (H), enfrenar
refresh afreskar, arrefreskar, rafreskar; **refresh oneself** calar (si) (v,
    Monastir dialect); **refreshing drink** rafreskamyento; **refreshment**
    rafreskamyento
refuge avrigo

refund (n) hazira (kanunn)
refusal negativa
refuse refuzar; refused dezechado
refute refutar
regain (n) pujita; regain health arremeterse
regard eguardo
regiment polk (Bulgarian Judeo-Spanish), regimento
region rejion; regional rejyonal
register (n) tefter (from T *defter*), rejistro; (v) kayd (T kanunn),
     rejistrar; registered rejistrado
regret (n) repentimyento; regret (v) repentir. regretar (F *regretter*);
     regretted regretado
regular arreglado, regular, regularyo; regularly regularmente
regulate arrizintar (Monastir dialect)
regurgitate (v) regoldar
regurgitation (n) regoldo
reheat arrekayentar
reign (v) reynar; reigning reynante
reimburse (v) rembolsar; reimbursement rembolso
reincarnation gilgul (H)
reinforce enfortecer; reinforce a belief enfeuzyar; reinforced
     enfortecido; reinforcement enfortesimyento
rejected dezechado
rejoice emrenear (T *imrenmek*); rejoicing alegria
relate to (v) denunciar; related to mutalik (T *müteallik*, kanunn)
relation relato
relative familiar, kosuegro, pariente, serkano; relatives parientes (arch)
relax (v) arrafganeár (T), deskansar, arrajlaneárse (T *rahatlik*),
     arrefulgar, asoltar, rafraganar; relaxation kef (T *keyif*); relaxed
     asoltado, flosho
reliability seguransa
religion relijion, relijyon
religious relijioso; religious scholars hahamim
relish asaborar
remade leshano
remains restos
remake the stitches of a sock, etc. remayar
remark (n) remarka; remark (v) remarkar
remedy (n) çare (T), melezina, remedio, kura; remedy (v) parar

remember akordar, arrekodrar, membrár; **remembered** membro,
     memoro, niembrô
remembrance recuerdo
remind of (v) recuerdar
reminisce arrekodrar
remission embio, remesa
remit remitir
remorse apezadumbre, apezadúmbre, remorso
remoteness leshura
removal ablasyon
remove sakar; **remove the chains** deskadenar; **remove the fleas**
     despulgar; **remove the lice** despyojar
renaissance renasyensya
render rendyer; **render a decision** asetensyar; **render bland** shavdear;
     render stupid embovar, emboveser; **render vain** envaneser
rendezvous apuntamyento
renew renovar; **renewed** renovado
renovate arrenovar
renown for good or bad reputasyon
renowned reputado
rent (n) arkilo, renda (Port), kira (T kanunn); (v) alkilar, arkilar
renunciation rrenunsya
repair (v) adovar, adobar, remendo; **repairman** adovador
reparation enderechamyento; **reparations** reparasyones
repeat asegundear, repetar (modern Spanish *repetir; F répéter*)
repellent askeozo
repent arrepintir (se), fazer tajlij; **repenting** repentimyento
replica replika
replicate replikar
report raporto; **reported** denunçio
representation reprezentasyon
representative reprezentato, rrepresentante
reptile remouilla, sierpe, syerpe
republic republika
repudiate repudyar
repudiation deshadura, get (H), repudyasyon
repugnance angustia, eskifozo
reputation nam, fama; **have a good reputation** tomar buen nam
reputed reputado

request (n) redja, ridja (T *rica*), ridja (T *rica*, kanunn), arzoal
(T *arzuhal*), epistola (Gr); (v) dimandar (Monastir dialect), pedir
rescue sokorrer
research (n) búshkita; researcher bushkadór
resemblance arremiransa, asemejansa, ayrada, dimyon (H)
resemble asemejar
resembling arremirante
resent asarse (lit: to be grilled), displazer a unu; resentment enkapado,
ensuña, garez (T)
reserve (n) rezerva, reserva
reside morár; resided estuuo
residence estancia, morada
resident morador, murador (Monastir dialect)
residing situado
residue reziduo
resign (v) demisyonar
resin rechina, rezina; wine with a small percentage of resin vino rechinato (*retsina*); resinous rechinato
resist dadanear (T *dayanmak*), rezistir; resistance rezistensya
resistant rezistente
resolve rezolver; resolved decidido, decizo (Ital *deciso*), entensyonado
respect (n) respekto, eguardo, hormet (T *hürmet*), reayet (T *riayet*);
(v) akatar, respektar; respectability nanuz (T *namus*); respected
onorado
respiration aliento (Fer Bib Gen), respirasyon, solup (T *soluk*), sulup,
soluk (T *soluk*)
respire respirar
response repuesta
responsibility responsabilidad
responsible responsavle, responsavlo
rest (n) deskanso, reposo, repozo; (v) arrefulgar, arrepozar, deskansar,
repozar; rest comfortably ferajlanearse; rest on arrimar
restaurant lokanda, locánta (T *lokanta*), likuanda T *lokanta*);
restaurant keeper lokantadji (T *lokantaci*)
rested arripuzadu (Monastir dialect), repozado
restroom betakiseé (H), bedakavód (H)
result (n) rezultado
resuscitated aribivio
retain retener

retake retomar
retell racontar (Passover Haggadah, Salonica)
rethink arrepensar
retire retirar; retired person tekaut, tekaud (T *tekaüd*)
retort (v) escrouchir
retreat (n) retirada, rincon
retribution enderechamyento
return (n) hazira (kanunn), atornada, buélta (n); (v) dolashear
    (T *dolashmak*), boltar, vuelar, aturnar (Monastir dialect), dar
    atráz, retornar, tornar
reunion adjunta, agunte, banda, tenida
reunite aguntar (Monastir dialect)
revamp remendar; revamped arremendado
reveal revelar
revelation revelasyon
revenge (n) vindikasyon, nekamá, vengansa, vingansa; take revenge
    rekavdarse
revenue avait (T kanunn), revinido, vardat (T *vâridat*, kannunn)
reverence reverensya
reverent reverendo
review revista
revise revizar
revision revizyon
revival arrebivimyento
revive arrebivir, arremanear; revive oneself arebiver(se) (T)
revocation revokasyon
revoke mandate or power dezotorizar
revolt (n) revuelta, solevantamyento; (v) revoltar; revolted rebolteado
revolution revolucion (Ferrara Siddur), revolusyon; revolutionary
    revolusyonaryo
revolve vuelar
reward recompensa
rheumatic rumatismal, ramatizmo, romatisma, rhumatizmo,
    rhumatizmo, romastismos
rhyme (n) rima; rhymed verse kompla
rhythm compás
rib (n) kostiya, costilla
ribbon cordéla, sherit (T), shirit (T *sherit*), sinta
rice arroz, rizoto; rice field arrozal; rice pudding sotlach (T *sütlaç*)

rich riko, zengin (T); riches azyenda, fortuna
ricotta cheese rikota
riddle bilmejeke (from T *bilmece*), endivina
ride (v) enbeneyar (T *binmek*)
ridiculous rezil (T)
riding suvido; riding backwards suvido al reverso; riding on horseback
    suvyente
rifle pishtol, rifle tufenk (T *tüfenk, tüfek,* kanunn)
right (adj) diestra; right hand derecha; right side derecha; righteousness
    çedaquá tsedaka (H), derechedad
rigid dich (T *dinç*); rigidity tejor
ring (n) aniyo, anillo; ring (v) son, sonar
ringworm tinia, tinya
rinse enshaguar
riot (v) solevantar; riots fesad (T *fesad*)
rise (v) amanecer (of the sun), subir, suvir; rising suvido
risk (n) riziko; (v) arrezikar, azardar, rizikar
ritual fast taanid, tani, tanid
ritual slaughter shehita; ritual slaughterer shohet, sojet, shohet
river dere (T), kuryente, koryente, rio
road camino, carrera, kamino, yol (T kanunn)
roam rodear, sorretar
roar brameár (v)
roast (n) rosto; (v) asar, assar; roasted asada; roasted meat kebap,
    rosto; roasted peanuts fustukes
rob (v) rovar, soydear
robes tongas
robust bábachko, babayit (T *babayigit, babaghit*)
rock (n) penia, piedra; rock the cradle balansar
rod (n) palo, vara, vàra
roll (n) rulo, rolo (F *rouleau*); (v) rodear
Romanian rumano
romantic romantico
romanticism romantismo
roof çati (T), tejado, tejo, viga
room oda (T kanunn), uda, oda (T *oda*)
root (n) raiz, kyok (T *kök*), rayiz, raiz; root (v) enraigar; rooted
    arraygádo, enraigado
rope cordele, kuedra

rose komca (T), konya (from T *konca* bud, rosebud), roza, triandafila
     (Gr *triandafilo*) rose bush rozal; rose bush rozero; rosebug mavlacha
rot (n) mófo; (v) amofar, amofeser, federse, pudrir
rotate çevirear
rotisserie asaderia
rotten amofado, çuruk (T *çürük*), kufyo, sapyo; rotten egg guevo
     bozeado
roughcast sova, siva (T *siva*)
round (adj) redondo, rodondo; (n) ronda
routine rutina, rutinyero (adj)
row (n) stifa
rowboat barka
rowdy kulanbey (T *külhanbeyi*)
rowing boat kayik (T)
rub (v) fregar; rub against arrefregar; rubbing with soap enshavonada
ruble rubla (Russian currency)
ruby rubí
rudder bar timon
rude abdal (T *aptal*), azpan, barbuzáen, çomak (T), kaba; rudeness bót
rug tapet
rugged arrijado, aspro
ruin (n) ruina, ruvina, rovina, çurukluk (T *çürüklük*) depedrisyon,
     estruisyon; (v) bodear (from T *bozmak*), bozdear, bozear
     (v, T *bozmak*); ruin one's health fendir; ruined (adj) aspur,
     desposivle, estrashado
rule (n) regla
rum brandy
rumor rumor; rumors ruidos
rumple enjandrazonar; rumpled enfregoneado, engroviñado
run (v) correr; take a risk aventurarse; run away fuyír, fuyír, huir; run
     up slanchyo; running aground varadura; running away huyendo
     (Moroccan Sephardic Ballad); running kuryendo, koryendo
runt mofto
russet royo, ruvio, ruvyo
Russian language rusesko, ruso
rust (n) ferroja, furroje (Gal *furruje*)
rustic yaban (T)
rusty ferrojenteado
rye (T) çavdar

S

Sabbath saba
sabotage (v) sabotar
saboteur sabotador
saccharine sakarina, zaharina
sack (v) sakear, soydear (T *soymak*); sacking sakeamyento
sacred sakarado, sakrado
sacrifice (n) alsayon, korban (from T *kurban*), korbán, sakrifisyo, sangreficio; (v) sakrifikar
sacrilege sakrilejyo
sacrosanct sakrosankto
sad erremo, triste
sadden atristar, desolar, enfyelar
sadness sehora, tristeza
safe salam (T *saghlam*), seguro; safe deposit boron; safety seguransa
saffron asafran, safran
sail (n) vela
sailor marinero
saint sadik (H *tsadik*)
saintliness çedaquá tsedaka (H)
saintly santo
salad salada, salata
salami salama, salami
salary aspaka (H), maish (from T *maash* literally), salaryo
sale vendidad
saliva kolondrina, kulina (Ital *aquolina*);
salt (n) sal; salt and pepper sal i pimienta; add salt saladura; without salt shavdo; salt marsh tuzla; worker in salt marsh tuzladji; salted tuna lakerda; a little too salty saladiko
salute (n) reverencia, selamet (T); (v) saludar
same mesmo, mezmo, mismo, steso (Ital)
samovar samovar
sample (n) egzemplar, eshemplaryo, campion, mostra, muestra
sanatorium sanatoryo
sanctuary santed, Santuvario, templo
sand arena
sandal sandal
sandwich sandvich, sanvich
sandy arenozo; sandy beach arenal

sapphire safir, zafir
sardine sardela; sardines sadrela; vendor of sardines sadrelero
satan satán, sheytan (from T *sheytan* devil)
satiated artar, arto (Fer Bib Gen), farto
satiety artadura
satire sita
satisfaction deletaçion, satisfaksyon
satisfied afartado
satisfy (v) akontentar, satisfazer
Saturday shabat (Judeo-Spanish), sabado (Modern Spanish)
saucepan tendjere (T *tencere*), tenghere, tendjere (Haketia, T *tencere*)
sausage salchicha, sarsiça
savage salvaje; like a savage sylvestre; savagery salvajeria
save (v) ekonomizar, salvar, arrizgatar (Port *resgatar*), avansar; save
    oneself (v) salvar (se); save oneself eskulterear (T *kurtulmak*);
    save souls abidugar almas; save time adyar (Port)
savings arrevánso
savior salvador
savor asaborar, saboerear
saw (n) siedra; (v) siar
say dezir, dizir; say again asegurar; as said before sovredicho; say
    good-bye dispartir (si)
sayings dichas
scalded eskaldado
scandal eskandalo, kyepazelik, kepazelik
scar (n) sikatriz, sikatriza; (v) enkorar, enkrostar
scare (v) espantar, asustar, atorvar, ispantar
scarf bambula, fishu, fular (F *foulard*), tokador
scarlet fever skarlatina
scarred enkorado
scatterbrained tirilo, shabsal
scattered desparzido
scenario shenaryo
scene (of a theater play) shena
scent bar (T *bahar*)
scholar meldahon
scholarly universitario
school (T kanunn) mektep, eskola, shkola (Serbo Croatian Judeo-
    Spanish); school teachers melamedim
science sensya, syensya, sencia, sensia; life sciences sensia de la vida

scientist savyo, sensyudo
scissors tijeras
scorn (n) desde, desdeñador
scorpion alakran, modrefuy, modrefuz
scoundrel kanalya, kyerata
scowling face mutra
scrap soruntluk, suruntluk
scratch (n) reskuño; (v) arraskar, reskuñar, acusar (Port *coçar*),
    araskar; scratched areskuniado, areskunyado, sarjado
scream (n) esclamaciiôn, esclamaçion, grito; scream (v) gritar; scream
    of pain gritos de dolor
screen perde (T)
screw (n) vida (T); (v) bulmá (T *burmak, burulmak*); screwdriver
    kachavida (Ital *cacciavite*)
scruple safek (H)
scrutinizer eskruteador
sea mar, pelagos
seagull babéka de mar
seal (n) sello, muur (T *mühür*, kanunn); (v) (with the official stamp)
    ensiyar; sealed emplombado
seaport liman (T)
search (v) bushkár, buxcar; search out arremoshkar; searcher
    eskarvador
seashore orilla de la mar (Ladino Bible of Ferrara, Kings)
seasons plazos; in this season (a) plazo
seat (n) silla (Ferrara Siddur)
second (adj) segundo, sekondo, sigundo; second (v) asegundar
secondhand dealer eskidji; secondhand clothes dealer palyadji (Gr
    paleos old)
secret enkuvyerta, secreto, sekreto; secretly (lit: behind the hand)
    atrasmano, baséter
sect sekta
sectarian sectaryo; sectarianism sektarismo
section zona
sector sektor
secure (v) stifar; (adj); (adj) seguro
security seguridad, segurita, sigorta, siguritad, tahvil (T kanunn); secu-
    rity measures medidas de siguridad
sediment reziduo
sedition fesad (T kanunn)

seditious fesaddji
seduce enfechizar; **seduced** embabukado
seductive sangrudo
see devizar, veer, ver; **without being seen** sin ke lo veygan
seed (n) sémen, simyente, tane (T); **seed** (v) asembrar; **seeded**
   asembrado; **seeding** asimyente
seem pareser; **seeming** paresiendo
seizure zabt (T kanunn)
self-assurance çalum (T *çalim*)
self-determination autodeteminasyón
self-esteem amor propryo
sell vender
semen matan (H), sémen, semiente, simyente
Semite semita; **Semitic** semitiko
send embiar; **send for** mandar; **send to hell** siktirear (T, vulgar, Judeo-
   Spanishized verb); **sender** mandador; **sending** embiamiento
senior señor
sensation sansasyon, sensasyon; **sensational** sensasyonal
sense senso, tino, sensio; **common sense** buen sensio; **artistic sense** sensios artistikos
sensibility sensivilidad
sensible sezudo
sensitive sensivle
sensual voluptuozo; **sensuality** voluptuozidad
sentence (n) frasa (phrase), gezera (H), hukyum (T *hüküm*);
   (v) sentenciár
sentiment sentimiento
sentry nobetchi (T *nöbetçi*, kanunn); **sentry box** kuliba (T *külübe*
   kanunn)
separate (v) estajar, apartar; **separate from** alezar de
separation apartante, appartadura, despartimyento, estajo; **separations**
   espartimientoa (Salonica Pesah Siddur)
Sephardic Sefaradi, Sefardi
September septembro, elul (H), ululu (Bab)
septentrion septentrionon
sepulcher fuesa
sequence sira (T)
sequester (v) sekuestrar, sokestrar; **sequesterer** sekuestrador
sequestration sekuestrasyon
Seraph adredor

serene aserenado
serenity tenaylik
sergeant (military) çaush (T *çavush*)
serious serioso, seryozo; seriousness seryo
sermon derasa (T), dirush (H)
serpent kulebro, syerpe
servant moso, mosu (Monastir dialect), dishipla, hademe (T kanunn),
    moshka, servidor, serviente, siruiente (Ferrara Siddur); servants
    moços criados
serve (v) hizmét, aprestaese, servir (T); serve a meal eskudiyar
service hizmet (T kanunn), servicio, servis, servisio
servitude esklavaje, esklavedad
sesame seeds susám (T)
session seduta (Ital), tenida
settle remamsarse (archaic Castilian); settle down estableserse; settle
    upon poner se; settled se remanso
seven siete, syete
seventeen dezisiete, dizesyete, dizisyete
seventeenth dizesyeten, dizisyeten
seventh setentaiyen
seventy setanta, setenta
sew cuzír; sewer caño
sewers lagum (T *laghim*)
sewing kostura
sex sekso, sexo
sextuple sekstuple
sexual seksual
shack çosa
shade solómbra, sombra
shadow nombra, solómbra; shadows tiñevla; shadowy tenebrozo
shady asolambrado, asolambrado, asolombrado
shake (v) manear, sakudir; shake violently estemperear; shake with fear
    estremeserse; shaken estempereado; shaking sakudida
shame picadu (Monastir dialect), verguenza, vervuensa
shameless alchak (T *alçak*), atrivido, azpan, sfacato (adj) (Ital
    sfacciato), sinvervuensa, utanmáz (T)
shape (n) forma, kalup; (v) formar; shaped finio; shapeless vana
sharp agudo, aspro; sharpen desmolar, tajar; sharpen utensils esmolar;
    sharpening stone desmoladera; sharpshooter mangu (Monastir
    dialect)

shave (v) arapar, (v) arrapar (Monastir dialect); **shaving** arrapada
shawl shal, shali (T *shal, shali*)
sheath fuzo
sheepfold mandra
sheet savaná
shelf platera
shell (n) casca
shelter avrigo
shepherd çoban, ganado, pastor
shield (n) escudo, eskudo
shine (n) lustre; (v) briyar
shining resplandeciente
ship (n) nave, navi (Monastir dialect), navio; **shipment** (n) manda;
      shipwrecked fundido
shirt camisa, kamiza, nagüita; **small baby shirt** kamizika
shish kebap shish kebap
shivering temblor
shock (n) çakeada, çakear (T *çarpmak*); çakeo
shoe (T *kundura*), kondurya, kondúrya, çapato, kalsado, papuchu
      (T *papuç*); **shoe(s)** sapato(s), tchapinas; **shoelace** sherit (T); **shoe
      polisher** boyadji (T); **shoe shiner** lustraji (T *lustraci*); **shoeless**
      deskalso, çelebi deskalso; **shoemaker** kunduryero, zapatero,
      remendon
shop botika, butika, butique (Monastir dialect), magazin (F *magazin*);
      shop assistant tezyahtar **shop owner** butikáryo; **shop window**
      vitrina; **shopkeeper** buticariu (Monastir dialect), ispicieru
      (Monastir dialect)
short kurto; **to be short of** mancar; **short walk** bueltezíka; **shorten**
      akurtar; **short-handled ax** eshjuela
shoulder (n) espalda, spalda
shout (n) grito
shovel paleta; **blow with a shovel** paletada
show (n) mansevedumre; (v) amostrar, mostrar
shower (v) dushar; **shower-bath** dush
showily vistozamente, vistozamente
showy shamatali, vistozo
shrew soysuza
shrimp karides (T)
shroud sudario
shrunken arresekado

shuffling maraze
shutter (v) quebrar, quebrantar
shutting in ensyerro
sick enfermo, hazino, hazinu (Monastir dialect), sufriente; sickly
    person holento; sickness hazinura, hazinura
side ladu (Monastir dialect), pare, pared, vera; at his side a su lado
    lado; from his side de su parte
siege (n) asédyo, sospiro
sigh (v) esclamar, esclamir, suspirar
sight mirada, vista
sign (n) siim (T *sim*, kanunn), siman (H), señal, signal, signo, tabela;
    (v) firmar
signal fenel (T *fener*), siñal; signals señales
signature firma
significance senso
signification sinyifikasyon
signs señas
silence cayadés (Monastir dialect), kayades, kayadez, keyadura,
    silensyo; silenced akayado
silent akedado, kayado, silensyozo
silhouette silueta
silk estofa, seda
silly zevzek
silver plata; silverware arjanteria
similar arremirante, paresido, semeja, semejante; similarity asemejansa,
    semejança; similarly altretánto (Ital)
simple bovankyón, bovarrón, semplice (Ital), sémplice
    (Monastir dialect), simpliche; simple-minded buenivle,
    prenismo
simplicity sempleza, semplisita
simplification semplifikasyon
simplify alivyanar, semplifilar, simplifikar
simply sencillamente
sin (n) peccado, pekado; (v) pecar, pekar
since desde, pues
sincere sinsero
sincerity frankeza, senserita, sinserita (from Latin *sin sera*)
sinew pelejo
sing (v) kantar, (bird) trinar; singer cancionero, cantador, kantador,
    sharkidji; female singer kantadera

sinister sinistre
sink deskaeser
sinner pecador
sinusitis sinuzit
sip (n) sorviko; take a sip dar un sorviko
siren sirena
sister ermana, hermana; sister-in-law cuñada
sit asyento; sit down asentar (se)
situate situar; situated assituado
situation hal (T), situasyon
six hundred seicentos, shesentos
six sesh, seys (Ferrara Siddur) sejen
sixteen dizesej
sixth secento, seksto, sesenta, shesenta
sixtieth sesentaiyen
sixty sesenta
size grandure (Monastir dialect)
skeletal eskeletiko
skeleton eskeleto
skeptic çatlak (T)
skewers shish
skid varadero
skies çielos
skill sheytaneria; skillful desbolvido; skillfulness desbuelvez
skin cuero, cueru (Monastir dialect), kwero
skinflint muñi muñi
skinny (fem) flaca; skinny (masc) flaco, flako; skinny flacu (Monastir dialect)
skipped saltàdech
skirt fostan, fusta
skull kashko, meoyera, meoyero
sky syelo, sielo; sky blue (adj) çeleste; sky full of stars estreyado; the skies (los) sielos
slacken arrafganeár (T)
slain matar
slander iftira (T kanunn), kalomnia; (v) kalomnyar; slanderer favlistan, kalomnyador; slanderous syerpa
slap in the face shamar (n) (from T *shamar*)
slaughter degoyar; slaughterer tajador; slaughterhouse salaná (from T *salhane*)

slave esclavo, esklavo, sieruo (Ferrara Siddur), siervo; **slavery** esclavedad, esklavaje

Slavic slavo

sleep (n) esfuenyo; (v) arrepozar, dormir, durmir; **sleeper** dormidor; **sleeping** (adj and n) dormido, dormyente, durmiendo; **sleeping pill** dormitorio

sleepy person durmido

sleeve manga

slender svelto

slice (of a fruit) tajo; **large slice of cake or fruit** tajon; (v) tajar

slide arresvalar

sliding arresvalada

slimmed sorvido

slipper pantufla, papuchu (T *papuç*), terlik (T), zapateta; **slippers** sapato(s); **slipper manufacturer** pantuflero

sloppy chapachul, cholpa

slow avagar; **very slow** avagariko; **slowly** davagar (Port)

slowness avagareza, fyakedad

slug bavóza

sly (de) embasho, de en basho en basho, debasho en basho, enganchado, ensavanado, hanef (H); **sly person** harif; **slyly** dabashamento; **slyness** maliñidad

small chico, chicu, chiquito, çiko, pequeño; **smaller** (más) chicuy; **smallness** çikidumbre, çikitura

smearing enkalo, untadura

smell (n) guezmo; **bad smell** negra golor; **smell** (v) goler

smile (n) rize (n, Monastir dialect), sonriza, sonrizo

smirking naz

smite ferir

smitten ferido

smoke (n) fumo, humo, umo, dúman (T); (v) fumar; **smoker** fumador, tiryaki; **smoky** fumozo

smuggler kachakchi (T *kaçakçi*)

snake culebra, syerpe; **snakes** culebros

sneaky samanalti (lit from T under the hay)

sneeze (n) sarnudo; (v) sarnudar; **persistent continuous sneezing** sarnudadero

sniffing sorvetina

snob snob; **snobism** snobismo

snore ronkar; someone who snores ronkador; noisy and continuous
    snoring ronkerio; lasting snoring ronkido; snorer sorvidor
snow (n) inyeve, ñeve, nieve; snowstorm ñovetina
snuff burnú tutún; snuffing sorvetina
so ansi, ansina, ansine (Monastir dialect), asi, avis, na; so that afim,
    para
soaked enadado; soaked with water papika
soap jabón, shavon
sobriety sobriyedad
soccer ball (T), futbal, futbol
society socheta (Ital *societá*), sosyeta
sociologist sosyolog
sociology sosyologia
sock kalsa; socks chorap (from T *çorap*), çorap (T)
soda gazoz, soda
sofa canape, sofa
soft afofado
soil (n) tavlada (Monastir dialect); (v) embatakar, ensuzyar; soil one's
    pants sortirse; soil oneself ensuzyarse; soiled embatakado; soiled
    engreshado, enkañado, ensuzyado; soiling enkono
sojourn estada, estansya, morár; short sojourn estadia
soldier asker, askyer (T *asker*), hayal (H), soldado; (coll) young
    conscript/young soldier askyeriko
sole (fish) lenguada, soleta
solely solamente
solemnity solenidad
solid bábachko, rezio, reziu (Monastir dialect), rezyo
solitary aleshado; solitary place solidumbre
solution solüsyon, solusyon
somber funebro
some algun, algunu, (pl) unos
somebody fulano; someone sistrano (used alone or together with
    fulano somebody), alguno, algunu (Monastir dialect); someone
    else otri
something algune coze (Monastir dialect); something scary que espanto
somersault takla
somnolence dormisina
son fijo, hijo, ijo; son-in-law yerno
song canto, romancillo, sharki; songs kantos

soot folin, tizna, tizón; covered with soot entizmadura, entiznado
soothe abatir, alivyanar
soothsayer falaja
sherbet shorbet, shurbet (T *sherbet*)
sorcerer ecizero, fechizeo, karmador; sorceress echizera, karmadora
sorcery chizo, echizeria, echizo, fechizeria, fechizo
sordid avarice çingenelik (T)
sore ulser; sores llagas
sorrow ansya, gam (T), sehora, sogeftos
sorry - I am very sorry regreto muncho
sort (n) turlu, (T *türlü*), felek; (v) asotir, deskartar, eskojer; sort by
    pairs apariyar; sorter eskojedor
so-so shirta ferta, sirta ferta
soul alma, neshama (H), ruah
sound sunido (Port)
soup chorba (T *çorba*), çorba, supa; soup bowl supyera
sour agro, vinagrozo
source manadero; source of the water fuente de las aguas; sources
    fuentes
south darom (H), meridion; southwest sudeste; southwest wind
    imbat (T)
souvenir recuerdo, suvenir
sovereign soberrana; sovereignty podesta, saltanat (T), soverenedad
sow (v) ensembrar, sembrar; sowing sembrado; sembradura; someone
    who sows sembrador
space aralik (T)
Spain Sefarad
Spanish (Judeo-Spanish) spanyol, spanyol
spanker harvador (kanunn); spanking çaketon, dayak (T), haftona
spare (v) ekonomizar
sparkle (n) çispa, senteya; sparkling fire brazináda; sparkling wine vino
    espumante
sparrow pashariko
spasm empido
speak avlar, pedrikeador; speak of (v) recontar; speak of somebody
    nombrar; speaker avlador
spear (v) alancear
special majsus (T *mahsus*)
species djis (T *cins*), espeça
spectacle spektakolo; entertaining spectacle shena

spectacular shamatali, shinanali
spectator spektador, spektator, spektatör
specter aparisyon
speech derasa (T), dirush (H), diskorso; **speeches** deskorsoz
speed prestes, velosidad, velosita; **with speed** kon prestes
sperm matan (H)
spicy espinosa
spider araña
spider web arañero
spill (v) derramar; **spill over** arreverter
spin (v) filar
spinach espinaka, spinaka
spindle fuzo
spine eskino, espina, espino, spina
spinner filador
spinning factory filatura
spiny espinosa esponde
spirit espirito, esprito
spit (n) eskupidijo, shish; **spit** (v) eskupir
spittoon eskupidor
spleen melsa
splendor resplandor
splinter (v) arrevantar
spoil bodear (from T *bozmak*), bozdear, bozear (v, T *bozmak*), federse;
    spoiled bozeádo, dañado, kufyo
sponge (n) esponja, spongdja, espondja
spongy afofado
spontaneous espontaneo
spoon cuchara, kuchara
sport espor, sport
sportive esportivo, sportivo
spot (n) mancha
spouse bula, bulísa, bulisú, espoza, espozada
spray arrufyar
spring primavera
sprinkle sarpicár
sputter farfuyar
sputum balgam (T)
spy (n) eshpion; **spy** (v) eshpionar, espionar; **spying** eshpiomluk,
    eshpionaje, hafiyelik, kuladeo

squad takum (T *takim* kanunn)
squalling çiyon
squander (v) despedrer, desperdrer; squanderer derritidor; squandering
   desfazedero, dezazimyento (more formal: *desfazimiento*), fina
squash kalavasa; small squash kalavasita
squat arrodiyarse
squeeze (n) apretón; (v) apretár, esprimir, appretar, estrinjar; squeezed
   estrinjado
squint (v) shashutear
squirrel (fur) sinjap (T *sincap*)
stab wound cutchiyada
stability stabilidad
stabilization stabilizasyon
stabilize (v) estabilizar, stabilizar; stabilized stabilizado
stable ahir (T), stavle
stage fright trak (from F *trac*)
staggered shashkin
stagnant - become stagnant remamsarse
stain (n) manche, tachon; (v) embatakar, manchar; stained
   entachonado, manchado
stairway escalera
stake (n) estaka
stale bayát (T)
stamp estampilla; stamp mark estampilla; stamped damgali, timbrado
stand (v) somportar, soportar, somportar
star (n) estréa, estreya; stars estrellas
starch (n) lishisten nishasta (T *nishasta*); (v) enkolar; starched
   enkolado
start (v) empesar, empessar, prisipiar; start again asegurar
starvation ambrera, fambrero, hambre
starving fameliko
state (n) estado, devlet (T kanunn), dovlet (T *devlet*), hal (T)
statement ifade (T from Kanun Name), takrir (T kanunn)
station estasyon
stationary estasyonaryo, estatistika
statistics statistica
statue estatua, imaje
statutes estatutos
stave (v) arrevantar, esfondar
stay (v) kedar, haftear

steal arrovar

steam (n) vapora; steamboat vapur (T *vapur*); steamy vaporozo

steel azero, çilik

stenographer estenografo

step (n) paso; step on pisar

stepmother mâdrasta

sterile esterilo

sterility esterilidad

sterilize esterilizar

stew gizado

stick (n) palo, tchibuk (from T *çubuk*); (v) apegar; stick in enkashar; stickiness espesor, espesura; sticky apegadozo, espesura muncho, pegadozo

stiff entezado; stiffness tejor

stigmatize estigmatizar

stiletto punchon, púnchon

still ainda (Port), ainde (Port *ainda*, Monastir dialect), aún, ayinda, dainda, inde inde; still more aun, indemás (Port *ainda mais*)

stimulate asigiyir

sting (n) punchada; small sting punchadika; bee stings bisba puncha; (v) punchar

stinginess tamahkyarlik (T)

stingy avaro, eskaso, tamahkyar (T)

stinking fedorento, fedyendo

stipulate estipular

stir (v) menear, meneyar; stirred maneado; stirrer siye di cunar (Monastir dialect)

stock market bórsa

stockings chorap (from T *çorap*), çorap (T)

stocky godron

stolen arovada, arrevatado

stomach estomago, tripa; stomach pangs (due to hunger) estilo

stone piedra, pyedra; precious stones piedras presyozas; stone (v) apedrear; full of stones pedregozo

stool banketa

stop (n) dezistimyento; (v) aretar, stankar, tupir

stop estanko; stopped aquedarse

store butika; store window vitrina; storehouse ambar (T), anbar (T); storekeeper butikáryo

stork grua

storm fortuna (T *firtina*), furtuna, tempesta; **stormy** fortunojo, orajozo
story (floor) tabaka (T), cunsejo (Monastir dialect), istorya, konseja,
    kwenta, maasé
stove orno, soba (T)
stow (v) stifar; **stowing** stifadura
straight dich (T *dinç*); **straighten** aplanar; **straightforwardness**
    derechitud
strained enguantado, entezado
strange adjaib (T *acaib*), bambashka (T *bambashka*); **strangeness**
    estrañedad; **stranger** estraúero, forastero, pelegrino, perigrino (Fer
    Bib Gen), yabandji
strangle aogar
straw paja, saman (T kanunn)
strawberry fragulo, frangula, fresa, fragwála (from Ital *fragola*)
stream kuryente, koryente
street blóko, kaye
strength fortaleza, fuersa (noble form of *huersa*), hwersa; **strengthen**
    enfortecer, enforticier
stretch out estirar
striated (wood or marble) damarli (T)
strict estrikto; **strictly** estriktamente
string of beads reste (Port *reste*)
strip (n) sherit (T); (v) soydear; **stripped** espojado
striped rigado
strive (v) lazdrar, penar
stroke dada, dade (Monastir dialect), golpe; **stroke of an ax**
    eshjuelada; **in a single stroke** una testreada; **stroke of the oar**
    remada
stroll (n) vuelta; (v) morhunear, morjunear, parziar (Moroccan
    Sephardic Ballad); **stroller** paseante
strong fuerte; **strongly afflicted** enfilendrado
structure estruktura
struggle (n) kombate; **struggle with** ograshar (T *ughrashmak*)
strut arrajlaneárse (T *rahatlik*)
stubborn empesuñado, testarudo; **stubbornness** enduresimyento, inat
stucco estukar
student alevo, çirak, dishiplo, elevo, elevu (Monastir dialect),
    eskolaryo, estudyante; **students** talmidim (H)
studious estudyozo

study (v) estudiar, estudyar; **study** (n) estudio, estudyo; **studies**
 estudyos
stuffed with food empapushar
stultified enterpesido, entudresido
stun estudeser, estudrir; **stunned** shabsal
stupefied enterpesido, entudresido, estempereado, shabsal
stupefy entonteser, entorpeser
stupid bovo, estupido, lonson, maredo, puerro, shashkin, tonto; **stupid**
 person (n) bovo; **stupidity** bovedad, buchukchulúkes (T *buçuk*),
 estrupidez, estupidita, estupidad, tontedad, torpedad, tronchedad;
 stupidities bavajadas; **stupid-looking individual** embolada, vaka
 embolada; **stupidly** a l'aznedad (T *eshekçasina*), eshek jasina,
 eshek yebi (lit: like a donkey would do) (T *eshek gibi*)
stupor tutuleo
stutterer peltek (T)
style one's hair peynar
subject of a state sudito; **subjects** suditansa, sudjeftos(Salonica Pesach
 Siddur), sujetos
subjugate majorgar, **subjugate** sodjeftar, **subjugated** sojuzgalda
submission sumisyon
submit someter, sumetir; **submitted** sodjefto, sofiguado, sumetido
subordination subordinasyon
subsist subsistir; **subsistence** mantenisyon, parnasa, subsistenya;
 subsisting estante
substance sostansya, sustansya, sostansya
substantial suntansyozo, sostansyozo
subterfuge brazón
subtract sustrar; **subtraction** subtraksyon
subway metro
succeed (v) riuxir, riushir, reushir, bedjereár (T *becermek*), bejerear
 (from T *becermek* to be able of), bijirear, lograr, parvenir
 (F *parvenir*); **succeeded** reusho
success azlaha (H), reushita, reuchita (F *réussite*); **succession of** seguita
such tal
suck (v) chupar, çupar; **sucking** çupadura
sudden apansiz (T); **suddenly** (en) supito, enbreve, ensupeto, ensupito
suffer sufrir; **suffering** (adj) dolyente, sufriensa, sufriente
suffice bastár

sufficiency abastansa
sufficient bastánte, sufiziente; sufficient quantity sufizensya
suffocate abafar
suffocation abafyamento, atabafo
sugar sheker (T)
suggest prupuzar (Monastir dialect), sugdjerar; suggestion sugdjestyon,
    sugjestion, sujesion
suicide suisidyo; commit suicide suisidarse
suit (n) vestido; suitcase valija, valije (Monastir dialect)
suitor baal adavár (H)
sulfur asufre; sulfured asufreado
sulkiness enkonshada
sultan sultan; wife of the sultan sultana
sum suma; large sum grande suma
summary hulasa (T hulâsa kanunn)
summer enverano, esverano, verano; summerhouse kösk (T köshk)
summit (n) tepe T), pino, Sima
summons ihzar (T kanunn)
sun sol; the sun rises esclaresse el sol; sunrise alvoráda, madrugada,
    maneser
Sunday alhad (Judeo-Spanish), domingo (Modern Spanish)
super rich rikon
superabundance çokluk bokluk
superstition eklavadura
supervision nezaret (T kanunn)
supplicant redjadji
supplication redja, ridja (T rica), sopliko; by dint of supplication kon
    rogativas
supply (n) komanya (T)
support (n) dayanak (T), suporto, entretenimyento; (v) davranear
    (T davranmak), padeser, soportar (Ferrara Siddur), sotener,
    suportar, adanear (from T dayanmak resist), sustentár; supporter
    sustentador
suppose supozar; supposed supuesto; supposedly (en) supuesto
supposition supozisyon
suppress supremir, suprimir; suppressed suprimido; suppression
    supresyon
sure seguro, siguro; surely decierto, seguramente, siguramente, vadáy
    (H bevaday); surety seguransa
surface sovrefaz, superfisia

surgeon djerah (T *cerrah* kanunn), kirugio, operador
surgery djerahlik (T *cerrahlik* kanunn), operasion, opersayon
surliness dañadoriko
surly fyelozo
surname alkunya (from Turkish *künye* register of names), nam,
  nombradiya, parachukli
surplus demazya, pujita; to be in surplus sovrar
surprise (n) surpreza; surprising adjaib (T *acaib*)
surround circundar, engreñar, entornar, rodear, saradear (T *sarmak*),
  sarear (v, T *sarmak*); surrounded enserklado; surroundings entorno
surveillance dolash (T *dolashmak* make a round), nobet (T *nöbet*)
suspect (v) shubelear
suspense (n) sospezo
suspension stanko
suspicion duvdo, desfeuzia, shube (T *shüphe*)
suspicious desconfiado, dubyozo, dudozo, duvdozo, shubeli
  (T *shüpheli*)
sustain adanear (from T *dayanmak* resist), sustentár
svelte esvelto; sveltness esveltez
swaddle (n) enfashadura; swaddle a baby empaldar; swaddled infant
  enfashado
swaggerer asoltador, fanfaron
swallow (n) kirlangitch, golondrina; (v) englutir, engrutir, sorver
swamp bára
swashbuckler kabadayi (T)
swear (v) jurar
sweat (n) sudor, ter (T); (v) sudar; covered with sweat sudado;
  sweating sudadura; cold sweats sudores jelas, yeladas
sweater fanéla
sweep (with a broom) barir; sweep chimneys esfuliñar; sweep the floor
  barrer, iscuvar (Monastir dialect); sweeping suruntluk
sweet dulce; sweeten endulsar, ensharopar; sweeten with honey
  enmelar; sweetened with sugar shekerli; sweetness dulsor; sweets
  dolse, dulsura
swell auflar; swell tremendously engodreser; swelling solevantamyento
swim (v) enadar, nadar; swimmer nadador; swimming natasyon
swindle (n) dolandirjilik (T, *dolandiricilik*); (v) dolanderear
  (T *dolandirmak*), dulanderear (T *dolandirmak*)
swindler batákchi (T *batakçi*), dalaveradji (T *dalaveraci*), dolandirji
  (T *dolandirici*), dubaradji, dulanderji (T *dolandirici*)

swindling dulandiridjilik (T *dolandiricilik*)
swing (n) báskula
Swiss sviserano
swollen auflado, topachudo
sword espada
sycophant parmaktchi
symbol siim (T *sim*, kanunn)
sympathetic sangrudo, sempatika(o), simpatiko
sympathy picadu (Monastir dialect), simpatia
symptom siman (H)
synagogue havra, kahal, kal, templo; synagogue beadle samas(s),
    samaz samas(s), sammaz, sammas de la Keila,
syndicate boréo
syntax dikduk (H)
Syrian Arami
syringe sheringa (T *shiringa*)
syrup jarope, sharope
system sistema

T

tabernacle tabernaklo
table meza; tablecloth mantel
tactfulness takto
tactic taktika
tail kola
tailor chastre, kroitor (Romanian Judeo-Spanish), shâstre
take tomar; take a bath bañar; take a shower dusharse; take advantage
    (v) avantajar; take away retirar, lyevar, yevar en prezo; taken
    away lyevado; take back arriftar; take care of okuparse; take
    clothes off dezmudar; take note anotár; take out kitar, sakar; take
    place asodesér; take possession empoderar; take revenge vengar
    (se); take root arraygar; take the pulse tokar el pulso; take with
    yevar en prezo; taken aback shashkin; taken prisoner catiuado
    (Fer Bib Gen); taking (a sample) toma; taking back a given
    promise arrenpentidizo, arrepentirse; taking possession
    emposesyamento
talc powder talko
tale cunsejo (Monastir dialect)

talent dono, talento; **talented** talentuozo
talk (n) avla; (v) avlar, çarlar, çarlear; **talkative** zevzek
tall boylí (T *boylu*)
talmudic school yeshiva
tamarind demirindi (T *demir hindi*, also *merendi*), tamarino
tambourine tumbana, pandero, **tambourine player** tanyedor, tañedor
tangerine mandarina
tango tango
tank tank
tannery tabaña
tap dadika
tape (n) shirit (T *sherit*), sherit (T)
tapeworm lamya
tar alkatran, katran
tarry (v) detadràrse
tart (adj) vinagrozo
task (n) lazerio, avóda, tahsa, tarefa
taste (n) guste, gusto, lezet (T), savor; (v) gustar; **tasteless** (savor de)
    çiçigaya, lezetsiz (T), shavda; **tastelessness** shavdura
tasty ensharopado, gostoso, lezetli, savrozo, savrózo
tattoo (n) tatuaje; (v) tatuar; tatruador
tavern taverna, meana, meane, meyane (T *meyhane*); **tavern keeper**
    rakidji (also raki merchant), tavernero, meanadji
tax darsyo, impuesto, taksa, vergi; **taxes** risumat (T *rüsumet*, kanunn);
    tax office maliye (T *maliye*); **tax stamp** timbro
taxation empozisyon, taksasyon, taksadura
taxi taksi
taxidermist empajador
tea (T) çay
teach adotrinar, dotrinar; **teacher** doskel, ensenante, hodja (T *hoca*),
    maestra; **teacher's job** hodjalik (T *hocalik* kanunn); **teaching**
    dotrino, ensenyamento
team taifa
teapot çaylik (T)
tear (n) lagrima; **shed tears** lagrimear; **soaked in tears** (speaking of sick
    eyes) lagrimozo
tear (v) arrasgar, rasgar, razgar; **tear off** arrankar; **tear open** esventrar;
    tear out arrancár
tease docuneár (from T *dokunmak*), taklear (T *takilmak*); **teasing**
    pisma

teat bicu (Port *bico*), tetadera
technical teknika
technician tekniko
telegram telegrama
telegrapher telegraphista
telepathy telepatia
telephone telefon; telephoned telefoneo
telescope teleskopo
television televizyon
telex telex
tell racontar; tell a secret mishiricar (v, Port *mexericar*); tell a story (v)
    kontar; tell aconsejar (Fer Bib Kings I)
telltale entregador
temper (n) gesto, nature (Monastir dialect)
temperament temperamento
temperance temperansya
temperature temperatura; at high temperature (a alta) temperatura; at
    low temperature (a basha) temperatura
tempest furtuna; tempestuous fortunojo
temple kal, Santuvario, templo; Temple of Jerusalem bedamikdash (H)
temporary moayar (T *muhayyer*); temporary illness kyefsizlik
    (T *keyifsizlik*)
temptation tantasyon, tentasyon
ten dies, diez
ten thousand diez mil
tenth diezen
tenant kyeradji
tendency enklinasyon, tendensya; to have a have tendency to tender
tender terno, tierno
tendon pelejo
tennis tenis
tenor tenor
tension sikinti (T)
tent çadir (T), tenda, tienda
tentative moayar (T *muhayyer*), tentativa
tenth dezeno, dyezen
tepid tivyar, tivyo
term eskapadura, termino
terminal terminal
terminate eskapar, terminar

termination acabamiento
terrace altarrassa, çadrak (T *çardak*), tarrasa
terrible terivle
terrify estremeser; **terrifying** estremesivle
territorial territoryal
territory territoryo
terror estremisyon, ispantu (Monastir dialect), temouridàd, temeridad,
    terror, timuridad (Monastir dialect)
terrorism terrorismo
terrorist terrorista
terrorize terrorizar
test (v) aprevar
testament sava, testamento
testicle tashak (T), besim (H); **having testicles** tashakli (lit)
testify atestiguar; atestar
testimony edut (H)
tetanus tetanos
textile tekstil, tesido; **textile dealer** merkador de tesido
textually tekstualmente
than ke
thank (v) agradecer, rengrasyar, rigrasjar (v, Port *regraciar*); **I thank
    you** rengrasyo te; **thankful** rekonosiente; **thankful
    acknowledgment** regrayamento
that (pronoun) ki, lo; (conjunction) que, akeyo; **that is** dehaynu (H)
thaw (v) desyelar; **thawing** desyelo
the al, (pl) lus, luz; **the other world** olam aba
theater play pies de teatro
theft rovo
their sus
them ellos
theme tema
themselves ellos, eyos
then alora (Ital), entonces, entonches, estonses
theologian teologo
theory teoria
there aim, alli, aya, ayi; **there he is!** ecce homo!; **there is** ay
thereby donde
therefore (conj) dunke, de prendimiento, por esto
thermal termal
thermometer termometro

these (masc pl) estos, (fem pl) estas
they si
thick bulaník (T), djodru (Monastir dialect); thickness espesor,
    espesura
thicket soto
thief ladron
thigh gámba, lombo, pyerna
thimble dado, dedal
thin delgado, delgádo
thing cosa, koza, siatranu (Port *sicrano*)
think pensar
third terçero, tersyo
thirst sed, sede; thirsty sediente
thirteen treje, treze
thirteenth trejen, trezen
thirty treinta, trenta, treynta (Ferrara Siddur)
this akel, aquel, aquello, aquesto, estu, (fem) esta, (masc) este; this
    is na
thistle cardo
thorn ispinu (Port *espinho*)
those who (prep and interrogation) kyen
thou tou
thought (n) pensada, pensamiento
thousand mil; thousands miles
thousandth - one thousandth un milesimo
thread (n) hilo, ilo, filo
threat amenáza
three tres
three hundred trezientos, tresientos
three thousand tresmil
thriftiness ekonomia
throat garganta
throne silla (Ladino Bible of Ferrara, Kings)
throw (v) etchar, echar, tirar; throw arrows asaetár; throw oneself into
    something yallear; throw to the side echar de lado; throwing
    etchando
thrust (n) desterràdos
thunder raya; thunderstorm borráska, burráska, oraje
Thursday penchembe, pershembe (T), juevez
thus (conj) dunke (Ital *dunque*)

thy tu, Tu
thymus móleja
ticket bilieto, posula (T *pussula*)
tickling koskiyas
tie (n) atadero, atadura; (v) atar; tie a knot ennnudar
tight estrinjado
tighten enkojer, estrinjar, siklear; tighten the belt siklear la cintura
    (T *sikmak*), stringar
tile (roof) teja
till fasta, fin, fista
tilted enklinado
timber kereste (T kanunn), kyereste
time tiempo, tyempo; vez; times vezes; from time to time (en) vezes; in
    the mean time mientris (Monastir dialect)
timetable orario
timid arrezistado, timido; timidity çekineo, timidez
tin (T) kalay, tin teneke; tin can tenikyel; tinsmith kalaydji (T)
tincture tintura
tinsel (used in embroidery) sim; tinsel for embroidery tel (T)
tiny minuskulo
tip (n) bahshish, bakshish (T *bakshish*), parabever, punta
tippet pelerina
tire carru (Monastir dialect), karrucha
tire out oneself desbelarse (v, T *bel* back, backbone)
tired kansado
tiring alenguaziko, fatigante, fatigozo
tissue komash, ropa, tesido
to a, ala, por, qué; to that end afim; to the ala
toast brindis, tostada; (v) torrar (Monastir dialect)
tobacco tutun (T *tütün*), tabako, tobako (synonymous *tutun*, T *tütün*);
    tobacco case tabatyera; tobacco dealer tutundji (T *tütüncü*)
together baraber (T *beraber*), djunto, endjuntos, enjunto, enjuntos,
    juntos, yuntos
toilet toaleta (F *toilette*), kabinet, (vulg) kenef
token (in a game) finkes
tolerable toleravle
tolerance tolerensya
tolerant tolerente, tolerante
tolerate (v) dadanear (T *dayanmak*), soportar (Ferrara Siddur),
    soportar, somportar, tolerar

tomato tomat
tomb tomba
tombola tombola
tome tomo
tomorrow amanyana
ton tonelada
tongue alguenga, eluenga, lashon (H), lingwa, luenga
tonsillitis agáya
too much demasia, demasiado, mutcho (muncho), tambien
tooth diente, dyente; small tooth dyenteziko; toothache dolor de
    muela; toothbrush furcha de dyentes; toothed dyentozo; toothless
    desdyentado
top (n) sima; on top en sima; top hat çapeo, çilindro
topic fechu (Monastir dialect)
Torah Atorá
torch torcha
torment (n) supplicio; torment (v) atormentar, fishugar; torment
    oneself atormentarse; tormented atormentado
torn into pieces despedasado
torn off arrankado
torrent arróyo, ravdon, torrente
torture (n) supplicio, iskendje (T ishkence); (v) torturar
totalize asumar, sumar
touch (v) tocar, tokar, asunar (Monastir dialect)
touch dukunear (T dokunmak)
towards verso, versu (Monastir dialect); towards the evening verso la
    tadre
towel tovaja, tuvaja
tower kula, tore
town villa; town-planner urbanista; town-planning urbanismo
toy jugete
track (n) pista; (v) depistar
trade (n) mircansie (Monastir dialect), tidjaret (T ticaret, kanunn),
    negosyo; trade guilds rofit (T esnaf, hirfet, taife), taife; trader mir-
    cader (Monastir dialect); tradesman esnaf (T kanunn),
    komerchante, negociante, negosyante, rofit (T esnaf, hirfet, taife),
    taife
tradition tradision, tradisyon; traditions komarka traditional
    tradisionel (F traditionnel); traditionally anadan babadan (T, lit:
    from mother from father)

trail (n) pista; trail of seguita
train shimén di fer (Monastir dialect, T *shimendifer*), treno
trained embezado
traitor traidor
traits embultura
tram tramvay
tramp desbeder
trampling batán
tranquil akedado, arrepozadiko (kedate) arrepozado, arripuzadu
    (Monastir dialect); **tranquilize** apasensyár; **tranquilizer** dikotes;
    tranquillity tenaylik
transfer (v) transferar, transmeter; **transfer of money** remesa
transformation troakadura, trokamyento
translate into Ladino enladinar
translation terdjume (T *tercüme*)
translator tardjuman (T *tercüman*), terdjuman (T *tercüman*)
transmit transmeter
transvestite tepdil (T *tebdil*), travestido, travestito
trap aselada
travel (n) viaje; (v) viajar; **travel agent** viajador; **travel allowance** yol
    parasi; **traveler** viajador, yoldji (T *yolcu*, kanunn), yuldji, yoldji
    (T *yolcu*)
tray tabla, távla; **contents of a tray** tablada
treachery hiyanet
treason hianetlik (T *hiyanetlik* kanunn), hiyanet, traisyon
treasure hazine (T), siyero; **treasurer** banquiero; **treasurer of the syna-**
    gogue gizbar (H); **treasury** hazine (T)
treat (v) tratar; **treat with disdain** pisotear; **treated** tajo; **treatment**
    tratamiento
tree árbol, arvole
tremble temblar, titireár (T *titremek*), tremblar; **trembling** temblante,
    temblor
tremor temblor
trespass ashirear (T *ashirmak*, kanunn)
trial préva, prova
tribunal djuzdju (Monastir dialect)
trick dalavera, dubara (T), shakera
trickster dubaradji
trifles buchukchulúkes (T *buçuk*)
trill trinar

trimming shirit (T *sherit*)
Trinity Trenidad
trinket bagatella
triple (adj) triple; triple (n) triplo; (v) triplar; tripled triplado
triumvirate triumvirato
triviality vulgaridad
trouble (n) skotura (Gr); trouble (v) disturbar; trouble (n) disturbo
troublemaker fitildji
troublesome torobolos
truly veramente
trumpet trompeta
trunk bavul (T), forseliko, sepet
trust (n) figúzia, boréo; trustworthy sadik (T)
truth vedrá, verdad, vidrad; truthful verdadero; truthfulness verasidad
try (v) aprovar; try to accomplish ograshar (T *ughrashmak*)
tube alkadrúz (Port), dreno, oluk (T)
tubercular entekiado
tuberculosis tekia, tikiya, tizia, tuberkuloza
Tuesday martez
tumble (n) takla
tumultuous sfacato (adj) (Ital *sfacciato*)
tuna palamida
tunic opa
tunnel lagum (T *laghim*), tunel
turban turban (F, originally from Persian *tübend*); turbaned sarikli
turbid bulaník (T)
turbot kalkan (T)
turkey biba
Turkey Turkia
Turkish (language) turkesko; in the Turkish manner turk, a la turka;
    Turkish Republic Republika Turka
turmoil shamata (T)
turn (n) vuelta, arrodeo, buélta (n); (v) tornar; turn in circles arrodear;
    turn oneself aboltar (se); turn over tornar; turning arrodeo;
    turnover (n, food) boreka; small turnover borekita; boreka
turtle tartuga
tutor maestro, tutor; female tutor tutris
tuxedo smoking
twelve doje, doze
twelfth dozen

twenty veynte (Ferrara Siddur), vente
twenty-five venteisinko
twin buchúk (from T *buçuk* half)
twist (v) arretuuerser, atorsar, entrelashar; twisted enkulevrado
two dos, doz
two hundred dozicntas (tos); dozyentos
two thousand dozmil
type (n) tipo
typesetter emprimidor, estampadir, mesadder (H kanunn)
typography estampa, tipografia
tyrannize tyranizar
tyrannical tiraniko
tyranny tirania
tyrant tirano

U

ubiquity ubiquidad, ubikuidad
ugliness fealdad
ugly feo, brúto (It *brutto*), marsik (T)
ulcer ulser; ulcerous ulserozo
ulcerate ulserar (v)
ulterior motive ramayu
ultimate ultimo
ultimatum ultimatum
ultraviolet ultraviyolet
umbilicus ombiligo
umbrella çadir (T), chadir (from T *çadir* tent, umbrella)
unaccustomed dezakostumdrado
unappealing person shavdo
unbutton desbotonar
uncertain duvdozo, shakureko; uncertainty dubyo
uncle tibio, tiyo
unclean suzio, suzyo
uncoiled desdevanado
uncomplicated semplice (Ital)
unconditional (T) mutlak
uncovered descuverto
unctuous mantekozo

undecided endechiso (Ital *indeciso*)
under debasho; under the authority of the police zabtiedje
  (T *zaptiyece*, kanunn)
undergarments ropa
underground passage lagum (T *laghim*)
undersecretary stosekretaryo
undershirt fanella, (woolen) fanela, (with wide sleeves) kazaka, (for a
  baby) kazakita
understand (v) entiender, antender, entender; understanding dáath (H),
  entendimiento
undertaker's man enterrador
underwritten sotoskrito
undesirable dezagradesido
undo (v) dizazer, desfazer, dezazer; undo the hair despeynar
undress desnudar
uneasy desrepozaso
uneducated individual bashiboósh (T *bashibosh*), kulibero
unfair haksíz (T)
unfavorable desfavoravle
unfolded desdublado
unfortunate desgraciado, desmazalado (from H *mazal* luck), fukara,
  zavalli (T)
unfriendly enemistozo, karaylan (T *karaoghlan*)
unglue despegar
ungrateful nankyor (T *nankör*)
unhappily barmimam (H)
unhappiness malor (F *malheur*)
unhappy malorozo (F *malheureux*)
unhook deskolgar
unicorn unikornyo
unification unifikasyon
uniform duz (T *düz*), uniforma, uniforme, yano
uniformity uniformidad, uniformamente
unifying unifikador
unimportant person hashfurro
uninhabited dezuzado
unintelligent (no le) kuadra muncho (lit: much understanding does not
  reach him)
union unyon
unique uniko

unit (n) unita
unite (v) englobar, unifikar, unir, aguntar (Monastir dialect); united
    unido
unity unidad
universal universal
universality universalidad, universalmente
universe universo
university universidad
unjust enjusto
unkept çurro
unknown person fulano
unleavened bread sessenia (from Salonica's Passover Haggadah)
unmask demaskar
unpleasant dezagradavle; unpleasant encounter eskontro
unqualified worker argat (Gr)
unravel desbrolyar
unreasonable desrazonivle
unscrew desvidar
unsheath desvaynar; unsheathed desvaynado
unskilled worker ergat (Gr)
unskillful gafa
unthankful engrato
untidy chapachul, cholpa
untie desñudar, dezatar; untied dezatado
until asta, hasta, kadar (T)
unto asta onde
unused sovrado
unusual bambashka (T *bambashka*)
unwelcome dezagradesido
up arriba, enriva; up to kadar (T); up to date à la page (F)
uplift alevantar, solevantar, solevar
uprising solevantamyento
uproar shamata (T), shimata (T *shamata*, kanunn)
uproot (v) arrankar, arrancár, desraigar, dezraygar; uproot a plant des-
    plantar; uproot violently deskarrankar
upset bulandereár; upset stomach bozéo
upside down alti ostu (T *altüst*), arrevés
upturn arezvalar
uranium uranyo
urbane urbano

urbanism urbanismo
urbanist urbanista
urbanity urbanidad
urbanization urbanizasyon
urbanize urbanizar
urchin (T *külhanbeyi*)
urea urea
uremia uremiya
urethra uretra
urgency urgensa, urjensiya
urgent urgente, urjente; **urgently** urgentemente, urjentamente
urinary urinaryo; **urinary infection** ijada
urinate (v) pishar, orinar, urinar, pichar
urine orina, urina, pisho
urn kantaro
urologist urologo
urology urologiya, urolojiya
us mos, mozotros, nos
usable utilizavle, utilizable
usage uzo
use kulanear (T *kullanmak*); **used** uzado; **use economically** templear;
     use the left hand estyedrear
useful util; **to be useful** (v) aprovechar; **usefully** utilmente
useless abes, batál, vano
usher (in court) muvashir
usual uzadu (Monastir dialect); **usually** uzualmente
usurer uzuraryo
usurpate uzurpar
usurpation uzurpasyon
usurper uzurpador
usury uzura
uterine uterino
uterus utero
utilitarian utilitaryo
utility utilita, utilitad
utilization aprovechamyento, utilizasyon
utilize kulanear (T *kullanmak*), utilizar
utopia utopiya; **utopian** utopiko

V

vaccine ashlama (T *ashilamak*)
vagabond (n) esmouido, andaréte, desbeder, serseri (T), sorretero
vagina macho
vague shakureko, wéko
vain abes, kibir (T), orgolyozo, vana, vano
vainglory vanaglorya, vanagloria
valiant brávo
valley valle
valorize avalorar; valorized avaliado
valuable valorozo
value (n) valor; value (v) avaliar; to have value valer
vamp up remendar
vampire vampiro; female vampire vampiresa
van furgon
vandal vandalo; vandalism vandalismo
vanilla vanilla, vaniya
vanity envanesyimento, vanidad
vapor vapora; vaporous vaporozo
variability variabilidad, varyabilidad
variable variable, varyable
variation variasyon, varyasyon
varicose veins varises
varicosity varikozidad
variety sheshit (T *çeshit*), turlu (T *türlü*), variedad, varyedad, varyeta
various (pl) muchus (Monastir dialect)
varnish (n) lustro, arrelustrear
vary variar
vase vaza
veal hijo de vaca (Fer Bib Gen)
vector vektor
vectorial vektoryal
vegetable zarzavá, zarzavat (T); vendor of vegetables zarzavatchi
     (T *zerzevatçi*), zarzawá; vegetables virdure (Monastir dialect);
     vegetable casserole guvetch
veil (n) velo; veiled velado
vein damar (T), vena
velocity velosidad, velosita

velvet katife, velur
venality venialidad
vendor vendedor
venerable veneravle, venerable
veneral venereo
vengeance nekamá, vindikasyon
vent-hole abaca (from T *baca* chimney)
ventilate desbafar, ventilar; ventilated ayregozo
ventilation desbafamyanto, ventilasyon; ventilation duct abaca (from T
    baca chimney)
ventilator ventilador
verbose verboso, verbozo
verbosity corrençias
verdict veredikto
verification verifikasyon
verify avedredear, averdadear, averiguar, verifikar, de cierto
verily decierto
versatile versatil
verse verso
versed in versado
versification versifikasyon
version version
vertical dich (T *dinç*), vertikal
vertigo mareo, sheshereo (from T *shashirmak* get confused)
very good bravo
very little estrechiko
vest jaketa, yeléc (T *yelek*, Monastir dialect)
vibrate (v) vibrar
vibration vibrasyon
viceroy virrey
victorious vencedor
view (n) vista
vigilance vijilansia
vile alchak (T *alçak*), jinganelik (T *çingenelik*), pusht (T), rezil (T)
vilification pushtluk
villa kösk (T *köshk*), vila
village chief kyeaya, kyehaya (T *kâhya*)
villain villano; villainy bashéa
vinaigrette vinagreta, viunegreta
vindicate vindikar

vindication vindikasyon
vine higuera (Ladino Ferrara Bible), vinya, viña (lit)
vinegar vinagre; **vinegary** vinagrozo
vineyard higuera (Ladino Ferrara Bible)
violate esbivlár, violar
violation esbivlamyento, violasyon
violence adolme, violensya
violent furyente, sanginaryo, violente
violet (flower) menekshe (T), violeta; (adj) violet
violin kyeman, keman (T *keman*); **violinist** kyemanji, kemandji
   (T *kemanci*)
virago kulibera
virgin galana, moça (Ladino Bible of Ferrara, Kings), vierj
virologist virolojista
virology virolojia
virtuosity virtuozidad
virtuoso virtuoso, virtuozo
virus virus
visa viza
viscosity viskozidad
viscous viskozo
visibility visibilidad, vizibilidad
visible visible, visivle
visit (n) vijita, visita; **visitor** musafir (T), vijitador
visual visual, vizual
vital vital; **vitality** vitalidad, vitalita
vitalize vitalizar
vitamin vitamina; **vitamin-supplemented** vitaminado
viticulture vitikultura
vitriol kyezap, kesab
vituperate vituperar
vivacious enguerkado, vivaracho
vivacity despertez, vivasidad
vivid vivido
vixen soysuza
vocabulary palavra, vokabulario
vocal vokal
vocalization vokalizasyon
vocation vokasyon; **vocational** vokasyonal
vociferate vosiferar

vociferation vosiferasyon
vodka vodka
voice bos, boz, boze, son
volatile volatil
volcanic volkaniko
volcano volkan
voltage voltaje
voltmeter voltimetro
volubility (neg) esboro
volume tomo
voluminous bultózo, voluminozo
voluntarily voluntaryamento
voluntary voluntaryo
voluptuous voluptuozo; voluptuousness voluptuozidad
vomit (n) vomito, gomito; (v) gomitar, vomitat, gomitar
voracious voraz; voraciousness vorasidad
vote (n) voto; (v) votar
vow (n) sueto
vowel vocal
vulgar basho, kaba
vulgarity vulgaridad
vulgarize vulgarizar
vulnerable vulneravle
vulva vulva, vulvar

W

wadding wata
wage page (n)
wagon araba (T), furgon
waistcoat yeléc (T *yelek*, Monastir dialect)
wait asperar, esperar
wake up despertar, espertar (se)
walk (n) paziar (Moroccan Sephardic Ballad), vuelta; (v) caminar, kaminar; walking kaminando; walking by pasandu
wall pare, pared; wall painter enkaladoe
wallet juzdám, juzdan (from Turkish *cüzdan*), sakula
walnut muez; walnut tree muezozjal, muezezero
want querer; wanted dezeado

war gerra
ward off (v) parar
warden in a lunatic asylum gullabi (T)
warm cayente, kayente
warn (v) acavidar (Port *cavidar*)
warrantor fiansa
warranty garansia
wart barruga; small wart barrugita
wash (v) labar, lavar; wash oneself labarse, lavarse; wash with soap
    enshavonar; washing-machine washer (Engl)
waste (n) fina, fira
watch (v) bekleár (T *beklemek*), kuladear (T *kollamak*); watch ora;
    watch chain kostek (T *köstek*), leguentina; watch dealer saatchi;
    watch repairman saatchi; watchmaker saatchi
watchman nobetchi (T *nöbetçi*, kanunn)
water agua, su (T); waters aguas; water carrier saka (T), suyudji, saka
    (T); water reservoir shadrivan (T *shadirvan*); water vendor suidji;
    watering arregadúra; watering can arregador
watermelon karpuze, karpuz (from T *karpuz*)
wave (n) dalga (T), onda
wavy ondozo
wax (v) arrelustrear
way fechura, mode; in such a way that de manera ke; ways mezos,
    modoz, munchos mezormany, pasajes
we mosotros, mozotros
weak zaif from T *zayif*), debil; weak voice bozzezika; weaken
    enflakeser; weakness flochura
wealth aziendas, rikeza, riqueza
weapon arma, armo
wear vestir, vistir
weather tiempo, tyempo; good weather bien tiempo
weave entressar
weaver tesedor; weaver's loom telar; weaver's workshop telar
wedding boda; wedding canopy talamo, tálamo (Salonican spelling);
    wedding ring aniyo de kidushim
Wednesday çarshamba (T *çarshamba*), myerkolez, miercolez
weed (n) çaramella; weed the grass desyervar
week semana; duration of a week semanada; weekly (n) ebdomaderyo
    (from F *hebdomadaire*), semanal; worker/employee with weekly
    pay semanero

weigh (v) pezár
welcome akolyo (Ital *accogliere, accoglienza*), baruh aba, bienvenido,
    buirum; welcome! (interj) buyrún, byenvenído; welcoming (n)
    byenvenída
well now! artik
well (n) pozo
well-adjusted potrivita (Romanian Judeo-Spanish); well-disciplined
    talum; T *talim*); well-fed arto (Fer Bib Gen); well-off person
    siñoron
were ivan
westernize frankear; westernized enfrankeado
wet (adj) mojado, amohado, amojado, lemli (from T *nemli*), remojado;
    wet (v) arremojar, mojar, amojar; wetting mojo
whale balena
wharf skala
what kualo, ke?; what happened kualo se paso; what is your name?
    komo te yamas; what was it? ke fue; what? whatever it is nasilisa
    (T *nasilsa*); whatever kualunke (Ital *qualunque*)
wheat arina, trigo; wheat flour semola
wheel çark (T), carru (Monastir dialect), galgal (H); wheelbarrow
    arabeka
when cuando, kuandu, quando
where ande (Haketia), onde, andi, aonde; Where are you? ado tu;
    whereby onde
which ke; which was que fue
whiff baforada
while inmientris, intrimentis (Port)
whim arrojada, bót
whimpering gimoteo
whimsical sherilop
whiner choron
whip (n) asote, shamar (from T *shamar*), kamdjik (from T *kamçi*);
    whip (v) asotar
whisper (v) çuçutear; whispering çuçuteo
whistle (n) çuflar, çuflet (v) chuflár; small whistle çufletiko
white blanko; whitened emblankesido
who (prep and interrogation) kyen; ken (Port *quem*, modern Spanish
    equivalent: *quien*), que, quién
whole entero, salam (T *saghlam*)
wholesale dealer toptandlji, engroso, toptan

wholly enteramente
whom ken (Port *quem*, modern Spanish equivalent: *quien*)
whore puta
whose cual (dil)
why deke, porque
wick fitil, kandil
wicked maldicho/a (archaism, modern Spanish equivalent is *maldito*),
    negro, rashá (H)
wide ancho
widow bivda, embivdada, viuda; widower bivdo, embivdado
width anchura
wife espoza; wife of a rabbi rubisa (H)
wig peluka/peruka
wild arsiz (T), ferose, sfacato (adj) (Ital *sfacciato*); wild animals
    animales feroces
will volontad, voluntad, veluntad
willingness volontad, veluntad
willpower voluntad, veluntad
win (v) ganar
winch winc (Engl, also from T *vinç* with similar meaning)
wind viento; wind blow ruah; windpipe gaznéte; winds ayres
window ventana, yan, ghan; window-glass jam
wine vino, wine tester savoreador
wing ala
winter inuerno, invierno
wipe one's nose amokar (se)
wire sim, tel (T kanunn)
wise person meoyudo
wish (n) deseo, dezaeyo, sueto; (v) dessear, kerer, suetar (F *souhaiter*)
wish (n) hazak baruh (H); wishes kere; (v) orar; wish-come-true deseo
    cumplido
witch brúsha
with con, kon; with me migo konmigo; with oneself konsigo; with you
    contigo
withdraw çekinearse, retirarse; withdrawn from tajada
wither (v) amurchár (Port *murchaer-se*, Monastir dialect)
within (adv) ende, dedyentro, tok (H kanunn)
without sin; thout any doubt seguramente; without any money fulus
    (T); without shame desverguensa; without strength desjuersado;
    without zeal despasyenado

witness ed, edut (H), shaed (T *shahit*), testiguo; witnessing shaedlik; to
     be a witness to atestiguar; atestar
wolf lobo, lovo
wolfram volframo
woman kadun (T *kadin*); woman's robe fostana
womanizer findirizero, zampara T)
wonder (n) maravia; (v) sorretar
wood bósko, leña, madeira, madera, madero, share (Monastir dialect);
     piece of wood lenya; wood cutter leñador; wood scrapings talash;
     woodcutter baltadji, kortaleña; wooden floor dusheme;
     woodsman baltadji
wool lana; woolen lanozo
word palabra (Moroccan Sephardic Ballads), byérvo, palavra, vierbo
     (vs. *verbo* in modern Spanish); word by word tekstualmente
work (n) avóda, lavoro (Ital), lazerio, obra, ovra, trabajo; do burden-
     some work lazdrar; (v) lavorár; ovrar; trabajar; work hard çalis-
     hear (T *çalishmak*); work hard penar; worker lavorante,
     lavurador (Monastir dialect), obrero; workman amele
     (T kanunn), artezáno; workmanship artezaneria; works of the
     devil guerkeriyas; workshop tezya (T *tezgâh*, kanunn)
world mundo, olám (H); worldly person laico
worm guzano; small worm guzaniko; worm-eaten enjaryentado, haryeno
worn out sorvido; worn out shoe sapateta
worried penseryozo
worry (n) merekiá (from T *merak*), merrekiya, skotura (Gr); (v) dert
     (T *dert*), freirse
worse peor; worsen empeorear, engangrenarse, enkangrenar
worship (v) encorvar
worst daabeter (T *daha beter*), peor
worth - to be worth valer; worthless hashabi; worthless person kelepur
     (T *kelepir*); worthless sample kilipur ciego
worthy diño
wound (n) yara, ferida, yága; (v) yaredear, yaraladear, ferir, vulnerar;
     wounded ferido; wounding yaradeadura (T kanunn)
wrap (v) embrujar; wrapped embuelto; wrapped in paper empapelado
wreath sania
wrestler pelivan (T *pehlivan*)
wring (v) despapar
wrinkle (n) rija, ruja; wrinkled (fabric, paper) embolsado, arresekado;
     arrijado, carapicado

wrist pulsu (Monastir dialect)
write eskrivir; **written** eskrito; **written command** emir name
(T *emirname* kanunn)
wrong malefisyozo; **the wrong way** tersene (T *tersine*); **to be wrong**
estar en el lyero, yerarse; **wrongdoer** malezador (Judeo-Spanish);
wrongdoing malefisyo

X

X rays rayos X
xenon xenon
xenophobe xenofobo; **xenophobia** xenofobia
xenophobic xenofobo
xylophone xilofono

Y

yard (measure) yarda
yawn (v) bostejár, bustejar, bustijar (Port *bocejar*); **yawning** bostíjo
year anio, ano, año, anyo; **the year to come** leshana aba (from H next
year in Jerusalem)
yeast levadura, maya
yelling gritaron, gritalon
yellow amariyo
yesterday ayer
yet dainda
yogurt yagur; **yogurt soup** tarator
yoke yàga
you te, ti, tou, ty, vos
young chico (Monastir dialect), mansevo; **young boy** çikito; **young
child** çikito; **young girl** brúna, demuazel (F *demoiselle*),
ninia/niña; **young girls** mutchatchas; **young man** caballero,
delikanli (T), donzel, manseviko, manzebo (Moroccan Sephardic
Ballad), niño, varón; **young plant** fidan; **young woman** muchacha
your güestro, ti, tous, tus, tuyo, vuestro
yours suyo (a polite address instead of *tuyo*, addressing somebody in
the third person), tuyo, tuyos, vuestros
yourself ti mismo

yourselves vozotros, vosotros
youth jyovintud (Ital *gioventu*), mansevez

Z

zeal ardor, hiba, zelo; zealous zeloso
zenith pir
zeppelin zepelin
zero nula (Monastir dialect), zero
zodiac zodiako
zone zona
zoologist zoolojista
zoology zoolojia, zoolojiya

LADINO PROVERBS AND POPULAR SAYINGS

A

A damla damla se inche la bota Drop by drop, the barrel fills up.

A Dio santo i alavado Oh! God! Saint and elevated.
Used to express frustration, such as the inability to obtain a response, or an exclamation of anger and protest.

A la barragana la noche le viene la gana To the vigorous woman, the envy comes at night.

A la mar entra, sale seco He enters the sea and comes out dry.

A la mar se va, agua no topa He goes to the sea but does not find water.

A su boka ke no kaygas May you not fall in his (her) mouth.

A su kavesa klavo no entra In his head, a nail does not penetrate.

A tu muher no le digas lo ke ganas Do not tell your wife what you earn.

Abasha un eskalon para tomar mujer, suve un eskalon para eskojer un amigo Go one step down to take a woman, go one step up to choose a friend.

Abashar es kolay subir es guch Going down is easy; coming up is hard (T *kolay* easy, *güç* hard).

Agora veras de ke palo se aze mi kuchara Now you will see from what stick my spoon is made of.
Now you will see from what material I am made of.

Ajalun de tu madre, de tu siño de tu This does not exist, this has never existed.

Aki va korrer sangre Blood will start running.
Referring to a violent discussion, or a confrontation which may turn violent, as the adversaries do not seem to be ready to compromise.

Al buen entendedor pokas palavras abastan To one who understands only a few words are needed.
Given as a warning.

Al bueno se le enbeneyan enriva They ride on top of a good person (*enbeneyan* is a Judeo-Spanish adaptation of Turkish *binmek* ride on).

Al desmasalado le kaye el bokado From the mouth of an unfortunate person the little piece of food falls out.

Al guerko lo kita del yelek He is so capable that he takes the waistcoat from the devil.
Said of a very intelligent individual.

Al judio el meoyo le viene mas tadre To the Jew the brain comes later.
He comes to his senses later.

Al kuchiyado una kuchiyada mas To the one who has been stabbed, one more stabbing.

Al lado del seko se va i lo mohado yanar The green burns along with the dry (translated from Turkish *kurunun yaninda yash ta*).
The innocent suffers with the guilty.

Aldikera burakada Pocket with holes.
Big spender.

Allado de lo seko, se va i lo mojado Next to the dry, the wet also goes away.

Aller (ir) a Bismarck Going to Bismarck
Going to the toilet. Expression of Sephardim with a strong affiliation to the French. Bismarck was very unpopular in French circles after the French-German War of 1870–71.

Amiral de agua de dulse Sweet water admiral
Individual with high pretense but no real power.

Amistad de yerno, sol d'envyerno The friendliness of a son-in-law lasts as little as the warmth of the winter sun.

Añade de oro en nariz de puerko Gold ring in the nose of a pig (from the Bible).

Ande ay dos Judios, el uno es el prezidente el otro el vekil Where there are two Jews, one is the president and the other is the minister (*vekil* Turkish minister).

Ande mete los pies, yerva no krese Where ever he puts his feet, the grass does not grow.

Arvole tohumu seed of tree.
Stupid person.

Asibiva tus pulgas! May your fleas live!
Ironical wish to express doubt on the validity of a statement made by the interlocutor.

Ate ermano kon el guerko asta ke pasas el ponte Make yourself a brother with the devil until you have crossed the bridge safely (translation of a Romanian proverb, also from the Turkish proverb *köprüyü geçene kadar ayiya dayi diyeceksin* until you cross the bridge you shall call the bear uncle).

Avlar la verdad es perier l'amistad To tell the truth is to lose the friendship.

Ayer salio de la kashkara del guevo He just hatched from the egg yesterday.

Aze lo ke te digo, i no lo ke yo ago Do what I tell you, not what I do.

Azerse del sodro Someone who feigns deafness to avoid answering.
It was rumored that Inönü, the second President of the Turkish

Republic (1938-1950) *would feign deafness when he did not want to answer a question, hence his nickname of El Sodro (the deaf).*

Azerse pishman de la ora ke nasio Being sorry of the hour one was born; wishing not to be born.

Azno de natura ke no entiende su eskritura Donkey by nature who cannot read his own writing. Translated from French *âne de nature qui ne peut pas lire son écriture.*

Azno kayado por savio kontado A silent donkey can pass for a knowledgeable person.

Azno vistido (enkalsato) Dressed up donkey (with shoes)
Stupid man.

B

Bendicha tripa de madre ke tal ijo partio Blessed be the belly of the mother who has given birth to such a son.

Bien darsha el senyor haham komo ay ke lo sienta The rabbi preaches well as if anyone were listening
Voice screaming in the desert.

Bien de los cielos mal de la tierra Good from the skies, ill from the earth.
Spoiling a good opportunity by inappropriate actions.

Bivir i ver Live and see.

Boka de leon te koma i no lojo de persona Better that you be eaten by the mouth of a lion than by the envious, evil eye of another person.

Boka de miel, korason de fiel Mouth of honey, heart of bile.

Boka por ermozure Mouth for beauty
Said of someone who is beautiful but silent.

Buen pipino Good cucumber
Unexpected bad news.

Bueno komo el pan bueno Good like good bread.

Bueno komo la fiel del guerko Good like the devil's bile
Very evil.

Bushkar alguja en la paja Look for a needle in a haystack.

Bushkar kon kandela Look with a candle
Look with attention.

C

Chokluk bokluk Too much abundance brings too much garbage
A well balanced measure of things, or moderation is the only source of true enjoyment. In the late 16th century, the ostentatious display of wealth and jewelry by Jewish women made Sultan Murad III so angry that he was ready to take action against the Jewish community, but could be calmed by his Grand Vizier Sokullu.

Coha que se vido con tavan boyali Coha, who saw himself surrounded by painted (T *boyali*) ceilings (T *tavan*).
Coha (Djoha), a humorist figure in the Judeo-Spanish folklore, is usually living in poor conditions but suddenly find himself raised from rags to riches when he gets a painted ceiling, a status symbol in the milieu of newly rich people.

Come degoyado Eating the meat of a beast which has been slaughtered by cutting the throat.
Usually a burlesque expression for a paper tiger, somebody who threatens but does not puts his threats into action. The expression also used to scare misbehaving children in the same way as one would say "the werewolf is coming."

Como una rapoza Perfidious like a fox.

D

Da le kmamino Give him the road
do not pay attention to him.

De la kavesa gole el pishkado the fish smells bad from the head
corruption starts at the top. Translated from Turkish *balik bashtan*
kokar.

De la roza sale una espina y de la espina sale una roza From the rose
comes a thorn, and from the thorn comes a rose.

De lo contado se yeva el gato From what is so scarce the cat steals
(even) more.

De lo haram no se ve hayre From ill-gotten gains no profit comes.

De los kayadikos es de espantar One should fear the silent ones.

De onde te vino esta para, de ajalun de tu padre? From where, from
which unsavory origin did this money come to you?

De su solombra no ay ken se aproveche One cannot benefit even from
his shadow.

De una pulga azer un gameyo To make a camel from a flea.

Del tiempo de Abdulhamit From the time of the Sultan Abdulhamit II
(1876-1909).
From quite old times.

Del tiempo de Antiochus From the time of Antiochus IV Epiphanes
(2nd century B.C.).
From very early times.

Deshar la savor en la boka Leave the taste in the mouth before one
has finished enjoying it.

Detras del rey avlan Behind the king they speak badly of him.

Dia entero korte havyari The whole day he cuts caviar
the whole day he does nothing.

Dies amigos es poko, un enemigo es muncho Ten friends are too little,
one single enemy is too much.

Dime kon ken vas, te dire ke sosh Tell me with whom you go, and I'll
tell you who you are.

Djusto komo el gancho Just like a hook
Unjust person.

Dos Judiyos, tres kehiloth Two Jews, three communities.
Two Jews, three opinions.

Dos pies en el kayik Two feet in the boat.
Person ready to travel.

E

Echar con syete yaves To go to bed with seven keys.
*Hide very securely an object; remove something from uncontrolled and
indispensable use.*

Echar el kalpak Throw away the hat.
Accept with enthusiasm.

Echar gaz a la lumbre Throw gasoline on the fire
provoke fights

Echar la kara al lagum Throw the face to the sewer.
Make someone feel ashamed.

Echar una bombada Talk nonsense.

El azno, Jan azno The donkey, Jan donkey.
Treat someone as a lord.

El fierro se bate kuando esta kainte One must strike the iron when it is hot (from French *il faut battre le fer quand il est chaud*).

El gameyo no ve su korkova, ve la de su vijino The camel doesn't see his hump, he sees that of his neighbor. Another version of the this proverb is el gameyo no mira su korkova, ma mira la delfrente The camel does not look at his hump, but he looks at the one in front of him.

El guerko kito los pies, el los metio The devil took his feet off, he put them in a very intelligent person.

El gwerko se lo yeve May the devil take him.

El haham por onde kere bolta la oshika When the rabbi cannot answer a question, he turns the page and speaks of other things. *This is Jewish humor about rabbis.*

El judio bive riko i se muere prove The Jew lives rich and dies poor.

El kagalon se burla del pishalon (vulg) Someone who defecates too much mocks the one who urinates too much.

El ke apromete en devda se mete Someone who promises puts himself in debt (from the French proverb *qui promet en dette se met*).

El ke muncho save muncho se yerra Someone who knows too much errs too much.
A lesson of modesty.

El ke oye a su mujer es bovo, el ke no la oye es loko Who listens to his wife is stupid, who does not listen is crazy.

El ke se kema en la chorba, asopla el yogurt Someone who got burned from the soup blows on the yogurt (translated from the Turkish proverb *çorbadan agzi yanan yogurdu üfleyerek yer*).

El ke toca sangre no muere de fambre Those who manipulate blood by profession (the butcher) are in no danger of starving.

El ken ken da al prove empresta al Dio Someone who gives to the poor lends to God.

El ken de otro aspera ya puede asperar Who waits (for help) from another (person), can keep waiting.

El ken kere la roza, kere i el punchon Who wants the rose, also wants the thorn.

El ken tiene nada de azer se pelea kon su mujer Someone who has nothing to do fights with his wife.

El ken ve el palasio del rey deroka su chosa Who sees the palace of the king destroys his slum house.

El livro es el mijor amigo The book is the best friend.

El mal no viene solo A bad thing does not come alone.

El ojo kome mas ke la tripa The eye eats more than the belly.

El onor no se merka kon paras The honor cannot be bought with money.

El padre le dio una vinya, el ijo no le dio ni un razino The father gave him wine, the son did not even give him a raisin.

El padre mantiene diez ijos y dies ijos no mantienen un padre The father maintains ten sons, but ten sons cannot maintain a father.

El rey esta hazino, al vizir le chan la ayuda The king is sick, the minister gets the enema.

El selo de los savios puja la sensia The envy of the scientists pushes forward the science.

El zadelik se ve en su kara the nobility is visible in his face. *Said of a noble person.*

En kada dado un marafet In every finger another talent. *A very skillful person.*

En su boka ke no kaygas May you not fall in his/her mouth.
A very slanderous person; a scandalmonger.

Ermuera es dolor de muela A daughter-in-law is a pain the tooth.

Es bueno i bovo He is good and stupid.

Es de buena famiya He is from a good family.

Es de dos karas He has two faces.
A hypocrite.

Es de la sulukule Person with the character of a Gypsy (allusion to Sulukule, Istanbul's Gypsy quarter).

Es judio i estambolli He is a Jew and from Istanbul.
He is a Jew of the most authentic kind.

Es kara de pokos amigos He is a face of a few friends.
A person hard to befriend.

Es kavesa de apio de Odesa He is a head of celery from Odessa. *A rather stupid person.*

Es su kostiya She is his rib.
She is the right wife for him.

Es sulu bamya He is a wet okra.
Someone not very serious.

Es un vaziyo An empty person.
A person with little brain.

Esta mas de aya ke d'aki He/she is more there than here.
He/she is moribund.

Es una polvora He is gunpowder.
A strong person.

Esta persona es una guerta This person is a garden
A person whose presence is a pleasure.

Esto es ley de Moshe This is Moses' law.
A just cause.

Esto no es boka, esto es makina This is not a mouth, it is a machine.
A person who talks too much.

F

Fin ke al riko le veyene la gana, al prove le sale la alma Until the rich get the wish (to help), the poor has lost his soul.

Furtuna muncha dertes munchos Too much wealth, too many worries.

Fuyir a pie deskalso Run away on foot without shoes.

G

Guadravos de kaza i ora mala To be safe from accidents and bad times. Also guadro voz de kaza i de ora mala May you be guarded from accidents and bad moments.

Guay de mi i sovre de mi Pity on me and upon me.

Guay de mi ke ya me kemi Poor me who has burned myself.

Guay de su madre Beware of his mother.

H

Hadras i baranas ostentation

Haftona salio del ganeden Spanking came out of heaven.

Hahan de mezikas Rabbi of the many tables. *A rabbi who at the occasion of weddings, bar mitzvahs, or memorial services goes from house to house in one same evening, partaking in meals at each place. Used for a person who invites him/herself to many tables.*

Hanalel el papel From the man's name Hanalel, which rhymes with *papel* paper. *Worthless paper or document.*

Harif komo judio Smart like a Jew.

Harrif para mal Smart for evildoing.

Harva kulo ke no pedo (vulg) Beat the behind which did not fart. *Make it work out the hard way.*

Hayre que no veya de su vida Let him get no goodness from his life. *A curse.*

I

I un siuego lo ve Even a blind man can see it.

Ija de judio no keda sin kazar A daughter of a Jew does not stay without marriage.

Ijo de un perro Son-of-a-dog.

Ijos chikos kantarikos de miel, ijos grandes kantarikos de fiel Little sons pitchers of honey, big sons pitchers of bile.

Ijodun judio Son of a Jew.

J

Janna detras de Mejulla Janna behind Mejulla.
A person following docilely and stupidly another, persons who are inseparable.

Judio bovo no ay Stupid Jew there is not.

Judio de kazal tizon de guinan Jew of out-of-town bramble from hell.
Said by the Jews of Istanbul who came from Thrace after anti-Jewish riots.

Judio i Estanbolli Jew and from Istanbul.
Very intelligent person.

Judio santo meleh aolam Holy Jew king of the world.

K

Kada gayo kanta en su kumash Every rooster sings in its coop.

Kada koza en su tiempo Everything in its time.

Kada uno por si, i el Dio para todos Everyone for himself, and God for all.

Kaminos de leche i miel Rods of milk and honey.
Everything going one's way.

Kara de abistru Ostrich-faced.
Person who never laughs.

Kara de mutra Scowling face.
Sour-faced person.

Kara de zargana Evil person.

Kavesa de agranada Head of pomegranate.
Very intelligent person.

Kavesa de arnaut Head of Albanian.
Very capricious, stubborn person.

Kavesa de boshnak Head of Bosnian.
Stubborn person.

Kavesa de piedra stonehead

Kaveyos largos, meoyo kurto Long hair, short brain.
Anti-feminist description of a woman.

Kazika de Moshe Rabeno The house of Moshe Rabeno
A house where there is continuous coming and going. Moshe Rabeno was a real person in the Jewish settlement of the Golden Horn.

Kemar lo seko i lo vedre Burn the dry and the green.
Chastise the innocent with the guilty.

Ken beve vino, perie el tino Who drinks wine loses his mind.

Ken bien te kere te face yorar He who loves you much will make you cry (equivalent Spanish proverb **ken mas tiene mas kere** the more one has, the more he wants; equivalent to Castilian *cuanto más tienes más quieres*).

Ken de verde se vistio en su ermozura se atrivio A woman who dresses in green does so because she is confident of her beauty.
The expression comes from the idea that green is a difficult and risky color to wear for a woman, unless she is really beautiful.

Ken kon gato djuga areskuniado sale Whoever plays with a cat ends up scratched.

Ken mokos manda, bavas aresive (vulg) Who sends nasal mucus gets back slime.

Ken nasc kon mazal i ventura, ken kon potre i kevadura Some are born with good luck, others are born with a hernia and bad luck (equivalent to Spanish *unos nascen kon estrella, otros estrellados*).

Ken se aharva kon sus manos ke no se yore Someone who strikes himself with his hands let him not cry (translated and modified from the Turkish saying *kendi düshen aglamaz* someone who falls by himself does not cry).

Ken (el ke) se kema (la boka) en la chorba asopla (en) el yogurt. Someone who has burned his mouth with soup blows on the yogurt (translation of the Turkish proverb *çorbada agzi yanan yogurtu üfler*).

Kita mete bulasete Someone who provokes intrigues.

Kiter al rey, meter el vizir Take off the king, pick the minister. *Someone who talks about politics without knowing anything.*

Kitar de una aldikera, meter a la otra Take from one pocket and put it in the other.

Kitar la alma Take away the soul. *Put to much pressure on someone.*

Kitar ojos Take away the eyes.

Kome, beve i alava el Dio Eat, drink and praise God.

Komer komo un pasharo Eating like a bird.

Komerse los guesos Eating one's own bones. *Not to make a profit in business.*

Kon parientes poko ilaka Avoid business dealings with relatives.

Kon ti no lo vas a yevar You will not be able to take your fortune to the grave.

Kopollu kopek kopollu Son-of-a-dog (from Turkish *kopekoglukopek*).

Kuando el guerko no puede ir algun lugar, embiya el vino para ke aga su misyon When the devil cannot go to a certain place, he sends wine to accomplish his mission.

Kuando el padre da al ijo, riye el padre, riye el ijo; kuando el ijo da al padre yora el padre yora el ijo When the father gives to the son, the father laughs, the son laughs; when the son gives to the father, the father cries, the son cries.

Kuando la gayne pare un guevo, esperta el kazal entero When the hen lays an egg, it wakes up the whole village.

Kuando la preiada dezeyo, la mar se seko When a pregnant woman craves for something the sea dries up.

Kuando searapan las moshas When the young ladies will shave their face.
Never.

Kuando se kere eshuegra kon ermuera? When is there much love between the mother-in-law and the daughter-in-law?

Kuando suve el azno eskalera? When does the donkey climb a stairway?

Kuando ya sos azno, todos te se embinayan ariva When you are a donkey, everybody rides on you.

Kuelevra morio a su esfuegra The snake has bitten its mother-in-law.
The snake attacked somebody more poisonous and dangerous than itself.

Kulo de mal asiento (vulg) Buttock of bad sitting.
Unpleasant person, bad character.

Kunyadika kulevrika! Sister-in-law, a snake!

L

La boka aze, la boka dezaze The mouth does, the mouth undoes.

La bolsa del riko se vazia i la del prove no se inche The purse of the rich empties itself and that of the poor does not fill.

La boz no se siente The voice cannot be heard.
Somebody very silent, usually a married woman in the presence of her husband.

La kara preta The dark face.
His face darkened.

La karne es tuya los guesos son miyos The flesh is yours, the bones are mine (translated from Turkish *eti senin kemigi benim*).
Expression used by the Ottoman Sultan Murad II in entrusting the young Crown Prince Mehmed, the future Fatih Sultan Mehmed, Mehmed the Conqueror to his tutor, meaning that the tutor should be very tough with the prince in educating him)

La kavesa ke no le ayerge May his head never reach there.
May he never be able to achieve what he is plotting.

La kavesa me se izo un davul My head became a drum.
My head is full, I am tired from listening to this eternal talk

La limpieza es media rikeza Cleanliness is half riches.

La manseveza es una vez; el ke no se la goza loko es Youth happens only once, the person who does not enjoy it is crazy.

La mejor kura es la pasensya i la kayades The best cure is patience and silence.

La mujer fragua la mujer deroka The woman builds, the woman destroys.

La mujer i el vino kita al ombre del tino The woman and the wine make a man loose his mind.

La noche todos los gatos soon pretos At night all the cats are black (translated from French *la nuit tous les chats sont gris*).

La palavra es de plata i la kayades de oro. Speaking is silver, silence is gold (translated from French *la parole est d'argent et le silence est d'or*).

La pasemcia es madre de la siensia Patience is the mother of science (knowledge).

La pasencia es pan i siensa Patience is bread and science (knowledge).

La primera mujer es la mejor The first wife is the best one.

La roza tyene pinchones ke areskunyan The rose has thorns that scratch.

La sereza tyan alavada, alko ssalio guzanada The cherry so much praised in the end turned out to be worm-eaten.

La toz i la provedad no se pueden eskonder One cannot hide the cough and the poverty.

Las palavras bolan, las eskrituras kedan The words fly, the writings stay (translated from French *les paroles s'envolent les écrits restent*).

Las paredes tienen oyidos The walls have ears (translated from French *les murs ont des oreilles*).

La vida ki nu mus manke That is all right, as long as we are alive.

Le salio piyango He won in the lottery
He was lucky.

Lo ke le quedo es la tinia i la turkedad What is left to her
(after her husband's death) is ringworm and being Turkish.
Lo ke kere la mujer kere el Dio What the woman wants, God wants it.

Lo pujaron a los sielos The prices skyrocketed.

Lo que ve la sfuegra What the mother-in-law sees.
*Limiting house cleaning to the most obvious and exposed places, just
enough to quite down an inquisitive mother-in-law.*

Lodo toka oro se le aze Mud he touches, it becomes gold in his hands.

Loka la madre loka la ija Crazy the mother, crazy the daughter.

Los dos pies en un sapato Put the two feet in one shoe.

Los panios dan honor Nice clothes bring honor.
*It is said that Nasreddin Hodja, the Turkish hero of folk tales, once
went shabbily dressed to a banquet; nobody paid attention to him.
Nasreddin Hodja left the party, went home, put on his most beautiful
fur coats and returned to the banquet; he was this time received with
great honors and invited to sit at a most prominent place around the
banquet table; he imperturbably started to put the food in the sleeve
of his fur coat, saying "Ye kürküm ye!" (Eat my fur! Eat!). When the
people at the banquet asked him with surprise: "Hodja! What are
you doing?", he quietly answered: "All the honors and greetings have
been for the clothes I am wearing, it is therefore the right thing to do,
that my clothes which have been so deserving of your welcome also
get the food!"*

Los pipinos se alevantaron a aharvar a los guartelanos The cucumbers
rose to beat up the gardeners.

Los sielos estan yorando The skies are crying.

Luna en kinze moon on its fifteenth day.
Very beautiful young girl.

M

Madrasta el nombre le abasta stepmother, her name is already enough (to express how bad she is).

Mal i malanyiko Bad and bad year.

Makina ya tiene, kuzir no save He/she has a sewing machine, does not know how to sew.

Marido lo kero presto lo kero Husband I want; fast I want it.

Mas al dip mas yagli More at the bottom more oily.
The more you dig and more you find out.

Mas da el prove ke el riko The poor give more than the rich.

Mas vale un pasharo en la mano ke siente bolantos A bird in the hand is worth more than a hundred flying ones.

Me lo yevatas de la boka You took it out of my mouth.
I was precisely on the point to say what you are saying.

Merkader de agua de dulse Buyer of sweet water.
Poor buyer.

Mezura los kaldirimes One who measures the sidewalks (from Turkish *kaldirim*).
Jobless, unemployed.

Mujer buena es la ke poko avla A good woman is one who speaks little.

Mujer kon meoyo, mazal i repozo A woman with brains, good luck and rest.

Mujer no es kamiza ke se troka A woman is not a shirt that you can change at will.

Muncho bien te kero, ma mi bolsa no tokes I love you very much, but do not touch my purse.

Munço plata Too much silver.
Too much money.

Muy bueno ser no es bueno It is not good to be too good.

N

Na to kafa na to mermeri So is the head, so is the
marble (from Greek).
Head as hard as the marble; stupid.

Negra la kulpa mas negra la deskulpa Bad the guilt, worst the excuse.

Ni a la mujer kreyete, ni a la mar te yuveneyes Do not believe in the
woman, do not put your trust in the sea.

Ni ajo komi ni la boka me fiede I neither ate garlic nor do I have bad
breath.

Ni bive ni desha bivir He neither lives nor does he let live.

Ni el guerko no kita kon el judio Not even the devil can have the
upper hand with the Jew.

Ni friyo ni kalor me izo It feels neither cold nor hot for me (translated
from French *il ne m'a fait ni chaud ni froid*).

Ni gayo kanto ni perro grita No rooster sings, no dog barks.
A very far away place unsuitable for living.

Ni mulkes en Turkiya ni mujer de Romanya He does not have
property in Turkey nor a woman from Rumania.
A have-nothing.

Ni preto ni blanko ni zerzuvi Not black not white not purple.
Colorless.

Ni su bien ni su fiel Not his goods nor his bile.
Nothing from that person.

No kayo la asukar al agua The sugar has not fallen in the water. *The case is not yet lost; the illness is not as bad as it looks at first glance.*

No se le siente la boz One cannot hear his/her voice. *A very silent person.*

No tiene verguensa en la kara He/she has no shame in the face. *Impudent person.*

Novio lo kero presto lo kero I want a fiancé, I want it fast.

Nunkua es tarde para bien azer It is never too late to do good.

O

Ograsheyar kon perros Struggle with dogs. *Struggle with bad persons.*

Ojos de guerko Devil's eyes. *Person who sees everything.*

Ojos por ermozura Eyes for beauty only. *Look without seeing.*

Onde el rey (la reina) va kon sus piezes Where the king (the queen) goes with his (her) own feet. *The toilet.*

P

Paciencia es pan i ciencia Patience is bread and science.

Pagan los justos por los pekadores the just pay for the sinners.

Paredes tienen orejas The walls have ears.

Perro ijo dotro Dog son of another.

Pi dishitez muerte mereces You only said p and you already
deserve death.
An out-of-proportion adverse reaction to a very small word or action.

Polvora ingleza English powder.
Strong person.

Por una pulga kemar una kolcha For a flea to burn a bedspread.

Primero el Dio God first.
God willing.

Puedo no puedo kon mi mujer me tomo I can, I cannot I take it on
my wife.

R

Refran mintirizo no ay. Proverbs don't lie.

Repuesta en su ora vale mil dukados A timely answer is worth one
thousand ducats.

Rey muerto no aze gerra A dead king does not make war.

Ropa ingleza English tissue.
Quality merchandise.

S

Sakop vaziyo no se tiene enpies An empty bed does not stand upright.

Salir de la kashkara del guevo Freshly hatched.
Young person who likes to give advice.

Salir limpio Come out clean.

Sangre ajena Alien blood.

Sangre buyendo Boiling blood. Ardent, audacious, quick to get angry.

Sangre fria Cold blood.

Santo Meleh Aolam Holy King of the World.

Se alimpyo seko i verde He cleaned himself up dry and green. He lost everything.

Sfuegra de barro Mother-in-law of clay. *A man hung a clay portrait of the mother-in-law whom he disliked in the kitchen, and the portrait fell on his head; thus not even the real thing, a mother-in-law of clay is any good.*

Si bushkas muncho en la mujer, ni aproves a kazarte If you look for too much in a woman, do not even try to get married.

Si es kismet koshuegraremos If it is written in our fate, we shall enter in a kinship by marriage.

Si mansevez saviya, si la vejes podia If youth knew, if old age could (translated from French *Si jeunesse savait si vieillesse pouvait*).

Si le dates la mano te toma el braso If you give him the hand, he takes your arm.

Si le kontas una koza amanyana ya lo topas en la gazeta If you tell him something, tomorrow you already find it in the newspaper.

Si me oyiyas otro gayo nos kantava If you had listened to me another rooster would be singing for us.

Si no ay un buen pleto, no ay una buena pas Without a good fight, there is not a good peace.

Si sos judio inaneate If you are Jewish, believe in it. (Tinanmak)

Si tu enemigo es una orniga, kontalo komo un gameyo If your enemy is an ant, count it like a camel.
Do not underestimate your enemy.

Si yo no para mi, ken para mi, i si no agora kuando If I am not for myself, then who will be for me.
Proverb of rabbinical origin, attributed to Hillel in Pirkei Avot literally Ethics of the Fathers, a treatise of the Mishnah which contains the ethical maxims of the early rabbis.

Sos riko sos mi tiyo You are rich, you are my uncle.

Subir es guch, abashar es kolay Going up is hard, going down is easy.

Sumo no le sale Juice does not come out of him.
Someone so stingy that even a little juice does not come out of him.

Suvir la sangre a la kavesa Have the blood rise to the head.
Let one bring himself to a violent explosion of anger.

T

Tahi taha todo una mishpaha The whole family went jogging.

Tanto bien te kero fin ke te kito el ojo I love you so much until I snatch off your eye.

Tanto esacureso que es para manecer It has become so dark that the sun will rise again.
Face with optimism in the future the present dark clouds.

Tanto lavora el provi k'el riko si enrikese The poor employee works so hard that the rich man gets rich.

Tanto va el kantaro a la fuento alkavo se rompe So many times the pitcher goes to the fountain that it finishes by being broken (from French *tant va la cruche à la fontaine qu'elle finit par se casser*).

Te dishe ke no te vaz azer benadam no to dishe ke no te vaz azer vezir I told you that you will not become a gentleman, I did not tell you that you will not become a minister.

Tener el pie ugurli Have a lucky foot.

Tener kavesa de chefalo Have the head of a gray mullet. *To be empty headed.*

Tener la mano apretada To be tight-handed. *To be stingy.*

Tener mano avierta Have an open hand. *To be generous; a big spender.*

Tener mano burakada Have a hand with holes. *To be a big spender.*

Tener un bulto en el korason Have a weight in the heart. *Feel uneasy.*

Tierra mana leche i miel Land of milk and honey. *Eretz-Israel.*

Todo lo ke briya no es oro Everything that shines is not gold (from French *tout ce qui brille n'est pas or*).

Todo lo muncho bulaneya Too much of anything gives nausea.

Todos los guevos no se meten en el mesmo sesto Do not put all your eggs in the same basket.

Todos saben kuzir samarra, ma los pelos los embarassan Everyone pretends that he knows how to work on furs, and to assemble pieces of fur with a needle, but the hairs are a hindrance. *As long as he/she has not tried it, an inexperienced person imagines that he/she can do something as good as an experienced craftsman.*

Tomar al shuki Make fun of somebody.

Topo la Amerika Find America.
Find that all is well.

Tornar kon los mokos enkolgango Come back with mucus hanging
from the nose.
Fail miserably.

U

Un loko, un bovo i un shudula A crazy one, a stupid one and a
worthless person.

Una muchacha buena A good girl.
Used in Bosnia to mean a prostitute.

Una paja detiene un molino A single hay fiber can block a mill.

Umo sin fuego no ay There is no smoke without fire.

Unos tienen las echas, otras la fama Some have the deeds some have
the fame.

V

Vender el sol para merkar la kandela To sell the sun to buy a candle.

Ver al guerko See the devil
Hurt too much.

Viejo no kere murir paramas ver i oyir The old man does not want to
die in order to hear and see more.

Vistidos emprestados no kaintan Borrowed clothes do not keep you
warm.

Vizino bueno es mijor ke parientes A good neighbor is better than relatives.

Y

Ya dyo savor de lakavasa It gave the taste of squash.
Give a headache.

Ya konosko las koles de mi guerta I do know the cabbages of my garden.

Ya lo tomaron a anchor They took this lightly.

Ya se pisho (vulg) He pissed.
He repented.

Yerno bueno es el ke ke ve ke la esfugra se esta kemando i la salvo A good son-in-law is one who sees his mother-in-law burning and saves her.

BIBLIOGRAPHY

Altabé, D. F., Atay, E., and Katz, J. *Studies on Turkish-Jewish History: Political and Social Relations Literature and Linguistics.* The Quincentennial Papers. New York Sepher-Hermon Press, Inc. for the American Society of Sephardic Studies, New York, 1996.

Atkins, B. T., Duval, A., Lewis, H. M. A., Milne, R. C., Carpenter, E., and Maxwell, F. *Collin's Robert French Concise Dictionary French-English, English-French.* Paris: Harper Collins Publishers, 1993.

Barokas, D.N. *Autobiographical Sketch. Sephardic Storm Lamp. Ladino, Judezmo and the Spanish Jewish Dialect.* Tract Number-XI-pp. 43–45. New York: The Foundation for the Advancement of Sephardic Studies and Culture, 1976.

Bérard, R. R. *Sepharad. Le monde et la langue judéo-espagnole des Séphardim.* Mons (Belgium): Annales Universitaires de Mons, 1966.

Turkish-English Dictionary Ingilizce-Türkçe Sözlük. Princeton: Berlitz, 1988.

Turkish-English-Dictionary. Princeton: Berlitz, 1998.

Bicerano, S. *Relatos i Refleksiones.* Istanbul: Gözlem, Gazetecilik Basin ve Yayim A. S., 1994.

Bunis, D.M. *A Lexicon of the Hebrew and Aramaic Elements in Modern Judezmo.* Jerusalem: Magnes Press Hebrew University and Mirgav Yerushalayim, 1993.

Deleon, J. *Ancient Districts of the Golden Horn (Balat, Hasköy, Fener, Ayvansaray).* Istanbul: Gözlem, Gazetecilik Basin ve Yayim A. S.

Deleon, J. *Pera Hatirati (Ani, Arshiv).* Istanbul: Gözlem, Gazetecilik Basin ve Yayim A. S.

599

Del Rosarío Martinez, González M.ª. *Un marido entre dos mujeres. Novela anonima en ladino*. Transcription and study of the anonymous novel in Ladino. Biblioteca Nueva Sefarad. Volume IV. Barcelona: Ameller Ediciones, 1998.

Denoeu, F., Sices, D. and J. B. *French Idioms*. Hauppauge (New York): Barron's Educational Services, 1996.

Díaz-Mas, P. *Los Sefardies, Cultura i Literatura*. VI Cursois de Verano en San Sebastian VI. Udako Ikastaroak Donostian. San Sebastian: Servicio Editorial Universidad del Pais Vasco, Argitarapen Zerbitzua, Euskal Herriko Universiataria, 1988.

Díaz-Mas, P., and Sephardim, P. *The Jews from Spain*. Translation by Zucker, G. K. London: The University of Chicago Press, 1992.

Harris, T. K. *Death of a Language. The History of Judeo-Spanish*. London and Toronto: Delaware University Press, Newark and Associated University Presses, 1984.

Hony, D. C., and Fahir, Iz. *A Turkish-English Dictionary*. Oxford at the Clarendon Press, 1967.

Juhasz, E. *Sephardi Jews in the Ottoman Empire. Aspects of Material Culture*. Jerusalem: The Jerusalem Publishing House, Hamakor Press, 1990.

Langenscheidt's New College Spanish Dictionary. Berlin: Langenscheidt, 1990.

Lazar, M. *Ferrara Bible. The Ladino Bible of Ferrara. The Complete Old Testament*. Initial edition, 1553. Culver City (California): Labyrinthos, (reprint) 1992.

Lazar, M. *The Ladino Mahzor of Ferrara. Prayer Book for Rosh Hachanah and Kippur*. Initial edition, 1553. Culver City (California): Labyrinthos, (reprint) 1993.

Lazar, M. *Ladino Pentateuch*. Initial edition, 1547. Culver City (California): Labyrinthos, (reprint) 1988.

Lazar, M. *The Ladino Siddur of Ferrara*. Culver City (California): Labyrinthos, 1995.

Lazar, M. and Dilligan, R. *Siddur Tefillot. A Woman's Ladino Prayer Book. A critical Edition*. Culver City (California): Labyrinthos, 1995.

Levi, A. *The Jews of the Ottoman Empire*. Princeton: The Darwin Press, in cooperation with the Institute of Turkish Studies, Washington, D.C., 1992.

Love, C. E. *Larousse Concise French-English Dictionary*. Paris: Larousse-Bordas, 1998.

Luria, M. A. *A Study of the Monastir Dialect of Judeo-Spanish Based on Oral Material Collected in Monastir Yugoslaviaa*. New York: Instituto de Las Españas en los Estados Unidos, 1930.

Muniz-Huberman, A. *La Lengua Florida. Antologia sefardi (compilladora)*. Mexico: Universidad Nacvional de Mexico, Faculdade de Filosofia y Letras, Fondo de Cultura Economica, 1989.

Nehama, J. *Dictionaire du Judéo-Espagnol avec la collaboration de Jesús Cantera*. Madrid: Consejo superior de investigaciones cientificas, Instituto Benito Arias Montano, 1977.

Nihat Özön, M. *Küçük Osmanlica-Türkçe Sözlük*. Istanbul: Inkilâp Kitabevi, Yayim Sanayi ve Ticaret A.S., 1995.

Passy, A.M. Sephardic Folk Dictionary English-Ladino/Ladino-English. Self-published, 1994.

Pequeño Larousse Ilustrado. Paris: Libreria, 1964.

Shaul, E. *Folklore de Los Judios de Turkiya*. Istanbul: Isis, 1994.

Spyers, A. and G.P. Quackenbos. *Spyers and Surenne's French and English Pronouncing Dictionary.* New York: Appleton and Company, 1864.

Stillman, Y. K., and Zucker, G. K. *New Horizons in Sephardic Studies.* Edited by Walter P. Zenner. SUNY Series in Anthropology and Judaic Studies. Albany (New York): State University of New York Press, 1993.

Varol, M.-C. *Balat, Faubourg d'Istanbul.* Les Cahiers du Bosphore III. Istanbul: Editions Isis, 1989.

Rabbi Yishak Yerushalmi. *Kanun Name de Penas. Letras de Muestro Sinyor el Rey. Y"H sigun lo eskrito se deve de afirmar 5620.* Cincinnati: Sephardic Beth Shalom Congregation and Hebrew Union College-Jewish Institute of Religion, 1975.

Webster's Dictionary of the English Language. New York: Gramercy Books, Avenel, 1994.

Hagggada Shel Pessah (Passover Prayer Book). Initial edition, Salonica, 1895. Salonica: Ekdose Isralikitis Koinotetos Thessalonikes, (reprint) 1970.

LaVergne, TN USA
07 December 2010
207705LV00004B/88/P

9 780781 806589